舞风秋海

陈欣——著

Wind Dance Autumn Sea

Billson International Ltd.

Published by
Billson International Ltd
27 Old Gloucester Street
London
WC1N 3AX
Tel:(852)95619525

Website:www.billson.cn
E-mail address:cs@billson.cn

First published 2025

Produced by Billson International Ltd
CDPF/01

ISBN 978-1-80377-132-8

©Hebei Zhongban Culture Development Co.,Ltd All rights reserved.

The original content within this product remains the property of Hebei Zhongban Culture Development Co.,Ltd, and cannot be reproduced without prior permission. Updates and derivative works of the original content remain the property of Hebei Zhongban. and are provided by Hebei Zhongban Culture Development Co.,Ltd.

The authors and publisher have made every attempt to ensure that the information contained in this book is complete, accurate and true at the time of printing. You are invited to provide feedback of any errors, omissions and suggestions for improvement.

Every attempt has been made to acknowledge copyright. However, should any infringement have occurred, the publisher invites copyright owners to contact the address below.

Hebei Zhongban Culture Development Co.,Ltd
Wanda Office Building B, 215 Jianhua South Street, Yuhua District, Shijiazhuang City, Hebei province, 2207

作者陈欣

丹凤朝阳　唐山标志性建筑，总高度70米。基座净高9.23米，铜雕净高60.77米，重447吨。

Danfeng Chaoyang Tangshan landmark building, the total height of 70 meters. The clear height of the base is 9.23 meters, the clear height of the bronze sculpture is 60.77 meters, and it weighs 447 tons.

唐山市丰南区河头老街望月楼
Wangyue Building, Hetou Old Street, Fengnan District, Tangshan City

锦绣天地 Splendid World

内容简介 Content Introduction

《风舞秋海》一书，取名于书中一篇题为《风舞秋海》的散文，大气恢宏，气势磅礴。

在度夏圣地秦皇岛海域的秦始皇求仙入海处参观游览，有一尊高大的巨型秦始皇帝（公元前259—公元前210）立身石雕像，那么气宇轩昂，雄视天下，威震四方。也许，在全中国这是秦始皇最大的一尊石雕像了。这位从公元前230年到公元前221年，用十年时间征服了海内四方的中国始皇帝，面对茫茫沧海，既有他真心还想再活五百年的愿望，更有他四海一统的勃勃雄心和霸主的胸怀大略。

在这里，始皇帝极目远望，凛然威风，衣带飘摆。千古一帝像是在呼唤着崭新乾坤，再现盛世，呼唤中华重振雄风，威扬四海。

中华考古证明民族文化已有8000年发展的脉络，确凿历史文字记载已经5000多年的发展进程。中国，历史辉煌，文化辉煌，成就辉煌。到2024年，新中国成立75周年之际，新时代，新征程，中国，还将更加辉煌。所以，《风舞秋海》书名寓意中华古国强势崛起，大善至诚，一带一路，构建人类命运共同体构想，砥砺奋进，实现中华民族伟大复兴的中国梦。

《风舞秋海》一书中的作品是作家陈欣在不同时期，在国家、省、市级报纸、杂志、电台、新媒体发表过的散文作品。

The book "Wind Dance Autumn the Sea" is named after an essay entitled "Wind Dance Autumn the Sea" in the book. It is magnificent and majestic.

In the summer holy land of Qinhuangdao sea area of Qin Shihuang Qianxian to visit the sea place, there is a tall giant Qin Shihuang Emperor (259–210 BC) standing stone statue, so imposing, majestic, majestic 4 square. Perhaps, this is the largest 1 statue of Qin Shi Huang in all of China. From 230 BC to 221 BC, the first emperor of China, who conquered all directions in the world in ten years, faced the vast sea, he not only had his sincere desire to live for another 500 years, but also had his ambition to unify the four seas and his overlord's mind.

Here, the first emperor looked at him from afar, awe-inspiring, and his clothes were floating. An emperor through the ages is like calling for a new world, reappearing the prosperous times, calling for China to revive its glory and its prestige.

Chinese archaeology proves that the national culture has been developed for 8000 years, and the development process has been recorded for more than 5000 years. China has a glorious history, a glorious culture and brilliant achievements. By 2024, the 75th anniversary of the founding of New China, the new era, new journey, and China will be even more brilliant. Therefore, the famous the book "Wind,, Dance, Autumn and the Sea" implies the strong rise of the ancient Chinese country, the great, good and sincere, the belt and road initiative, the concept of building a community with a shared future for mankind, forge ahead and realize the Chinese dream of the great rejuvenation of the Chinese nation.

"Wind Dance Autumn the Sea" a book of works is the writer Chen Xin in different periods, in the national, provincial and municipal newspapers, magazines, radio, new media published prose works.

与时代对接 与时代共情 Docking with the Times and Empathy with the Times（序）(Preface)

关仁山 Guan Renshan

  陈欣，是我的同乡，也是我的好朋友。他热爱文学创作，是一位始终不渝、坚持不懈、笔耕不辍的作家。早在20世纪80年代陈欣在央企党委宣传部工作时，就在报纸杂志上发表文学作品。90年代他的文学创作方兴未艾并屡屡获奖。特别是他的散文诗《仲夏情思》获得1993年《当代文坛》杂志举办的全国首届当代文坛力作选拔赛上，一举荣获全国首届当代文坛力作选拔赛诗歌创作一等奖。也正是因为《仲夏情思》这首获得一等奖的散文诗，《人民文学》杂志社当年在"京都之春""京都之夏""京都之秋""京都之冬"几次文学笔会向陈欣发来邀请，但陈欣由于工作关系皆未能前往的情况下，《人民文学》在创刊45周年之际，再次向陈欣发出笔会邀请。当时的《人民文学》杂志散文诗编辑"绿风"在北京见到陈欣时笑着说："陈欣啊，你的散文诗《仲夏情思》写得那么好，今天，我终于把你给找到了……"陈欣十分感动。最美好的感情下是心灵的相惜，喧嚣的尘世里他们因文字相知相敬相近，当他得知《人民文学》杂志散文诗编辑"绿风"，通过全国首届当代文坛力作选拔赛获奖作品集《中国新诗人千家》一书，欣然发现、认真了解、不离不弃联系自己的时候，那一种赏识和肯定使他决心在文学路上经历各种坎坷，克服各种困难，并从中觉醒和成长。他知足而上进，执着而坚定，文学有他生命的梦想。

  陈欣为人热情，干事专注。这些年来，他把所有心血都倾注在了新闻工作和文学创作上，让自己及作品像星星一样在浩瀚的夜空中不息地闪光。四十年来，陈欣在国内外、国家、省内外各种报纸杂志、广播电视等媒体发表了许多文学作品。悠悠岁月，日积月累，成绩斐然。对陈欣的写作精神和文学创作精神，我钦佩而且赞赏。他的作品就像他的人那样憨厚广博，大气爽朗，能登大雅之堂，亦可融入民众和水土一方。

  陈欣的散文集《风舞秋海》，是2021年由北京日报出版社出版的，很受读者青睐和好评，应广大读者要求不得不在2024年再版。当我通读了陈欣的《风舞秋海》书稿后，感觉到在陈欣诗化的散文里，有高山仰止，也有辽阔无垠。有大气磅礴，也有静水浮波。散文中有小桥流水般的柔情流淌，也有高昂的激情澎湃，显现着深沉沧桑，往日烟云。从文章来看，他有一颗坚强的、具体的、无处不在的世俗心。时代的喧嚣足以粉碎一切，在浮躁的物质世界，我们在失去一种具有生气和情谊的温暖情愫，他试图将这一切寻找回来。

在《风舞秋海》这本散文集里，集纪实散文、抒情散文、游历散文、微散文于一书。人文历史、山川风物、世间情暖皆现字里行间。从中我们会掂量出陈欣散文创作的厚重，随着阅读的深入，也会看到陈欣的散文创作水平和散文写作技巧的至高点；散文集里情感流露有的低回婉转，有的荡气回肠，让读者领略一派男儿心肠；散文里显露着大国威风，也有家国情怀；洋溢着锦绣山河之美，升华着乡恋故土之情，其间洒落着博爱之光。从文章里，体现了作家的担当和责任，他走进了诗意而深情的文学世界，同时也理解了文学是如何与生活、社会和时代产生相互联系。

文学与时代对接，与时代共情。陈欣的散文创作涉及不同创作题材，涉猎不同知识层面和领域，丰富自己丰富写作，从未彷徨徜徉，那是一种精神的别样。陈欣的散文集《风舞秋海》，能够让读者在阅读过程中感到一种博大浩瀚，一种可贵难得，一种蓬勃力量。在快速变化的时代，作家需要一双热情冷静的眼睛，这样才能将时代看得真切，洞见生活本质。所以，他将笔触对准了广阔的社会，研究经济问题和民生问题，以不回避的姿态，揭示社会关系的复杂性，提出解决问题的方法，发人深省。

《风舞秋海》一书的再版，证明了读者对《风舞秋海》的喜爱和文字的价值。让我们在散文集《风舞秋海》的大散文、大视野、大胸怀里，在陈欣诗一样优美的散文里领略泰山挺拔，一览东海浩荡；放眼长河奔流，登上长城望远；回首华夏辉煌，看今日中华崛起，万古流芳！

2024年1月6日

（作者系中国著名作家，中国作协主席团委员，河北省作家协会主席）

Chen Xin is my countryman and my good friend. He loves literary creation and is the 1 writer who has always been unswerving, steadfast in his and has never stopped writing. As early as the 1980 s, when Chen Xin worked in the Propaganda Department of the Party Committee of central enterprises, he published literary works in newspapers and magazines. In the 1990 s, his literary creation was in the ascendant and won many awards. In particular, his prose poem "Midsummer Love" won the first national contemporary literary masterpiece selection competition held by "Contemporary Literary World" magazine in 1993, and won the first prize of poetry creation in the first national contemporary literary masterpiece selection competition in one fell swoop. It is also because of ". Summer "Love", a prose poem that won the first prize, "People's Literature" magazine was in "Kyoto Spring" and "Beijing" all "Summer", "Autumn of Kyoto" and "Winter of Kyoto" have sent invitations to Chen Xin several times, but Chen Xin was unable to go because of his work. On the 45th anniversary of its publication, People's Literature once again sent invitations to Chen Xin. Pen will invite. At that time, the prose poem editor of the People's Literature magazine "Green Wind" in Beijing met Chen Xin and said with a smile, " Chen, your prose poem" Midsummer Love "is so good, today, I finally found you..." Chen was very moved. Under the of the most beautiful feelings, it is the heart to cherish each other. In the noisy world, they know each other and respect each other because of words and. When he learned that the prose poem editor of the magazine People's Literature "the green style", through the national first contemporary literary masterpiece selection competition award-winning works "Thousand Chinese New Poets", he gladly discovered, carefully understood and never gave up contact with himself, that 1 kind of appreciation and affirmation made him determined to go through all kinds of ups and downs on the literary road, overcome all kinds of difficulties, and awaken and grow up from it. He contented and motivated, persistent and firm, literature has the dream of his life.

Chen Xin is enthusiastic and dedicated. Over the years, he has devoted all his efforts to journalism and literary creation, making himself and his works shine like stars in the vast night sky. Over the past 40 years, Chen Xin has published many literary works in various newspapers, magazines, radio and television and other media at home and abroad, the country, the province and abroad. leisurely leisurely years, accumulated over time, outstanding achievements. I admire and praise Chen Xin's writing spirit and literary creation spirit. His works are as simple and honest and broad as his people, with a hearty atmosphere, can be elegant, and can also be integrated into the of the people and the soil and water.

Chen Xin's collection of essays, "Wind, Dance, Autumn and in the Sea", was published by Beijing Daily Publishing House in 2021. It was very popular with readers,, and and praised. At the request of readers, it had to be republished in 2024. When I read through Chen Xin's manuscript "Wind Dance Autumn the Sea", I felt that in Chen Xin's poetic prose, there are mountains and boundless expanse. There are majestic, there are still water floating. In the prose, there are small bridges and flowing tenderness, but also high passion surging, showing the deep sinking vicissitudes, the past smoke and clouds. From the article, he has a strong, concrete, everywhere secular heart. The hustle and bustle of the times is enough to crush everything. In the impetuous material world, we are losing 1 a warm feeling of vitality and friendship. He tries to find all this back.

In the prose collection "Wind Dance Autumn the Sea", documentary prose, lyrical prose, traveling prose and micro prose are collected in one book. Humanities and history, mountains and rivers, and warmth in the world are all between the lines. From this, we will weigh the weight of Chen Xin's prose creation. With the deepening of reading, we will also see the highest point of Chen Xin's prose creation level and prose writing skills. Some of the emotions in the prose collection are low-level and tactful, while others are stirring, allowing readers to appreciate a school of men's heart. The prose shows the prestige of a great power and the feelings of family and country. Overflowing with the beauty of splendid mountains and rivers, sublimation, the hometown love, the light of fraternity is sprinkled in the meantime. From the article, it reflects the writer's responsibility and responsibility. He walked into the poetic and affectionate literary world, and at the same time understood how literature is interrelated with life, society and the times.

Literature is connected with the times and empathies with the times. Chen Xin's prose creation involves different creative themes, dabbles in different knowledge levels and fields, enriches his rich writing, and never wanders. That is the difference of 1 spirit. Chen Xin's prose collection "Wind Dance Autumn the Sea" can make readers feel 1 a kind of broad and vast in the reading process, 1 a kind of valuable difficult to, and 1 a kind of vigorous power. In the era of rapid change, writers need to 1 a pair of warm and calm eyes, so as to see era clearly and see the essence of life. Therefore, he focused his brush strokes on the broad society, studied economic issues and people's livelihood issues, revealed the complexity of social relations with an unevasive attitude, and proposed solutions to problems, which was thought-provoking.

The reprint of the book "Wind Dance Autumn Sea" proves the reader's love of "Wind Dance Autumn Sea" and the value of the text. In the prose collection "Wind, Dance, Autumn and the Sea", let's enjoy the tall and straight of Mount in and the vast East China Sea in the prose as beautiful as Chen Xin's poem. Looking forward to the long river, climbing the Great Wall and looking far away; Looking back on the glory of China, see the rise of China today, immemorial!

6 January 2024

(The author is a famous Chinese writer, a member of the Presidium of the Chinese Writers Association, and the chairman of the Hebei Writers Association)

目　录

第一辑　那一方水土风华
The first series that one soil and water scenery

十月辉煌　/　002

October splendor　/　208

遥望新疆　/　006

Looking at Xinjiang　/　214

中国最萌摩天轮——"唐山之光"　/　007

China's cutest Ferris wheel ——"Tangshan Light"　/　215

不散乡愁敲击家乡回响　/　008

does not disperse homesickness hit home echo　/　217

曹操与常新不老的新军屯　/　010

Cao Cao and the New Juntun of Changxin　/　219

辽国汉臣韩昌与韩城　/　012

Han Chang and Han Cheng of Liao Kingdom　/　223

晚霞醉卧龙　/　014

Sunset Drunk Wolong　/　226

漂亮伏击战催生新路开　/　015

Beautiful ambush war gives birth to a new road　/　227

开滦依然　/　016

Kailuan remains　/　229

"八神"落三庄　/　017

"Eight of God" falls to Sanzhuang　/　231

钱塘观潮 / 018

Qian Tong Tide Watching / 232

海南"五腿蛙" / 019

Hainan "5 leg frog" / 233

神游乐 / 020

Shenyule / 234

冬天回味夏日的煤河香 / 020

Winter aftertaste summer river coal fragrance / 235

历代君王与丰润县 / 022

Monarch and Fengrun County in Past Dynies / 236

新军屯集有传说 / 023

New Juntun Collection Has Legends / 238

历代唐山属地 / 024

Tangshan Dependencies in the Past Dynasties / 239

神秘龙潭坨 / 024

Mysterious Tuo of Longtan / 240

千金冶城话今昔 / 025

Qianjin Yecheng Words Past and Present / 241

遵化今昨 / 026

Zunhua yesterday / 242

石市观畸 / 026

Shishi City View Abnormal / 243

追忆尉迟恭大黑马甸智取神马 / 027

Remembering Wei Chigong's Big Dark Horse Dian / 244

三女河 / 028

Three Women River / 245

宋徽宗留迹大安乐庄 / 029

Song Huizong's Remained Da An Le Zhuang / 247

唐宗清帝与唐山与钓鱼台 / 030
Emperor Tang Zong and Qing Dynasty and Diaoyutai / 248

南海北山古丰润 / 031
Nanhai Beishan Ancient Fengrun / 249

喜峰口——《大刀进行曲》的溯源地 / 032
Xifengkou -- The Origin of the Broadsword March / 251

赵国华与心香书院 / 033
Zhao Guohua and Xin Xiang Academy / 252

传于唐抵于今的净觉寺 / 034
Jingjue Temple, which was passed down from Tang to today / 253

老马识途——典故源于唐山 / 035
The old horse knows the way -- the allusion originates from Tangshan. / 255

沧桑还乡河 / 035
The vicissitudes of life return river / 256

梁久功与白官屯 / 036
Liang Jiugong and Bai Guantun / 257

两个蜜桃吃三天 / 037
Two peaches for 3 days / 258

青山关上水门闸 / 038
Qingshanguan Sheung Shui Gate Gate / 259

歪老板的老歪饭店 / 038
Wacky owner's old Wacky Hotel / 260

走进鼓浪屿 / 039
into Gulangyu Island / 261

景忠山的驴 / 040
The Donkey of Jingzhong Mountain / 262

雾灵山览奇 / 041
Wuling Mountain Lange / 263

雾灵山上十八潭 / 043

Wuling Mountain Upper Eighteen Tam / 265

傲岸青山关 / 044

Aoan Qingshan Pass / 267

雄伟泰山 / 045

Majestic Mount Tai / 268

大连灿烂的笑容 / 047

Dalian's Bright Smile / 271

关帝庙　净觉寺　田中角荣留下史话一段段 / 049

Guandi Temple Jingjue Temple Kakuei Tanaka left a historical passage / 274

今昔铁匠庄 / 050

The present and past blacksmith village / 276

萝卜坨 / 051

Turnip / 277

煤河　老铁道　白梁桥　黑石碑　大铁锚 / 052

Meihe Old Railway White Beam Bridge Black Stone Anchor / 279

煤河记忆 / 053

Memories of Coal River / 281

大钿，玲珑美丽的世外桃源 / 054

big twinkle, exquisite and beautiful Xanadu / 283

北武当 / 055

North Wudang / 284

一路风情 / 057

All the way style / 286

梦回唐朝 / 060

Dream Back to Tang Dynasty / 291

唐山，腾飞吧涅槃的凤凰 / 062

Tangshan, take off the phoenix of nirvana / 293

风舞秋海 / 063
wind dance autumn sea / 294

回归 / 064
Regression / 296

皇家窖藏金顶饮 / 065
Royal Cellar Jinding / 297

草原行：康巴诺尔、南天门、卧龙图、闪电湖、
Prairie Row: Cambanor, Nantianmen Gate, Wolong Tu, Lightning Lake, Nine Curves and

九曲十八弯 / 066
Eighteen Bends / 299

"中央大街"的俄罗斯风味 / 079
the Russian flavor of "Central Street" / 315

秋访白羊峪 / 080
Visit Aries Valley in Autumn / 317

白玉山上回眸旅顺口的血泪往昔 / 081
Baiyu Mountain Looking Back at the Blood and Tears of the Past / 319

第二辑　那一方名人风云
The second series of celebrities on that side

雨中访曹公 / 084
Visiting Cao Gong in the Rain / 322

一代才子张佩纶 / 085
generation of gifted scholar zhang peilun / 324

张爱玲与《红楼梦》的不解情缘 / 087
Zhang Ailing and the Indissoluble Love in A Dream of Red Mansions / 327

编剧张爱玲 / 090

Screenwriter Eileen Chang / 331

大刀张凤鸣怒打马县长 / 093

Zhang Fengming, the broadsword, was angry with the and hit the horse county magistrate. / 336

程普与东吴三代君王 / 094

Cheng Pu and the Three Dynasties of Eastern Wu / 337

卢舍那大佛下的遐思 / 095

The Reverie under the Giant Buddha of Lusana / 339

丁开嶂与铁血会 / 096

Ding Kai and Iron and Blood Meeting / 341

皇后诗人萧观音 / 097

Queen poet Xiao Guanyin / 343

老李，英名永驻 / 100

Lao Li, Yingming Yongzhi / 347

英雄无畏排除炸弹 / 101

Hero fearless to eliminate bombs / 349

李清照与"花"与"酒" / 103

Li Qingzhao and "Flowers" and "Wine" / 351

留以清丽照后人 / 105

"Li San thin" / 357

"李三瘦" / 107

1 Beach Gull Heron / 359

一滩鸥鹭 / 108

Screen Uncle Dong Hao / 360

屏幕叔叔董浩 / 109

Sun Fengming, the First to Let Pingju Go Abroad / 364

率先让评剧走出国门的孙凤鸣 / 112

73将士在天英灵俯瞰神州83年 / 113

73 soldiers overlook China in 83 years / 366

金国开国候大刀王信墓迷之千古 / 115

Jin Guo Founding Waiting for Broad Sword Wang Xin Tomb Eternally / 368

清朝第一位汉族皇妃 / 116

The first Han imperial concubine of the Qing Dynasty / 370

高第，经历明三帝 / 118

Gao Di, Experienced Three Emperors of Ming Dynasty / 373

聂耳，与国歌并寿而永垂不朽 / 119

Nie Er, with the national anthem and forever / 376

鲁奖《良宵》张楚 / 120

Lu Award for "Good Night" Zhang Chu / 377

鸡毛信使李盛福 / 121

Chicken Feathers messenger Li Shengfu / 379

新华部队突围在狂风暴雨中 / 123

Xinhua troops break through in the storm / 382

第三辑 悟我心语
The third part of my heart

当写作融入生活 / 128

When writing into life / 386

感谢恩人和自己 / 130

Thank you and yourself. / 389

我心中的毛泽东 / 132

Mao Zedong in my heart / 391

梦中，点燃凤凰泪 / 133

Dream, lit Phoenix tears / 393

昨夜星辰 / 134

Last night's stars / 394

那一年我在中央人民广播电台为灾区捐款点歌 / 134

That year, I donated songs to the disaster area at the Central People's Broadcasting Station. / 395

命运 / 135

Destiny / 396

构思谋篇列车上 / 136

Conceive a piece on the train / 397

多事麦秋那些帮过我的人 / 137

Mai Qiu, those who helped me / 398

写作，作家弥足珍贵的生活方式 / 139

Writing, a writer's precious way of life / 400

仲夏情思 / 141

Midsummer Love / 403

复旦大学作家班，我心中永远的楼兰 / 142

Fudan University writer class, my heart forever Loulan / 404

感悟初冬 / 143

Perception of Early Winter / 406

爱人即爱己 / 144

Love is love yourself / 407

携一抹阳光向善行 / 145

Carry a ray of sunshine to do good / 409

第四辑 别样情怀
The fourth series of different feelings

让情感的光芒闪烁文章中 / 150
Let the light of emotion flash in the article / 414

中国五大姓溯源 / 151
Tracing the Origin of 5 Chinese Surnames / 415

集信，别有情趣 / 152
Collection of letters, don't have fun / 417

看书 / 152
Reading / 418

山村夕阳 / 153
Mountain Village Sunset / 419

我给老爸一叶平凡小舟 / 154
I give dad a leaf ordinary boat / 420

闲云孤鹤 / 155
Idle Cloud Solitary Crane / 421

为了青山那边的小姑娘 / 156
For the little girl on the other side of Castle Peak / 422

诗——我的恋人，我的爱 / 157
Poetry-my lover, my love / 424

父子情深 / 158
Father and son deep / 425

苦乐痴迷道诗心 / 159
Bitter and Happy Obsession Tao Poetry Heart / 426

阅读欢矿 / 159
Huan Mine Reading / 427

那一份关怀 / 160
that 1 care. / 428

景忠山观松 / 161
Guansong, Jingzhongshan / 429

矿工的美弥足珍贵 / 162
The beauty of the miners is precious / 430

妈妈做的倭瓜花儿咸食香 / 163
Mom made pumpkin flowers with salty food / 432

八月十五其乐融融 / 164
Happy 5 August / 433

怀念儿时的"井倍儿凉" / 166
Miss childhood "well Beier cool" / 436

48年前，我们是唐山第一支中学生抗震救灾队伍 / 167
48 years ago, we were the first middle school student earthquake relief team in Tangshan. / 437

月色长城 / 172
Moonlight Great Wall / 444

难忘父亲演奏过的《彩云追月》 / 174
Unforgettable father played "clouds chasing the moon" / 449

48前爸爸那翘望期盼的眼神 / 175
The look in my father's eyes before 48 / 450

笛声响 / 177
flute sound / 452

黑色的歌——为矿工们而作 / 178
The song black —for the miners / 453

阴雨天里那颗颗暖人的心 / 178
the warm hearts in rainy days / 454

给树松绑 / 180
Untie the tree / 456

第五辑 向阳而歌

The fifth series of songs to the sun

向东方　/　184

To the east　/　460

仲夏旭日　/　184

Midsummer Rising Sun　/　460

七月的太阳　/　185

The Sun in July　/　461

你已把我占据　/　186

You have occupied me　/　462

可知我心　/　186

know my heart　/　462

日全食　/　187

total solar eclipse　/　463

天狗　/　187

Tiangou　/　464

不再追随　/　188

No longer follow.　/　464

夕阳　/　188

Sunset　/　465

圆明园　/　189

Yuanmingyuan　/　465

经纬依然　/　189

The longitude and latitude are still　/　466

精灵　/　190

Elf　/　466

一篇获奖散文诗成全了好姻缘 / 190

The 1 award-winning prose poem made a good marriage. / 467

人性的光芒 / 192

The Light of Humanity / 469

朋友，我想对你说 / 193

friend, I want to say to you / 471

拾级七步有乾坤 / 194

Pick up the seven steps have dry Kun / 472

益寿园唱美 / 196

Yishou Garden Sings Beauty / 474

那年去《人民文学》参加笔会 / 197

That year to "people's literature" to participate in the pen / 476

常忆父爱 / 199

Often recall the love of father / 479

从《陈欣作品选》到《风舞秋海》 / 200

From "Selected Works of Chen Xin" to "Wind, Dance and Autumn Sea" / 480

作家陈欣文学艺术成果索引 / 202

Writer Chen Xin Literature and Art Achievement Index / 483

后记 / 204

Postscript / 486

第一辑
那一方水土风华

十月辉煌

1949年10月1日，毛泽东主席庄严向世界宣布"中华人民共和国中央人民政府今天成立了"。礼炮28响。从此，中国屹立在世界东方。

中国人民志愿军，1950年跨过鸭绿江，抗美援朝，打败野心狼，天下美名扬！

20世纪60年代，两弹蘑菇云在大西北升腾，卫星上天使得《东方红》的乐曲声在寰宇经久回荡；第一座武汉长江公路铁路两用大桥，天堑变通途，公路汽车奔驰，铁路列车鸣笛向前方！

一种中近台两面快攻的打法震惊乒坛，在26届（1961年）、27届（1963年）、28届（1965年）世乒赛上，中国人接二连三获得男子单打冠军。鲜红的国旗，在赛场高高飘扬。

20世纪90年代中后期，中国人是世乒赛、世界杯和奥运会男单"大满贯"得主，是男子单打冠军、男子双打冠军、混合双打冠军、男子团体冠军，是乒乓球的标签，是国乒的信仰。让外协在乒乓球领域知道了国乒这个词，让国乒的统治地位不断稳固，让乒乓球不再是一个运动项目，而是国乒的标签深深地印上。

不尽长江从天际走来，源远流长，2006年三峡大坝之水喷薄而出日夜放声歌唱。

亘古不尽的滔滔黄河，从西到东一泻千里，小浪底沉沙阵阵涤荡，奔流入海荡气回肠。

青藏铁路挺进高原之上，那条天路翻山越岭延伸到日喀则身旁，条条巨龙为藏家儿女带来吉祥安康。

中国曹妃甸天然钻石级深水良港，2005年开建，湾阔水深凭船渡，北方大港焕新潮。作为环渤海天然"钻石级"港口，唐山港已建成"一港三区"，下辖京唐港区、曹妃甸港区和丰南港区，成为国家首批渤海沿岸唯一可靠泊40万吨散货船的港口。今天沐浴海上霞光，港口雄开万里流，开通国内外贸易航线110余条，通达全球70多个国家和地区近200个港口。设立内陆港21个，开通至蒙古国乌兰巴托、俄罗斯莫斯科等多条中欧班列，构建了覆盖三北、连通蒙俄、直达欧洲的国际物流运输体系，使得连接全球的货源有了充分保证。2022年货物吞吐量已达8471.6万吨，稳居世界沿海港口前列，成为世界一流综合贸易大港。千帆竞发，百舸争流。北方大港，乘势而上。到2035年，曹妃甸港将成为港产城深度互动融合的第四代国际大港。

2008年，百年奥运、百年世博，让中国人尽情舒展了百年的梦想，华夏子民豪气真爽。

"娜"之花怒放巴黎，网球大满贯，奥网——法网，一路飙狂。

"东风41"人称"快递"，尽领风尚。嫦娥在2014年蛇年冬月（12月14日、15日）飞临广寒宫，玉兔在虹湾区巡视徜徉。

有一种冠军，叫中国女排；有一种情怀，叫中国女排。中国女排艰难起步，平稳过渡，雄霸一方。中国女排，在1984年洛杉矶奥运会、2004年雅典奥运会、2016年里约奥运会上，唯一具备站上领奖台的坚实力量。如绚丽彩虹绽放，震惊世界，势不可挡。

"中国天眼"——500米口径球面射电望远镜，中国自主知识产权、世界最大单口径、最灵敏的射电望远镜。1994年提出构想，历时22年建成，2016年9月25日落成启用。综合性能是射电望阿雷西博的十倍之强，中国人观察宇宙不再迷茫。到2023年已发现脉冲星数量超过740余颗。这样的数字，透着中国天文的响当当！

常驻苍穹的天宫一号，2013年6月11日17时38分，太空拥吻宇宙飞船神舟十号，携手遨游太空不懈求索，更圆世界航天第一人"万户"那六百年的宇宙梦飞翔。天舟一号与天宫二号，2017年4月22日12时23分，太空拥吻，顺利完成自动交会对接。2021年4月29日的海南文昌，长征五号B遥二运载火箭搭载空间站天和核心舱发射升空。2022年底，问天实验舱和梦天实验舱将发射。酒泉卫星发射场，2021年6月17日9时22分，搭载神舟十二号载人飞船的长征二号F遥十二运载火箭点火发射。此后，神舟十二号载人飞船与火箭成功分离，进入预定轨道，顺利将聂海胜、刘伯明、汤洪波3名航天员送入太空，15时52分，神舟十二号载人飞船与空间站对接成功！从此，太空班车开启，中国航天员的太空出差、太空快递将是平常来往长期轮换驻留。2021年10月16日0时23分，中国神舟十三号载人飞船在酒泉卫星发射中心搭乘长征二号F遥十三运载火箭发射升空，乘组成员包括翟志刚、王亚平（女）、叶光富3名航天员。"中国神箭"又一次离弦，让中国空间站完成人员"换班"。2022年6月5日17时42分，神舟十四号飞船成功对接于天宫核心舱径向端口，陈冬、刘洋（女）和蔡旭哲进入中国太空站。2022年12月2日，神舟十五天空员费俊龙、邓清明和张陆顺利进入中国太空站，中国航天员首次太空会合。2023年5月30日18时22分，翘盼已久的神舟十五号航天员乘组顺利打开"家门"，欢迎远道而来的神舟十六号航天员乘组景海鹏、朱杨柱、桂海潮入驻"天宫"。离开祖国家园扶摇直上八百里路云和月，中国太空站三仓三船沐浴不尽阳光。中国空间站，21世纪担当大任，载人漫游太空巡航！

天宫遨游，嫦娥揽月，天问探火，2022年又有墨子号实现1200公里量子传输，夸父一号开启太阳探测之旅。中国人仰望苍穹，心情舒畅。

港珠澳大桥在2018年1月1日全线灯光闪亮，10月23日正式开通。55千米全球超长大桥飞架辽阔伶仃洋，珠港澳大湾区建设浮波踏浪向前方。

2012年9月25日，我国第一艘航空母舰辽宁号交付中国人民海军。2019年12月17日我国第一艘国产航空母舰山东舰在海南三亚某军港交付海军。2022年6月17日上午11时，中国第三艘航空母舰"福建舰"下水。耗时17年，中国进入了三航母时代！21世纪，中国海军飞跃发展，并直接步入到电磁弹射时代，真正的跨越式发展。大航母跨岛链，迎风破浪西出太平洋，双航母深海远航。

2020年伊始，新冠病毒暴虐武汉、湖北，胖妞运-20从天而降，四万官兵和白衣战士迅速就位医院、方舱。激战四个月，大疫无处藏。中国有社会主义制度，有伟大的中国共产党，有众志成城的无比力量，任何困难战无不胜，人民幸福健康！同年，全中国脱贫共小康。

中国天问一号火星探测器携祝融号火星车，2020年7月23日在文昌航天发射场由长征五号遥四运载火箭发射升空，经过长达七个月，累计202天，4.75亿公里的漫长飞行，2021年5月15日7时18分，成功着陆于火星北半球乌托邦平原南部预选着陆区上，孤胆英雄，单枪匹马，踏行在那遥远星球之上。第一次自主进行火星探测任务，接触火星土壤。将来，星际旅行也是中国的设想。

奋斗者号潜航器于2020年11月10日，成功坐底最深处10909米的海沟，创造世界载人深潜的新纪录！聚焦海底寻宝藏。

探月工程嫦娥五号探测器，2020年12月1日23时许成功着陆月面上，经过约19小时月面工作，机械臂表取和钻具钻取两种方式多点、多样化自动采样。12月2日22时，顺利完成月球表采样1731克并保存封装。

探月工程嫦娥五号返回器于2020年12月17日1时59分，在内蒙古四子王旗预定区域成功着陆，标志着我国首次地外天体采样返回任务圆满完成。嫦娥六号于5月3日在中国文昌航天发射场发射升空并进入地月转移轨道。探测器经过轨道修正、近月制动，顺利进入环月轨道飞行。此后，探测器经历着陆器和上升器组合体、轨道器和返回器组合体的分离，在鹊桥二号中继星支持下，着陆器和上升器组合体实施环月降轨及动力下降，于6月2日精准着陆在月球背面南极-艾特肯盆地预选区域并开展采样。中国成为第一个从月球背面取回岩石的国家，并对以后的地外天体采样充满希望。

中华目标是星辰大海，磅礴大气揽月上九天，抱定初心捉鳖下五洋。向海图强、向天图强，向太空图强，成就令全球瞩望。

冬奥之约在2022中国虎年立春，盏然烟花在鸟巢绽放，北京冬奥，冰雪健儿疾驰雪野，飞越山岗，纪录争创，夺金摘银，群情激昂，尽情豪放，中国精神随国旗升起共升华，中华民族无尽畅想。全球观众心绪潮涌，世界冰雪澎湃激荡。歼—35呼啸天宇，万里长空展翅翱翔。

2023年6月15日13时30分，长征二号丁遥八十八运载火箭在太原卫星发射中心拔地腾空，成功将41颗卫星依次释放，准确定轨，提升中国一次发射卫星数量到最多的新台阶之上。

2023年8月29日，华为Mate60 Pro全球首款支持卫星通话的大众智能手机，横空出世。可在没有地面网络信号的情况下，拨打接听卫星电话，对美西方半导体极限打压发起绝地反击，堪称重磅。

中国，5000年前，正智慧面对大洪水荡荡，4000年前，青铜器正趋于辉煌。3000年前，正思考哲学，2000年前，拓土开疆。1000年前，家国无比富足金黄，现在，中国与世界顶尖一较短长。

西电东送，促进经济快速增长。西气东输四线并驾齐驱，龙头昂扬。南水北调滋润华夏，功倍万古永流芳。东数西算，中国又一次在广袤的国土展开大规模的跨区域资源调配顺畅。新丝绸之路，正今非昔比焕发光芒，一带繁花一路开向前方，奋发慨而康。

神州大地，锦绣山河，普照缕缕金色阳光。黄河长江，纵情歌唱。人类的财富，世界的遗产，雄伟的长城，绵延万里起伏跌宕。

中国承载着祖祖辈辈中华先祖的希望，中国实现着中华民族生生不息的理想，中国正强劲迈向富国兴邦。

新中国75年振翅飞翔，56个民族的铮铮铁骨，支撑着中华不曾断档的强盛梦想，14亿人民不懈奋斗为的就是这不尽的荣光。

中国，始终屹立于世界东方，虽经风霜，却不改荣光。我们，正见证着她的又一次伟大复兴。再次崛起，是五千年文明的归航。

中华崛起，倡导人类命运共同体，引领幸福全球共享。

十月，日出江海，梦起东方，长空万里，浩浩荡荡，中国前程更加灿烂辉煌。

注：

中国曹妃甸：唐山曹妃甸世界级深水大港。

万户：明朝人，被誉为"世界航天第一人"。

《十月辉煌》，气势恢宏，大气磅礴。时间跨度从20世纪到21世纪。写出了中华人民共和国白手起家，发愤图强，砥砺前行，百折不挠，实现中华民族伟大复兴的信心、决心和所取得的巨大成就。前沿性科技、世界级工程、重量级突破，令国人自豪、骄傲；令世人惊叹、震撼！通读全诗让读者看到了一个举世瞩目的中国，赞叹东方大国强势崛起，势不可挡。更看到新世纪、新时代中国实现中国梦，创建人类命运共同体的构想、魄力和美好愿望！

这一经典作品深受读者喜爱，更得到了各报纸杂志的欢迎，《中国辉煌》最先以《十月放歌》为题目2017年在《唐山劳动日报》发表。自2019年8月在《精短小说》杂志发表后，陆续被《作家艺术家阳光传媒》《作家文苑》报《唐山文学》杂志转载。还收入了山花出版社出版的《长歌》一书。时至今日八次续写。

遥望新疆

在我很小的时候，参加中国人民解放军的老舅，20世纪60年代服从命令去了遥远的新疆。到了我记事儿时，老舅带着恋人，也就是我的舅母，回到我们这个在曹操当年攻打乌桓前招募操练新军并屯田，随时为前线提供兵源和粮草的地方——河北省唐山市丰润区新军屯来探家。

也许是老舅在新疆的缘故吧，从那时起，我就关注着新疆。20世纪60年代没有电视，但从当时的画报杂志上，我看到了一些关于新疆的画面。也时常从收音机里听到《克拉玛依之歌》《咱们新疆好地方》等旋律优美的歌曲。因而，羡慕老舅去了这迷人的地方。在老舅返回新疆时，我问姥爷，新疆离咱这有多远？姥爷说，坐火车要七天七夜才能到。噢，这么远啊。这样的时空距离，对于小小的我来说好远哪，那时我在想，长大了我也能到这地方该多好哇。看着老舅他们乘坐的汽车远去，直到消失在视线尽头，我仍在望着，久久不回头，像是在追寻遥望着神奇的新疆。

20世纪六七十年代，群众性的文艺活动相当普遍，豪放、大方、洒脱、欢快的新疆歌舞和文艺节目，在内地广泛演出。透过这些，刚上学的我，从中贪婪渴望的遥望着民风热情畅达的新疆。

参加工作后，我的新疆梦依然。《塔里木河》《达坂城的姑娘》是我口中的保留曲目，通过歌唱，抒发心中想往，遥望美丽诱人的新疆。

改革开放后，国家提出开发大西北，我在上大学和进行业余写作的同时，在书籍中翻阅着汉唐时新疆丝路花雨的繁荣，又结交了新疆的文朋诗友，通过这些，遥望充满活力的新疆。

1995年以来，从中央到地方的各种新闻媒介都大量宣传新疆维吾尔自治区成立以来，在农垦、交通、冶金、石化、毛纺、边贸、文教等方面所取得的巨大成就，通过这些，我遥望着欣欣向荣的新疆。

2000年伊始，国家再次提出开发大西北并真正付诸实施。新疆，我的梦乡，我的向往。我终于遥望到我的新疆，西气东输的龙头已翘首东海，你正迎着新世纪的曙光，开动时代快车冲出亚洲；你的蓝天之上银燕翱翔振翅飞向世界的四面八方。

新时代，开发建设一带一路，让新疆重振中亚雄风，更加繁荣向上！

"我走过多少地方，最美的还是我们的新疆"。巴哈尔古丽那清丽动人而高亢的歌声已唱遍华夏神州，更吸引了中国乃至世界的目光，遥望新疆，问询新疆，随之投身，投资建设新疆。

忆往昔，峥嵘岁月稠。七十年，建设发展，各族儿女共圆中国梦。新疆，天山南北，大美新疆，你这充满神奇和蓬勃生机，充满旺盛活力和美好希望的地方，正如东方红日，你的未来绚丽美好令世界瞩望。

中国最萌摩天轮——"唐山之光"

在唐山市丰南区惠丰湖永丰岛上，一座通体洁白，被誉为"中国最萌摩天轮"的"唐山之光"轮摩天轮，高高矗立。"唐山之光"摩天轮底部基座在湖心岛上的惠、丰二桥之间，呈"二龙戏珠"之势。摩天轮基台为汉白玉环面湖梯形观光台，台下的湖中建有声光瀑布和音乐喷泉，与湖北面的大型音乐水幕喷泉隔水相望，交相映辉，成为镶嵌在京东大地的一颗璀璨明珠。

惠丰湖摩天轮建筑一始就闻名遐迩。其"二龙戏珠"巧然天成的独特魅力，更让世人望眼欲穿，久久期盼。摩天轮，在甲辰龙年七月的阳光下，腾空旋转，银光烁烁。湖水荡漾，白云缭绕，美轮美奂。阳光洒在泛起层层涟漪的湖面上，舟船穿梭。惠丰湖边百花竞放，争妍斗艳，摩天轮扶遥直上，徐徐转动，气势恢虹，慰为壮观。

仰视摩天轮，被它的恢弘气势深深地震撼。它高高耸立在惠丰湖心岛上，像一位巨人俯瞰着整个城市，那庞大的身躯，既撑得起唐山标志性建筑的头衔，又体现出一方水土守护神的宏伟气魄。

摩天轮升至最高处，视野辽阔，无垠大地上的无限风光尽收眼底，高空瞭望欣欣向荣的城市、津唐运河两岸的锦绣景色，河头老街大唐盛世的繁荣，仿古建筑楼、舫、庭院，赤檐灰墙，雕梁画柱。宽阔大路上花团绵绣，人流如潮……似梦似幻的飞天感觉，让人身心早已抛开了尘世的喧嚣，进入了一个如梦如幻的童话世界。

如果说白天乘坐摩天轮是一种奇特的体验，那晚上的摩天轮更是引人入胜，别有一番风趣。夕阳西下，夜幕降临，摩天轮像一个巨型的光环，悬空旋转，夜唐山的迷人景色使人目不暇接，美不胜收。惠、丰二拆玉带拱卫，灯光闪耀，像两条飞龙架着"天眼"，邀月揽天。音乐喷泉，声光瀑布，曼妙绮丽。惠丰湖湖面灯光闪烁，游船画舫穿桥而过。游轮的二层平台上，演艺人员载歌载舞，吹拉弹唱，热火朝天。天眼南边的大桥上，银花火树，车水马龙，川流不息。河头老街河道两旁,灯排林立,华灯万盏。廊桥五座沿河伫立,河上灯火通明,熠星映月,金碧辉煌。真可谓是"地上景似锦,苍穹摩天轮,人间仙境现,云中转飞人"。

被誉为"中国最萌摩天轮",作为唐山新地标的"唐山之光"——惠丰湖摩天轮,亦可称之为"京东之光""冀东之光",是一张美丽而又充满魅力的城市名片。

不散乡愁敲击家乡回响

"乡愁"。说到乡愁,我还真是一抹乡愁不散于心中。在一首民歌里的那句"谁不说俺家乡好",一直是我对家乡的念念不忘。我深深地爱着生我养我的家乡,牢牢地记着家乡的人和事。

我的家乡是古老的丰润,曾经北依莽莽燕山,南临滔滔渤海(1961年以前),腹地是广阔的大平原,西南是水草肥美的湿地。这方"丰泽润美"的土地,拥有四千年的历史,两千年的建县史,古称土垠,是一个历史悠久且文化底蕴深厚的古老县域。

光阴荏苒,历史的长河奔流不息,泛着粼粼波光,从三女河、老庄子、杨官林、白官屯、韩城等地出土的石器、骨器、陶器、铜器证明,早在新石器时期,人类就已居住并繁衍生息于此地。从中国古代唐、虞、夏时幽州一路走来的丰润,大地上流淌着还乡河、陡河、泥河,滋润哺育着这一方水土一方人。历史上素有"南无锡、北丰润"之说的丰润,称得上是文化昌明、人才辈出。悠悠岁月里,三国时期曾有过历经东吴三代君王的开国重臣程普;大清国度里没落成一介草民的曹雪芹,老家就在丰润,可就是曹雪芹凭借《红楼梦》这一巨著,登顶了世界级文学巨匠的高峰;晚清那句"南有孙中山,北有丁小川"的话里,丁小川指的就是当时北方国民革命的重要领袖丁开嶂;还有中国早期马列主义的传播者——安体成、国际著名作家张爱玲。新中国成立后涌现了剧作家宋之地、评剧皇后白玉霜、音乐指挥家李德伦、历史学家扬向奎、作家管桦、陈大远、诗人李瑛,等等,这一个个身上闪耀着人性、思想、智慧、勇敢、艺术光芒的杰出人才,是中国各个不同历史时期的著名人物,是国家的骄傲,历史的骄傲,时代的骄傲。

历史的长河,舟帆船影,大江东去,浪淘尽千古风流。生在丰润,就要了解丰润,就要写丰润的山水、人文、人物、往事,还要让更多的人知道丰润。踏着先人的足迹,沐浴着历史的阳光,我曾经在20世纪90年代,骑着自行车,挎着行军壶,背着干粮,独自一人在丰润的乡间行进，两脚勘踏在河流两岸的堤坝之上，头顶烈日爬上北山（燕山）。也曾下到"黑山沟"（张佩纶的墓地所在处），也曾坐在大王庄的街头（大清山东巡抚赵国华的老家），也曾走在古时通往燕京那千年大道已经走成河的土路中，风尘仆仆寻访流年，仔细倾听记录那曾经的人和事，汗流浃背穿越在时光隧道之间。更曾经，90年代在丰润县大齐坨村的田野里，深入早在20世纪60年代已遭掘的大清两广总督张人骏的地下洋灰（水泥，老百姓习惯叫"洋灰"）墓穴，查看墓室结构……

那段时间，只身迎接朝阳升起腰带山，一人送一马平川落日圆。白天辛辛苦苦，晚上孜孜不倦。脑子里回放着汉唐宋元明清时的景象，笔下书写着过去时光的激荡与轩昂。银城铺（赵武灵王始建的土垠城）、大黑马甸（尉迟敬德获神马的地方）、三女河（传说民女跳河的地段）、新军屯（曹操军屯的地点）、韩城（韩昌建帅府、设立点兵场的地方）、龙潭坨（有传奇色彩的村庄）心香书院（清代有名的书院，大清山东按察使赵国华所建）……

程普、尉迟敬德、曹操、宋徽宗、韩昌、曹雪芹、张佩纶、赵国华、张爱玲……

要写的事源源不断，要写的人纷至沓来。这些丰润过去的事情和传说；这些过去丰润的历史和人物，以及与丰润有关的故事、历史、人物，都是丰润历史发展的见证，都是丰润成长之树上独一无二的片片树叶，而且是其他地方所没有的，色彩缤纷的。那年那月那苍茫，那人那事那时光，流于笔端，跃然屏幕，呈现在国家、省、市各级报纸之上。

我的一本书里面，记述着过去南管海北管山的大丰润古往今来的一些人和事，还有一些让人难以忘却的历史瞬间。

我走过了许多地方，静下心来想一想，我还是最爱我的家乡，乡风乡情乡音，一直在我心海里荡漾。家乡历史风云里的那些人和事，是我久久的不能遗忘。我在书的前言里以题为《我拿什么奉献给你》这样写道："赤裸裸来到这世上，苍天却给我以滋润的雨露和温暖的阳光；游云给我以向往与遐想；大地给我赖以生长所需的五谷杂粮；山峰让我领略挺拔高昂；江河让我得知血脉流长。可是，我这一微乎其微的宇宙尘埃，拿什么来奉献给你——大地、上苍。只有将我这一点微不足道的认知、领悟、情感，还有一颗感恩的心，流于笔端，虔诚奉上。

故乡，这片古老而又永远年轻的土地，是我出生、成长、学习过的地方。我深深地爱着生活在这里的人们，还有这块可爱的一方水土。弹指一挥间，再回首：故乡大道宽广，新城大钟声传四方，处处新气象。十八离家老大还，我曾经豪情万丈，归来更让我心情激荡。借此也把这本书献给亲人、师长、同窗，献给亲爱的故乡。"

*丝丝*乡愁，淡淡萦绕。已是夏日，树影婆娑，晚风习习，我将继续以文字敲击家乡的回响。

曹操与常新不老的新军屯

丰润县志载："三国时期曹操曾在此地屯兵招募新军。"

"凿渠通海谋略深，曹公北上起征尘。无终平霸安百姓，募兵留迹新军屯。时逢大雨阻军道，幸得田涛为路人。卢龙古寨旌旗过，柳城平虏尽称臣。"这是大明朝万历年间，一个名叫常元庆的知州来到新军屯时留下的抒怀诗句。诗中提到的曹公就是东汉丞相曹操，是一个妇孺皆知的人物。他统一中国北方、推广屯田制，对巩固国家疆界、扩大版图都有一定的贡献。

东汉献帝（刘协）建安年（公元190—219年）间，丞相曹操在江下实施屯田制取得成功后，便在全国特别是边塞地区大力推广屯田制，或募兵垦荒或募民种田。就是政府利用军队驻扎的地区种地，或招募农民来种田，目的都是为取得军队给养、垦荒戍边。建安五年（公元200年），曹操统大军打败袁绍。建安十年（公元205年），袁绍子袁尚败走河北逃往乌桓，投靠乌桓单于楼班幼。

东汉时期的乌桓民族以游牧射猎为主，驰骋旷野，生性凶猛，能骑善射，疆域辽阔。那时，今天的卢龙至北京以北也就是当时的上谷、辽东、辽西大片土地皆属乌桓。当年曹操最初谋划在建安十二年（公元207）夏秋间由卢龙塞出击乌桓时，就考虑到战争前线的后续兵源和粮草供应问题。

那时的新军屯（今唐山市丰润区新军屯）有古道穿泥河跨浭水（今还乡河）分别可达通州、燕京（今北京）及中国北方。地处广阔肥沃平原，往北8里（今唐山市丰润区郑八庄村）是河面宽阔的泥河，往西8里（今丰润区大坎村）还是奔流不息入渤海的泥河，往南8里是大片的沿海滩涂湿地沼泽，从地理位置上讲，是募兵屯田、养精蓄锐、保障前线粮草供应及兵源提供的好地方。从战略意义上讲，对日后攻打乌桓有极其重要的战略意义。于是，曹丞相就在这里设立军屯招募新兵，边屯田边练兵，以备战时兵源补充。在以后打败乌桓，统一北方，加强东汉统治的过程中，可以说，新军屯发挥了地理和兵源优势，在某种意义上起到了积极重要的军事作用，在历史发展的进程中留下了一笔，对中国北方的统一做出了自己的贡献。这就是新军屯，一个常新不老的地方。

在历史的长河中，新军屯（早有村，名不可考）几经兴废，但汉代以来新军屯的建筑基址一直未变。整体布局是在一个地势较高的正十字街区之上。这种建筑地势选择方式，在建筑学上是汉代开创并开始流行的。所以，新军屯自古有"天上下雨四街流，百姓吃粮不用愁"的说法一直流传到今天，也更印证了新军屯始建于汉代和地势较高的史实。旧时的新军屯整个城区呈正方形，意在堂堂正正，面向四面八方，人称"方城"。城区以十字路口为龙头，东南西北四条主大街，八条次道，二十四条胡同，古时有四座城门分别为紫气东来门、鎏金西兆门、南极生辉门、拱星北辰门（均毁于抗日战争时期）。城门由古老厚重的双扇炮钉大木门、石门槛和两侧雕琢精美的石门礅构成，简洁、明快，便民通行。城门之上有城门楼，高大雄势，四门上金色辉煌的大字彰显着独特的地域文化，展现着古城的俊俏与凝重。连接四门的是端正的石砌码基、砖砌的城墙，体现着当年曹操屯兵屯粮的安全防范意识。在古城内有一道奇特的景观和现象：四条主街、次街与胡同贯通，形成了路路纵横交错、巷弄左右逢源、进出方便自如的格局。城门关闭后，人们可以穿行于城内胡同之间，来往于各家各户，行走于大街小巷之中。更令人叹为观止的是，不熟悉地形地貌的外地人，只要沿着任何一条街巷行进，不用担心迷路，准能返回原地。这一奇特现象，不知是先民设计理念超前，还是因地制宜顺势而建，抑或是出于战事的考虑，能进能出、能攻能守。

有关形似迷宫但又不是迷宫的布局，至今仍是一个难解的谜团。这些印迹着岁月沧桑的古街古巷，有的至今犹存，有的却早已毁于战火、"文革时期"或唐山大地震。在坚固雄伟的城郭外，有一条宽、深各约2米的环城壕沟，城壕上还有吊桥，是预防外敌入侵、完全出于防范采取的安全措施。在城外距四街城门约300米处均设有一座大石板桥，每座桥长3米、宽3米、高3米，它既是通往古城市井的必经之路，又是环城水系。每到雨季，环城水流潺潺，满沟鱼虾浮游，显现出生态自然的和谐与靓丽。新军屯东西南北四街街头均有一座庙宇，东门外的三官庙供奉福、禄、寿三仙；西门外的火神庙，供奉灶王爷；南门外的观音庙，供奉观世音菩萨；北门外的关帝庙，供奉关帝。这些修建于唐代的庙宇，为信奉各路神仙的信众提供了朝拜敬香的一块神奇的净地。至今民间仍然流传着："四庙镇街头，水往四处流。官家不长久，富贵不到头"的顺口溜。

故城西门外还有一座著名的"心香"书院，是清朝时的山东知府赵国华亲自选址并督建的。新军屯街市建筑颇具古风，房屋飞檐斗拱，前廊后厦，雕梁画栋。市面上买卖商号、酒烧锅、中医堂、医药铺、酒馆儿、饭馆儿比比皆是，商贾云集。使之成为明清以来丰润南半县较大的集镇。

20世纪60年代初，随着丰润县第一化肥厂在新军屯建成，当时的人民公社书记张济民，组织并带领人民群众把古老的护城河重新开挖出来，河水环绕小城流过，最终西经泥河入渤海，使小城焕发青春再现风韵。可惜的是，1976年大地震把这座古老的城镇夷为平地，地上建筑一切皆无。但在党和政府的关怀支持下，一座社会主义新型小城镇又在这里崛起，20世纪90年代，当时的镇党委在上级领导的支持下，积极争取国家把新军屯列为丰润县两座重点规划小城镇之一。2002年借助唐山至通州省级公路拓宽改造的机遇，又将东西大街路面由原来的20米扩展到40米。笔直宽阔的道路两旁，一座座造型新颖，建筑新潮别致的楼房拔地而起，七层楼高的钟楼高高矗立。政府、医院、购物大厦、百货大楼、小学、初中、高中教学大楼，一座比一座建筑漂亮，新型社区住宅楼不断建起，充满一派勃勃生机。为适应小城经济建设和交通发展需要，还修建了一条南外环路。今天的新军屯，是一个集文教卫生、工业农业、商业贸易、电信邮政为一地的建制镇。高楼林立，交通便捷，市容市貌一天天美起来靓起来，跻身于中国名镇行列之中。唐（山）通（县）、新（军屯）宝（坻）公路从城中穿过，与城东相距7.5公里是京哈高速公路出口，与城西相距2.5公里是丰润天津快速公路。唐山市116路公交车，丰润区内8路、2路公交车都在这里经过，是一个远近闻名的重镇名市。建于汉，兴于明、盛于清的新军屯历经风雨岁月千百年，逐渐步入繁荣与富庶。

今天试想，孟德公当年初建新军屯时，也许并未对新军屯的将来想得太多，只是出于战争需要把它当作一个军事基地。孟德公若能看到今天新军屯的新面貌和喜人景象，也许会心潮起浮，感慨万千，挥毫再写一首《万里行》吧。

辽国汉臣韩昌与韩城

从唐山市中心向西10公里处，有个叫韩城的地方。原属丰润县，丰润区，今属唐山市路北区。根据20世纪70年代筹建开滦东欢坨矿开挖地基时，当地的出土文物考证，早在我国春秋战国时期，这里就已经有人居住并形成了村落，因年代久远村名已无从查考。但在文字材料中我们还可以看到有关于韩城的只言片语。清代的《丰润县志》古迹篇中有这样的记述："韩城镇，《奉使行程录》，镇有居民可二百家，并无城。"另有《遵化通志》载：金大安元年（公元1209年）改永济县为丰润县，同时设立韩城镇，为当时的蓟州玉田县辖。

说到韩城，不能不提到历史上的韩德让。韩德让也就是从古到今人们所熟知的韩昌。他的祖籍是玉田，他的祖上早就入辽为民，虽为汉人，却含辛求进且慢慢混出了一点儿名堂来。其祖韩知古，其父韩匡嗣，均为辽国大官，渐渐的韩家在大辽国也算是名门望族了。大辽国的统治者较为开明，允许臣民与汉人通婚。所以，才有日后的萧太后少年时曾经是韩德让的未婚妻这档子事儿。

大辽国统和元年六月（公元983年），幼年的辽圣宗（耶律隆绪）即位，萧太后听政执掌国事。这位历史上叱咤风云的铁娘子，可说是义气重情。萧太后没有忘记早年自己曾经许嫁韩德让（韩昌），那时正巧景宗（耶律贤）求婚，她心里非常清楚皇权大如天，不可冒犯。无奈，她只得嫁入宫中后来便成了皇后。怎奈，老夫少妻不长久，景宗死（大辽国乾亨四年九月，公元982年），萧太后怀念旧情，召韩德让（韩昌）入宫中为萧太后所宠，总领宿卫。使其成为自己的得力助手，私下对韩昌说："吾常许嫁子，愿偕旧好，则幼主当国，亦汝子也。"此时，韩昌处于监国地位，统和元年加封韩德让（韩昌）开封同三司，兼事政令，并让他积极参与南下攻打大宋的大小战役。大辽统和二十二年九月（公元1002年），大辽和北宋订立了历史上有名的澶渊之盟后，喜形于色的萧太后觉得，韩昌（韩德让）在攻打大宋的战役中和迫使大宋议和的事情上功劳不可磨灭，欣然赐韩德让（韩昌）辽国姓耶律，还改封韩德让（韩昌）为晋王，到这时，韩昌官至大丞相，总知南北院枢密使，集军政大权于一身。统和二十八年（公元1010年）又赐名隆运。这样，韩昌（韩德让）的辽国姓名就是耶律隆运了。在萧太后的关照下，耶律隆运（韩昌，韩德让）地位在大辽国的亲王之上。在大辽国自统和元年到统和二十年间（公元983年—公元1002年）六次对北宋的大规模战争中，萧太后大多是让韩昌（韩德让）参赞军机，在南下攻打大宋的大业之上，给予韩昌（韩德让）以广阔的空间和才能发挥的极大平台，使得韩昌（韩德让）能够在疆场驰骋自如，充分展示发挥了他大战运筹帷幄的军事才能和征战谋略。

由于当时连年不断的辽宋战争，在大辽强大的南下攻势下，北宋不得不屡屡败退，使得大辽国和北宋王朝的交界地不断向南移，两国交界曾在今天的天津海河、河北霸县（今霸州市）、山西雁门关一带。那时，当大辽国军队打到今天的韩城所在地之时，身为大辽国三军大元帅的韩昌，望着缓缓南流的猪龙河和南面指日可待的大宋土地，不禁心生感慨，打到祖籍家乡啦。因为，韩昌祖籍玉田，当时这里正为玉田辖地，可谓是"荣归故里"。心胸舒展，长出一口气，休整一下，养精蓄锐，以利再战。随即安营扎寨，大军营盘扎在了这里，号令三军将士和当地百姓，人人运土搬砖，堆砌起了一座高大气派的辽军点将台（今韩城小学）。韩昌（韩德让）还在自己的帅府驻地建起了一座雄伟的韩昌府，以示光宗耀祖和灭宋的气概。

随着岁月流逝，光阴荏苒，千百年弹指一挥间。韩昌府早已无迹可寻，点将台上的原有建筑也已荡然无存，可高高的点将台依然犹在，点将台上早已建成了韩城小学，点将台下的练兵场已成为韩城小学的大操场和韩城第一幼儿园。

历史一段段，人物一个个，历史的大舞台上走马灯似的你方唱罢我登场。转眼间，辽衰金盛。金时，今丰润地为永济县，今韩城属永济县。到金卫绍王时，为避金卫绍王完颜永济之名讳，朝廷下令改永济县为丰闰（明朝改为润）县。想必，金卫绍王完颜永济，在金大安元年（公元1209年）改永济县为丰润县并设韩城镇时，也许，就是基于这段历史流传才定名此地为韩城。

晚霞醉卧龙

前不久，我的一个朋友出版了一本名叫《卧龙圆梦》的图书，浏览其中，被其感染，总想一见卧龙真颜。为了便于游览，查阅了一些关于卧龙山的有关资料。得知，卧龙山在遵化市区东南二十公里的娘娘庄乡，连绵起伏的山峰，酷似巨龙横卧。山间林木苍翠，清泉圣水。果树拦腰，松柏戴帽，是一个令人神往和瞩目的地方。长久以来，由于当地的人们从山南看其龙头酷似一只鞋底的模样，所以，俗称鞋底山……看到这些，兴致顿起，于是，邀上作家协会的好友一行十三人，在9月12日下午4点，从唐山市西山口驱车前往，一路疾驶。到达境内，马不停蹄，驱动车轮，加油在蜿蜒、曲折、迂回的卧龙山山路上行驶，直达山顶的腾龙寺前停下。下得车来，站在山上俯视四周。眼见得卧龙山由西向东，自古山势为龙，有形有势，雄奇磅礴。满山松柏繁茂，郁郁葱葱；山花烂漫，争奇斗艳；怪石嶙峋，奇特峥嵘。

遵化市卧龙山旅游开发有限公司经理王洪成接待了我们。并向我们介绍了卧龙山的来历，他说："相传，东海龙王受玉皇大帝之旨，巡视天下，体察民情，观其民间疾苦。当游历此地上空的时候，只见灾荒遍野，民不聊生。随即派其第九子貔貅来此安抚。貔貅耕云播雨，遍洒雨露甘霖于人间。从此以后，这里的穷乡僻壤变成了山清水秀、美丽富饶的山乡。为保一方百姓平安，貔貅变化成一座山，日夜驻守于此，忠诚守护着这一带的百姓，由于形似卧龙，故取名卧龙山。"

站在腾龙寺外东面的空地上，时年76岁的王洪成老人指引我们远看四面的山峦说："从这里向东南西北远远望去，可以看到六重山峦，层层叠叠状似莲花，腾龙寺所在的山头正处在连花心的位置，腾龙寺就建在了这莲花心儿上。"听了老人的提示，我环顾四周，仔细欣赏，还真的是像老人说的一样，酷似莲花瓣一般的层层山峦，包围着我们脚下的山峰。我们跟随老人走进腾龙寺，王洪成老人指点着山下的一处处景点，向我们做着介绍。我们顺势看去，不禁感叹，大自然的鬼斧神工造就了卧龙山的龙头峰、龙脊峰、龙腹峰、龙乳峰、龙尾峰，五峰相连，如巨龙横卧吞吐于山海之间。可叹时间短暂，意犹未尽，未能看遍景点，游遍卧龙山，遍览风光。

今年的秋天来得早，9月12日的傍晚，在卧龙山中那美丽的晚霞里，我们仍然感觉到丝丝凉意。但西方天边那红彤彤的晚霞，沐浴着大地上的群山和寺院，映照在腾龙寺的红墙和金黄琉璃瓦上，显得是那么的灿烂辉煌，那么的沁人心扉，让我痴迷，让我深深地陶醉。

漂亮伏击战催生新路开

唐山至新军屯的公路，是唐山至通州这条省级公路的重要路段，也是唐山市通往市辖西部地区及天津市一些村镇的必经之路。然而，八十年来，这条与八路军游击队的一场伏击有极大关联的公路经历了几多变迁，才有今天这宽阔平坦的模样。

20世纪40年代，在中国人民艰苦卓绝的抗日战争时期，日本帝国主义在疯狂残害中国和亚洲人民的同时，妄图扑灭中国人民包括唐山人民的抗日火焰，建立所谓的大东亚共荣圈。然而，拖不垮打不烂的唐山人民，在中国共产党的领导下，不屈不挠展开了灵活机动的游击战，抗击着日本侵略者。唐山的冀东八路军游击队曾多次在韩城的日军据点以西设埋伏袭击日军，而直接关系到这条道路部分路段改道的原因，是游击队一次成功袭击日本军车车队的战斗。

那是1942年冬季的一天，八路军游击队事先根据有关情报得知，日军有几辆运送人员和物资的军车要从唐山市里开往新军屯的日军据点。为了消灭日军破坏他们的给养供应，我们的八路军游击队，便在沿途的西欢坨村中路段严密布置悄悄设下埋伏，等待从唐山市里开往新军屯日军镇据点的日本军车。当时唐山到新军屯的道路，都是一路穿庄而过的，这也为伏击提供了掩护。这天上午十点多日军三辆军车开进埋伏圈，指挥员一声令下，游击队员们拉响地雷、投掷手榴弹、手枪步枪一起开火。真是晴天霹雳，如同天降神兵，打得日军措手不及，根本来不及组织下车反击，军车忽然起火。燃烧的军车上鬼子兵无一幸免全部死亡，三辆军车上的物资被全部烧毁，这次战斗给日军带来一次不小的打击，人力财力物力上都造成了损失。从此，穷凶极恶的日军一怒之下，下令把唐通路上韩城至新军屯这两处日军据点之间的一段十八里的道路全部改道出庄，以免再遭伏击。于是，强迫大量民工改修新道。从东欢坨一、二、三、四村、西欢坨、小庄子、王道庄等村庄里全部统一改到庄南，并严令沿线各个村庄的老百姓不准在道路两旁种植高粱、玉米等高大农作物，以防里面藏匿八路军游击队再次伏击日军。从哪儿以后，唐通线上韩城至新军屯这段路便迁出了村外。直至中国人民打败了日本帝国主义，道路两旁才重现高粱玉米等高大作物的影子。现在，80多岁的老人们回想起那时的情景，还历历在目，讲起那时抗日的事情也津津乐道。

新中国成立后，国家和政府多次拨款对这条唐通线上的唐山到新军屯路段进行调整、翻新、拓宽。从一开始的黄土路到后来的石渣路，再到柏油路。1976年唐山大地震之后，唐山市政府为了适应城市、社会、经济、建设发展的需要，又把穿过刘火新庄、郭家庄、袁家庄、韩城这一段一并调到村南和原唐山市第二农机厂南门外，并将路面加宽取直，还把这条路定为文明路段。

改革开放后由于唐山的不断发展建设，特别是2003年，在唐山西外环高速公路修好的同时，重又把刘火新庄至韩城镇这一段路再次一律在庄南开辟新路，与唐山市北新西道直接对接，拓宽路面为双向四车道。在新的形势下唐山经济建设形势的迅猛发展，2012年，唐山市政府又一次拓宽刘火新庄至韩城镇这一段路为双向六车道。2023年，再次对唐通线韩城段进行升级改造。从而，使这条唐通线上的重要路段，进一步发挥了对唐山市城乡建设、货物贸易流通、公路运输等事业的促进作用。也更加充分地发挥了这条省级公路，在京津冀经济一体化和协调发展上的积极作用和潜在能力。在抗战胜利79周年之际，回首艰苦卓绝的十四年抗日战争，展望新中国建设成就，憧憬中国梦和中华民族伟大复兴，不免心生慰藉。

开滦依然

望高天流云，看煤河长流，追寻开滦（1878年—2024年）跨越三个世纪历史岁月的回响。

长队毛驴驮来的银子，大清朝子民的汗珠子，见证着中国人不息的自强。中国大地上第一台蒸汽机车的第一声汽笛，拉开了中华民族工业的徐徐大幕。开平煤矿滚滚的乌金，燃烧起腾腾火焰，鼓舞着晚清北洋舰队那亚洲第一大舰队的雄威强壮。

建设新中国、抗美援朝、建设中国特色社会主义、实现中华民族伟大复兴，各个阶段无不有你——开滦的卓绝贡献，从未断"特别能战斗"的歌声嘹亮。

十九世纪建起的第一座开滦矿务局办公大楼，至今高高矗立在海河之滨倾听海河的日夜吟唱。

秦皇岛港东升的朝阳，目睹中国第一个煤码头的建立与兴旺、唐山港煤码头昼夜奔忙、曹妃甸港区更在迎接中国第一大煤码头的辉煌。

蔚州实现煤电路一体化；内蒙古大草原已看到开滦骑上奔驰的骏马；开滦之歌在伊犁河畔回荡；加拿大的土地上也有开滦的旗帜在高高飘扬。

一轮朝阳升起，一只鹏鸟展翅，一艘航船扬帆。多少年风雨兼程，多少次鼓起勇气放飞，多少回阳光下无尽的畅想。

看，长天云卷舒，地广马奔驰。开滦，与时俱进奋发昂扬。做大做强，搞活开放——圆146年开滦雄浑的梦想。

开滦，21世纪青春依然，活力依然，浩气依然。"新时代"新步伐，面向未来，一路充满灿烂热望。

"八神"落三庄

传说，古代丰润县一个村庄上住有八位神仙，所以，人们就把这村庄叫做八神庄。

八位神仙由于长居此地，时常感到有些寂寞。于是，八位神仙坐在一起大家一商议，便决定结伴出游。在一个晴朗的日子里，他们出发了。众神仙一路飘然而行，不觉来到一个叫四姓庄的地方，有位神仙建议停下来歇歇脚。大家就在一棵古树下席地而坐，赏景闲谈起来。歇了一会，几位神仙起身要走，不想有四位神仙由于喜欢这里的乡间景色，执意不肯再走。无奈，另四位神仙只得告别他们继续前行。他们走了一段路，又来到一个村庄歇了下来。过了一会儿，他们中的一个灶神，提出继续向前赶路，可另三位神仙却不想再走了，只是笑望着灶神，灶神看着他们问："你们怎么光笑不走哇？"三位神仙答道："我们看这里的风光也不错，打算住在这里了。"灶神一听急了："原来你们都商量好啦！那好，你们不走我走！"说完，他自己气呼呼地走了。他独自没着没落地走了一程，感到有些乏累，也觉得没啥意思，这时，不远处正好有个村庄，在夕阳残照下映入他的眼底，灶神索性住在了这个村上，从此，该村遂得名灶神庄。住四神的庄就叫四神庄，住三神的就叫三神庄，八位神仙的出发地就叫八神庄了。现在，这几个村庄都在，皆属唐山市路北区管辖。

2024年1月8日

钱塘观潮

"八月十八潮,天下壮观无。"钱塘潮乃天下奇观,去年农历八月中旬,我出差杭州,有幸一睹,实为幸哉。

那天,我们一大早就从杭州驱车前往海宁县的盐官镇。这里濒临杭州湾,海潮至此汹涌澎湃。镇东南海堤为观潮胜地,有观海台、观潮亭、镇海塔等建筑。潮头到此齐列一线,为"海宁宝塔一线潮"之壮景。我们来到这里已是人山人海,费了九牛二虎之力,好容易把车开到一家旅馆。江边,等待观潮的人中,黑皮肤、黄皮肤、白皮肤;金发、白发、黑发……真是万头攒动。

钱塘潮中午一次半夜一次。夏令时十三点,我们直视前方。在天水一线处,像是一条银龙横卧,随后有很大的声音传来,继而,雪浪冲天、海水倒立。一堵近三米高的褐黑色水墙呼啸而来,齐头并进,如万马奔腾,让人感到惊心动魄。难怪有人观潮后在诗中这样写道:"转瞬水墙筑海上,轰雷闪电鬼神愁!水墙流滚滚齐头涌,汹涌奔腾若貔貅。"

钱塘潮为什么如此壮观呢?这是因为杭州湾出口处,地形是个喇叭口。海潮涌来,潮锋宽度急骤收窄,能量集中,流速加大,致使潮头越来越高,出现这翻江倒海的壮景,据当地人说:近年来,由于海湾地区进行围海造田,大潮的壮观度不及以前了。但对于我这个从未见过大江大浪的内地人来说,如此景色还是叹为观止的。

1987 年 10 月 4 日

海南"五腿蛙"

人都说天底下三条腿的蛤蟆不好找,可我倒是见过了五条腿的青蛙。

那是1981年,我在海南岛海口的时候,星期天没事,时常去逛公园。一次看过孔雀开屏之后,不觉来到一个笼罩前,笼下一池清水,有一人工砌成的小石洞露出水面。咦!这是啥动物?怎么不见动静?抬头去看笼上挂着的牌子,哈,原来写的是青蛙。再细看下文却使我耳目一新,大意是:此蛙,是世所罕见的"五腿青蛙",雄性。若今后有发现此类青蛙者,敬请送至园来,以配成双,繁衍后代,供人观赏云云。

说实在的,这五条腿儿的青蛙还是真的从来没有见过。我们几个人瞪大双眼等待观看,可就是不见它出来,真急人。等了好一会,大神青蛙终于出世了。只见它站在小洞边,好一副大模大样的架势:后两腿蹲,前双腿撑,下颚底下又多出一腿撑于石上。我们看了好笑的纳闷,莫非是这青蛙头太重才多出一条腿儿来撑着?大家见此怪模样不觉哈哈大笑起来。哪料得,这一笑可坏了,青蛙把下颚那只腿往前一伸,稍后的两只前腿合十,两后腿一蹬,一头扎进了水中。不一会儿又浮出水面,瞪着两只大眼睛看着眼前的世界。我们静静地观其形态,它与一般青蛙一样,只是前单腿随右侧前腿行动。怪哉,怪哉!令我们一饱眼福。只是遗憾,那时手里没有相机拍下这难得的镜头。

1989年9月9日

神游乐

每个人都有自己的业余爱好，我的一个业余爱好是收集旅游图。一段时间我在物资供应单位工作，外出机会多，而且面广地域宽，采购点和厂家遍布全国。

正是由于有这一有利条件，每逢我出差办事，除留心各地风土人情，习俗传统外，还注意购买当地旅游图，以备收藏。本单位别的同志出差办事或开会，我总忘不了让他们捎回一张旅游图来。日积月累，现在，我的写字台抽屉里已存了差不多两抽屉各地旅游图、旅游交通、旅游食宿图等。其中，有繁华都市，有偏僻城镇；有名山大川，有幽谷仙境；有美丽海滨，有浩瀚大漠；有革命圣地，有名人故居。每当茶余饭后，闲得空来，我总要打开抽屉翻翻这些旅游图，也使得疲劳的心绪得到一点调剂。现在，我收藏的旅游图遍布祖国江南塞北，长城内外。踏丝绸之路可去西域，登万里长城可东到渤海，乘北上列车可到内蒙古、新疆，坐南下客轮可到天涯海角。真可谓安坐斗室，便可神游九州，美哉，乐哉。

1989 年 12 月 17 日

冬天回味夏日的煤河香

立冬之后又过小雪几天了，初冬的风刮起来，城市中的杨树、柳树、法国梧桐等树上还长着许多叶子，一片片黄黄的杨树叶和银杏树叶飘荡着。抬头看天，蓝蓝的，飘着几丝游云，感觉有些瘦冷。楼下，剪草机秋末剪过的草坪犹如一张偌大的地毯般铺展开着，仍然有些毛感的柔美，草地间有些败落的红黄白紫各色月季花，还在不愿舍弃最后一缕暖阳，挣扎着绽放在阳光下。一簇簇西粉莲的花朵又是那么惹人眼目深情而鲜活的开放着，甬道边垂柳的柳丝摇荡在微风之中。站在房间里，瞩目阳光下的静静煤河，回味她夏日的芬芳。

煤河，这条开挖于大清帝国光绪六年（公元1880年），东西横贯于当今胥各庄（清，河头镇）这座小城的人工河流。沐浴晨光，泛着粼粼波光，静静地向西流淌。那还是7月初的一个清晨，我走向煤河边的带状公园。

这个时节，正是合欢花盛开的时节。还没走近河边的绿化带，阵阵沁人心扉的合欢花香味儿就扑鼻袭来。不觉中，深深吸了几口气，以让身心感受这浓郁的芳香。走到合欢花树下驻足，抬头仰望。树枝上，稀疏绿色的小叶间，开满了一朵朵粉红色放射状球形合欢花，绒绒的花球淡而鲜艳，花蕊紧凑而奔放。树下小空场里，一群中年男女，随着音乐舞动手中的三尺长剑，那么张弛有节，轻松自然。

继续往前走在河边，只见一棵合欢花树的枝杈探向岸下，绽放的合欢花，显得那么烂漫。一位老者安坐在这美景之中，放竿垂钓，那么自在悠然。站在不远处欣赏，这个镜头像是一幅画很是好看，说是煤河一景，可谓理所当然。

煤河两岸绿化带里的树木间甬道边，一片片草坪布满，草坪上一棵棵小草，像是一个个小矮人儿似的站在那里挺直傲岸，头上还顶着一个个晶莹剔透的小露珠儿，在晨光中显得十分逗人可爱。我不禁蹲下身来仔细观看，一阵青草香的气息迎面升起，这是一种大自然的气息，置身其间，一种心足意满。不远处，一位老人正在强身练拳，腾挪闪展。在这个氛围里，人和自然和谐相伴。

漫步在河边的树木草地甬道中，间或可见一片片矮株的小花，在这盛夏之时，它们不甘寂寞，粉色的红色的踊跃开放，离地不高却开得很是旺盛，并散发着一股股淡淡的花香，奉献美丽于人间。与其临近的小空场儿上，一群运动装的女人们在整齐排列着时而跳动，时而有节奏的拍打身体的不同部位，时而舞动腰身。看着她们个个面带笑意，正像那一朵朵小花一般，快乐而淡然，平淡而灿烂。

站在煤河带状公园，自西向东极目纵观。社区高楼分立两边，人们生活平静恬淡。今日的煤河已是144年了，虽无清末的帆影舟船，但滨河大道笔直而宽，带状公园里的花草树木一派生机盎然，华北平原上的冀东小城和小城人的梦想画卷，也在这盎然芳香中得到不断舒展和实现。

历代君王与丰润县

丰润，是今天唐山市的一个区，古称土垠县。说到土垠县，又涉及战国七雄之一赵国的赵武灵王（公元前325年—公元前299年在位）。赵武灵王在公元前325年成王，在赵国大胆进行军事改革，胡服骑身，强军兴国，攻灭中山，打败林胡、楼烦，建立云中、雁门、代郡，其疆域包括今山西中北部、陕西东北部、河北西南部及河套地区，国势大盛。也就是这位赵武灵王，通过强国之间的换地形式在浭阳河（今还乡河）上游建筑了土垠城（原址在今唐山丰润区银城铺，垠城演绎银城，后演变银城铺），后为土垠县城。

公元前202年，汉高祖刘邦（公元前206—公元前193）置土垠县，县城就是土垠城。北齐（公元550—577年），高洋（古渤海人，即今河北井县人）这位北齐的建立者，公元550—559年在位时，改元天保，任用汉人，改定律令。连年出击柔然、突厥。土垠城废于兵燹，天保八年（公元557年），迁民聚堡，设永济务，取"粮草丰盛，永济不断"之意，属徐无县。金世宗完颜雍大定元年（公元1161年）由完颜福寿等发动政变，拥其为帝。改元大定。元年十二月派重兵侵宋。五年（公元1166年）南宋被迫求和。战争结束后注意发展农业生产，在位二十九年，农业、手工业都有不同程度的发展，仓廪有余，号称"小尧舜"。大定五年（公元1166年）动土兴建永济县城，即今丰润县城。大定二十七年（公元1187年）改永济务为永济县。完颜雍第七子完颜永济于泰和八年（公元1208年）即位。次年（公元1209年）改元大安。金卫绍王完颜永济大安元年（公元1209年）为避卫绍王完颜永济之名而改丰闰县。元世祖忽必烈至元二年（公元1265年）将丰闰县并入玉田县，四年又复丰闰县，二十二年（1285年）立丰闰署。朱元璋灭元建明（公元1368年），改元洪武。洪武元年（公元1368年）改丰闰为丰润，取"丰泽润美"之意，属顺天府蓟州。自此始有丰润县名。

1995年4月14日

新军屯集有传说

在唐山市丰润区，有一个建村较早的一个地方——新军屯。有文字记载显示建于东汉，东汉丞相曹操还在此建立军屯。这里的开设集市年代较早，是一个传统的集镇，当地百姓赶集的风俗也由来已久。

相传，早年间朝廷要在新军屯一带设立集市，促进当地和周边地区的农副产品贸易。当时新军屯村西4里许，有一村名杨家庄（现在还有），与新军屯村的地理位置、交通条件、村落规模、人口数量、物产等，均不相上下。为了能设集兴本村一方水土，新军屯和杨家庄两村展开了激烈的竞争。朝廷的地方官一时也难以定夺，后来，决定让两个村取同等体积的沙土各一份，以其净重，决一雌雄。哪村的沙土重，就在哪村设集。结果，新军屯村的沙土重于杨家庄村的沙土，杨家庄无奈败北。于是，在新军屯设集，一、六为集日。农历初一初开集市之时，新军屯东街的旱船，西街的小车会，南街的龙灯，北街的高跷，一齐出动，以庆开市大吉。来自宁河、玉田、遵化和丰润北部的商贾云集新军屯进行交易，盛况空前。

集市上有大豆、玉米、高粱等各种农作物产品和农村生活用品的买卖，以及鸡鸭鱼猪羊的交易，还有骡、马、驴、牛这些农用牲畜的买卖。由于新军屯往西、南两个方向的地势较洼，古来的就盛产芦苇，所以，过去这里集市上的芦苇和苇席（家家必备的炕席）交易也占一定比重。

集市娱乐也较丰富，其中杂耍较多。像杂技、武把操儿（武术）、气功……用新军屯人的话说就是"打把式卖艺的"。

集市上，一顶白布棚里一把木椅子，一只烧炭的炉子上面一个黄铜的盆子，铜盆子的水里边泡着白手巾，这就是老百姓说的剃头棚儿，集市上不可或缺的，那年头赶集上店的老百姓剃头的很多。集市上摆摊儿卖膏药的也不少。集市上卖布衣布袜之外还有卖小孩虎头鞋、虎头帽的、吹糖人儿、卖泥人儿的。磨剪子锵菜刀的，是一条板凳，一头绑着磨石，一头挂着小水桶，外加一把锵菜刀的锵子。从民国至20世纪60年代初还有看西洋景的。逢庙会赶集期间，许多大人孩子一拨一拨地轮流坐在一条长板凳上，围在一个大器具外，通过放大镜向里看。里面是拉着细绳子把一张张图片拉下来，因此也叫拉洋片。

21世纪的今天，过去集市上的一些场景已经不复存在了，但赶集这一民间风俗没有改变，赶集买卖的物质极大地丰富了，赶集的形式、规模、内容也在不断融入了现代元素，逐渐丰富、扩大、完善。

1995年10月2日

历代唐山属地

在漫长的社会发展过程中,唐山市今境的属地也留下了一条千姿百态变化的轨迹。夏、商、西周、东周时,唐山属孤竹国地。春秋为山戎地。战国时属燕国地。秦时为辽西郡地。西汉时属幽州右北平郡夕阳县地。东汉、魏、晋时皆属辽西郡地。北齐时属肥如县地,隋时为卢龙地。唐武德初年属临榆县地,后改石城县,属平州地。辽、金时均属石城县地。元初石城县并入义丰县。明代,义丰属永平府,洪武二年省义丰入滦州地。清为直隶省滦州地。民国初属直隶省渤海道,后为津海道,属滦县第八区。现今,唐山市为河北省直辖市。

1995 年 8 月 23 日

神秘龙潭坨

在唐山市丰润区新军屯镇东南 1.5 公里的地方,有个小村庄名叫龙潭坨。关于这个村的村名,还有三个传说。

娘娘庙。相传,村中赵姓家族曾出了三个娘娘,娘娘死后,为了纪念娘娘,赵姓族人在村里建起三座庙。所以,人们就把这个村子叫做了娘娘庙。

龙潭坨。当时建庙开挖地基时,有人挖出了一个古磬,古磬上面刻有"龙潭坨"的字样,后来,人们也把该村叫做龙潭坨。

龙潭。又相传,古时村中有一家姑嫂相依为命,嫂子勤俭且明大义。小姑从小爱吃鱼,每饭必备。尽管家中不宽裕,嫂子还是千方百计弄来鱼做给小姑吃。后来,家境实在困难,买不起鱼,但小姑不体谅。无奈,嫂子晚上独坐院子里仰天哭泣。天上神仙听到哭声下得凡来,问清缘由,甚是感动，便交给嫂子竹竿一根，嘱咐道：要鱼时，就用竹竿指一下水缸，便会水涌鱼跃，鱼够用了便轻呼"停"，就水回鱼止。

神仙说完飘然而去。嫂子一试，果然灵验。日久天长，嫂子捞鱼被小姑偷看到了。一日，趁嫂子下地干农活之际，小姑拿起竹竿，在院中乱指，不想，这一只可了不得了，平地竟出现一个深不可测的地穴，一股又急又猛的地下水奔涌而出。嫂子闻讯从地里赶回，奋不顾身抢救小姑，却被大水淹没了。不一会，一条飞龙驮着嫂子腾出水面而上天空。这时，地面上的水也返回了洞穴。为此，人称此洞为龙潭，村随洞名，遂称龙潭坨。

这些美丽的传说，给冀东小村龙潭坨披上一层神秘色彩，随着社会主义新农村建设步伐的加快，小村的将来一定会更加迷人。

1995 年 9 月 13 日

千金冶城话今昔

古冶，今唐山市的一个区，古孤竹国地。相传，是千金冶城之地。唐代，这里已人丁兴旺，并曾建有北大寺（原址在今北寺公园）。从辽代到清代（907 年—1911 年）属滦州。随着开滦林西矿的筹建（1879 年）和投产（1889 年），唐胥铁路延伸至古冶（1889 年）并建古冶站。民国时属滦县，曾建古冶镇。现在的古冶集铁路、公路、商贸、煤炭等业于一身，是唐山市东部城乡最大的物资集散地和交通枢纽，205 国道线上的重镇，京线上的重要区段，并有开滦矿务局下属的林西、吕家坨、范各庄、唐家庄、赵各庄矿等大厂矿铁路专用线与之接轨。

改革开放给古冶带来生机，为使古冶经济更快发展，国务院批准将古冶由处（办事处）升区，同时将东矿区入古冶区。相信，早已扬名中外的古老的古冶将会充分发挥其地理、交通、能源和知名度等优势，在社会主义市场经济的大潮中腾飞、再造辉煌。

1995 年 5 月 12 日

遵化今昔

今隶属于唐山市的县级市遵化市，古称徐无，西汉（公元前206年）始置，历代沿用其名。到北周（公元前557—581年），废入无终县。新朝（王莽代汉建新，公元8年—23年）称北顺亭。唐朝（公元618年—907年）始筑土城，建四门。五代后唐（公元923年—936年）朝廷为巩固北方，教化臣民，始名遵化县，意为"遵守朝廷教化"。洪武年间（公元1378年），由于当时明朝加强北方统治的需要，将遵化县城在原来基础上向西、北两面扩大近一倍。清朝（公元1644年—1911年）因在其境内建清东陵，由县升州，改名遵化直隶州。此时，遵化城市繁荣。为供大清皇族朝臣游玩，还在遵化城东北角护城河外兴建了龙泉公园，抗日战争前尚存。民国2年（公元1913年）复改遵化县。

在改革开放大好形势的推动下，遵化充分发挥自身交通、物产、旅游等优势，经济迅速壮大，各业蓬勃发展。1992年，国务院正式批准遵化撤县建市。从而，遵化以更大的步伐前进在具有中国特色的社会主义大道上，并将以新的姿态迈进21世纪。

1995年5月19日

石市观畸

石家庄动物园里，人们早已司空见惯的豺狼虎豹象狮熊自不必说，单说园内的畸形动物馆，就足以让你观后尽得其乐。那里有两个畸形动物展馆。

第一馆门口是一只黑白花色的五腿猪，第五只腿长在右后腿上。挨它一侧的是一头黑色雄性六腿牛，第五、六只腿均长在其右前膀上，一大一小约一尺长。再侧是一头雌性黄色五腿牛，第五只腿长在其前右腿腋下。还有一只三爪雄鸡，第三支爪长在其右腿根部，向外方向伸着。紧挨着的是一只人行鸡，走起路来昂首挺胸，站立于天地间，俨然一副大丈夫的气派。第二馆里有一条三条腿的雌性狗，后二前一，前一只腿下关节向右弯曲着地。在三腿狗旁是一只三条腿雄性山羊，后腿两只前腿一只。其后是一只五腿雌性绵羊，第五只腿长在其头右上方，像耳朵一样耷拉着。这里也有一头五腿黄牛，第五只腿长在其左膀上。看完这些，觉得造物主还是公平的。即使是"节外生枝"吧，但也让它们左右搭配。虽多肢少足，可却丝毫没有影响它们的吃喝拉撒睡等一切同类俱有的功能发挥。它们在这里，更免去了觅食、看家、劳作之苦，水来开口，饭来开吃，饱食终日，无所用心，安然自得，倒也悠哉。

1995年7月7日

追忆尉迟恭大黑马甸智取神马

尉迟敬德，在中国历史上是一个家喻户晓的人物。大唐初期的著名大将。尉迟敬德（公元585—658年），名恭，字以行。隋朝大业末年，从军高阳，随刘武周为偏将。唐朝武德三年（公元620年）降唐，引为右一府统军。曾从李世民击王世充军，参与镇压窦建德，刘黑闼起义军。武德九年（公元626年），"玄武门之变"因助秦王李世民杀太子李建成及齐王李元吉有功，授左卫率，寻升右武侯大将军，封吴国公。唐贞观十九年（公元645），随唐太宗李世民东征攻打高丽，诏以本官行太常卿，为左一马军总管。马上皇帝唐太宗李世民一生珍爱随他征战四方的六匹坐骥，为此，而产生了艺术精湛举世无双的"昭陵六骏"那栩栩如生的战马石雕。皇帝且如此，更何况是"战将爱战马"的将军呢，尉迟恭就是一个爱马如痴的人。当年，尉迟恭随唐太宗李世民御驾亲征高丽（今朝鲜）从都城长安一路向东进发，兵至今唐山市丰润区阎家铺时，御令安营扎寨，休整人马，屯兵于此。

一天早上，大将尉迟恭起床来走出军中大帐，忽见大营南方不远的地方，有一匹油黑油黑的高大野马饮水于潭。

霞光中，野马全身乌黑闪亮，若如神马一般。马上将军尉迟恭一眼便喜欢上了这匹野马。心想，好一匹漂亮威武的神马哟。古来驰骋疆场的战将酷爱良马，这是在讲的。于是，尉迟恭立即搬鞍任镫，飞身骑上战马急速飞奔而去，可神马早已无踪影。尉迟恭乘兴而去，败兴而归。但从此后，对神马更加日思夜想的尉迟恭并不甘心，不得神马，誓不罢休。下令士卒在营中高筑看台，天天早上登台瞭望。预设圈套，埋伏兵丁，决心将神马捉为己有。

一日清晨，尉迟恭登上土台例行瞭望，忽然眼前一亮，又见神马在潭边饮水，尉迟恭大喜若望，传令伏兵将其拿之，最终使得尉迟恭如愿以偿。后来，人们在尉迟恭拿马处建起了村庄，人们为了纪念这段历史传说，特立石碑以示后人铭记，更起村名"拿马甸"，再后来又更加贴切的改称为"大黑马甸"。

古时的大黑马甸青草葱葱，潭水清纯。直到现在，黑马深潭犹在，可供人们追忆，但石碑早已坠入深潭之中不可考。在经济蓬勃发展的今天，大黑马甸村恰似一匹神马，前进在社会主义小康村建设的康庄大道上。

2005 年 5 月 13 日

三女河

在唐山市丰润区城南偏西 15.4 公里的地方，有一条河流叫泥河，河南岸有个村庄名叫"三女河"。多么温馨美好名字，但她却经历了一段段痛苦和辛酸的往事。据《丰润地名志》载，该村建于明初。至于村名的来历，村中有几个版本的传说：元朝末年兵荒马乱，一伙贼兵兽性发作，对三个姑娘穷追不舍，追至此地，三个姑娘走投无路，前是河水，后有淫兵。为保洁身三个姑娘毅然投河自尽，遂得村名"三女河"。

又传说：先前有一屠夫，妻子早亡，家中有三个女儿。屠夫嗜酒如命，致使家境破败一贫如洗。为使自己能够经常有钱讨得酒喝，便不顾亲情圆图将女儿一一草率许人，且不论人品德行。大女儿许配了一个病秧子，连拜堂成亲都是找的替身，可偏偏此时，忽报"少爷身亡！"而后，新娘受尽婆婆的百般凌侮。在一个漆黑的夜晚，新娘来到母亲的坟头，哭诉心中凄苦。婆家派人前来找屠夫要人，新娘不从，欲到庵中削发为尼，老尼姑惧怕势力，拒绝收容。真是叫天不应，入地无门，到了这种地步，新娘一狠心纵身跳入泥河……

二女儿被屠夫许配了一个年过五十的老员外，二女儿不甘落入虎口，抗婚出逃，找到自己的心上人。谁知老员外派人把他们双双抓获，并将二姑娘押回府中，勾结官府把年轻人发配充军。心上人从此离去，二姑娘心灰意冷，觉得自己不再有活着的意义。大婚之日，即是二姑娘的绝望之时，二姑娘又伺机逃走，寻着大姐的足迹，投入泥河……

三女儿倒是被屠夫许配给了一个青年人，这个青年后来还当了县令，人们都说这是一段好姻缘，比她两个姐姐都强。可谁知这好人没好命，好景并不长，这人官升情变，开始了喜新厌旧，攀上了金枝，在为官之地又与一知府的千金小姐成了婚。三姑娘得知，进城找到夫君问询，狼心狗肺的夫君反将三姑娘投入监牢。

多亏好心的禁卒婆将三姑娘偷偷放出牢房。县令得报急忙派人一路追赶，三姑娘急不择路跑到泥河边，望着滔滔河水，回头看看追上来的衙役，无路可走，情急之下，纵身投入了泥河之中。

后来，人们出于对三姐妹忠贞不辱和反抗封建婚姻而投河自尽的贞烈行为的敬意，专门在村中关帝庙中塑了三女的立像，并取村名"三女河"。

今日三女河已今非昔比，进入 21 世纪，随着唐山军用机场改为军民两用机场，唐山机场也以所在地名更名为三女河机场。由于经济和城市建设发展、京津冀协同发展的需要，三女河机场又经过几次改扩建。三女河已快速融入京津冀一体化进程，插上了奋飞的双翼，带着昔日三女的美好愿望翱翔天宇，奔向更加美好的明天。

2024 年 1 月 1 日

宋徽宗留迹大安乐庄

大安乐庄，一个多么安乐祥和的庄名，但她却记述了北宋抗金的一段悲壮，述说了一代君王渴望治国安邦的向往。

大安乐庄地处唐山市丰润区城西偏南 5.3 公里的地方，北临还乡河，是宋金当年交战的前沿地带。相传北宋抗金失利，皇帝宋徽宗被掳往五国城，在番兵人马的刀剑铁蹄伴随下，宋徽宗踏上了去往北国的路途，当宋徽宗走在还乡河上的木桥时，远望茫茫北国，回首故国山河，低头眼见脚下西去的河水，心想水皆东流，唯此水西流，不禁触景生情，倍感思乡，凄然而叹。

然而，就是这位被金军俘虏的皇帝，也曾御驾亲征前线指挥千军万马，抗金保国。据当地人说，那时宋金交战，宋徽宗巡营至此，正值夜深人静，营灯高照，万家入梦，心情感慨道："东安乐，西太平，南沧桑，北还乡。"从而，这个原本古称安各庄的村庄，遂改称安乐庄，又因后来村西新建一庄，便在庄名前加一"大"字为大安乐庄。如今的大安乐庄，真正走上了社会主义新农村建设的小康路，人们过上了安乐祥和的幸福生活。

1996 年 12 月 11 日

唐宗清帝与唐山与钓鱼台

公元645年，也就是唐朝贞观十九年。那一年，唐太宗李世民亲率十多万大军东征高句丽（今朝鲜半岛北部），在途经今天的唐山市区时，在一座山上驻扎休整。因山上有城，所以叫大城山，因为李世民曾在此停留过，后来就被当地百姓称为"唐山"，大城山是山也是城，以此算来至今唐山建城已经是1379年了。

北京有个钓鱼台，唐山也有个钓鱼台，且唐宗、清帝本皆与此有关联。这里的唐宗不是唐高宗，而是后唐明宗（公元926年至932年在位）李嗣源。他称帝前因战功官至蕃汉内外与步兵总管，曾屯兵"唐山"，也就是今天唐山市的大城山，闲暇时常常来到山下陡河垂钩钓鱼。

清帝就是清高宗乾隆帝，就是这位中国历史上叱咤风云的乾隆皇帝，在乾隆六十年（公元1795年）出巡路过此地时，随行大臣向他述说了后唐明宗在此钓鱼的传说，清高宗心悦，欣然按此传说命名此地为钓鱼台，从而沿用至今。

2024 年 7 月 18 日

南海北山古丰润

丰润县原本是中华大地上一个大而古老的县域，最先是战国七雄之一赵国的赵武灵王通过强国之间的换地而得到燕国的一片土地，并在其上建造了规模宏大的土垠城（《丰润县地名志》载），正式设县于西汉。大汉王朝继承秦朝郡县制度，建土垠县，县城设在土垠城。今唐山市丰润区银城铺，就是当时的土垠县城的所在地。传说，古土垠城气势雄伟而壮观，彰显了一代霸主赵武灵王的非凡气度，更有海市蜃楼时常出现而成为战国时闻名于燕赵的"银城晓市"。

在中国古代历史长河里，不断的战争和朝代更迭中，丰润几经兴废，不同时期隶属于不同郡县，直到金世宗大定六年（公元1166年）才动土兴建今县城，因丰润县域地处燕山冲积平原，一马平川，风调雨顺，物产丰富，又取"粮草丰盛，永济不断"之意定名永济县。到金卫绍王大安元年（公元1209年）为避卫绍王完颜永济之名讳更名为"丰闰"。又到明洪武元年（1368年）定名为"丰润"至今，取"润泽丰美"之意。翻开《中国历史地图集》，可见古时丰润县地域的辽阔，莽莽燕山、滔滔河流、广阔平原、无垠大海尽置其辖。从明代中期的丰润县志记述的"燕山障郡""更水朝京""龙石兆雨""仙洞题金""韩室砚润""秦岭荆伏""朝峰偃月""腰带横云"更可看出古丰润的地广物丰山河壮美。直到清光绪年间的县志仍载：丰润县有两卫，镇21个。今天津宁河县的丰台镇和今天唐山的开平那时皆属丰润。过去的丰润县是一个行政辖区南管到渤海北管到燕山的大县。民国时期建立唐山市，从丰润县划出了一部分。新中国成立前夕（1937年）设立滦阳县，从丰润县划出了南半部至沿海，中华人民共和国成立后重归丰润县。

中华人民共和国成立后，中国第一个平原果园也是亚洲第一大平原果园，即唐山果园的兴建又是全域从丰润县划出。设立开平区从丰润再度划出一部分。

1961年6月，丰润丰南再度分而治之，因其是丰润县的南半部，所以取名丰南县，再度使丰润县一分为二，县境南部及沿海尽归丰南。

唐山大地震后正式建立唐山市丰润新区，丰润县又划117.5平方公里归唐山市。继而，唐海县于1982年9月成立，又一部分丰润县辖地划给唐海县。

以后，唐山军用飞机场改为军民两用机场，又把三女河划出。2013年老庄子镇、韩城镇相继划归唐山市高新开发区和唐山市路北区。2014年岔河乡划归唐山市丰南区。

今天，唐山丰润新区与丰润县合并为丰润区，虽然，古丰润"北枕燕山，南为海川，傍泥河，环滦水"之景已是面目皆非了，燕山还在枕，但海川不复存了。好在还有傍泥河，环滦水之景，仍不失为京东重镇，境内还有中国北车集团（中车集团唐山厂）、冀东水泥等大型国有企业。她正以新的姿态和步伐，融入环渤海经济圈，随境内电气化铁路和京哈高速公路，乘中国北车集团的快速动车，奔向京津冀协同发展的新天地。

1997年9月3日

喜峰口——《大刀进行曲》的溯源地

喜峰口，位置在唐山市迁西县城兴城北31公里处，万里长城上的一个重要关口。而她的名字随着一幕幕历史剧的上演而流传于民间。元朝有诗云："天教此地适相逢，父曰从天坠吾子。"是说昔日有人子戍边久未还乡，家父寻访至此与子相遇，喜泪横飞，抱子大笑，乐极而死。因此故事的长久流传，民间便将原为"松亭关"的这一关口慢慢称为"喜逢口"了。

明永乐年间改为"喜峰口"。明景泰三年（1452年），为抵外敌，筑城建关，名曰镇远楼，楼高四丈。关口有明嘉靖年间所建来远楼。喜峰口有三道关门，牢固难攻，俗称"三关口"。古来历代重兵守关。1933年日军进关，宋哲元部在此固守，并与日军展开激烈的白刃战，锋刃的大片刀杀退日军两次猛攻，敌千余人。所以，当时人们又称"砍头口"。著名的抗日歌曲《大刀进行曲》就是根据这一战例创作产生的。1944年，我方伏兵喜峰口两侧一个排，消灭日军200多人。

今天，我们重温古松亭关的往昔岁月，回顾她抵御外敌的光荣历程，别有意义。

1997年10月7日

赵国华与心香书院

书院是中国封建社会一种特殊的教育组织，始于唐代，当时为藏书、修书之所，后来作为授徒讲学之所。唐山曾有过10所书院，清末名宦赵国华创办的心香书院就是其中之一。

赵国华，清直隶省丰润县大王庄人。生于1838年（清道光十八年），少年刻苦学习，1863年（同治二年）考取进士，曾在山东任知县、知州、知府等职。在任克己奉公，效力朝廷。在山东为官期间，赵国华曾回老家丰润县新军屯大王庄小住两年。他关心家乡教育，想创办一个书院，便于其间筹备资金，选定师资，踏勘院址，最后把院址定在新军屯的福兴寺。

古时新军屯就是丰润南半县的最大集镇，十字形街区，24条大胡同，商农并盛，交通便利，南可去天津，西北可到北京，东可达山海关，书院建在新军屯在各方面都具优势。

书院各项事宜筹备就绪时，赵国华为书院起名为"心香书院"。心香书院在当时各县书院中独具特色，该书院完全是私立，其宗旨为"吾党僻居村塾，限于方隅，各守一塾之说，积而相延，得此而振拔之，不但室气有所宗，亦得风俗之羽翼也。"即为交流思想，培养人才，为乡邑增光，为朝廷养士。按唐山其他书院例，书院应设"山长"，负责主持院务及讲学，而心香书院不设"山长"而设"师位"，将京师国史《文苑传》中第一名丰润籍人谷霖苍列为师位之首，以下还有18位奉祀乡贤。

1894年（光绪二十年），57岁的赵国华离世。废除科举后，心香书院又于1923年（民国十二年）开办了男子师范讲习所，首开丰润县男子师范教育之先河。20世纪90年代，丰润县新军屯镇又在心香书院的原址上建起5层楼的现代化初中教学楼，为新军屯镇第二中学。

2001年1月8日

传于唐抵于今的净觉寺

净业觉悟真空寺，就是今天的净觉寺，是一座素有京东第一寺之称，有着1000多年历史的平原寺院，坐落在唐山市玉田县蛮子营村。清清的石榴河（还乡河的一段，当地称呼石榴河）河水静静地从净觉寺前面向西流过，像是慢慢述说着净觉寺往日的辉煌与沧桑。

净觉寺在历史的长河中，屡屡经历战火，虽几建几废，但兴衰从容。时至今日，整个寺院现存的建筑为大清雍正元年（1723年）重修的。据寺内清乾隆年《重修碑记》载："帷兹净觉寺，僧众师祖居于此，传始于唐，阅乎五代炎宋，历元明而抵于今。"

在寺院外从远处直观净觉寺，山门殿前面是新建的牌楼式建筑，山门殿和寺墙之内的全部建筑由黄、绿琉璃瓦覆盖，在灿烂的阳光下显得那么的金碧辉煌。

走近山门殿，砖雕斗拱，石砌圆窗，工艺是那么的精湛。进入殿内，那用中国建筑绝技无梁特艺建成的砖拱券顶，浑然天成，仰面望去，像是向人们昭示着宇宙苍穹的深邃无限。殿中两尊高大的"哼哈"二将，守卫在金色大肚弥勒佛两边。

虽是清代泥塑又经"文革"时期的破坏，但仍色彩依然，神态逼真，令人胆寒之余又倍感泥塑大佛的神采可爱。

山门殿与正殿之间的碑楼下是三通清代《重修碑记》。碑楼后面，东西两侧是晨钟暮鼓的钟鼓楼。钟楼大钟敲响后声音厚重悠远，敲响鼓楼大鼓鼓声荡荡。

正殿香阜宫门前是一对高大石狮，殿脊高耸，龙凤双飞，雕刻剔透。殿内高大的千手千眼佛全身金黄，十八罗汉分列两厢。更可称奇的是正殿与东西配房之间的侧门楼，石雕嵌壁，花鸟如生。东西角门，东面雕龙，西面雕凤，所雕龙凤活灵活现，故称"龙凤门"。

再往后便是壮观雄伟的大雄宝殿，殿门前石柱抱厦，四大独根石明柱上栩栩如生的盘龙浮雕别具一格，精湛技艺，堪称一绝。大殿之内供奉着几尊金身大佛，令人仰视。

走出净觉寺，仔细回味它的寺名，原是取佛教净业觉悟真空之意。再回眸，净觉寺精美别致，独具匠心，风格新颖独特，真不愧为"京东第一寺"啊。

1998年3月29日

老马识途——典故源于唐山

老马识途是一个古老的成语。它的出处见于《东周列国志·齐桓公定兵破孤竹》一节，专门记述了这一成语典故。当年令支国（今迁安市为故国地）攻打燕国，燕国求救于齐国。齐桓公大军北进，灭了令支国，令支国君奔逃孤竹国。齐桓公又兵至孤竹国都无棣城。兵临城下，孤竹国君为阻止齐军，用宰相己律之计，于黄昏诱齐军入迷谷，使齐军人马皆惊，毛骨悚然，前不知去向，后不晓退路。情急之下，齐相管仲献计说老马能够识别来时的路，便将军中老马摘去笼头缰绳一一放行，齐军将士随行其后，最后终于大队军马走出迷谷。

瀚海为地名，俗称迷谷。此地为沙碛之地，每到傍晚阴风刮起，人隔咫尺不能相见，入此谷定死无疑。所以，齐军中孤竹国计而迷失方向。今天，人们用老马识途来比喻富于经验的人能在日常工作和生活中起到引导作用。"老马识途"这一典故源于唐山这片古老的土地。

1998年12月27日

沧桑还乡河

还乡河，又名环香河，全长160公里。她的源头在唐山市迁西县新集乡泉庄村，经新集、夹河、新庄子等村镇，累累西流到唐山市丰润区岩口村入丰润境，往西流入丘庄水库，后向南流至丰润城，又西流过丰润区白官屯镇到玉田县蛮子营村入玉田县境，又西南流经鸦鸿桥、窝洛沽、河涧头等村镇，再西南流入天津市宁河区入蓟运河。大段西流水域集中在丰润境内，全长60公里，流域面积460平方公里。

古时人们称河为水。北魏郦道元所著《水经注》中的浭水（也为庚水、巨梁水），即还乡河。古时的丰润，特别是北宋时期，一直是边陲要地，于今还乡河南岸仍有大令公庄和小令公庄。旧《丰润县志》上说，这两个地方分别是北宋名将杨继业和他的儿子杨延昭驻军把守的地方。到宋徽宗时（公元1101年—1125年），金兵经常南下烧杀抢掠。擅长书画的徽宗皇帝曾御驾亲征，扎营于浭水（还乡河）南岸的小谷庄、东安各庄西边这一地段，徽宗皇帝住在安各庄沙岩寺指挥抗金。旧《丰润县志》介绍：宋徽宗夜晚巡营，大营内外无鸡鸣犬吠，甚为寂静，心中深为感慨，即兴赋诗："东安乐，西太平，南沧桑，北还乡。"所以，为了记住这段历史，小谷庄和安各庄也就从此改名为太平庄和安乐庄了。

靖康二年（公元1127年），金兵又不断出兵南下，宋钦宗执意求和，导致金兵生俘宋徽宗（赵佶）、宋钦宗（赵恒）并掳往五国城（今黑龙江依兰）。当宋徽宗骑马立在浭水桥（今还乡河大桥上游300米处）上，回首家国河山，触景生情，倍感凄凉。《燕山丛录》载：宋徽宗凄然曰："过了大漠，吾安得似此水还乡乎？"不食而去，人们也便把浭水称作还乡河了。

历史一段段，如眼前云烟。但今日还乡河畔的人们，建设着美好的家园，过着安康喜乐的生活。令宋徽宗泪眼蒙眬的"思乡桥"早已不复存在了，两座长102.6米，高5米，桥面净宽7米的还乡河大桥飞架两岸。河畔有左家坞村，更以还乡河水酿造了"不药不煮即以鹿，生贮于瓮，初淡有风致辞，久则香郁"的历史名酒浭阳酒（曾名曹雪芹家酒），伴随着还乡河两岸的人民走向新时代。

2001年6月9日

梁久功与白官屯

清雍正年间，家境贫寒的梁久功，为了有吃有穿讨一条生路入选老公（也就是当了宫廷里的太监），从丰润县一个叫梁家坟的村子来到大清皇宫，负责照看年少的乾隆。随着乾隆即位和岁月的积累，梁久功的名气在朝廷上下已经很大了。民间传说当时曾流传着这么一句话："宫里的事情中不中，先去问问梁久功。"由此可见梁久功在宫中的地位非同一般。

经历了两代皇帝的梁久功看尽了荣华富贵，遍闻了宫中明争暗斗争权夺势的事情，不免也心起非分之想。于是，网罗了一帮死党密谋造反，篡权夺位，并秘密选定拟在丰润白官屯建国都。

据传说，都城的东门在丰润县令公庄的沙岩寺，西门在岳王庙（遗址无从查考），南门在丰润县白官屯镇的黑马甸村，北门在丰润县田富庄乡的福兴寺。因宫中一些人对此已有察觉，有忠臣面奏了乾隆皇帝，乾隆帝果断决策，将梁久功推出午门之外斩首。

2002 年 3 月 3 日

两个蜜桃吃三天

蜜桃好吃，"深州蜜桃"更好吃。

深州蜜桃，是河北深州市的地方名产，素以个大皮薄、味甜多汁驰名于世。在老辈子，深州蜜桃那可是朝廷贡品，果不下树，早已清点，如数进贡，劳动人民根本吃不到。

说来奇怪，在深州也只有三四亩地才真正出产这种蜜桃。其中还有一段民间传说哩。相传，一次，王母娘娘在去见玉帝的途中，因天气炎热，感到口干舌燥，便命随从人员停下小歇，拿出仙桃圣果来润喉止渴。圣果体大肉肥，汁多甘甜，一个果子下肚，感到心满意足，顺手扔下桃核。可巧，果核落在深州境内。从此，这枚桃核在此发芽生根开花结果。

耳听不如眼见，一次，我出差去深州，晚上出来散步时，忽听小贩吆喝"深州蜜桃"，便迎上前去。只见蜜桃顶呈红色，底部微黄，小西瓜般大小，一个就二斤重。我买了两个，回到招待所，洗过后一吃：滋！一股桃汁喷溅出去。哇，真甜哪！深州蜜桃名不虚传，肉厚核小，我吃了半个就饱了。我在深州住了三天，到第三天临走，才把第二个大蜜桃吃完。现在再想起深州蜜桃来，它的滋味还是那么甘美绵长，回味不尽。

1988 年 10 月 30 日

青山关上水门闸

在唐山市迁西县上营乡青山口村的绵绵青山之中，高高矗立着一座雄伟的青山关，就是在这座青山关上，有从居庸关到老龙头这条漫漫长城中唯一保存下来的一座"水门闸"。

水门闸的建筑，是借助于一道山口的自然地形坐西朝东，高三丈宽两丈的拱形门洞，其南北两边联结着高高的城墙，门闸由黄铜铸就，所以，人们又叫它铜门闸。大闸一放，真如铜墙铁壁一般，把青山关城紧紧关在了长城之内。

之所以叫水门闸，是因为它既可以挡住和积蓄门西面大山之上下来的山水，又可在山洪到来之时，打开铜门泄下山洪。另外，它的一个重要军事作用是可以用来开门泄洪，水淹来犯之敌，攻防自如，得心应手。戚继光曾在 1568 年，也就是明朝隆庆二年，在青山关城之上击退敌之前锋后，带兵冲出水门闸，追杀敌军。

1644 年，爱新觉罗氏由山海关进入，进而统一整个中国，长城随之也失去了往日的重要和功能，水门闸也是如此。只可惜，这座既可蓄洪泄洪又可防敌御敌的水门闸，在清朝光绪十三年（1887 年）夏，被爆发的山洪冲垮，铜门无了踪影，只剩高大宽阔的门洞还在，可以让人去凭吊它的昔日辉煌。

2002 年 3 月 21 日

歪老板的老歪饭店

人们都听说过天津有狗不理包子，北京有王麻子剪刀，却大概不晓得唐山市还有一家"老歪饭店"吧。

"老歪饭店"是一家个体饭店，坐落在新军屯镇。店主姓李，名叫学勤。因其脖子生得歪歪的颇像那古时的玉田县令许九经，故而人称"歪老板"。起初，对于这个"雅号"，李老板听起来非常难为情，感觉非常别扭，心说话，你们这不是同着瘸子说短话吗？甚至有些愤愤然。可久而久之，耳朵灌满了也就默认了。

本来，老歪饭店并不这个名字，当时位于新军屯镇中心的十字街头，后来迁到镇东唐山6路公交车站附近。欣逢乔迁之喜，许多老顾客前来捧场，建议"新饭店要有新字号"。在嘈杂的议论声中，店主灵机一动：对！你们不是总叫我歪老板吗，我还就叫它"老歪饭店"了。第二天，他即请人题写店名。在开市大吉的鞭炮声中，他不慌不忙地挂起了"老歪饭店"的大横匾揭开了大红布，四个朱红大字显得异常夺目，吸引了不少凑热闹的顾客。

"老歪饭店"名歪实不歪。店里有家常便饭、经济小吃，还可供上下班的工人喝上两盅，尤其"歪老板"的服务态度，更让顾客三九生暖。因此，生意越办越兴隆。

1987年1月25日

走进鼓浪屿

张暴默的那首《鼓浪屿之波》的歌曲，曾勾起过许多人对这个南海小岛的无限向往。

前几年的一个夏天，我和朋友由厦门坐轮渡到了有海上花园之称的鼓浪屿这个美丽岛屿。

小岛环抱在碧海之中，蓝天白云下，林木葱郁，景色秀丽。这里的建筑有异域风格，且各不相同：有澳洲式，有希腊式，有印尼式，有中西合璧式……

过去鼓浪屿人到南洋、西欧、澳洲等地谋生的较多，当他们重返家乡后，便把他们的侨居的海外建筑风格带到了这里。

鼓浪屿四周的海浪声，仿佛是永不休止的音乐。也许因此，这里的人们特别钟爱钢琴，钢琴人均拥有率居全国之首。到2000年，全岛已有600架钢琴。所以，人们又称鼓浪屿为琴岛。一年夏天，这里举行广场音乐会，当地政府曾组织百台钢琴同奏《鼓浪屿之波》，让人们尽情享受琴声与海浪声形成的那股天地人琴的强大和弦之美。

行走在鼓浪屿的大街上，你看不到有机动车。问当地人才知道，这里的机动车只有消防车和环境卫生车，只是因为当地对环保的十分重视，才为这里环境保护打下了良好的基础。

仲夏夜里，走在日光岩下，望满天星光闪耀，踏阵阵海涛，听琴声如潮，看美丽浪漫的鼓浪屿风情，真是一种超然享受。

2001 年 7 月 1 日

景忠山的驴

生在平原，长在平原的我，却从小爱上了山。去过泰山，上山途中看到了泰山挑夫负重而上，额头上坠地成八瓣的滴滴汗水；到过峨眉山，见到了峨眉群猴与游人讨要食物的逗人劲头与贪婪；然而，早在2002年来到唐山市迁西县境内的景忠山，我却看到了景忠山驴的一种坚韧、一种聪慧、一种悟性。

在茫茫燕山的怀抱之中，景忠山就像一个美丽的少女亭亭玉立在那里。漫山的翠绿苍松让我深深地感觉着幽谷清风的气息，给人与痴恋。听人说和查看历史得知清朝康熙大帝曾多次驾幸景忠山，又听说山中有明朝的"三忠祠"山顶还有宏伟壮观，金碧辉煌的碧霞元君大殿，于是，乘兴而去。

进了景忠山的山门，一步步拾级而上，穿过四帅殿，绕过御佛寺，慢慢向山上行进。走了一段时间，觉得有些喘，我便在一个平台上稍事休息。不经意间一回头，忽见一头驴站在我身后，一队毛驴上山而来，背上驮着木工们打好的建造房屋用的窗户框，它后面的驴儿们分别驮着几大桶水和米面。我赶紧闪到一边让路，正在我观看时，驴的主人吆喝了一声，驴子们就继续前行了。打头的驴先是向左侧斜拾级而上，走到一个平台后又迈步向右侧斜走去。这一左一右的侧斜的前进方式，写成了一个又一个的正反Z字形。独自前行的我，起初还是心不在焉地看着这些上山而去下山而来的驴儿们，看着看着忽然想到这景忠山的人也太聪明了，往山上山下运东西，用驴驮而不用人去挑，这是何等的机敏哪，古往今来省去了多少背负青天肩挑担之苦哇。我若有所思的继续向上走，在山路石阶的一处平台上停下脚又歇了一会儿。放眼望去，远近山峦叠苍驻绿，置身其中真是心旷神怡。赏景之余，不断思索，而后得出的结论是：这样上山省劲。驴背负重载，若沿着石阶直接向上，无疑会使物体产生垂直向下的重力，有一种沉重感。

而斜向侧行迂回前进，则可缓解或减轻驮在背上重物的这种垂直压力，会有一种较为轻松的负重感。哦，原来这驴也有如此灵通的悟性，而且在它的驮运实践中，能觉察并运用了力学道理。就这样避重就轻的年年岁岁，朝朝暮暮的往返在景忠山那1872级石阶之上。由此，我也想到，这普普通通的毛驴儿都能超乎人们想象的聪明。那么，自古以来人们就常说的"蠢驴""笨驴"似乎也应该得到正名了吧。

2004年12月19日

雾灵山览奇

承德市兴隆县的雾灵山属燕山山脉，是燕山山脉最高峰也是燕山主峰，一亿多年前造山运动和第四纪冰川的共同产物。亿万年的桑海变迁，生生息息的万物轮回，造就了雾灵山诸多的雄奇与灵秀，神秘与安详。游历雾灵山，我深为其奇所感染。

奇一：雾锁"歪桃"日升腾

海拔2118米的"歪桃峰"是雾灵山的主峰，因其远看状似一个歪嘴大桃而得名。这里是观看云海日出的最佳地点，早上五点半，等待观看雾灵山日出的男女老幼们聚拢在夏末秋初的歪桃峰上，望着眼前雾灵山那茫茫云海，微波荡漾，海水般的涌上山来。站在峰顶放眼望去，是一望无际的白茫茫、雾蒙蒙、莽莽森林和千山万壑，都被其吞没，一切显得那么的气势磅礴。渐渐的东方云雾由微红变成淡紫红色的云霞，继而，云霞里隐现出半轮朝阳；云霞的色彩逐渐变成大红，随之而来一轮朝阳跃然而上。这时，总面积14247公顷的雾灵山区，笼罩在朝阳的方丈光芒之中。秋雾如海，苍山莽莽，人们看到一个蔚为壮观的雾灵山日出。

奇二：刺雾穿云"仙人塔"

由于雾灵山生成年代久远，反反复复的大自然沧海桑田变迁，岁月消磨，风化侵蚀，使得雾灵山出现了许多奇峰异石，"仙人塔"就是其中一个典型。雄浑伟岸的"仙人塔"高48米，横宽9米，厚度为5米。它突兀耸起，即像擎天柱立，更像凛凛仙人，洞察尘世万象。传说，明代刘伯温把降服的黑龙打入海眼并栽下此塔。人都说面对仙人塔搂一搂，能够活到九十九，所以，来到这里的游人们无一不搂一搂仙人塔，以求长寿。

奇三：龙潭瀑布挂峭壁

雾灵山茂密的森林和各种植被，涵养了丰富的水源，使她溪水潺潺，潭瀑相连，龙潭瀑布就是其中一个。它距龙潭水面20多米高，从寸草不长、没有树木的峭壁之上倾泻而下。仰头望去，犹如白帆直挂。潭水清澈见底，站在潭边，捧上一捧送到口中倍感清爽甘甜，满有农夫山泉的味道。

奇四：雾灵林海色彩迷离

森林覆盖率达80.29%的雾灵山区域属温带森林生态系统，融南之秀丽，北之伟岸于一体，常年温度平均7.6℃以上，最热月温度平均17.6℃。树木葱郁百草丰茂，有高等植物1870多种，从春到秋，600多种花卉相继开放，花香不败。被誉为"华北物种基因库""京东绿色明珠"。秋到雾灵山呈现在你面前的是一片壮丽的秋天景色：山势雄伟，峡谷峭立，溪流曲涧，沟壑幽深，层峦叠嶂，林涛阵阵，色彩迷离。间或，鸟鸣声声，松鼠在树上树下跳跃。满山所有树木的黄色、红色、绿色、紫色会给你无限的沉醉与痴迷。

2006年10月24日

雾灵山上十八潭

俗话说山不在高，有水则灵。而我来到的雾灵山却是海拔2118米，有燕山主峰、京东第一高峰之称的雾灵山。可就是这样高的一座山，仍是山有多高水有多长。从上到下源源不断，源远流长，充满了水的灵性，让人流连忘返。

在雾灵山一百多个景点和众多的潭瀑之中，你不能不看的是那二九一十八潭。十八潭顺山而下，一潭一景，美不胜收。为了便于写作，我拿出本子一一记下潭名。第一潭是香杨潭，潭的两侧满是山林，其中长有杨树。潭下是一桥，名叫枫叶桥。秋来游潭，红褐色的枫叶飘落在你的肩上、飘落在潭水里，满有一番浪漫的情趣，油然的诗意而升。潭水过桥倾泻而下流进入一潭——泻潭，潭名不言而喻。潭下有一泉，泉边茂密的森林中长有柳树，所以名为柳叶泉。走过柳叶泉下的碉楼台，只见一潭起名卧龙潭。卧龙潭面积较大，潭水较深，使人总是觉得潭水里面卧有苍龙似的。此潭顺势而下直挂岩石生生不息，成为乾坤瀑。乾坤瀑较有气势，站在瀑前，望高天游云，宽阔静淡；看山林流水，雅致怡人。乾坤瀑下就是八音瀑。站在八音瀑边，听林涛阵阵，流水潺潺，鸟鸣声声，蝉鸣连连，倍感大自然和谐奏鸣的那一份悠然。八音瀑，经八音桥入楸潭，楸树林在潭边茂盛地成长着。潭水顺楸子桥流过，水边山石上朱红大字写着"饮水思源"。再往下是之字瀑，取瀑形似之字而得名。站在瀑下，往上看，湍急的之字瀑由于受到山石的阻碍，真是飞珠溅玉般的美妙。于是便有了下边的飞珠瀑，飞珠溅落又成了溅玉潭。潭水顺丁香桥流下挂在山石之上，恰似银龙降落人间，人们便给它起了一个好听的名字——银龙瀑。银龙瀑水过楸林桥右一股流经石上而下，左一股进入石洞再流出，汇入阴阳潭，再直接流下，形成一潭，由于水面较宽，所以流速减慢，显得静悄悄的，此潭得名缓潭。缓潭之下就是香泉了，香泉之下是净潭，潭边长满白桦树，下边就是白桦桥，桥下潺潺流水聚集成了新月潭。新月潭下是美丽的虹潭。此潭上空时有彩虹出现，是水还于天，天还于地的自然现象美丽的反映。水流继续前行，进入浴潭。水面平静且不深，炎热夏天，是洗浴的天然良好场所。下面是瀑水潭、映月潭。一路下来，我在本子上记录了所有潭和瀑的名字，山林秋晚，望天上人间两月相映，是一种美的享受。

2004年12月29日

傲岸青山关

在东起老龙头，西至居庸关这条始建于战国，修建连结于秦朝，最后修筑和扩建于明朝的千古长城上，有一个坐落在河北省唐山市迁西县（1947年9月，迁安西部被划为迁西县）上营乡青山口村的青山关。自朱元璋率领农民起义军推翻元朝起，元蒙残余依据蒙古草原和东北各地屡谋复兴，不断侵边扰民，威胁北京。嘉靖三十八年（1559年）数万蒙古骑兵在兀良哈部酋长率领下突破潘家口，渡滦河，在玉田、迁安大肆进行疯狂抢掠。1567年，明朝穆宗即位第一年，也就是隆庆元年（1567年），便把抗倭名将戚继光调入北方任命他为蓟州、昌镇、真保三镇总兵，总理"内三关"军务，总兵府设在今迁西县的三屯营。戚继光一到任，便对这一带的长城进行了修建和加固。明《迁安县志》载："铁门关、董家口、城子岭口、青山口、榆木岭口、擦崖子等关塞，加固加高城体，关口之内增设屯兵驻守的关城，石筑城墙，高一丈五六尺，大城周长千余丈，小城三四百丈。"1568年，戚继光坐镇蓟州的第二年元月，朵颜部酋长辇狐狸、长昂等率兵袭扰蓟州镇，戚继光闻讯飞身上马直奔青山口，击退敌军前锋，带兵冲出青山关追杀敌军，直打得敌军屁滚尿流，溃败而逃。

现在的青山关，是古老长城之上一个保存比较完好的长城关口。这里，在从南到北再折向西的绵绵群山中，至今还矗立着一座座修建于明朝的空心敌楼。长城在这里随着山峦的起起伏伏，层层向上。敌楼由大块青砖与白灰垒砌筑成，里面可通人马，四面有箭口，围阔大概十六七丈吧。从台底算来，高可三丈有余。这里，有我国古长城上唯一现存的一座水门闸，当地人叫它铜门闸，闸门全铜铸造，放下闸门水泄不通，即可蓄洪又可御敌，打开闸门即可泄洪又可水淹敌军，可谓一举四得，可惜的是，这座铜门闸在光绪年间被暴发的山洪冲走。这里还完好地保存着一口搬倒井，据说，康熙微服私访曾在这里饮马，但苦于没有水桶。康熙命人将井搬倒，马便顺坡而下喝足了水，驮着康熙帝继续前行。可是，日军侵华期间，命当地百姓把搬倒井砌成了竖井。青山关里有一座小城，名叫元宝城，这座建于明朝的小城以横贯南北的厚实的长城为屏障，坐北朝南，南北各有一座高大拱形城门。仰望南门，至今还清晰可见"青山关"三个大字刻于门额之上，城门气宇轩昂，尽显宏伟傲岸的雄风。小城里还有建于明代的青山寺、士兵住房、石碾等古代建筑。小城不大，却历览了中国历史沧桑，中华分和统一的变迁。

2005年9月23日

雄伟泰山

泰山，1993年我曾走进过你。2007年5月中旬，泰山槐花飘香的时节，我再次走进了你。登临中天门，眼前依旧感觉是那样的开阔，苍莽跌宕的群山在脚下起伏连绵，你胸怀里一块巨大岩石上面，写着遒劲有力的四个大字"五岳独尊"。

读史书得以知道，岳官的职称与名山的山名统一起来且形成制度，始于汉武大帝，汉宣帝正式确定东岳——山东泰山，西岳——陕西华山，中岳——河南嵩山，南岳——安徽天柱山，北岳——河北大茂山。以后，隋代改南岳为湖南衡山，明代改北岳为山西恒山，最后始成今日之五岳，但自汉至今五岳之首始终是你——泰山。

那还是1978年的时候，世界自然保护协会副主席卢卡斯，受托于联合国教科文组织来泰山进行考察。考察之后，他称赞泰山——你是"自然与文化遗产融为一体的典范"。这一年，泰山，你以雄伟壮丽，风光旖旎，历史悠久，文物众多，即是中华民族的象征，又是中国历史文化的局部缩影的特点，作为全人类文化的重要遗产之一，被联合国教科文组织的《保护世界文化和自然遗产公约》将泰山名胜列入《世界遗产清单》。

泰山，你峰峦嵯峨，溪谷纵横，松柏蓊郁，琼阁掩映。你的人文景观之美体现在你的内涵与外在之上。随着孔子"登东山而小鲁，登泰山而小天下"之后，你的名望就越来越高了，你渐渐成了"崇高""伟大"的象征。古人称你为"岱宗"。看字典才知道"岱"含大山、长辈之意，那你就是中国大山的长辈。你雄踞山东省中部，虽然是1545米的海拔，却被称为"天下第一山"，地位在华夏名山中很高。历代封建帝王把你视为"神"的化身。史书记载：从大秦到大清，竟有72位皇帝对你进行封禅，文人墨客也多以游泰山为快，并以诗词歌赋、题字来歌颂你——泰山。因此，在你宽广的怀抱里留下颇多的文物古迹。从你脚下的岱庙到山顶的碧霞寺，无数的碑刻和古建筑，使你成为一座名副其实的文物宝库。山下的岱庙，规模宏大，是中国少有的几个主要宫殿式建筑群之一；碧霞寺在中国是独一无二的金属构件与土木砖石融为一体的特殊建筑。

泰山，要想一览你的真容颜，必须全程登攀。那一年，一心要从你山脚下的岱宗坊到南天门，我实实在在地登上7000余级石阶，才到达玉皇顶，一睹你的极顶风光。浏览你的风景名胜及文物古迹，我坚持在岱庙、岱麓、红门路、天外村路、岱顶、岱阴及灵岩寺、神通寺、娄敬洞山、徂徕山之间走走停停地走马观花。艰苦历练了自己，也历览了你那300多座峰峦崖岭、

260多条溪谷瀑流、34处古寺庙、110多处古遗址、2500多处碑刻。泰山啊，收获颇丰中我惊奇地发现，其间你既有太古代寒武纪国际地质剖面地层，又有地质学上的新发现——涡柱结构及重力滑动结构；我看到了上古周天子巡狩泰山、会盟诸侯的遗址——周明堂，又看到了春秋时的泰山齐长城——中国最早的兵事防线；我走近历代帝王封禅告祭的故址登封台，也近距离仰视了中国最早的纪功刻石——秦泰山刻石；大字鼻祖刻文经石峪《金刚经》让我大开眼界，唐玄宗的《纪泰山铭》更让我感受到洋洋大观之铭的气魄；四门塔，让我领略了中国现存最早的地上石建筑的风采，宋天贶殿让我看到中国古代三大宫殿式建筑之一的恢宏雄伟；古刹灵岩寺，让我觉悟了自唐代就号称"域中四绝"之首的绝处所在，岱庙在祠庙建筑中的最高规格让我懂得东岳神府的名副其实；我看到了道教壁画之最的《泰山神启跸回銮图》，也看到了海内第一塑——灵岩寺罗汉彩塑；还有清代帝王御赐的镇山三宝——沉香狮子、温凉玉圭和黄瓷釉葫芦等。面对这些，泰山，你真的让我目不暇接，流连忘返。我的泰山哟，在这极短的时日里，怎能让我去细细品味，慢慢咀嚼你那相映生辉着泰山的雄伟壮丽呢？

泰山，你的自然景观之美体现山体的高大和形象的雄伟。你周围环绕的是河海、平原，与泰山主峰突兀，山势陡峻，山峦叠起形成了强烈的对比，崛起了"一览众山小"的高旷气势。近500里的泰山基础宽厚绵延，形体集中，你给我一种安稳、厚重之感，成就了我"稳如泰山""重如泰山"的自然心理感受。

地质考古的结果证明，你在二十五亿年前的太古代是被海水淹没的，岁月蹉跎，时光荏苒，你渐渐抬升出海面，你在三千万年前新生代中期的喜马拉雅山运动影响下，才有了现在的模样。我触摸着你，世界上最古老的岩石——泰山石，而你的山体却又是世界上最年轻的，从未停止过生长发育，直到今天，我的泰山啊，你仍以每年0.05毫米的速度成长着。

泰山，你从远古走来，悠远的历史已经证明，你挺拔昂扬，雄伟壮丽，充满中华民族的精神。泰山，你一如既往走向遥远未来，无尽的岁月必将更加证明，你会更加挺拔壮丽，昂扬雄伟，与中华民族一起傲立在世界的东方！

大连灿烂的笑容

在电视里常常听到张行那美好悠扬的歌声："千里万里走不出爱的晴空，我是大连灿烂的笑容……"张行的歌声常常引领着我对大连的无限想往。

灿烂广场

2007年6月初，我终于来到这座引人注目的美好城市，从而，得以一睹这座城市灿烂的笑容。大连以广场著称，全市有52个广场，名列榜首的当数星海广场。

星海广场，建成于1997年7月30日香港回归祖国之际，是亚洲最大的公众广场。广场内圆直径199.9米，寓意公元1999年大连市建市100周年；外圆直径239.9米，指2399年时大连将迎来建市500周年；广场中心部分借鉴北京天坛圜丘的设计理念，由999块大理石铺装而成，红色大理石的外围饰以黄色大五角星，有星有海，是"星海湾"的象征，红黄两色更象征着炎黄子孙；大理石面分别雕刻着天干地支、二十四节气、十二生肖等图案，还雕有9只造型各异的大鼎，每只鼎上各有一个魏碑体的大字，共同组成"中华民族大团结万岁"；广场周边的5盏大型宫灯，各高12.34米，由汉白玉柱托起，光华璀璨，与华表交相辉映……

广场往南行500米，是蓝色的大海，临海是百年城雕所在，100双脚印寓意大连走过的百年沧桑，天真的儿童雕像寄托着大连人民的希望，面向海天敞开的石雕大"书"则显示这座城市开放向上的胸怀；城雕不远屹立着百年灯塔。

这座既彰显中华古老文明，又充满现代意识的广场，中央大道红砖铺地，两侧绿草如海，每隔20米设一个航标灯造型的石柱灯，象征着中国大连正面对大海，走向世界，走向灿烂明天。

灿烂北大桥

滨海城市大连有许多的桥梁，但有一座漂亮的桥梁建筑不得不提，那就是北大桥。之所以建造这座大桥，为的是纪念中国大连市与日本北九州市结为友好城市。大桥近海临山横跨山谷，桥身通体洁白，桥型既雄伟壮观，又新颖别致，虽然是一座旱桥，却给人一种美的视观感觉。

大桥1987年5月1日竣工后成为大连南部海滨风景区的一道灿烂景观。

灿烂金石滩

距大连市中心58公里有一处声名赫赫的金石滩，金石滩的石头比金子还要贵重，因为它是中国乃至世界独一无二的，极其罕见的，地球不可再生的。金石滩号称"奇石的园林"，大片大片粉红色的礁石、金黄色的石头，像巨大的花朵分别被称为玫瑰园、金石园。

粉红色的礁石是7亿年前藻类植物化石堆积而成的，石碑上的"玫瑰园"三字是我国著名的作家老舍的夫人所写。玫瑰园方圆千余平方米，由一百多块高达数丈的奇巧怪石组成，涨潮时，它们衬着湛蓝的海水，映着白云飘浮的蓝天，像花儿开得格外惹眼。朝落时，踏着光华如玉的鹅卵石，信步其间，仿佛走进一个梦境般的世界。

金石园发现于1996年，于当年发现兵马俑的过程相似；施工单位发现这里的石头颜色造型特别，便报告给度假区委员会。俗话说："精诚所至，金石为开"。经过金石滩人半年多连续不断地发掘，使得一片占地3万平方米、在地下沉睡了6亿多年的沉积岩石得见天日。金黄色的岩石如龟似象，雄伟多姿，被称"海蚀动物园"。置身园中，曲径通幽，别有洞天。这里是金石滩著名的自然奇石地质景观之一金石园。金石园占地面积3万平方米，为风化海石积聚地。这里奇石林立、曲径通幽、造型各异、巧夺天工。这里有一线天、登天洞等景观，更加险峻和奇特。

据地质科学考证，金石园形成于距今6亿年前的震旦纪，与金石滩闻名于世的龟裂石属于同一时期。金石园的岩石成分为石英砂岩，属海进体系中典型的滨外碎屑堡岛系统的沉积层，岩石形态千奇百怪，如龟似象，如鹿似犬，被人们称为海蚀动物园。因为它是金黄色的，所以大连人民就称为"金石园"。

在大连还有好多灿烂的景致、美好的去处值得一看，我们在以上景点中就可以"一斑窥豹"。

在此再次提起张行那美好悠扬的歌声："千里万里走不出爱的晴空，大连是我灿烂的笑容……"张行的歌声也许会导引你对大连产生兴趣，生出遐想，进而，一种耳闻不如眼见的念头油然而生，促使你走进大连，一睹大连灿烂的笑容。

关帝庙　净觉寺　田中角荣留下史话一段段

关帝庙，这里说的是新中国成立前丰润县新军屯北街的关帝庙。古往今来，丰润新军屯不但是曹操曾经屯兵的地方，而且是古县丰润的一个中心镇，地理位置自古一直很重要，四通八达的交通区位优势使之成了历代兵家必争之地。日本侵华后，就把新军屯当成了据点盘踞，并派一支日军小分队驻扎在新军屯北街关帝庙里，同时在"官井"（水井）旁修筑了炮楼。

净觉寺，是从古至今一直位于玉田县城东南偏北44里处，一个叫蛮子营村的东边，还乡河与沙流河交汇处的净觉寺。净觉寺始建于唐朝，取名于佛教净业觉悟真空。公元1842—1855年曾进行四次大规模的重建、扩建、修缮。现存均为清代建筑。占地18540平方米，属于皇家寺庙，被称为"京东第一寺"。

田中角荣，1938年当时驻扎在新军屯北街关帝庙日军小分队的队长，后来在20世纪70年代曾担任日本首相。让他万万没想到的是，1938年7月6日、7日，冀东武装起义先后在滦县港北村、丰润县岩口镇爆发。接着，在以李运昌为首发动的冀东大暴动中，一夜间将新军屯北街"官井"旁的日军炮楼夷为平地，日本兵死的死，逃的逃，田中角荣也负伤仓皇出逃。被吓蒙了的田中，胆战心惊一时找不着北，慌不择路径直朝玉田方向逃窜。为转移暴动队员们的视线，田中跑了一段路后，又抄近路直奔玉田县蛮子营跑去。因为他老远就发现了金碧辉煌的净觉寺，所以不顾一切地朝寺庙直奔而去。当时寺门正好大开，他慌忙跑进寺院山门殿，看到殿内面目狰狞、令人生畏且很高大的哼哈二将，不禁毛骨悚然，田中角荣灵机一动躲到了背后。随后赶到的暴动队员们在寺内各个角落进行大搜捕，但谁也没想到田中角荣躲到了哼哈二将的身后。暴动队员们误判他是从庙中跃墙潜逃了，便又继续前往捉拿。

经过这次漏网的田中角荣，后来在他的思想里坚定地认为，是净觉寺山门殿里的哼哈二将护佑了他，他才得以大难不死逃过一劫保住了性命。也正因如此，才有他日后的从商从政和在日本政坛上的发展，历任众议院议员（第16期）、邮政大臣（第12代）、大藏大臣（第67—69代）、通商产业大臣（第33代）、内阁总理大臣（第64、65代）。1972年，田中角荣出任日本首相，同年9月底访问中华人民共和国，签署了具有历史意义的《日中联合声明》，实现了中日邦交正常化，主动让大和民族和中华民族淡化积怨，面向未来，携手世界之林，因此被称为"中国人民的老朋友"。

深秋是个容易让人怀旧、产生千思万念和别样情怀的时节，下野后的日本首相田中角荣，是一个亲历日本侵华战争并参与、感受日本帝国主义最终战败、亲手签字《日中联合声明》、亲身见证中日两国关系走向正常化的特别经历的人。

作为中华人民共和国和日本两国的友好使者，田中角荣在1985年深秋带着对中国人民的诸多忏悔，专程从日本东京再次来到中国，并特别来到他曾经驻扎过的丰润新军屯，与当年曾给驻扎在新军屯北街关帝庙日军小分队当过伙夫的新军屯村民李宝中一起叙旧。离别时，田中还把随身携带的一个精致的日本产打火机赠送给李宝中，以示友好和忏悔。后来，田中又专程来到玉田县的净觉寺虔诚朝拜了哼哈二将，追寻他避难时那惊魂动魄难以抹掉的记忆。

时光流转到21世纪的今天，新军屯北街的关帝庙和日军炮楼早已不复存在，但作为丰润区的一方重镇，新军屯正在蓬勃发展，已成为全国重点镇。

在玉田县经济快速发展的今天，净觉寺也得到很好的修缮，门口竖立了典雅秀丽的古式牌楼，铺设了5000多平方米的广场。如今这座千年古刹一洗破旧不堪的龙钟老态，真正恢复了昔日风采，再次焕发青春，寺内香烟缭绕，敬佛、参拜和旅游的人们络绎不绝，保持着京东第一寺的美誉。

田中角荣这位具有特别经历，对中日友好做出过决定性贡献的中国人民的老朋友，1993年病逝于日本东京。

今昔铁匠庄

铁匠庄，这庄名让人一听就有一种实在、踏实、勤劳的感觉。

说起铁匠庄来话就长了。清光绪十七年间的《丰润县志》上记载，铁匠庄属丰润县胥各庄管辖。相传，铁匠庄的原址是董各庄董家坟地的看坟小屋，后来，从外地搬来了一户打铁的人家在此落户，慢慢地，这里也就叫铁匠庄了。那还是大清国康熙六十年（1721）的事儿呢。

在近代这不算长的历史时光里，铁匠庄反复归属于不同时期的乡镇所管辖。民国初期，铁匠庄属丰润县第三区下辖的行政村；到了民国36年（1947），政府把原丰润的南半部划分出来，设立了浭阳县。这样，铁匠庄就被浭阳县清庄湖乡管辖了；其后铁匠庄几经更换隶属，就不一一述说了。直到1954年7月随丰南重新划归丰润县，属丰润十九区辖；1956年7月属丰润县侉子庄乡辖；1958年9月到了人民公社时期，属丰润县胥各庄人民公社侉子庄管理区辖；1961年6月随丰润、丰南再度分置，铁匠庄属丰南县侉子庄人民公社管辖；1988年12月，属丰南县侉子庄镇辖；1994年4月，属丰南市银丰镇辖；2004年属丰南区丰南镇辖。

2012年12月，丰南区政府将原址坐落在京山铁路拐弯处，东临青年路，东北与西板桥村相望，西临铁路百米之多，南与侉子庄二村相连，北邻铁路500米的铁匠庄进行了居民搬迁，其中大部分村民迁入银丰小区，少部分村民迁入金盛花苑社区。从此，拥有近三百年历史的铁匠庄，结束了它的以往融入了欣欣向荣的都市新城区。

2017年7月

萝卜坨

萝卜坨，一个满含中国农耕文化味道的名字。它曾经是丰南区丰南镇下辖的一个村庄——萝卜坨村。

据《丰润县志》载："明朝年间建村……"相传，明代张姓自山东来此立庄。也有传奇这样说："当时立庄的附近的一处高地上生长着一棵大萝卜，其个甚大，一个人要围着它锄耪一天，才能把这个大萝卜周围的地锄耪一遍。"所以，在明朝第三代皇帝明成祖朱棣（1402—1424年在位），为燕王时，发动靖难之役，起事攻打侄儿建文帝，夺位登基之后在此重新迁民建庄时，顾借此得名"萝卜坨"。

就是这样一个富有传奇色彩的小村庄，自古以来，却频繁更迭隶属，大清朝时，萝卜坨属于丰润县胥各庄镇管辖；中华民国期间属于丰润县第三区管辖；中华人民共和国成立后，属于丰润县第11区管辖，1958年属于丰润县胥各庄公社小稻地管理区管辖，1959年属于丰润县韩城公社管辖，1961年属于丰润县小稻地公社管辖，1984年3月属于丰润县小稻地乡管辖，1993年3月属于丰润县岔河镇管辖；2009年6月划入丰南区丰南镇管辖。

在丰南城区建设统一规划中，丰南区加快了萝卜坨村农村改造进程，于2010年7月13日全面启动拆迁改造工作。2011年4月，村民返迁楼建设正式破土动工，并以极快的速度，良好的质量于2013年6月全面竣工。坐落在胥各庄西城，范围东至国文路，西至源盛路，南至春阳街，北至友谊大街，拥有 13 栋居民楼的一个社会主义新农村拔地而起。昔日的"萝卜坨"村，沐浴着夏日灿烂的阳光华丽转身为"萝欣苑社区"。

煤河 老铁道 白梁桥 黑石碑 大铁锚

煤河，是 1878 年，经大清帝国政府批准开挖的运煤河道，有史以来一直被官方和民间称为"煤河"，是位于今丰南境内一条全长 35 公里长的人工河。关于煤河，过去的《丰润县志》曾有这样一段记述："……长约七十余里，宽十数丈，引芦河之水，随潮汐上下，设闸储蓄，波平浪静，四时不涸，商艘客船，樯密如林，来往洋轮疾于奔马而起，浚之处名河头，方圆数十亩，波水澄清，两岸洋楼花坞；目不暇尝，稍西桥旁，列肆鳞比，人烟辏集，居然一水陆埠头也。"

煤河于 1881 年春开挖，几乎与谎称"快车马路"的唐胥铁路同时在同年夏季竣工，河底宽 1.5 丈，河面宽 6 丈，深 1 丈，河道有铁石水闸，控制水位，总占地约 6500 亩，工程造价 11.5 万两白银。至此，路与河的连接，使唐山真正意义地走出了封闭，走向了广阔的发展之路。

从此之后，煤河之上舟楫的迷人环佩，帆樯飘逸神韵。喧嚣的煤河码头，横河卧波的九道桥，繁华着因煤而兴因河而盛的冀东小镇——河头。

一百多年后的 2002 年，丰南区历时两年花费 4000 万元完成了煤河治理一期工程。

如今，经历了一百四十二年之久历史的煤河，已是碧水含青、鱼翔浅底，两岸花团锦簇，杨柳依依，健身路径曲径通幽，一片旖旎风光。沿河带状公园镶嵌着四件宝贝：老铁道、白梁桥、黑石碑、大铁锚。已经成为煤河之上的一道亮丽风景。

老铁道：煤河带状公园东段，至今还特意保留有两条原始松木道枕的标准轨距铁道，一左一右由东北向西南斜向展现在人们面前。向人们展示着中国第一条准轨铁路铺设并使用于胥各庄，这里是中国近代工业辉煌的起点。这是一条建设于大清帝国光绪七年（公元 1881 年）唐山至胥各庄的铁路，虽然，愚昧迷信的慈禧太后，生怕火车头的轰鸣与笛声惊动了清东陵地下长眠的先祖，当时不让火车头运转，但即便是马拉装满煤炭的车厢，也依然把优质的开滦煤炭运出了海，装上了海轮驶向海外。同时，大清帝国的北洋舰队使用的就是开滦煤炭，熊熊燃烧的炉火鼓舞着条条战舰，冲向日本侵略者的战舰！回望历史，唐胥铁路的铺设和使用，不但推动了历史车轮的前进，带动了中国近代工业的发展，还为中国人民抗击外来侵略做出了不可磨灭的贡献。这一点，在某种意义上说，是中国的大美，是中华民族的大美。

白梁桥：这是坐落在胥各庄滨河东路南北向横卧在煤河之上的一座架设在原桥之上附加的钢结构桥梁，通体白色，远看近看都很美观，不但提高了原桥的档次，更增加了桥梁的景观效应。

黑石碑：这是一座不规则扁长形的碑记石，全黑色碑石，碑体表面光滑闪亮。无论碑体还是碑文，都充满凝重和深远。记录着中国第一条专门运输煤炭河流的人工开挖和日后治理的始末，昭示着这"煤河"是中国近代民族工业产品走出唐山、走向世界的起点。

大铁锚：大铁锚的所在之处，就是现在丰南第一中学隔河相望的对面。无论春夏秋冬，风霜雨雪，大铁锚都傲然挺立在那里，静静伫立在天地间。但它的凝视里，有历史烟云，有朝代更迭，有兴衰荣辱，更有美好的未来。

煤河记忆

煤河，1878年，经大清帝国政府批准人工开挖运煤河道，史称"煤河"，位于今丰南（清朝属丰润县地）境内，是一条全长35公里长的人工河。今天的胥各庄镇毗邻的就是原来的"河头"镇，"河头"作为开滦煤炭水路外运先河，有过她一时的繁华。"河头"也曾是丰润县政府的所在地。关于煤河，过去的《丰润县志》曾有这样一段记述："……长约七十余里，宽十数丈，引芦河之水，随潮汐上下，设闸储蓄，波平浪静，四时不涸，商艘客船，樯密如林，来往洋轮疾于奔马而起，浚之处名河头，方圆数十亩，波水澄清，两岸洋楼花坞；目不暇尝，稍西桥旁，列肆鳞比，人烟辏集，居然一水陆埠头也。"

开平煤矿从1878年开矿后，当时的上海轮船招商局总办、候补道台唐廷枢，受朝廷总理大臣李鸿章委托，统揽开平煤矿事宜，但他已敏感地觉察到，筑路的阻力足可以将这一新兴产业扼杀掉，他只能重新设计并几次调整运输方案，最终议定，由胥各庄到阎庄之间开挖一条70里长的河道，引蓟运河水。而胥各庄至唐山一段，地势渐高，引水造河显然不宜，所以改修"快车马路"，与之相接。这就是后来的煤河和唐胥铁路。煤河1881年春开挖，几乎与谎称"快车马路"的唐胥铁路同时在同年夏季竣工，河底宽1.5丈，河面宽6丈，深1丈，河道有铁石水闸，控制水位，总占地约 6500 亩，工程造价 11.5 万两白银。至此，路与河的连接，使唐山（当时是桥屯镇）真正意义地走出了封闭，走向了广阔的发展之路。

144 年历史的煤河之上，曾经的迷人环佩，帆樯飘逸神韵。喧嚣的煤河码头，横河卧波的九道桥，繁华着因煤而兴因河而盛的冀东小镇——河头。

从煤河在这片充满生机的土地上诞生，丰南就张开了宽广的臂膀，以博大的胸襟容纳着天下的人流物流。繁荣的航运拉动了商贸的飞速发展，刺激了工业的蓬勃兴起。煤河不仅创造了一方富土，更孕育了丰南人民敢为人先、勇创大业的奋斗精神。丰南不能没有煤河，丰南不能放弃煤河！于是，一百多年后的 2002 年，丰南区成立煤河治理指挥部，开始了煤河历史上最大规模的治理。全区人民自愿捐款，仅一周时间，就收捐款 3000 余万元。历时两年，共投资 4000 万元，完成了煤河治理一期工程。

如今，经历了清朝、民国、共和国历史进程的煤河，已是碧水含青、鱼翔浅底，两岸是沿河带状公园，花团锦簇，杨柳依依，健身路径曲径通幽，一片旖旎风光。

长天流云，历史悠悠，唐山、开滦、河头（胥各庄）都不会忘记这条把优质的开滦煤炭运送装上海轮驶向海外。同时，大清帝国的北洋舰队使用着开平煤矿的煤炭，熊熊燃烧的炉火鼓舞着条条战舰，冲向日本侵略者的战舰！回望历史，煤河的开挖和使用，推动了历史带动了中国近代民族工业的发展，还为中国人民抗击外来侵略做出了不可磨灭的贡献。这一点，在某种意义上说，是中国的大美，是中华民族的大美。在中华民族伟大复兴，努力实践中国梦的今天，我们更不会忘记这条代表国家光荣与梦想的河流……

2017 年 7 月

大钿，玲珑美丽的世外桃源

2015 年 6 月间，我采风到玉田农村住了一段时间，在那里，除了写作，还有一个意外的收获，就是发现了"大钿"这块儿优雅美丽的田园。

天天早上出去转转，是我长久以来的一个习惯。6 月 5 日的晚上，老天下了一夜的雨，快到天亮时停了。6 日的早上 5 点，我下楼来到大街上，渐渐向这个村庄南面走去，沿着晚上被雨水冲刷干净的乡间水泥路，穿行在长满绿油油的玉米和已经泛黄的小麦的田间。因为刚刚下过雨，早上的天空格外的晴朗。呼吸着田野里清新的空气，田园风光我一边走一边欣赏。目光远及之处，一个高台，上面还有一个亭子，隐隐约约映入眼帘。我伫立遥望，然后顺路寻去。十多分钟的工夫来到近前，只见门口写着："大钿生态农场"。

走进门口，往里望去，草地、石刻、甬道、垂柳、池塘、假山、高台、凉亭……整洁清爽。

甬道两边垂柳丝丝，门口右侧一大块汉白玉石上镌刻着："大钿生态农场"的金色大字。其南面是草坪，草地间栽有柳树，还散落其间一块块大小不一的石刻。草坪右边是一排整齐的背西向东的蓝顶木屋。再往南依次是梅花鹿、鸵鸟、孔雀、山鸡、矮马、矮黄牛、驴、山羊，还有鸡、鸭、鹅、猪等各种动物的栏舍，虽然是圈养，但有专人饲养它们，所以各个显得都干净精神，很是招人喜爱。

门口左边是一道人工木质的回廊，廊前是一个小型人工湖，湖心亭和小船在里面，湖水的南面就是人工堆砌的假山，山上的平台有墙，墙上有长城一样的垛口，像古城似的平台上，还有一个木质的凉亭。阳光下，这一切都倒映在湖水之中，显得清静悠然祥和。顺水上栈桥走进湖心亭向水面望去，一群红色的鲤鱼在水中欢快地游动嬉戏，不时地露出水面。南面假山上一条人工瀑布直泻下来，让人感觉到一股夏日凉爽。从湖心亭出来拾级登台而上，像是在登邯郸古丛台一样的感觉。来到台上，四外环顾，上下打量，让人眼前豁然开朗。蓝蓝的天上飘着白云，白云下面一望无际的庄稼地里，小麦一片金黄，玉米一片翠绿。在希望田野上的不远处，看得见的是新农村一栋栋一排排的新楼房，红色楼顶在晨光中显得那么鲜亮好看……

站在假山平台上登高望远风光无限，这在当地人来看，早就习以为常已是不显什么，但对于我这一过客来说，那就是新大陆的发现。没想到，在玉田县邢庄这块土地上，竟然还有这样一个环境宜人，清静优雅的生态农场，好比世外桃源。大钿生态农场——让人惊喜欢颜。

北武当

站在山脚下，迁西石门山，就展现在我们面前。这座山峰因其南向有一巨大峭壁酷似一道石门，因而得名石门山。

相传，春秋战国时期，群雄崛起，天下纷争，连年混战。此地更是水深火热，民不聊生。道教祖师老子听说石门山里藏有无数珍宝，便欲取出救济苍生。然而，打开石门需要一把特殊的钥匙。一天，老子云游来到石门山，在一农户的葫芦架下，将一只奇特的葫芦施以法术，并与农夫约定七七四十九天后来买取。

那农夫十分狡黠，见老子行为怪异，猜中老子欲买葫芦的意图，趁老子不在，便在四十八天时将葫芦摘下，打开了石门。石门开了一条缝，农夫果然见到里面财宝无数，顿起贪心。为怕石门关闭，便用葫芦顶在门缝处。可怜葫芦不坚而碎，石门复闭，财宝没有取出。第二天老子来了，葫芦却不在了，老子得知详情，叹息道："亿万年机遇，得而复失，可惜了。"遂点化一只神犬，终日守护石门山。

岁月悠悠，日月轮回，时至今日，石门山又有了一个威武的名字——北武当。

当你站在山顶，你会看到海拔七百多米的北武当，四十座雄奇的山峰矗立在栗乡腹地，守望在滦河东岸，依偎喜峰雄关，与长城比肩。登顶极目，画境栗乡尽收眼底；开怀舒胸，诗意山水倾注心间。

古老中国，江南海北，遍布佛道名山；塞外川中，神仙洞府纷呈。熙来攘往，尽是寻求之客；云卷风流，皆为名利之行。然而，当你来到迁西北武当，必然令你产生这样的感叹：原始生态，生发别样情怀；涤荡胸中块垒，竟是这造化自然。

行走在布阵奇峰，林立怪石，十一个天然洞穴散落其间的50里北武当山中，让人感到步步景不同，你会听到一景一传说。这里的赤色花岗岩体，显眼夺目；山上飞瀑流泉，腾空素练。守门天犬，不倦千载任劳任怨；灵性神龟，伏地反省，万冬忏悔无眠。山岭之上有蟠龙，往古来今，犹记张坤事迹；山头卧虎，李广雄风依然彰显。天降四兽，一如既往千万年，把守道教仙山。将军顶盔，武威世间，直慑敌胆；隐仙洞里有仙人，逸性迥异世情。玄山洞口，悠闲对弈合和二仙；玉兔峰下，日月两轮奇松在山间。岚风迎晓，披霞浴火满青山；日落时分，宛如碧水淌玉流莹的，正是那余晖送晚。是处皆妙、天趣大成美景。避开繁华喧嚣，亲近美好自然，来此北武当山，放眼赏景，不尽气定神闲，不啻神仙。

北武当，古迹满山。唐王征东，娘娘山中诞龙种；李俅修仙，仙人洞里成了仙。圆觉寺院，曾见香火旺盛，缭绕云烟；玉皇道场，还有遗址再现。老子山山如道祖；老子洞洞似仙宫。玄武峰上，大帝未老；观音山中，菩萨年轻。佳境天成，步移景换。

有诗人赞石门山："远近高低放眼量，侧峰横岭装画廊。浓妆淡抹佳绝景，错把栗乡为梦乡。"

下得山来，转身回望神秘的苍莽层峦，犹抱琵琶半掩面。落日辉煌，我在静思，当今的北武当，虽然还藏在深闺人未识，但美好前景无限……

2017 年 7 月 5 日

一路风情

2007年7月26日，我们一行50人前往内蒙古旅游，我们一路北上。从河北省的唐山市经停迁安市白羊峪、承德外八庙、塞罕坝到内蒙古的古克什克腾旗草原，的确让人领略了沿途不一般的生态，不一样的风情。

长城月色

来到迁安市的白羊峪已是傍晚时分，旅游车太大开不到山顶，人们只得走下车来，拿着各自的行囊，徒步山间小路向山顶的住地走去。山路左边，是一道较高的山梁，山梁上一道长城横亘，一轮落日悬在一个箭楼的右上方。是岁月和人为的因素，使这道长城让我今天看来显得有些寂寞、残破。但从另一个角度去看，夕阳下，长城既让我看到她的悲壮，又让我看到她的傲然。在我的视线里可以看到五个箭楼，箭楼间的城墙已无明显的垛口。岁月蹉跎，箭楼虽是缺牙少口，但依然屹立在那里，显得高大而不可侵犯。山上的大树不多，但满山灌木，显得郁郁葱葱，生机勃勃。

吃过晚饭，同宿去打牌，我则坐在窗前的石鼓凳上看眼前的长城。夜幕下的长城在山梁上东西走向，多半轮在山雾中显得有些昏黄的月亮，悬在白羊峪长城之上，给我一种雾蒙蒙月朦胧的苍凉之感。遥想明朝、秦朝，甚至更早的战国的长城卫士们，就是在这样寂静的一个个夜晚，或披星戴月，或风雪交加，或电闪雷鸣，或伸手不见五指，都要时刻睁眼竖耳，机警注视所有草木动静，警惕着胡马铁蹄的声响。为保家卫国，耐得住那一方寂寞与冷清、那一份孤独与苦楚，在长城沿线辛苦戍边，保卫着长城内500万平方公里的家国河山。

旅游团的团员们在住地的歌厅里纵情高歌，深情演唱。我则望着白羊峪的夜空、群山、长城、月色，心里想，不知道那时的戍边将士们是否有过篝火欢歌、胡琴弹奏、家乡小调。白羊峪，你让我想了很多很多……

普陀舞姿

世界上最大的皇家寺庙群就是承德的外八庙。大清朝40座皇家寺庙有32座在北京城，其余8座在承德，俗称外八庙，实际是十二座。外八庙是当今世界上保存最好、规模最大的皇家寺庙群。其中，普陀寺是极具特色的一座藏式寺庙。因其仿建西藏拉萨布达拉宫且小于布达拉宫，所以，人们又习惯于叫它小布达拉宫。参观普陀寺，除了让我感受到藏式佛教寺庙建筑风格和藏传佛教文化精深之处的同时，还让我意外的欣赏到了一场别具特色的藏族歌舞演出。演出中，藏民族特有的高原民族那嘹亮高亢的歌声，震撼着我的心灵，藏民族那粗犷大方、奔放洒脱的民族舞蹈，舞动着空气与阳光，也舞动着场上的气氛和观舞者的快乐与激昂。通过歌舞，我看到了藏族人民今天生活的幸福和欢畅。通过歌舞，我看到了藏族人民对美好未来的追求和向往。

草原驰骋

旅游大巴从承德出发沿着武烈河顺伊逊河北上，穿越著名的塞罕坝国家林场，行驶在林海之间，我们边听松涛边看白桦林继续前行，离内蒙古自治区克什克腾旗草原也就不远了。克什克腾旗在内蒙古西拉木伦河上游，与河北省接壤，明朝时为克什克腾部，清朝初期正式设旗。

在大草原上，对于我们这些同车到来的唐山人来说，都想纵身上马一试身手，体会一下在一望无边的内蒙古大草原上纵横驰骋，放马奔腾的感觉。蒙古妇女从马厩里牵出一匹马，也许是一般游客都不会骑马的缘故吧，马的主人按惯例都要牵着游客骑的马向草原进发。不会骑马的我，却非想自己一试身手。于是，软磨硬泡的说服马主，没让马的主人给我牵马进草原，任镫扳鞍翻身上马，自己骑马穿过南北向的大道，走向草原。我的前面有二十多匹马，背上驮着游客由马的主人牵引前行。走上一处山包，我勒住马，立马高岗之上，放眼展望远无边际的大草原，这天堂般的大草原哪，是那么的旷达、辽阔、壮美。顿时，一种豪放奔驰的欲望驱使我情不自禁脱口一个"驾"字，胯下的枣红马立即小跑起来。此时我想起导游的话："骑马时要前脚掌点镫，屁股似坐非坐，双手轻松持缰。"于是，再"驾"一声。马儿加速奔跑起来，我的耳边呼呼生风，马儿快速向草原深处跑去……

跑了很远，我"吁"了一声勒住马缰，马儿收住撒开的四蹄。在广阔无垠的大草原上，回首我身后的草原，看到那些坐勒勒车、骑四轮摩托仍在慢慢前行的游人们，在很远处星星点点镶嵌在绿色的草原上。我有点不放心这些同来的兄弟姐妹，怕是发生出其不意。于是，掉转马头，纵马持缰折了回来，看到大家平安无事，我心里也踏实了，看看大家我笑了。高兴得再次调转马头，双脚后跟一磕马肚子大喊一声"驾"！马儿撒开四蹄重新奔向远方……

信马由缰，在大草原上豪情奔放，那是一种心灵的激荡，那是一种激情的释放，那是一种驾驭的体验和能力的检验。豪爽性格的我在这里更加爽朗，草原上驭马奔驰的成功更坚定了自我信心。

马儿奔驰到一个湖边我"吁"了一声，马儿停下。立马湖边，望着蓝蓝的湖水和远方无边无际的茫茫草原，一辆辆散落其间的勒勒车和一个个游人走马，我再一次策马踏上回返的路程。当姐妹兄弟们看到我在马背上的得心应手的同时，我们不约而同地相互招手致意。

跑马溜溜的草原，任你溜溜的跑哟。只要你坚定了信心，没有办不成的事哟。内蒙古克什克腾旗生态完美的大草原啊，是你给了我机会、成功、快乐。是你告诉了我："自信就会成功，坚持创造永恒。"

"云外天"塞罕坝

农历盛夏六月，我们来到著名的塞罕坝林场。12米长的大巴进入了总面积达2324平方公里的塞罕坝国家森林公园，简直就像一叶小舟航行在茫茫大海里一样。汽车穿行于掩映在茂密森林之中的森林公路上，平原长大的我，坐在车窗前看林间公路两旁高大笔直的松树和间或的白桦树，感觉着塞罕坝莽莽大森林的凉爽、清新。树木一棵棵迅速掠过，车窗前的树木又很快扑到眼前继而迅速掠过。汽车向前疾驶，连绵不断让我目不暇接的林涛树海，耳边不觉回荡起现代京剧《智取威虎山》里杨子荣"打虎上山"，那高亢嘹亮的唱段："穿林海，跨雪原，气冲霄汉……"大有一种昂扬豪迈的劲头。

导游告诉我们，由于生态良好，这里的野兽有野猪、黑熊、狼、松鼠等。山货有灵芝、蘑菇等。他还特别向我们介绍了一种名贵的中药材，塞罕坝第一花——金莲花。夏天灿烂的阳光下，金黄色的花朵开放在绿色的草原上，很是好看。他说："非典期间，这种中药材非常紧俏，价格昂贵。这种药材，还有清咽利喉消炎的作用。"一路旅程中，导游滔滔不绝地为大家讲述着天上人间的故事，历史长河的典故，人文地理的奇处，自然环境的绝妙神奇。不知不觉中，我们来到了塞罕坝林场总场所在地。这里规划还是很好的，大路宽阔笔直平坦，两旁高楼、酒店、宾馆、商业楼比比皆是。我们的汽车开进了金字高悬的"云外天宾馆"。走下车来入住宾馆，看看腕上的手表，已是下午5点多钟了。打开淋浴喷头，洗去一路征尘和一身的疲惫。躺在床上，放松了自己的筋骨与身心。

傍晚7点钟，宾馆外走进来一队文工团员，全部蒙古族穿戴，他们在宾馆的天井里铺上了红地毯，摆上了音响，架起了架子鼓。我们喜出望外，分别在宾馆的院子里摆好的五桌丰盛宴席前坐下。开场了，身穿蓝底金花蒙古袍的高大蒙古族小伙子用蒙古语开场白。蒙古族姑娘用汉语说："来自远方的朋友们，欢迎你们的到来，我们要把纯正的马奶酒，豪放的歌声，热烈的舞蹈献给亲爱的朋友们，与你们一起度过一个火红热烈的篝火晚会！"

天井中央，篝火燃起，映红了宾馆里的天地人楼。一段奔放的蒙古族舞蹈之后，一个蒙古族姑娘热情地唱起："远方的朋友，请让我为你斟满马奶酒，这酒纯正，这酒醇厚……"

蒙古族姑娘们手捧哈达，端着银制的酒壶和银碗，来到大家面前，为我们一一献上哈达，一一斟满马奶酒。我按照蒙古族习俗，用中指沾酒分别敬天敬地，然后，把这一碗盛满民族盛情的香醇马奶酒一饮而尽。

晚会进行着，文工团的一位蒙古姑娘上来唱起了《向天再借五百年》这首歌。我惊愕地发现，她虽然是个姑娘，却把这首歌唱得大气豪放，荡气回肠，一展乾隆盛世帝王的气度，舒放霸主皇帝的浩荡胸怀。让我感到心灵震颤，倍感欣赏。不禁为她热烈鼓掌，然后，拿起一束鲜花献给这位才华的歌者。

一首歌儿悠然唱起，一个蒙古族小伙子深情地演绎着著名歌手腾格尔那一首亲切的《蒙古人》。这个高大的蒙古汉子，脚蹬一双蒙古长靴，一身蒙古长袍，一头披肩长发，在他的歌声里浸透着对蒙古家乡的情和爱。我看着他充满自豪和赞美的表情，听着他悠扬的歌声，沉醉在一种深情里。我非常敬重他对家乡的情和爱，因为我也有家乡，我也有对家乡的情和爱。所以，身在千里之外他乡的我，情不自禁地起身走上前去与这位蒙古族歌手紧紧握手，合影留念。晚会进行到高潮，文工团员们走下舞台与我们手拉手，围着熊熊燃烧的篝火，跳起了热情欢快的集体舞蹈。在我们旅游团员里有满族、回族团员，在这激情的夜晚，我们汉满蒙回四个民族的人们，在一种畅达、欢快、热烈、友好的气氛中，度过了一个团结、美好、友谊、和谐的夜晚。云外天的篝火格外的红，塞罕坝的情谊格外的浓。

梦回唐朝

在唐山南湖的西岸，南湖大道与学院南路交叉口的东南侧，那座始建于大唐帝国时代，2010年重新复建，2016年建成并于2016年唐山世界园艺博览会开幕之际对外开放的"唐山龙泉寺"。在21公顷土地上，形成了拥有建筑面积4.1万平方米的大型寺庙，整组建筑凸显着大唐风范，彰显着唐朝国度那大气、弘放、豪迈的风格和气概，傲然挺立在四月阳光明媚春花烂漫的唐山大地上。

上午 10 点的天气晴朗，阳光正好。我来到唐山龙泉寺，站在寺前，看着这座作为今天冀东地区第一大道场的唐山龙泉寺，不禁让我仰望并回顾龙泉寺的前世荣耀。龙泉寺始建于公元 644 年，此时的大唐帝国已经建立 27 年之久，正处于大唐贞观盛世期间，也就是唐太宗（李世民）贞观十八年，那时的唐朝，国家强盛，人民安康。唐太宗时期开疆拓土的得力大将军尉迟敬德亲临监修龙泉寺这一寺庙，时至今日已有 1300 多年的历史。悠悠岁月，时光荏苒，寺庙前的一条大沟静静的东西向横亘在那里，如今隐约可见，是自古出关的老道，也由此验证了"千年的大道走成河"这句中国古老话语的千真万确。现在，古道已成为龙泉河的一部分。

这里的龙泉寺不失为古代中国北方地区一处重要的佛教活动场所，历史上曾经有过重修。1971 年，人们在拆除龙泉寺正殿的时候，在庙宇脊檩的嵌的上首发现有用毛笔写的文字："明万历年重修"。下款是三个人名，有两个为"洪X"，这也许是佛人的法号。直到 20 世纪 30 年代的一天，一场大雾中，寺庙里最后一个老和尚在寺中圆寂了，从此结束了这座古老庙宇里有和尚的历史。

复建后的唐山龙泉寺山门前广场，利用现有一处较高平台的地形，形成了进入寺院主体前的集散空间，其北侧为寺院的主体。龙泉寺这座寺院是坐北朝南的坐落，主体建筑位于高出周边 10 米左右的平台之上，平台南北长 300 米，东西宽 250 米，据说，现在的规模比原来龙泉寺还要大 3 倍。从南到北的主要建筑有山门、天王殿、观音殿、大雄宝殿、藏经阁，依次递进向里形成了五进式禅寺院落，营造出传统的寺院空间效果。在建筑风格和整体布局上保持了大唐帝国那种开明奔放，大方气派，阳光磊落，昂扬向上的气势。身临其境，自然被周围简洁厚重明朗的氛围，感染思绪。浸浴在唐朝的建筑，唐朝的色彩，唐朝的草木其中，面对着唐朝气宇轩昂的高大殿宇，凝视泡钉大门，仰视金身佛像。感受唐朝气息，闻到唐朝味道，触及唐朝国度。

不觉时已下午，站在龙泉寺，眯缝着眼睛看天，阳光飞跃时空，从唐朝一直照耀到今天，让人感觉到了一种飞扬畅达，仿佛有了一种梦回唐朝的穿越感，一种挺拔傲岸的鼓舞，散发一种只争朝夕的精神。

在灿烂阳光下我走出寺院，回头环顾唐山龙泉寺，仰慕寺院那宏伟的气派，感叹不愧是冀东地区一座大型的佛教道场，顺春光畅想，龙泉寺不但继往开来，更将重新焕发中国北方地区唐山龙泉寺这一古老重要的佛教活动场所的往日辉煌。

唐山，腾飞吧涅槃的凤凰

唐山有座凤凰山，过去叫双凤山。因为唐山地带在一千年前属于大辽国，辽圣宗耶律隆绪的仁德皇后萧氏，乳名菩萨哥，辽道宗的宣懿皇后萧观音。辽国中晚期兴起了崇佛热潮，隐居在凤凰山一带的萧姓族人出资在山上建造了菩萨庙，为齐天皇后萧菩萨哥铸造真身造像，还在菩萨庙下开掘洞穴，供奉萧观音石象，逢年过节敬香祭祀，以示怀念。因为他们祭祀的是两位皇后，便给原本无名的小山起名双凤山。直到20世纪70年代才被改称凤凰山。

唐山这座有凤凰城之称的一百多年的重工业城市，京山铁路纵贯其中，两大国企开滦、钢厂；两大城区路南路北，分列左右两边，像一双翅膀一样，振翅唐山不断向前。正在唐山蓬勃发展之时，1976年7月28日发生了7.8级大地震毁灭了唐山，但是这座英雄的城市，正如凤凰涅槃，浴火重生，时至今日，这座城市于1991年成功举办第二届中华人民共和国城市运动会之后，已先后获得联合国人居奖、中国优秀旅游城市、国家级园林城市、全国双拥模范城市等荣誉。自2016年4月29日2016年举办唐山世界园艺博览会盛大开园，下半年第25届金鸡百花电影节、中国—中东欧国家地方领导人会议、中国—拉美企业家高峰会还将在唐山举办。这一次次的机遇，无疑又给唐山的经济文化和城市建设与发展增添了无形的双翼，必将助力唐山腾飞。

站在世园会一号门，抬眼向南望去，让你无不震撼的感觉，宏大设计的整体造型，那就是一只巨型的展翅奋发的凤凰：十三巨大羽毛造型的凤尾舒展上翘，唐山规划展览馆的建筑造型恰如凤身和展开的双翼充满着动感与力量，在前，就是那高昂的凤头，引领着高飞的凤凰……

走进巨型凤凰雕塑前的市民广场，站在南湖边上，环顾2016年唐山世界园艺博览会园区布局，国际国内两片园区分立一湖碧水东西两边。这让我感到，这不再是无意的巧合，也不是简单的平面设计，是世园会设计师独具匠心的设计构思，巧妙利用地理环境的精巧用意，这样又是一双巧夺天工的凤凰双翼。

登上龙台阁，居高临下俯瞰，画面顿时不禁让我惊叹：一只巨大的凤凰跃然眼前，昂头振翅，奋飞向前！唐山啊，唐山。你不就是这只展翅高飞的凤凰嘛。

蓝蓝的天空极为晴朗，灿烂的阳光正好照耀。南湖上的大型喷泉在音乐声中腾升起舞。好风凭借力，扬帆好行船。唐山，美丽的涅槃凤凰，向着美好的明天飞翔吧！

2016年4月

风舞秋海

下午4点钟,大巴车行驶在昌黎县境通往北戴河海滨的水泥公路上,天高云淡,晴空万里。道路两旁垂柳的枝条,既像舞者杨丽萍那双绵软的手臂,又像一匹匹绿色的丝绸,荡漾在风中是那般的飘柔,让人感觉到一种美妙的温馨。不觉中车已进入黄金海岸,透过车窗和路边的树木可以看到大海,海面风平浪静。海边的人们各自悠闲的玩儿着自己想玩儿的,看着自己想看的。蓝蓝的天,白白的云,蓝蓝的海,金色的沙滩,红色的楼顶,给人一种浪漫悠闲的情致。不一会儿车就到了海滨疗养所。这里坐北朝南,打开窗子就见路边那一望无际的大海,那么宽广,那么博大,海风吹来是那么惬意。

北戴河海滨的夜晚月明星稀,疗养员们有的去夜市,有的去海边。我则到疗养所里的舞厅来唱歌看跳舞。变幻迷离的灯光,让人迷奇又沉醉,间或低回缠绵间或奋发向上的舞曲,使得偌大一个舞厅时而温情脉脉时而激情荡漾。忽然,视频和音箱里影现出的图像和音乐是由周冰倩和她演唱的歌曲《今夜无眠》,顿时,全场人员群情激扬,纷纷起舞,男男女女的舞步是那么的协调轻盈,心情和笑容是那么的开朗洒脱。秋夜,这里却春风阵阵。

来这里的第三天,所里组织大家去秦始皇求仙入海处参观游览。在这里,有一尊高大的巨型秦始皇帝(公元前259—公元前210)立身石雕像,那么气宇轩昂,雄视天下,威震四方。也许,在全中国这是秦始皇最大的一尊石雕像了。这位从公元前230年到公元前221年,用十年时间征服了海内四方的中国始皇帝,面对茫茫沧海,既有他真心还想再活五百年的愿望,更有他四海一统的勃勃雄心和霸主的胸怀大略。在这里,始皇帝极目远望,凛然威风……

在秦皇的注视下,我们走过栈桥登上秦皇1号游轮,向大海深处进发,船上还有新疆维吾尔族青年男女在演出歌舞节目,让我有幸一睹西域歌舞的遗风。游轮迎着海风前进,我手扶船舷,面向大海,背对美丽海岸,队友几次为我拍照,留下在宽阔海洋上那风飘额发和衣衫的飘逸与浪漫,领略秋日那舒爽宜人的海风。

傍晚,我独自来到海边坐下,看拣贝壳的人们。肤白体胖的俄罗斯妇人仍在海里游着。不远处,归来的船只忙着卸货,不时有海鸥在晚霞中飞舞。海浪哗哗地拍打着岸边的礁石,对对情侣在沙滩上留下串串脚印。夕阳西斜残照,海面涌起浪花……

疗养最后一天的清晨,我信步来到海边等待日出。这片秦皇瞩目的千古沧海又要迎来新的一轮红日。海鸥在浅海觅食,游人在礁石上等待朝阳。忽然有人惊呼:太阳出来了!火红的太阳先是半个，一会儿就是一整个儿地从大海里跳了出来继而冉冉升起。再回首，秦皇迎风远望，衣带飘摆。千古一帝像是在呼唤着崭新乾坤，再现盛世，呼唤中华重振雄风，威扬四海。

  秋天的海起风了，浪大起来。中华民族伟大复兴的中国梦，澎湃而来，不可阻挡！

2005 年 2 月 19 日

回归

  怎能忘，强人践踏我河山，纵火圆明园，耻辱我祖国，掠我母怀抱之子——香港！

  香江流淌，不息母子长久离散的牵肠，风动海浪，不停母子凝眸望。

  悠悠岁月，殷殷情怀，深深期盼，沧桑依然，从不断一个半世纪遥远的思乡。国力强，国运昌，江河唱，海激荡。大不列颠兴叹望洋，一九九七收香港，炎黄子孙心欢畅。深情地喊一声——香港！你终于实现了太久的向往，回归祖国，东方之珠，你会更加辉煌。

  向上、繁荣的香港，二十七年紫荆花灿烂绽放。港珠澳超常大桥卧波踏浪跨越大洋，国家创建大湾区将托举一个更加活力的香港。

1997 年 7 月 1 日为香港回归而作
2024 年 7 月 1 日香港回归 27 年修改

皇家窖藏金顶饮

借段故事开个头：1681年4月，康熙帝北巡来到今天的平泉大吉口安营扎寨，并在这里的围场沟狩猎。时近响午追捕猎物时，饥肠辘辘的康熙忽然闻到一阵酒香，循味儿望去，见一茅屋前，一白胡子老者正在酿酒。康熙赶过去问老者，可有充饥之物？老者端过一碗酒，一碗羊杂，两个芝麻烧饼。康熙帝兹拉一口酒，吧嗒一口菜。酒香沁心脾，烧饼填饱肚。康熙帝吃得那叫一个香。康熙问老者，此地叫啥地儿？这酒叫啥酒？老者答：此地叫八沟，酒是八沟酒。

1711年，承德行宫初具规模，康熙帝亲自命名为"避暑山庄"，传旨用他念念不忘的平泉八沟酒大排筵宴，赐封并御笔亲题"山庄老酒"四字。还钦选皇家御用酒窖来存储，源源不断的平泉八沟老酒，就储藏在避暑山庄最早的皇家窖藏之地——"上用库"，"山庄皇家窖藏酒"就此而来。

回头咱说2007年7月26日，我们一行50人前往内蒙古旅游。中途，我们在世界上保存最好、最大的皇家寺庙群承德外八庙游览。大清朝40座皇家寺庙有32座在北京城，其余8座在承德，所以俗称外八庙，实际是十二座。外八庙是当今世界上规模最大的皇家寺庙群。其中，普陀寺是极具特色的一座藏式寺庙。因其仿建西藏拉萨布达拉宫且小于布达拉宫，又称小布达拉宫。参观普陀寺，除了让我感受到藏式佛教寺庙建筑风格和藏传佛教文化精深之处的同时，还让我意外的欣赏到了一场别具特色的藏族歌舞演出。演出中，藏民族特有的高原民族那嘹亮高亢的歌声，震撼着我的心灵，藏民族那粗犷大方、奔放洒脱的民族舞蹈，舞动着空气与阳光，也舞动着场上的气氛和观舞者的快乐与激昂。通过歌舞，我看到了藏族人民今天生活的幸福和欢畅。通过歌舞，我看到了藏族人民对美好未来的追求和向往。

看完演出，大家陆续来到普陀寺金顶游览拍照。普陀寺金顶金碧辉煌，金光闪闪，大气恢宏，游人纷纷拍照留念。大家都照，自然也少不了我。背靠金顶，手扶琉璃瓦连拍几张，至今珍藏。

那时在金顶上，游人还可以停留。（出于对古代建筑和文物的保护，现在不行了。）连续几个庙宇游览下来的我们也感觉有些乏累，于是铺上一块携带的布在金顶露台上，从包里掏两瓶山庄老酒打开，一只烧鸡撕扯开来，哥几个在金顶叙说承德外八庙的宏大壮阔，气派非凡。在山庄品山庄老酒，品一口酒香沁人心脾，美意满怀。虽然，阳历7月正是农历六月，天气正热，但我们带着牛仔式宽檐帽，吃手撕烧鸡，喝山庄老酒，畅想着乾隆皇帝那时在这被称为"小布达拉宫"的普陀寺里大摆盛宴，用山庄老酒热情招待西藏六世班禅那热闹、排场的盛大场面。

可说是乾隆帝密切同少数民族首领与大清王朝关系的一种睿智，因此，"山庄老酒"也不愧是大一统国家多民族和睦相处的"融合剂"，更是中华古国繁荣昌盛，民族团结的最好真实物证。

天上阳光灿烂，普陀寺上老酒回甘。往事一段段，难忘皇家窖藏金顶畅饮那一段。

草原行：康巴诺尔、南天门、卧龙图、闪电湖、九曲十八弯

三年来，张北草原一直计划去一下，这里的草原最美的时段就是7月下旬到8月上旬这段时间。向东、佃福、海霞、春淋也一直盛情邀约。2023年8月4日早上9点钟小张开车我们从家里出来，车至高速路口入高速直接导航奔承德外环线，一路向北，到承德地界一路向西，目的地张北康保，来一次魂牵梦绕的草原行。

五小时车程到达高速路千松坝服务区，我们在这里稍事休息，吃了点东西。服务区对面的山峦平缓苍翠，是天路的一部分，天路绵延百里，横跨承德、北京、沽源等张家口地区。满眼绿色，非常养眼，天地间充满生机。

40分钟后启动汽车，前往沽源，一路奔驰向康保。

下午3点30分许到达康保县，与海霞联系上。4点14分海霞再与我们联系，她问我们现在的位置，我发过去后海霞说，很好，也就不过15分钟就到了，海霞发来我们要入住的酒店位置。于是，我们按位置导航100迈前进。20分钟后，海霞、樊佃福、杜向东，相继打来电话问我们到哪里了。40分钟、60分钟、一小时后，他们觉得不对，不断打电话询问我们的位置。

接下来又是20分钟、30分钟、40分钟、50分钟……这之间，我们的车子看导航显示已经围着中都草原绕了一大圈。途中经过了张北县沙沟镇、公会镇，康保县的土城子镇等等。海霞、樊佃福他们看了我发的位置恍然大悟是海霞发的位置有问题，但我们在这两个多小时的光阴里，驰骋草原公路，观光中都草原，是意想不到的收获。下午5点26分，海霞发来位置共享，引导我们到达会合地点。

康巴尔诺尔

下午6点11分,海霞、樊佃福、杜向东和我们终于相见。大家简单相叙,海霞提议,趁太阳还没下山,先到康巴诺尔国家湿地公园去看一下,顺便照几张相。大家响应,启动汽车一同前往。

康巴诺尔国家湿地公园里的康巴诺尔湖,像一面洁净的天空之镜,白云蓝天倒映在湖里,这里是遗鸥的天堂,遗鸥在湖面的天空上飞翔,美极了。

"砂锅小火锅"

晚上,老樊带大家来到一家康保特色饭店"砂锅小火锅"涮康宝羊肉,喝康保老窖美酒。羊肉片宽厚地道,货真价实,蘸料齐全而且味道极好。店老板还是一个上过央视星光大道的康宝民间二人台演员。老板很随和,和大家喝了一杯酒,还现场为大家唱了一段地道的康保二人台。

康保县的华夏精短文学华北张家口分会的贾海燕,看到了8月4日晚上,我发到朋友圈在康巴诺尔国家湿地公园里的康巴诺尔湖边的照片,打来微信电话确认我已到康保后,8月5日早便赶来与我们会合。早上8点,在康保城北的一个康保小肥羊的餐馆,我们8人一起来吃早餐,先是一碗热乎乎的康保奶茶,奶茶表面飘着点点油花,喝上一口,微咸但洋溢着奶香。隔了一小会儿,上来一盘两小块儿白饼(白面火烧),刀切十字,一块儿四瓣,用筷子夹上一小块儿白饼,放在碗里的奶茶里泡一会儿,放到嘴里吃上一口,奶香茶香油香白饼香一股脑地涌现满口,味道特好。

敖包相会

吃完早餐,两辆车开足马力前进,目的地——南天门。途中,路边有一座敖包,头车停下,于是大家一同下车拍照留影。

南天门

康保一景南天门。这是一道自然天成的石门口,左右天成两山,中间空过,是一道天然的大门口,门口里面是座山,门口朝南,所以叫做南天门。

卧龙图生态氧吧度假区

匆匆游过南天门，我们驱车赶往卧龙图生态氧吧度假区。沿途草原风光无限，高大洁白的风力发电机塔上三片叶扇不停地旋转。草原、风车、蓝天，一幅美丽的画卷。

来到卧龙图生态氧吧度假区，已经是上午11:15了，大家赶紧走进草原一闻草香花香，在开放式蒙古包里歇凉拍照。贾海燕一直担任讲解，向我们介绍草原和草原上生长的各种花，这些花都是中药材。我想骑马，但马场还在这片草原的最北端，我徒步20分钟来到马厩，和马的主人询问骑马如何计费。马主说："一圈四里地，80元。"我问："自己骑行可以吗？"马主说不行。没有达成协议，我徒步回来。大家一起快步走出卧龙图生态氧吧度假区，到大门口一起合影留念，合完影已经是12:30了。大家赶紧上车往康保城里赶。下午一点多我们赶到城里，恰好赶上2023年康宝草原马拉松举办，城里饭店各个爆满。我们从下午1:40转到2:20终于在一家罗跃东饭店二楼坐下，贾海燕招待了一桌丰盛的康保特色午餐，真诚待人的贾海燕恨不得把康宝所有好吃的美食都摆上桌面，诚意满满令人感动。一顿特色而丰盛的午餐后，下午3点半大家上车赶路，驶离康保，前往中都草原。

海霞诚恳邀请一对七十多岁的中都夫妻俩临时加入了行程。这里，还要专门介绍一下他们夫妻俩：刘润杰，77岁，张北法院，法警队政委，1960年参加工作，1969年参军，在某部队转战在内蒙古乌拉特前旗、湖北宜昌、承德、新疆那拉提，为修筑我国战备工事和天山公路，献出自己的青春。任副排长，多次立功。转业后从事法警工作，并取得审判证书。退休后，仍然发扬雷锋精神，帮助困难战友，积极参加参加文艺宣传，旧楼改造，支农助农等社会活动，被人们称为"活雷锋"。

赵月莲，76岁，原张北县文化局局长，1965年上张北师范，1968年毕业留在张北从事群文工作50多年，现在还担任离退休干部党支部书记，县关工委副主任，社区文联主席，张北师范校志编委。参加，"中华优秀传统文化座谈会"，第四届河北燕赵音乐文化研讨会。

热心的夫妻俩，我们都亲切地叫他们姐姐姐夫。夫妻俩带我们前往中都博物馆，但赶到时博物馆已经到了下班的时间。于是，我们掉头前往向东表弟的草原海阁。

草原风光美

两天的沿途采风，大家从康巴诺尔国家湿地公园，到康保南天门，翻山越岭，到卧龙图，张北大道至简，汽车驰骋，一百二十迈，一路观光，草原无际，葵花金黄，荞麦花雪白，山脉丘陵，长途越野。

草原海阁

下午 4 点 20 分，我们的车队开进了在小三营北面的草原海阁，大家卸下行囊，走进房间，暂住草原海阁。

骑马

大家安排好住宿后，纷纷出来感受这里的阳光、蓝天、空气。

当夫妻俩听张家口分会会长海霞说我计划骑马，夫妻俩觉得身为张北人，要尽地主之谊，一展张北人的坦荡豪爽义气，非要请我出去骑马，一再说服，盛情难却，便同意并感谢。老哥哥起动汽车 8 分钟来到小三营对面的草原跑马场。大姐先行扫码付费要了一匹马，我又扫码付费要了两匹马，请他们夫妻俩一同骑马。77 岁的姐夫不上马，于是，76 岁的姐姐飞身上马，梁丽萍（男）老弟也搬鞍任镫骑上一匹马。梁丽萍这个乐观，善良的哥们，我很喜欢。我也搬鞍上马，骑行草原。这一张立马挥手的照片是张家口分会会长海霞抓拍的。

傍晚，6 点 20 分，我们骑马回来车子开进草原海阁院子里，走进屋子，打开淋浴喷头，洗去一路征尘。

草原海阁烤全羊

晚上，杜向东特意准备了烤全羊，开席之前，我因地制宜的按蒙古族礼仪，端起一碗奶茶，中指蘸奶，一敬天，二敬地，三再敬自己，并感谢杜向东的盛情款待，感谢有这样的机会大家相聚在中都草原的草原海阁，祝大家晚上开心，相聚快乐，开怀畅饮。

大家大快朵颐烤全羊，大碗喝着 52 度中都白酒。酒过三巡，军人出身，公安战线退休的姐夫刘润杰，走出蒙古包拿起话筒，一首《骏马奔驰保边疆》高声唱起。虽然已经 77 岁了，但声音洪亮，气势高昂。姐夫的爱人，76 岁原张北县文化局局长，在张北从事群文工作 50 多年的大姐赵月莲随即起舞，一对快乐夫妇载歌载舞风采不减当年，歌声嘹亮，舞姿优美，大家为之点赞。

一席烤全羊，一碗香奶茶，一首心中的歌，大家吃着、喝着、唱着，尽在无限欢乐中，放声高歌到午夜才散席。

草原的月亮

凌晨4点醒来，窗外明月当空。草原的夜空特别晴朗，夜晚还能看得见白云相伴月亮。起身披衣出门，手机拍下草原的月亮。回到屋里来，老樊的呼噜依然。4：30分，我便冲了个冷水澡。5时，隔窗看到梁丽萍（男）老哥们儿在院子里擦车，我便出去在院子里的地方桌边小方凳上坐下。一会儿，刘润杰、赵月莲夫妇也出来，我们一同坐在地方桌边唠嗑。

奔向中都博物馆

早上，7点30分，杜向东在草原海阁外已经办好了早点，招呼大家赶紧吃饭，计划之后赶往习近平主席到过的德胜村，然后去中都博物馆。为对德胜村有所了解，我先在百度上百度了德胜村，小村很美。但临到出发一看时间已经不够，于是改变计划，直接前往中都博物馆。

姐夫刘润杰、大姐赵月莲夫妇俩头车开路，四驱车一百二十迈一路急行。

我在这里穿越时空，一睹马背民族，快马弯刀，横扫欧亚，先后攻灭西辽、西夏、花剌子模、金朝，创建中国历史上版图最大元朝时期的文字记述，实物展览，疆域展示。若元朝北部延伸至北冰洋，则有2267万平方公里。

在这座位于张北县城南山路以北、察哈尔大街以东，总占地69亩，建筑面积9202.68平方米，上下两层的元中都博物馆，是我国第一个蒙元历史专题性博物馆，也是全国第一个以单一朝代为主题的博物馆。元中都博物馆的建成，对蒙元发展史研究的确具有非常重要的意义。

我快步先于大家在前一人迅速浏览了馆里展示的所有内容并拍照之后，走出元中都博物馆，站在博物馆对面，眼望蓝天白云，遥想元帝国辉煌时期的盛况，于是打开手机百度，资料显示：

元朝的前身为大蒙古国，1206年成吉思汗铁木真建国时领有大漠南北与林木中地区（即尼布楚地区），经由历代蒙古诸汗的经营及三次西征后，最大疆域的面积高达3300万平方公里。

东起日本海、东海，西抵黑海、地中海地区，北跨西伯利亚，南临波斯湾，占了世界土地面积的22%，超越了五分之一，为20世纪时苏联的1.5倍，现今俄罗斯的1.9倍，为当时横跨亚欧大陆的超级大国。

公元一二七一年，忽必烈下旨改国号为元，次年二月，改中都为大都，并在此建都。元朝依然拥有庞大的多达一千三百七十二万平方公里的领土，领土北至北冰洋，东至朝鲜半岛、西至帕米尔高原，南至缅甸东北部和泰国北部，总面积比现在的中国还要大四百一十二万平方公里。

根据元朝的地图来看，元朝的疆域主要是包括两个国家，也就是中国和俄罗斯，俄罗斯是西伯利亚那块比较大，而这块地素来是中原王朝不太在意的，此外还有缅甸和中南半岛许多国家的小部分，韩国也有一部分，锡金、不丹、克什米尔等地区也在内。

过了一段时间，大家也参观完毕从博物馆里出来。我在心里深深感谢赵月莲大姐和海霞会长，给大家创造这么良好的机会和文化旅程，了解张北，了解中都，了解元朝。

从4日下午到6日上午这之中的一系列活动安排，行程策划，我也看到了海霞会长的层次、水平、人脉、格局。使我坚信华北下辖分会里，有一个非常有能力的会长，那就是她了。

8月6日上午近11时，三辆车在加油站加完油，姐夫刘润杰、大姐赵月莲夫妇俩，还是头车开路，我们驱车来到赵月莲大姐在张北县城里的家，大姐专门送了我两本她著的书，并告诉我说：明天她要到省城开一个会，就由姐夫开车和我们一起到沽源。

沽源午餐

时间紧，我们一一和大姐握手告别，随后，又是姐夫一马当先开车前行，四驱车一百二十迈一路疾驶。下午1点多到达张家口分会秘书长于春淋预定在沽源县城的一个饭店，秘书长和县里的两位部长早已等候多时。大家见面一一握手相互认识后，由于时间太晚了，便赶紧走进餐厅。大家各自在桌前坐好，杯子里倒满白酒。春淋是曾经的滑冰健将，有视野，有见识，也有格局。她说因为我是哥哥让我先说，那我也就先说说吧：虽然我们路上开足马力一刻不停，由于路途远我们初来乍到来的还是晚了，好在春淋和两位老弟耐心等着我们。大家初次见面相聚在沽源，是一个莫大的缘分。所以，远道而来的我们举杯敬春淋和两位老弟，感谢你们的等待和款待，大家共同举杯庆祝相逢。之后，春淋端起酒杯说：早就盼着陈大哥来草原，今天终于等到了。在这里，我和我的两个好兄弟共同举杯欢迎陈大哥和在座的各位兄弟姐妹，大家再一次共同举杯一饮而尽。由于我和姐夫、小张、丽菊都不喝酒，所以，向东和佃福主动担当和春淋的两个好兄弟推杯换盏，相互干杯，不觉间，已是四杯酒下肚，喝得不亦乐乎，气氛很好。

翻江倒海

当大家喝得正在兴头之时，我忽然感觉肚子不得劲儿，<u>丝丝隐痛</u>，而后明显疼起来。但大家正在开怀畅饮之时，我也不好影响氛围，默不作声，强装作态。是春淋察觉我脸色不对：陈大哥我给你倒上葡萄酒吧。这个时候，我的肚子里翻江倒海的绞痛。我强装镇静地站起身说：不倒了春淋，大家慢慢喝着，我先出去一下……大家看到我脸色蜡黄，赶快让开给我出路，我急忙来到洗手间……

之后，大家也就收拾了，一同来到外面。春淋觉得天儿热，我可能是中暑，于是拿来藿香正气水让我喝下。然后，大家分别上车去沽源。车子走了不多时在路边停下来，春淋和海霞他们都下车去了对面门市。小张说：他们到药店和超市干啥去了？我在车里昏昏沉沉的，也无暇顾及。

一会儿春淋从药店里拿来了藿香正气水，大山楂丸，还有别的药。告诉我怎么服用，并让我再喝一瓶藿香正气水。之后，大家上车继续赶路去沽源。

海霞说，我可能是早上洗冷水澡阴着了。

闪电湖

闪电湖，一个美丽而充满遐想和冲击力的名字。百度上说：闪电湖地处河北沽源，是滦河上游最大的湖，因入湖前的河流为闪电河而得名。闪电湖面积不小，湖水不深，清澈见底，水草飘摇，偶尔能看见小小的虾子自由游弋，黑色和洁白的水鸟在水面上敏捷地起落，把这黄昏里的湖泊点缀了生动、阳光是金色的，把草原也涂抹成了金色地毯，只身湖边，感受微风习习，心在这样的夕阳里飘摇成了水底那株柔软的水草。在天苍苍、野茫茫的草原上闪现出这样敞亮清澈美丽的湖水。据说在高高的天空上她看上去就像一道银色的闪电，当地人叫它闪电湖或闪电河。虽然这个名字的来历已无从考证，但是在这在天苍苍、野茫茫的草原上能有如此美丽的风景，怎能不让你感叹大自然的伟大。

车队接近闪电湖景区，高高的闪电湖景区大门真的是充满了冲击力。山顶上一只金鹰展翅欲飞，下面"闪电湖"三个大字红色醒目。

安排住宿晚餐

下午5点多我们到达闪电湖，春淋的朋友是闪电湖景区的经理，在酒店大厅东墙挂有巨幅鲲鹏展翅图，从这一点看得出，老板胸怀大志，干事业出色，有抱负。

安排好了房间，春淋很热心想安排大家漂流，我看看时间已经6点多了，建议让大家先在景区转转吧。

傍晚7点，大家聚到餐厅吃饭，春淋的侄女是餐厅经理，热心周到，服务上乘。一桌子丰盛的美味佳肴，春淋还特意带来美酒给大家品尝。我倒上一杯水陪大家一边说笑，一边进餐。

发烧

春淋发现我并未夹菜，便问我：陈老师你怎么不夹菜呀？我说：因为一直以来我不吃晚饭，另外我也感觉有些热。春淋忙把手放在我的脑门上：哎呀，真是的，陈老师你发烧了。正在喝酒的姐夫看着我说：老弟没事的，我车里有感冒胶囊，我给你拿去，吃上就好。姐夫很快拿来给我，我便和大家打了招呼让大家吃好喝好，自己先行撤退了。一出餐厅门口，我觉得浑身发冷，直打哆嗦，心里告诉自己：陈欣，你真的病了。在这沽源夏夜的晚上，我却赶紧抱紧胳膊，急忙回到宿舍，倒上白水，迅速吃上两丸感冒胶囊，穿着衣服躺在床上盖上被就晕乎着了。

姐夫叫门来

不知我迷糊了多长时间，听到有人打大声叫门，估计是昏睡中人家叫了我几声也没醒来吧（后来听海霞说，姐夫叫了五六声）。当时我好懒啊，浑身发烫，真的不想起。便问：谁呀？只听有人说：检查房间的。我一听是姐夫的声音，虽然高烧中，但还是一阵高兴，因为，这是刚刚认识一天的姐夫哇，而且是我身在异乡的酒店里发烧之时看我来了，我心里一阵热乎。迷迷瞪瞪地起来开门。门开了，姐夫看着我问：现在怎么样？我说还是烧。这时的我，不意间手碰到自己的大腿都感觉很烫。

春淋捧来蛋糕侄女送来药

跟在姐夫身后的是春淋和海霞，春淋满面笑容地捧着一个蛋糕进来：陈老师，今天是我侄女的生日，我侄女特意给老师送上一个蛋糕。

我感动地说：谢谢春淋，也谢谢你的侄女，太好了。可是春淋我现在可能更烧了。春淋用手一摸我脑门：哎呀我的老师啊，你真的好烫啊。她拿起手机就拨通了她侄女的手机：你那里还有感冒药吗？手机里传来她侄女声音：有感冒颗粒和布洛芬，还有……春淋说：赶紧都拿上来，陈老师高烧了。一小会儿，春淋的侄女，侄女的姑娘，还有一个服务员一同上来，把三样药交到春淋手上。这时，和我一同来草原的小张也进来。我这人泪点低，看着眼前的姐夫、春淋、海霞、春淋的侄女、侄女的姑娘、服务员、小张七个人，我哽咽了。因为，这是我身在千里外的沽源闪电湖景区度假酒店里独自高烧之时，大家看我来了。虽然在高烧，但这这种情谊却深深地感动着我。可是，我还得控制。因为，这么大个人了，不能把眼泪流出来，咽喉一阵灼热。我望着大家无言地沉静了五秒钟：谢谢大家……又说不出来了。还是春淋反应得快：陈老师，我拿快壶给你坐一壶开水吧，准备吃药。说着去拿快壶接水。坐上快壶后，又去试试淋浴水的温度。回来说：陈老师，淋浴水的温度还是可以的。这时，水也坐开了，她倒了半杯说：陈老师一会儿就吃刚拿上来的药吧。我看你也挺不精神的，等吃完药就躺下吧，我们先走。

半夜醒来

大家走后，自己很担心紧张，这要是重了可咋办？新冠病毒流行四年来我还没有阳过呢，是不是阳了呢？明天会怎样呢？胡思乱想，心里没底。于是，恨病吃药，我便把春淋侄女拿来的几样药搭配着同时吃下，浑身酸软，晕头晕脑地倒头睡去。

迷糊中，让尿憋醒了，起来小解。之后，觉得走路脚下有根了。坐到床上，看看时间是夜间11点41分。为了快好，我又吃了一遍药后躺下继续睡。

早上走步遇到春淋

再次醒来已是早上5点了，这也是我夏天通常早上出去走步的一贯时间。下床站起身来感觉比半夜起来时身子轻松多了。心里话儿说：看来是老天有眼，朋友情浓，药力发威，成全了我没有病重啊。试着挥挥胳膊，踢踢腿感觉还好。于是，走进浴室打开淋浴喷头，温度正好的洗澡水奔流直下，冲去了我一夜的病痛和满心的不安、愁绪。洗漱完毕，换上衣服，打起精神，穿上鞋子，下楼坚持一贯的户外走步去了。

闪电湖湿地草原的早晨，很是凉快，这样的温度，要是昨晚的我，肯定是要冷得打哆嗦的。感谢老天、朋友、感冒药，合力让我恢复了活力。我呼吸着散发着草原清香的空气，迈着轻松的脚步，顺着闪电湖草原栈道向闪电湖边走去。

边走边浏览手机微信内容的我，忽然看到春淋在群里发布的早餐时间，想到她已经起来了。便发过去几个字：春淋在哪里？马上接到回复：我在闪电湖草原栈道入口前小广场练功。我回头见她在向我招手，我往回向春淋走来。她问我：陈老师起得早哇，身体感觉怎么样？我说：感觉没事了。春淋欣喜地说：真哒？太好了！我说：看你在群里发通知，咱们七点吃早饭？春淋说：是的老师。

海霞的善良

你在这练功，海霞呢？我问春淋。她现在也该起来了，陈老师打个电话告诉她咱俩在这儿等她出来。春淋说。我把手机拨通了：海霞在哪里？那头说：我在下楼。你怎么样？我说：重了，得去医院了，春淋送我去，正准备走呢。那头说：到医院？那等等我，和你一块儿去，好照顾你一下。我说：不用了，还得陪床啥的，麻烦，让春淋送我一个人去吧。那头急了：不行，你一个人去怎么行？还烧得那么厉害呢？我说：那好的，下来吧，我和春淋在小广场等你。

海霞急匆匆地来找我们，来到跟前见我精神如昨：哎，不是要去医院吗？怎么看着你没事似的？我说：您是福神，托您的福，我没事了。海霞说：你呀，急死我了。还是吓唬我呀！我说：就是在人没有任何准备的时候，才能显示一个人的本真呢。

虽然是开了个玩笑，但这样没有任何心理和思想准备的情况下的临时对话，却实实在在地显露了人性本来的善良，显示了朋友真情。

这次草原行，在闪电湖旅游度假酒店发烧的遭遇，使我切实感到了老天眷顾、确切感悟了朋友真情、切身感受了药物的威力，让我终生难忘。

特别感谢

这次高烧迅速得以平复，实在要感谢姐夫、春淋的侄女送药及时，如若不是，那可以想象后果如何。所以，陈欣在此再次向姐夫、春淋的侄女说一声：谢谢！我将永不忘怀！

早上大家吃完早饭，回到宿舍收拾衣物，整理行囊，下楼交房卡，准备出发。这次出发也就意味着不再到别处去了，因为小张在已经出来第四天了。于是，我们在沽源闪电湖景区度假酒店的超市门前照了一下像，便各自上车，还是姐夫开车前行，向滦河神韵风景区，也就是闪电九曲十八弯进发。

滦河神韵风景区

我们的车队开进滦河神韵风景区大门，春淋带我们走进转佛山大门。

转佛山祭坛

我们顺着山势拾级而上一会工夫到达山顶，在山顶，我们看到了远古先民建起的祭坛。

转佛山祭坛大约建于5000年前新石器时期，于2012年被发现，祭坛有别于敖包，是用石块一层高于一层往上垒砌，每层往里收缩，其间留有约60厘米宽的平面，每层都是非常规则的圆形。

祭坛是原始人对太阳的敬畏和崇拜，是沽源先民用于祭祀天地、草木神灵的。

祭坛为滦河神韵增加了远古历史的见证。

这座古老祭坛，是古人祭拜山神和风、雨、雷、电等神灵的地方。科学考察发现，山的西北处草原湖东岸有大量的石磨、石锄、石刀等石器，山的西南处有古人类居住的半穴式房屋，这些发现充分说明早在远古时期这里就有人类居住。

我们在此与远古的先人对话，告诉他们我们来了，在祭坛边合影留念，让这沽源古老的山川河流，大地草原记住我们来过。

闪电河

最具神韵，游人如织，仿古亭榭立于白云间，长廊曲悠是观赏滦河神韵的最佳点。闪电河蜿蜒流转、九曲十八弯，像一道道闪电闪现于草原之上，今夏雨水丰足，闪电河更具诱人之美。在这如梦如幻的闪电河九曲十八弯上，我们的华夏精短文学华北张家口分会秘书长于春淋高举大旗与大美闪电河的九曲十八弯完美组合，相得益彰。

华夏精短文学华北分会副秘书长杜向东高举大旗，让我们鲜红的旗帜飘扬在沽源这古老山河土地和草原的上空。

转佛寺

海霞，2019年以前曾经多次来过转佛山，对转佛山、转佛寺昔日的境况有深刻的印象。据有关资料显示，转佛山景区有一座转佛庙，转佛庙是察哈尔正白旗的牛羊群庙。建于康熙四十九年（1710），由查干固什喇嘛筹建的藏传佛庙。朝廷赐名为"镇远寺"。转佛庙（镇远寺），因其门前有转佛殿所以称为转佛庙，庙建在花根山下，山叫成了转佛山，上边的村子也叫成了转佛山村。据说，原庙前转佛殿所供奉的佛在闪电河河道上的水磨上，故民间有水推磨转佛之说。转佛庙从兴建到北迁在沽源经历了一百多年的风雨历程，佛像北迁后，庙宇房屋被民间所用，民国期间毁于战乱。

让人痛惜的是，2020年新冠疫情期间，经当地政府同意，转佛被请走了。现在转佛寺里已没有转佛、转佛亭里也已没有能够转动的四方佛。就连大雄宝殿屋脊上的二龙戏珠、殿前的一对石狮子也没有了踪影。这对沽源古迹和宗教文化的传承绝对是无法用金钱来计算的一大损失。

从转佛寺原址可以看出古人的智慧，就像今天水力发电的原理一样，利用闪电河九曲十八弯的水流动力作用和简单机械动力转换原理，促使昔日转佛寺的转佛亭里的四方佛能够转动，不得不为古人点赞。

心存遗憾和希望

游历完没有佛的转佛寺回到没有佛的转佛山顶的长亭里，望着美丽婉转，风韵无限的闪电河九曲十八弯，心中不由得产生遗憾和失落。唐代诗人刘禹锡所著的《陋室铭》，含义为：山不在于高，有了神仙就出名气。潭水也不在于深，有了龙就显得有了灵气。1980年湖北应山县中华林场观音寺发现一块唐代石碑，碑文起首两句是："盖闻山不在高，有僧则名；寺不在大，有神则灵。"碑文背后署"大唐贞观四年（630）三月勒石"字样。由此想到，倘若，真的有一天经过文化宗教部门、当地政府的重视，社会贤达、有识之士的执着奔走，转佛重回转佛寺，那么转佛山就名副其实了，转佛寺也就实至名归了，转佛亭重置四方转佛，并能在闪电河九曲十八弯的盛水期重现四方佛自转的盛况，那该功在当今，利在后世，功德无量的一大好事啊。更可为沽源古迹和宗教文化的传承添上浓重的一笔，并流芳千古。

三河源

沽源三河源指的是滦河、黑河、白河三条河。沽源这个河北省北部，闪电河上游古老县域，是滦河、白河、黑河三河的发源之地，全域水域面积达6.1万亩，有湿地面积达到70万亩，是游牧文化和农耕文化交融交汇地带，是游牧文化和农耕文化交融交汇地带。

滦河，是渤海独流入海的河流，古名濡水，因发源地有众多温泉而得名。濡后讹为濡。濡、滦音相近，后唐朝演化为滦，元朝又称"御河"或"上都河"。发源于河北省丰宁县，流经沽源县、正蓝旗、多伦县、隆化县、滦平县、承德县、兴隆县、宽城满族自治县、迁西县、迁安市、卢龙县、滦县、昌黎县、在乐亭县南兜网铺注入渤海。河流全长，河北省政府网站称888公里，《河北省志·自然地理志》称877公里。

滦河源远流长，沿途接纳了众多支流，其中流域面积大于1000平方公里的有9条，即小滦河、兴州河、伊逊河、武烈河、老牛河、柳河、瀑河、潵河及青龙河。支流中流域面积最大的是伊逊河，长度和水量最大的是青龙河。

滦河也是河北省北部东部的主要水源，有著名的引滦入津工程，将河水引入天津市区。

虽然资料显示，滦河发源于丰宁，但在坐东面西的转佛寺西门左侧置一块大石，上写"滦河源"三个大写红字。深深感叹，滦河，从这里出发，不但滋润了河北、内蒙古、山川草原大地，还引入天津，以缓解直辖市用水瓶颈问题。

神奇美丽的闪电河九曲十八弯

站在转佛山顶，环顾山下的草原、河流，抬头仰望蓝天白云。下山，我们就要各奔东西了，几天的采风旅游，马不停蹄，奔驰几千里，开阔了眼界，增加了知识，丰富了阅历，感受了风土人情，收获了真情实意。有感动，有快乐，有享受，有所得。团结、友谊、真诚，成就了草原之行。我们在转佛山的栈道上合影留念！

多想在草原久留，可挡不住这行程脚步。日程紧张，计划之中的张家口市里没能继续进发。好朋友王昆，深表遗憾。我深深理解，并请放心，长天流云，草原常在。张家口大境门，我的朋友，王昆，有期后会。大姐赵月莲，姐夫刘润杰、海霞、杜向东、于春淋、樊佃福、贾海燕，相逢来日。

最后，一首深情悠扬美好的草原歌曲《离别草原》的一段歌词作以结尾，待到他日风吹草低骏马驰，更是大家欢笑时。

离别草原

作词：张峰

作曲：贾一英

难忘你的回首

难忘你那一眸

难忘草原的笑容

难忘花落随风走

今宵酒醒何处

已是华灯高楼

不见天边的弯月

只听那喧嚣如流

想起草原的清秀

走过那小河溪流

记得你深情的挽留

不忘流泪的嘱咐

多想在草原久留

可挡不住这行程脚步

盼望还有相见的时候

让我们紧紧相守

"中央大街"的俄罗斯风味

单位放假五天,加上双休日,又是一个"七天长假"。人们喜欢冬天去南方旅游,然而,我和朋友们一商量去了哈尔滨。

11月下旬的哈尔滨,气温比唐山冷得多。虽是乘坐大巴行驶在高速公路上,但一路奔来的旅途劳累,还是让大家在宾馆里洗完澡,吃过晚饭便倒在床上睡去。

初尝大马哈鱼子酱

早就听说哈尔滨的"中央大街"是以异国风情著称的一条大街,由于历史上沙俄帝国曾经占领哈尔滨,所以,这条大街的建筑充满了拜占庭风格、俄罗斯风格,特别是这里的美味更是充满着俄罗斯风味。想到这些不免要去亲口尝一尝,于是,我们这几个睡不着的哥们儿蜂拥而出。夜幕下的哈尔滨,男男女女老老少少的人们,或漫步在闪闪烁烁的霓虹灯下,或进进出出于购物中心,或饮酒、谈笑于饮食娱乐场所,一派浪漫休闲的情调。

我们走在大街上,在这冰天冻地的寒冷季节里,居然看到还有冰棍在买。大家路过一家餐厅,名字叫作"华梅西餐厅",导游告诉我们,这是一个名叫楚吉尔漫的俄籍犹太人创办的,还欣喜地告诉我们,这里的鱼子酱是比较便宜的。说到鱼子酱,我们这些唐山人是很少有人想起它。走进餐厅落座,叫上五份面包鱼子酱。不叫不知道,一叫才知道,全世界都著名的大马哈鱼子酱在这里才40元钱一份。拿过一片面包抹上鱼子酱,撒上洋葱沫,再加上一片面包,咬一口。嘿!味道那叫一个美。那是一种葱甜中带着鱼子香的味道。您要问为啥要撒洋葱沫?就是因为洋葱的味道可以折去鱼子的腥味。

第一次吃银雪鱼加奶油

放下第二天的旅游观光不说,再说一道美味——银雪鱼加奶油。这又是一道欧洲人非常爱吃的美味佳肴。我们来到一家名叫波特曼西的餐厅坐下,当服务员端上一盘银雪鱼后,又在我们每个人面前摆上一个小盘,小盘上放一个长方形容器,之后,里面一一放一块银雪鱼,然后再叫上奶油，这道菜就算上完了。我们打开带去的张裕葡萄酒并倒上一杯之后，吃上一口鲜嫩而香甜的银雪鱼加奶油，呷上一口葡萄酒，感觉是与吃中餐那的确不一样。

走出这家波特曼西餐厅，遥望北方的夜空，心里不禁感到一阵凄凉。我在想，若不是沙皇俄国从大清帝国的版图上强行侵占一百多万平方公里的中国领土，我们今天品尝俄罗斯风味的地方也许就不是在这里了。我仰头看看天上的月亮，此时的嫦娥一号正在进行绕月探测。是否有朝一日，强盛的中国能够讨回历朝历代被列强侵占的所有中国领土呢？曾经出现过强秦、大汉、盛唐和打遍欧亚的大元朝代的中国，秦皇、汉武、唐宗、宋祖、天之骄子的后代们，是否有朝一日，还要让万邦来贺堂堂中华呢？是否今天所有中华儿女们都在考虑这个问题呢？我想应当会吧……

秋访白羊峪

深秋，前往冀东迁安，在白羊峪林场住了七天。仅凭月酒长城的景象，就足以令人心满意足了。

白羊峪长城，山雄关险，自古为兵家必争之地。白羊峪又称白羊关，以雄闻名，当地有一段声名远播的大理石长城，格外罕见。

如今的白羊峪山雄水美，融江南秀色、北国风光于一体，古迹胜景遍布，比如"列岫联珠""西山灵雾""凌岩古井""仙洞石床"等。殊不知，白羊峪长城的古老与雄浑、威武与沧桑，早已融会贯通、深入人心了。

傍晚时分，徒步出行，脚下是一道山梁，长城蜿蜒而上，落日悬在一座敌楼上方。这一独特视角，令人读到古老建筑的雄壮。敌楼虽已老旧，却依然据守在那里，即便早已远离了战争与杀伐，砖石的筋骨也透着高大雄伟、不可侵犯的气势，这恰是钢铁长城坚强意志的体现吧。

遥望那座神威楼，明朝游击将军张世忠，曾专门题写楼名。神威楼的神奇之处，在于它不像其他敌楼那样骑在城墙上，而是挂在城墙外，凸显了明朝将士抵御外敌入侵的勇气与决心。

走近细观，神威楼是一座砖石结构的硬山顶建筑，犹如一座仿木的二层楼，建筑风格奇特雄伟、别具一格。

神威楼上上下下，每一块青砖之间，都抹着石灰泥，一直砌到檐椽下，这是中国古代典型的砌墙方式。背面外墙中间，开了一道箭窗，既可通风采光，又能观察敌情，还便于发射弓箭等。在箭窗下有两个礌石孔，专门用来发射礌石，打击敌人。箭窗与礌石孔，成"品字形"排列，既有高低错落的美感，又有战斗实用性。

第二天，前往人称"马圈""阅兵城"的谎城。山中晨雾相伴，湿气很重。登上谎城制高点，俯瞰雄关，不由心生感慨。古今风霜雨雪，战乱破坏，如今雄关犹在，易守难攻。漫步城中，惊叹于这座与众不同的"军用袖珍城"。首先，它可以迷惑敌人；其次，便于屯兵和储存粮草、马匹。这种军事防御的独创方式，堪称中国兵法的出奇之处。

居高临下，驻足古往今来关内通往塞北的咽喉之地，顿觉，这才是真正的"一夫当关，万夫莫开"呀。

有史料记载：白羊峪长城，始建于北齐（550年至577年），时均为石砌，宽仅三米。明朝初期，徐达于要隘修筑关口城。后来，蓟辽总督谭纶、蓟镇总兵戚继光等多次组织加固，重要地段用砖包修，宽度增至五六米，并增设敌楼、炮台等军事防御设施。另有文献说：白羊峪长城为战国时燕国所建，明朝时修复加固，其中城楼21座，保存完好的长城4552米……

这些资料，无声地讲述着白羊峪长城的前世今生，其中最值得骄傲的是独一无二的大理石长城。大理石长城长约1.5公里，由棕红色大理石作基石，这在长城建筑史上可谓绝无仅有。这段长城在高山险峰之巅熠熠生辉，成为见证历史的奇丽瑰宝。

一轮明月，照耀千年。白羊峪的长城、群山、月色，仍在脑海中浮现，让人不由思绪万千……

河北日报 2023年10月27日 11:08

白玉山上回眸旅顺口的血泪往昔

登上白玉山顶，远眺这个依山傍海，气候宜人，风光绮丽的旅顺口军港，回想它的去日沧桑，峥嵘岁月。

翻开历史的篇章才知道，旅顺口在东晋时叫马石津，唐朝时称都里镇，辽金后当地人称这里为狮子口。明朝洪武四年（公元 1371 年），朱元璋命大将马云、叶旺率军从山东半岛渡海，登陆狮子口一举收复辽东半岛。为这次纪念渡海征战的顺利，朝廷颁旨改狮子口为旅顺口。

打开地图可以看到，旅顺口坐落在辽东半岛最南端，突出于黄海、渤海之间，隔渤海海峡与山东半岛相对，三面环渤海，背靠旅大半岛，是优良的海港。旅顺口扼守渤海咽喉，历来战略地位重要。

回眸历史，清光绪四年（1880 年），走出康乾盛世，步入衰变的大清帝国面对世界列强，不得不做强国力，壮军威的努力，兴办北洋水师，在旅顺口建造船坞，修筑炮台，建立军事港口。但时隔十五年，清光绪十九年中日甲午海战爆发了。日军在距乾隆末年（1795 年）99 年（1894 年 11 月 22 日）之时击败中国守将徐帮道占领旅顺口，在三昼夜惨绝人寰的大屠杀中，两万多中国人民惨死在日本人血淋淋的屠刀之下。后在俄法德三国的干涉下，日本无奈把旅顺口归还给中国。

旅顺口这个兵家必争之地，历史上可谓是豺狼前脚刚走，北极熊就后脚踏来。1897 年 12 月，沙皇俄国的军舰突然闯进旅顺港，强占了旅顺及大连。1898 年 1 月，又派兵到篦子窝，就是今天的皮口一带设卡征粮，俄军的强行勒索，激起了民愤，当地百姓奋起反抗。残忍的俄国毛子竟武力镇压，杀害 100 多名中国老百姓。1898 年 3 月 27 日，也就是光绪二十四年，沙皇俄国向清廷强租旅顺港为军港，迫使清政府派李鸿章与沙俄驻华代办巴布罗福在北京签订了《旅大租地条约》，4 月出兵金州（今金县），5 月 7 日，又在圣彼得堡签订了《续订旅大租地条约》，进一步确定了沙俄帝国在旅顺大连的独占权和建筑铁路权。11 月勘划旅大租借地，从而，中国东北全境沦为沙俄的势力范围。

但是，对旅顺口夺而未获的小日本贼心不死，仍然对辽东半岛特别是旅顺口虎视眈眈。在日本人朝思暮想的阴谋策划中，日俄战争终于在旅顺口爆发。历时一年多的争夺战里，日俄双方损失惨重，战争打得十分惨烈，以至于俄军把军舰上的加农炮都拆到了山上的工事上用了。1905 年 1 月 1 日战争结束，日军占领旅顺口。在这次战争中日俄双方损失惨重，日军死亡多于俄方，66800 多人，就连日军司令乃木希典之子乃木保典也战死在这里。

1945 年 8 月抗战胜利，旅顺口回到祖国的怀抱。但是，直到 1955 年 5 月，这里的所有事务才由中国全面管理。

走下白玉山，徜徉在翠绿的山峦，漫步在清爽的海滨，游走在秀丽的风光里，心中仍不免有些隐隐作痛。在这不堪回首的一百多年里，列强们对我们这个几经强盛、也曾四方来贺的五千年文明古国和中华民族接二连三的欺压凌辱，他们在给中国人民留下无比辛酸记忆的同时，也对中国早已犯下了种族灭绝罪和反人类罪。

在夏日灿烂的阳光下，站在甲午古炮前，展望遥远海疆，再次想起"落后就要挨打"这句话是千真万确的。中国只有强盛，才能站在世界的东方，中华民族才能挺起腰板，奋发昂然。

第二辑
那一方名人风云

雨中访曹公

到北京的第三天，老是觉得有一件事不办不妥，一定要去看看祖籍同是丰润的老乡、中国古代的文学巨匠——曹公曹雪芹。于是，下午我迎着阴冷的雨丝向北京植物园走去。曹公的故居坐落在植物园内，我撑伞走在园中的甬道上，裤脚和皮鞋都已被雨水打湿。不觉间走近曹雪芹故居，故居前的古槐下我停住脚步。

抬头仰望古槐，古槐沧桑凝重，疑问古槐是否在向我述说曹公那"西窗剪烛风雨昏"的往事。可否想让我了解曹公那段"残杯冷炙有德色，不如著书黄叶村"的清贫时日。

黄叶村的柳树枝条在雨中飘飘摇摇，曹公的塑像淋在雨中湿漉漉的，紧锁眉头、低头沉思。看雨中的曹雪芹塑像，让我感到这才是曹公的真实再现，曹公是在思索，在思索人生。

遥想乾隆盛世的豪门公子哥，怎能料想家道败落，更无奈流落京郊"抗风轩"里"举家食粥酒常赊"的窘境。然而，正是这么一笔大富大贫、人上人下的宝贵人生经历的财富，启发了一代文学天才的灵感，成就了文学骄子一部驰名中外伟大而不朽的文学巨著《红楼梦》。

茅橼蓬牖的"抗风轩"里，瓦灶绳床，凄萧寒冷。也就是这样的人间彻冷，焕发了伟大作家奋笔著书的热望，书写出人间不朽的切肤之作，让人们世世代代去研读、去探究。

浮华时的曹雪芹，是祖宗手掌心儿里的一块"宝玉"，宗族里地位至高的"正统"少爷，众美女心里的情哥哥；家境败落的曹雪芹，不是翰林院里的大学士，不是一品道台，不是江南织造的世袭官员，只是大清朝的一介草民，但曹公心不草，才不草。没有封建权利却有丰富阅历，没有封建学位却有丰富人生经历，没有封建横通的平台却有真实水平。大彻大悟贫富、学衔、功名皆如烟云，在艰苦环境中铸就了字字珠玑的不朽华章，呕心沥血了一把浸透辛酸泪的文字。

因此，到如今曹公仍是当之无愧的文学巨匠。站在雨中的"抗风轩"门口看古槐烟柳，瞩目曹公，头上没有桂冠顶戴，面前没有金钱豪宅，身边没有美女香车。但曹公作为思想者写作者，却以博大的胸怀，盛满宇宙真经。偏居京郊樱桃沟，"卧雪黄叶村，红楼梦不休"。超凡脱俗，站在人间之上看人间；高居生活之上看生活；立于生活高端观察生活。思考深邃，专心锤炼"石头"文字，提升自己的思想境界，艺术境界。

曹雪芹（约1715年5月28日—约1763年2月12日）于乾隆二十九年（1763年）的大年三十夜里离开忧伤悲哀的世界，但曹公的英灵250多年来一直在人们的心间，高居九天。

雨中站在曹雪芹故居前，我不禁在心里念出一首小诗：凉风冷雨植物园，黄叶村里黄花卷，雪芹故居荒犹然，曹公在此叹苦短，身在草庐淡人间，远来乡音道寒暖。

《雨中访曹公》刊于《唐山劳动日报》，永久收藏于"浩然文学馆"。

一代才子张佩纶

在中国近代史上与张之洞、左宗棠齐名，被李鸿章评价为"丰才啬遇"的晚清重臣、大官僚张佩纶，素以做官清正才思敏捷而深受朝野称颂。

张佩纶，字幼樵，今丰润（清直隶丰润）区欢喜庄乡大齐坨村人，1848年（清道光二十八年）11月24日出生在浙江杭州的一个官僚家庭。父亲张印瑭早在清嘉庆己卯中举，道光乙未进士。历任浙江景德、建德、海宁、桐庐知县，杭州府知府，安徽按察使等职。且为官清廉，一身正气、两袖清风，多有惠政，颇得民心。咸丰年间，李鸿章回乡间创办团练时曾得到按察使张印塘的支持，两人可称世交。张佩纶6岁时父亲病故，寡母毛氏带领张佩纶兄弟6人生活在清直隶丰润县大齐坨村。佩纶排行在3，从小天资聪颖，7岁时就能背诵唐诗百余首，9岁拜丰润县李轶老先生为师攻读诗书百家，老先生十分喜爱这个聪明的孩子，特许他免费入学，亲赐字"幼樵"。少年出生在经常到书摊借书，阅后掩卷成诵，回家即手书成卷，数千字文章一挥而就，编号藏于箱中，到晚年竟集藏亲手自录者达百余卷。李老先生称赞佩纶说："张氏门中有幸，幼樵实在有过目成诵之才！"同治年间民间也有"风流才子张丰润"之说。青年张佩纶24岁考中进士，其后历任侍讲、右庶子，署左副都御史、侍讲学士、总理衙门行走等职。初入仕途便一帆风顺、平步青云。他与宝廷、张之洞、陈宝琛三人一起，奉同治皇帝的师傅、工部尚书、军机大臣李鸿藻为宗主，以刚直不阿、主持清议为己任，面对吏治腐败，敢于上疏直言，评议朝政，弹劾大臣，指斥贪官。风头之健，一时无两。在短短几年里，连续劾下工部尚书贺寿慈、户部尚书董恂等一批高官。还敢于为庚辰午门案中的护军张目说话，逼使慈禧太后更改主张。从而煊赫一时，满朝侧目，人们称之为"翰林四谏"、"清流党人"。时人袭毓磨在《清流党之外交观》中指出："清流党之势最盛，实有左右朝野舆论之权。"

光绪初年，李鸿章竭力倡办工矿企业，对开矿山、建铁路等新生事物进行尝试，遭到了守旧派的大肆围攻。这时，张佩纶与张之洞等人一起，宣传"时艰之亟，实以洋务为大端"，挺身支持洋务派的变法主张，强调要"采西法以敌西人"。张佩纶还和吴汝纶、刘铭传一起起草了《筹造铁路以图自强折》，率先提出了修建铁路的计划。为近代中国的铁路建设，起了积极的先导作用。

张佩纶做官后，慈禧太后也曾多次在养心殿召见他。一次，太后令他背诵"万年历"，他竟然倒背如流，高兴得太后连声称赞："幼樵真是无书不读也。"1884年（清光绪十年），由于中法关系日益紧张，马尾海战开战不过半小时，福建水师就几乎全被法国炮舰炮轰击沉了。1885年（清光绪十一年），朝廷下旨将37岁的福建会办海疆事务、授三品衔，与船政大臣何如璋一道指挥抗法事宜的张佩纶，从严遣戍到张家口、伊利等地，充军三年以赎其罪。当时，外患连起，朝廷屡遭败局。残喘的大清王朝，沦落到破鼓万人擂的地步，日本公使竟然草书一联戏弄清廷："张长弓，骑奇马，琴瑟琵琶，八王八，王王在上，单戈成战。"慈禧太后传满朝文武，竟无一人出对。后来李鸿章荐举当时（1884年，清光绪十年）已充军发配到伊犁的张佩纶就对。佩纶不远千里回京后立刻对出下联："伪为人，袭龙衣，魑魅魍魉，四小鬼，鬼鬼居边，合手即拿。"泱泱大清国让一个罪臣回来应对，才算出了一口恶气。

1888年（清光绪十四年），张佩纶总算结束了三年的流放生活，返回天津，投入李鸿章幕下，主管文书。当年5月，李鸿章将大女儿李鞠藕许配给他续弦，并于11月15日为自己的女儿和张佩纶在天津隆重举行了婚礼。李鞠藕时年23岁，而张佩纶已年届40，而且是一个流放归来一无所有的罪臣，但是，李鞠藕正是由于以前非常敬仰张佩纶的才华，偏偏挑选了他，且留下了一段当时文人称羡的佳话。

婚后的夫妻二人相濡以沫，伉俪情深。在张佩纶日记里，常有"以家酿与鞠藕小酌，月影清圆，花香摇曳，酒亦微醺矣"。"鞠藕小有不适，煮药、煎茶、赌棋、读画，聊以遣兴"。"鞠藕生日，夜煮茗谈史，甚乐"这样的记载。生动说明了两人的日常生活充满爱和情趣。在金陵（南京），称得上才子佳人的夫妻二人不但生育了1子2女，校订完成了张佩纶在流放期间所写的《管子注》二十四卷、《庄子古义》十卷，创作了《涧于集》《涧于日记》等多部著作，还合写了一本食谱、一部武侠小说。1903年（清光绪二十九年），张佩纶因肝病离世于南京，终年56岁。妻子李鞠藕1912年死后与之合葬在丰润县东北部黑山沟村的秦王山下。

1988年4月17日

张爱玲与《红楼梦》的不解情缘

祖籍丰润——张爱玲——读《红楼梦》、研究《红楼梦》;祖籍丰润——曹雪芹——筹划《红楼梦》、写作《红楼梦》。张爱玲祖上在清廷为官;曹雪芹祖上在清廷为官。这些跨越年代并无太紧密联系但却有共同点的因素,有意无意地在冥冥之中铸就了张爱玲与《红楼梦》的不解之缘。从1934年她写《摩登红楼梦》到1977年《红楼梦魇》一书出版,张爱玲几十年红楼情丝不断,令人感叹。

据传记,母亲离家出走,父亲张廷重为之撰《摩登红楼梦》的回目,是历史事实,而且张廷重还是给张爱玲讲解《红楼梦》的启蒙老师。张爱玲自己说:从十二三岁时看《红楼梦》,看到80回以下,只觉得:"天日无光,百般无味"!真真令今天的人们感到震惊,不禁暗自叫绝,数十年来愚笨的我看了张爱玲的书才第一次听人说出"天日无光,百般无味"这么样的八个大字!也就是这八个字就给高鹗伪续"后40回"拍了板,定了论。

有文章说:据可查知的年月行踪来看,张爱玲1920年生于上海,到3岁时迁居到天津,时为1922年。她住天津一直到9岁时(1928)方又返回上海。在这小学生时期,她已经喜欢阅读中国古典小说《红楼梦》和《三国演义》了。在十二三岁的女孩子中,找几个能像张爱玲这样一眼能感到《红楼梦》原著与伪续的极大区别的实例,恐怕是凤毛麟角也难找到。可见她的天赋是高层次的,"官能"是个直感性的,是她独自具备的重要的"本领",从事文学艺术,没有这本领,是不会有什么创造或研究上的业绩的。张爱玲以作家的身份名扬寰宇,除她在直感官能上的优胜条件之外,更有思想家与治学者的特长。人才的难能可贵,大抵是以"多才多艺""不拘一格"的兼美者为最不易逢。张爱玲从"直感"始,却以"治学"终。这充分体现在她晚期的学术性很强的著述——《红楼梦魇》。到1961年冬天,张爱玲在港为电懋电影公司编写《红楼梦》《南北一家亲》等剧本。

1968年,张爱玲在台北《皇冠》发表《红楼梦未完》。1969年,得陈世骧教授之识,任职加州大学伯克利分校"中国研究中心",继续《红楼梦未完》之研究。

1976年,张爱玲出版自己的第二部散文集《张看》,同时发表《三详红楼梦》。1977年,张爱玲《红楼梦》评论文集《红楼梦魇》一书出版。

1995年9月8日夜,恰逢中华民族传统的团圆节日中秋节,瞩目中国文学界的才女张爱玲一个人在美国洛杉矶西木区公寓内孤独地离去,享年七十四岁,传奇在寂寞中默默拉下了帷幕。

中国的才女客死在异国他乡，生前指定林式同为遗嘱执行人。9月19日，遗体在洛杉矶惠泽尔市玫瑰岗墓园火化。9月30日，骨灰由林式同、张错、高全之、张绍迁、许媛翔等人携带出海，撒向浩瀚无际的太平洋。

中国和世界从前没有张爱玲，以后也不会再有张爱玲，张爱玲是此世间的绝响！2012年北京十月文艺出版社也出版了张爱玲的《红楼梦魇》一书。《红楼梦魇》是一本华丽新版的著作。红学大师周汝昌隆重推荐：只有张爱玲，才堪称雪芹知己，我现今对她非常敬佩，认为她是"红学史"上一大怪杰，常流难以企及。张爱玲之奇才，心极细而记（记忆力）极强，万难企及，我自惭枉作了"红学家"！

《红楼梦魇》是张爱玲一生中的一部重要作品。从1966年张爱玲定居美国至1995年离世，期间以十年的时间研究《红楼梦》，此书正是张爱玲经过多年研究之后的红楼学术结晶。书中共收入其七篇研究文章，包括《〈红楼梦〉未完》《〈红楼梦〉插曲之一》《初详〈红楼梦〉》《二详〈红楼梦〉》《三详〈红楼梦〉》《四详〈红楼梦〉》《五详〈红楼梦〉》。

有评论说《红楼梦魇》像迷宫，像拼图游戏，又像推理侦探小说。张爱玲形容自己考据《红楼梦》是一种疯狂的情形，故得句"十年一觉迷考据，赢得红楼梦魇名"。《红楼梦魇》是张爱玲十余年间对《红楼梦》的考据与研究。《红楼梦魇》是张爱玲给世界留下的一本珍贵的红学著作。

传奇女作家张爱玲从不讳言她对《红楼梦》的喜爱，甚至花费了十年时间写出了一部《红楼梦魇》，其考证的细腻、感悟的独特，令很多红学家都大为惊异。张爱玲对《红楼梦》的熟悉程度简直到了令人咋舌的程度，她在《〈红楼梦魇〉自序》中是这样描述的，"每隔几年又从头看一遍"，"我唯一的资格是实在熟读《红楼梦》，不同的本子不用留神看，稍微眼生点的字自会蹦出来"。这篇序很重要，代表着张爱玲十年的红学收获和治学心情，是了解作家张爱玲的文心的一把金钥匙。这篇序代表了她的文笔风格。特色是很平实，不玩弄笔花，扭捏一些"文艺性语言"。真正的"白话"，朴素的心音。张爱玲不仅熟悉《红楼梦》，甚至已然把《红楼梦》当作了自己生活的良药，"偶遇拂逆，事无大小，只要'详'一会红楼梦就好了。"对于这样一个从小就徜徉在《红楼梦》奇幻的艺术境界中的作家来说，其小说创作受到《红楼梦》的影响是再自然不过的事情。当年，《紫罗兰》主编周瘦鹃先生，在刊首语《写在〈紫罗兰〉前头》中就细致地描摹了他初读张爱玲小说《沉香屑》的感觉："一壁读，一壁击节，觉得它的风格很像英国名作家Somerset Maughm的作品，而又受一些《红楼梦》的影响，不管别人读了以为如何，而我却是'深喜之'了。"正因如此，读张爱玲的小说，总会有似曾相识的感觉，甚至产生错觉。毫无疑问，在张爱玲的心中有一个情结，这就是红楼梦情结。这"心中的感情纠葛，深藏心底的感情"，是一种对《红楼梦》的喜爱成为张爱玲心中挥之不去、萦绕于心的一种强烈的感情，并深深影响到她小说的创作。

张爱玲迷《红楼梦》是一种近乎疯狂的状态——读红、续红，十四五岁创写《摩登红楼梦》、研红，十年写就《红楼梦魇》，因此形成了张爱玲纠结在心的复杂情绪。大凡一种复杂情绪的形成原因也是很复杂的，先天性情禀赋、后天教养熏陶、社会环境的浸染、亲友交往的影响等等，如果用最简单的办法去探究其形成的根源，可以从主客观两个方面去分析。主观地说，张爱玲有个不寻常的家庭。众所周知，张爱玲的身世还是非常显赫的，到她父亲这一辈虽然已经家道中落。父亲是个遗少型人物，生活上声色犬马，母亲则生就一副反骨，于是，这样一对南辕北辙的夫妻两人注定要以离异收场，所以张爱玲有一个不快乐的童年和少年。父母失和给张爱玲造成极大的伤害，父母又同时成为张爱玲文学创作的启蒙老师。父亲张廷重虽然生活堕落，但家学渊源，文学根底甚厚，常在闲暇时给她讲解《红楼梦》，为之撰写《摩登红楼梦》的回目。母亲黄素琼每天早晨也必定叫女仆将张爱玲抱到她床上背书，后来又把她送入新式小学读书，继而升入中学、大学接受现代教育，使张爱玲同时受到西方文化的影响。也就是说，张氏家庭虽然有着浓重的封建气息，但还是受到时代潮流的影响。于是，张爱玲既拥有深厚的中国文化根底，又能很好地理解西方文化，这使她可以自如地将两者融会贯通，从而形成自己独特的风格。客观地讲，这个家庭对张爱玲的影响远不止如此。张家是个大家庭，成员之间关系复杂，父母离异，继母入门，由此构成了诸多剪不断、理还乱的多角关系：父亲与前妻、续妻之间，张爱玲与父亲、继母之间，以张爱玲为核心而构成的母女之间、姐弟之间、姑侄之间，再加上亲戚之间，甚至家中的仆人之间等等，现实中，张家这个没落的贵族家庭已经俨然是一个贾府了。因此，复杂的家庭生长环境，大家族生活的经历，直至后来生活上富贵与困顿的强烈对比，在大起大落的浪尖谷底之间，张爱玲心理的落差以及对世态炎凉的感悟也就比常人深刻得多。

这样特殊的生存境遇，不仅使张爱玲形成了罕异的性格，也使她很容易在《红楼梦》中找到与曹雪芹相同的感受：盛世繁华之中掩盖不住没落和衰颓，于热闹之处眼见荒凉与沧桑。于情于理，张爱玲怎么会不喜欢《红楼梦》呢？

纵观张爱玲的生活经历以及与曹雪芹甚为相似的性情禀赋，这就不难理解张爱玲对《红楼梦》的极度喜爱之情了。那种洞彻人类普遍生存困境的荒凉感，家世荣辱兴衰的失落感，是两位天才作家可以跨越时空的最好切合点，也是其文人品格的天然共性，正所谓"相知无远近，万里尚为邻"，所以红学家周汝昌不无感慨地说："只有张爱玲，才堪称雪芹知己。"

《张爱玲与〈红楼梦〉的不解情缘》一文，2016年收入中国电影出版社出版的《唐山与中国电影》一书。

编剧张爱玲

祖籍唐山丰润的张爱玲，天分极高，见识也广，是难得的天才作家，也是不可多得的编剧。

生活在大城市的张爱玲自小就与电影有不解之缘，在小说和散文中她屡屡提到电影，写作技巧显然也受到电影的启发。她短暂的编剧生涯始于战后上海，走喜剧路线，将家庭伦理化悲为喜，幽默抵死却又感人至深。后来为香港电懋公司编剧，题材虽然仍是婚姻与家庭，却在电影里建立一个与小说截然不同的世界。

张爱玲的小说本身就带有"纸上电影馆"的特点，其编剧的电影同小说又不完全相同，电影的表现更为直接、商业，在20世纪繁华奢美生动的跃然于荧幕。

张爱玲编剧在上海

十分喜欢看电影的张爱玲，早在她的《十八春》中就借主人公的口说，上海的好处，"一是买东西，一是看电影"。看电影常常是她笔下恋情发展的场景、转折点乃至于一个男人可靠与否的象征。她在《花凋》中，写一个病入膏肓的女子出门去买安眠药自杀，没买成，就茫然坐上黄包车兜了个圈子，在西菜馆吃了顿饭，在电影院里坐了两个钟头。之后，她就改变了念头要重新看看上海。

孤身一人这样静静观察上海，是张爱玲在大多数时间里做的事，并以她极其独特的笔触，给《泰晤士报》、英文月刊《二十世纪》写了不少的影评，像对一片叫好声中的电影《渔家女》，她却在文章里这样说，我们走的是死胡同，因为《渔家女》的英雄是美术专门生。西洋美术在中国始终是有钱人消闲的玩意儿。……"渔家女"的恋人教她读书，不过是传统士大夫"教姨太太读书"……

而在她写《乌云盖月》的影评文章里，倒是引起了她的赞扬，"中国电影的题材通常不是赤贫就是巨富，对中产阶级的生活很少触及，这部片子是个例外，对这个阶层的生活有敏锐的描绘。"

1946年抗日战争胜利后，她转向电影剧本写作，经柯灵介绍认识编导桑弧，桑弧是她在电影界的启蒙者。1947年，她写了《不了情》和《太太万岁》。张爱玲初次为桑弧写了电影剧本

《不了情》，被拍成"文华电影公司"的创业作，还选了当时最红的刘琼和陈燕燕演出，影片当年卖座极佳。在《惘然记》后记中，张爱玲写道："1947年，我初次编电影剧本，片名《不了情》……"

她一度也完成了《金锁记》的剧本，但由于时局动荡以及女主角张瑞芳患病而拍摄搁浅。像小说一样，女人在这些电影里是极其重要的，她在另一篇影评里不无调侃地说，如果不谈情节和配搭的吸引力，中国电影明星真正有票房的，全都是女的。

桑弧随后再找张爱玲写出剧本《太太万岁》，张爱玲把这家庭生活喜剧写得流畅风趣，编入一连串误会巧合和逗笑噱头，是华人少数好莱坞式的"神经喜剧"（Screwball Comedy）。

1952年张爱玲离开上海，也算是一次永别了，去往香港。张爱玲编剧在香港电影资料馆的《张爱玲电懋剧本集》，册1开篇，前言中第一句话就是："香港有幸，文学与电影史上皆有张爱玲的名字。"《回顾〈倾城之恋〉》的首句："珍珠港那年的夏天，香港还是远东的里维拉……"虽然，台湾和香港在张爱玲眼里都属"边城"，这样的命题更体现在《重访边城》中。可是，是张爱玲意象的孤岛情结。香港对她来说是很有情结的，有很多的境遇堪比上海，有些生命的轨迹在此重叠。香港对于张爱玲，不只是她生命中的首次背井离乡，也不只是她中年返回的一次短暂停留；张爱玲对于香港，更不仅是时代洪流的匆匆过客，是孤岛文化的一部分，是距离她有爱有恨的彼岸最近的地方。

张爱玲是在经济困境中来到香港并再一次接触电影的，在电懋公司任职的宋淇介绍她去写剧本，不但可以拿最高的稿酬，还同时担任剧本审查委员会委员。

1957年的《情场如战场》改编自美国舞台剧《温柔的陷阱》，情节紧凑，节奏明快，戏里戏外充满了爱的狂想和悬疑，很符合张爱玲对爱情的想法："我以为人在恋爱的时候，是比在战争或革命的时候更素朴，也更放肆。"

虽然是电懋特色的文人电影，但也入乡随俗，有了浓厚的香港市民文化的气质，影片由当红明星林黛、张扬、陈厚主演，主题曲："情场如战场，战线长又长，你若想打胜仗，战略要想一想。你若要打败仗，最好是先投降，楼房买一栋，汽车送一辆，只要你口袋肯帮忙，不怕她不欣赏……"也是那时间风靡香港大街小巷的。因为电影的成功，上映后打破了当时香港华语片的卖座纪录。

张爱玲为电懋编写剧本，首先在基本价值观上必须与多数观众相一致。她之所以能够与香港观众或者干脆说香港市民在某些方面产生共鸣，编出一个又一个为他们所欢迎的剧本呢，首先因为她懂得他们。张爱玲的剧作惟妙惟肖地描绘了"小奸小坏"的众生相，这里有他们的笑，他们的爱，他们的烦恼，他们的幸福。张爱玲对此有很深的理解。可以说这些剧本展现了张爱玲的另一面：她并不像很多人想象的那样孤芳自赏，她对于与自己不同的，甚至是截然相反的东西也有所理解，有所包容。其次，张爱玲是一个很会编故事的人，她的剧本确实都编得很巧妙。

这些剧本多为喜剧，人们从中可以看到她的好玩、轻松和聪明。

不过，接下来《红楼梦》的改编却让她心力交瘁，因为老板并没有读过原著，只想要一个少男少女又哭又闹的爱情故事。倒是在这期间轻松写就的几个剧本都顺利投拍，并票房大卖。那时，已经做了老板的前女星李丽华见张爱玲的时候，特意打扮得很漂亮，接待也算隆重，但香港编剧的地位却和大陆时期无法同日而语，导演和主演都可以任意要求编剧来修改剧本，但即使这样，张爱玲从1956年到1964年，张爱玲还是为香港电懋影业公司编写了十个剧本，拍摄了八部，剧本都保存至今，就是《人财两得》（1958年1月上映，影片佚）、《情场如战场》（1957年5月上映）、《桃花运》（1959年4月上映，影片佚）、《六月新娘》（1960年1月上映）、《小儿女》（1963年10月上映）、《南北一家亲》（1962年10月上映）、《一曲难忘》（1964年7月上映，影片佚）、《南北喜相逢》（1964年9月上映），其中有些是原创的，有些是改编的。中"南北"系列电影席卷了港台地区，《南北和》放映六十天，卖座为全年第二名。没拍的两部中，《魂归离恨天》原稿还在，很遗憾《红楼梦》已经遗失。从1957年到1965年给"电懋"编剧近10年之久。直至1965年，张爱玲编写了最后的剧本《魂归离恨天》，本来是为野性难驯的叶枫量身创作，但它还没有来得及交到导演手上，"电懋"董事长陆运涛就遭遇空难，"电懋"改组成"国泰"而宋淇离职，张爱玲也从此脱离电影编剧，走进了她的隐遁人生！

后世的影响

1943年《倾城之恋》出版了，这部爱情小说书写了467页，是张爱玲最脍炙人口的短篇小说之一。也是一篇探讨爱情、婚姻和人性在战乱及其前后，怎样生存和挣扎的作品。

《倾城之恋》是一个动听而又近人情的故事。《倾城之恋》里，从腐旧的家庭里走出来的流苏，香港之战的洗礼并不曾将她感化成为革命女性；香港之战影响范柳原，使他转向平实的生活，终于结婚了，但结婚并不使他变为圣人，完全放弃往日的生活习惯与作风。

1984年8月2日，由香港邵氏兄弟有限公司制作的电影《倾城之恋》在香港上映。影片改编自张爱玲同名小说《倾城之恋》，讲述了香港沦陷后，范柳原和白流苏之间的爱情故事。影片是由许安华执导，周润发及缪骞人主演的一部爱情片。

2009年，由梦继任导演，邹静之担任编剧，根据张爱玲同名小说《倾城之恋》，改编了34集同名电视连续剧《倾城之恋》，并于同年3月14日在央视八套（CCTV-8）播出。陈数、黄觉、王学兵等人主演，该剧讲述发生在20世纪30年代上海和香港两地的一段华丽而苍凉的传奇爱情故事。

1995年9月8日夜，恰逢中华民族传统团圆节日中秋节，74岁的张爱玲在美国洛杉矶西木区公寓内孤独地离世，传奇在寂寞中默默拉下了帷幕。但是，随着张爱玲文学作品的陆续被改编成影视作品，她强大的艺术生命力依然在延续，光华依然在强势绽放！

《编剧张爱玲》一文，2016年—一文2016年，收入中国电影出版社出版的《唐山与中国电影》一书。

大刀张凤鸣怒打马县长

大清光绪年间（1875年—1908年），当时的丰润县小张各庄村一个叫张凤鸣的人，在光绪元年（1875年）自己办起了一个有三四十人的"大刀张河北梆子戏班"，自任班主，演出于宁河、丰润、玉田等地的村镇城乡，深受百姓的广泛欢迎。

张凤鸣由于从小习武，特别是精通大刀技法。所以，人送外号"大刀张"。

清朝时的乡村百姓，走亲访友，赶集上店大多是徒步而行，有交通工具的就是骡马驴等脚力了。张凤鸣每每外出总是骑着一头高大的白驴。因而，人又送他"大白驴张凤鸣"之称。由于张凤鸣自幼练武养成了一种惩恶扬善，路见不平拔刀相助的性格，且性情耿直深为乡里赞扬。光绪三十一年（1905年）的一天，张凤鸣从丰润县三女河村写戏回来。当张凤鸣骑着大白驴走到丰润县黄花港村时，只听前面一阵锣响，抬头一看，正见一群班头衙役一边高喊："闲人回避"，一边鸣锣开道。张凤鸣一打听原来是丰润县新来的马县长下乡巡视来了。提起马县长张凤鸣早有耳闻，这个马县长是个专横无理，飞扬跋扈，鱼肉百姓的县太爷。正巧这天对面相逢，张凤鸣决意不给让路。马县长见有人竟敢前头挡道，便让衙役们把张凤鸣叫到轿前问话："你是啥庄儿的？"张凤鸣说："看坟的，没庄。"

马县长又问："你叫啥名儿？"张凤鸣答："黑班头，没名儿。"马县长一听这不明明是个找碴儿的刺儿头嘛，于是，一声令下："给我打！"众衙役蜂拥而上。但得见张凤鸣面不改色心不跳，坐在大白驴上抓起一个衙役，一撒手，扑通一声将其摔在地上。顺势跳下大白驴来施展武功，一通拳脚把这帮狗仗人势的衙役们打得落花流水之后，箭步轿前，揪出马县长痛打一顿。身为一县之长挨了草民一顿狠揍，怎能咽得下这口臭气。于是，回到县衙后，把全丰润县养大白驴的人都捉拿归案，人人过堂。这时候已年过50的大刀张凤鸣，只好将自己苦心经营了20多年的"大刀张河北梆子戏班"含泪解散，只身下关东躲灾避祸去了。直到1910年中华民国建立后,马县长终于调离丰润县,年事已高的大刀张凤鸣才回到了家乡。民国二十年(1930年)75岁高龄的大刀张凤鸣离世而去,但他的故事却一直流传到今天。

程普与东吴三代君王

我国的大型工具书《辞海》有词条载:"程普,三国右北平土垠人。字德谋。"西汉东汉时期的土垠,即土垠县,也就是今天的唐山市丰润区。

东汉末年,诸侯崛起,群雄纷争,各立为王。最终魏、蜀、吴三足鼎立分天下,形成这样的局面,在吴国有一位功不可没的大将军,那就是程普。为什么说程普功不可没呢?因为程普早年任州郡吏时,曾随吴国的孙坚(公元155年—公元191年)在平中元年(公元184年)镇压黄巾军起义,与孙坚一同讨伐董卓。

初平二年(公元191年),孙坚率军击刘表时,中了刘表将黄祖之箭而亡。孙坚死后,程普随孙坚子孙策(字伯符)为将,因在大小战斗中屡建显赫战功,被封为吴郡都尉。后迁丹阳都尉。程普英勇善战果敢,一次,孙策军被敌军围困,处境十分险恶,程普率骑兵死死护卫主公孙策并一马当先,东挡西杀奋力突围。因在这次战斗中程普舍身救主有功,被拜为荡寇中郎将,领零陵太守。建安四年(公元199年),程普再随孙策征讨刘备,破卢江郡。建安五年(公元200年)孙策遇刺身亡,程普又辅佐孙策的弟弟孙权(字仲谋)称帝。孙权在位其间,曹操曾于建安十三年(公元208年)亲率大军20万浩浩荡荡南下攻吴,想统一中国。这时候,分别占据长江中下游的刘备和孙权联合拒曹,并以5万人的联军与曹操决战于赤壁(今湖北省嘉卓县西北)。吴军主帅周瑜与程普为联军的左右都督。程普协同周瑜及其他战将一起,采用火攻战术大破曹军,这就是中国历史上著名的"赤壁之战"。从而奠定了三国鼎立的局面。作为东吴的开国元勋同时更是三朝元老之一的程普,是东吴朝野内外,军政两界德高望重,举足轻重的人物,所以,东吴人都尊称他为"程公"。

2005年6月10日

卢舍那大佛下的遐思

早想瞻仰举世闻名的卢舍那大佛，一饱大唐圣佛的眼福。还是在春风荡漾的日子里，龙门石窟文化的灿烂，引领我来到河南洛阳龙门石窟，一睹大佛姿容。

晴朗的天空下，我站在大佛下仰望高高在上的卢舍那，仔细端详。卢舍那大佛坐姿背向大山，面向世间，体态丰盈，面容饱满，双耳垂肩。大佛嘴角微翘，双目微笑，头微俯，螺形发髻高梳。高大的卢舍那佛像既有一种栩栩如生的动态美感，又诠释给人们一种庄严，睿智，神秘，含蓄。盛唐是一个崇尚光明并充满光明的朝代，不以苗条纤秀为美，开明开放富强是唐朝这个中国繁荣朝代的标志，这些在卢舍那大佛身上都有所体现。人说卢舍那大佛是武则天的"报身像"。由此我想到武则天（公元624年—公元705年），武则天自起名"曌"。姓，不用辨。则：在辞海里有乃，即，只，而，若，之，那么的含义；天：在辞海里有颠，天帝，天空，依靠，精神源本的含义。曌，不言而喻，光照乾坤。而卢舍那的译意正好为"光明遍照"。

当年武则天十四岁时（唐太宗贞观年间，公元638年）便被唐太宗（李世民）选入宫中为才人。历史资料显示，武则天不但天生姿色好，且通晓文史，还写得一手漂亮的章草字，在盛唐这个诗的国度里武则天的诗文也还好。《全唐诗》等录有武则天58首诗。其中的一首《如意娘》这样写道："看朱成碧思纷纷，憔悴支离为忆君。不信比来常落泪，开箱验取石榴裙。"唐太宗死（公元649年），武则天遁入空门，入感业寺为尼。唐高宗（李治）即位后，永徽五年（公元654年）复召武则天回宫立为昭仪，得宠于唐高宗。永徽六年（公元655年）立为皇后，时年三十一岁的武则天已身经两帝，一次为尼，两次入宫了。由于唐高宗即位后一直有病，武则天在立为皇后以后便参与了朝政的处理和决策，时人将武则天与唐高宗并称为"二圣"。所以说，武则天对大唐的社会繁荣发展不能说不无贡献。

卢舍那大佛开凿于贞观二十三年（公元649年）。也就是唐高宗即位后的第一年。也许这是唐高宗为给武则天献礼而专门开凿的。时为昭仪，二十五岁的武则天捐钱两万贯，这里不能说唐高宗和武则天之间没有达成一种默契。佛像一凿就是25年，直到唐高宗上元二年（公元675年）才告完工。这座高高的卢舍那大佛就是则天皇后的形象与仪表及容姿，大佛的头部就是武则天二十五岁时容貌的再现。此时的则天皇后已是五十岁的人了。今天看来，这卢舍那大佛大有母仪天下的威严与风度。可是，则天皇后却是在卢舍那大佛这座则天皇后报身像建成后近十年（公元684年）才临朝称制。在这期间，则天皇后在弘道元年（公元684年）废中宗（李显）立睿宗（李旦）又废睿宗，亲理朝政，改元光宅。到公元690年，则天皇后直接自称圣神皇帝，国号为周。改元天授。此时的武则天除唐高祖（李渊）外，已经历了大唐四位皇帝。从此成为封建社会和中国历史上唯一一位女皇帝。武则天以千古一女帝的气魄、睿智、才华和坚毅，纳谏用贤，协助唐高宗，扶助中宗、睿宗和亲自治理国家50年。是武周皇帝开创了殿试的先河，亲自考试贡士；是武周皇帝允许九品小官和百姓自行荐举；是武周皇帝改官制，规定五品官可升入士流；是武周皇帝减赋税、轻徭役；是武周皇帝督修了《姓氏录》。这些都是大唐国度开明、开放，公平、公正，社会稳定繁荣向上的延续和体现。直到武周皇帝死后近50年唐玄宗（李隆基）后期，才出现了安史之乱，大唐盛世的光环才略显暗淡。

人人皆有志，想当皇帝更无可非议。谁都想当个好皇帝，可当皇帝不易，当个女皇帝更不易。人皆向上进取，没有一个皇帝想败了家国河山，武周皇帝年近八十时仍是如此，并保持了江山一统稳定繁荣的局面。

太阳虽红，但有黑子；阳光普照，但仍有照不到的苔藓。武则天，一代女皇帝虽历尽艰辛，图治家国社稷，也有一些时弊。这也正是每一个朝代都不可避免的，因为任何事物都是正反共存的，对立统一的。曌字之意，则天之意，卢舍那之意，都有光照普天的意思，这也正是武皇帝和历代君王的本来愿望。

在卢舍那大佛那慈祥可亲、丰颐柔和、秀日宁静中，蕴含了多少为人、为女人、为人妻、为人母、为万人俯首，为众敌称臣的人上人的亘古一女帝之喜忧哀乐，酸甜苦辣。阳光下，再次回望卢舍那大佛，品味很多，很多……

2005年11月11日

丁开嶂与铁血会

丁开嶂原名丁作霖，字小川，大清直隶省（今河北省丰润区南青坨村）人。生于清同治九年（1870年），卒于民国三十四年（1945年）。20岁时中秀才，后入京师大学第一班。

丁开嶂在清末时期，是一个中国北方赫赫有名的人物，充满铁血情怀和民族气节。

光绪二十六年（1900年）沙俄乘八国联军侵入中国之机出兵占领我国东北，之后日俄开战。

战争爆发第二年，丁开嶂在张家口地区与铁血会首领秦宗周、丁关弟一起，进一步扩大铁血会力量。1907年丁开嶂在东三省、绥远、热河、察哈尔、内蒙古、外蒙古（中国历史领土名，今蒙古国及唐努乌梁海）、河北、山西等地，以摆斋戒洒为名发展铁血会组织，又在家乡当时的丰润县南青坨村创立了北振武社。还把原来旨在抗击沙俄的铁血会更名为北洋铁血会，亲任总理，下设京东、京北、边外、关东四个支部，分28路领袖。1911年设立铁血会军部于天津法租界的小白楼，建立了拥有9.5万人的四部军。

1912年1月2日，铁血会宣布滦州独立。清通永镇总兵王怀庆与第三镇统制曹锟于1月4日向滦州合力大举进攻，军内将领岳兆林、张建功率部叛变，腹背受敌的铁血会付出了极大牺牲，最后终于失败。丁开嶂回到天津马上集齐四部军将领议事，决定于壬子年除夕午夜时分，精选各部将士入京，分别出击清廷衙门并由四部军所在地方树旗宣告独立。1912年2月3日，丁开嶂改铁血会军部为军政府，各路铁血会将士一致推举丁开嶂为中华民国北方军政府临时大元帅。那时的中国是南有孙中山北有丁小川。在全国南北革命形势的逼迫下，清宣统皇帝被迫宣布退位。至此，誓与清廷不共戴天的铁血会于1913年自动解散。

2002年3月24日

皇后诗人萧观音

萧观音（1040—1075），大辽国女诗人。兴宗重熙二十二年（1053）为燕赵王（耶律弘基）的王妃。清宁元年（1055）耶律弘基继位为道宗，立为皇后，次年十一月上尊号懿德皇后。

大辽重熙九年（1040）五月五日酉时，在辽西京（今大同）皇宫附近的一座花园式的建筑里，随着一阵清脆的婴儿啼哭，一个女婴来到了世上。这个女婴就是辽兴宗（1032—1055）母后钦哀皇后（萧耨斤？—1057）的弟弟；当朝国舅爷萧惠（983—1056）和夫人秦晋国长公主的女儿——萧观音。

历史上的萧观音算得上是个美才女，明眸皓齿，美丽清秀，眉不描自黑长，唇不描自若含丹，而且琴棋书画样样通，骑马射箭拉硬弓。兼备中原女子的才貌和北方女子的强悍。在大辽国历史上，萧观音以能诗尚武著称。留传至今的诗作有《伏虎林应制》《君臣同志华夷同风应制》《同心院十首》《绝命词》等。

随着萧观音一天天长成了大姑娘,她的美貌和才气也传遍西京(今大同),王公贵族的公子哥们也纷纷前来求亲。为给女儿找到一个如意郎君,在兴宗重熙二十二年,萧观音十四岁那年(1053),萧观音的父母想出一个主意,设下考题由萧观音自己亲自考试上门前来求婚者。谁和女儿的意,谁就中选。无奈,西京少年大多平庸之辈,半个月过去后,无一过关。萧观音倍感失望,无意再考。忽然一天,来了一位姓韩和一位姓萧的公子哥。萧观音一看他俩,个个相貌不凡,精神俊朗,不禁心里暗喜,于是说:"小女子自幼喜欢吟诗,我写几个字,请两位公子读出一首诗来。"萧观音面带嘲讽,心怀得意而窃喜地信手写来:色青黄花乱香,风为去日能长。

萧观音写完后说:"这是一首唐诗,两位公子只要能写出这首诗来,小女子就认为两位公子是才子。但不熟读唐诗,恐怕添不出全诗来。"

不承想,韩、萧两位公子拿过来看后,竟不约而同地迅速写出唐诗:"草色青青柳色黄,桃花离乱李花香。东风不为吹愁去,春日偏能怨恨长。"

萧观音又经过弹琴(古筝)、骑马射雕两道关考试两位公子,虽然韩、萧两位公子不分上下,但最终选择了萧公子,可万没想到萧公子却是当朝皇帝辽兴宗的儿子耶律弘基。

耶律弘基(道宗)于清宁元年继位,清宁二年(1056)的秋猎,道宗与皇后(萧观音)一同前往黑山。这次秋猎,道宗御猎一只猛虎,皇后猎获一只黑熊。

道宗高兴下令摆宴,席间,道宗对群臣说:"众爱卿,朕今日杀虎林伏虎,美宴之上有酒有肉,岂能没有歌舞、诗词,让南朝人笑我北朝无人?"随后对皇后说:"爱卿何不吟诗一首,为朕助兴。"

皇后稍加思索后挥毫写道:"威风万里震南邦,东去能翻鸭绿江。灵怪大千都破胆,那叫猛虎不投降。"这就是那首气吞山河,睥睨天下的《伏虎林应制》。

这一年萧观音十六岁,虽为年轻女子,却有如此气魄和胆视,不能不让人叹服。从以上这首诗里,我们充分感受到了诗人充满阳刚、气魄雄浑之美,但在萧观音的一首《怀古》诗里,又能让我们充分感受到女诗人阴柔美的另一面:"宫中只数赵家妆,败雨残云误汉王,惟有知情一片月,曾窥飞鸟入昭阳。"读后细细咀嚼品味,我们又会感到一代佳作之美。更有《同心院十首》,娓娓道来,婉怨而真切:

扫深院,闭久金铺暗。游丝落网尘作堆,积岁青苔厚阶面。扫深院,待君宴。
拂象床,凭梦借高唐。敲坏半边知妾卧,恰当天出少辉光。拂象床,待君王。
换香枕,一半无云锦。为是秋来展转多,更有双双泪痕渗。换香枕,待君寝。
铺翠被,羞杀鸳鸯对。犹忆当时叫合欢,而今独自相思眠。铺翠被,待君睡。
装绣帐,金钩未敢上。解却四角夜光珠,不教照见愁模样。装绣帐,待君贶。

迭锦茵，重重空自陈。只愿身为白玉体，不愿伊当薄幸人。迭锦茵，待君临。
展瑶席，花笑三韩碧。笑妾新埔玉一床，从来妇欢不终夕。展瑶席，待君息。
剔银灯，须知一样明。偏是君来生彩晕，对妾故作青荧荧。剔银灯，待君行。
热熏炉，能将孤闷苏。若道妾身多秽贱，自粘御香香彻肤。热熏炉，待君娱。
张鸣筝，恰恰语娇莺。一从弹作房中曲，常和窗前风雨声。张鸣筝，待君听。

就是这样一首婉约而倾心的优美之词，想不到竟招祸到身。原来，《同心院》曲谱只有宫中伶人（旧指以唱戏为职业的人）赵惟一和一个叫单的宫女能奏。而单的哥哥单登是辽国叛臣重元的家属贬为奴，皇后认为不能近御。单登怀恨在心，便利用其妹单与奸臣耶律乙辛通奸的关系，向其妹诬称皇后与赵惟一私通，证据就是《怀古》诗中"赵""惟""一"。但老奸巨猾的耶律乙辛认为仅此还不能治皇后于死地。于是命人伪作《十香曲》，假称是宋朝某皇后亲作，若得皇后亲笔御书，将是双绝存世。善良直爽的皇后不加思索便把《十香曲》和《怀古》抄在了一起。殊不知，奸臣耶律乙辛如获至宝，心怀鬼胎的迅速将皇后手迹呈送道宗皇帝并进谗言。顿时，一股醋意促使震怒的道宗不问青红皂白，不做冷静分析，听信谗言，执意相信皇后与赵惟一行为不轨。盛怒之下，大发皇威，御赐自己曾经深深爱过的皇后自缢。无奈何，美丽、善良、刚烈而又多才多艺的萧皇后，愤恨奸臣、小人伴君侧，愤恨自己的夫君不明善恶，一气呵成，写下《绝命词》后毅然自缢。天祚乾统元（1101）六月得昭雪，追谥"宣懿皇后"移葬永福陵，今内蒙古巴林右旗白塔子北。

词云："嗟薄祐兮多幸，羌作俪兮皇家。承昊穹兮下覆，近日月兮分华。托后钧兮凝位，忽前星兮启耀。虽衅累兮黄床，庶无罪兮宗庙。欲贯鱼兮上进，乘阳德兮飞天。岂祸生兮无朕，蒙秽恶兮宫闱。将抛心兮自陈，冀回照兮白日。宁庶女兮哀顿，对左右兮摧伤。共西曜兮将坠，忽吾去兮椒房。呼天地兮惨悴，恨古今兮安极。知吾生兮必惑，又焉爱兮旦夕。"好一首告天地之分明，还清白于世间的《绝命词》啊，坦荡抒情意，明白告上苍，凄凉别天地，令今人读来仍恨道宗帝。虽是《绝命词》，却洋溢着疾恶如仇、刚直不阿，一派女丈夫的气概；绝不失大气、昂然、凄美。读罢掩卷，深深感叹，前不见古人，后不见来者。读诗和古人交谈，让人觉得：萧观音，貌美、诗——更美！

2007 年 4 月 6 日

老李，英名永驻

他就是电影《英雄儿女》里王芳唱的"老李和老赵"中的老李。这是笔者六年前听丰润新军屯镇大街上群众讲的。于是追寻到新军屯光荣院对老李进行了采访。

毛主席说："你干得太漂亮啦"

1948年12月5日，党中央毛主席指挥我军两个兵团及地方部队100万人发起了平津战役，第一仗是新保安战斗。当时，李克增（即老李）在我华北野战军第195师59团8连2排3班任爆破组长。临战，师首长找到李克增说："你们的任务就是炸掉敌人所有的堡垒，为大部队总攻扫清前进道路上的障碍。任务十分艰巨。"李克增马上回答："为消灭敌人打胜仗，死也心甘！"首长高兴地说："好！我们军队就需要你这样的战士。"

12月22日，战斗打响了。李克增带领两名战士携带四个炸药包，还拿着一把掐铁丝网用的大铁钳，向国民党军的堡垒摸去，我军的机枪猛烈地向敌方射击，以掩护他们前进。国民党军堡垒里的机枪更是疯狂地向外扫射，弹雨中，李克增和战友们越壕沟跨河道，机智敏捷迅速地接近了敌堡垒，在敌人狂吼的机枪扫射下，点燃了炸药包的导火索。随着一声巨响，三个敌堡在漆黑的夜幕中炸开了花。李克增抖掉身上的石土呼叫身边的战友，但没有回声。两个战友已经牺牲了。这时，还有一个敌堡仍在狂妄的向外射击阻止我军前进。李克增怒不可遏地爬向敌人最后一个堡垒，放好炸药包，点燃导火索，然后快速撤离。随着又一声巨响，我军前进道路上最后一颗钉子被拔掉了。此时，正是大部队总攻的时间。我军立即以排山倒海之势压向敌军阵地，围歼了新保安国民党军第35军军部和两个师。

平津战役首战告捷，党中央毛主席从西柏坡发来贺电，并专门接见了战斗英雄汇报团成员。毛主席握着李克增的手高兴地说："你干得太漂亮啦。"李克增精神抖擞地回答："主席，下次任务我一定完成得更好。"毛主席亲切地拍着李克增的肩膀说："好！"为表彰战功，军委给李克增记大功一次，毛主席还亲自将一支钢笔和一个笔记本赠给李克增。

用扁担和饭勺活捉 5 个美国佬

笔者十分敬佩这位时已七十多岁的老英雄,又请他讲讲当年在抗美援朝战场上的英雄事迹。当老李讲到电影《英雄儿女》中王芳唱的故事时说,当时他是炊事班长,一天老李和两个姓赵的战友去给阵地上的战士们送饭,途中突然发现前面有五个美国兵,他们马上轻轻放下饭菜隐蔽观察。从外观动态上他们断定这几个背着枪的美国兵是被打败的散兵,只要智取定能抓获他们。于是,老李拿着扁担,另两个战士拿着饭勺悄悄摸上去,距离都很近了,但敌人没有发现他们。三人交换一下眼色,猛地冲上去大喊一声:"缴枪不杀!"这突如其来的喊声,吓破了敌人的胆,美国兵头也没敢回的就乖乖地放下枪、举起手,当了俘虏。

笔者问老英雄,这段故事是否有人采访过,李克增说,在部队时,团首长曾经带着一个作家采访了他。

1955 年,国家给老李安排了工作,但老李坚决要求回家乡,参加社会主义新农村建设,到家后他当上了生产队长。1976 年大地震后,政府按国家有关规定接老李到县市级光荣院去安度晚年,但老李舍不得他长大和参加革命的地方,于是就住进了新军屯光荣院。在这里他还自己主动种了三亩菜园子,以保证光荣院生活用菜。

为充分了解老李光荣的过去,笔者近日又去丰润县新军屯光荣院看望他。令人遗憾的是,老李已于 1997 年农历十二月三十日因病与世长辞。

老李没有别的留在世上,笔者只抄录了他的简历:1926 年农历正月初一生人;1947 年参加中国人民解放军;1948 年加入中国共产党,曾任爆破组长;1950 年参加抗美援朝战争,曾任炊事班长;1955 年 1 月 25 日复员回乡;48 年党龄。

2000 年 11 月 5 日

英雄无畏排除炸弹

65 年前,志愿军王贵成功排除炸弹。王贵这位 1929 年出生,1948 年入伍成为中国人民解放军的老战士,参加过中国人民解放战争、抗美援朝保家卫国的战争,经历了无数次大大小小的战斗，有讲不尽的硝烟战火，说不完的战斗故事。

2017年6月2日早上8点，我再一次来到果园乡光荣院拜访王贵老人家，听他讲那过去的战斗故事和感人的事迹。

89岁的王贵老人一说起战斗岁月便精神抖擞，很是健谈，兴致勃勃地讲述起来，让我觉得有惊无险的一段故事是在朝鲜战争期间发生的。老人说："那是1952年9月的一天，正在进行的是朝鲜黑桥战斗。"当时王贵在中国人民志愿军防空军独立四十二营指挥部，这天的上午9点左右，从营部的东南方向飞来60多架敌机，围绕着营部在上空盘旋了三圈后，分批向下俯冲扫射，然后爬高返回并投弹。几次的轮番俯冲、扫射、投弹、爆炸，使得营部被毁。敌机飞走后，趴在地上的王贵站起来抖掉一身的泥土，定下神，看到眼前土里露出一只手，他马上去扒，原来是营部的话务员被炸弹掀起来的土埋在下边，好在埋压时间短，话务员没有窒息，还好营部附近的军车也庆幸没有炸毁。等营部清点人数平静下来后，大家发现一枚定时炸弹就在离大家的不远处戳在土里。这是明摆着的重大隐患，如不排除将是全营志愿军战士生命的威胁。战争时期，朝鲜国有专业的"朝鲜人民起弹组"，每三人一组，负责战地炸弹排爆。但部队要联系他们，等他们到来还要一段时间。王贵这时心里想的是全英志愿军战士的生命保障，看住眼前的定时炸弹，和时间一分一秒地慢慢流逝，心情急切。于是他主动向营长请求，要自己亲自去排除定时炸弹。此时此刻，营长看着眼前这个侦查副参谋的王贵，没有答应他的情求。但为了营部全体志愿军指战员们的生命安全，王贵坚持一再请求营长批准他去排除这颗定时炸弹。没办法，营长最后问他："你有把握吗？"王贵说自己仔细观察过朝鲜人民军起弹组的排爆过程，对他们的方法步骤都记在心里了。营长告诉他："保重。"

王贵向营长端正地敬了一个标准的军礼，带上当时拆卸定时炸弹所需的钳子、扳子、锤子，静静地接近了这颗美军投下的定时炸弹，他先是拿起锤子仿照朝鲜人民军起弹组人员的动作，用锤子在炸弹胆体表面敲击三下，随后把耳朵贴近弹体，侧耳静听炸弹内部的动静，听了一分多钟，炸弹里面没有任何动静。为了拆弹方便，也为了大家的生命安全，万一发生不测时，他可以趴在定时炸弹上，用自己的生命保护大家的生命安全，他把定时炸弹放倒在地上，再拿起板子，拧松的螺丝……

王贵小心翼翼地进行着拆弹工作，远处隐蔽起来的志愿军指战员们，都在手心里为王贵捏着一把汗，因为大家知道这是一件十分危险的事情。从来没有接触过定时炸弹拆卸的王贵，额头上沁出汗珠，王贵深知重任在肩，责任不一般，心中只有一个念头，那就是：用我一个人的牺牲，换取营部全体指战员的生命安全。所以，谨慎小心，认真周密，一丝不苟的安全操作。慢慢地，慢慢地，他终于稳妥地把这枚定时炸弹的引火棒，从定时炸弹弹体上拆卸了下来。直到这时，王贵才抹了一把脸上的汗，然后爬起来，当他站起身高高举起定时炸弹的引火棒时，营部全体指战员欢呼雀跃，跑过来拥抱王贵……营长也紧紧握住他的手说："你不愧是最可爱的人哪。"之后,营长站在高地上对大家高声说:"我们大家要学习王贵不怕死的精神、为大家伙的生命安全,不怕牺牲自己的大无畏精神!"

这样生与死的经历虽然过去了65年,但说到这里,王贵老人脸上还是浮现出自豪欣慰且开心的笑容。因为,在那特殊的年代、特殊的环境、特别的战斗里,他确实是想用自己一个人的牺牲,来换取营部全体指战员的生命安全。这段实战故事里的事,渗透着我们一个中国革命军人的精神和本质,我深深为之而感动着。

老英雄送我到光荣院院里的五星红旗处时告诉我:"这面国旗和旗杆,都是我花钱买来的,我们不能没有国家,国旗就是国家的象征,我们看着国旗心里就踏实……"

我仰望着高高飘扬的国旗,心里想,这面红旗浸透了老英雄的爱国心情,更饱含着一个中国革命军人深知共和国来之不易的情怀。我看一下老英雄,再一次深深为之而感动着。

2017年6月6日

李清照与"花"与"酒"

一代词人李清照曾被尊为藕花神,供奉于济南大明湖畔的藕神祠。她曾作《如梦令》,描述她少女时代在济南的欢乐生活:"常记溪亭日暮,沉醉不知归路。兴尽晚回舟,误入藕花深处。争渡,争渡,惊起一滩鸥鹭。"宋时,济南城西确有"溪亭"。从唐山直下济南,来感受体味李清照的花与酒。

在李清照的作品里也为我们留下了爱情甜美的故事。这个爱情故事,经李清照妙笔的深情润色,成了中国人千余年来的精神享受。请看这首《减字木兰花》:"卖花担上,买得一枝春欲放。泪染轻匀,犹带彤霞晓露痕。怕郎猜道,奴面不如花面好。云鬓斜簪,徒教郎比比看。"这是李清照婚后的甜蜜,是对丈夫的撒娇,从中也透出李清照对自己美丽的自信。

人不能没有爱,如花的女人不能没有爱,感情丰富的才女更不能没有爱。正当她的艺术之树在爱的汁液浇灌下茁壮成长时,丈夫到外地上任为官了。夫妻团圆,难舍难分,不等今日去且盼春来归。看这首送别之作《一剪梅》:"红藕香残玉簟秋,轻解罗裳,独上兰舟。云中谁寄锦书来,雁字回时,月满西楼。花自飘零水自流,一种相思,两处闲愁。此情无计可消除,才下眉头，却上心头。"

别绪离愁，爱深思切，另是一种甜蜜的偷偷地咀嚼。但是，李清照绝不是一般的只会叹息几句"贱妾守空房"的小妇人，她在空房里修炼着文学，直将这门艺术练得炉火纯青，于是这种最普通的爱情表达竟变成了夫妻间的命题创作比赛，成了他们向艺术高峰攀登的记录。所以，她写下了《醉花阴·重阳》："薄雾浓云愁永昼，瑞脑销金兽。佳节又重阳，玉枕纱厨，半夜凉初透。东篱把酒黄昏后，有暗香盈袖。莫道不消魂，帘卷西风，人比黄花瘦。"这是赵明诚在外地为官时，李清照寄给他的一首相思诗。彻骨的爱恋，痴痴的思念，借秋风黄花表现得淋漓尽致。史料上说，赵明诚收到李清照这首词后，先为情所感，后为词的艺术力所激，发誓要写一首超过妻子的词。于是三日闭门谢客，得词五十首，将李清照词杂于其间，请友人陆德夫评点，不想陆德夫说只有三句绝佳："莫道不消魂，帘卷西风，人比黄花瘦。"赵自叹不如。这个故事流传极广，可想赵李夫妻二人是怎样在相互爱慕中享受着琴瑟相和的甜蜜。这也令后世一切有才有貌，却得不到相应质量爱情的男女感到一丝的悲凉。

李清照自己在《金石录后序》里追忆那段生活时说："余性偶强记，每饭罢，坐归来堂，指堆积书史，言某事在某卷第几页第几行，以中否胜负，为饮茶先后。中即举杯大笑，至茶倾覆怀中，反不得饮而起。"这是何等的幸福，何等的欢乐，怎一个"甜"字了得。蜜一样的生活，滋养着她绰约的风姿和旺盛的艺术创造。

女词人李清照，借酒抒情，是她隽永清丽的词风。"昨夜风骤雨疏，浓睡不消残酒。试问卷帘人，却道海棠依旧。知否，知否？应是绿肥红瘦！"好个《如梦令》简洁明了地描述了词人那"浓睡不消残酒"的醉态，以及"应是绿肥红瘦"的情怀。

从写作激情到酒后的真情则是毫无做作的宣泄。"故乡何处是，忘了除非醉。沉水卧时烧，香消酒未消。"这首《菩萨蛮》是作者饱尝了战乱流离漂泊之苦的叙述。前半阕是冬去春来，阳光虽微，风却柔和了，我换上了夹衫，仍有一丝未尽的寒意，梅已凋残，我的心已破碎，为了逃避思乡之苦只有醉，睡前燃上的炉火沉香已烧尽，而我的酒意却没退。正如素有惊人绝句的女词人所述"学诗谩有惊人句"，道出了一个弱女子，只能纸上谈兵空有才气。而眼前却要随世事沉浮！

说起李清照于酒的缘分，也正如词人与词的关联，这原本就是心海与情感的交融，生活与生命的欢歌，更加升华了李清照人品，虽然经历了一场再嫁匪人、离异系狱的灾难，但是李清照生活的意志并未消沉，诗词创作的热情更趋高涨。她从个人的痛苦中解脱出来之后，把眼光投到对国家大事的关注上。绍兴三年（1133年）五月，朝廷派同签书枢密院事韩肖胄和工部尚书胡松年出使金朝。李清照满怀激情地作古诗、律诗各一首为二公送行。诗中有"欲将血泪寄山河，去洒东山一抔土"之句，表达了反击侵略、收复失地的强烈愿望，充满了怀念故国的情。一杯薄酒论短长，无限深情寄思乡。这些个满腹愁肠，欲语还说的语言，怎能道得尽词人盼望国泰民安,思念家乡的真实写照!其实,婉约的词人骨子里却有着不为众人所意想的豪放,"至今思项羽,不肯过江东"便是她的风采。

留以清丽照后人

在济南趵突泉公园东北侧有漱玉泉,是济南七十二名泉之一,泉水清澈见底,池底泉水不断涌出,轻轻溢出池外,跌落石上,水石相激,淙淙有声,犹如漱玉。相传早年李清照曾在泉边洗漱,因而得名漱玉泉。在漱玉泉的后边,就是旷世才女李清照的纪念堂。

2007年槐花飘香的5月,我怀着崇拜敬仰的心情走进了这个供奉着一代伟大词人的殿堂,来一睹词人风韵,在词人遗落的文字里,寻觅词人的芳踪香魂。

纪念堂前的一副对联这样写道:"大明湖畔,趵突泉边,故居在垂柳深入;金石录里,漱玉集中,文采有后主遗风",是已故老先生郭沫若手书的。上联是指李清照故居的所在地;下联是对其词作成就的赞扬。

史料上说,北宋神宗元丰七年甲子(公元1084年),李清照出生在一个上层士大夫家庭。李清照"自少年便有诗名,才力华赡,逼近前辈",北宋文坛名家晁补之这样称赞。元符三年(1100)左右,李清照写了长诗《浯溪中兴颂诗和张文潜》,受到当时人们的好评。轰动京师的《如梦令》(尝记溪亭日暮),是李清照十余岁时的作品,"当时文士莫不击节"。

被世人称为"易安体"的是指李清照的词,今日读来,倍感独具婉约道情的风格。创作特点因李清照在北宋和南宋时期生活的变化而变化。今天读来,我们仍可明显看得出前期写悠闲生活为多,后期作品自辟途径,运用白描手法形式,悲叹身世,虽情调感伤,也从中流露出对中原的怀念,但语言与她的为人一样既铿锵又清丽。

北宋建中靖国元年(1101),18岁的李清照,与当时在太学当学生的21岁的赵明诚结婚。

历史上的宋王朝经过167年"清明上河图"式的和平繁荣之后,金人一锤砸烂了都城汴京(开封)的琼楼玉苑,还掠走了徽、钦二帝,赵宋王朝于公元1127年匆匆南逃。李清照在山东青州的爱巢也树倒窝散,一家人开始过漂泊无定的生活。南渡第二年,赵明诚被任为京城建康的知府,不想就在这时发生了一件国耻又蒙家羞的事。一天深夜,城里发生叛乱,身为地方长官的赵明诚不是身先士卒指挥戡乱，而是偷偷用绳子缒城逃走。因此，他被朝廷撤职。李清照在这件事上却表现出大节大义，很为丈夫临阵脱逃而羞愧。赵被撤职后夫妇二人继续沿长江而上向江西方向流亡。当行至乌江镇时，真性情的李清照得知这就是当年项羽兵败自刎之处，不觉心潮起伏，面对浩浩江面，吟下了这首雄浑奔放的千古绝唱《夏日绝句》："生当作人杰，死亦为鬼雄。至今思项羽，不肯过江东"。丈夫在其身后听着这一字一句的金石之声，面有愧色，心中泛起深深的自责。

公元1129年，最令李清照伤心的是在流亡途中49岁的赵明诚死了，46岁的一代才女李清照倍感孤独无助，陷入痛苦的困境中。追忆往昔，她抱憾终生的是和赵明诚一起度过二十九个春秋的回忆与悼惜的历历往事。

在李清照孤苦伶仃、担惊受怕、痛苦迷茫的时候，一个时任右承奉郎的张汝舟出现了，李清照不胜张汝舟甜言蜜语的攻势，确实被张汝舟俘虏了。李清照经历了和赵明诚神仙伴侣般的浪漫爱情生活，又连遭国破家亡的厄运，这种命运的巨大反差让她不顾一切地向往着甜蜜、温馨的家庭生活，绍兴二年夏（1132），李清照嫁给了张汝舟。然而，张汝舟追求、迎娶一位46岁的李清照，决然不是为了李清照的容貌，更不是李清照以为的张汝舟看中了她无与伦比的才华，而是想得到李清照的金石收藏品。本性浅薄、暴虐、恶俗的张汝舟婚后暴露无遗，让李清照欲哭无泪。张汝舟看到李清照的古玩字画也没有自己想象的那么丰富，而且李清照还不愿相让，张汝舟大为失望。最后，张汝舟恼羞成怒，开始对李清照拳脚相加，甚至想将她打死，除去这个年老色衰的包袱，得到她的财物。

华帐前，红烛下，兼具顽强、独立、智慧、刚毅性格的李清照看着这个厚颜无耻的小白脸，幻想破灭了，怒火中烧。此时的李清照悲恨交加，联想到张汝舟把李清照娶到手后得意之时，竟将自己科举考试作弊过关这种大逆不道的事拿来夸耀的卑劣嘴脸。李清照决心立即检举上告张汝舟利用欺瞒手段获取官职的罪行，告发这个奸计小人。但是，依照当时宋朝的封建法律，女人告丈夫，无论对错输赢，都要坐牢两年。此时的李清照已对感情不抱任何幻想，觉得在感情生活上绝不凑合，她宁肯受皮肉之苦，也不受精神的奴役。一旦看穿对方的灵魂，她便表现出无情的鄙视和深切的懊悔。曾经沧海难为水，心存高洁不低头。李清照视人格比生命更珍贵，哪里受得这种窝囊气，便决定与他分手。她曾在给友人的信中这样写道："猥以桑榆之晚景，配兹驵侩之下材。"她是何等刚烈之人，宁可坐牢也不肯忍辱苟且。她坚持独立的人格，坚持高质量的爱情。当时，李家和赵家还有很多人在朝为官，在他们的帮助下，李清照仅仅坐牢九天就走出牢门。

绍兴二年秋（1132），李清照终于达到目的，离异成功。李清照快刀斩乱麻结束了这两个月的噩梦婚姻，全身心地投入先夫赵明诚《金石录》的编写中去了。

读过这段史料，让我看到一个千年以前宋代反封建的新女性。南宋时期，李清照的作品表现出高度爱国精神。"明月松间照,清泉石上流",李清照是从骨子里追求民族气节和政治上的坚定,追求人格超俗的,她总是清醒地持着一种做人标准,顽强地守着自己的节操。在未遭大难,生活还比较稳定时,已看出她高标准的人格追求。正如"生当作人杰,死亦为鬼雄"所说。还有"欲将血泪寄山河,去洒东山一抔土"之句,表达了她反击侵略、收复失地的强烈愿望,充满了怀念故国的情。以后的李清照就更加超群拔俗了,在世事纷扰中出淤泥而不染。她是站在高阁之上,穿越时空,俯视众生的,所以有一种特殊的寂寞在《忆秦娥》中清楚道来:"临高阁,乱山平野烟光薄。烟光薄,栖鸦归后,暮天闻角。断香残酒清怀恶,西风催衬梧桐落。梧桐落,又还秋色,又还寂寞。"

绍兴十三年(1143年)前后,60岁左右的李清照将赵明诚遗作《金石录》校勘整理,表进于朝。开禧元年(1205)刻书。过了十余年,大约在绍兴二十六年(1156年)或者以后,无子无女的李清照,怀着对死去亲人的绵绵思念和对故土难归的无限失望,在极度孤苦、凄凉中,悄然辞世,享年至少73岁。

"李三瘦"

到了济南,前来趵突泉北的漱玉泉李清照纪念堂看望李清照。却原来,只知李清照词中的"三瘦",殊不知一代词人的汉白玉雕像也可称得上"三瘦"。颈瘦、腰瘦、身瘦,雅称别号"李三瘦"。这个雅号是较为奇特且不好理解的。

为什么人送雅称别号"李三瘦"给李清照呢?要说"三瘦"必须从李清照的词说起。之所以"三瘦",是因为在李清照的词里以"瘦"字入词,来形容花容人貌,并创作了三个因"瘦"而名传千古的动人词句。

捧读《凤凰台上忆吹箫》:

香冷金猊,被翻红浪,起来慵自梳头。任宝奁尘满,日上帘钩。

生怕离怀别苦,多少事、欲说还休。新来瘦,非干病酒,不是悲秋。休休!

这回去也,千万遍阳关,也则难留。念武陵人远,烟锁秦楼。惟有楼前流水,应念我、终日凝眸。

凝眸处,从今又添,一段新愁。

里面的"新来瘦,非干病酒,不是悲秋"之句,让大清文人陈廷焯读的如痴如醉,叹之为绝妙,评价为"婉转曲折,煞是妙绝";当代词学大师唐圭璋也无不感慨地说:"'新来瘦'三句,申言别苦。较病酒悲秋为尤苦。"

词主要描写伤春怨别和闺阁生活的题材,特别是表现了女词人李清照善感多情的个性。如《如梦令》描写惜春怜花的感情:

昨夜雨疏风骤,浓睡不消残酒。

试问卷帘人,却道海棠依旧。知否,知否,应是绿肥红瘦。

就是这句"知否,知否,应是绿肥红瘦",使得黄蓼园在他的《蓼园词选》中情不自禁地说:"'绿肥红瘦',无限凄婉,却又妙在含蓄,短幅中藏无数曲折,自是圣于词者。"

李清照在丈夫赵明诚外出时因相思而作的怨别词《醉花阴》,更是情深意挚,一格别具。《醉花阴》以新颖的构思,高雅的意趣,描写了李清照在"佳节又重阳"时,倍感孤寂内心情感,于是自喻黄花道:

薄雾浓云愁永昼,瑞脑销金兽。佳节又重阳,玉枕纱厨,半夜凉初透。

东篱把酒黄昏后,有暗香盈袖。莫道不销魂,帘卷西风,人比黄花瘦。

这不是一般男女词人的代言体怨词就能比得了的。传说,李清照写好《醉花阴》一词后,给分居两地的丈夫赵明诚寄去,"明诚自愧弗逮,务欲胜之",便闭门3昼夜苦心写作,得15阕,与李清照的词混在一起请来友人陆德夫赏鉴。德夫品读再三之后说:"只有'莫道不销魂,帘卷西风,人比黄花瘦'三句绝佳。"

瞻仰李清照汉白玉雕像,回味李清照"三瘦"词《凤凰台上忆吹箫》《如梦令》《醉花阴》,字字句句,情切切意长长,怎是一个"瘦"字了得,真可谓人"瘦"字"瘦"情不"瘦"。

"李三瘦"你让我饱览了你的情不"瘦"。

一滩鸥鹭

李清照借酒抒情,彰显其隽永清丽的词风。"试问卷帘人,却道海棠依旧。知否,知否?应是绿肥红瘦。"这首《如梦令》简洁传神,描述了词人"浓睡不消残酒"的醉态,每句话都细微缜密、直抵人心。"故乡何处是,忘了除非醉。沉水卧时烧,香消酒未消。"这首《菩萨蛮·风柔日薄春犹早》,是她饱尝战乱之苦的倾诉,词意含蓄隽永,展现出女词人灵魂深处的悲愤、不安和强烈的思乡情绪。

李清照与诗词的关联,原本就体现了生命与情感的交融。虽历经磨难,但她的意志并未消沉。她从个人痛苦中跳脱出来,将目光投射到国家大事上。

1133年春,宋高宗派人出使金国,李清照作诗送行:"欲将血泪寄山河,去洒东山一抔土。"作者以悲壮豪迈的诗句,表达了反击敌军收复失地的强烈愿望,充满了爱国主义激情。

在李清照这位婉约词人的背后,始终隐藏着不为人知的豪放。她挥笔写下的"至今思项羽,不肯过江东",再次体现了柔情女子的英雄气魄。

屏幕叔叔董浩

在唐山人中一说起董浩——央视少儿节目著名主持人,大家都会情不自禁地引以为豪,因为是家乡人嘛。虽然董浩是1956年出生于北京市海淀区,但他祖籍在唐山市的丰润区。这个体内流淌着丰润这块丰泽润美土地血脉的董浩,在北京出生、成长、上学、工作、退休。

董浩作为中央电视台少儿节目主持人,数年前,随着迪斯尼的《米老鼠和唐老鸭》搬上中国电视屏幕,他的声音便为全国的小朋友所熟悉,可爱的米老鼠形象也使董浩在少年儿童心目中留下了深刻的印象。此后数年,他一直活跃在少儿节目之中,不仅为全国瞩目,甚至受到国外的关注。一个重要因素,是他作为男性主持人,为温馨的少儿天地注入了一种健朗、豁达的气息。董浩曾说:无论国内国外,从事少儿教育的多为女性,她们的细腻、亲切,给孩子们留下了温馨的记忆。然而,社会不仅仅是靠温馨就可维系的,特别是在中国,独生子女家庭的现状,更需要一种刚性的教育与影响,需要一种创造力的培养。否则,面对飞速发展的世界和日趋激烈的竞争,这些21世纪的主人将无法担负起中国未来的命运,社会也将因人群的性格弱点使发展受到限制。国外的一些媒体和机构对此也表现出了极大的兴趣和关注,在国内,董浩是继孙敬修之后,在该领域第二个具有影响力的男性公众人物。

建国初期第一批书法家中就有董浩的父亲董静山,当时我国著名的书画店铺荣宝斋等都挂有他的字。董浩从小生活在这样的家庭里，耳濡目染，幼年时就对写字，画画非常感兴趣。但天有不测风云，1960年董浩刚刚4岁时，父亲突患心肌梗塞离开了人世。好在董浩还有一个美术功底不错的妈妈，妈妈从小就教他练毛笔字，整个童年，董浩就沉浸于色彩的天空里，当时他的理想就是成为一个跟父亲一样的书法家。但命运就是这样，有时候会给你一种两难的选择，这种选择使你必须对你的某一个钟爱学会放弃。1977年董浩参加了北京人民广播电台招考播音员的考试。他在一千多名考生中脱颖而出，从此开始了自己的播音，主持生涯，之后他成为了著名的节目主持人，但是他并没有放弃对书画的兴趣。

董浩从1978年开始在新闻、专题、文艺播音工作中获得长足进步，并在全国获奖，1987年以前他播音的通讯、配乐散文、北京新闻、对话等近二十篇节目得到广院专家的称赞，被选作示范教材外，还开始了小说连续广播、散文、短篇小说、广播剧、诗歌朗诵等方面的实践。在1980年以后开始与郑熔、毕克、李梓、扬成纯、金乃千、周正、赵忠祥、雅坤等同志们合作，自己的主持、播音风格日渐成熟，逐渐形成"深沉但有激情、庄重又不失幽默、自然真诚"的董浩风格（张颂老师语）。他朗诵的七十五讲《荆棘鸟》（澳大利亚小说）获"1990年全国长篇小说朗诵金奖"，并在中央人民广播电台重播，被同行专家称为"第一次将影视配音的角色表现与主观叙述相结合的成功例子"。

1985年与著名配音演员杨成纯、冯宪珍合作的诗体长篇小说《叶莆根尼·澳涅金》《茵梦湖》《弥尔顿的抒情诗》《今夜有暴风雪》《白比姆·黑耳朵》等作品也都获奖。

从80年代初开始先后为中央电视台解说大型重点系列专题片：《大潮》《走出低谷》《二战纳粹罪行录》《周恩来》的解说风格受到中央文献研究室领导的好评，使自己风格趋于稳定。

1978年到1989年我们的董浩叔叔先后推出了主持、人偶相结合的"滑稽头与董叔叔"的串联主持（1989年底）。此行被为专家称作"第一次人与偶在操和作语言造型方向的完美结合"，后来又相继推出《大青蛙讲故事》《挂历先生》《乐百氏智慧宫迷》《新一代影迷宫》《家小庭魔术系列》《牡丹乐园》《周周开心》《董浩叔叔信箱》等全国少儿喜爱的节目。从1989年年底以"董浩"的形象出现在屏幕上，正式成为"全国第一阿舅"，受到孩子们和家长们的喜爱。他因此也拒绝了多次成人专题、文艺节目工作调动的诱惑。誓做第二个"孙敬修"，积德行善，自得其乐。

董浩叔叔1993年曾策划、组织编导一周期的《和爸爸妈妈一起看》栏目，通过这一年的实践，提高了能力，为今后自编自导自制自己主持的展发做好准备。1993年底与团中央领导同志共同策划并主笔《于关筹备成立中国儿童电视台的策书划》，以团中央名义上报中央，到得有关领导的大力支持和关注，被为称儿童频道成立的"前奏曲"，尽做"孩子头儿"的义务。

1996年以后曾以"风车王"的形象主持《大风车》，以"董嘟嘟"的形象表演《校园幽默剧》。还主持了几百期的《芝麻开门》，全国小朋友和高年级学生深深喜爱。

董浩叔叔除栏目主持外，这年些主持了历届现场直播的"六一会晚"、"三优晚会"、"MTV"、"卡拉OK"等大赛晚会、"罗华庚金杯赛"（2年一次，主持了5次）、"校园风、全国中小学文生艺汇演晚会"（直播）等大型综艺晚会，圆满完成主持任务，以上节目均获奖。

1998年与少工委、中少报社共同推出"董浩叔叔小祝朋友早日成才CD邮品纪念卡册"，中国关心下一代委员会有关领导题词："今日小苗明日栋梁"，他本人主要策划、主讲6个传道统德教育故事，主唱6首爱国教歌育曲。此活动受到有关领导的称赞。他本人书及卡的稿酬均于98年"六一"通过"希望工程"捐给百色地区的孩子们（以捐书的行式）。对此董浩叔叔一直不许过于宣传。

2009年11月，董浩为《阿童木》宣传而现身重庆。谈起陷入经济纠纷的昔日央视同事，董浩不胜唏嘘；说到自己的处世秘诀，他透露，为了捍卫对主持人这一职业的使命感，专注于儿童主持这个圈子，1990年到现在，他已推掉9个亿的广告代言收入。这让大家从中看到了董浩叔叔的职业道德和自身品德。

董浩叔叔从1988年到2010年连续主持央视"六·一"晚会《和祖国一起成长》，为少年朋友们带来了无尽的开心快乐。2011年，参与百集动画片《董浩叔叔讲故事》的动画配音与项目运作。2012年1月，主持辽宁卫视少儿音乐成长节目《天才童声》。2013年，主持厦门卫视益智挑战类节目《鸡蛋碰石头》。2014年8月，主持青海卫视、贵州卫视双星联播的《爸爸请回答》。10月，参加北京吉利学院举行的"华氏传媒学院名师名家庆典晚会"，获聘特聘教授，讲授"董浩播音与主持"。

正是这些节目的播出，给亿万青少年观众及家长带来知识、启迪、快乐和人生指南。董浩叔叔努力的工作，辛勤的汗水，换得了广大影视观众的赞许和领导、社会的认可，获得了许多个人荣誉：1985年与著名配音演员杨成纯、冯宪珍合作的诗体长篇小说《叶莆根尼·澳涅金》《茵梦湖》《弥尔顿的抒情诗》《今夜有暴风雪》《白比姆·黑耳朵》等作品也都获奖。《办公室的故事》获得1987年《飞天奖》、最佳译制奖，《大鸟在中国》也在国际展播中获得大奖。2005年央视十佳主持人。2009年11月14日晚，2009中国播音主持"金话筒奖"颁奖盛典在北京电视台大剧院隆重举行。来自全国各地的百余名播音员、主持人欢聚一堂，共同庆祝"金话筒奖"的又一次精彩亮相。中央电视台张泉灵、杨锐、董浩，北京电视台刘文燕、河北电视台于辉等10人获得电视播音员主持人奖。

2015年6月，在新版中国少年先锋队队歌的MV中，董浩自曝2015年即将退休。2016年1月7日下午，董浩，这个央视著名主持人发文宣布退休，称"别了，话筒"，董浩在深情道别的同时，还晒出在《回声嘹亮》为自己办的退休告别专场节目中泪洒舞台的照片，董浩在文中不无感慨的写道："感谢央视，感谢70、80、90、00后以及所有的观众对我的厚爱！今天晚上央视3套文艺频道，19:30分播出的《回声嘹亮》为我制作了1个多小时的退休告别专场！

我演唱了《掌声响起来》和《我爱蓝色的海洋》，李思思代表当年的孩子拥抱了我，我泪洒舞台！别了！话筒！我会在书画舞台上给你们新的惊喜！"

董浩叔叔就是董浩叔叔，走下银屏的董浩叔叔会让我们在今后的书画舞台上看到一个更加豁达爽快，带给人们开心快乐的董浩叔叔。

《屏幕叔叔董浩》一文，2016年收入中国电影出版社出版的《唐山与中国电影》一书。

率先让评剧走出国门的孙凤鸣

孙凤鸣（1880—1942），清光绪六年至中华民国三十一年，号岐山，绰号"孙瞎子"。是中国评剧重要发祥地之一的清代丰润县泊家港（今唐山市丰南区大新庄镇薄港村）人，与成兆才同一时期的评剧创始人。孙凤鸣自幼喜欢莲花落（中国评剧的前身），十几岁入乐亭崔八班（此班为最早的班社）学艺，志攻丑行，因表演诙谐，肚囊较宽得"东发亮"艺名。

1901年，21岁时的孙凤鸣，与成兆才等人进京演出拆出戏。1912年32岁时，孙凤鸣带着三个弟弟孙凤岗（东发红）、孙凤龄（开花炮）、孙凤利，在天津成立了"凤鸣班"，又被称为"孙家班"，在天津进行演出评剧，同时授徒花莲舫、李金顺、白玉霜，造就了中国评剧第一代女演员和评戏著名旦角。1917年，孙凤鸣继续拓展演出空间由天津南下山东济南、青岛等地演出。

"孙家班"在1920年来大连演出时受到了热烈的欢迎，想看他们的演出，那可是一票难求，这使孙凤鸣感到大连是一块适合评剧发展的风水宝地。1922年，孙凤鸣经过再三思索，便带领"孙家班"部分演员正式扎根大连，改"凤鸣班"为"岐山戏社"，也就是中国评剧史上有名的"南孙班"。建立自己的评剧基地，开创了中国评剧以社养科班的先河。"南孙班"的学员招收特色是招女不招男，生旦净丑全由女孩承担。因为招女童成功率高，少数女童是代培，多数女童经过七八年科班训练，大多都能成为主角。在大连20年的"南孙班"共开了四科，培养了70多名坤角，像花小仙、花月仙、花灵霞、白玉霜、筱彩凤、筱金凤、筱银凤、筱玉凤、筱桂花、筱麻红、筱菊花、筱丽华等人都成为红极一时，成为以后中国评剧的名角。其中涌现出有为评剧发展兴盛做出贡献的筱桂花、筱麻红、筱灵芝、金灵芝等中国评剧史上的著名旦角。当时，像花莲舫、李金顺、刘翠霞、金灵芝这些已在东北有一定名气的成年主角只有到"南孙班"来"镀金"深造，取得"南孙班"的"文凭"和亲授师父，才敢在外面称唱奉天落子，够成"名牌"。

那时的《五女哭坟》在大连一上演就场场爆满，由于白玉霜、筱桂花、黄翠舫、筱麻红、筱菊花等演员系数参加演出。而小科班的小演员们各个基本功扎实，准纲准词儿，唱念做打，手眼身法步，无一不精，走到哪里红到哪里。

在大连家喻户晓的"南孙班"不仅名震东北三省，还上北京、跑天津、下上海、去海外。"南孙班"的筱桂花、筱麻红、筱彩凤、筱玉凤、花灵霞还在1929年和1934年两次东渡日本名古屋、大阪，为唱片公司灌了《黄代女游》《金钗钿》《珍珠衫》等评剧唱片。1934年和1935年，孙凤鸣应日本荣利唱片公司邀请携筱麻红等先后两次赴日本灌制唱片，录制《二县令》《黄氏女游阴》《白玉楼卖画》《杜十娘》《秦雪梅吊孝》等十几出戏的唱段，扩大了中国评剧在日本的影响。可以说是孙凤鸣的"南孙班"率先让评剧走出了国门，是孙凤鸣让中国的评剧名扬海外。

1942年，这位为中国评剧发展做出过卓绝贡献的评剧大师，逝世于辽宁兴城，终年63岁。

73将士在天英灵俯瞰神州83年

1941年，在抗日战争熊熊烈火越烧越旺的冀东大地上，活跃着一支抗击日本军队的有生力量——中共新华部队。在这支部队的接连打击下，日本帝国主义的侵略阴谋在我冀东地区屡屡遭到失败。为扑灭我抗日烽火，这一年日本侵略者纠集了驻山海关、唐山、北平（今天的北京）等地的鬼子兵，对我冀东地区进行了惨无人道的"五一"大扫荡。活动在丰润、玉田、宁河一带的中共新华部队，为了保存实力，当时奉命由宁河向丰润北部山区转移。纵队长李云鹏、政委邓文彪的率领着部队，全体指战员边打边走，在经过七天七夜的艰苦战斗后，于当年5月11日这一天，由李前庄村转移到河浃溜村，刚进村的新华部队官兵们还没来得及吃饭，得到密报的几千名鬼子兵就由四面八方向河浃溜村包围过来。为了保护村里百姓的生命安全，部队决定由村内转移到村南苇坑隐藏，政委邓文彪带领一部分战士占领了东窑坑，纵队长李云鹏带领余下部队占领了南窑坑。日军进村后发现新华部队已占领了南窑坑，随即便发起了进攻，我军战士们在政委邓文彪和纵队长李云鹏的指挥下，沉着应战，连续打退日军的多次进攻。

日军在多次进攻遭到失败后，气急败坏地又从新军屯、鸦洪桥等地调来了大批鬼子兵，支援的日本鬼子到达后立即占领了河渿溜村东的两块坟地，在日本军官土田邦的指挥和多座坟头的掩护下，又向我军发起了更加猛烈的进攻。在敌众我寡的危急时刻，我军战士越战越勇，誓死坚守阵地。在激烈的战斗中，我军战士战地发挥，机智地用窑厂的办公桌、棉被泼上水，制成流动工事夺下鬼子的机枪，当鬼子接近我军阵地时，我军用机枪、步枪、手榴弹一齐射向鬼子群，又连续打退敌人的三次进攻，并击毙了日军指挥官土田邦。在敌我实力相差悬殊的情况下，我部队全体战士英勇顽强，奋力拼杀，最后因弹药不多，战士们端起刺刀冲向敌群，同敌人展开了殊死搏斗，有的战士竟拉响了手榴弹与敌人同归于尽。

直到下午五点多钟惨烈的战斗还在继续，天下起了大雨，日本鬼子兵经不起雨淋，一个个缩成了一团，我新华部队一个营乘机集中起来向东南方向发起冲锋，胜利突围由索辛庄向崔家屯方向转移。

这次河渿溜战役共打死敌军350多人，新华部队有包括纵队长李云鹏在内的78名将士不幸壮烈牺牲，使日军付出了数倍于我军的惨重代价。为了纪念在河渿溜突围战中牺牲的73名革命先烈（其中有丰润区李前庄的李云鹏等5名烈士由其家人埋回了老家），1946年，河渿溜村在村南建立"河渿溜烈士陵园"。

陵园东西坐落，面积约544平方米。正门有"为有牺牲多壮志，敢教日月换新天"的诗句。园内正中有6米高的纪念塔，塔上题词为"中共新华部队七十三将士战役英灵塔"。还有烈士墓一座，安葬着新华部队七十三将士的忠骨。1995年4月被原丰润县委、县政府命名为县级爱国主义教育基地之一。

壮烈的河渿溜战役已过去83年，安眠在陵园内的新华部队73将士在天英灵俯瞰神州83年，每年的清明节，周边各乡镇的中小学都组织学生前去扫墓，凭吊烈士，在使烈士英灵得到慰藉的同时，也使青少年们不忘历史，激励他们努力学习，增强本领。许多群众也自发地来以不同形式表达哀思。该基地自一九四六年建成以来教育了一代又一代的人们。河渿溜烈士陵园是丰润区爱国主义教育基地，在世界反法西斯战争胜利80周年之际，它的意义显得更加显著河重要。

2023年7月

金国开国候大刀王信墓迷之千古

在今天唐山市的丰南区胥各庄镇有一个古老的村庄还依然存在，他的庄名就叫四王庄。

据有关史志记载，这是一个建庄较早历史较长的村庄，早在大唐玄宗时代人们就在这里定居建庄了。史志资料显示，唐玄宗先天元年（721年），这里就建立了村庄，由于当时的村庄在大唐朝的一条要道之间，所处地理环境较好，交通便利四通八达，人们出行十分的方便，所以，人们根据这一特点就把村庄的名字起为"四往庄"。意思就是从这里出发，东西南北无所不至。

历史的不断发展，续写着这个村庄的历史与演变。到了南宋时期，中华大地上西夏、金、齐、西辽、大理多国并存，真可谓群雄四起。强盛一时的金一再南下攻打南宋王朝，在攻打南宋的军队中，有一位将领作战勇猛，所向匹敌，屡立战功，将军姓王名信。时光流转到金世宗大定十一年（1171年）时，金世宗为了表彰王信，封大刀王信为镇国将军、开国候。而王信的家乡就是四往庄，至此，庄以将军为荣，为了纪念这位王侯，就把四往庄改名为四王庄了。王信死后，金朝廷还专为王信在其家乡四王庄西北处建起一座宏大壮观的陵墓。据有关资料和村中老人讲，陵墓由南边两座，北边一座呈品字形排列的三座墓组成，墓高一丈，坐北朝南。北边的墓前有龟趺驮石碑，高有丈余的石碑上刻有"金国开国候大刀王信墓"。墓边有石庙，墓地还有神道，神道两旁由南向北各排列雕刻工艺出神入化，栩栩如生的石像生，石羊、石马、石牛、石人立在两旁，仪仗队一般肃立。特别是第三组石雕马，双眼圆睁，紧闭双唇，四蹄粗大，强悍威武，昂首而立。第四组石雕武将，头戴战盔，身披铠甲，双目微合，目露柔光。左手按在腰间，右手握住跨在右腰的战刀，脚穿战靴，俨然是一位威风凛凛的大将军。第五组石雕文臣，头戴官冠，腰挎宝刀，脚穿朝靴，酷似金国一品大员。但大墓在1967年7月被打开时，却发现南边两座墓是空的，北边一座墓里的大石棺椁里也只有一块刻有人名的青砖和一具羊的遗骸，没有其他任何陪葬物，墓主人葬在何方，谜底至今不得揭晓。

清朝第一位汉族皇妃

在中国历史上，满族1644年入主北京建立清朝，为了显示征服者的威严，曾严禁满汉通婚。但随着政治形势的变化，清朝皇廷迫切需要缓和满汉矛盾，稳定京畿大局。清顺治五年（1648年）农历八月二十八，清世祖从长治久安出发，毅然颁布圣旨："朕欲满汉官民，互相辑睦，令其互结婚姻。……嗣后凡满洲官员之女，欲与汉人为婚者，先须呈明尔部。……至汉官之女，欲与满洲为婚者，亦行报部；无职者听其自便，不必报部。其满洲官民娶汉人之女，实系为妻者方准其娶。"这是清朝初年处理满汉关系的一项重大举措，对整个清朝的历史进程中产生了重大而深刻的影响；而第一位汉族皇妃是从京东滦州选娶的。她是滦州明碑村（今属滦州镇）石维岳的孙女、石申的女儿，后被封为"恪妃"。

这里需要说明的是：顺治五年当顺治皇帝颁布"满汉通婚"谕旨的时候，滦州石申之女还仅有7岁，远未到结婚的年龄，所以圣旨特地写明："石申之女，及笄承恩。"

"及笄"是说女孩子到了用簪子梳挽发髻的时候；到15岁用簪子梳挽，已成年可以婚嫁的年龄。圣旨是预先宣布：等到滦州石申的女儿长到15岁时，就迎娶入宫，承受皇恩。

清光绪年间的《滦州志》记载："顺治十三年，丙申。侍读学士石申女，受封为贵人。"……"后封恪妃"。正好是8年之后。

顺治皇帝的圣旨中原本规定："满洲官民娶汉人之女，实系为妻者方准其娶。"意思是：满人娶汉女必须作为正妻（不准娶为妾妇），以表尊重；防止出现"满妻"欺负"汉妾"的局面，影响满汉关系，用意是好的。但皇帝本人不在"官民"之列，他早有皇后，按宫制，滦州石氏之女只能封妃，不是"正妻"。

为此，顺治皇帝"制外施恩"，对恪妃给予特许的优宠和礼遇：

第一，特封恪妃的生母赵氏为"淑人"，特许赵淑人进宫伴女；第二，特许赵淑人坐汉式彩轿进宫，"入西华门下轿入室"；第三，特许赵淑人对女儿"行家礼"；第四，"恩赐宴席彩缎"，特许恪妃母女穿汉装，用汉族饮食。这在等级森严的"皇宫大内"本来都是不可想象的，是孝庄太后和顺治皇帝特许的优遇。

当时，连皇后之母也不能随便进宫伴女，即使偶尔恩准进宫时，也要以臣下之礼步行下跪，按宫制先向女儿叩头。滦州恪妃母女却可以日夜陪伴，坐轿进宫，行家人之礼。西六宫的满蒙女性完全采用入关前的贵族装束，都是"两把头""盆底靴"，独有恪妃母女身穿汉族绸缎，真可说是绝无仅有，鹤立鸡群。

难得的是，滦州恪妃在这种特殊的优宠之中却不骄不躁，恭谨有礼，充分显示着汉族书香门第的美德。后来她被封为"恪妃"（恪，读 ke），意思是"谨慎而恭敬"，正是她贤淑性格的写照。她是给汉族妇女和滦州人增了光的。

顺治皇帝特别是他的母亲孝庄皇后，破天荒地冲破了祖制立了这位汉族皇妃，是由于看到了恪妃的父祖两代的人品业绩和广远的声望。更迫切的是弥合满汉矛盾，稳定大局，安定人心。因此，倡导"辑睦满汉"成了当务之急；而要"辑睦满汉"，并且深入到亲情血缘，自然莫如婚姻，所以顺治五年颁布了《满汉通婚》圣谕。

那么要选哪一家呢？石维岳明朝为官清名满天下，但明末蒙冤，清廷对其礼葬昭雪，对其子石申高才点翰林委以重任，已在全国传为佳话，有着广远的示范力，因而，第一位汉族皇妃石申之女就成了首选。石维岳明末蒙冤而清初昭雪，石申又是本朝高官，其女心怀感激，自然水到渠成。

恪妃住西六宫的永寿宫中，故生前称她为"永寿宫妃"查阅文献顺治皇帝亲笔撰写的《孝献皇后行状》原文这样写道："顺治十七年（1660年）春，永寿宫（妃）始有疾，后（指孝献皇后）亦躬视扶持，三昼夜忘寝兴。其所以殷殷慰慰解悲忧，预为治备，皆如侍今后者（全都像侍奉当今皇后一样），后所制衣物，今犹在也。""孝献皇后"是顺治最宠爱的满族内大臣鄂硕的女儿董鄂氏，死后封为"孝献庄和至德宣仁温惠端敬皇后"，通称"孝献皇后"。她生前封至"皇贵妃"，身份比"贵妃"和"妃"的身份要高。她以"皇贵妃"的身份却能三天三夜侍奉病中的"永寿宫妃"，"就像侍奉当今皇后"，殷切安慰，缝制衣服。一方面体现了这位董鄂妃之贤淑，一方面也说明恪妃在西六宫中确实很受尊敬。

传说住在永寿宫的恪妃经常在看书、写字。孝庄皇后问她是什么书？写的啥？恪妃回禀：这书叫《治家格言》，都是至理名言哪。并念给孝庄皇后听："毋以己长而形人之短，毋以己拙而忌人之能"，意思是说："不要用自己的长处去耻笑别人的短处，不要因为自己手拙就嫉恨别人的贤能。"

孝庄皇后听说这个话，不觉想起后宫里钩心斗角。这个《治家格言》太好了！从此就让恪妃在后宫教《治家格言》《女儿经》，以后又教《女论语》，教写字画画。清顺治十八年（1661）正月初七半夜子时，顺治皇帝病逝，年仅 24 岁，恪妃年轻丧夫。

清康熙六年（1667 年）九月皇帝东巡之前，恪妃已经染病，日重一日，到十一月三十日不幸西归，年仅 26 岁。

高第，经历明三帝

高第，字登之，生卒不详，有资料显示其生卒在1560左右—1639左右，古滦州（今河北省唐山市丰南区安集寨）人。

据《明实录》《滦州志》载：崇祯十二年（1639），放回滦州。不久去世，享年82岁。又据新华出版社1990年6月出版《丰南县志》载："……崇祯十二年（1639），放还乡里，建白云楼为'东山别墅'。面壁著书，著有《太极良知》《抚云书稿》《籁真》（诗集）等。82岁去世。"以上两条记载，共同点就是高第于崇祯十二年（1639）回老家、82岁驾鹤西去准确无误。再据新华出版社1990年6月出版的《丰南县志》载："高第，字登之，本县安机寨人。生卒年约在明隆庆（1560）至清顺治初年（1644）之间。"加以推断，高第82岁去世当为明崇祯十五年，后金（清）崇德七年，也就是1642年，距清顺治初年（1644）仅一年之隔。

这样算来，高第一生赶上明朝五位皇帝：嘉靖、隆庆、万历、天启、崇祯。从万历十七年（1589）高第中乙丑科进士，任临颍（今河南省漯河市临颍县）县令，到崇祯十二年（1639），放还乡里，在大明朝的为官路上经历了万历、天启、崇祯三个皇帝。

纵观高第为官历程，虽然天启五年（1625年）夏，努尔哈赤攻打宁远，边关告急。熹宗派高第经略蓟辽军事。本为一儒生不懂军事的高第，到任后，以关外不可守为由，不听袁崇焕等主战派的苦苦相劝，竟拆除了锦州、右屯、大凌河等地的工事，"驱屯兵入关，委弃米粟十万余，而死亡载途，哭声振野，民怒而军益不振。"袁崇焕坚持不撤，仍固守宁远。阉党主要成员崔呈秀向熹宗参奏高第畏敌撤退，被撤职。从万历十七年（1589）高第任临颍，到天启五年（1625年）夏这段时间内，高第还是勤政清廉，敬业奉公，尽忠职守，为官一任造福一方的。特别是明天启元年（1621年），宦官杜进忠掌管湖广税收，对百姓横征暴敛，贪赃枉法，这时，已升为湖广布政使司参政的高第迅速将其撤职，深得民心。不久，即升为陕西省按察司、都察院左都御史、巡抚等职。据《永平府志》，《滦州志》等记载，他又私人出资七千两银子，助给（给养）边将的抚赏，在军中朝中口碑很好。也就是说在巡抚大同期间，高第又从自己的俸禄中捐银7000两，用于犒赏军卒。在此之前，万历三十八年（1610）二月，高第从大同知府转为山东按察副使。万历四十一年（1613）三月，高第考满，再从山东副使升为湖广右参政（从三品）。关于他此段期间的事迹，《湖广通志》说："高第……分守荆西，修学宫及魁星楼、尊经阁。捐资区画，不烦民力"，高第自己出钱，捐资助学，帮助当地培养人才。这与高第为官理念有极大的关系，在高第心里怀有辅佐朝廷治理国家的雄心壮志，有为官清廉的理念。这也就导致高第廉洁，为官之初就把缴上来的赋税根本不拆封，直接送到开封府上，由此杜绝了耗羡的弊端。当时的明政府规定：地方官征收的地方赋税，有一定数额归其所有。高第考虑国家正处于内忧外患之际，国库空虚，怎能中饱个人私囊？因此，每年的赋银均如数上缴，分文不取。

这样，可能由于征税方面的政绩比较突出，万历十九年（1885）高第"转户曹，権浒墅关"，也就是派去了苏州钞关收商税。

天启三年（1623）升兵部左侍郎，五年（1625）夏，升兵部尚书。努尔哈赤攻打宁远，边关告急之时，朝廷派高第经略蓟辽军事。但不懂军事的高第，竟下令拆除锦州、右屯、大凌河等地的军事工事。导致阉党成员崔呈秀向熹宗奏高第畏敌撤退，被撤职。

正因此，影响了高第的仕途。当崇祯十二年（1639），高第回到故乡，身居白云楼"东山别墅"里，回想他眼前过往的三代皇帝，才问心无愧，面壁著书，在他的《太极良知》《抚云书稿》《籁真》（诗集）里放入一种释然。

聂耳，与国歌并寿而永垂不朽

眼看就要国庆节了，不免想起国歌，也忽然想起那年去云南拜谒人民音乐家聂耳墓的情景。

在云南昆明西山太华寺与三清阁之间，有一片缓坡，松柏森森，绿树丛中，长眠着我国一位伟大的人民音乐家，他就是中华人民共和国国歌《义勇军进行曲》的作曲者——聂耳。

那是2007年夏秋之交去云南旅游，在去龙门景区回来的路上，我没有随着游人鱼贯而去，半路左拐一个人走入蹊径，怀着无比崇敬的心情，前来拜谒聂耳。在大山脚下苍松翠柏间，音乐家的墓地呈琴状，主体为琴盘，墓穴琴颈，道上七个花台，呈琴键状，象征着七个音阶；道上的24级石阶，示意着他仅活了24岁。琴盘顶部，七块晶莹的墨石上，分两行横书"人民音乐家聂耳墓"。墓地设计新颖，构思精巧，既富于特点，又显得庄严大方。

我敬慕地站在音乐巨子的墓前，默读着聂耳的生平：聂耳，原名守信，字子义，一作紫艺。1912年生于云南昆明一个清寒之家。自幼喜爱音乐，能演奏多种乐器。中学时代即加入中国共产主义青年团，参加革命活动。1930年到上海，在一家商号当店员，次年考入"明月歌舞社"

任小提琴师。1933年由田汉介绍加入中国共产党。此后，积极参加左翼音乐、戏剧、电影工作，并以"黑天使"为笔名发表艺术评论，抨击靡靡之音，提出替"大众呐喊"的主张。1935年，取道日本赴苏联。不幸于7月17日在日本神奈川县藤泽市鸪沼海滨游泳时溺水逝世。

日本人民为纪念聂耳，1954年11月1日，在藤泽市鸪沼海岸聂耳遇难的附近，建立了聂耳纪念碑；1963年重建"耳"字形的花岗石纪念碑，郭沫若书题"聂耳终焉之地"六个大字，日本戏剧家秋田雨雀先生撰写介绍聂耳生平的碑文。

肃立在聂耳汉白玉雕像前，凝思伟人的经历，追思音乐之子的步步惊雷。耳畔回荡聂耳那一首首铿锵有力的歌曲：《义勇军进行曲》《前进歌》《毕业歌》《开路先锋》《码头工人歌》《新的女性》，等等，集中表现了那个年代工农群众在旧中国阶级压迫下的苦难和反抗，特别是在"九·一八"事变后，唤醒了中国人民抗日救亡的坚强意志，吹响"中国革命之号角"，擂响"人民解放之鼙鼓"。其中，《义勇军进行曲》于1949年9月27日，经中国人民政治协商会议第一届全体会议决议，作为中华人民共和国代国歌。1982年12月4日，第五届全国人民代表大会第五次会议，正式定为中华人民共和国国歌。

"闻其声者莫不油然而兴爱国之思，庄然而宏志士之气，毅然而同趣于共同之鹄的。聂耳乎巍巍然，其与国歌并寿而永垂不朽。"这是郭沫若在《聂耳墓碑文》里，对这首歌和歌曲创作者的感知与肯定。

湛蓝的天空上，洒下灿烂的阳光，我再次向聂耳墓三鞠躬，留恋地走下台阶，了却心愿。

鲁奖《良宵》张楚

鲁迅文学奖：当今中国具有最高荣誉的文学奖之一，由中国作家协会主办，每四年评选一次，已成为衡量一个作家乃至一个地区文学创作水平的标尺。2014年8月11日届鲁迅文学奖正式公布，我市滦南县作家张楚以短篇小说《良宵》荣获第六届鲁迅文学奖短篇小说奖。

《良宵》授奖词：张楚的叙事绵密、敏感、抒情而又内敛，在残酷与柔情中曲折推进，虽然并不承诺每一次都能抵达温暖，但每一次都能发现至善的力量。

《良宵》以细腻平实的手法描写了一位颇有来历、看惯人世浮沉的老人与一个罹患艾滋病的失怙男童之间感人至深的情意,在寂寞的人物关系中写出了人性的旷远。在一个短篇的有限尺度内,张楚在白昼与夜晚、喧哗与静谧之间戏剧性地呈现当下的复杂经验,确立起令人向往的精神高度。

《良宵》首发于《民治新城市文学》2012年夏季号,然后发表于《天涯》2012年第6期及《小说月报》2013年第1期。《良宵》里的孩子是艾滋病患儿,女人是生活中遭受情感困惑的曾经红极一时的戏曲名旦,对于两人来说,现实的"恶时光"无处不在,但他们却在彼此的真诚里迎来了心灵的"良宵"。阅读这部小说和其他的作品一样,总是在悲惨甚至有些惨烈的人生里读到悲悯,这融合着作家的人生观,作家的作品反映了作家的世界观。《良宵》描述了年华已逝、魅力犹存的程派名旦,不满世情淡薄,隐居山村,在旁人的不解与恐慌中,与身患艾滋病的孤儿建立起忘年之交的故事。作者以深厚的内功逼近了人性的脆弱与坚韧、黑洞与光亮。

张楚:中国作家协会会员。在《人民文学》《收获》《十月》《当代》等杂志发表过中短篇小说。著有中短篇小说集《樱桃记》。曾获"大红鹰文学奖""人民文学奖""河北省文艺振兴奖""河北省青年文化建设奖"。2011年入选"未来文学大家TOP20"。被《人民文学》和《南方文坛》评为2012年"年度青年作家"。

张楚大学期间学的专业是财税,毕业后在滦南县国税局工作至今。张楚已迈过不惑之年,他说能获得鲁迅文学奖,觉得无比荣幸。2015年已经开始,羊年春节就要到了,张楚说,虽然我的《良宵》,还有一部短篇《野薄荷》和一部中篇《七根孔雀羽毛》,在省内外文坛引起很大关注,但作为基层的文学工作者,将继续扎根生活,用诚实的笔触写出属于这一方土地的精气神,用坦诚、宽容的心灵来歌颂人世间永恒的爱和美德。

鸡毛信使李盛福

1930年2月的一天,今属河北省唐山市丰南区的崔坨村的一个贫苦人家里,一个男孩出生了,1938年,这个小男孩懂事了;1942年3月,日本鬼子进村了,1942年8月,这个男孩当上了儿童团长。这个男孩看到了八路军组织发动农民群众建立革命根据地,成立民兵组织、妇女会、儿童团的热情与活力。也看到了日军在村庄进行大扫荡,到处烧、杀、抢掠、奸淫无恶不住的暴行。更在他幼小的心灵里，埋下了对日本帝国主义仇恨的种子。这个男孩，就是日后大名鼎鼎的鸡毛信使李盛福，著名电影《鸡毛信》里的主人公儿童团长原形就是李盛福。

老英雄曾被授予"解放奖章"并受到中央领导亲切接见。

巧送"鸡毛信"

在抗日战争时期，八路军传递的信件中有一种叫做"鸡毛信"，就是在信封的右上角插上一支鸡毛，表示信件的重要性，必须飞速送到目的地。1942年8月，12岁的李盛福在解放区参加儿童团，并担任由140多名儿童组成的儿童团团长。那时的儿童团在李盛福的带领下，每个星期5人一组，不论白天黑夜，轮流负责把"鸡毛信"从丰南县解放区送到6公里外滦南县的八路军手中。儿童团员每一次都义无反顾、机智勇敢地把一个个情报安全及时地送达目的地。儿童团员不知经历了多少次，也不知经历了多少考验。每次他们都表现得十分勇敢，想方设法把信件送出去，为八路军打击日军提供了及时准确的情报。

有一次，一封"鸡毛信"要急送到解放区，李盛福便和3名儿童团员洋装玩耍，一路前行。正当他们走在半路时，迎面走来了10几个日伪军，为使情报不落在汉奸的手中，情急之下，李盛福机智地把"鸡毛信"藏在身边的草丛中，然后装着和其他3名伙伴在地里挖野菜。然而，这些日伪军瞪大一双双贼眼，并没有轻易地放过他们，还用木棍殴打李盛福和他的伙伴，威逼他们交出情报，并承认是"小八路"。强忍着疼痛的李盛福和小伙伴们，咬紧牙关就是不说，最后日伪军没办法无奈地放过了他们。看见汉奸走远了，李盛福和伙伴们马上找出埋藏在草丛中的"鸡毛信"，小心地揣在怀里，以当时孩子们所能达到的最快速度把情报送到八路军手中，出色地完成了任务。

助战得胜利

李盛福带领下的儿童团，在做好传递"鸡毛信"的同时，还积极协助八路军站岗、放哨，在八路军与日寇交战时，帮助扛运弹药，包扎伤员。1944年秋季的一天，李盛福和儿童团员在村头站岗时抓获了一名日伪军密探，经审讯确认其是个作恶多端的汉奸，随即被八路军枪毙了。第二天上午，由于汉奸告密，日寇出动了200多人马疯狂地向解放区袭来，解放区迅速集中兵力，出动4个连约500名八路军战士同日寇展开了激烈的战斗。在战斗中，李盛福带领儿童团员冒着枪林弹雨，及时为八路军战士补充弹药。经过4个多小时浴血奋战，把这200多名日军全部歼灭。这次战斗的胜利，儿童团员功不可没，受到了解放区八路军的夸奖。

急送情报

那是 1945 年 2 月 27 日的早晨，东方的天空刚蒙蒙亮，李盛福和驻扎在村里的八路军战士帮老百姓扫地、挑水。这时接到哨兵报告，看见远处有大批日本骑兵正向村庄袭来。面对突如其来的袭击，八路军战士临危不惧、英勇作战，子弹打光了，就用刺刀拼；炊事班战士没有枪，就用木棍的尖头刺向日寇的胸膛。在战斗中，有一位八路军战士头部中弹，流血不止。李盛福立即为他包扎伤口，这位身负重伤的战士艰难地对李盛福说："我快不行了，在我的口袋里有一封秘密情报，请你转交给党组织。"李盛福对这位战士说："请放心，我一定把情报送到党组织。"刚说完，这位战士就牺牲了。这次战斗非常残酷，从早上 6 时一直持续到下午 3 时才结束，日寇被打死 80 多人，参战的八路军战士 120 多人到最后只剩下 9 人。义愤填膺的李盛福，眼见着一个个战士的英勇牺牲，牢记那位战士的嘱托，满怀对日本鬼子的满腔仇恨，挥泪告别，拔腿上路，把秘密情报迅速送到党组织。

现在老英雄在广东汕头军区干休所，已经 85 岁的离休老战士李盛福现在依然身体硬朗，精神爽朗。

2015 年 8 月

新华部队突围在狂风暴雨中

在 1938 年冀东大暴动时，中国共产党组织起来一支党的武装——中共新华部队。就是这支活跃在冀东大地上的抗日部队，自组建之日起就接连不断的沉重打击日本侵略军，使日本帝国主义侵略占领中国的阴谋在我国冀东地区屡屡遭到失败。被视为日本推行"大东亚共荣圈"的重要障碍，当作必除的眼中钉肉中刺。

1941 年，为了扑灭冀东抗日战争的熊熊烈火，消灭抗击日本军国主义军队的有生力量——中共新华部队，打击冀东人民的抗日精神。日本侵略军对冀东地区进行了惨无人道的"五一"

大扫荡，集中调集了驻北平（今北京）、山海关、唐山等地的鬼子兵，对这支抗日队伍进行疯狂的围追堵截。

转移

中共冀东党组织为了保存抗日实力，当时命令中共新华部队，逐步放弃丰润、玉田、宁河一带的平原地区活动，由宁河县向丰润县北部的燕山深处转移。

但是，日军一路尾随，穷追不舍。总队长李云鹏（又名李印鹏）、政委邓文彪率领部队，经过七天七夜的艰苦战斗，全体指战员边打边走，终于在1941年的农历五月十一日这天上午九点，由丰润县李前庄村转移到河浃溜村。可是，刚刚进村的新华部队官兵们还没来得及吃饭，哨兵报告：得到密报的几千名鬼子兵就由四面八方向河浃溜村包围过来。危急时刻，关乎百姓的生命和财产的安危。为了保护村里百姓的生命安全，部队决定由村内迅速转移到村外以南的窑坑隐藏，政委邓文彪带领一部分战士占领了东窑坑，总队长李云鹏带领余下部队占领了南窑坑。

激战

纷至沓来的日军赶到后发现新华部队已经占领了南窑坑，随即便发起了进攻，新华部队战士们在总队长李云鹏的沉着指挥下，积极应战，连续打退日军的多次进攻。

在发动多次进攻却遭到失败后的日军，气急败坏地又从丰润县新军屯、丰登坞、玉田县鸦洪桥等地调来鬼子兵，增援来的日本鬼子到达作战地点后立即占领了河浃溜村东的两块坟地，日本军官土田邦指挥日军，在多座坟头的掩护下又向新华部队的阵地发起了更加猛烈的进攻。敌众我寡的危急情况下，面对着武器优良且穷凶极恶的日本兵，新华部队战士越战越勇，誓死坚守阵地。在激烈的战斗中，战士们战地发挥，机智地把窑厂的记账用的账桌，蒙上泼了水的棉被制成流动工事，冒着敌人的枪林弹雨机智前进，夺下鬼子的机枪，当鬼子接近我军阵地时，新华部队官兵用机枪、步枪、手榴弹一齐射向蜂拥而上的日本鬼子，又连续打退敌人的三次进攻，并击毙了日军指挥官土田邦。在敌我兵力相差悬殊的情况下，中共新华部队全体战士英勇顽强，奋力拼杀，因弹药不多，战士们最后端起刺刀冲向敌群，同敌人展开了殊死的肉搏战，有的战士竟拉响了手榴弹与敌人同归于尽。直到下午五点多钟惨烈的战斗还在继续，可就在这时天下起了大雨，战斗暂时停歇。

突围

　　日本鬼子经不住暴风骤雨的抽打，缩成一团避起雨来。新华部队抓住这一有利时机，政委邓文彪指挥突击兵力乘机集中起来向东南方向发起猛烈冲锋，胜利突围。之后，新华部队的战士们在砖窑一位老乡带领下，绕过敌人的哨卡，由索新庄、南卜、塔六庄方向崔家屯方向撤退。

　　这次河淡溜战斗共打死日军 350 多人，中共新华部队有包括总队长李云鹏在内的 78 名将士壮烈牺牲，使日军付出了数倍于我们的惨重代价。然而，日军还打肿了脸充胖子，到处宣扬"全歼新华部队"的胜利。可是只过一个月，新华部队这支冀东人民的子弟兵不仅又迅速恢复壮大起来，而且继续发扬骁勇善战的传统，英勇驰骋在冀东大平原上，到处重创日本侵略者。

　　为了纪念在河淡溜突围战中牺牲的 78 名中共新华部队将士，1946 年，河淡溜村在村南建立"河淡溜烈士陵园"。陵园东西坐落，面积约 544 平方米。正门有"为有牺牲多壮志，敢教日月换新天"的诗句。园内正中矗立着 6 米高的纪念塔，塔上题词为"中共新华部队七十三将士战役英灵塔"。还有烈士墓一座，安葬着新华部队七十三将士的忠骨（有丰润区李前庄的李云鹏等五名烈士由其家人埋回了老家，所以，是七十三将士），把这抗日的壮歌深深地埋进历史的记忆。

2015 年 8 月 3 日

第三辑
悟我心语

当写作融入生活

大地震的经历留给了我无尽的记忆与思索,唐山人百折不挠、执着进取、坚忍不拔、感恩社会的精神刻也深深影响着我的家庭生活。

由于从事工作的关系,新闻写作和文学创作早已不经意地成为我生活中的一部分。因为新闻的时效性,是不容缓的,最快速地形成稿子才行。文学创作灵感是无时无刻的,且稍纵即逝,不及时抓住便丧失了写作的源泉。

20世纪80年代中期唐山地震后恢复建设中,人们的生活并不富裕,别无它好的我哪怕是吃着饭呢,写作灵感来了,也要马上撂下碗筷记上几笔,并不爱好写作的妻子,觉得我把工作和创作都融入了家庭生活,是十分不乐意的,每每见此情景定是白上几眼。

打牌、抽烟、玩麻将,我从不沾边;言情、武打、玄幻之类的书籍、电影、电视剧,是我从来不好戏儿的,实在没事儿了就是坐在沙发上看看书或电视新闻。记得一次,星期日妻子要出去买东西。临出门告诉我,把速热器插上弄一壶开水。妻子走后,我接上一暖壶自来水来到北阳台,暖壶里插进速热器并插上电源插销。之后,便到南屋看地方志去了。不知过了多长时间,我忽然闻到一股塑料烧焦的味道,怦然想起北阳台的暖壶的水,急忙跑过去一看,那速热器的塑料壳已经瘫痪,暖壶里的热水还在往外喷呢,我赶忙拔掉了速热器的插销。但随后却办了傻事,竟然接了一舀子自来水倒进了沸腾的暖壶里,暖壶立即就爆了,弄得满阳台都是暖壶胆的玻璃,所幸没有伤到我。

还有一次傍中午我正在屋里写东西,突然听妻子说:"陈欣快下楼买瓶醋去,我弄鱼没醋了。"我倒是听话,急忙跑下楼来,可正好看见楼下摆着一个书摊,见到书一切都忘在脑后了,停下脚步蹲在书摊前,一门心思地看起书来。也不知过了多长时间,听到妻子在我身后说:"陈欣,咱上楼吃饭吧。"我一回头猛然想起叫我买醋的事,赶忙说:"你让我买的醋我还没买呢。"妻子一笑看着我说:"鱼我都炖好了,上楼吃饭吧。"坐在饭桌前,我们一边吃饭一边唠。妻子说:"我在阳台上看着你下楼到书摊儿哪儿就站住了,我一琢磨呀,这下子买醋的事儿你是忘脑袋后去了。也不跟你废话了,我关上气灶,自己下楼买去吧。这不,鱼也炖好了,啤酒也给你倒上了,奖励你忘了买醋,来,干一杯吧……"

1988年的冬天,我在当年接送开滦林西矿、范各庄矿上下班工人的林西小火车站站台上等待小火车发车时,忽然,离站台较远的东边一个冰冻的大坑里传来嘈杂的叫喊声,许多人跑去围观。这时，小火车鸣笛启动了，我上了火车去矿上上班。到下午回来时听说，是一个在冰上玩的小孩掉进冰里了，一个男人顾不得脱掉衣服奋不顾身跳进冰水里施救，一番救助小孩得救了，但施救的男人精疲力尽，沉入了水底。因此，我写下了纪实短剧《悲剧》，并在1989年7月，我的纪实短剧《悲剧》获得"中国首届微型作品编辑出版大展"优秀奖。

我的同事曾经见义勇为救了一位姑娘，事件突发，本不相识，事后也未曾联系的两个人，可就是阴差阳错的让他们成了夫妻。就此我写了小小说《丑丈夫》，并在海南省文学人才函授学院获奖。

20世纪90年代，我进入了散文诗创作的高峰期。1992年5月我到秦皇岛一日游是在海边看到一个小伙子伫立海边若有所思……回来就写下了散文诗《仲夏了，去看海吗？》，投到香港《世界散文诗作家》杂志。1992年6月，我的散文诗《仲夏情思》获海南省《当代文坛》编辑部举办的"全国首届当代文坛力作选拔赛"诗歌创作一等奖，并被收入由方梦泉主编的《中国新诗人千家》丛书，还先后被天津经济广播电台、《唐山团讯》等媒体播发转载。1993年，陕西青年自修大学校刊《窗》创刊号，专版发表了我的获奖散文诗《仲夏情思》，还有我的创作谈《让感情的光芒闪烁在文章中》，并加编者按。更是因为这首获得"全国首届当代文坛力作选拔赛"诗歌创作一等奖的散文诗《仲夏情思》，创刊于1949年10月25日的新中国第一份纯文学期刊，在中国当代文学（新中国文学）的历史上，无论从哪方面来看都堪称最为重要、最为突出也最具权威性和代表性的文学刊物《人民文学》，也邀请我参加了《人民文学》创刊45周年座谈会。

生活的点点滴滴，激发了我的创作灵感，一次次收获了荣誉。从此，我的文学创作也更加一发不可收了，常有作品在从国家到地方不同级别的报纸、杂志、广播电台上都有刊发播出，有的或收入文学作品专集或获奖。甚至，1993年我的散文诗《仲夏了，去看海吗？》《你已把我占据》分别在当时英国统治的香港的《世界散文诗作家》第五期、第七期也接连发表，并获"繁荣杯"世界散文诗大赛优秀奖。关于我的词条也先后收入著名诗人阿红（王占彪）主编的《当代诗歌爱好者名录》、著名作家姚雪垠主编的《未名作家和诗人名录》、著名作家、诗人方梦泉主编的《当代文学新人集录》等辞书类书籍。复旦大学的何淑云教授，也一直指导鼓励我进修复旦大学中文系作家班。1994年，我读完上海复旦大学中文系作家预备班，被优先录取为上海复旦大学中文系作家班正式学员。

2007年，著名作家、河北省作家协会主席关仁山，得知我的《陈欣作品选》一书即将由作家出版社出版时，当面叮嘱我说："书出版后，一定送我一本！"著名作家、河北省作家协会副主席谈歌先生，更是先前欣然亲笔为我题写了《陈欣作品选》这一书的书名。2009年，印刷《岁月回响》一书。2015年到2022年这段时间，组织《陈欣新闻作品集一至四》（1985年—2022年）。2017年1月，18万字的《梦回唐朝》一书由"团结出版社"出版。2018年1月，《携一抹阳光》

一书由"四川民族出版社"出版。2021年1月，散文集《风舞秋海》一书由"北京日报出版社"出版。

唐山市作家协会、河北省作家协会、中国煤矿作家协会、中国散文学会。这是我经历了1976年"7·28"唐山大地震之后，在写作这条漫漫长路上，不断进行写作的同时，相继迈进的一个个写作人之家并成为其会员。写作伴随着我的生活，俨然成了我的日常生活的一部分。

2023年伊始蓦然回首，看看自己走过来的路倍感欣慰，感叹坚持可以成就一切。一个城市的精神影响着这个城市的人，我们唐山人，也正是凭着抗震精神，一直的努力追求和奋斗，把这座废墟之上的家园重新建设成了今日这样美好靓丽，进步文明的沿海城市。48年前，我从震灾中走来，继而，把写作融入生活。48年后，作为一个震后与唐山共同成长起来，并参加其建设发展的唐山人，感到欣慰。因为，我的生活中有写作，写作中有收获也有成果！

感谢恩人和自己

今天是感恩节了，在此感恩一路走来我遇到的好人，也感谢自己对写作的不离不弃。

那是20世纪80年代的一个夏秋之际吧，当时的科党支部书记招呼他对面办公室的我到党支部，进到党支部只听书记说："陈欣你认识这两位大姐吗？"我看着她们说："不认识。""那我跟你说吧，这位是咱们矿广播站的贾大姐，这位是冯大姐。"书记说。"她们一是来认识一下你，二是给你送奖品来了。"接着贾大姐说："你的散文《铁马骑士》写得很不错，获得这次矿广播站征文活动一等奖，因为和你不熟，今天特来看看你，把这对大红腈纶枕巾奖品顺便给你拿来了。"

当时，我在《开滦矿工报》已经上了许多稿。继而，我在地级市的市委机关报《唐山劳动日报》上也不断上稿，稿件屡投屡中促使我又把稿投向了《中国煤炭报》，结果，稿件在1985年7月份的《中国煤炭报》一版发表了。看到报纸时我那个高兴啊，因为这是在全国发行的《中国煤炭报》上发稿了。于是打电话给当时在开滦矿务局工作的表兄说："大哥，你找一下这天的《中国煤炭报》，那上边一版有我的稿，这张报纸等你歇礼拜给我爸拿去看看。"又星期天休礼拜了，我装作没事似的啥也没跟老爸说，等晚上吃完饭，妹妹小声对我说："爸说你哥蔫了吧唧的还中，在全国发行的《中国煤炭报》一版发稿了……"

此后，我在坚持新闻写作的同时，又开始了文学创作。1989年7月，我的纪实短剧《悲剧》获得"中国首届微型作品编辑出版大展"优秀奖，小小说《丑丈夫》在海南省文学人才函授学院获奖。

20世纪90年代，我进入了散文诗创作的高峰期。1992年6月，我的散文诗《仲夏情思》获海南省《当代文坛》编辑部举办的"全国首届当代文坛力作选拔赛"诗歌创作一等奖，并被收入由方梦泉主编的《中国新诗人千家》丛书，还先后被天津经济广播电台、《唐山团讯》等媒体播发转载。1993年，陕西青年自修大学校刊《窗》创刊号，专版专页发表了我的获奖散文诗《仲夏情思》和我的创作谈《让感情的光芒闪烁在文章中》，并加编者按。

从此，文学创作也一发不可收了，常有作品在从国家到地方等不同级别的报纸、杂志、电台上刊播或收入文学作品专集或获奖。1993年我的散文诗《仲夏了，去看海吗？》《你已把我占据》分别在当时英国统治的香港的《世界散文诗作家》第五期、第七期也接连发表，并获"繁荣杯"世界散文诗大赛奖。关于我的词条也先后收入著名诗人阿红（王占彪）主编的《当代诗歌爱好者名录》，著名作家姚雪垠主编的《未名作家和诗人名录》，著名作家、诗人方梦泉主编的《当代文学新人集录》等辞书类书籍。1994年，我读完上海复旦大学中文系作家预备班，被优先录取为上海复旦大学中文系作家班正式学员。

2007年出版《陈欣作品选》，2009年印刷《岁月回响》，结集我在各级报纸发表过的500多篇新闻作品剪辑的《新春文稿集》；加入唐市作家协会、河北省作家协会、中国煤炭作家协会、中国散文学会……所有这些，现在想来，这一切还真是都与良师益友有关。记得1986年的一天，我正在宣传部写稿子，同事说有人来电话找我。我一接听着温文尔雅的普通话，竟是素未谋面唐山师范学院中文系的牟云江教授。爱惜人才的牟教授详细告诉了家里住址、电话、约我到家里来坐。原来，牟教授当时从《矿工报》上看了我的小小说《春耕烟》，很感兴趣，几经打听要见我。我既欣慰又为难，感觉自己的水平低不便高攀，几次婉言谢绝。但是牟老爱才，每次唐山市作家协会开会都亲自通知我参加，一来二去，成了我强化提高的良师益友。复旦大学的何淑云教授，也一直指导鼓励我进修复旦大学中文系作家班。以至于一些名家都是先看了我的作品，才看上我这个人的。著名作家、河北省作家协会主席关仁山，当得知我的《陈欣作品选》即将出版时，当面叮嘱我说："书出版后，一定送我一本！"著名作家、河北省作家协会副主席谈歌先生，更是先前欣然亲笔为我题写了这一书名。

这一切成果的取得同时也得益于企业的锻炼和自己的坚持。这也充分说明，人在成长的道路上，无论爱哪行干哪行，如何走好自己的路，坚持是必须的。坚持就会取得成绩，努力就会有所收获，蓦然回首，会欣慰所获所得所有成果。

我心中的毛泽东

亲爱的朋友们，还记得1976年9月9日这一天吧。是的，中国人怎会忘记这个举世沉痛的日子呢？9月9日，这是中国人民的一种特殊情怀。那时我还是个中学生，地震后正在忙着重建的校园。忽然，校广播喇叭里传出撕裂心肺的哀乐声。老师在下面向正在上房梁的同学们招手，要全体同学到校园的树林里集合："伟大的马克思列宁主义者、中国共产党，中国人民的伟大领袖、和导师毛泽东主席，因病医治无效，于1976年9月9日零时10分，在北京逝世……"

噩耗传来，字字句句剧烈震颤着我们一颗颗纯洁、执着、热爱领袖的心。哀乐声起，师生们全哭了，失声痛哭了。那一刻我的心碎了。毛主席离开我们了？我无声地在心里问自己。巨大的悲痛汹涌而来，我咬住嘴唇，泪水如破堤之水，夺眶而出。我泪眼蒙蒙的仰望那灰蒙蒙的天空，寻找着伟人星座的方位……

一个女同学极力拍打着树干哭诉："毛主席呀，毛主席，我们刚刚从地震的废墟里爬出来，学校还没有盖好，您怎么就走了呢？不看看我们重建后的校园了？……"

我的一个男同学冷不丁站起来，双脚使劲踩着土地呼喊："毛主席，我们爱您哪！"与我并肩席地而坐的一个女同学叫杨贺云，平时一个泼辣的女孩子，一听到这惊天动地的消息，痛心疾首地大喊一声："毛主席，您不能走哇！"随后，便晕了过去。

是啊，亲爱的朋友们，20世纪70年代，中国人民对毛主席是极其热爱的，有谁能抑制住这极大的悲痛呢？尤其是我们这些"7·28"唐山大地震劫难余生的学生们呢。我们生在新社会，长在五千年来中国第一面五星红旗之下，是唱着《东方红》长大的呀。是毛主席派来亲人解放军，救唐山人于天塌地陷的大灾之中啊，毛主席离开了我们，我们怎能不悲伤，怎能不哭天抢地？

巨星陨落，举国哀悼。珠峰垂泪，长江呜咽，呼伦贝尔在哭泣，腾格里大漠在哀鸣。在告别领袖的日子里，工厂听不到机械歌唱，田野看不到拖拉机的尾烟，军营内默默无声，学校静悄悄。哀笛长鸣，中国版图全境一片哀悼的海洋。

也就在此刻，降半旗下的中国人民，把心头对伟人的思念和悲痛，化作了无限的力量，抱定信念，祖国四个现代化一定要实现，社会主义道路一定要走下去！朋友们，亲爱的朋友们，没有忘记吧，这是当时八亿中国人共同的心声啊。在我们这座城市里，几个地方都有高大的毛主席立像，立像高瞻远瞩，浩气荡荡，领袖的风范至今仍感召鼓舞着亿万中国人民。每年9月9日，我都要去看看他老人家，一表哀思和怀念。在毛主席逝世48周年之际，我的情感愈加浓厚，我的思念愈加强烈，我再次来站在毛主席立像前，良久良久，我凝望着毛主席高大魁梧的体魄，思绪万千……

48年过去了，您的光辉思想依然闪烁着光芒，人民对您的情感依然没有改变。毛主席，敬爱的毛主席，您在天之灵可会感知到：这就是领袖的威望，伟人的魅力！毛主席，人民不会忘记您，历史不会忘记您。中国不会忘记您，世界不会忘记您。您仍与江河同在，与日月同辉，生命永恒。

2024年9月9日

梦中，点燃凤凰泪

深邃的夜，做了一个深邃的梦，我在深邃长河中不懈挖掘远古的迷，寻觅久远的传说源。（想重圆那温馨的梦中世界）我发现一颗晶莹的彩石，却不知该为何物，拿来放在千倍镜下，未能扩散那石的美丽，又置于凹凸镜前仍不能影现那石的美丑昔日，再把那石放在阳光下久久凝视，仍无变化，断定是一块顽石而已。心又一动拿来聚光镜不懈照耀，慢慢地，那石逐渐膨胀，扩大，伸展，壮观终于呈现：莽原，茂林，青山秀水，万物丛荣，百羽朝贺，共庆盛世。突然，天崩地裂，地动山摇，西伯利亚火山创史纪的炸响，喷涌。弥漫了山川，截阻了河流，笼罩了大气层，窒息，窒息，百羽在奋力拼搏中仰望凤凰，凤凰振翅力帅百羽冲破混沌，但终于精疲力竭，掉下悲惨无望的泪。泪映照着凄凉，拼搏和悲壮，埋入火山灰中，成为一个远古的琥珀。

啊，这点燃的是凤凰泪，呈现的是昌盛，喜庆和悲壮，带来的是思考和怀念。据说恐龙也绝种于这次灭顶之灾的火山大喷发。

1989年

昨夜星辰

晚风习习，我坐在秋日的法国梧桐下，仰望繁星璀璨，勾起无尽遐想。这广袤深邃的苍穹啊，隐没了多少壮烈，分娩了多少新天体，看尽了多少沧桑世纪，经历了多少裂变聚合。这广阔无限的星光宇宙啊，令我上下求索，令我万千思绪。

一颗流星划过，拖着尾巴消失在深远的夜空。没人知道它有没有遗憾和遗愿。它的稍纵即逝，谁知它的去向，它的隐秘，它的甘苦。

茫茫天宇，风云变幻，日月穿梭，明暗交错；阳光普照，星河横流；观不尽的景观，看不完的现象，层出不穷的新发现，这是生命的往复，希望的所有，更是痛苦的根源。

眼望闪烁星斗满天，我想起那远古的新生的，昨夜的今晚的，逝去的未来的——星辰。它们有或没有情、恨、恩、怨？有或没有迷茫，困惑，希望？哦，有吧，混沌既朦胧，爆炸即分离，运动既是组合诞生。万物皆同，有吸引，有结合，有孕育，有亡故……昨夜星辰带着这一切离去，今夜星辰带着这一切存在。

1989 年

那一年我在中央人民广播电台为灾区捐款点歌

那是 1991 年夏天的事了，江苏、安徽等多个南方省份发生严重的水涝灾害，那时，在开滦矿务局范各庄矿基层工会工作的我，十分关注新闻。每天看着屏幕上被肆虐洪水冲毁的长堤、良田、村庄，不禁心里直颤，更不禁回想起 1976 年 7 月 28 日唐山发生的大地震……一种相怜、同情、支援、鼓励受灾人民的心情油然而生。于是给我喜欢收听的中央人民广播电台"今晚 8

点半节目"写了一封信，并寄上一些钱，托该节目转交受灾最重的江苏省，并为灾区人民点了一首歌。

一星期后的一个晚上，当晚21时，收音机里的报时钟声刚刚响过，中央人民广播电台节目主持人、著名播音员雅坤，那庄重、亲切的声音便从收音机里送到我的耳边："开滦矿务局范各庄矿工作的陈欣同志，不知您是否在收听我们的'今晚8点半节目'。您的来信和给灾区人民的汇款我们已经收到，我们将回信把处理情况通知给您。在这里，我代表'今晚8点半节目'组的全体同志和灾区人民向您表示感谢，并为您播放一首由韦唯演唱的《爱的奉献》。下面就请您与全国听众一起收听。"

歌声响起，我的心里一股热流涌起。"只要人人都献出一点爱，世界将变成美好的人间……"

是啊，世界需要爱心，人人需要爱心，人人都有爱心。作为一个受过大地震洗劫的唐山人，一个接受了全国人民爱心援助的唐山人，现在又援助他人的唐山人，听到这歌声怎能不在热流涌动呢？我想，这动情的歌声，也一定打动、鼓舞着灾区抗灾自救的人们，感动激励着所有的人奉献爱心。我特别记下了这难忘的时刻——1991年7月23日21点。从此，每每听到《爱的奉献》这首歌，心里总有别样的感觉。

1998年8月20日

命运

不知你可否有过这样的时刻。早已被人情世故，事业坎坷，颠簸碰撞的不堪疲惫的你，像倦累的泳者，很想找到一片松软沙滩，背负其上，嘘一口长气，叹息人活得太累。这短暂的人生路，你步步紧追，却步步不济，进而显得步履维艰，感叹命运不佳。

我有过这样的时刻。我不会吸烟，没有在烟云缭绕中冥冥苦想的境遇，有倒是常常独自坐在靠窗的写字台前，望着窗外的蓝天游云，羡慕那份悠然，那份广阔灿烂。也不觉耳畔回荡起法国浪漫钢琴王子理查得·克莱德曼那震颤心灵的《命运》钢琴曲，并不自觉地按下组合音响的放音键。顿时，我周身四处的空间，全被那立体感，深沉铿锵的旋律所萦绕——咚咚咚咚……咚咚咚咚……理查得手点键下，却弹奏出命运的严峻，冷酷与浩然，你会看到汹涌海涛逼来，让你紧迫，令你筹措，强你去搏。之后，你会随着节奏的舒缓，感觉亮丽，畅达，展望，更有不忍回首的牢记，最后驻足搏击那坚定有力的旋律上而倍感振奋。继而，一种少年壮志不言愁的情怀悠然而升，站起身来推开窗扇，放眼长空，想到雷鸣电闪之后不是长久的阴霾密布；春天过后不是秋，只有山势险峻，才显得探险者风采，只有波涛翻卷才显大海宽阔。于是一种博大宽广充满你胸怀，一种蓬勃自信充满你心中，一种豪放无畏使你浩气荡荡。

此刻，你会领悟——命运就是搏击，命运之舵在你自己手里掌握，只有搏击才能进取，只有不断进取才是人生意义。

2003 年 1 月 4 日

构思谋篇列车上

外出坐车是个苦差事，一坐就是几个小时，甚至几天几夜，单调枯燥。可我偶然发现，这却是写文章谋篇构思的好时机。

记得那是 1984 年夏，领导要我去内蒙古赤峰办事，当晚动身。午夜星河，人物皆静，车上旅客大都进入梦乡，我却毫无睡意，忽然记起前段时间想写的一篇反映矿工生活的小小说，于是顿生灵感，便开始构思，开头、结尾、层次安排、主题思想……到赤峰时，腹稿出来了，定名"春耕烟"。到招待所里马上动笔，一气呵成，在《开滦矿工报》上发表后受到好评。

一次去锦州，天上下着绵绵细雨，我坐在靠车窗的位子上等待发车。这时，一顶红黄两色小伞下一对情侣依依不舍。汽笛长鸣，列车出站，姑娘才含情脉脉地离去。这一镜头使我联想到千百个家住农村甚至外省的矿工，他们与妻儿老小长期分居，只有一年一度的探亲假才得以团聚。他们的爱该是多么深沉。当他们起程返矿的时候，那依依惜别之情不难想象。曾有一位矿工家属，每年丈夫探亲假期满回矿，她总要送出十里地……想到这里，灵感来了，车到锦州，腹稿已成，连夜写就散文诗《笛声响》，刊于《开滦矿工报》。

由此，就形成一种习惯，每每长途外出必有新篇问世。纪实短剧《悲剧》，腹稿形成于从秦皇岛开往石家庄的列车上，此剧本获中国首届微型文学作品大展赛鼓励奖。小小说《丑丈夫》成熟于去太原的列车上，发表后海南文学人才函授学院颁发荣誉证书。散文诗《经纬多少》诞生于去天津的列车上，被评为 1989 年度《中国合作经济报》优秀作品。短诗《幸福之星》孕育在开往西安的列车上，被收入《中国新诗人千家》一书，并获当代诗人、作家优秀作品奖。

坐车构思，是一种乐趣，一种享受。它已成为我旅途生活中不可缺少的一个组成部分。

1992 年 6 月 20 日

多事麦秋那些帮过我的人

1985 年 6 月的麦收，那是一个让我难以忘记的金色麦秋。中华人民共和国成立以来第二次分田到户的这个麦秋让我感到困惑，更让我遇到了众多好心人。

1985 年 2 月，母亲的嗓子老是感觉异常，说话吃东西总觉得不对劲儿。到咱唐山好几家医院都检查过了，也许是当时医疗设备和技术不过关吧，都不能确诊得了什么病。大家都怀疑是喉癌，母亲为此思想压力很大。但到现在我还清楚地记得，最后，还是开滦医院的一位陈大夫，建议我们去一下天津总医院查一查。那时已经是 5 月份了。

家里 5 个孩子我是头大，其中，两个妹妹一个弟弟都在上学，几个月里一直在为母亲看病而奔走于工作和医院之间。当时我在宣传部担任宣传报道组组长，我们这个一万多人的国企单位还是业内屈指可数的通讯报道先进单位。我这人要强，恐怕耽误工作。为了不影响这块工作的连续性，我向部长说明家在农村，母亲得病要去天津总院，父亲养了一百多只蛋鸡，还有几亩地又临近麦秋的实际情况，提出下基层工作的要求，以减轻领导对工作的担心。部长看看我一笑说，在家里我也是老大，我知道当老大的不易和辛劳，工作我来抓，你放心地去联系天津总医院去吧。这样的领导多好，我深深体会到，工作上遇上好领导真好。

我的一个同事听说这事儿找到我问："天津总医院有关系吗？""没有。""那这样吧，我一个表嫂在那儿是一个科主任，我给你写封信带上去找表嫂吧。"就这样，怀着期待来到天津总医院。"表嫂"很是亲切地忙前忙后的帮我们，就是在"表嫂"热心帮助下，通过一系列检查，母亲的病情很快弄清楚了，原来是声带息肉，但必须做切除手术。在母亲这病的检查和治疗上，我的领导、同事和"表嫂"，可以说是我母亲的贵人。

眼看就麦秋了，父亲把所有正在下蛋的鸡卖给了万里香烧鸡店，专门来天津肿瘤医院陪护母亲。

从天津坐在回家的列车上,我望着车窗外一望无际金灿灿的滔滔麦浪,想着家中地里麦子,心里有些犯难,因为走出校门进了企业门的我没干过真正的农活,但这时也必须干了。当时的农民很辛苦,因为没有小麦收割机,所有的小麦全是一镰镰地从地上割下来,再装车拉到麦场里用打麦机脱粒,然后在地上晾晒,费时费工费力。记得中国作家协会主席铁凝曾经写过一篇名叫《麦秸垛》的小说里,有过农村麦秋忙碌的描写。第二天我正要和两个妹妹下地割麦子,刚要出门时,迎面走进来我单位的三个哥们儿:"大哥,我们哥几个帮你割麦子来了。"看着兄弟们,我心里一阵热乎乎的。此时,真是好兄弟什么也不要说了。是弟兄们的到来,真的给了我希望和力量。

在医院的母亲父亲也惦记着家里的麦子,母亲带着喉管就急忙返回来了。当父母回到家里看到已经收割的麦子,心里也踏实了……

年年春秋,年年麦收。眼下又逢麦收时节,看着麦田里一辆辆大型的小麦联合收割机往返穿梭于大地之上忙着收割小麦,吃进去大片金黄的麦秸麦穗儿,却把奔流不息的小麦颗粒之河倾泻在同行的汽车车斗里,真是省时省工省力,道道工序一气呵成。每每这时我就触景生情满心感慨:机械化真好,农业现代化真好,今天的时代真好。

蓦然回首,这个麦收的事已是过去三十多年了。回想当时,无论是心理上还是思想上,我都有一定的压力。因为母亲的病突然来临,农活我又没有历练,真的是犯怵,一切都是硬着头皮去干的。但是通过这件事可以用上两个词:"感谢、感恩。"感谢的是,这个麦收锻炼了我;感恩的是,陈大夫、我的部长、同事、"表嫂"、工友,你们都是世上的热心人好人。陈大夫、我的部长,虽然你们已经逝去,但在我心里一直把你们深深地牢记;同事、"表嫂"、工友,你们如我的亲兄弟帮我度过艰难,祝你们生活开心,健康如意。

2016年6月15日

写作，作家弥足珍贵的生活方式

居于中国古典四大名著之首的《红楼梦》，是一部具有世界影响力的人情小说作品，举世公认的中国古典小说巅峰之作，是集传统文化之大成的中国封建社会的百科全书。不但有藏、蒙、维吾尔、哈萨克、朝鲜多种文字的译本的《红楼梦》，在国内有数以百万计的发行量，而且有英、法、日、韩、俄、德、西等20多个语种的择译、节译、全译本，《红楼梦》早已成为世界人民共同的精神财富。1910年版的《英国百科全书》称赞：《红楼梦》是一部非常高级的作品，它的情节复杂而富有独创性。在2014年，英国《每日电讯报》发布"史上十佳亚洲小说"排行榜，《红楼梦》位列第一。早在17世纪中后期就翻译了中国元曲《赵氏孤儿》的法国，文学评论界更赞扬曹雪芹具有敏锐的目光，高度的同情心，机敏的才智和幽默，深刻的洞察和再现包括整个社会自下而上的各阶层的能力。

在大清康熙、雍正两朝做了58年江宁织造的曹家祖孙三代四人，使得曹家盛极一时。少年时代的曹雪芹，在南京经历了一段富贵繁华的贵族生活，曹家在雍正六年（1728年）因亏空得罪被抄没，曹雪芹一家迁回北京。回京后，他曾在一所皇族学堂"右翼宗学"里当过掌管文墨的杂差，境遇潦倒，生活艰难。

曹雪芹在《红楼梦》开卷第一回第一段《作者自云》这篇自序中，自述说他是依托自己早年在南京亲历的繁华旧梦而写作此书。因流落北京西郊，碌碌无为，一事无成，面对乡野生活悠闲自在，风光宜人，回忆起年少时曹府里所有的女孩儿，觉得她们的见识才气远远超过自己，不禁深自愧悔。祖上辛勤创下这份家业，自己身在福中，却不务正业，没有听从父母老师的管教，以致长大后无一技之长，半生潦倒。历历在目的往日家族生活，经历的人人事事，自谦才疏学浅的曹雪芹不甘贾府上下，主子仆人的一切湮灭无闻。及此一念，荡漾心旌，一切困难不在话下，文思泉涌，下笔如神将这段经历和悔悟用市井白话写成小说。

晚年移居北京西郊，生活更加穷苦，"满径蓬蒿"，"举家食粥"。《红楼梦》一书是曹雪芹在贫困之中创作的。创作年代在乾隆初年到乾隆三十年左右(1737—1765)。正是这段清贫岁月，曹雪芹却因《红楼梦》的写作在艰辛苦难的生活中平添了充实无限，更给后世甚至是全人类留下一笔巨大的文化遗产，也在300年来的世界文学领域赢得着独特的赞誉。

托尔斯泰的长篇小说《安娜·卡列尼娜》1877年首版发行，领导俄国革命的列宁曾反复阅读，以至把封皮都弄得起皱了。他说：托尔斯泰在自己的作品里能提出这么多重大的问题，能达到这样大的艺术力量,使他的作品在世界文学中占了一个第一流的位子。《安娜·卡列尼娜》在那个时代的俄罗斯引起了"一场真正的社会大爆炸",它的每个章节都引起了整个社会各个阶层的注视,仿佛事情关乎涉及每个人最切身的问题。全社会公认它是一部了不起的巨著,它所达到的高度是俄国文学从未达到过的。作家陀思妥耶夫斯基兴奋地评论道:"这是一部尽善尽美的艺术杰作,现代欧洲文学中没有一部同类的东西可以和它相比!"他甚至称托尔斯泰为"艺术之神"。

19世纪70年代的1870年,托尔斯泰眼看俄国乡村遭到资本主义势力的入侵,目睹"到民间"去等活动的开展,怀揣对新的思想危机和新时代的探索,计划要写一部出身高等社会的有夫之妇失足的小说,并打算把这个女人写得可怜而无罪。

1872年,在距托尔斯泰的农庄五俄里的地方,有个妇女名叫安娜兹科娃,当她发现自己的情人另有新欢,向自己儿子的家庭女教师求婚时,一气之下带上一些换洗衣服去了图拉,后来又返回村子,毅然决然地投身在货车车轮下而死。目睹了这出悲剧的托尔斯泰,心灵深受触动。于是在1873年动笔,1877年完成了《安娜·卡列尼娜》的写作。

在写作生活中,托尔斯泰这个居住乡下的寄生贵族,细心观察,仔细记录着俄国封建农奴制度迅速崩溃,封建贵族地主日趋腐化堕落的思想与新兴资产阶级人文思想发生的激烈地对撞;书写着在政治、经济制度,思想、道德观念急剧变化中,欧洲资产阶级人文思想的启蒙、人性的自觉不自觉地觉醒,人们要求人性解放、恋爱自由、婚姻自主越来越高的呼声。他频繁访问神父、主教、修道士和隐修士,并结识了农民、独立教徒康·修斯塔夫,完全接受了宗法制农民的信仰,以完美与和谐的艺术,以史诗的笔调在小说《安娜·卡列尼娜》中,描写了资本主义冲击下俄国社会生活和人们内心世界的躁动不安,展现了"一切都翻了个身,一切都刚刚开始安排"的时代特点,广泛表现了19世纪70年代处在新旧交替时期的俄国社会。把19世纪批判现实主义推向顶峰,树起了一面高耸入云的丰碑,100多年来,以《安娜·卡列尼娜》写作的巨大成功,不断地得到人们的肯定、推崇,它的成就与影响无疑是俄罗斯前无古人后无来者的,这也是作家写作生活极具事半功倍效果的充分体现。

仲夏情思

我独自徘徊在沙滩，海风吹来，轻轻撩起我一缕额前散发，像在数我又添几许皱纹。脚下多情的波浪，舔湿我的鞋子和裤脚，海面涌起浪花，隐现我往事记忆……

仲夏了，去看海吗？仿佛又听你在说。是啊，曾是这浪漫季节，在海边，你歌如潮，情如海。歌中唱，你期待白马王子迎面来，一同到那遥远的地方去流浪。故事美丽令人陶醉，怎奈书生气，未留意醉翁之意……

秋叶落，顿开茅塞。

是寒冬热烈的思恋，才有这不冻的海……

仲夏了，去看海吗？

一路耳膜鼓动，走过秋冬春。蓦然回首，面对澎湃海洋，面对红男绿女，激不起我欢欣情绪，诱不出我一丝笑意，举足信步向茫然……

你说我是生活的强者。可在爱的二元一次方程式前，我是低能儿。退潮后，我拾到一枚金贝壳，是你丢给的。洒脱岁月有了一个它，才醒悟夏娃情感……今又仲夏，来看海吧，我请你同行。

看不安的海，骚动的海，激荡的海……

天依蓝，海依蓝；阳光依然，沙滩依然，仲夏，这里一片灿烂热望……

《仲夏情思》一文在1993年《当代文坛》杂志举办的全国首届当代文坛力作选拔赛上，一举荣获全国首届当代文坛力作选拔赛诗歌创作一等奖。收入《中国新诗人千家》丛书。在天津人民广播电台播发，《窗》《唐山团讯》转载。

1993年，陕西青年自修大学校刊《窗》创刊号，专版专页发表《仲夏情思》和创作谈《让感情的光芒闪烁文章中》并加编者按。也因为这篇美文，作者被邀请参加《人民文学》创刊45周年座谈会。

复旦大学作家班，我心中永远的楼兰

辉煌汉唐时期，亚欧大陆间那条繁荣的丝绸之路上，有一个美丽富饶令今人仍魂牵梦绕的西域文明古国——楼兰。据专家考证主要是由于周围自然生态系统和环境的人为变化，是导致这个美丽国家带着她灿烂的文化神秘消失的原因之一。时至今日，楼兰故地尚可去寻访，而楼兰古国早已荡然无存。虽然，我早已是中国散文学会会员、河北省作家协会会员、唐山作家协会会员，但是，上海复旦大学中文系作家班，就如这楼兰古国一般，永远成为我心中可想不可求的楼兰。

1992年6月，我的一首题目为《仲夏情思》的散文诗，在海南省《当代文坛》举办的文坛力作选拔赛上获得诗歌创作一等奖，并收入当年香港金陵书社出版公司出版的《中国新诗人千家》一书。当时的《唐山团讯》也转载了这首散文诗，天津经济广播电台还播发了这首散文诗。当年的《人民文学》主编就是因为看到了《仲夏情思》这首散文诗，专门邀请我参加了《人民文学》创刊40周年文学笔会。因此，1993年，我报名参加了上海复旦大学中文系作家预备班函授学习，主修诗歌创作，偏重散文诗创作。时至今日，我仍清楚地记得，我的指导老师何舒云教授，每次都是把我的诗稿仔细批阅后寄我。批语浸满教诲真情，让我受益匪浅，也更加激励我去努力创作，散文诗写作水平迅速提高。这一点，也许让老师频感欣慰。后来，我却让我亲爱的指导老师很感遗憾，也更让我倍感痛失良机，抱憾不已。

那是1994年7月，上海复旦大学中文系根据我在中文系作家预备班的学习写作情况，经过严格考查、审核、选拔之后，我被录取为上海复旦大学中文系作家班正式学员。我的指导老师亲笔写信向我表示祝贺，并寄来"上海复旦大学中文系作家班录取通知书""上海复旦大学中文系作家班学员登记表"等。

能到中国名牌学府去读作家班，这不是一个人人都能有机会的事。已在报纸杂志上发表过不同体裁和题材文学作品的我，虽曾经过了不懈的努力，但仍感到欢天喜地。可那时我的家庭经济情况支持不了我的学业，不禁心情一落千丈。上作家班要到上海复旦大学全日制就学，公寓化住宿。若自费上学，再无工资可开，我的经济实力也是难以承受的。心里矛盾重重的我，思前想后还是做出了一个极不负责任的保守选择——放弃这一难得的就学深造的机会。

1994年9月初，上海复旦大学中文系作家班开学了。我虽填好并寄去了学员登记表，却人未到校。无疑，作家班要找我这个人，更要找我的指导老师问个清楚。于是，我的指导老师来信给我,向我讲述作家班开学的情况,询问我未能到校学习的原因,告诉我能来的话晚到几日也要来。并在信尾婉言写道:"今后若有较满意的作品照样可以寄给我,我们永远是朋友。"看得出,我的老师在默默的惋惜中充满着无限疼爱与期待的心情。

下班回到家里,我反复读着老师的来信,而后,静默凝立在靠窗的写字台前,仰望着高天流云思维却像是停滞了。良久,我按下音响的放音键。顿时,我周身四处的空间,全被法国浪漫钢琴王子理查德·克莱德曼弹奏的著名钢琴曲《命运》那铿锵有力的旋律所萦绕。我注视着窗外残淹的夕阳,黄昏如血。1994年9月,让我遗憾终生。现在想来,这件事的结果有主客观两方面的原因,但最主要的还是自己没有辩证地把未来和学业放在环境和时间之上的高度,来思考和观察去上海复旦大学中文系作家班学习的问题。更因此懂得:人生的机会并不太多,要好好经营把握,因为,命运之舵掌握你自己手里。

感悟初冬

立冬之后11月15日,翻开月历一看11月22日就是小雪了,初冬的风刮起来,松树就不用说了,城市中的杨树、柳树、法国梧桐、枫树等树上还长着许多叶子,一片片黄黄的杨树叶和银杏树叶飘荡着,中国槐苍绿的叶片间还挂着一串串槐树角。抬头看看天,蓝蓝的,还飘着几丝游云,感觉有些瘦冷。楼下,剪草机秋末剪过的草坪犹如一张偌大的地毯般铺展开着,仍然有些毛感的柔美,草地间有些败落的红黄白紫各色的月季花,还在不愿舍弃最后一缕暖阳,顽强绽放在阳光下。一簇簇西粉莲的红色花朵又是那么惹人眼目深情而鲜活地开放着。甬道边垂柳的条条柳丝,摇荡在微风之中只争朝夕。南面小楼上,爬满的植物叶子由于初冬的来临虽然有些暗,但还依然有的黄、有的绿、有的红,依然保持着深秋的景色。

时光荏苒,但这可以说是深深秋之景却并不让人感觉破败萧瑟。蓝天白云,阳光普照,红花绿叶,长柳拂肩。在这样的时日,花儿仍在最后烂漫的绽放,充满生命延续的欲望,激荡着生命焕发生机,霜叶渲染,火红荡漾,怎能不让人心生感慨。看着眼前的这些景色,不禁让人感叹,真是万物生长靠太阳啊,这世间的所有生命,永远不懈的争朝夕,天地间的万物,享受阳光,生机不泯。对生存情有独钟,充满渴望。

并不寒冷的初冬风儿再次刮起，送来厚重的色彩斑斓，送来深沉成熟，送来遐思无尽。初冬的风，让人感悟生命意义，珍惜往日情怀，保重幸福今天，追求美的未来。

站在这天空蓝蓝、游云雪白、银杏金黄、枫树红火、松树苍翠、柳丝摇摆的天地间，皮衣微鼓初冬的风，眼底尽收依旧深秋的景，倍感荡气回肠，心怀畅想。让思绪装满对美好的思念；心若在情就在，寰宇间阳光不败，温暖和大美永远人间澎湃。

1999 年 11 月 15 日

爱人即爱己

"只有学会爱别人，才能学会爱自己，别人才能会爱你；只有学会关心别人，才能学会关心自己，别人才能会关心你"。从孩子稍一懂事，我和妻子就这样言传身教的教育孩子，引导孩子，关爱孩子。所以，孩子从小就学会关爱别人。

记得儿子那年刚刚 4 岁时，骑 50 型摩托车的我又买了一辆 125 型珠江摩托车，换挡提速快，骑着过瘾。但妻子心里却是着实地不放心，最怕我骑飞车。所以，天天在我上班出门前嘱咐两句："慢点儿骑。"一天一天的老是这么说，儿了也记住了，每天早上一见我拿起头盔要走，他都要跟到门厅对我说："爸爸，摩托车您慢点儿骑。"

父子天性，小小几岁的孩子竟如此牵挂我，能不让我加倍喜欢他吗？本来儿子就很惹人爱，又这样的乖，我更从心里喜欢他了。每天骑车上路前，儿子还要让妈妈抱到阳台探出头对我说声："爸爸，再见。早点回来。"

骑在车上，我心里记着儿子的话。童心无邪，话虽简单，却是一份真爱亲情，能不让我感动吗？它让我心里感到实在是热乎。人是有感情的，对每一份情和爱都会珍惜，更何况这是年龄幼小的乖儿子的一份真爱呢？所以，行车中，我总是谨慎地操纵着摩托车的变挡、刹车、油门、转向。虽是大车，但从不太快，宁停三分不抢一秒。因为，天真可爱的小儿子心系着我的安危，盼望着我早点儿回家，我的平安会给他幼小的心灵带来抚慰和欢欣。

"爸爸，摩托车您慢点骑。"我常记着儿子这句充满真爱的话，天天下班回家，总要把儿子轻轻抱起亲亲，让儿子惦念的童心得到亲切的回报。

现在儿子长大了,他所在学校的教学楼前,迎面悬挂着一个大大的"爱"字,"爱"这种伟大的教育也许与我的教育方式相符。有时我在家,儿子常会对我说:"爸,您教导我的对。只有爱别人,才能爱自己,别人才会爱你;只有关心别人,才会关心自己,别人才能关心你。我给了同学爱和关心,同学给我的也是爱和关心;我给了老师爱和关心,老师给我的还是爱和关心。爱和关心相互激励着我们,爱和关心温暖着我们。"儿子是这样说的,也是这样做的,更是这样感受到的。正因如此,在学校里,儿子已好几次获得"团结友爱奖"了。

2001 年 11 月

携一抹阳光向善行

我国的传统文化著作《三字经》的第一句就是:"人之初,性本善。"老祖宗的话是智慧的,作为写作者,我对此深信不疑。所以,一直以善为念。

善无处不在,记得在 1972 那年初冬,爸爸骑自行车带我从唐山回家。在路过一条河的一个石桥时,爸爸看到一个在河岸边拣树枝儿的老太太,不慎跌倒滚下了干枯的河沟,但一直没有松开抱着树枝儿的双手。爸爸打上自行车梯下到沟里扶起老太太问她:"天儿这么冷怎么还出来拣树枝儿哪?"老太太说:"家里冬天没有多少煤,拣点树枝儿烧炕暖和。"爸爸听后没说啥,只是从兜里掏出两块钱给她说:"快回家吧,天儿冷别冻坏咯。"事后我问爸爸:"爸把老太太扶起来了,怎么又给了她两块钱(那时的两块钱可是很顶用的)哪?"爸爸说:"她日子穷不好过,帮点儿是点儿吧。"爸爸的善举给我留下了深刻的印象。

1988 年冬天的一个早上,我坐公交车上班。头班车人多,我从来不和大家抢座,总是最后一个上车。车开动了,一个女乘客叫我,要把座让给我。我说谢谢,您坐吧,我就不坐了。无奈,她老是叫我非要让我坐不可。我一看怎么也想不起来她是谁,但她一把把我拉过去:"大兄弟,你还认识我是不?坐下来我跟你说,你是我们家的大恩人……"弄得一车人全看我,我当时还挺不得劲儿。我只好坐下来听她说。原来呀,我小时候居住的镇子上也还有茶馆呢。天天早上爸爸妈妈让我到茶馆打一暖壶开水,2 分钱,家里人刷牙洗脸的热水就够了。一天早上我在排队等候打水,我前面有四五个人。这时,一位妇女神情紧张地走进茶馆,着急地请求我前面那几个人让她加个塞先打一壶,说孩子在医院急等用开水,但没人让她加塞。该我了,我说你先打吧。她马上接上暖壶,打完连连说了三声谢谢,然后连颠带跑地回医院去了。她说:"你先让我打了那一壶开水,就保住了我儿子的一条命……你的模样没有变,还和小时候一个样,所以我一眼就认出你来了,你是一个大好人哪。"那年我9岁,时隔20年没想到她还一直记着我。等她说完了,我真真觉得在这世上啊,你为别人做一点善事,人家会记你一辈子的。也就是这件事,深深触动了我并让我坚定要坚持做善事。出发点很简单,那就是:"助人为乐!"

记得那是1991年夏天的事了,江苏、安徽等南方省份发生了严重的水灾。我看着电视屏幕上被肆虐洪水冲毁的长堤、良田、村庄,不禁心里直颤,更不禁回想起1976年7月28日唐山发生的大地震……一种相怜、同情、支援、鼓励受灾人民的心情油然而生。于是给我当时我很喜欢收听的中央人民广播电台"今晚8点半节目",写了一封信,并寄上一些钱,托该节目转交受灾最重的江苏省,并为灾区人民点了一首歌。

一星期后的一个晚上,21点的报时钟声刚从收音机里响过,中央人民广播电台节目主持人、著名播音员雅坤那庄重、亲切的声音便从收音机里送到我耳边:"陈欣同志,不知您是否在收听我们的今晚8点半节目。您的来信和给灾区人民的汇款我们已经收到,我们将回信把处理情况通知给您。在这里,我代表今晚8点半节目组的全体同志向您表示感谢,并为您和灾区人民播放一首由韦唯演唱的歌曲《爱的奉献》。下面就请您与全国听众一起收听。"

歌声响起,我的心里一股热流涌起。"只要人人都献出一点爱,世界将变成美好的人间……"

是啊,世界需要爱心,人人需要爱心,人人都有爱心。作为一个经受过大地震灾难洗劫的唐山人,一个接受了全国人民爱心援助的唐山人,现在又援助他人的唐山人,听到这歌声怎能不在热流涌动呢?动情的歌声,一定打动、鼓舞着抗灾自救的人们,感动激励着人们奉献爱心。我特别记下了这难忘的时刻——1991年7月23日21点。从此,每每听到《爱的奉献》这首歌,心里总有一种别样的感觉。

2016年4月份,唐山世界园艺博览会拉开了序幕。我应邀组织部分作家、画家、书法家一行十一人,进行世园会采风。一日世园会,闻遍全球香。花香浓厚,阳光正好。为世园会泼墨作画,挥毫书法,激扬文字,书写文章。

我们就此建起了一个微信群"作家艺术家阳光艺苑",初衷就是建阳光的群,聚阳光的人,营造阳光的氛围,做阳光的事。在开展进行文学、书法、国画、朗诵等文化艺术交流的同时也搞公益活动。

2016年夏天,我省部分市县遭受水灾,我和部分作家艺术家阳光艺苑成员,毅然决然地走上街头,在唐山市中心地带百货大楼前参加义演义卖赈灾活动。

为激发人们的爱国热情,强化人们的爱家情节,在古老传统节日中秋佳节和第六十七个中华人民共和国国庆节到来前的9月25日,我组织策划了"中秋情中国心"诗歌朗诵会。来自唐山各地区的部分作家、诗人、画家、书法家欢聚丰南图书馆，借长空浩荡共抒中秋情，借秋风万里同表中国心。

10月16日我和朋友去迁西罗屯看朋友时，听说一个12岁的农村小女孩宏颖患了脑髓瘤，举家借债花了十八万元治疗依然没有治好。为此，我和朋友一起专门发起组织了一场"感恩生活，为爱起航"的义演义卖爱心捐赠活动，募集善款帮助小宏颖筹集作第二次手术的医药费。

而我们的活动中，一位和妈妈一起来的7岁小女孩让我深深感动，她竟然把自己1000元的压岁钱，全部当场买了书画作品。大家问她为什么把压岁钱全都义买了书画，她说："就是想多添上点儿钱，让小姐姐快快治好病。"

2016年11月12日，我到革命老区走访当地人民，实地了解农户生活状况。

我们一行人爬坡越岭往返30多里，相继来到庞庄、刘庄、柴家湾等几个山村进行走访。大家看到，在清澈的还乡河边和美丽的玉带山旁，这里曾经是冀东抗击日本侵略者的根据地，这里的人民有着勤劳勇敢的革命传统。但是山村百姓的生活还不算富裕，为此，大家还带去了大米送给贫困户。

为了激发人们向前进的信心和精神，在2016年即将结束的12月18日，我又发起了与丰南区文化馆联合举办的"唱响明天"大型公益演出，以此激发人们对美好生活和美好明天的向往，焕发昂扬饱满精神迈向前方和新的一年。

阳光的人，阳光的氛围，阳光的心。自"作家艺术家阳光艺苑"2015年建立以来，阳光人奋发向上，积极进取。大家在参与社会公益活动的同时，努力参加各种文学艺术活动，各种体裁不同内容的文学作品、书法作品、国画作品分别在市、省、国家级报纸杂志上发表刊用，并在不同层次的大赛上取得名次和成绩。更有26人出版了个人文学作品专集。推荐1309人相继加入了中国散文学会、中国诗歌学会、中国煤矿作家协会、河北省作家协会、河北省美术家协会、河北省诗词学会、唐山市作家协会、唐山市音乐家协会、唐山市书法家协会、唐山市美术家协会、唐山诗词学会、华夏精短文学学会等等。

长天流云，人间爱心浩荡。我一人之力虽然微不足道，但我将坚定走文学、国画、书法、诵读、歌唱、表演、舞蹈等艺术交流活动与公益相结合的道路，尽己之力携一抹阳光一心向善，广泛团结更多的人奉献才智和爱心，汇入公益大潮，帮更多的人享受温暖阳光。

2024年1月18日

第四辑
别样情怀

让情感的光芒闪烁文章中

文章，特别是文学作品中的抒情作品，若作者对某个事物没有真情实感，那么，是写不出好作品的，这是我通过在陕西青年自学大学学习和创作实践中得到一点体会。

参加自学前，我主要给报社撰写新闻稿件或写些小小说等，三年学习毕业后，我潜心自己的创作，短诗、小说、散文、散文诗等都写，有时也写些新闻稿给广播电视和报纸。在日常生活中，往往一些事情使我产生喜怒哀乐，这种现象反映到文学作品里就构成了抒情的基础。如一次我出差去锦州，天上下着绵绵细雨，我坐在靠车窗的位子等待发车，这时，一顶红黄小伞下一对情侣依依不舍，一声汽笛长鸣，列车出站，姑娘含情脉脉地看着车上情人随列车缓缓离去，这一镜头使我联想到千百个家住农村甚至外省的矿工，他们与妻儿老小长期分居，一年一次的探亲假才得以团聚，他们的爱该是多么的深沉，当他们起程返矿的时候，与家人的惜别之情并不难想象。

曾有一位矿工的妻子，每年丈夫探亲假期满回矿，她总要送夫十里……想到这里，灵感来了，车到锦州，腹稿已成，连夜写就散文诗《笛声响》，刊于《开滦矿工报》，诗中写出了热恋情人的惜别之情和心理状态。

在1991年初夏之时，我来到北戴河海滨，然而却触景生情，想起了一位曾经深深爱过我的姑娘，就是在这美丽海滨向我表露了心迹，可并未如愿以偿得到一个玫瑰色的梦，她苦恼，因为她已偷偷爱我两年了。梦难成，对于一个痴情姑娘来说是一个极大的打击。她恨她无能，她恨我无能，她恨我无情，恨人为什么要有爱有情！对于爱的猛醒，可以说是一种觉悟，当我悟出真谛的时候，心里好不是滋味，一种歉疚的心情，促使我写下了《仲夏情思》这首散文诗，以表情怀。初稿题目为《仲夏了，去看海吗？》，1991年在香港《世界散文诗作家》第五期上发表，后来再经润色更名的《仲夏情思》则被收入《中国诗歌大辞典》一书和中国新诗人千家一书，获得1992年由海南省当代文坛杂志社举办的文坛力作选拔赛诗歌创作一等奖，并先后被天津人民广播电台经济台选播，《唐山团讯》转载。

通过这些使我感觉到，用真情去写，是铸就美好文章的基础。

此文为散文诗《仲夏情思》作品的创作谈，刊登于陕西青年自修大学校刊《窗》。

中国五大姓溯源

据中科院遗传研究所研究员杜若甫先生最新研究成果表明，当今中国人数最多的五大姓为李、王、张、刘、陈。姓氏文化是我们文明古国文化的一个组成部分。姓的起源与演变复杂多样，一般与古代封国、官名、族号、自然、器物、颜色及天干、地支等有关。

李姓始祖为帝少昊的后裔皋陶。皋陶是尧时的司法主管——大理。商纣时，皋陶的子孙理征因执法如山得罪了纣王被处死。理征妻携子利贞逃生，时值李子成熟之季节，一路奔命饥不择食的母子俩，以李子饱腹得保活命。大难过后，为答谢李子的活命之恩，母子俩改姓理为李，从此有了木子"李"姓。

王姓由来众说纷纭，各种资料其说不一。一说出自姬姓，周文王第十五子毕公高之后；一说出自妫姓，为帝虞舜之后；另一说出自子姓，为商朝王子比干之后。

张姓始祖当为少昊之子——挥。

挥儿时就挥刀舞枪，且聪明过人勇猛无比。他发明了古代战争中最主要的武器——弓，并因此封官"弓正"监造弓箭，赐姓为张。

刘姓其说有二。一说源于祁姓。

尧帝姓伊祁，其子孙有一支以祁为姓，被封刘国，所以，这些子孙便以刘为姓。一说晋襄公死后，子还小，朝臣立襄公弟雍为君，并派一人士会去秦国接雍归晋，襄公遗孀缪嬴天天哭闹，弄得群臣无措，只得立太子夷皋为君。执政大臣赵盾也不得不率军拦阻雍由秦回晋，护送雍回晋的秦军见此不义之事，便刀兵相见，但吃了败仗，士会也随秦军逃往秦国。几年后回晋任职的士会，却把家留在了秦国，后来便成了刘氏——意为"留"。

陈姓始祖当为舜。在舜当天子之前，尧把两个女儿嫁给他，他的子孙居于妫汭河边一带，便以妫为姓。武王伐纣灭商，封舜后裔妫满为陈侯，其域为古陈国之地。其后人以陈为姓。

1995 年 4 月 26 日

集信，别有情趣

我集信，是因学习引发的。以前，参加刊授大学学习和人民文学创作中心学习，每次辅导老师寄回作业及批阅评点，我总是认真研读，从中领悟真谛。久之，辅导老师的回信增多，我忽然想到，这就是老师的授课笔录，保存下来大有裨益，于是便注意收集。

因上学和在一些书报杂志上常有作品发表及获奖，我的名字被收入几家名录。继而，一些商贸、信息、报刊、出版、征稿、招聘、赠阅、笔会等信件纷纷飞来。这样，又为我扩大了集信范围和内容。现在，我的集信大致可分求学类、通联类、征稿类、笔会通知类、赠阅类、文朋诗友类、友情类、恋情类、家书类，算来也千余封了。正是由于这些信件在手，常有某日某种情绪上来，对往日某段时光、情怀留恋时，便翻阅有关信件，以得安慰。

另外，对查阅一些省、市、报社、杂志社及各类朋友的通讯地址、邮编、电话号码等均可信手拈来。这些信件伴随于我的生活之中，倒也美哉幸哉。

1995 年 9 月 29 日

看书

一有空，我就想看书。上街最多是去书市和书店，还是看书。我特别爱看历史书籍，所以，一看就没钟点儿，也让妻着实的生气。

那是一个礼拜天，我一边在家里看地方志，一边用速热器烧开水，暖壶放在北阳台后插上电就到南屋去看书了。不想，这书一看下去就把水忘了，直到我嗅到满屋的塑料烧焦的味儿，才猛然想起水来，急忙跑出去拔掉电源。但速热器已彻底烧坏了，只剩两条金属杆子，水也烧干了。更糟的是我居然犯傻，接了一舀子凉水倒进暖壶想冷却，适得其反，嘭的一声，暖壶爆了，满阳台的水银玻璃碎片，好在没伤着我。这时，妻从楼下上来，见此情景不禁大声说："你准又看书来着。哎，真没法儿，你这人一见书是啥都忘喽哇"。可说归说，妻的话锋一转，"反正东西都坏了，好了，我来收拾吧。"

又是一个礼拜天。中午，妻在炖鱼，突然喊我快到楼下商店拿瓶醋来，我跑下楼去正好看到有个卖书的，嘿，又啥都忘了，蹲在路边就看上了，不知看了多久，妻找下来站在我身后："你真着人稀罕哪！让你买醋你来看书。""呦，我的错，我去买。""我早就买来啦，我一想你就是看书来了。快回家吧。"

来到楼上屋里，妻端上鱼一本正经地说："第一，你烧坏了我的暖壶还有速热器；第二，你耽误了我炖鱼，你功劳不小哇，说，今儿个该咋办？"我看看妻一乐。

妻又说："这样吧，为了奖励你误事有功，本宫赐你一瓶啤酒吧。往后可不能一看书就误事了，中不中？"我一边点头一边说"中"，心里暗自称道妻的大度宽容。

2001年3月19日

山村夕阳

那是一个夏秋之交，我出差在一个山村小旅店住下。旅店西不远有座不算高的山，傍晚，我便和同事一同向山间走去。走上一处地势较高的山石前，只见山下人家袅袅炊烟，黄牛白鹅，黛瓦白墙，绿树夕照……眼前景象宛如一幅清静悠然的美丽国画，让人品味不尽。

忽然，我的视线里走进一个姑娘的倩影。但她拄着右拐，上着白地黑格外套，下穿一条冷色调长裤，显得修长苗条。她站在山腰的山路边，一动不动地凝望着西方天空的太阳和那灿烂的晚霞。不知多久，我们走下山时，她仍立在原地，神情十分专注且带有一丝哀婉。

我们在那旅店住了一星期，天气很好，每天上山都能在山上看到那位看夕阳的姑娘。我心里不禁纳闷，她怎么一个人天天站在这山路上看落日呢？写作人的探求心里决定我向她问问缘由。

"姑娘，你们这儿的傍晚景色很不错啊。"我轻声说。姑娘对我微微一笑，略带凄凉地说："这儿的夕阳好,这儿的夕阳红啊。"姑娘扶着身边的小松树说:"我和它一同看夕阳已经3年了。"说到这,姑娘眼里转了泪花。

"为什么?"我诧异地问。

"三年前的一个傍晚,我们拉山货的拖拉机突然刹车失灵,从山路上冲下来,正当惊恐我茫然不知所措时,坐在车斗里的山二叔猛地把我推下拖拉机,但是,与此同时拖拉机连同司机和山二叔却……"

一阵沉默后,姑娘调整一下自己的情绪接着说:"当时,我只是右腿骨折,可山二叔却命丧山谷了。如果不是山二叔,我也不会今天站的这里了。所以,伤稍微好一点,刚能下床,我就在这拖拉机滚下山谷的地方为山二叔栽下这棵松树,每到傍晚就和它一起看夕阳。"

我看看姑娘、看看小松树、看看那山谷、看看那漫天的晚霞,没再问关于山二叔的事,只觉得这晚霞里充满着生者对逝者的哀思,这夕阳里装满着逝者对生者的希望。只觉得那一种纯洁的人间亲情,在晚霞中升华。

1997年8月24日

我给老爸一叶平凡小舟

电视里的广告天天一个劲儿地嚷:"今年爸妈不收礼呀,送礼要送脑白金哪。"一对儿小假人儿在电视屏幕里跳儿跳的天天这样说,听着就让人烦气,我给爸妈送礼,今年我就是不送脑白金。

23岁时,我的新闻稿件已被多家市级以上电台、电视台、报纸等新闻媒介采用,文学作品也多有发表。一次爸爸问我,你成天地写,也给我写篇小说看看。当时我自信地说:"写,那还不好说。"后来便几次发表了小说。每每爸爸看了,嘴边总是挂着微笑。去年猴年农历八月十八是老爸72岁的生日,酒席宴上我对老爸说:"等到了年三十我想送您一件礼物,您猜是啥?"老爸看着我猜不出来。我说送您一本书,书名就叫《陈欣文集》。过去您没有一一看过我发表过的作品,这回,您可以坐在家里系统地看看我写的东西啦,这对您来说也许是个安慰,爸您说行吗?患脑血栓十几年的老爸摸着满头白发说:"中,中。"前些天我终于把一些作品通过电脑整理出来，封面设计朴实无华，上写一行小字："沧海横流，一叶平凡小舟"，下面立排"陈欣文集"几个大字。

2005年1月12日我把它打印装订成书，到了大年三十这天中午，我给老爸倒了一杯葡萄酒，然后对老爸说："这本彩印带插图的《陈欣文集》，作为过年礼物送给您吧。它是您期望的结果，您自己有空的时候看吧。"老爸拿起书说："对，对，我是得好好看看。"看着老爸患病以来少有的高兴的样子，我的心里十分宽慰。

闲云孤鹤

平时我有个爱好——逛书店。午后徒步走进一家书店，在音像部见货架上有张名为《一意孤行》的CD。

忽然记起《电子报》上有过介绍，不过已是5年前的事了，这次被我撞见丝毫没有犹豫就掏钱买下。下午回到家里，立刻放入CD机中。音乐响起，顿时，一种久违的感觉油然而生，于是兴起，便连听了三四遍，直到妻叫我吃饭才告一段落。

我尤其喜欢那首《闲云孤鹤》。在古琴曲中配以一些西方乐器辅助，曲子的编排，乐器的配伍，加上乐手精湛的演奏技巧，使曲中那苍凉凄美的意境体现得淋漓剔透。

曲子的节奏、韵味，让人感觉是那样的幽怨动人，恰似一支仙乐，一个个音符从耳朵轻轻飘入，而后徐徐落入欣赏者的心田，心里便生出一股荡漾的清流，顺着血管流遍全身，让人感到微微的凉意和一丝的苦涩。曲子像是婉约派的一首词，愁思万缕，幽怨孤独；又像是一篇抒发乡愁的散文，让你不忍放手看了又看；更像国画的一幅山水长卷，画中苍山碧水，孤舟独钓……充分展现了民族乐器独特魅力的《闲云孤鹤》，更显示了作者的一种异乎寻常的情怀。它让人深切体会到"莫把幺弦拨，怨极弦能说"的含意。

沉浸在乐曲的意境里，像是看到了一位虽居于山中陋室却胸怀天下的老人。

听着这曲子，仿佛老人就坐在你面前，对你讲述着段段苦楚的人生历程：年少时寒窗映雪，遍览群书。中年历尽艰辛得以一展才略，后因事与愿违无端遭贬而归隐山野，以至茕茕孑立，万念俱灰，颇有怀才不遇，报国无门的悲凉。历经一切后，暮年老人心思静若秋水却偶有涟漪。

老人娓娓动听的道来，高潮处激昂澎湃，低落时怅然垂黛，让你不由得不为老人慨叹。

《闲云孤鹤》似一池清泉，净化了我繁杂的心绪。这几日，那深沉励志的古琴声时时萦绕于耳畔，由此而初晓古人"绕梁三日"用词之精妙。

窗外，残阳夕霞，给世间不泯的光华。

2005 年 12 月 24 日

为了青山那边的小姑娘

2002 年 1 月 19 日的这天早晨，6 点钟的天空已经发亮。开滦集团东欢坨矿业公司汽车队司机郭仕银，已驱车赶在了去往迁西的路途上了。这是一条他向山村失学孩子献爱心并寄托希望的路，他开车来过不止一次。

2000 年初的一天，郭士银刚刚资助一名贫困学生上了河北大学，又听说迁西县上营乡青山口村有个叫王迎春的小姑娘失学了。于是，驱车一百多公里赶到小姑娘家了解情况。当得知小姑娘因父亲有病家庭困难交不起学费而辍学时，心里一阵的不是滋味儿，不禁掏出 500 元钱放到小姑娘父亲王振峰的手中说："让孩子上学去吧。"此后的日子里，郭士银每年资助王迎春一千元上学，还经常买些学习用品和衣服，以便让小姑娘更好地学习。开滦集团东欢坨矿业公司党委、工会也对此事颇为关注。这天东欢坨矿业公司党委副书记李大为、党委宣传部长孙彦彬和郭士银一起，驱车 170 多公里，来到迁西县上营乡坐落在万里长城青山关脚下，一个叫青山口村的王迎春小姑娘家里，给小姑娘送来两件御寒的羽绒服和书包、笔、纸、本等。开滦集团东欢坨矿业公司党委副书记李大为等坐在王振峰家的土炕上，与小姑娘及她的父母一边拉着家常，一边了解小姑娘的学习情况。当大家得知小姑娘今年在初中二年级 150 名学生中成绩排在前六名时，都为小姑娘和她的父母感到高兴。李大为语重心长地嘱咐小姑娘："要好好学习，将来没有文化不行，学习要再有长进，再有进步，争取将来考上重点大学。"当小姑娘穿上郭士银给她买来的鲜红的羽绒服时，王振峰夫妇激动地说："你说这个，我们原本素不相识，无亲无故的，资助上学不说，还给迎春买这些个使的用的，迎春说了，要用好的学习成绩来报答好心人。说实话，我们真是感激不尽……"

当大家起身要走的时候，王振峰一家人非要留大家在家里吃饭不可。最后，还是李大为副书记说了一句话："饭我们就不吃了，只要小姑娘的学习成绩好，就是对我们最好的报答，也是我们最大的愿望。祝小姑娘学习进步。顺便给你们拜个早年儿，祝你们全家幸福。"

一家人恋恋不舍地把好心的人们送出了农家小院儿，大家也带着对小姑娘及她一家人的美好祝福，驱车走上返回的路程。汽车渐渐走远了，但大家却把对小姑娘的一片美好希望和祝福留在了小山村，留在了青山口村那背负万里长城的绵绵青山中……

诗——我的恋人，我的爱

还是在我幼小的年龄，艾青、贺敬之等前辈的诗和夏青老师的毛泽东诗词朗诵，就启发了我对诗歌朦胧的爱。步入社会后，读诗、写诗，写诗不成却写起小说来了，小说发表后仍又写起诗来。发表、获奖，进而体味到，诗——是我抒发情感的最佳形式。回想起这些情景，苦乐甜辣又一起涌上心头，好像就在我的眼前。现在，我们可以说诗的春天已经到来。开放的时代，解放了思想也解放了诗歌创作。社会需要发展，时代需要发展，这些发展，都伴随着诗歌的兴盛与发展。

中华民族在人类文化发展史上曾有过几次辉煌的贡献，今天，我们的祖国正经历着一场伟大的复兴，这就更需要大批时代的歌者。改革大潮激荡着华夏神州，时代充满呼唤，充满创新。

亲爱的朋友们，那潮头的歌声不能让歌者去独领风骚，也不能让那些风云人物去独显风流，我们要汇入大潮开发幻想，抒发浪漫情怀，迎着七彩阳光，开拓亮丽架起彩虹，让盛唐之梦重圆！

亲爱的朋友们，那无际海洋大潮起伏，正是弄潮的好天地；望漫漫长路，任重而道远。趁我们正激情满怀，为诗坛繁荣作出贡献吧。

中华五千年历史长卷，无一时期不有诗的沉郁悠扬伴随历史的滚滚车轮前进；无一时期不饱含了诗人的豪放、忧伤、苍凉、激昂。

这些在诗经、楚辞、唐诗、宋词及以后各个时代的作品中都有充分的体现。他们的忧患来自国破山河在，城春草木深；他们的豪放来自堂堂中华坐看四方来贺。今天，恰逢中华腾飞的年代，我们要吸吮中华诗歌的丰富营养，蓄积对祖国真挚的爱，注入我们创作的心海，写出华美的诗章，富饶中华伊甸园。

亲爱的朋友们，十月霜染万重山，看香山红叶，坐爱枫林晚。这是成熟的季节，这是收获的季节，这是诗的季节，让我们拿起笔来，面对五千年诗的国度，奉献我们执着的爱，写出时代的放歌，描绘美丽写出美好诗篇！

1989 年 10 月

父子情深

天天忙着上班，一去就是一天，只有到了晚上，才和妻子儿子在一起吃一顿热乎乎的团圆饭。冬季天黑得早，下午五点半钟就黑黑的了。一天傍晚回到家，在屋里看动画片的儿子闻声喊着爸爸跑出来。我抱起儿子亲亲后放下。妻正忙着做饭，我仰面躺在床上觉得一阵轻松。儿子又坐在沙发上继续看动画片，我合上双眼闭目养神。不知多会儿，儿子转过脸把小嘴儿贴在我的脸上亲了一口，然后说："爸爸，您为啥不睁着眼呀？"听着儿子细微观察后的疑问，我赞叹儿子人小心细，便想逗逗他。于是，佯装没精神地说："爸爸要死啦。""爸爸为啥要死呢？""天天给你挣钱累的。""我不让你死！""不让我死我也要死啦。"这下急坏了儿子，他动画片也不看了，开门跑进北屋，趴在床上呜呜地哭起来。妻子听到儿子在哭，忙从阳台上跑进北屋，问儿子哭啥。儿子抹着泪抽泣着说："我爸爸说他要死啦！"妻一听是这么回事，抱起儿子来到南屋说："你爸是跟你闹着玩儿呢，你看你爸乐了吧！"

我也忙说："儿子，爸跟你闹着玩呢，好儿子，爸爸有你这样的好儿子，爸爸怎么会死呢？来，爸爸抱抱。"一番解释后儿子才不哭了，在我的肩膀上擦着他的泪水。

妻怪罪地说："孩子一天到晚才见你一面，跟你这么亲，往后，你别跟孩子这么闹了啊。"想来也是，儿子还不到五周，每天早上他还没醒我就上班走了，但儿子哪怕是还在蒙眬中，也要公式化地说一声："爸爸再见，早点回来。"可一直盼到晚上才能和爸爸待一会儿，听到这样的话，他幼小的心灵怎会不痛苦呢。再一想这就是父子情深哪。

2000 年 3 月 31 日

苦乐痴迷道诗心

五千年华夏文明，造就了我们这个古老而伟大的诗的国度。从《诗经》到《离骚》，从唐诗到宋词，无一不是我们中华民族的骄傲和瑰宝。但是，这一朵朵璀璨的文明之花却像我们面前香喷喷的白米饭一样："谁知盘中餐，粒粒皆辛苦。"

从古到今，中华民族的诗人词家数不胜数，但在他们流传千古的美好诗句中，无不浸透着每一位辛勤作者的一番番心血。他们在艰苦卓绝的写作实践中，深深体会到作诗写词的艰辛刻苦，更体味到心境入诗意境入词后得到满意作品之时的那一份欣喜与慰藉。

诗人刘威有诗写到"都由苦心无休日，已证前贤不到心"的苦苦寻觅；卢延让则写出"吟安一个字，捻断数茎须"的冥思苦想；李频也道出了"只将五个字，用破一生心"的一番良苦诗心；杜荀鹤更是痴迷地写出诗人"生应无辍日，死是不吟时"的不懈诗心。贾岛不禁流露出"两句三年得，一吟双泪流"这犹如晚来得子般的喜悦心情。而僧归仁更是大有一诗得意忘万忧的劲头儿："日日为诗苦，谁论春与秋；一联如得意，万事皆忘忧。"

遥想春秋战国，群雄争霸；强秦大汉，唐宗宋祖；一景景盛世，一幕幕诗情。在白发三千丈，豪情向天冲的浪漫情怀中，放歌中华民族的起落衰兴，诗人写诗的苦乐情怀也尽伴其中行。

阅读欢矿

欢矿，人说，你怀胎未足月就生下了脆弱的希望。的确，你在计划经济时期由国家规划，改革开放时期由开滦建设，市场经济时期中走在边生产边建设的路上。

欢矿，你曾独自伫立在黄土地上。更因地质、水文、技术、资金等困难，使你一度艰难强忍"流产"前的阵痛。想一想，也曾使我泪眼汪汪。

欢矿，看到你今天挺拔伟岸的模样。我要说，你先如破土的豆芽，弱小曲折，而后是顶天立地的坚强。从1976年到1994年（1994年8月18日建矿），从年产400万吨的宏大设计，到停贷留守，再到建矿生产，历经18个年头的急切盼望。

欢矿，是雄鹰谁不想飞翔，只不过是羽毛未能丰满翅膀。蓄势待发，为的是奔向目标远大的前方。年产50万吨、80万吨、100万吨、120万吨、185万吨……还要追逐300万吨的辉煌。虽然，这只是普通的一步一步，但你是开滦做大做强又添新生力量。它预示着一首雄壮的进行曲，将在黄土地上空唱响！

欢矿，你给我无尽畅想。

那一份关怀

天气的不正常，使得许多人都患了感冒。或许我也是感冒吧，白天就觉得浑身的不好受，晚上回家吃完饭后更是觉得上下不得劲，于是，连新闻联播都没看就睡了。

事先没有察觉的妻子收拾完桌椅碗筷，来到屋里见我已睡着了才觉得不对劲。忙问："哥们儿，你是不是感冒了？"我说："可能是，哪儿都不得劲儿。"妻急忙拿来感冒药——给我吃上，又让我喝了一些白开水，算是心里踏实了许多。

深夜两点多钟，我忽然咳嗽得厉害，不但我自己咳嗽醒了，也把熟睡的妻给咳醒了，妻赶紧爬起来又是倒水，又是给我吃咳特灵的一阵子忙活。等安定下来，妻坐在我的床边说："可怎么才好哇，都老夫老妻的了，我这做妻子的既要把你当丈夫的当孩子看，又要把你当孩子的管，真让人操心哪。"

妻子的话让我想起在一本书里的话：新娘，自打和她的丈夫结婚，就代替了丈夫的亲娘来尽关心呵护的职责。还有一本书里说：其实，妻子的角色是双重的。她既是妻子又是母亲。在日常生活的不自觉中，她就把妻子的爱和母亲的爱同时带给了丈夫。

细想想，书里说得对。对于这份爱，不能不说这份爱可贵、伟大。

景忠山观松

　　来迁西县景忠山是为了赶庙会，而那满山的松树却深深地吸引了我，目光所及的地方只有松。无论是陡崖峭壁，幽深峡谷，还是山路两旁小亭边，满目青山皆是松，绿色成了景忠山的基调。

　　漫步在林间小道，山谷中一阵阵夹杂着松果香气的清风，轻轻掠过我的面颊，让我感到风的轻柔，闻到松的芳香。置身其间，不觉让人倍感超脱，气定神闲，心旷神怡。

　　山风徐徐吹过，送来松的生气和灵秀，也带来风的幽柔和活力，山的壮魄和挺拔。山风松天成合一，使得这风景如诗如画，让人痴迷沉醉。

　　一棵孤傲的仙鼠松，毅然挺立在陡峭山路中一块仅有的平坦之所，挺直擎天。

　　高大的树冠倾向石阶一旁，显出它特有的高洁苍翠。在它的周围没有千年古松与之媲美，只有一群参差不齐的小松树，仰着头，像是期望它的呵护。仙鼠松带领着孩子们俯视着脚下平庸的树，用它的坚韧抵住世间的浮华。

　　它粗壮发达的根系，悄无声息的嵌入山石间，离开尘世的嘈杂，吸吮山的阳刚之气，使生命得以不折不扣的延续。一蓬油绿的松针叶错落有致地叠成松鼠的形状，远远望去，酷似一只翘起尾巴正在品食人间美味的仙鼠，让人顿生欣爱。结实的树干让人感觉一种傲骨凌风，脚踏青山，头顶苍穹。用它的高大，挺起人间正道历览岁月沧桑。不知仙鼠松经历了多少年的风雨洗礼，才有今天这般坚毅，任凭山势险峻，山风劲吹，根却依然牢牢地植入山石缝隙之中；树干依然高高挺拔；树冠依然浓密硕大，为游人遮一缕阳光，挡一丝风雨，目睹寒来暑往，暮鼓晨钟的繁华与稀落。

2003 年 7 月于景忠山

矿工的美弥足珍贵

在人类发展史上，煤矿工人，是创造光热文明的伟大力量。

多彩的世界，人类文明也是多种多样的，但人类的心灵是相通、美好可共的。我在不同省份，不同区域的不同煤矿所见过的矿工，虽然他们的自身背景、地方语言、各自素质、从事煤炭行业的年限各有差异，但对光明、温暖、幸福、安宁生活的渴求是相差无二的。这一点可以从他们的憨厚、笑容、眼神，以及他们对人们的友善中得到充分展现的。这让我在异地他乡，井上井下，大罐里矿车上，歌厅食堂都倍有感受，也让我对人与人之间的温馨、亲切、理解、和谐充满信心和希望。

矿工，是光和热的追求者、采掘者，更是创造者、奉献者。他们用自己的勤劳勇敢、善良智慧、坚忍不拔、真诚宽厚等种种内在美，用辛勤的汗水、乌黑的面容，明亮的眸子，磊落慷慨等外在美，丰富了这个世界，照亮了人们的心田。

这些年来，能够常常接触和感受矿工不同风格的美，我感到非常的快慰，同时也为那些多姿多彩的美而感叹，矿工的美弥足珍贵。

1976年7月28日，矿工李玉林独自开车到北京向党中央毛主席报告唐山大地震的灾情。他的行动让我感到一种博大之爱的美，感受到紧急关头一种民族责任感的美。

1979年，开滦范各庄矿一个名叫刘少云的井下工人，在掌子面上发生险情时毅然喊道："我是共产党员，你们先撤！"大家都撤了，他却被砸坏了肾脏。他的舍己救人让我感动。那是一种英雄的美。

1984年6月2日上午，在地下封存了5亿多年的奥陶纪淡水，突然，随着采面老塘顶板的冒落在2171工作面汹涌而出。当时的范各庄矿综采四队队长常来，在组织工作面职工撤到安全地点清点人数时，发现老工人曾宪义没有上来，马上返回去寻找。当常来拉着老曾来到上风道地下水透点时，比人腰还粗喷涌的水柱拦住了去路。生死关头，常来毅然双手用力把老曾推过水柱，同时大喊："老曾，你快……""常来……常来……常来……"老曾和矿工们千百遍声嘶力竭的呼喊，随着汹涌残酷的水流吞没了常来而被吞没。为救矿工兄弟而永远长眠煤海深处的常来，让我感受到生死之间，一个煤矿生产一线干部那种为人民大众而忘我的共产党员的形象美。

凡此种种，在矿山生活的路途上听到遇到的美尚有许多。有矿工的粗犷豪放美、诚实守信美；

有开拓工，掘进工的锐意进取美、勇往直前美；有割煤机手神情专注，驾驭自如的铁马骑士美；有液压支架工顶天立地，铁掌擎天的美；有矿灯女工笑如银铃，体态轻盈的美；有青年矿工一路高歌《矿工万岁》青春昂扬，荡气回肠的美……

回想着看到的一个个人，经历的一件件事，品味着种种不同的美，深深感到在人生的长河中这些美的珍贵。我不禁要深深感谢那些矿工，是他们让我感受到不同地方、不同环境、不同年龄、不同文化、不同修养的矿工之美，并促使我用笔写下他们，记录下他们美的人生片段。看着从我眼前走过的一个个矿工上井、下井、工作、生活、畅饮、欢歌……我真诚祝福他们幸福美满，祝愿矿山充满美好。

妈妈做的倭瓜花儿咸食香

生产队，对于今天的孩子们来说无疑是一个陌生的词汇，同时也是一个遥远的年代，但是对于那个时代的孩子——我们来说，也有幼小心灵里别样的记忆。其中，我就有一段童年记忆至今还能给我带来美好的回味。

农业社生产队时代，农民们全凭在生产队上班劳动挣工分养活一家人，农村孩子的父母全要去下地干农活，我的妈妈也不例外。

我五岁那年，妈妈白天都要去生产队上班，我只能自己在家待着，可那时的家里又没啥好玩儿的东西，天天一个小孩子在家里没着没落（lao）的，孩子的活泼天性不得不在孤寂中泯灭。所以，每当妈妈要出门上班儿我就恋恋不舍地拽着妈妈的衣角，扬着小脸望着妈妈。我是家里头生头长的大儿子，妈妈当然也是从心里惦着我，但在那个时代是为了生计那也是没办法的事。总是对我说好孩子听妈妈话，下班儿回来妈给你做好吃的啊。可这话一天两天管用，时间一长了也不好使了。盛夏时节，地里的玉米高粱这类大型农作物需要人们去除草施肥管理，劳力缺乏，妈妈不上班不行。当后半天妈妈扛起锄头又要去上班的时候，我有些无助地看着妈妈，不想让妈妈走，妈妈哄我也不管事，妈妈无奈地在堂屋呆呆地望着南面炎炎烈日下的院子。现在想起来，当时妈妈对儿子的疼爱之心和对生活的操劳之心一定在激烈斗争着。也正是这种心理斗争，促使妈妈急中生智。儿子，你看那儿的倭瓜花儿好看吗？小小的我点点头。妈给你摊一块儿倭瓜花儿的咸食吃中呗？中。于是，妈妈迅速放下锄头跑到南院儿，掐了三朵嫩黄色的倭瓜花儿，洗了一根葱，一同用刀飞快切碎，打上面糊放上五香面和盐面儿（那时是没有鸡精、味精的）一块儿搅拌，大锅下面一把柴火燃起，锅里倒点儿油，油热了把面糊往锅里一摊。一小会儿，用铲子一翻，哇！油黄黄的，香喷喷的一大块倭瓜花儿咸食看着就好吃。妈妈把咸食铲在盘子里说，儿子，等凉了再吃啊。说完拿起锄头，锁上门就匆匆上班去了。

岁月如梭，好几十年一晃就过去了，虽然时光荏苒，但小小年纪吃的妈妈摊的那一块倭瓜花儿的咸食，一直觉得很好吃，很香。成家以后的日常生活中时常想起这一道美味，也曾经几次让妻子摊咸食吃，但是，城市高楼大厦里是找不到那嫩黄色的倭瓜花儿的，所以，飘香久远的倭瓜花儿的咸食再也没有吃到过。

妈妈的恩情，儿时的记忆，美味的回忆，一直缠绕在我心中并挥之不去。前些天，在回老家看老妈时和妈妈说起了这件事。年近八十的老妈仍像当年一样高兴地说，妈出去给你掐几朵倭瓜花儿来，切上葱花儿放上五香面儿和盐面儿，再给我大儿子摊上一大块倭瓜花儿咸食吃啊。炎热的天儿，堂屋里大锅下又是燃起一把柴火，同样锅里倒了一点儿油，油热了，妈妈依然像年轻时一样，把搅拌了倭瓜花儿、葱花儿、五香面儿和盐面儿的面糊往锅里一轮均匀地摊好。一小会儿，用铲子一翻，哇！又是一大块油黄黄的，香喷喷的倭瓜花儿咸食，妈妈把咸食还是铲在了盘子里说，儿子，等凉了再吃啊。不过，这次我是和老妈一起品味了倭瓜花儿咸食的，回忆了当年的情景。只是安度晚年的老妈那拿起锄头，锁上门就匆匆上班去了的情景早已一去不复返了。倭瓜花儿咸食，童年的美味，妈妈的爱，永远在我心中存留。

八月十五其乐融融

"床前明月光，疑是地上霜，举头望明月，低头思故乡。"中国伟大的现实主义浪漫诗人李白这千古流传的不朽诗句，凝结了多少游子思乡的情怀，又集结了多少故乡亲人的期盼和凝望的眼神。

每逢佳节倍思亲，这是人之常情。只不过每个人思念的人各有不同。每年的大节小节，我最想念和惦记的是我的妈妈。爸爸去世已经七八年了，妈妈一个人在家。妈妈已经是78岁的人了，但老人家精神很好，记性也好，身体还好。有这几好，我这当儿子的十分满足。因为，老人家的健康就是儿女们的福分。

在中国，像妈妈这个年龄的老人们，大多经历了中国的抗日战争、解放战争、抗美援朝战争、三年严重困难，俗称："瓜菜代"；还经历了唐山大地震、新时期的分田到户、改革开放、新农村建设。这么多的经历和阅历，无不是他们这一代人宝贵的精神财富和人生财富，也使得他们思想开明，心思淡然，情绪通达。因为他们经历了不同时期的生生死死，是是非非，纷乱嘈杂，真理反思。我很珍重妈妈的经历和人生，尊重妈妈的为人和生活。

作为儿子，对妈妈唯一最大最好的报答就是一个字："孝"。简单明了，为人之道。俗话说："七十有个家，八十有个妈。"这话真的是不假。一个人从小到大，直到满头白发，无论何时何地，世上最惦记你的人，还是一个妈。无论到啥时候，妈关怀、想着儿子的心总也放不下。这一点，我是颇有感触和体会的。所以，我对妈妈是实心实意的伺候，认认真真的服侍。每当和妈妈一起说话的时候，感觉心里就踏实、就高兴、就乐见这样的情景。每次回老家和妈妈坐在炕上，面面相对地说着话时，总是要和妈妈说上一句："妈咱娘俩这样说着话儿您老看多好哇。"的确，有妈就是好。可以倾诉，可以放赖，可以装懒；可以得到妈妈的慈祥、谅解、关爱。世上只有妈妈好，虽然是歌里唱的，但却是一个放之四海而颠扑不破的真理。

妈妈很自强，不和我们住，坚持要自己吃住。没办法，只好依着妈妈，但我会时常接妈妈来家小住。每次妈妈来了，我都是尽心尽力让妈妈吃好、住好、玩好。从早上的刷牙、洗脸、吃饭，到晚上的泡脚、铺床、拿尿罐儿，我都是件件做到做好。妈妈老是觉得我一大老爷们儿，不让我为妈妈做这些。但我是儿子，应该为妈妈做。日子长了，妈妈也就不说什么了。一天妈妈对我说："儿子，你们哥几个就你细心，对爸爸妈妈都是这样，妈心里知道你的心意，挺好的。"

去年中秋节前，我就把妈妈接到家里来。妻子也是忙前忙后地料理着天天的吃喝，老妈很高兴。到了八月十五这一天中午，一家人围坐在一起，面对着满桌的美味佳肴，我给妈妈倒上了葡萄酒，妻子和儿子端起酒杯，在中国传统的团圆节到来之际，我们共祝愿妈妈身体好，中秋节开心快乐！妈妈乐着举起杯，看着儿子儿媳和孙子高兴地说："好。也祝你们节日快乐，祝我大孙子学习进步！"

八月十五的夜晚，中央电视台的中秋晚会，准时开始，妈妈和我们坐在沙发上，甜蜜的哈密瓜，脆甜的金丝小枣，香香的瓜子儿摆满了茶几。央视的节目热闹亲切，家中的氛围充满亲情。期间，我和妈妈来到阳台上，望着天空上圆圆的月亮，我对妈妈说："您老看多好，节日好，圆月好，一家人好，我们有老妈更好。"妈妈说："是好，看着我儿子一家，吃得好住得好心情好对妈好，妈的心情也更好……"我望着妈妈，心里想，妈妈开心快乐就好。圆月在天，映照着妈妈充满喜悦的笑脸，我也在心里祝福妈妈，更祝妈妈健康长寿。

八月十五，妈妈、儿子、儿媳、大孙子，团员幸福，充满开心，其乐融融。

2015年9月26日

怀念儿时的"井倍儿凉"

爷爷居住的地方历史较长，是一个古镇。有文字明确记载，始建于东汉，东汉丞相曹操在此建立军屯。但此前这里早已形成村落，年代已久远名不可考。可以说始于东汉，兴于明，盛于清。直到20世纪70年代古镇风貌依然，大十字街，四通八达，三十二条胡同，关闭城门后，城内居民家家户户往来自如，井然有序的街区，镇上明清建筑全然尚存。只可惜，1976年唐山大地震时这里变成一片废墟，使得古镇一切荡然无存。但是，那里还留有我的一丝童年记忆。那就是"崔克思"的"井倍儿凉汽水儿"。

"崔克思"，实名崔文光，独臂，身体魁梧。笑容常挂在脸上，一对可爱的笑眼儿，说话幽默风趣。因蓄有马克思式的胡须，人送美名"崔克思"。

儿时盛夏市面上的消夏冷品有"冰糕"，还有"冰棍儿"。二分钱一根儿。喝的冷饮就是"冰镇汽水儿"，五分一瓶。就是一个大盆里用凉冰镇着一瓶瓶的汽水。尽管那个年代物质不丰富，"冰棍""冰镇汽水儿"单调简单，但十分畅销，人们都爱吃这样的"冰棍"，喝这样的"冰镇汽水儿"。

每每夏天，镇上四街店铺、门市前卖"冰棍儿""冰镇汽水儿"的比比皆是。南来北往的人们，也纷纷停下脚步买上"冰棍儿""冰镇汽水儿"解渴祛暑。

在古镇东大街的大石桥北侧崔家大院临街的大门口前，一顶白色凉棚下，一张四方的八仙桌，四边放着四个老式的凳子，后边还有几条老式长凳。布棚前挂着一个纸板儿招牌，上面写着"井倍儿凉汽水儿"七个大字，很是惹人眼目，特别招人。这就是"崔克思"的"井倍儿凉汽水儿"。人家特别之处不是冰镇，而是水镇。街上行走、办事、路过的人们，大多驻足坐在凉棚里喝上一瓶"井倍儿凉汽水儿"解渴祛暑。

"崔克思"卖的汽水儿为啥就叫"井倍儿凉汽水儿"呢？原来呀，"崔克思"也就是崔文光的父亲是在旧社会做大买卖的，所以，崔家大院是一个买卖人家的住所，坐北朝南五进式院落。院里有一口深深的大石井。深井里的水那是天然凉凉的，把汽水儿用铁桶沉到井里一段时间再提上来，人们喝起来那是真真的凉快。我儿时专门顶着火辣的日头，从南街跑到东街花五分钱买一瓶"井倍儿凉汽水儿"喝着过瘾。

时下，继京津冀高温红色预警之后，依然持续高温，真正是夏日炎炎，热浪滚滚。这时候，真的好想念儿时在"崔克思"买的那"井倍儿凉汽水儿"。今天，虽然是社会进步了，科技发达了，生活水平提高了，但是，那一种纯天然无污染的"井倍儿凉汽水儿"的味道是彻底没有了。现在，虽然好几十年过去了，但那时一个小小子儿，穿着那个时代的"塑料凉鞋"，穿着裤衩和挎梁背心儿，咪咪着一对小眼睛，顶着一个人火辣辣的太阳，从古镇南大街，颠颠儿地跑到东大街，去买一瓶"井倍儿凉汽水儿"喝的情景，还时常清晰地显现在眼前。

48年前，我们是唐山第一支中学生抗震救灾队伍

48年弹指一挥间，时光流逝，但唐山人永远不会忘记自然界这一给唐山造成毁灭的刻骨铭心的大劫难之日，日月穿梭，但1976年7月28日，是我一生都不能忘却的日子。

亲身经历了举世罕见的1976年7月28日唐山大地震的我，时至今日仍然感到心在颤抖。大地震不仅给我留下了心灵的震颤、精神的惊恐和失去亲人的痛苦。而且，更让我深深感受到了一个未成年人，在灾难来临之时却与家人天各一方，独自一人承受天塌地陷这样的大灾大难所带来的那份惊恐、凄凉、孤独、自立、期盼、不安、惦念。每当我想起那极度恐怖无助的一幕，我始终有一种说不出的滋味和感觉。

支农南坨村

1976年唐山大地震的前三天，也就是7月25日，学校组织400多名师生来到当时的丰润县小张各庄公社南坨村参加抢荒（拔草）劳动，就是与老天争时间抢时间，给生产队拔棉田里疯长的杂草。

这里，曾是兴盛于大清和民国时期丰润县南半县一个赫赫有名的大地主家族的庄园。庄园建筑显得高大气派，气势非凡。庄园中的一座座深宅大院里，一洞洞讲究的石砌的月亮门，仍是那么考究精致；一条条长条石铺就的步行道，还是那么干干净净整整齐齐地躺在那里，两边是满院落的大块青砖铺地；院子里的拴马石和水井台，都是经过精心雕刻的，依旧显得那么赏心美感。庄园里一座座建筑的台基很高，房屋建筑形式都是前出廊后出厦的，传统的飞檐斗拱，雕梁画栋，全木质门窗的造型透着一种古香古色的中国美。就连房上的烟囱，也是飞檐凉亭式

的精巧造型设计。院子里和回廊下，当年摆放的大瓷缸、大花盆，还原封不动地摆放在原地，让人依稀可见庄园主人往日的富有与辉煌。

我就是在这片古老的土地上热诚地参加这里的支农劳动、洒下了真诚的汗水、经历了史无前例的唐山大地震，而且，我们这支支农劳动的学生队伍，在大地震发生后的第一时间变为抗震救灾队伍，在那里开展了唐山大地震中最先的学生抗震救灾活动，还有我的八个高中同学震亡在那古老的村庄里。

瞬间的凄惨

这个南坨村大地主庄园里，有各自独立的八大院落，是一座晚清时号称"八大堂"的大型庄园。虽是长堤垂柳河水环抱，但1976年7月27日这个盛夏之夜的特别闷热天气，还是让人久久难以入睡。午夜过后，我和四个支农男学生趴在村党支部副书记家东屋的炕上，拖着疲惫的身躯在窗外阵阵热风的吹拂中渐渐入睡。睡梦中，屋里靠北墙的板柜上码到房顶的好多黑色泥坛泥罐，突然间噼啪作响坠地摔得粉碎。惊醒的我由于当时不知道是地震，还以为是大黑天来了土匪在打砸北窗呢。紧接着整个三间平房的北墙全部向外轰然倒去。还是小组长林秀良脑子清醒："地震，快下炕！"并跳下去拉开房门，窜到院中，我们几个学生也急速跑了出去。西屋的村支部副书记已破窗而出，小腿被窗玻璃划出尺许的口子，流着鲜红的血。他的妻子、儿子也在院里，只有女儿身着内裤乳罩羞于见我们几个毛头小子，双手抱着双肩胳膊护着乳房不肯出来。副书记着急地大吼："快出来，再不出来，房子倒了砸死你！"副书记的妻子也在喊："闺女，你快出来吧，都啥时候了，别管穿不穿衣裳了，听话快出来，要不等会儿再震房子倒了就把你埋里边儿了。"姑娘无奈，这才羞答答地依然抱着两肩护着乳房光着脚从屋里走了出来。

我转眼望向村庄，蒙蒙天幕下偌大的庄园甚嚣尘上，烟尘弥漫，一片鬼哭狼嚎般的凄厉杂乱。昔日满庄园气势恢宏的千百间高屋大厦，一个个深宅大院，一扫去日挺拔傲然，坍塌在震颤的大地上。这突然到来的灾难，使我有生以来第一次感受到了灭顶之灾的毛骨悚然，第一次感受到大灾难毁灭的力量，第一次目睹凄惨与悲凉和自然灾害的不可抗拒……

投入救援

灰色的天空下着凉凉的丝丝细雨。房东一家人的平安无事，使得我们五个学生也放心了。我与秀良想到分别住在全村各处的同学和老师们，于是，便把临来带去换洗用的衣服拿上去找他们。我们俩来到当时为支农师生做饭的伙房处，正见一个光脊梁的男人边声嘶力竭地喊救命，边使劲撬一根非常粗重的大房梁。秀良和我拣起两根大橡子，打上嵌，帮那男人撬沉重的房梁。果然奏效，梁的一头翘起，那男人趁势钻进去上半身，拉起他喘息着的80多岁的老母亲。之后，我们一同把老人抬到空地儿。男人从废墟里扯出一块炕席，盖在他老母亲赤裸的身上。又拉住我们的手说，谢谢你们小哥俩，要不我妈就该让那大房梁给压死了……

我俩刚要迈步向别处走去，数学老师幺树行忽然迎面疾步走来，一下把秀良我们俩紧紧搂在怀里："哎哟，我的孩子们哪，你们都没事吧，我的孩子……"

这种真挚的师生之情现在想来仍然令我十分感动。老师问我们去干啥？我俩说去找找别的同学，看看他们怎么样。老师说，那去吧，我也去找找其他学生去。

我俩往西过一堵残墙，只见一群女生正蹲在一块哭，走近一问，是两个男生还埋在废墟下边。我急了：这个时候你们还哭！快扒！快！女生们这时才醒过神来了，一个个顾不得只穿内裤背心赶紧和我们并肩扒起来。因为这里的房老、砖沉、瓦重，且我们手中并无锹镐用具，所以，我们的双手都磨出了血，但总算扒出了一个男同学。他面部发青，嘴里、鼻子里、耳朵里尽是土，没知觉。又抓紧去扒第二个男同学，不知多久，好容易扒出来，像是早已没救了。有个女生说："看看吧，要是醒来哭了就有救。"果然，那男生慢慢醒过来，哭着说我找我妈去……大家流下泪水长出一口气，也把悬着的心放下了。冷不防，一个叫杨贺云的女同学，迅速解下我腰间系着的确良汗衫，穿在身上掩住她青春的乳峰。冲我一笑，陈欣这汗衫我穿了。

秀良的两件衣服分别给了另外两个女同学，之后，我们又向别处寻去。正走着，一个只穿内裤的女老师迎面走来："陈欣，你手里拿的是啥衣裳？"我说是裤子。"给我。"说罢，女老师把裤子拽了过去两下蹬上。"呀！紧点儿，凑合着，你们走吧。"我俩继续往前走，又碰到我初中的同桌左向阳同学，在落难的庄园里，从房倒屋塌的惊恐中走出来的他，像见到亲哥哥一样地痛哭着说："陈欣，我姐姐被砸死了。"我忙问，扒出来了吗？左向阳说，扒出来了。我抱住左向阳，望一眼整个毁灭的庄园，拍拍左向阳的肩无奈地安慰说："那就别哭了，向阳啊，这是天灾呀，咱们也没办法……"

天已大亮，天空仍然雨下个不停，而且是大雨如注。全村各处不管老师还是学生，都冒雨努力在坍塌的房屋下、残垣断壁中寻找营救埋在其中的村民们。这是唐山大地震发生时，第一支在第一时间投入抗震救灾的队伍，而且还是一支中学生抗震救灾队伍。这群还不知家中亲人生死的400多名支农师生，在雨中忘我抢救着当地的村民，在大瓦砾中寻找着遇难的父老乡亲们。

吕凤安、裴凤伍、韩广新、张志刚、王俊琪他们5人住的是一处青砖瓦房，房东一家住东屋，他们几个学生住西屋。强烈的震感把他们从睡梦中震醒，几个同学相继从窗户极速跳出去，房子也随着坍塌了，所幸没有被埋住。

地震发生后，顿时村子里哭声、喊声连成一片。东屋房东的小孩在废墟中撕心裂肺地号叫着，他们几个同学赶紧从瓦砾堆中扒人。当他们把房梁、檩子等搬开后，看到的是惨不忍睹的一幕：

房东夫妇被同一根檩子砸中头部已经死亡，两个小孩在父母中间因父母的身体支撑才幸免一难。

他们把两个小孩救出后，孩子不停连喊带哭地叫"妈妈"。时间不长，来了一位五十多岁的大婶，见此情景，她大哭几声，表情木然地把两个孩子接过去，原来这是小孩的姥姥。

他们几个向生产队队部走去，他们同宿舍的王俊琪的家人来找他，才得知他母亲已经在地震中遇难。王俊琪的家就在南坨村东500米的青庄坞村，两个村子紧相连。27日中午他们几个同学还到过王俊琪家，他母亲摘了好多西红柿来招待他们几个呢，想不到……

我和秀良继续向前寻找着，忽见一堆人围着。走近一看，一名村里的"赤脚医生"在为一个刚刚从废墟里扒出来的我们的女同学打强心针。她一边推针管里的药一边无奈地边说："没救了，那也打一针吧。"意思是尽心了。天上的雨，不停地打在她凝结在17岁时青春的脸上。

正当老乡和同学们为之惋惜之时，忽然有人哭嚎着喊道："哎呀我的儿子，你姐姐砸死了……"一听这话众人马上回头一看，只见一个中年男子正抱着他的儿子哭诉着。原来，他从新军屯骑自行车赶来看看在南坨支农看到儿子没事，一下子控制不住失去女儿的痛苦，抱住儿子号啕大哭起来。同学们忙围拢过来问新军屯、新军屯中学咋样了。中年男子瘫坐在地上哭天抢地地说："孩子们哪，新军屯都平了。"这一下同学们的情绪顿时沸腾紧张起来，因为学生们都对家人的一切情况都无从知晓，急切、盼归、惦记、焦虑、不安……心里滋味杂陈。

在南坨东边的欢喜庄村，张玉臣老师还带领着20多名学生驻村进行农村工作调研活动。7月27日那天晚上，闷热闷热的天儿，男孩子们一丝不挂的还嫌热呢。和老师一屋同住的两个学生刘瑞春、张爱国。把衣服全都洗了，光溜溜地睡在炕上。

老师睡觉比较轻，地震刚一颤就醒了，并马上连喊带叫地招呼他俩起来，一起跳出了敞着的南窗。人刚落地，就听身后一声闷响，回头只见房子的中间墙拍在了他们睡觉的炕上。要是晚出来一秒后果不堪想象。俩学生安然无恙，但老师的屁股被窗户的下闸子刮出了一道深深的口子，裤衩也刮破了。

在西屋的房东老太太由于地震的惊吓已经昏过去了。特定环境下也顾不得这个那个的了，刘瑞春、张爱国赤身裸体地跑进塌了半边的房子里把老太太抬到院子里来。

紧张稍稍平静，已经是夏天的4点了，天亮了。站在院子里放眼向整个村庄望去，欢喜庄村全都平了。他们师生三人赶紧帮邻近群众在废墟里扒人。在一家村民倒塌的房子下面，他们和老乡一起扒出一个压在房檩下的老人，抬到空地儿，他可能受了严重的内伤，一会儿就咽气了。他们又去找其他的学生，一处住有女生的房子倒了，里面还有一个女同学埋着。由于房倒屋塌找不到裤衩护体，刘瑞春和张爱国就找了两件女同学的上衣系在腰间遮挡住下身和大家一起抢扒。五六个同学扒了好一阵子，才把这个女学生从废墟里拔出来，但人已没救了。

舒海和一块住的四个同学还好都跑出来了，跑出来之后房子就倒了。他们就赶紧到老乡家帮着扒人去了，有一家人正在扒埋在废墟里的孩子，扒着扒着就看见那男孩的脸了。大家加紧扒，终于拔了出来，但是，这个13岁男孩儿由于窒息时间较长，还是死了。

汗水、泪水、生命奉献在这方水土

阴雨中，没吃没喝却十分紧张的抗震救灾中不知不觉已是下午，这里的救灾抢险工作基本告一段落，满身泥水的师生们向南坨村小学的操场上集结，全体师生清点、核实，有8名同学遇难，20多名师生伤势比较重，轻伤的很多。8名震亡学生的名字是李宝、左慧芳、唐玉梅、冯瑞艳、赵桂芬，还有几个同学的名字已经回忆不起来了，年仅17岁的他们，震亡在这两个从明朝就有历史记载的古老庄园和村庄里。以往朝夕相处活蹦乱跳的八名同学，此时，他们的遗体静静地躺在一刻不停的大雨中，支农师生们的泪水和雨水一起滴入这庄园的土地。

站在雨中讲话的周尚义校长高声说："老师们，同学们，这里乡亲不会忘记我们。因为我们不但在这里支农参加地里的繁重劳动，还在大地震发生的时候，积极抢险救灾，及时抢救了埋在倒塌房屋里的群众。现在师生们大都脱离了危险，除党团员全体老师和伤残师生外，其余同学可以上路回家了……"

我们这群十六七岁的学生，像一个个找不到家的小燕儿一样，望着一个个毁灭的村庄，全然不知自己父母兄弟姐妹的生死存亡，满心急切地踏上回家的路途。

48年前的我们没有汽车，没有自行车，只有心中记忆着母亲所在的方向，噙着双眼的泪水，大声呼喊着妈妈，撒开了双腿，冲着一个方向疯狂奔跑。回家的路上，空中回荡着我们这些高中生们对自己亲人们的一声声急切地呼唤……

我们所经过的村庄，各村的受灾情况不大一样，有的村房屋倒塌的很少，而多数村庄受灾非常厉害，街道两边到处是用炕席苫着的遇难者的遗体，到处是伤者的呻吟声和失去亲人后家属的痛哭声。这些村子里的村民，有的正用牲畜车、担架或直接用人背着往学校或大队部运送伤员；有的正在用竹竿、木棍、炕席、塑料布之类的东西搭一个个简易的小棚来遮挡风雨。在一个村子通往一条大沟的土路上，我们看到一辆牛车横七竖八拉着好多尸体，有的用苇席卷着，有的用塑料布裹着，后面跟着几个拿着锹镐的青壮年人。当时因为没有运输工具，几家合用了生产队的一辆车将遇难亲人的遗体掩埋掉。

当时，有的同学还不足16岁，天又一直下着雨，道路泥泞，因为没有鞋，下午3点多了还没走到家。虽然又渴又饿，但归心似箭，并没有走不动的感觉。路途上，吕凤安和裴凤伍走到一块白薯地里，见四周没人，每人偷偷地扒了一块白薯边走边吃。那个年代，纯真的学生偷吃一块白薯也觉得是非常耻辱的事情。下午4点大多数同学终于回到家中与家人团聚。

"7·28"唐山大地震过去48年了，人们不会忘记，在里氏7.8级的唐山大地震，导致24.2万多人死亡，19.4万多人重伤，7200多个家庭全家震亡，上万个家庭解体，4204个孩子成为孤儿。

大劫难，我们在南坨、欢喜庄；"7·28"，我们在南坨、欢喜庄；这古老的庄园和村庄，我们终生难忘。"7·28"，我们是唐山第一支学生抗震救灾队伍！

2024 年 7 月 28 日

月色长城

来白羊峪是 2007 年 9 月，在白羊峪林场住了七天。看长城、爬长城、拍长城，全办到了心里较为满足。

钟情白羊峪长城，一是白羊峪长城山雄关险，堪称天下第二关。二是这里声名远播的大理石长城，万里关山十分罕见，是长城的精髓所在。

虽说今天的白羊峪是山雄水美，融江南秀色、北国风光于一体，交相辉映。

二十八景星罗棋布，步步有景，景景宜人。有"列岫联珠、西山灵雾、凌岩古井、仙洞石床、旱龟断流、九龙戏珠、三羊开泰、石猴攀壁、七松登高、凤落梧桐"等古迹胜景。但我看中的是白羊峪长城的古老与雄浑、威震与沧桑。

来到白羊峪已是 9 月的一个傍晚时分，徒步山路向山间的住地走去。边走边向山路左边望去，是一道较高的山梁，山梁上一道长城横亘，一轮落日悬在白羊峪长城一个敌楼的右上方。是岁月和人为的因素吧，使这道长城让人们看来显得有些寂寞、残破。但从另一个角度去看，夕阳下，长城既让人看到它的悲壮，又让人看到它的傲然。在视线里可以看到五个敌楼，敌楼间的城墙已无明显的垛口。岁月蹉跎，敌楼虽是缺牙少口，但依然屹立在那里，显得高大而不可侵犯。

山上的大树不多，但满山树木，显得郁郁葱葱。真是暮色苍茫看劲松，巍峨长城晚霞中。

我们的住处在古长城白羊河水关西侧的山腰上，第二天我早早起来，站在住室门口向南面的长城望去。那里有一座明朝游击将军张世中题写楼名的神威楼。

这座神威楼还真有它的神奇之处，不像别的敌楼一样骑在城墙上，而是挂在城墙外（北侧），凸显了明朝将士抵御外敌入侵的勇气与决心。在人们眼里，从结构上看，它像是在附近墙上增添的一座砖质仿木硬山顶的房子，远远望去像是一座古代仿木二层楼似的，在众多的敌楼中神威楼建筑奇特雄伟、别具一格，令人刮目相看。目光所及的地方就是神威楼，所以，早就穿戴好准备上山去见神威真容颜。

当走近神威楼，我看到神威楼上上下下的每一块青砖与青砖之间，都沾和着明朝建筑工匠抹上去的白灰泥一直砌到檐椽下，这是典型的中国古代的砌墙方式。我看到，背面外墙中间开了一个箭窗，通风采光、观察敌情、向敌人发射弓矢、开炮、放枪，是一个一窗多用的地方。还有两个雷石孔在箭窗下，专门用来发射雷石打击来犯近至楼下的敌人的，箭孔与雷石孔成品字形排列，既有建筑美感，又有整齐的高低错落感和战斗的实用性。楼内简拱上的门额中嵌有石质门匾，阴刻楷书"神威楼"三个大字，左上款"游击将军张世忠题"，右下款"万历丙申仲夏吉立"。看着大字和提款，我感到一种威武在眼前，一种民族的精神在升腾，一种骄傲在心中。门券对面宇墙上砌有影壁，下有须弥座，镶嵌一块记事碑。

走出神威楼站在阳光下再看神威楼，建筑奇特雄伟的神威楼历经风雨400多年，依然挺立在山脊之上。神威楼除门窗外没用一根木头，楼顶上没有一片青瓦，但砖制的仿木结构是那么的惟妙惟肖，并且增加了敌楼的坚固程度。我觉得，这不但显示了明朝防御工程的设计精美，形式考究，建筑坚固，且实用化，人性化，还显示了中国人的建筑智慧和建筑技艺的高超。

次日清晨，我再次出门向被人称为"马圈""阅兵城"的谎城进发。山中晨雾一路陪伴，到达山顶时，山雾已经湿透了我的头发和衬衫。登上白羊峪长城古白羊水关东侧制高点上的谎城，立于漫漫雄关之前，不由得让我心生感慨。顿时觉得，虽经古今风霜雨雪，战乱遭劫，但如今谎城雄姿犹在，易守难攻，可望而不可及。走在城中，漫步在3000平方米的空间。让我看到这是一座一方面可以用来迷惑敌人，另一方面可集中储存粮草、马匹、士卒的军用袖珍城，不愧是白羊峪长城防御体系中的一种独创，也是中国人运用兵法战术的出奇之处。

我居高临下，俯视着白羊峪口山雄关险，在这古往今来关内通往塞北的咽喉之地，感觉那"一夫当关万夫莫开"的气势。环顾四周山高峰险，山巅之上长城蜿蜒，烽火台（马圈）、水关、都察院等古代边关防御体系完整地汇集在此。

一天的学习结束之后，吃过晚饭，同宿去打牌，我则坐在窗前的石鼓凳上看眼前的长城。夜幕下的长城在山梁上东西走向，多半轮在山雾中显得有些昏黄的月亮，悬在白羊峪长城之上，给我一种雾蒙蒙的苍凉之感。遥想燕国、秦朝……

直到明朝在这里的戍边将士们，就是在这样寂静的一个个夜晚，或披星戴月，或风雪交加，或电闪雷鸣，或伸手不见五指，都要时刻睁眼竖耳，注视长城外敌人的动向，警惕奔马铁蹄的声响。为保家卫国，耐得住那一方寂寞与冷清、那一份孤独与苦楚，那一种艰辛与坚守。在长城沿线英勇戍边，保卫着长城内的家国河山。

住在白羊峪林场的旅游的人们在住地的歌厅里纵情高歌，深情演唱。我在山中月下琢磨着有关白羊峪长城的记述。有资料这样说："白羊峪长城始建于北齐（公元550—577年）时均为石砌，宽仅3米。北周灭北齐后略有修补。明朝初期，徐达置各于要隘修筑关口城；隆万年间，谭纶和刘应节等蓟辽总督、戚继光等蓟镇总兵官组织多次加固，重要地段用砖包修，宽度增至5—6米，并增设敌楼、炮台等军事防御设施。"另有资料这样说："白羊峪长城为战国时燕国所建，明朝时修复加固，其中城楼21座，保存完好的长城4552米。"

我不去探究哪一种说法对错，但两种说法的共同点是"明朝时修复加固了长城"。最值得我们骄傲的是让万里长城格外增添光辉的白羊峪"大理石长城"。

这段3华里长的大理石长城，由珍贵的棕红色大理石作基石，在中华万里长城建筑中绝无仅有，是长城的精髓，用今天的话来说是珍品。就地取材用大理石修建长城，当时的长城建筑指挥者和建设者，也许并没想到他们建筑的这段既大方又美观，且壮观坚固的长城，在高山险峰之巅修砌得整整齐齐，熠熠生辉，堪称长城一绝。时至今日，已成为国家乃至世界防御工程范围内的艳丽瑰宝。

望着白羊峪的夜空、群山、长城、月色，深谷，我心里在想，白羊峪这块历来的兵家必争之地，春秋战国，大秦御匈，清兵入关，奉军入关，日寇入关，白羊关一直是要道。古往今来，历史苍茫，岁月悠悠，长城穿越时空近3000年，沧桑历览日月星辰，明月从战国时一直照耀到今日，不知道各个不同历史时期的戍边将士们是否有过篝火欢歌、筝琴弹奏、畅饮美酒、家乡小调、狂放劲舞。白羊峪的月色长城，白羊峪的长城月色，你让我想了很多很多……

白羊峪泉水如珍珠般的涌出来，一条清澈的静静白羊河水自北向南穿过关口，四季长流。看着白羊峪这般青山绿水，风景雄浑秀丽，如诗如画的雄关山水，着实让我感叹白羊峪无愧于"北国江南"的美誉。随着人们的生活富裕，在当地政府和有识之士的努力下，白羊峪重振雄风，古朴典雅，日臻宏大。白羊峪已进入一个新境界，呈现一派大好风光。我看到了昔日雄关的风采，正伴随着国人的"中国梦"和迁安的腾飞一同迈入小康时代，走向更加美好的未来！

难忘父亲演奏过的《彩云追月》

随着年龄的增长，我对父亲的思念越来越强烈。在许许多多的儿时记忆里，其中有一段老是像电影一样，时不时地萦绕在我的脑海，闪现在我的眼前，回荡在我的耳边。

20世纪60年代，我老家的北院、南院都长有大树，直到70年代末才伐掉，树大成荫，夏天夜晚，树下乘凉唠嗑，人们乐在其中。在税务所工作的父亲，有时和同事们吃完晚饭，就会聚在我家南院的大树下面，铺在地上的大凉席上坐着几个大人说着我不懂得的话题。有时父亲也会给同事们演奏或二胡或扬琴的民族乐器，大家都很喜欢听父亲的乐器演奏。一天晚上，父亲和同事们在外面吃完晚饭后一起回到家来。简单说了几句话，他们便拿上凉席往南院大树下的地上一铺，父亲的几个同事坐在其上，父亲高兴地拿来小提琴，站在树下，把小提琴架在左肩和左下颚之间，冲大家一笑便拉响了小提琴。父亲拉琴时的姿态洒脱优雅，弓走弦上，琴声婉转悠扬，大家人人听得都很陶醉。

那时的我，完全不知道这曲子是啥曲子，只知道很好听，很优美。直到20世纪80年代我才知道，父亲演奏的这支最早见于清代，源自清代广东民间粤音曲谱，系著名的粤音曲谱的《彩云追月》，其风格轻快独特，描写了小市民平凡生活的轻松写意，彰显了典型的广东民间音乐风格。李鸿章任两广总督时曾将此曲抄送大内演奏。

20世纪30年代由中国作曲家任光（1900—1941）整理重编，成曲于1935年。

1960年，彭修文根据中央广播民族管弦乐团的乐队编制重新配器。

《彩云追月》，父亲用小提琴演奏过这首描写人们心目中的月宫仙境的中国名曲，我一直记忆犹新，但父亲已在天国。追思父亲，遥想，在天国可能也会演奏这美妙动听的乐曲吧……

48 前爸爸那翘望期盼的眼神

唐山大地震已经过去48年了，但我一直没有忘记1976年7月28日那天下午，父亲站在十字街翘首张望，期盼我平安归来的眼神。

大地震发生的时候，我和同学们一起正在丰润南坨村参加支农劳动。1976年7月27日这个盛夏之夜天气特别闷热，直到午夜过后，我和同屋的5个支农学生，才在窗外阵阵热风的吹拂中渐渐进入了梦乡。睡梦中，突然响声大作，我们所在的3间平房整堵北墙全部向外轰然倒去，我们几个同学也迅速地跑了出去。

住在西屋的村党支部副书记已破窗而出，小腿被窗玻璃划出尺许长的口子，伤处皮肉翻卷，鲜血淋漓。副书记的妻子、儿子、闺女都安然无恙。

我与同学林秀良想到分别住在全村各处的同学和老师们，便去找他们。我们俩经过当时为支农师生做饭的伙房处，正见一个光脊梁的男人边声嘶力竭地喊救命，边使劲撬一根非常粗重的大房梁。秀良和我拣起两根大椽子，打上嵌，帮那男人撬沉重的房梁。这一招果然奏效，梁的一头翘起，那男人趁势钻进去上半身，拉出他那位惊慌失措连连喘息的80多岁老母亲。之后，我们一同把老人抬到空地儿。细雨中，男人拉住我们的手说，谢谢小哥俩，要不是你们帮忙，我妈就被那大房梁给压死了……

我俩往西走过一堵残墙，见一群女生正蹲在一块哭，走近一问，是两个男生还埋在废墟下边。我一听就急了："这个时候你们还哭！快扒！快救人！"

这时她们才像如梦方醒，赶紧和我们并肩扒起来。因为房老、砖沉、瓦重，且我们手中并无锹镐用具，所以，我们的双手都磨出了血，但总算扒出了一个男同学。他面部发青，嘴里、鼻子里、耳朵里尽是土，没知觉。我们又抓紧去扒第二个男同学，不知多久，好容易扒出来，好像是已经死了。有个女生迟疑着说："听大人说过，这种情况只要哭了就有救。"奇迹还真发生了，那男生竟慢慢苏醒过来，"哇"的一声哭了，抽搭着说："我找我妈去……"大家这才长出一口气，把悬在喉咙里的心放回原处。

我俩再往前走，路上又碰到我初中时的同桌左向阳同学，在这落难的庄园里，房倒屋塌的惊恐中走出来的他，像见到亲哥哥一样，紧紧地抱住我："陈欣，我姐姐被砸死了。"我忙问："扒出来了吗？"左向阳说："扒出来了……"我无奈地安慰他说："向阳啊，这是天灾呀，咱们也没办法，你就别哭了……"

我们继续向前寻找着，忽见有一堆人聚拢在一起。过去一看，是村里的"赤脚医生"在为一个刚刚从废墟里扒出来的女同学打强心针。她一边推针管里的药，一边无奈地说："没救了，那也打一针吧。"意思是尽心了。这个女同学仰天躺在地上，天上的雨，不停地飘落在她17岁青春的脸上。

时至下午，救灾抢险工作基本告一段落。满身泥水的师生们向南坨村小学的操场集结。李宝、左慧芳、唐玉梅、冯瑞艳4名震亡同学的遗体也被抬来。烟雨迷蒙中，校长铿锵有力地说："老师们，同学们，这里的群众，这里的乡亲是不会忘记我们的。因为我们不但在这里支农，参加地里的繁重劳动，还在大地震发生的时候，和这里的群众一起抢险救灾，及时地抢救了埋在倒塌房屋里的群众。现在师生们大都脱离了危险，经研究决定，党团员留下，继续参加抢险救灾。全体老师留下，也参加抢险救灾。受伤的师生为防止伤情恶化也得留下，等待救治。其余同学可以回家了……"

回家的路上我们没有汽车，没有自行车，只有对家人的惦记，只有浸满双眼的泪水，撒开双腿向着家的方向狂奔。阴沉沉的天空中，回荡着我们这些学生们对自己亲人的一声声急切地呼唤……

等我回来一看，到处废墟一片没有一处挺立的房屋，好在昔日的街道还分明。我远远看见爸爸站在十字街头张望着，我跑过去却看见爸爸手里拄着一个棍子，再看右脚上缠着纱布。原来是在从废墟里扒我姥爷的时候，让枣核钉子穿透了脚掌。但他看到儿子回来了还是喜出望外的，仔细看看我说，回来就好……

48年了，爸爸当时那种盼望儿子归来的眼神，时常浮现在我的眼前。我理解当时心里着急的爸爸不知道儿子的情况如何，可自己有伤又动不了，能做到的只有等待、盼望。所以，我一直忘不了48年前爸爸那翘首期盼儿子归来的急切眼神。

2024年7月28日

笛声响

凌晨，下着小雨。人们打着各色雨伞，进出于车站。车站里，电机车的汽笛，不时地鸣叫……

月台的水泥地面上，两行带雨水的脚印，时疏时密，像首诗，像首歌……

玲抬头，深情的双眼望着华，华——年轻的矿工，也低头凝视着玲那深情的眸子，这眸子使他再次联想到乌金那晶莹颗粒。华想对玲笑一笑，倏地看到那"颗粒"上漾着一汪"清水"，笑意在脸上蓦地消失了。玲低下头，刘海遮住双眼，紧紧挽着华。

华想对玲说些什么，却一时找不到话题。小雨飘在天地间，落在月台上……笛声响。玲想：若是发车的笛声永远不响；车就永远不会进站了，那么我……他们心里这么想，谁也不敢先看一眼对方，无声的雨，沉默的人，任时间分分秒秒的流逝……

车窗里，华向着那"黑颗粒"笑了。

玲扬起手，像是一盏明亮的矿灯，华扬起手臂，像是那高擎的割煤机摇臂……

1986年7月10日

黑色的歌——为矿工们而作

烧一辈子煤的人不一定知道矿工的模样，认识矿工的人不一定懂得煤海深沉厚重的胸膛。只知道没有煤的燃烧就没有温暖如春的厅堂，就没有奔腾的钢流和钢花怒放……

矿工们喜欢阳光，却天天在阳光下乘罐来到井下，和着机械的隆隆作响，采掘滚滚乌金闪亮。

若说天上最炽热火红的是太阳，那地上最炽热火红的就是矿工们的心房。掌子面上那一个个忙碌的矿工，他们像不像一轮轮周身散发着光和热的太阳？

消夏时节，悠闲的人们在歌厅酒吧潇洒，浪漫海滨红男绿女。而矿区大地上一座座井架高耸，一个个天轮飞转，像一艘艘航船，正扬帆远航。

大年三十，井下没有佳肴美酒，没有爆竹烟花，没有轻歌曼舞。却有割煤机的高唱，却有满载原煤的矿车一趟趟，却有矿工们的神采飞扬……

其实，矿工就如航海水手，无论春夏秋冬忙碌无暇。在海上什么样的波澜壮阔、什么样的艰难险阻、什么样的悲壮与激情都会遇上。当你细心倾听过矿工们那心中深沉激昂的歌，你会倍感曲折、畅想而又荡气回肠。

阴雨天里那颗颗暖人的心

天天上午坚持走步，2023年7月4日早上5点，像往常一样走出小区大门一路向北慢步而去。不想，一个半小时后在回来快到家的路上天上下起了小雨，我在树下躲了一会见雨势不停就就近来到一个公园的凉亭里避雨。就是在避雨的时段里有三段对话让我感受到了暖人的心。

走步大约40分钟后到了河边大桥顺甬道往下走，一抬眼又看到了那些河边、甬道边的树木，由于刚栽种时为防止被风刮倒而在树干上绑上木框，再附上三根木棍作为支撑。几年时间过去了，树木长势良好，支撑树木不倒的松木棍已不知去向，但绑在树干上的木棍四框却被用铁丝死死绑在树干上。树木长得快，但有木棍四框这段明显困住了，木棍四框上下两端凸显鼓包，而被木棍四框束缚的地方不能正常生长，甚至铁丝已勒入树木之中。见此情景，我的心里不禁有一种痛苦挣扎很不舒服的感觉，于是手机拍下发到圈里。没有想到，一位善良的微友看到了朋友圈的镜头，打来电话商定明早开车拉我一起到河边去解决树木被捆绑之痛。这个电话，让我替树木感到心暖和欣慰。

约好一起去做善良的事，善良的人，善良的心。

朋友清早互道一声好，天天如是。不例外，阴雨天也不断档。恰在我刚进公园凉亭避雨坐定看手机时，一条早上问候祝福显现出来。我惯例语音回复："早安吉祥！我在走步回来时，天上下起了小雨。在公园小亭里避雨，天儿挺凉快，也祝你开心愉快！"

凉亭里我在手机上翻看各个群里的信息，凉亭外阴雨缠绵不停。一会儿电话响了："哥哥你好，现在在哪儿呢，刚好我出来办点事儿，发个位置我顺便去接你把你送你回家。"阴雨丝丝中带来的风都是凉凉的，但此时此刻，接到这样一个的话，确实让我心里热热的。风雨中，朋友要开车来接我送一程到家，这是何等的情谊呀。但我不忍心让朋友冒雨来接我送我，于是说，一会儿雨停了我就回家了。谢谢，别开车来了，我再等一会儿……

真诚的人，友爱的心，风雨无阻的友情暖人心。

放下手机看看天，雨还在下且没有停的征兆。想想离家也不远了，紧走几步往回赶吧。可是，不出凉亭不知道，一出凉亭才感觉到这小雨下得还挺密，急忙跑到路边的大梧桐树下走，但这雨下时间长了梧桐树也在滴雨。好在离家不远的未来城就在前面，疾步走到一条走廊处。刚站定，手机响了：爸在哪儿？我说在咱们小区对过路北未来城的一个走廊下。我说。好，那我就不动车了，走过去送伞吧。儿子说。

不一会儿，密密麻麻的雨丝中见到一米八高的儿子，长裤白T恤，左手里拿着一把伞，右手打着一顶大伞，在马路对过向我走来。见到我说：我的个爸呀，看天气不好就带把伞出来。好了，怕你冷，拿来长袖上衣穿上吧。把大伞给你，咱们回家。

雨中走来的儿，懂事的儿，心怀一颗爱父的心。

给树松绑

天天早上坚持走步的我，7月4日早上5点，像往常一样出了小区大门一路向北慢步而去。走步大约30分钟后，来到了南湖大道南坡下的龙泉河南岸顺大桥边的曲径往下走，一抬眼又看到了河边和甬道边的那些火炬树，由于刚栽种时为防止被风刮倒，人们在树干上绑上木框，下面再附上三根松木棍作为支撑固定。几年时间过去了，树木长得很快，支撑树木不倒的松木棍儿已不知去向，但绑在树干上的木棍四框却依然被铁丝死死绑在树干上。树干的其它部位照常生长，但有木棍四框这段明显被束缚住而不能正常生长了，木棍四框上下两端凸显鼓包，甚至，更惨的是有的铁丝已深深勒入树木之中。让人看了觉得像人被五花大绑，绳勒入骨惨不忍睹。见此情景，我心里不禁有一种痛苦挣扎很不舒服的感觉。

于是，第二天，也就是2023年7月5日清晨，我带着螺丝刀5点30分准时来到河边，在一棵棵树干上一一拆掉被铁丝死死绑在树干上的木框，解决掉树木的被捆绑之痛。

在我拆卸这些树干上的木框的时间里，不时有往来于河边散步的人们停下脚步围观。当他们明白我是在为树松绑时，有的对我友善一笑，有的向我竖起大拇指，有的说："一看你就是个善良人，虽然这些树不会说话，但你的善良天地可鉴。为你点赞！"面对这些友好的人们我也报之以微笑，以示感谢，继续为一棵棵树木解除捆绑之苦。虽然我的头上身上沾了不少的树叶和尘土，螺丝刀的手柄因为铁丝绑得紧，紧勒着树干很费劲儿而弄坏了，我的右手大拇指也有些出血。但是，经过两个多小时的时间，还是为17棵火炬树解除了被捆绑之痛苦。从今以后，它们就再不会被束缚，可以放开了自由生长了。

2023年7月7日清晨5点30分，我这回带了电工钳子再次来到河边，继续为火炬树一一拆掉被铁丝死死绑在树干上的木框。在这期间，有一位在河边散步的老者停下脚步问我："你是园林的？"我说不是。"那你咋管这事儿啊？"我说看着这些树受罪我心里边不好受。老者一笑说："你真是个大善人。"并竖起大拇指说："你是这份的。俗话说，人在做，天在看哪。你这大好人一定有好报哇。"说完微笑着走了。剩下的几棵火炬树，我也解除了它们的被捆绑之苦。怀善心，做善事，成善为。大善无言，存于天地间。

最后，回到大路边完成最艰巨的给树松绑任务。因为，这里的树高树粗，铁丝绷得更紧。为这里我不知名的七棵树松绑费时费力，右手的中指和无名指上也磨出了两个大泡，但还是坚持为它们松完了绑。

放下钳子站在大树旁看着眼前这些被我松绑的树木,我也为这些树木感到欣喜和欣慰。自言自语说,你们自由啦,以后的日子里茁壮成长吧……

回家的路上,晴空万里一片湛蓝,阳光灿烂,我的心里也一样充满灿烂阳光……

第五辑
向阳而歌

向东方

  又是朝阳映碧海辉煌，独步沙滩，寄我欢欣想往，立蓝色之岸，身影修长。向东方唱支歌，荡气回肠。啊，我的太阳。

1983 年

仲夏旭日

  仲夏凌晨，我站在海边礁石上，眺望远方海平线，怀着一个热切期望——看日出。
  北戴河海滨鸽子窝前的海涛声，摧动着钟表的时针，激动着人们的心，召唤着欲升的红日。
  亘古的大海，亿万年的深沉，亿万年的无私，亿万年的厚道；孕育了生命的细胞，奉献了爱子太阳，托付着人类生存的大船。
  日月星辰，朝夕往复，唯有太阳亮彻大地和海洋。眼前大海躁动，一轮朝阳喷薄而出，冉冉而升，人群沸鼎海欢腾。彩霞绚丽，朝阳升起，人们在她的光芒下走向前方，心中留下美好。太阳最红，阳光最暖，阳光下大地明媚山河壮美。
  仲夏日出，我终生难忘。

1985 年

七月的太阳

七月的第一个清晨，一片朝霞，绚丽了天空的东方。

我站在海边礁石上，把海平线眺望，看日出，是我怀着的一个热切的期望。

日月星辰，朝夕往复，唯有太阳亮彻大地和海洋。

耳畔轻轻的海浪，多像南湖之上上共产党人在悠闲地划桨。

眼前被哥伦布称为"金子城"的一轮朝阳，在大海的激荡之下喷薄而出，冉冉而上。

人群沸腾了，大海沸腾了。人们欢呼看到了海上日出，大海欢呼这就是光明。

共产党像太阳，照到哪里哪里亮。

这歌词填进了陕北老农的歌声里，从此便唱出了《东方红》是那么的嘹亮。

七月的太阳，灿烂辉煌，在这个季节，诞生了中国共产党。

太阳渐渐升高，光芒照耀井冈山、延安、西柏坡、天安门城楼一片灿烂阳光。

香港紫荆花怒放、澳门荷花盛开、西域古国再现妖娆，人们在她的光芒下心里留下美好，喜悦走向前方。

太阳最红，阳光最暖。21世纪的中华大地分外妖娆，锦绣河山更加壮丽，五千年古国更加繁荣兴旺。

七月的太阳，我终生难忘。

荣获1989年7月《中国开发报》举办诗歌大奖赛一等奖。

你已把我占据

　　在烂漫季节，不期而遇一个落落大方的你，很想了解你，疑惑这是一见钟情，却未走近你。过了十个世纪，环境聚集了我和你，虽事过境迁，但记忆的录像没有抹去你，岁月风霜没有凋零你，还是一个那么洒脱，美丽，可爱的你。许是生活的偏爱，在那个无味的夏季，我看到一个不甘寂寞，不甘无为，不甘消沉，青春勃发的你。不知因我，不知因你，你我相会总是那么温馨甜意。我想象中的是你，我爱慕中的是你，想帮助我的是你，想倾诉于我的是你，想无间于我的是你。你你你，让我难忘怀的你。

　　1992年刊登在香港《世界散文诗作家》。

可知我心

　　面对东方红日，我久久凝视。你辉煌诱人。初向你倾诉，我是那么清纯，要献你一腔我的热血与童贞。

　　沿着起飞你的弧线，我穿过莽原、丛林，跨过山河、海川，尽尝艰辛……

　　数年留恋，苦苦追寻，我亦欢喜我亦忧。

　　久阴的时空，崩溃了我的思念，令我不忍让你负重我爱，向你道珍重，心却已碎……

　　一个亮丽的晴朗，见你爱明媚依然，说是时刻没有忘却，邀我同步背离寒冷冬季。我死灰样沉寂的心哟，重被你爱点燃，破窗拥抱你，展望明天会更好，但我复圆的心，渴望中倍感疲惫，再不愿在祈盼与等待的海洋里漫游，虽然你是我爱。

1993年

日全食

  两千五百年的等待，冰原雪域里，时针一丝丝的过滤着阴冷天幕上的黑太阳，得以让我仔细透析你的五脏六腑七情六欲；麻木的双腿支撑着我贯注全神的双眼，凝神倾听你动情的诉说……

  深墨镜下，品味你的孤独情怀，领悟你积蓄久远的希望，竟在瞬间破灭，月亮背后隐现你的热切和不堪回首的往昔。更顿悟，你给我那么多漫长无奈的等待的所在。缓缓复出，象征你滴血的坎坷心路……

  再有日月慧地球（太阳月亮彗星地球同在这次日全食中出现）同在要等两千五百年啦，明白了你壮美的过去，理解了你苍茫心境，天真、失落、自信、奔放……啊，我的太阳，让一切尽在无言中吧……

1997 年 3 月 9 日

天狗

  一个圆满之后，月就稍稍隐没了，日光捣碎我心，痛苦的泪淌成殷红的血……

  为何你要化痴情为泡影，红日啊，你是灿烂的魔鬼，我要做天狗，吞吃你的残酷，日全食的到来，即是清风送明月……

1994 年

不再追随

　　遥望夕阳，我步履蹒跚，走在铺满红尘的小路上，啊，我迷恋了多少年华的太阳哟，你光芒初露，我便心潮澎湃，向往你那灿烂。你看似憨厚，渡海可吻，却未等我下海就腾升，继而高远，灼热、凌空万物。我疾步山巅打起手蓬，构想起飞你的航线。春夏秋冬伴我孤帆船影。

　　望火红晚霞里残淹的落日，我无奈叹息之余也庆幸你的落没，这会令你冷静沉思，领悟并未超凡脱俗。也许，明朝你再度辉煌，却难起动我伤感痛苦的心车，没有追随的怠速。

2001 年 8 月 30 日

夕阳

　　孟春，远方小岛一个少年凝立，西方红日映红那天那云，更映红少年的脸庞，一切呈现玫瑰般灿烂。仲夏黄昏，夕阳悬在地球的边缘，延缓坠落时刻，一个青年赶在路途遥远处。

　　季秋晚霞里，残阳如血，枫红、草绿、白杨叶金黄，青年望眼在天涯，一片片云朵浸晚情，说不尽去日惆怅，留下静谧，留下孤独，留下深刻。世上只有一个青年。

圆明园

圆明园，我凝眸你面前，你苍凉俯瞰，明媚灿烂。圆明园，维纳斯留下一个观念：孤独的美丽，会被耻辱；绝世的纯洁会被强暴。圆明园，伟大的痛苦，壮丽的悲哀，你含泪注目，破碎的童贞，渴望阳光温馨玉体，重领风骚，辉煌 21 世纪。

写于 1994 年 1 月《人民文学》创刊四十五周年笔会

经纬依然

望高天流云，追寻你歌絮蓝天情醉云的那个季节。

柔风，小草，流水，曾窃听你我亲亲心语，掩藏你我厮磨的脚印，偷录了你我缠绵的吻。忽然不测飓风来，茫茫然迷失了你的身影。

目睹一轮夕阳的孤独，耳闻一只归鸟的哀伤，经历冬夜热切漫长的思念，我努力拯救残淹的炉火，企盼温馨一片。多少次风中徘徊，多少次雨中放飞，多少次阳光下远望。

一行大雁衔春天红日飞来。一只大雁引颈振翅，依呀问我该是经纬多少？

哟，这久违的声音啊，是我失落了几多日夜爱的问询，牵挂了我几多岁月的不了情。

北方，经纬依然，依然。

1986 年

精灵

一个宇宙的精灵，漂游在浩瀚太空，回荡着阵阵寻觅的呼唤。

盘古开了天地即化作山河，夏娃产下众生便失踪，金字塔下木乃伊，秦皇墓边千军万马世称奇，巴比伦的衰亡，玛雅人的破落。宇宙飞船、UFO，不懈求索。

游荡、游荡，数万光年一日还，却不见我同类的生息地，看不到文明皇冠的光芒。

遥远有座金子城，灿灿不息照苍穹，奔向她，述说一切疑问。

注：哥伦布寻找印度时，在海上称太阳为金子城。

2001年8月30日

一篇获奖散文诗成全了好姻缘

1993年在《当代文坛》杂志举办的获得全国当代文坛力作征文大赛上，我的散文诗《仲夏情思》获得了征文大赛诗歌创作一等奖。然而，就是这篇获奖作品引来了2000年的一段故事。

那年春节刚过单位都上班了，当时我在党委宣传部工作，午饭时间刚要下楼去食堂吃午饭，办公桌上的电话铃声响了。拿起电话接听："请问陈欣在吗？"我说我就是，你是？"我是二邢，给大哥拜年来了。"他是我一个朋友小邢的弟弟，原本没有太多联系，我赶紧下楼迎他并去饭店……

饭桌上我们边吃边唠。他说："哥你知道我为啥给你拜年来吗？"我说哥哪知道哇，这么多年你哥我俩倒是常来常往，今天你这是？

他满脸欣喜地说："哥，我是专程前来感谢大哥你的。"我说啥事儿值得让老弟这么神圣仪式感啊？他说："那值得。前一段时间吧我处了一女朋友，我们相互之间感情很好，她人不错的，对我也不错，时间长了慢慢地也就想到结婚了。可她和家里人一说之后她父母不同意，说是我买不起房，将来结了婚住在哪里呀？哥你知道我的情况，我是真的买不起房。这也确实是个问题，我也不怪她的父母。但也无奈，谁让我没钱呢，自己心里很是郁闷。一天下了班，我百无聊赖地躺在床上漫无目的地瞎翻东西看。忽然翻到哥你在1993年写的那一首散文诗，就是那年哥你获得全国当代文坛力作征文大赛诗歌创作一等奖的那首散文诗《仲夏情思》，还记得吗？"我说记得呀。"哥，你说我这个穷小子那才是癞蛤蟆想吃天鹅肉呢，躺在床板上，望着房顶，没钱买房还舍不得心爱的姑娘，咋办？咋办？？你兄弟我看着手里哥这篇《仲夏情思》散文诗冥思苦想，忽然灵机一动。哥诗里的内容就充分表达了我的心情。我清楚地知道此时的自己啥也没有，对我心爱的姑娘，只有一颗真诚的心奉上，只有让我的一颗心去打动她吧。思来想去，决意一搏。傍晚到电话亭给她家里打了一个电话，约她晚饭后出来，我把憋在心里话和她说完就没事儿了。她如约而至，我们来到陡河边边走边聊，找了一块长着青草的地方坐下。我对她说，我是真的买不起房，这也确实是个问题，我不怪你的父母。可是我也是确实舍不得你呀，真稀罕你，心里咋也撂不下，那也无奈，只有我自己心里郁闷，写了一首诗想念给你。听完之后，你可以走你的，我把对你的爱留在心里就是了。当我读着的时候，她静静地听着，听着听着她哭了：这是你写的？那就别念了，就凭你这颗心，我们家里反对我也嫁给你。没有房我们可以共同努力去挣钱攒钱将来买，有你的爱我就知足了……"

1999年10月，他们结婚了，农历正月就给我拜年来了。他也实话告诉了妻子说：那一篇感动你的诗，是我的一位好大哥写的，内容代表了我的心声，所以，我借来向你表白了。

听完他的故事，虽然他欺世盗名了，但我心里还是不禁感到欣慰，我那一首曾经获得当代文坛力作征文大赛诗歌一等奖的散文诗《仲夏情思》，竟然成全了一段好姻缘，也算是一件很好的事！

人性的光芒

中央电视4频道的《发现之旅》栏目曾经报道：我国考古人员在对黄河故道的考古挖掘中，惊奇地发现凝固于七千多年前的人性文明的一幕：一个女性双膝跪地，头惊恐地仰望着苍穹，双臂把一个幼童拢在怀里，双手紧紧抱着幼童，幼童紧紧依偎在她的怀中。

根据考古环境人们推断，这是当时人类遇到了突然袭来的抗拒不了自然灾害——特大洪水。但人性的本能特别是母性的本能是保护孩子。所以，这位生活在远离今天文明社会七千多年前的伟大母性，面对灭顶之灾的时候，本能的保护自己的孩子免受伤害。虽然，时至今日母子俩只以骨骼存在，但仍闪烁着远古人性可歌可泣的光芒……

时光飞逝，公元 2008 年 5 月 12 日 14 点 28 分这个全世界铭记的时刻。相似的情景再现于四川省汶川县北川的一个家庭里：楼房倒塌的危难之时，一位母亲双膝跪地上身前倾，双手撑地，护住她的孩子。2008 年 5 月 13 日中午救援队员在这座废墟下实施救援时，看到这令人感动的一幕。虽然母亲已经停止了呼吸，地上一个三四个月的小女孩安然无恙。是她的母亲用躯体挺住了塌下来的天，这定格在历史瞬间的一幕，让看到的每一个人怎能不动容，怎能不心颤，在能不潸然泪下……

救援人员在小孩的小花被里发现一个手机，手机的屏幕上留着母亲写给孩子的遗言："亲爱的宝贝，如果你要活着，请记住我爱你……"看到这里，我不禁要喊：母亲伟大，人性伟大！人性永放光芒！

四川省汶川县的一所学校里：在山崩地裂，房倒屋塌，课上师生生命受到极度威胁的危急时刻，讲台上的老师疾呼学生逃生保命，就在楼房倒塌的瞬间还在召唤学生躲在讲台下。四个学生的生命保住了，但老师双手召唤学生的姿势和生命却永远凝固在了这一时刻。

在电视报道中我看到：是一位遭到震灾袭击以至骨折的市民，把一个周岁左右的小女孩送到临时医院。而当小女孩的亲生父母来到医院时人们才惊愕地知道，小女孩在地震发生时与姥姥在一起。只是姥姥在惨剧发生的刹那间，奋力将小女孩抛出屋外，才保住了这个幼小的生命，可是老人却遇难了。

2023 年 12 月 18 日 23 时 59 分。甘肃省临夏回族自治州积石山县发生 6.2 级地震。12 月 21 日 14 时许，在海东市民和县草滩村 2 号点一处民宅，消防指战员在奋力挖掘，寻找失联人员。随后，一个令人悲伤的场景出现，泥土中 3 个成年人围成一个圈看似在保护着什么，救援人员用手快速将周围的泥水刨开，抬出 3 个成年人后发现他们用棉被包裹着 2 个小孩。

看到这一幕后，在场的消防救援人员无法抑制悲恸，眼含隐隐的泪水，细心地用手捧出泥水，又怕太慢，只能加快手刨的速度。待人员全部挖出后，现场进行了集体默哀。

一件件，一幕幕，古往今来，从今至古，在人类发展壮大的过程中，无不闪烁着人性的光芒。人性与生俱来，与生命同在，代代相传。人类之所以繁衍至今，与人性的存在关系至密，是人性的光芒，照耀灾难的夜空，指引生命成长，是人性穿越时空的一脉相承，才有这生命永生不息的高昂赞歌。

朋友，我想对你说

常听人这样说也常看人这样写，什么人生如歌啦，岁月如水呀。要我看，这做成一件事依然是如歌似水。转眼几年过去了，蓦然回首，出书的念头念念如故。2006 年底，公司高层领导以朋友的角度关心了这件事，并以极大的热情聚集各方力量支持书的出版与发行。这对我来说是一种无形的鼓舞。因为，一个写作的人，他最大的希望就是要把他对事物的观察、认识、求索，用他自己的语言和表达方式告诉给他的读者。正如我在《陈欣作品选》的前言里所写到的："苍天却给我以滋润的雨露和温暖的阳光；游云给我以向往与遐想；大地给我赖以生长所需的五谷杂粮；山峰让我领略挺拔高昂；江河让我得知血脉流长。可是，我这一微乎其微的宇宙尘埃，拿什么来奉献给你——上苍、大地。只有将我这一点微不足道的认知、领悟、情感，还有一颗感恩的心，流于笔端，虔诚奉上……"

出书，对写作者来说，既是自己对读者的一个小结性的交代，也是对自己的一个阶段性的总结。但是，从计划出书到真正出书，在这个过程里，却让我结交了许多的朋友，从各级作家协会到出版社，朋友们的行为让我感知，大家为我支付了太多的心血。同时，我更接受了许多热心朋友的帮助、支持和鼓励。现在，书已由作家出版社出版，面对我这些真诚的朋友们，我在不停地问自己：我拿什么奉献给你？思前想后，还是说一句真诚的话来表达吧："只有将我这一点微不足道的认知、领悟、情感，还有一颗感恩的心，流于笔端，虔诚奉上。"

拾级七步有乾坤

在唐山市丰南区府所在地胥各庄贯通东西的十里文化大街上，有一栋充满文化色彩的建筑——七步楼，在冬日阳光照耀下十分显眼。

站在全部地上四层，但中间两层楼外墙用近百幅不同风格书法"集古轩博物馆"字样装饰的七步楼前，一种不可抗拒的文化气息扑面而来，让人感觉别具一格！走近再看，只见七步楼的大门口挂着华夏精短文学学会华北分会、丰南区文化驿站、丰南区非遗客厅、丰南书法家协会牌子。不觉间一股吸引力强烈袭来，不禁拾级七步推开大门，走进"七步楼"一看究竟。进得门来只见左侧是翟氏锔瓷展品室，过道两旁还有天湖画院、丰南文苑和作家文苑编辑部。抬眼往里径直看，迎面是古香古色充满中国建筑特色的四扇雕花木门。看到这些，让你顿觉，这里俨然是古老与现代的交汇点，是一个文化聚集地。

在引导员的引导下，我来到七步楼地下填补了丰南区古玩市场空白的丰南古玩城。这里，金石玉器、古玩古籍、文物摆件、琴棋书画、古今现代工艺品，珠光宝气，琳琅满目，让人目不暇接。在这里人们可以看到文物活起来了，悠久的历史站起来了。还让人们看到，这里是传统工艺与现代文化展示的平台。这里还有古老的茶馆，供人歇息饮茶，谈古论今。遥想过去，畅想未来。

从地下古玩城上到地上二楼，灯光明亮，视野开阔。刚刚一进门口，令人惊叹的场面就出现在眼前，那些不同年代的陶瓷藏品，大的小的、高的矮的，遍布整整一层楼的地板上，让人目不暇接。排列整齐，堪比秦始皇兵马俑。连著名红学专家王家惠、著名中国作家张金池来此参观之后都深感震撼。

这里的陶瓷收藏有两大闪光点，一是，这里"唐山窑"陶瓷收藏最全，且红楼梦题材的唐山陶瓷瓷绘稀罕至极，有的堪称孤品。二是，河北省唐山市非遗项目丰南翟氏锔瓷代表性传承人的锔瓷器品展。古老的锔瓷技艺，把那些破碎残损的古今瓷器修补完好重现于世，使即将失传的瓷器的"锔活儿"得到传承延续。值得一提的是，翟氏锔瓷还举办了全国唯一一次锔瓷展。

这里还有建国到90年代的器具、物品、书籍、生活用品、标识、书籍、报刊的收藏展示。让人重温那逝去的年代、过去的时光和生活。

进得另一种风格的三楼，是集会议室、明清家具、珍贵器物、陶瓷、文献展示于一体的，显得气派、华贵、雍容、时尚，彰显出传统和现代文明的魅力。进入这样的境地，让人觉得不虚此行，难得难得！

走进四楼，这里是集学习培训、文化活动，会议、讲座于一身的多功能活动室！灯光、音响、场地，一应俱全。

随着"七步楼"的崛起，唐山市丰南区多了一处古今交融、传统文化和现代文化并存的场所。成为丰南地区、唐山市乃至河北省集文化产业、休闲娱乐、文化传播的亮点。影响的不断扩大，也使得全国各地的文史、文化、画家、书法家、旅游、玩家纷至沓来，慕名到这里参观交流。

"七步楼"所在的胥各庄，已有一千多年的历史，镇内曾有一座洪阳寺，始建于唐太宗贞观年间（公元627年—649年），远近闻名，影响广泛。且早在清咸丰年间，这里就成了中国北方最大的猪鬃加工出口基地，所产"火炬"牌猪鬃饮誉海外；清光绪二年（1876年），北洋大臣李鸿章委派上海轮船招商局总办唐廷枢以官督商办的方式，创建了开平矿务有限公司。为方便煤炭运输，1881年春在胥各庄开挖煤河，同时，一些民船利用煤河之便，载运石灰、陶瓷、粮食等生活日用品，往来津唐之间，成为当时交通运输动脉。1990年，胥各庄跻身全国"百强乡镇"行列，1991年在河北省亿元乡镇排名中名列第一。

2006年在国家统计局评定出的全国小城镇综合发展水平"千强镇"第十位，成为长江以北地区唯一进入前十名的乡镇，被誉为"江北第一镇"。2008年在中国乡镇综合实力500强评比中，位列第八名。

这里，是中国近代工业的摇篮。中国第一条标准轨距铁路——唐胥铁路，从这里延伸远去！胥各庄机车修理厂，生产出中国第一台蒸汽机车——"龙"号机车。1881年11月8日，自唐山起至胥各庄的唐胥铁路正式通车。随着两端不断延伸，构成了四通八达的铁路大动脉。唐胥铁路的建设，极大地促进中国近代民族企业的发展，拉开了中国铁路建设的序幕。胥各庄是1976年唐山大地震的重灾区，也是当时世人瞩目的焦点……

雪后初晴，阳光灿烂。走出"七步楼"，在冬日暖阳下回望"七步楼"，"七步楼"，是丰南区文创界的新地标性建筑，"七步楼"也必将承前灿烂文化，启后发扬光大。沐浴中华文化之光，绽放烂漫文化之花！

益寿园唱美

一个偶然的机会，我们闯入了"益寿园"这个占地6500平方米又名"亚热带室内风情园"的大型室内生态养生园。

园里迎面映入眼帘的是一座朝东背西的假山，山顶瀑布倾泻而下，山上北侧一棵长势良好的迎客松迎接着大家。山下人工湖湖水中红、花、白、金等各色观赏鱼，来来往往畅游在湖水和园内环流水系中，那么悠闲自在。

随着人们走上小桥，见桥下面流水清清。我疑问这水源是从哪里来的？身边游人示意提示牌：温泉馆、园中水系的水源都是唐山水源保护区内地下四百多米的深层水，富含钠、氧化物、重碳酸盐、硫酸盐、镁、碳酸钙、锶、钙、铁、硒、钾等几十种对人体有益的矿物质及多种微量元素，对关节炎、心脑血管疾病、神经功能性疾病等有良好的疗效，还有美白护肤、延缓皮肤衰老等作用，具有极高的保健理疗价值。没想到，在这大平原上还丰富蕴含着这么好的水源哪？

过了小桥，眼前就是飞檐吊脚的逸仙亭，给人以时光穿越，阳光飞扬的感觉。一进园人们见到的景象，看到的环境那简直是仙境一般。徜徉园中，亭间小息，欣赏美景，如神似仙。"逸仙亭"再佐之王勃《滕王阁序》中的名句"画梁朝飞南浦云，珠帘暮卷西山雨"。与园中的左水右山和花草树木的所有景物就是绝佳配伍。走在长廊里让人感觉是穿行在历史的岁月之中。

回首向南，亭南相对是一条古香古色的九曲回廊，红柱黛瓦，曲折蜿蜒，充满着中国古典园林的建筑美。廊的迎头横梁彩绘之上悬挂有"养生长廊"金字匾额。"养生长廊"配以八段锦、五禽戏和其它中华养生素材彩绘，使人们对养生耳濡目染可起到潜移默化的作用。大红圆柱上书写对联是赵朴初所写的"同修仁德，济世养生"相辅相成。

园区运用园林景观和水系营造出了人与自然和谐的环境，充满了亚热带自然风情。风光秀丽，景色宜人，植被茂盛，四季如春，园中的水、空气、湿度皆为上乘，因完全以亚热带气候为基底，园内温度一直保持在18°C—25°C、湿度40%—70%RH，堪称：天、地、人合一，浑于自然的佳境，更是隐匿于闹市中的世外桃源。

处于园子中间位置的亭子，即迎晨纳暮，视野开阔，景色宜人，又畅怀寄情，面对老年大学，流水绕亭，似歌浅唱，鱼游浅底，自在悠然。亭子名为"唱晚亭"佐以"渔歌晚唱炊烟起，晨钟报晓书声嘹"的对联，意境极佳。

园区北边有羽毛球乒乓球运动场地，使人感到充满活力。园区西侧是健身区，各种健身器的存在，给人以运动向上的感觉。园中南侧的中心小广场，在亚热带植物簇拥和草坪环绕之中。园中最南端是棋牌室、书画室、影音室更满足了今天人们对于精神娱乐生活的追求。

一番游览后要回去了，来到园门，看见园名"益寿园"想起古有一句话叫做"颐养天年"。置身于此，修身养性安得其乐，还能强身健体，延年益寿。夕阳绚丽，晚霞笼罩益寿园，花香鸟语，惬意之极。

那年去《人民文学》参加笔会

事情还要从1992年的4月份说起，海南省《当代文坛》杂志编辑部给我发来一封"全国首届当代文坛力作选拔赛"约稿信。当时手头没有现成的作品，突然收到约稿信一时也没有灵感。约稿信就放在了办公桌的抽屉里了。

过了几天，我在办公桌右上角的零散文件栏里找材料时，一份打印后还没有发出去的散文诗《仲夏了，去看海吗？》出现在眼前。拿过来一看，觉得当作征文也行。仔细看看，自己还想再斟酌一下题目。于是，几天的构思选题皆不满意。终有一天，灵机一动计上心来，脑子里浮现了一个理想的题目《仲夏情思》，一阵欣喜，马上从兜里掏出圆珠笔写在手心上。来到办公室打开电脑，立即把《仲夏了，去看海吗？》这一题目修改为《仲夏情思》，迅速装上信封，写好收信地址寄往海南省《当代文坛》杂志编辑部。

1992年6月的一天，我收到了海南省《当代文坛》编辑部的报喜书。散文诗《仲夏情思》获海南省《当代文坛》编辑部举办的"全国首届当代文坛力作选拔赛"诗歌创作一等奖，并被收入由方梦泉主编的《中国新诗人千家》丛书。散文诗《仲夏情思》还先后被天津经济广播电台、《唐山团讯》等媒体播发转载。1993年，陕西青年自修大学校刊《窗》创刊号，专版刊发表了我的获奖散文诗《仲夏情思》，还有我的创作谈《让感情的光芒闪烁在文章中》，并加了编者按。更是因为这首获得"全国首届当代文坛力作选拔赛"诗歌创作一等奖的散文诗《仲夏情思》，创刊于1949年10月25日的新中国第一份纯文学期刊，在中国当代文学（新中国文学）的历史上，无论从哪方面来看都堪称最为重要、最为突出也最具权威性和代表性的文学刊物《人民文学》，也邀请我前往北京去参加《人民文学》创刊45周年座谈会。

那是1993年12月初,《人民文学》编辑部给我发来《人民文学》笔会（暨《人民文学》创刊45周年座谈会）邀请信。1994年1月1日是星期六的下午,来自全国各地除台湾以外的专家、教授、作家、诗人、评论家、记者、编辑等370多人齐聚当时的铁道部党校。这天晚上在铁道部礼堂开的见面会,每个人相继到台上做了自我介绍。礼堂的舞台很大,当我上台做完自我介绍要往台下走时,大舞台上较为靠后的主席台座位上,一位戴眼镜的大个子编辑叫住我,示意我过去,我走过去握了他的手。他微笑着说:"陈欣你好。我是人民文学散文诗编辑绿风,我给你介绍一下各位领导。这位是人民文学主编刘白羽、程树榛,副主编崔道怡、王扶,这位是评论家雷达、吕同六……"在我和各位名家一一握过手之后绿风老师说:"陈欣怎么这么难请啊?"他这一下把我问愣了,我说没有哇。他又微笑着说:"没有吗?那去年的京都之春笔会邀请函收到了吗?"我说收到了。"京都之夏笔会邀请函收到了吗?""收到了。""京都之秋笔会邀请函收到了吗?""收到了。""京都之冬笔会邀请函收到了吗?""收到了。""那怎么都没来呀?""单位忙一下子出来一星期领导不批准。""那这次怎么来啦?""因为《人民文学》这新中国第一份文学杂志,我太喜欢了。另外,《人民文学》上发表的报告文学《哥德巴赫猜想》写得太好了!"我们就这样一问一答地说着。主编刘白羽、程树榛,副主编崔道怡、王扶、评论家雷达、吕同六列位都看着我们微笑。"陈欣,知道我是从哪里找到你的吗?""不知道。"他拿出一本《新诗人千家》,"这本书里的《仲夏情思》是你写的吧?""噢,是的。"他一笑,"你怎么写得这么好?就是因为你这篇获得一等奖的散文诗,我非要把你召唤到北京来不可!"我恍然一笑,"谢谢您老师!""好,先回台下座位吧,抽空我到你宿舍去。"绿风老师微笑着说。

这次人民文学笔会及座谈会在北京进行了一个星期,期间,听讲座、搞座谈、到圆明园、颐和园、长城采风,之后每人写一篇文学作品,最后联欢。

就是因那一篇获海南省《当代文坛》编辑部举办的"全国首届当代文坛力作选拔赛"诗歌创作一等奖的散文诗《仲夏情思》,创造了与《人民文学》主编副主编、中国著名评论家零距离接触这样的良好机缘。

常忆父爱

父亲节就要到了，这不禁让我再次想起儿时的一件事情。记得那是我上小学三年级时暑假的一天早上，独睡的我想起床，可不知怎么，这腿就是回不过弯来，膝盖还疼。我喊来爸爸，爸爸一看也不知道是咋回事儿。问我哪儿疼，我说膝盖和腿都疼。于是，爸爸给我揉了好一阵子肌肉、腿和膝盖，才算好了一点儿。我起身穿好衣服，洗漱吃饭。

为此，那天爸爸都没去上班，专门带我去了二院，也就是现在的唐山市骨科医院。地震前的唐山市没有今天这么多大大小小的医院。爸爸和我到了二院排了一段时间的队，终于轮到医生给我看病了，医生左瞧瞧右看看，还用小锤子敲了敲我腿的各个部位，最后推了推架在鼻梁上的眼镜说："昨天是不是到河水里去洗澡了，没事儿，就是着了点儿凉。记住，往后别再到水里玩得太久，不然的话就要得关节炎和风湿病了。"我看着大夫点点头。爸爸听了这话看看我笑了。现在想来，可能是爸爸当时心里不清楚我的腿究竟是咋回事，医生这么一说心里豁亮了，一团疑云散开，所以才开心地笑了。

从二院出来已是中午。爸爸领我转着玩，来到西山口南面当时的老长途汽车站对过的饭馆儿，爸爸看着饭馆儿对我说："咱爷儿俩中午不回家吃了，你想吃点儿啥就跟爸爸说。"说实话，改革开放前的每一个家庭都是不富裕的，爸爸一个人在工商所工作，全家七口人的日子并不宽松。那时候的孩子不像现在的孩子们，山珍海味吃个遍。因为没吃过啥好吃的，所以，才说不上来想吃啥，也就是不知道啥好吃。爸爸看着我不知所语茫然的样子说："那就给你来块儿大饼卷肥肠吧。"哎哟，这猪肥肠可是那时候过年才能够吃到的呀。我毫不犹豫地说："中。"

爸爸买来大饼卷好肥肠递给我："儿子，吃吧。香着呢。""爸不吃？""儿子，爸有烩饼。""那咱爷俩一人一半儿。""傻儿子，等你长大到了我这个岁数的时候，你就知道爸爸的心了。吃吧，你还要长身子骨呢。"一口口的大饼肥肠嚼在我嘴里，香在我心里。时至今日，每每回想爸爸当时慈爱而高兴的样子，心里就一阵酸，想流泪。俗话说："父子天性。"当我也有了儿子的那天起就深深理解了这句老话的丰富含义。爸爸虽然已经去世了，但通过一件件小事体现出来爸爸那一点一滴的父爱，让我在心里铭刻到今天仍念念不能忘怀。父亲节前，我又买来大饼卷上肥肠，放在老爸的遗像前，恭恭敬敬地给他老人家寄上哀思和心意。

大饼卷肥肠，味道真香。香味飘飘的同时，沐浴着父爱之光。我对我的儿子经常提起这悠悠往事一桩。

从《陈欣作品选》到《风舞秋海》

2007年到2024年间，我先后出版了《陈欣作品选》《岁月回响》《梦回唐朝》《携一抹阳光》《风舞秋海》五本书。并整理1984—2023年在各级报纸上发表的新闻文稿，剪辑结集《陈欣文稿集》一至四集。

20世纪90年代，我进入了散文诗创作的高峰期。1992年6月，我的散文诗《仲夏情思》获海南省《当代文坛》编辑部举办的"全国首届当代文坛力作选拔赛"诗歌创作一等奖，并被收入由方梦泉主编的《中国新诗人千家》丛书，还先后被天津经济广播电台、《唐山团讯》等媒体播发转载。1993年，陕西青年自修大学校刊《窗》创刊号，专版发表了我的获奖散文诗《仲夏情思》，还有我的创作谈《让感情的光芒闪烁在文章中》，并加编者按。更是因为这首获得"全国首届当代文坛力作选拔赛"诗歌创作一等奖的散文诗《仲夏情思》，创刊于1949年10月25日的新中国第一份纯文学期刊，在中国当代文学（新中国文学）的历史上，无论从哪方面来看都堪称最为重要、最为突出也最具权威性和代表性的文学刊物《人民文学》，也邀请我参加了《人民文学》创刊45周年座谈会。

从此，我的文学创作也更加一发不可收了，常有作品在从国家到地方不同级别的报纸、杂志、广播电台上都有刊播，有的或收入文学作品专集或获奖。甚至，1993年我的散文诗《仲夏了，去看海吗？》《你已把我占据》分别在当时英国统治的香港的《世界散文诗作家》第五期、第七期也接连发表，并获"繁荣杯"世界散文诗大赛优秀奖。关于我的词条也先后收入著名诗人阿红（王占彪）主编的《当代诗歌爱好者名录》、著名作家姚雪垠主编的《未名作家和诗人名录》、著名作家、诗人方梦泉主编的《当代文学新人集录》等辞书类书籍。复旦大学的何淑云教授，也一直指导鼓励我进修复旦大学中文系作家班。1994年，我读完上海复旦大学中文系作家预备班，被优先录取为上海复旦大学中文系作家班正式学员。

2007年，著名作家、河北省作家协会主席关仁山，得知我的《陈欣作品选》一书即将由作家出版社出版时，当面叮嘱我说："书出版后，一定送我一本！"著名作家、河北省作家协会副主席谈歌先生，更是先前欣然亲笔为我题写了《陈欣作品选》一书的书名。2009年，印刷《岁月回响》一书。特别是2018年3月26日，18万字的《梦回唐朝》一书，由团结出版社正式出版。2019年7月，《携一抹阳光》由四川民族出版社出版。2021年1月，散文集《风舞秋海》，由北京日报出版社出版。在这四年间，我连续出了三本书。期间，还组织剪辑《陈欣文稿集一至四》（1984—2022年）。

2022年7月24日上午，唐山市首届中发伟业"马嘶文学奖"颁奖典礼在丰南宾馆举行。中国作协主席团委员、河北省作协主席、著名作家关仁山出席活动并讲话。然后，为小说类、纪实文学类获奖者颁奖、散文类获奖者颁奖。

我的散文集《风舞秋海》获唐山市首届中发伟业"马嘶文学奖"。授奖词这样写道："陈欣散文集《风舞秋海》，是一部深沉隽永之作，书中有岁月的沧桑厚重，有小桥流水的柔情流淌，有澎湃的激情荡漾，更有感人肺腑的博爱之光！全书涉猎广泛，题材丰富，一册在手时有珠光闪烁，让人们感到一种执着的坚守，一种蓬勃向上的精神！"中国作协主席团委员、河北省作协主席、著名作家关仁山为我颁发了荣誉证书和奖杯。

2024年1月，应国内读者要求，《风舞秋海》一书由北京日报出版社再版。中国作协主席团委员、河北省作协主席、著名作家关仁山，还为《风舞秋海》再版，亲自作了题为《与时代对接，与时代共情》的序言。

2024年1月，《风舞秋海》译成英文版。

唐山市作家协会、河北省作家协会、中国煤矿作家协会、中国散文学会，这是我经历了1976年"7·28"唐山大地震之后，在写作这条漫漫长路上，不断进行写作的同时，相继迈进的一个个写作人之家并成为其会员。

蓦然回首，看看自己走过来的路倍感欣慰，感叹坚持可以成就一切。一个城市的精神影响着这个城市的人，我们唐山人，也正是凭着抗震精神，一直在努力追求和奋斗，把这座废墟之上的家园重新建设成了今日这样美好靓丽，进步文明的沿海经济强市。48年前，我从震灾中走来，48年后，作为一个震后与唐山共同成长起来，并参加其建设发展的唐山人，我骄傲，我更为唐山而骄傲。祝唐山这座创造凤凰涅槃奇迹与梦想的环海经济强市，转型发展。唐山向海，凤舞秋海，继往开来，奔向美好的新代。

作家陈欣文学艺术成果索引

1989年7月15日，纪实短剧《悲剧》获甘肃省西峰市（现在的西峰区）举办的"中国首届微型作品编辑出版大展"赛优秀奖。

1989年7月，小小说《丑丈夫》获海南省文学人才函授院颁发"荣誉证书"。

1989年7月，诗歌《七月的太阳》荣获《中国开发报》举办诗歌大奖赛一等奖。

1992年2月，被海南省中国民族文化城学术创作中心评为"91中国桂冠诗人"。

1992年3月，被海南省《大特区诗刊》评为"91中国诗星"。

1992年6月，散文诗《仲夏情思》获海南省《当代文坛》编辑部举办的"全国首届当代文坛力作选拔赛"诗歌创作一等奖。该散文诗被收入由方梦泉主编的《中国新诗人千家》丛书。散文诗《仲夏情思》还被天津人民广播电台播发，《唐山团讯》转载。

1992年8月，散文诗《仲夏了，去看海吗？》在香港《世界散文诗作家》第五期发表，并获"繁荣杯"世界散文诗大赛优秀奖。

1992年10月，散文诗《你已把我占据》在香港《世界散文诗作家》第七期发表。

1993年，陕西青年自修大学校刊《窗》创刊号，志版专页发表获奖散文诗《仲夏情思》和创作谈《让感情的光芒闪烁文章中》并加编者按。

1994年1月，因《仲夏情思》一文，陈欣被特邀到北京参加《人民文学》创刊45周年座谈会。

1996年，散文《7·28八大堂庄园纪实》一文收入中国国际统计出版社出版的《我心中珍藏的故事》一书。

2000年5月29日，散文《遥望新疆》被新疆人民广播电视台采用。

2007年7月，出版《陈欣作品选》。

2009年10月，印刷《岁月回响》。

1985—2015年组集《新春文稿集》。

2010年11月，《唐山大地震第一支抗震救灾学生队伍》获唐山市宣传部"情系唐山"优秀征文奖，《人性光芒》获唐山市宣传部"情系唐山"征文纪念奖。

2010年12月，获开滦集团公司党委命名"2009年度优秀新闻宣传工作者称号"。

2011年12月，获开滦集团公司党委命名"2010年度优秀新闻宣传工作者称号"。

2014年10月27日，纪实《和谐刘现庄 老年人的幸福天堂》在新华网发表（15:05:55）。

2014年10月27日，纪实《和谐刘现庄 老年人的幸福天堂》在中国日报网发表（15:13:00）。

2014年11月12日，纪实《走进刘现庄——刘现庄新农村建设践行社会主义核心价值观见闻》（16000字）在河北共产党员网发表（15:49:37）。

2016年4月，发表在《唐山劳动日报·文荟》的散文《雨中访曹公》一文，被"浩然文学馆"永久收藏。

2016年7月，纪实《40年，我从唐山第一支学生抗震救灾队伍中走来》（9285字）、《贾邦友：地震，带领井下矿工安全上井是我的职责》（4096字）被收入唐山市委宣传部编辑的《40，抒怀》一书。

2016年8月，《张爱玲的爱恨情仇》（3280字）、《董浩叔叔》（3026字）被收入中国电影出版社出版的《唐山与中国电影》一书。

2017年6月，在《矿工老哥》杂志发表小说《真命爱人》。

2017年9月，《唐山大地震，第一支学生抗震救灾队伍》一文被收入唐山丰润区作家协会编辑的《心痕》一书。

2018年3月，《梦回唐朝》一书由团结出版社出版。

2019年7月，《携一抹阳光》由四川民族出版社出版。

2019年10月，自由诗《中国辉煌》被收入《长歌》（山花杂志社出版）一书。

2021年1月，散文集《风舞秋海》由北京日报出版社出版。

2021年9月17日—31日，小说《真命爱人》在费城《海华都市报·文学世界》连载。并在《作家文苑》报发表。

2021年10月，小小说《咸阳有佳缘》《小英子》《歌恋》《春耕烟》《槐》《重归于好》在《作家文苑》报发表。

2021年11月，长篇小说《虎女》在《作家文苑》连载（待续）。

2022年7月，散文集《风舞秋海》获得唐山市首届马嘶文学奖。

2023年1月9日，小小说《帝都缘》获得《当代作家》杯文学艺术大赛一等奖。

2023年6月18日，散文《皇家窖藏金顶饮食》获得《我与皇家窖藏的故事》征文二等奖。

2023年10月7日，《河北日报·布谷》上刊散文《秋访白羊峪》。

2023年12月24日，荣获唐山市丰南区作家协会"年度人物"荣誉称号。

2023年12月29日，《河北日报·布谷》上刊散文《一滩鸥鹭》。

2024年1月，散文集《风舞秋海》由北京日报出版社再版。

2024年1月，《风舞秋海》译成英文版。

后记

散文集《风舞秋海》一书自 2021 年出版之后，一直有全国各地没有拿到《风舞秋海》一书的广大读者要求再版，感谢大家对我的鞭策和鼓励。今天《风舞秋海》一书终于再版整理就绪，里面辑录了我在 20 世纪 80 年代到 2023 年这段时间里，在国内外报纸、杂志、电台刊登发表过的部分不同题材的散文作品。一段时间以来，缠绕在我心头的一件心事，总算有了一点儿着落。要特别感谢河北省作家协会关仁山主席的关心和大力支持帮助，多次过问本书整理情况，并亲自为《风舞秋海》再版作序。在此，再次表示感谢！

我想，书中所写，能对社会和广大读者有所裨益，进而产生共鸣和认同，那将是我所高兴。

陈欣

2024 年 1 月 6 日

Wind Dance Autumn Sea

The first series that one soil and water scenery

October splendor

Twenty-eight gun salutes. Since then, China has stood tall in the East of the world.

The Chinese People's Volunteers crossed the Yalu River in 1950, fought against the United States and aided North Korea, defeated the ambitious Wolf, and became famous all over the world!

In the 1960s, two mushroom clouds rose in the northwest, and the satellite made the music of "The East is Red" reverberate throughout the world. The first Wuhan Yangtze River highway and railway dual-purpose bridge, the rift becomes open, the highway cars run, the railway train whistles to the front!

A two-side fast attack style shocked the world of table tennis. At the 26th (1961), 27th (1963) and 28th (1965) World Table Tennis Championships, the Chinese won the men's singles champion one after another. The bright red national flag, flying high in the stadium.

In the middle and late 1990s, the Chinese were the winners of the Grand Slam of men's singles at the World Table Tennis Championships, the World Cup and the Olympic Games, the champion of men's singles, the champion of men's doubles, the champion of mixed doubles and the champion of men's team, which is the label of table tennis and the belief of the national table tennis team.

Let the foreign association know the word "national table tennis" in the field of table tennis, so that the dominance of the national table tennis is constantly stable, so that table tennis is no longer a sport, but the label of the national table tennis is deeply printed.

The Yangtze River has a long history. In 2006, the water from the Three Gorges Dam burst out and sang day and night.

The endless flowing Yellow River, from the west to the east one thousand miles, the bottom of the small waves of sand bursts of cleansing, rushing into the sea.

When the Qinghai-Tibet Railway reaches the plateau, the sky road extends over the mountains to the side of Shigatse, and the great dragons bring good luck and well-being to the Tibetan children.

China Caofeidian natural diamond class deep water port, opened in 2005, the bay is wide and deep by boat, the northern port huan new trend. Today, basking in the glow of the sea, the port opens 10,000 miles, opening more than 110 domestic and foreign trade routes, and reaching nearly 200 ports in more than 70 countries and regions around the world. China has set up 21 inland ports, launched a number of China-Europe freight trains to Ulaanbaatar in Mongolia and Moscow in Russia, and built an international logistics and transportation system covering the three North regions, connecting Mongolia and Russia and directly to Europe, thus fully guaranteeing the supply of goods connected to the world. In 2022, the cargo throughput has reached 847.16 million tons, ranking firmly in the forefront of the world's coastal ports and becoming a world-class comprehensive trade port.

Thousands of boats compete in the race. Grand Port of the North, riding the wave. By 2035, Caofeidian Port will become the fourth generation of international port with deep interactive integration of port industry and city.

In 2008, the centennial Olympics and the centennial World Expo, let the Chinese people enjoy the stretch of the centennial dream, and the Chinese people are really proud.

"Na" flower in full bloom Paris, tennis Grand Slam, Olympic Open - French Open, all the way crazy. "Dongfeng 41" is called "express", and it is full of fashion. Chang 'e flew to the Moon Palace in the winter months of the Year of the Snake in 2014 (December 14 and 15), and the jade rabbit wandered in the Rainbow Bay area.

There is a champion, called the Chinese Women's volleyball team; There is a feeling called the Chinese Women's Volleyball team. The Chinese women's volleyball team had a difficult start, a smooth transition, and dominated one side. The Chinese women's volleyball team is the only solid force to stand on the podium at the 1984 Los Angeles Olympic Games, the 2004 Athens Olympic Games and the 2016 Rio Olympic Games. Like a rainbow blooming, shocking the world, unstoppable.

"China's Eye of the Sky" - 500-meter aperture Spherical Radio Telescope, China's independent intellectual property rights, the world's largest single aperture, the most sensitive radio telescope. Conceived in 1994, it took 22 years to build and was inaugurated on September 25, 2016. The comprehensive performance is ten times stronger than the radio telescope Arecibo, and the Chinese are no longer confused in observing the universe. By 2023, more than 740 pulsars have been discovered. Such figures reveal the brilliance of Chinese astronomy!

Permanent Tiangong-1 in the sky, June 11, 2013 17:38, space kiss spacecraft Shenzhou 10, hand in hand to travel in space unremitting pursuit, more round the world's first space man "Wanhu" that 600 years of cosmic dream flight. Tianzhou-1 and Tiangong-2, April 22, 2017 12:23, space kiss, successfully completed automatic rendezvous and docking. On April 29, 2021, a Long March-5B carrier rocket carrying the space station and core module blasted off in Wenchang, Hainan province. By the end of 2022, the Sky Experiment module and the Dream experiment module will be launched. At 9:22 am on June 17, 2021, the Long March 2F carrier rocket carrying the Shenzhou-12 manned spacecraft was fired and launched at Jiuquan Satellite Launch Site. After that, Shenzhou-12 manned spacecraft successfully separated from the rocket, entered the scheduled orbit, and successfully sent Nie Haisheng, Liu Boming and Tang Hongbo into space. At 15:52, Shenzhou-12 manned spacecraft docking with the space station successfully! Since then, the space shuttle has been opened, and the space business trips and space express deliveries of Chinese astronauts will be regular long-term rotation stays. China's Shenzhou-13 manned spacecraft blasted off from Jiuquan Satellite Launch Center at 12:23 am on October 16, 2021 aboard a Long March 2F carrier rocket. The crew includes Zhai Zhigang, Wang Yaping (female) and Ye Guangfu.

The "Chinese arrow" has once again left the string, allowing the Chinese space station to complete the "shift" of personnel. At 17:42 on June 5, 2022, the Shenzhou 14 spacecraft successfully docked at the radial port of the Tiangong core module, and Chen Dong, Liu Yang (female) and CAI Xuzhe entered the China Space Station.

On December 2, 2022, Shenzhou XV astronauts Fei Junlong, Deng Qingming and Zhang Lu successfully entered the China Space Station, marking the first space rendezvous of Chinese astronauts. At 18:22 on May 30, 2023, the long-awaited Shenzhou 15 astronaut crew successfully opened the "home" and welcomed the Shenzhou 16 astronaut crew Jing Haipeng, Zhu Yangzhu and GUI Haichao to enter the "Tiangong". Leaving the motherland and soaring up to 800 miles of clouds and moon, the Chinese space station three Cang three ships bathed in endless sunshine. China's space station, the 21st century to play a big role, manned space cruise!

Heavenly Palace travel, Chang 'e moon, sky ask fire exploration, 2022 and Micius to achieve 1200 km quantum transmission, Kuafu No. 1 to open the journey of solar exploration. Chinese people look up at the sky and feel comfortable.

The Hong Kong-Zhuhai-Macao Bridge was illuminated on January 1, 2018, and officially opened on October 23. The 55km global ultra-long bridge flies over the vast Lingdingyang, and the construction of the Zhuhai-Hong Kong-Macao Greater Bay Area floats to the front.

On September 25, 2012, China's first aircraft carrier, the Liaoning, was delivered to the People's Navy. On December 17, 2019, China's first domestically built aircraft carrier Shandong was delivered to the Navy at a military port in Sanya, Hainan province. At 11 am on June 17, 2022, China's third aircraft carrier Fujian was launched. After 17 years, China has entered the era of three aircraft carriers! In the 21st century, the Chinese Navy has developed by leaps and bounds, and directly stepped into the era of electromagnetic catapult, a real leapfrog development. Large aircraft carrier across the island chain, facing the wind and waves west out of the Pacific Ocean, double aircraft carrier deep sea voyage.

At the beginning of 2020, when the new coronavirus ravaged Wuhan and Hubei, Fatuniu-20 fell from the sky, and 40,000 soldiers and soldiers in white quickly moved into hospitals and shelters. After four months of fierce fighting, the epidemic had nowhere to hide. China has the socialist system, the great Communist Party of China, and the incomparable strength of unity. We can overcome any difficulties, and the people are happy and healthy. In the same year, the whole of China was lifted out of poverty.

China's TiAN-1 Mars probe with the Zhurong rover was launched from the Wenchang Space Launch Site on July 23, 2020 by a long March 5 carrier rocket. After a long flight of up to seven months, 202 days and 475 million kilometers, at 7:18 am on May 15, 2021, the Chinese Lunar New Year's Day spacecraft was launched. Landing on a pre-selected landing zone in the southern part of the Utopian plains in the northern hemisphere of Mars, a lone hero, a single man, treading the distant planet. The first autonomous mission to Mars, touching the Martian soil. In the future, interstellar travel is also a Chinese idea.

On November 10, 2020, the submersible Striver successfully sat in the deepest trench of 10,909 meters, creating a new record for manned deep diving in the world! Focus on the ocean floor for treasure.

The lunar exploration project Chang 'e-5 probe successfully landed on the surface of the moon at 23:00 on December 1, 2020. After about 19 hours of lunar surface work, the robot arm surface acquisition and drilling tool drilling are two ways of multi-point and diversified automatic sampling. At 22:00 on December 2, 1731 grams of lunar table sampling was successfully completed and the package was saved.

The Chang 'e-5 rover of the lunar exploration project successfully landed in the designated area of Siziwang Qi, Inner Mongolia at 1:59 on December 17, 2020, marking the successful completion of China's first extraterrestrial object sampling return mission. Chang 'e-6 blasted off from China's Wenchang Cosmodrome on May 3 and entered the Earth-moon transfer orbit. After orbit correction and lunar braking, the probe successfully entered the orbit around the moon. Since then, the probe has experienced the separation of the lander and ascender assembly, the orbiter and the returner assembly, and with the support of Queqiao II relay satellite, the lander and ascender assembly implemented the lunar orbit and dynamic descent, and accurately landed in the South Pole – Aitken Basin pre-selected area on the far side of the moon on June 2 and carried out sampling. China has become the first country to retrieve rocks from the far side of the moon and is hopeful for future extraterrestrial sampling.

China's goal is the star sea, the majestic atmosphere on the moon nine days, hold the initial heart to catch turtle under the five oceans. Looking forward to the sea map, looking forward to the sky, and looking forward to the space, the achievements are the expectations of the whole world.

About the Winter Olympics in 2022 Chinese tiger Year spring, full of fireworks blooming in the bird's nest, Beijing Winter Olympics, ice and snow athletes galloping through the snow, flying over the mountains, records, gold and silver, passionate, bold, the Chinese spirit with the national flag rising sublimation, the Chinese nation endless imagination. The mood of the global audience is surging, and the world's ice and snow are surging. The J–35 roared through the sky and spread its wings across the sky.

At 13:30 on June 15, 2023, the Long March II Ding Yao 88 carrier rocket lifted off the ground at the Taiyuan Satellite Launch Center, successfully releasing 41 satellites in turn, quasi-determining the orbit, raising the number of satellites launched in China to the largest new level.

On August 29, 2023, Huawei Mate60 Pro, the world's first mass smartphone to support satellite calls, was born.

In the absence of ground network signals, call and answer satellite phones, and launch a Jedi counterattack on the US Western semiconductor limit suppression, which is a heavy weight.

China, 5,000 years ago, was facing the great flood of wisdom, 4,000 years ago, bronze ware is tending to glory. 3000 years ago, thinking about philosophy, 2000 years ago, expanding the land. A thousand years ago, the country was rich and golden. Now, China is short and long with the world's top.

Transmission of electricity from west to east promotes rapid economic growth. The four lines of west-east gas transmission are running side by side, and the leader is flying high. Water from the south to the north to nourish China, the work times forever. Counting from the east to the west, China has once again carried out large-scale cross-regional resource deployment smoothly across its vast territory. The new Silk Road is now more radiant than before, with flowers blooming all the way ahead, brimming with courage and health.

The land of China, splendid mountains and rivers, shines continuously golden sunshine. The Yellow River and the Yangtze River, singing with abandon. The wealth of mankind, the heritage of the world, the magnificent Great Wall, stretching thousands of miles of ups and downs.

China bears the hope of generations of Chinese ancestors, China is fulfilling the Chinese nation's ideal of endless life, and China is strongly moving toward rich and prosperous country.

In the past 75 years, New China has flown with wings, and the 56 ethnic groups have made an unbroken effort to support China's dream of prosperity. The 1.4 billion people have worked tirelessly for this endless glory.

China has always stood tall in the East of the world, and despite the wind and frost, it has not changed its glory. We are witnessing another great revival of her.

Rising again is the homecoming of a 5,000-year-old civilization.

The rise of China advocates a community of shared future for mankind and leads the sharing of happiness around the world.

In October, the sun rises on the river and the sea, dreaming of the East, the sky is vast and mighty, and China's future is more brilliant.

Note:

Caofeidian, China: Tangshan Caofeidian world-class deep water port.

Wan Hu: Ming Dynasty people, known as "the world's first space man".

"October Splendor", magnificent momentum, majestic. It spans from the 20th century to the 21st century. It has written the confidence, determination and great achievements of the People's Republic of China to achieve the great rejuvenation of the Chinese nation, starting from scratch, working hard, forging ahead and indomitable. Cutting-edge technology, world-class projects, heavyweight breakthroughs, so proud of the people, proud; Wow the world, shock!

Reading through the poem allows the reader to see a world-renowned China and admire the strong rise of the Eastern powers, which is unstoppable. In the new century and the new era, China will realize the Chinese Dream and create a community with a shared future for mankind.

This classic work is deeply loved by readers, and has been welcomed by newspapers and magazines, "China Brilliance" was first published in Tangshan Labor Daily in 2017 with the title of "Singing in October". Since its publication in August 2019 in the magazine "Short Novels", it has been reprinted by the "Writer and Artist Sunshine Media", "Writer Wenyuan" and "Tangshan Literature" magazine. The book "Long Song" published by Mountain Flower Publishing House was also included. Eight more to date.

Looking at Xinjiang

When I was very young, my uncle, who joined the Chinese people's Liberation Army, obeyed orders and went to Xinjiang, far away, in the 1960 s. When I can remember, my uncle brought his lover, that is, my aunt, back to our place where Cao Cao recruited and trained new army and the fields before he attacked Wuhuan, and provided troops and food for the front line at any time-Xinjuntun, Fengrun District, Tangshan City, Hebei Province to visit our home.

Perhaps it is because Laojiu is in Xinjiang. Since then, I have been paying attention to Xinjiang. There was no television in the 1960 s, but from the pictorial magazines at that time, I saw some pictures about Xinjiang. I often hear melodic songs such as "Song of Karamay" and "Our Good Place in Xinjiang" on the radio. Therefore, I envy my uncle for going to this charming place. When my uncle returned to Xinjiang, I asked grandpa, how far is Xinjiang from us? Grandpa said that it would take seven days and seven nights to get there by train. Oh, it's so far. This kind of space-time distance, for the little me, is far away. At that, I was thinking, how nice it would be for me to be here when I grow up. Looking at Laojiu, the car they took far away until it disappeared at the end of the line of sight. I was still looking, not looking back for a long time, as if I were looking for the magical Xinjiang.

In the 1960 s and 1970 s, mass literary and artistic activities were quite common. Bold, generous, free and easy, and cheerful Xinjiang song and dance and literary programs were widely performed in the mainland. Through these, I just went to school, from which I greedily and longingly looked at Xinjiang, where the people are enthusiastic and open.

After taking part in the work, my dream of Xinjiang is still. "Tarim River" and "The Girl of Dabancheng" are the repertoire of the I say. Through singing, I express my thoughts and look at the beautiful and attractive Xinjiang.

After the reform and opening up, the country proposed to develop the Great Northwest. While I was in college and writing in my spare time, I read the prosperity of Xinjiang's Silk Road Flower Rain in the Han and Tang Dynasties in my books, and made friends and poetry friends in Xinjiang. Through these, I hope to a vibrant Xinjiang.

Since 1995, various news media from the central to the local level have to publicize the great achievements made by Xinjiang Uygur Autonomous Region in agricultural reclamation, transportation, metallurgy, petrochemical, wool spinning, border trade, culture and education since its establishment. Through these, I look forward to the prosperous Xinjiang.

At the beginning of 2000, the state once again proposed the development of the Great Northwest and put it into practice. Xinjiang, my dream town, my yearning. I finally look at my Xinjiang, the leader of the West-East Gas Pipeline is already in the East China Sea, you are facing the dawn of the new century, the era express rushed out of Asia; your blue sky above the silver swallow soaring wings to the world in all directions.

In the new era, the development and construction of the belt and road initiative will enable Xinjiang to revive the glory of Central Asia and become more prosperous and upward!

"How many places have I traveled, the most beautiful is our Xinjiang". The, beautiful and moving and high-pitched songs of Bahar Guli have been sung all over China and Shenzhou, attracting the attention of China and the world. They look at Xinjiang from afar, inquire about Xinjiang, and devote themselves to the construction of Xinjiang with the of. Recalling the past, the eventful years are thick. Seventy years of construction and development, the sons and daughters of all ethnic groups have realized the Chinese dream. Xinjiang, the north and south of the Tianshan Mountains, the great beauty of Xinjiang, this place full of magic and vitality, full of vitality and beautiful hope, just like the red day of the East, your future is brilliant and beautiful to the eyes of the world.

China's cutest Ferris wheel ——"Tangshan Light"

On Yongfeng Island, Huifeng Lake, Fengnan District, Tangshan City, a white Ferris wheel, known as "the most adorable Ferris wheel in China", "Tangshan Light" Ferris wheel, stands tall. "Tangshan Light" Ferris wheel base on the island in the middle of the lake between the Hui and Feng two Bridges, showing the trend of "two dragons playing with pearls". The base of the Ferris wheel is a white jade trapezoidal sightseeing platform with a sound and light waterfall and a musical fountain in the lake under the platform, which are across the water from the large musical water curtain fountain on the Hubei side and reflect each other, becoming a shining pearl inlaid in the Jingdong land.

The Huifeng Lake Ferris Wheel was famous from the very beginning. The unique charm of its "Two dragons playing with pearls" makes the world look forward to wearing it for a long time. The Ferris wheel, in the July sun of the year of Jiachenlong, was spinning in the air, and the silver light was shuffling. The lake is rippling and the clouds are curling. The sun was shining on the rippling surface of the lake, and boats were shuttling through it. Huifeng Lake side hundred flowers competing, competing, Ferris wheel support straight up, slowly rotating, imposing rainbow, comfort for spectacular.

Looking up at the Ferris wheel, I was deeply shocked by its magnificent momentum. It stands tall on the island in the heart of Huifeng Lake, like a giant overlooking the whole city, the huge body, both can hold up the title of Tangshan landmark building, but also reflects the magnificent spirit of the patron saint of soil and water.

Ferris wheel to the highest point, a wide field of vision, the endless scenery on the vast land can be seen, the flourishing city, the beautiful scenery on both sides of the Jintang Canal, the prosperity of the Tang Dynasty in the old street, the antique buildings, boats, courtyards, red eaves and gray walls, carved beams and pillars. On the broad road, flowers are embroidered and people flow like a tide... The dream-like feeling of flying, let the body and mind have already put aside the noise of the world, into a dream-like fairy tale world.

If riding the Ferris wheel during the day is a strange experience, the Ferris wheel at night is even more fascinating and interesting. The sun is setting, the night is coming, the Ferris wheel is like a giant halo, hanging and rotating, and the charming scenery of Tangshan at night makes people too dizzying and beautiful. Hui, Feng two Bridges with the arch, the lights shine, like two dragon frame "eye of heaven", invite the moon to the sky. Music fountain, sound and light waterfall, beautiful and beautiful. Huifeng Lake lake lights flashing, pleasure boats across the bridge. On the second floor platform of the cruise ship, the entertainers sang and danced, played and sang, and were in full swing. On the bridge to the south of the sky eye, there are white flowers and fire trees, and the traffic is heavy and flowing. Hetou old Street on both sides of the river, lined with lights, thousands of lights. Bridge five stands along the river, the river is brightly lit, glittering stars reflect the moon, resplendent. It can be said that "the ground is like Jin, the sky Ferris wheel, the fairyland on earth is now, and the cloud is flying."

Known as "China's most adorable Ferris wheel", as a new landmark of Tangshan, "Tangshan light" – Huifeng Lake Ferris Wheel, can also be called "Jingdong light" and "Jidong light", is a beautiful and charming city card.

does not disperse homesickness hit home echo

"Homesickness". When it comes to homesickness, I am really a touch of homesickness in my heart. In a folk song, "who doesn't say my hometown is good" has always been my memory of my hometown. I deeply love the hometown where I was born and raised, and I firmly and remember the people and things in my hometown.

My hometown is ancient and rich. It used to be bounded by the Mangmanyan Mountains in the in the north and the surging Bohai Sea in the south (before 1961). The hinterland is a vast plains and the southwest is a wetland with rich water and grass. This land of "Fengze Runmei " has a history of 4,000 years and a history of 2,000 years. It was called Tuyin in ancient times. It is an old county with a long history and profound cultural heritage in ancient.

As time goes by, the long river of history is flowing and sparkling. The stone tools, bone tools, pottery and bronze tools unearthed from Sannu River, Laozhuangzi, Yang Guanlin, Baiguantun, Hancheng and other places prove that human beings have lived and flourished here as early as the Neolithic period. From the ancient Chinese Tang, Yu, Xia Youzhou along the way to the rich, the earth flowing with the return of the river, steep river, mud river, nourishing the side of the, soil and. In history, it is known as "South Wuxi, North is rich", which can be called a prosperous culture and a large number of talents. In the long years, during the Three Kingdoms period, there was Cheng Pu, a founding minister who had experienced three generations of kings in the Eastern Wu Dynasty. Cao Xueqin, who became a grass-roots people in the Qing Dynasty, had a rich hometown, but Cao Xueqin reached the peak of world-class literary giants with his 1 masterpiece A Dream of Red Mansions. In the words of the late Qing Dynasty, "Sun Yat-sen in the south and Ding Xiaochuan in the north, ding Xiaochuan refers to Ding Kaizhang, the important leader of the Northern National Revolution at that time; and Zhang Ailing, the disseminator of Marxism-Leninism in early China-Ticheng and internationally renowned writer. After the founding of New China, playwright Song Zhidi, Pingju Queen Bai Yushuang, music conductor Li Delun, historian Yang Xiang Kui, writers Guan Hua, Chen Dayuan, poet Li Ying, etc., these people shine with humanity, thought, wisdom, courage, and artistic light of outstanding talents, are China's different historical periods of celebrities, is the pride of the country, the pride of history, pride of the times.

In the long river of history, boats sailing boats shadow, the great river goes east, and the waves go through the ages. Born in Fengrun, it is necessary to understand Fengrun, it is necessary to write about rich landscapes, humanities, characters, and past events, and let more people know about Fengrun. Following in the footsteps of my ancestors and bathed in the sunshine of history, in the 1990 s, I used to ride a bicycle, carry a marching pot, and carry dry food on my back. I walked alone in the rich countryside, surveying on both sides of the river with my feet. On top of my head, I climbed the Beishan (Yanshan) the day. He also went down to "Heishan Gully" (where Zhang Peilun's cemetery is located), sat on the street of Dawangzhuang (the hometown of Zhao Guohua, governor of Shandong in Qing Dynasty), and walked on the dirt road the thousand-year-old avenue leading to Yanjing in ancient times, which had to through the. Once upon a time, in the fields of Qituo Village,, Fengrun County,, in the 1990 s, we went deep into the underground tomb of Zhang Renjun, governor of Guangdong and Guangxi of the Qing Dynasty, which had been excavated and by as early as the 1960 s, to the of ocean ash (cement, which is used to be called "ocean ash" by ordinary people) to check the tomb structure...

During that time, I greeted the rising sun with the waist mountain alone, and one person sent a Ma Pingchuan sunset. Hard work during the day, at night tireless. In my mind, I play back the scenes of Han, Tang, Song, Yuan, Ming and Qing Dynasties, and write about the agitation and of the past. of Yincheng (the of Tuyin City built by King Zhao Wuling), of Dian of the Big Dark Horse (the place where Yuchi Jingde was to God), Sannu River (the location of the legendary folk woman jumping over the River), Xinjuntun (the location of Cao Cao Juntun), Hancheng (the place where Han Chang built Shuai Mansion and set up a military spot), Tuo in Longtan (the famous Qing Xiangyuan) Xiangyuan (the academy, the Qing Dynasty Shandong was built by Zhao Guohua, the inspector)...

Cheng Pu, Wei Chi Jingde, Cao Cao, Song Huizong, Han Chang, Cao Xueqin, Zhang Peilun, Zhao Guohua, Zhang Ailing...

There is a steady stream of things to be written and people to be written. These rich past events and legends; these past and rich history and characters, as well as stories, history, and characters related to rich, are all witnesses to the development of rich history, and they are all unique leaves on the tree of rich growth., And it is not found elsewhere, colorful. The boundless time of that year, that person, that matter, that time, was just at the end of the pen, jumping to the screen, and presented on newspapers at the national, provincial, and municipal levels.

In one of my books, I record some people and things from ancient times to the present in the past of Guanhai, South Guanshan, North, as well as some unforgettable historical moments.

I have walked through many places, calm down and think about it, I still love my hometown, the local style and local accent, has been rippling in my heart. Those people and things in the history of my hometown cannot be forgotten for a long time. In the preface of the book, I wrote with the title "What do I give to you?" "came to this world naked, but the of heaven give me moist rain and dew and warm sunshine. Traveling in the clouds gives me yearning and reverie. The earth gives me the grains I need to grow up. The peaks make me appreciate the high and tall. Rivers let me know that the blood is long. However, I this 1 tiny cosmic dust, take what to dedicate to you—the earth, God. Only my little cognition, comprehension, emotion and 1 grateful heart can be put into writing and offered with piety.

Hometown, this ancient and forever young land, is the place where I was born, grew up and studied. I deeply in love with the people who live here, and this lovely piece of water and soil. With a flick of one's finger, look back again: therefore, the avenue in township is wide, the new city bell is ringing in all directions, and the new atmosphere is everywhere. Eighteen away from home, the eldest brother also, I used to be full of lofty sentiments, return makes me more excited. This book is also dedicated to relatives, teachers, classmates, dedicated to my dear hometown."

Silky nostalgia, light lingering. It is already summer, the shadows of the trees are whirling and the evening breeze is blowing. I will continue to strike the echoes of my hometown with words.

Cao Cao and the New Juntun of Changxin

Fengrun County Zhi: "During the Three Kingdoms period, Cao Cao once stationed troops here to recruit new troops."

"the strategy of digging canals to the sea deep, Cao Gong went north to solicit dust. There is no end to the people of Pingba and An'an, and the of recruiting troops Xinjuntun. When the heavy rain blocked the army way, fortunately Tian Tao as a passer–. The ancient village of Lulong banners passed, and the of Liucheng Ping was. "" This is a lyric poem left by a Zhizhou named Chang Yuanqing when he came to Xinjuntun during the Wanli period of the Ming Dynasty. Cao Gong mentioned in the poem is Cao Cao, the prime minister of the Eastern Han Dynasty, a well-known figure. He unified northern China and promoted the system of cantonment, which contributed to the consolidation of the country's borders and the expansion of its territory.

Emperor Xian of the Eastern Han Dynasty (Liu Xie) During the of the year of Jian'an (190-219 AD), after the success of the farmland system under the river, the prime minister Cao Cao vigorously promoted the farmland system throughout the country, especially in the border fortress area, or recruited soldiers to reclaim wasteland or to raise people to farm. That is, the government uses the areas where the army is stationed to farm, or recruits farmers to farm, all for the purpose of obtaining army supplies and reclaiming wasteland and guarding the border. In the 5 year of Jian 'an (AD 200), Cao Cao's army defeated Yuan Shao. In the tenth year of Jian 'an (AD 205), Yuan Shaozi and Yuan Shang were defeated in Hebei and fled to Wuhuan, where they took refuge in the young of the building.

During the Eastern Han Dynasty, the Wuhuan people were mainly nomadic, shooting and hunting, galloping in the wilderness, ferocious in nature, capable of riding and shooting, and with a vast territory. At that time, large areas of land from today's Lulong to the north of Beijing, that is, Shanggu, Liaodong and Liaoxi at that time, all belonged to Wuhuan. At that time, when Cao Cao first planned to send Lu Longsai to attack Wuhuan in the summer and autumn of the 12th year of Jian'an (207 AD), he considered the follow-up source of soldiers and the supply of food and grass on the front line of the war.

At that time, Xinjuntun (now Xinjuntun, Fengrun District, Tangshan City) had an ancient road through the mud river across the river (now the return river). It was divided into to reach Tongzhou, Yanjing (now Beijing) and northern China. Located in the vast fertile plain, 8 miles to the north (to today's Zheng Bazhuang Village, Fengrun District, Tangshan City,) is a wide mud river, 8 miles to the west (to today's Dakan Village, Fengrun District, City) is still a mud river that flows into the Bohai Sea without interest, and 8 miles south is a large coastal beach wetland swamp. Geographically speaking, it is a good place to ensure the supply of food and forage on the front line and the provision of troops. From a strategic point of view, it is of great strategic significance to attack Wuhuan in the future. As a result, Prime Minister Cao set up a military camp here to recruit new recruits and train troops while cantoning the fields to prepare for war. In the process of defeating Wuhuan, unifying the north, and strengthening the rule of the Eastern Han Dynasty, it can be said that Xinjuntun gave full play to its geographical and military advantages, and in a sense played an active and important role in military. It left a stroke in the process of historical development and made its own contribution to the reunification of northern China.

This is Xinjuntun, a place that is always new and not old.

In the long river of history, Xinjuntun (there was a in village for a long time, and its name cannot be tested) has been abolished several times, but the building site of Xinjuntun has not changed since the Han Dynasty. The overall layout is above a high-lying positive cross block. This kind of architectural terrain choice way, in the architecture is the Han Dynasty to create and become popular. Therefore, since ancient times, there has been a saying in Xinjuntun that "the sky is and the rain is, and the people don't have to worry about food" has been spread to this day, which also confirms the historical fact that Xinjuntun was built in the Han Dynasty and has a higher terrain. In the old days, the whole city of Xinjuntun was square, which was intended to be open and upright, facing all directions, and was called "Fangcheng". The city is led by crossroads, with four main streets in the southeast and northwest, eight secondary roads and 24 hutongs. In ancient times, there were four gates, namely Ziqi Donglai Gate, Gold-plated Xizhao Gate, Antarctic Shenghui Gate and Arch Star Beichen Gate (all destroyed during the Anti-Japanese War). The city gate is composed of ancient heavy double cannon nails large wooden doors, stone thresholds and stone gate piers on both sides, which are concise, lively and convenient for people to pass through. There is a gate tower above the city gate, which is tall and strong. The golden characters on the four gates highlight the unique regional culture and show the handsome and dignified ancient city. Connected to the four doors of the is a correct stone —yard base, brick wall, reflecting the safety awareness of Cao Cao's army and grain. There is a peculiar landscape and phenomenon in the ancient city: 4 main streets and secondary streets are connected with hutongs, forming a pattern of roads criss-crossing, lanes lanes, and easy access. After the city gate is closed, people can walk between hutongs in the city, travel to and from each household, and walk in the streets and alleys. What is even more breathtaking is that outsiders who are not familiar with the topography of the can return to their original places as long as they walk along any street without worrying about getting lost. This 1 strange phenomenon, I do not know whether the ancestor's design concept is ahead of time, or according to local conditions and homeopathic construction, or out of the consideration of war, can enter and exit, can attack and defend.

The layout of a labyrinth, but not a labyrinth, remains a mystery. These imprints the ancient streets and alleys that have been in the vicissitudes of life for months. Some still exist today, while others have long been destroyed by the war, the "during the Cultural Revolution" or the Tangshan earthquake. Outside the strong and majestic city, there is a trench around the city with a width and a depth of about 2 meters. There is also a suspension bridge on the trench, which is a safety measure to prevent foreign invasion. Outside the city, about 300 meters away from the gate of the fourth street, there are 1 large stone bridges in the. Each bridge is 3 meters long, 3 meters wide and 3 meters high. It is not only the only way to the ancient city, but also the water system around the city. Every rainy season, the water around the city gurgling, full ditch fish and shrimp floating, showing the ecological and natural harmony and beauty. There is a temple in the east, west, north and south 4 of Xinjuntun, on the streets of Street. The Sanguan Temple outside the east gate is dedicated to the three immortals of Fu, Lu and Shou; the Fire Temple outside the west gate is dedicated to the Kitchen Lord; the Guanyin Temple outside the south gate is dedicated to Guanyin Bodhisattva; the Guandi Temple outside the north gate is dedicated to Guan Emperor. These temples, built in the Tang Dynasty, provide a magical place for worshippers of various immortals to worship incense. To this day, there is still a folk saying: "4 temple the streets of the town, and water flows everywhere. The official family is not long, wealth is not the head "jingle.

There are 1 famous "Heart Fragrance " academies outside the west gate of the old city, which was built by Zhao Guohua, the magistrate of Shandong in the Qing Dynasty, who personally chose the site and the. The buildings in Xinjuntun Market are quite antique, with cornices and arches, front porches and back buildings, carved beams and painted buildings. On the market, there are many shops, wine cooking pots, traditional Chinese medicine halls, medicine shops, taverns, and restaurants. It has become a large market town in the southern half of Fengrun County since the Ming and Qing Dynasties.

In the early 1960 s, with the completion of Fengrun County No.1 Chemical Fertilizer Plant in Xinjuntun, Zhang Jimin, then secretary of the People's Commune, organized and led the people to re-excavate the ancient moat. The river flowed around the town and finally entered the Bohai Sea via the Mud River in the west, making the town glow with youth and charm. Unfortunately, the 1976 earthquake razed this ancient town to the ground, and there was nothing on the ground. However, with the care and support of the party and the government, a 1 new socialist small town rose here again. In the 1990 s, the town party committee at that time, with the support of higher-level leaders, actively sought the state to list Xinjuntun as Fengrun County. One of the two key planned small towns. In 2002, with the help of the opportunity of widening and reconstruction of the provincial highway from Tangshan to Tongzhou, the road surface of the East and West Street was expanded from the original 20 meters to 40 meters. On both sides of the straight and wide road, buildings with novel shapes and fashionable buildings are rising from the ground, and the seven-story clock tower stands tall. Government, hospitals, shopping buildings, department stores, elementary schools, junior high schools, and Senior high school teaching buildings are 1 more beautiful than one building. New community residential buildings are constantly being built, full of vitality. In order to meet the needs of economic construction and traffic development in small towns, a South Outer Ring Road has been built. Today's Xinjuntun is a town that integrates culture, education, health, industry and agriculture, commerce and trade, telecommunications and postal services. There are many high-rise buildings, convenient transportation, appearance of the city, beautiful day by day, among the ranks of famous towns in China. Tang (Shantong) (County) and Xin (Juntun) Bao () highways pass through the city, 7.5 kilometers away from the east of the city is the exit of Beijing-Harbin Expressway, and 2.5 kilometers away from the west of the city is Fengrun Tianjin Expressway. The No. 116 bus in Tangshan City, and the No. 8 and No. 2 buses in Fengrun District all pass here. It is a well-known town a famous city. Built in the Han, flourishing in the Ming Dynasty and flourishing in the Qing Dynasty, Xinjuntun gradually entered prosperity and affluence after thousands of years of wind and rain.

Imagine today that when Meng Degong first built the new Juntun that year, he might not think too much about the future of the new Juntun, but just used it as a military base out of war needs. If Meng De Gong can see the new look of Xinjuntun today and the scene of people in, he may feel that the tide floating, and he will be filled with emotion and write another song "Ten Thousand Miles.

Han Chang and Han Cheng of Liao Kingdom

Ten kilometers west from the center of Tangshan, there is a place called Hancheng. Fengrun County was originally, Fengrun District, now belongs to Lubei District, Tangshan City. According to the textual research of the local unearthed cultural relics when the foundation of the Donghuantuo Mine in Kailuan was excavated in the 1970 s, as early as the Spring and Autumn Period and the Warring States period in my country, there were already people living here and forming villages. Because of the age of, the name of the village has been impossible to check. However, we can also see a few words about Hancheng in the written materials. In the historical sites of Fengrun County in Qing Dynasty, there is such a description: "Han Town," Fengshi itinerary Record ", Town has a resident who can hundreds of 2, and there is no city ." Another "Zunhua Tongzhi" contains that in the first year of Jin Da 'an (1209 AD), the of Yongji County in was changed to the of Fengrun County in, and Han Town was established at the same time, which was the of Yutian County in Jizhou at that time.

When it comes to Hancheng, one cannot fail to mention the historical Han Dirang. Han Dirang is also known as Han Chang from ancient times to the present. His ancestral home is Yutian. His ancestors have long been in the of Liao Dynasty for the people. Although he is a Han nationality, he has Xin and to make progress and gradually become a little famous. His ancestor Han Zhigu and his father Han Kuangsi were both of the great officials of the Liao State. Gradually, the Han family was regarded as a famous family in the great of the Liao State. The rulers of the Great Liao were more enlightened and allowed their subjects to intermarry with Han Chinese. That's why it happened that Empress Xiao was Han Dirang's fiancee when she was a teenager.

The Great Liao Dynasty and the first year of June (AD 983), the young Liao Shengzong (Yelu Longxu) took the throne, and the Empress Dowager Xiao was in charge of state affairs. This iron lady, who has been all-powerful in history, can be said to be righteous and sentimental. Empress Dowager Xiao did not forget to remember that in early years she had allowed to marry Han Derang (Han Chang). At that time, Jingzong (Yeluxian) proposed marriage. She knew very well that imperial power was as great as heaven and could not be offended. In desperation, she had to marry into the palace and later became the queen. However, the old husband and young wife did not last long, and Jing Zong died (in September, the fourth year of Ganheng in Liao Kingdom, 982 AD). Empress Xiao missed the old love and called Han Derang (Han Chang) into the palace to the favored by Empress Xiao and always led the Suwei. To make him his right-hand man, he said to Han Chang in private: "I often promise to marry a son. I wish to marry a son with, then the young master will be the country, and the will also a son." At this time, Han Chang was in the position of supervising the country. In the first year of the unification and the Kaifeng of Han Derang (Han Chang), together with the three departments of the, and the government decrees, and let him actively participate in the big and small campaigns of going south to attack the Song Dynasty. In September of the 22nd year of the Great Liao Dynasty and the Northern Song Dynasty (AD 1002), after the of the Great Liao Dynasty and the Northern Song Dynasty set to establish the famous alliance of Chanyuan in history, the delighted Empress Xiao felt that Han Chang (Han Derang) had made indelible contributions to the battle against the Great Song Dynasty and to force the Great Song Dynasty to make peace. Han Chang was gladly given Han Derang (Han De), han Changguan to the great prime minister, the general know the north and south council of the navy, the military and political power in one. In the 28th year of Tonghe (1010 AD), Longyun was given the name. In this way, Han Chang (Han Derang)'s Liao name is Yelu Longyun. Under the care of Empress Dowager Xiao, Yelu Longyun (Han Chang, Han Derang) was above the prince of the Liao Kingdom. During the six large-scale wars against the Northern Song Dynasty (AD 983-AD 1002) from the first year of the Great Liao Dynasty to the first 20 years of the

Great Liao Dynasty, Empress Dowager Xiao was mostly Counselor Jean Han Chang (Han Derang) army the plane, on top of the great cause of going south to attack the Song Dynasty, gave Han Chang (Han Dechang) a vast space and a great platform for his talents to play, enabling Han Chang (Han Dechang) to gallop freely in the battlefield and fully demonstrate his battle plan. Strategic military talent and strategy.

Due to the continuous Liao and Song wars at that time, under the powerful southward offensive of the Liao, the Northern Song had to retreat repeatedly, making the border between the Liao and Northern Song dynasties continue to move southward. The border between the two countries was in today's Tianjin Haihe, Hebei Ba County (now Bazhou City), Shanxi Yanmenguan area. At that time, when the army of the great Liao state hit the of today's Hancheng, Han Chang, as the grand marshal of the three armies of the great Liao state, looked at the Zhulong river flowing slowly to the south and the land of the great song dynasty just around the corner in the south, and couldn't help feeling deeply. He hit his ancestral hometown. Because, Hanchang ancestral home Yutian, at that time is to Yutian jurisdiction, can be described as "return to hometown". Stretch your heart, take a breath, rest and recuperate, and fight again in favor. Immediately, the camp was set up, and the of the large military camp was here. The officers and soldiers of the three armed forces and the local people were ordered to transport soil and bricks, and a 1 tall Liao army station (now Hancheng Primary School) was piled up. Han Chang (Han Derang) also built a 1 majestic Han Chang Mansion in his own Shuai Mansion to show Guang Zong's spirit of honing his ancestors and destroying Song Dynasty.

As the years go by, time flies, thousands of years in a flash. Hanchang Mansion has long been untraceable, and the original buildings on the point general platform have disappeared, but the high point general platform is still there. Hancheng Primary School has already been built on the point general platform, and the training ground under the point general platform has become the big playground of Hancheng Primary School and the first kindergarten in Hancheng.

A section of history, the characters one by one, the big stage of history, like a lantern, you sing my debut. In the twinkling of an eye, the decline of Liao Jin Sheng. Jinshi, now Fengrunxi is the of Yongji County, and now Hancheng is the of Yongji County in. When it came to King Jin Weishao, in order to avoid the of King Jin Weishao's name Wanyan Yongji, the court ordered to change the of Yongji County to Fengleap (changed to Run in Ming Dynasty) County. Presumably, when Wanyan Yongji, the king of Jin Weishao, changed the of Yongji County to the of Fengrun County in and established Han Town in the first year of Jin Da 'an (1209 AD), perhaps it was based on this historical spread that the place was named Hancheng.

Sunset Drunk Wolong

Not long ago, a friend of mine published a book called "Wolong Realizing a Dream". After browsing it, he was infected by it. He always wanted to see Wolong Zhen Yan. In order to facilitate the tour, access to some of the relevant information on Wolong Mountain. It is learned that Wolong Mountain is located in Niangniang Village, 20 kilometers southeast of Zunhua City. The undulating peaks resemble a giant dragon lying across it. Mountain trees verdant, clear spring holy water. Fruit trees in the middle, pine and cypress hats, is a fascinating and eye-catching place. For a long time, because the local people saw from the south of the mountain that the dragon head looked exactly like the 1 sole, so, commonly known as the sole mountain... Seeing these, they were very excited, so invited a group of 13 friends from the Writers Association of the to drive from the Xishankou of Tangshan City at 4 pm on September 12, and drove all the way. Arriving within the territory, driving the wheels without stopping, refueling on the winding, winding and circuitous Wolong Mountain Road, and stopping in front of Tenglong Temple on the top of the mountain. to get off the bus and stand on the hill looking down around. Seeing Wolong Mountain from west to east, the ancient mountain is a dragon, tangible and powerful, majestic and majestic. The mountains and cypresses are luxuriant and lush; the mountains and flowers are in full bloom, and the strange rocks are jagged and strange.

We were received by Wang Hongcheng, manager of Zunhua Wolong Mountain Tourism Development Co., Ltd. He also introduced the origin of Wolong Mountain to us. He said: "According to legend, the Dragon King of the East China Sea was ordered by the Jade Emperor of to inspect the world, understand the people's sentiments, and observe their suffering. When I traveled over this place, I saw famine everywhere and the people were in dire straits. He immediately sent his ninth son, Pi Xiu, to appease him. The brave plowed the clouds and sowed the rain, sprinkling rain and dew all over the world. Since then, the backwater here has become a beautiful and rich mountain village. In order to ensure the safety of the common people on one side, the brave changed into a mountain, and stationed in day and night, loyally guarding the common people in this area. Because it looks like Wolong, it is named Wolong Mountain."

Standing on the open space to the east outside the Tenglong Temple, the 76-year-old Wang

Hongcheng guided us to look at the mountains on all sides and said: "Looking from here to the southeast and northwest, we can see the six mountains, layered like lotus flowers. The top of the mountain where the Tenglong Temple is is located is in the position of the heart of the flower. The Tenglong Temple is built on this lotus heart." After listening to the old man's prompt, I looked around and appreciated it carefully. It was really like what the old man said, the layers of mountains like lotus petals surrounded the peaks at our feet. We followed the old man into the Tenglong Temple. The old man Wang Hongcheng pointed out a scenic spot below the mountain and introduced us. When we looked at it, we couldn't help sighing that nature's uncanny craftsmanship Wolong Mountain's leading peak, Longji peak, Longfu peak, Longyu Rufeng, Longwei peak, and the five peaks are connected, such as a giant dragon lying across the mountains and seas. It is lamentable that the time is short and the meaning is still not enough. I have not been able to see all the scenic spots, travel all over Wolong Mountain, and see all the wind and light.

This year's autumn came early. On the evening of September 12, we still felt cool in the beautiful sunset in Wolong Mountain. But the red sunset on the western horizon, bathed in the mountains and temples on the earth, reflected on the red walls and golden glazed tiles of Tenglong Temple, seemed so brilliant and refreshing, which made me obsessed and deeply intoxicated.

Beautiful ambush war gives birth to a new road

The highway from Tangshan to Xinjuntun is an important section of the provincial highway from Tangshan to Tongzhou, and it is also the only way from Tangshan to to the western part of and some villages and towns in Tianjin. However, in the past 80 years, this highway, which is greatly related to the 1 ambush of the Eighth Route Army attack team, has undergone many changes before it has the broad and flat appearance it is today.

In the 1940 s, during the Chinese people's arduous War of Resistance against Japan, while frantically the remnants and harmed the Chinese and Asian people, Japanese imperialism attempted to extinguish the anti-Japanese flames of the Chinese people, including the people of Tangshan, and establish the so-called Greater East Asia Co-Prosperity Circle. However, under the leadership of the Communist Party of China, the people of Tangshan, who were unyielding and unbreakable, launched a flexible guerrilla war against the Japanese aggressors the. The guerrillas of the Eighth Route Army in eastern Hebei in Tangshan have set up an ambush to the west of the Japanese stronghold in Hancheng for more times to attack the Japanese. The reason for the diversion of some sections of this road is that the guerrillas successfully attacked the Japanese military convoy.

It was a day in the winter of 1942. According to relevant information, the Eighth Route Army guerrillas learned in advance that the Japanese army had several military vehicles transporting personnel and materials from Tangshan City to the Japanese stronghold in Xinjuntun. In order to destroy the Japanese army and destroy their supplies, our Eighth Route Army guerrillas set up an ambush quietly in the middle section of Tuo Village in Xihuan along the way, waiting for Japanese military vehicles from Tangshan City to the stronghold of Town, Xinjuntun. At that time, the road from Tangshan to Xinjuntun all the way through Zhuang, which also provided cover for the ambush. At more than ten o'clock that morning, 3 Japanese military vehicles drove into the ambush. At the command of the commander, the guerrillas pulled mines, threw grenades, and opened fire with pistols and rifles. It was really a bolt from the blue, like a magic soldier from the sky. The Japanese army was caught off guard. It was too late to organize the anti-attack from the car. The military vehicle suddenly caught fire. All the devil soldiers on the burning military vehicles were killed, and the materials on the 3 military vehicles were all burned by the. This battle brought a big blow to the Japanese army, causing losses in human, financial and material resources. From then on, the ferocious Japanese 1 were angry and ordered to divert all the eighteen-mile road between the two Japanese strongholds, Hancheng and Xinjuntun on the Tang Road to avoid being ambushed again. As a result, a large number of migrant workers are forced to change the new road. From Donghuantuo 1, 2, 3, 4, Xihuan Tuo, Xiaozhuangzi, Wangdaozhuang and other villages all changed to Zhuangnan, and strictly ordered the people of all villages along the line not to plant sorghum, corn and other tall crops on both sides of the road, in case the Eighth Route Army guerrillas ambushed the Japanese again. From there, the section of the road from Hancheng to Xinjuntun on the Tangtong Line moved out of the village. It was not until the Chinese people defeated Japanese imperialism that tall crops such as sorghum and corn were reproduced on both sides of the road. Now, old people in their 80 s recall the scene at that time, and they still remember it vividly, and they also talk about the anti-Japanese things at that time.

After the founding of New China, the state and the government have allocated funds for many times to adjust, renovate and widen the section from Tangshan to Xinjuntun on the Tangtong line. From the beginning of the loess road to the later stone slag road, and then to the asphalt road. After the Tangshan earthquake in 1976, in order to meet the needs of the city, society, economy, and construction and development, the Tangshan Municipal Government transferred the section passing through Liuhuo Xinzhuang, Guojiazhuang, Yuanjiazhuang, and Hancheng to the south of Village and the original Tangshan City. Outside the south gate of the Second Agricultural Machinery Factory, the road surface was widened and straightened, and this road was designated as a civilized road section.

After the reform and opening up, due to the continuous development and construction of Tangshan, especially in 2003, while the outer ring expressway in Tangshan and Shanxi was repaired, the section of Liu Huo Xinzhuang to Hancheng Town was once again opened up a new road in Zhuangnan, directly connecting with Tangshan Beixin West Road, widening the road surface into a two-way 4 lane. Under the new situation, the rapid development of Tangshan's economic construction situation, in 2012, the Tangshan Municipal Government once again widened the section from Liuhuo Xinzhuang to Hancheng Town to a two-way road with six cars. In 2023, the Hancheng section of the Tangtong Line will be upgraded again. As a result, the section of this important road on the Tangtong line has further played a role in promoting urban and rural construction, goods trade circulation, road transportation and other undertakings in Tangshan. It has also given full play to the positive role and potential capacity of this provincial highway in the economic integration and coordinated development of Beijing, Tianjin and Hebei. On the occasion of the 79th anniversary of the victory of the Anti-Japanese War, looking back on the arduous 14-year Anti-Japanese War, looking forward to the achievements of the construction of New China, and looking forward to the Chinese dream and the great rejuvenation of the Chinese nation, it is unavoidable to be comforted.

Kailuan remains

Looking at the sky and clouds, watching the long flow of coal the river, tracing the echo of Kailuan (1878-2024) spanning the 3 century of years and months.

The silver carried by the long line of donkeys and the sweat of the people of the Qing Dynasty witnessed the continuous self-improvement of the Chinese people. The first whistle of the first steam locomotive on the land of China opened the curtain of the Chinese national industry. The Wujin rolling in the Kaiping coal mine was burning with flames, inspiring the Beiyang Fleet in the late Qing Dynasty to the majestic and powerful, the largest ship in Asia.

To build a new China, to resist US aggression and aid Korea, to build socialism with Chinese characteristics, and to realize the great rejuvenation of the Chinese nation, all stages have your-Kailuan's outstanding contribution, and the singing of "especially capable of fighting" has never been interrupted.

The first office building of the Kailuan Mining Bureau built in the 19th century stands tall on the shore of the Haihe River to listen to the of the River of the day and night.

The rising sun of Qinhuangdao Port has witnessed the establishment and prosperity of China's first coal terminal, the Tangshan Port Coal Terminal is busy day and night, and the Caofeidian Port Area is welcoming the glory of China's largest coal terminal.

Weizhou to achieve coal circuit integration; Inner Mongolia prairie has seen Kailuan riding a galloping horse; Kailuan song in the Yili River reverberated; Canadian soil also has Kailuan flag flying high.

A rising sun, 1 birds spread their wings, 1 ships sail. How many years of wind and rain, how many times to summon up courage to fly, how many back to the sun endless imagination.

Look, the long sky cloud volume Shu, to the wide horse Mercedes-Benz. Kailuan, advancing with the times with high spirits. To be bigger and stronger, to invigorate and open up the-to realize the dream of Kailuan in 146 years.

Kailuan, the 21st century youth is still, vitality is still, Hao Qi is still. The new pace of the "new era" is facing the future and is full of brilliant hopes all the way.

"Eight of God" falls to Sanzhuang

Legend has it that there were eight immortals living in village in Fengrun County in ancient times, so people called this village the Eight Gods Village.

The eight immortals often feel a little lonely because they live here for a long time. As a result, the eight immortals sat together and 1 deliberated, and decided to travel together. On a clear day, they set off. All the immortals drifted along and unconsciously came to a place called 4 Zhuang. One immortal suggested stopping to rest his feet. Everyone sat on the ground under the 1 old tree, enjoying the scenery and chatting. After a short break, several immortals got up to leave. I didn't want 4 immortals to refuse to leave because they liked the scenery of the countryside. Helpless, the other 4 gods had to bid farewell to them and move on. They walked some distance and came to a village to rest. After a while, one of them proposed to move forward after, but the other three immortals didn't want to go any more. They just smiled at the kitchen god. The kitchen god looked at them and asked, "Why don't you just smile and walk wow ?" The three immortals replied, "We see the scenery here is also good, and we plan to live here." Hearing this, the Kitchen God was anxious: "So you have all discussed it! Well, if you don't go, I'll go!" With that, he left himself angrily. He walked alone without landing. He felt a little tired and meaningless. At this moment, there happened to be a village not far away. Under the sunset, the Kitchen God simply lived in the village. From then on, the village was named Kitchen God Zhuang. The village where the 4 gods live is called four gods village, the village where the three gods live is called three gods village, and the place where the eight gods start is called eight gods village. At present, these villages are all under the jurisdiction of Lubei District of Tangshan City.

8 January 2024

Qian Tong Tide Watching

"August 18 tide, the world spectacular without ." The Qiantang tide is a wonder of the world. In the middle of August of the lunar calendar last year, I Hangzhou on a trip. I was lucky to have a glimpse of it.

On that day, we drove from Hangzhou early in the morning to Yanguan Town, of Haining County. This is on the verge of Hangzhou Bay, where the tide is surging. The east-south sea embankment of the town is as a tide-watching resort, with buildings such as sea-watching platform, tide-watching pavilion and zhenhai tower. Tide head to this line of, for the "Haining pagoda line tide" magnificent scene. We came here with a sea of people, and it took a lot of effort to get the car to a hotel. Riverside, waiting for the tide of the people, black skin, yellow skin, white skin; Blonde, white hair, black hair ... is really crowded.

Qiantang tide at noon once in the middle of the night. At thirteen BST, we looked straight ahead. At the Tianshui line, it looked like a silver dragon lying across, and then there was a loud noise, and then the snow waves surged into the sky and the sea stood upside down. 1 wall of brown-black water, which is nearly 3 meters high, roars and goes hand in hand, such as a galloping horse, which makes people feel thrilling. It is no wonder that some people wrote in the poem after watching the tide: "in a flash, the wall of water is built the sea, thunder, lightning, ghosts and gods are worried! The water the of the wall and the together. The surging is like a brave."

Why is the Qiantang tide so spectacular? This is because the exit of Hangzhou Bay, the terrain is a bell mouth. When the tide comes, the width of the of the tide front suddenly narrows the, the energy is concentrated, and the flow rate increases, resulting in the tide head getting higher and higher, and there is a magnificent scene of turning the river and falling the sea. According to the local people, in recent years, due to the reclamation of land from the sea in the bay area, the splendor of the spring tide is not as spectacular as before. But for me, a mainlander who has never seen big rivers and waves, the scenery is still amazing.

October 4, 1987

Hainan "5 leg frog"

People say it's hard to find a toad with three legs, but I 've seen a frog with five legs.

It was 1981. When I was in Haikou, Hainan Island, I had nothing to do on Sundays and often went to the park. After seeing the peacock open its screen once, I unconsciously came to a shrouded front. 1 pool of clear water under the cage, there was a small artificial cave exposed to the water. Huh! What animal is this? Why is nothing happening? Looking up at the sign hanging on the cage, ha, it originally said frog. A closer look at the following makes me refreshing, to the effect that this frog is a rare "5 leg frog" in the world, male. If you find this kind of frog in the future, please send it to the of the garden to make pairs and reproduce for people to watch.

To be honest, these five-legged frogs have never been seen before. Several of us stared and waited for the to be to watch, but we just couldn't see it coming out. It was really urgent. After waiting for a while, the great god frog was finally born. I saw it standing by the small hole, looking like a big model: the back legs squatting, the front legs supporting the, and the 1 legs supporting the on the stone under the lower jaw. We looked at it funny and wondered, is it because the frog's head is too heavy to an extra leg to support it? The of the big family laughed when they saw this strange appearance. What is expected, this smile can be broken, the frog jaw that leg forward 1, later two front legs folded ten, two hind legs 1 to push, plunged into the water. After a while, it surfaced again, staring at the world in front of him with two big eyes. We quietly observe its form. It is the same as a normal frog, except that the front single leg moves with the's right front leg. Weird, weird! It's a feast for our eyes. It's just a pity that there was no camera in my hand to take this rare shot.

1989 September 9

Shenyule

Everyone has his own hobby. One of my hobbies is collecting travel maps. For a period of time, I worked in a material supply unit. I had many opportunities to go out, and I had a wide range of areas, with purchasing points and manufacturers all over the country.

It is precisely because of these 1 favorable conditions that whenever I go on business trips, in addition to paying attention to local customs, customs and traditions, I also pay attention to buying local tourist maps for collection. Other comrades in this unit are on business trips or meetings. I always can't forget to them to bring back a tourist map. Over the years, now, my desk drawer has stored almost two drawers of travel maps, travel transportation, travel accommodation, etc. Among them, there are prosperous cities and remote towns; there are famous mountains and rivers, there are valleys and fairyland; there are beautiful seashores and vast deserts; there are revolutionary shrines and former residences of celebrities. Whenever I have free after dinner, I always open the drawer and look through these travel maps, which also makes my tired mood to adjust a little. Now, my collection of tourist maps all over the motherland Jiangnan Saibei, inside and outside the Great Wall. the Silk Road, you can go to the western regions of, climb the Great Wall east to the Bohai Sea, take the northbound train to Inner Mongolia and Xinjiang, and take the southbound passenger ship to the ends of the earth. It can be said that if you sit in a fighting room, you can travel around Kyushu, beautiful and happy.

December 17, 1989

Winter aftertaste summer river coal fragrance

After beginning of winter, there was a little snow for a few days. The wind blew in early winter. There were still many leaves on poplar, willow, French sycamore and other trees in the city, and yellow poplar leaves and ginkgo leaves were floating. Looking up at the sky, blue, floating a few silk cloud, feel a little thin cold. Downstairs, the lawn cut by the lawnmower at the end of autumn spread out like a huge carpet, still with some soft and hair feeling, and some red, yellow, white and purple rose flowers in the grass, still unwilling to give up the last 1 wisps of warm sun, struggling to bloom in the sun. Clusters of western powder lotus flowers are so eye-catching and affectionate and fresh open, the willow silk weeping along the aisle swaying in the breeze. Standing in the room, watching the quiet coal river in the sun, the aftertaste her the fragrance of summer.

Coal River, excavated in the 6th year of Guangxu of the Qing Dynasty (1880 A. D.), is an artificial river that runs from east to west through the small town of Xugezhuang (Qing Dynasty, Hetou Town). Bathed in the morning light, sparkling, flowing quietly to the west. It was still an early morning in early July, and I walked to the belt park by the coal river.

This season, it is the season of acacia flowers in full bloom. Before approaching the green belt by the river, bursts of refreshing acacia flower fragrance hit the nose. Unconsciously, I took a few deep breaths to let my body and mind feel the rich fragrance. Walk under the acacia tree and stop and look up. On the branches, among the sparse green leaflets, there are pink radial spherical acacia flowers. The fluffy flower balls light and bright, and the stamens are compact and unrestrained. In the small empty field under the tree, 1 group of middle-aged men and women danced their 3-foot swords to the music, so they were relaxed and natural.

Continue to walk along the river, I saw 1 acacia tree branches to under the bank, blooming acacia flowers, look so brilliant. 1 old man sat in this beautiful scenery, fishing with a pole, so carefree. Standing not far away, I appreciate it. This lens looks like a 1 painting. It is very beautiful. It is said that it is a scene of Coal River, which can be taken for granted.

On the side of the aisle among the trees in the green belt on both sides of the Coal River, lawns are covered one by one, and the grass on the lawn stands upright and proud like dwarfs, with crystal clear little dew beads on their heads, which looks very cute in the morning light. I couldn't help but squat down to watch carefully. A breath of green grass fragrance rose head-on. This is the 1 breath of nature. When I was in it, I 1 a kind of heart full of. Not far away, 1 old man was practicing boxing with a strong and moving around. In this atmosphere, people and nature are in harmony.

Walking in the trees and meadows by the river, you can occasionally see pieces of small flowers with short plants. In this midsummer, they are unwilling to be lonely. The pink and red flowers bloom enthusiastically, but they are not high from the ground, and they bloom very vigorously., And exudes a faint fragrance of flowers, dedicated to beauty in the world. In the small empty field adjacent to it, 1 groups of women in sportswear are arranged neatly, sometimes beating, sometimes beating rhythmically on different parts of their bodies, and sometimes dancing around their waists. Looking at her all with a smile on their faces, just like the small flowers, happy and indifferent, plain and brilliant.

Standing in the coal river belt park, from west to east polar eye throughout. The high-rise buildings in the community are separated from each other, and people's life is calm and. Today's coal river has been 144 years, although there is no late Qing dynasty sail shadow boat, but the riverside avenue is straight and wide, the flowers and trees in the belt park is full of vitality, the north China plain of Jidong small town and small town people's dream scroll, also in this full of fragrance has been continuously stretched and realized.

Monarch and Fengrun County in Past Dynies

Fengrun is a district of Tangshan City today, known as Tuyin County in ancient times. Speaking of Tuyin County, it also involves King Zhao Wuling (325 BC -299 BC) of the Zhao State, 1 of the Seven Heroes of the Warring States Period. King Zhao Wuling became the of the king of in 325 BC. He boldly carried out military reforms in Zhao. Hu Fu rode, built a strong army and rejuvenated the country, attacked and destroyed Zhongshan, defeated Lin Hu and Lou Fan, and established Yunzhong, Yanmen and Daijun. Its territory includes the central and northern parts of Shanxi, northeast Shaanxi, southwest

Hebei and Hetao. The country is prosperous. That is, the King of Zhao Wuling, through the form of land exchange between powerful countries, built the of Tuyin City in the upper reaches of the Yang River (now the Hometown River) (the original site was in the Yinpu, Fengrun District, Tangshan, and the city was interpreted Yincheng. After, the evolved into Yincheng), and later became the Tuxian County.

In 202 BC, Liu Bang (206-193 BC) of the Han Dynasty set up Tuyin County in, and the county seat was the of Tuyin Kencheng. In the Northern Qi Dynasty (550-577 AD), Gao Yang (from Bohai Sea in ancient, that is, from County in Jing, Hebei Province), the founder of the Northern Qi Dynasty, changed Yuan Tianbao, appointed Han people, and changed law when he was in office from 550-559 AD. Years of attack soft, Turks. The of the city of Tuyin was abandoned in Bingxian. In the eighth year of Tianbao (557 AD), the city of was moved to the of Jubao in. The set up the Yongji service, which means "abundant grain and grass, and continuous Yongji". The belongs to the of Xuwu County. In the first year of Jin Shizong's Wanyan Yongda Ding (1161 A. D.), Wanyan Fushou and others staged a coup and adopted him as emperor. Changed Yuan Dading. In December of the first year, heavy troops were sent to invade the Song. In the 5 year (1166 AD), the Southern Song Dynasty was forced to make peace. After the end of the war, attention was paid to the development of agricultural production. During his twenty-nine years in office, agriculture and handicrafts have developed to varying degrees ". In the 5 year of Dading (1166 A. D.), City in Yongji County was built, which is now City in Fengrun County,. In the 27th year of (1187 AD), Yongji was changed to, Yongji County,. Wanyan Yong's seventh son, Wanyan Yongji, took the throne in the eighth year of Taihe (1208 AD). The following year (1209 AD) was changed to Yuan Da 'an. In the first year of Da 'an (1209 AD), King Wanyan Yongji of Jin Wei Shao changed to Fengleap County in order to avoid the of the name of King Wanyan Yongji of Wei Shao. Kublai Khan of Yuan Shizu merged Fengleap County of into Yutian County in the 2 year of Yuan Dynasty (1265 AD). In four years, Fengleap County was resumed. In 22 years (1285), the of Lifeng Leap Department was. Zhu Yuanzhang destroyed Yuan Jianming (AD 1368) and changed to Yuan Hongwu. In the first year of Hongwu (1368 A. D.), Fengleap was changed to Fengrun, which means "Fengze Runmei " and belongs to Jizhou, Shuntian Prefecture,. Since then, Fengrun County has a name.

14 April 1995

New Juntun Collection Has Legends

In Fengrun District of Tangshan City, there is a place where the village was built earlier-Xinjuntun. There are written records show that was built in the Eastern Han, and the Prime Minister of the Eastern Han Dynasty Cao Cao also established a military village here. It is a traditional market town with a long history of local people's custom of going to the market.

According to legend, in the early years, the court set up a market in Xinjuntun to promote the trade of agricultural and sideline products in the local and surrounding areas. At that time, about 4 miles west of Xinjuntun Village, there was a village named Yangjiazhuang (still exists), which was comparable to Xinjuntun Village in terms of geographical location, traffic conditions, village size, population, and products. In order to be able to set up a village of Jixing, there is a fierce competition between Xinjuntun and Yangjiazhuang. The local officials of the imperial court were also difficult to decide for a while, and later, they decided to let the two village take 1 of sand with the same volume, and fight it out with their net weight. Set up in any village where the sand is heavy. As a result, the sand in Xinjuntun Village was heavier than the sand in Yangjiazhuang Village, and Yangjiazhuang had no choice but to lose. As a result, a gathering was set up in Xinjuntun, 1. six as the gathering day. When the market opened at the beginning of the first day of the lunar calendar, the dry boats in the east street of Xinjuntun, the car club in the west street, the dragon lanterns in the south street and the stilts in the north street were all dispatched to celebrate the opening of the market. Merchants from Ninghe, Yutian, Zunhua and Fengrun North gathered in Xinjuntun for trading, an unprecedented grand occasion.

There are soybeans, corn, sorghum and other crop products and rural daily necessities, as well as chickens, ducks,, fish, pigs and sheep, as well as mules, horses, donkeys,, cattle and agricultural livestock. As the terrain of Xinjuntun to the west and south is than that of depression, reed is abundant in ancient times, so the reed and reed mat (a necessary kang mat for every family) trade in the market here also accounted for a certain proportion.

Fair entertainment is also more abundant, in which more juggling. like acrobatics, martial arts (martial arts), qigong ... in the words of the new army tun people is "playing handfuls".

In the market, there was a wooden chair in the white cloth shed, a brass basin on the 1 charcoal stove, and a white handkerchief soaked in the water of the copper basin. This was what the common people called the shaving shed. It was indispensable in the market. In those days, many people who went to the market shaved their heads. There are also many stalls selling plasters in the market. In addition to the of cloth, clothing, cloth, and socks, there are children's tiger-headed shoes, tiger-headed hats, sugar-blowing people, clay figurines. The one that sharpens the scissors and the chopper is a bench with a magic stone tied one end, a small bucket hung on the other, and the and of a chopper. From the of the Republic of China to the of, there were still people watching western scenery in the and early 1960 s. During the temple fair, many adults and children 1 set aside 1 to sit on a long bench in turn, surrounded by 1 large utensils, and looked in through a magnifying glass. There is a pulling a thin rope to pull down pictures one by one, so it is also called a foreign film.

Today in the 21st century, some of the scenes in the market in the past no longer exist, but the 1 folk customs of the market have not changed. The material of the market has been greatly enriched, and the form, scale and content of the market have been constantly integrated into modern elements, gradually enriched, expanded and improved.

October 2, 1995

Tangshan Dependencies in the Past Dynasties

In the long process of social development, the territory of Tangshan City has also left a trail of with various changes. During the Xia, Shang, Western and Eastern Zhou dynasties, Tangshan was a solitary bamboo land. Spring and Autumn for the mountains Rong. During the Warring States period, it belonged to the land of Yan. When the Qin Dynasty was in Liaoning County. Western Han is Youzhou Right Beiping County Sunset County. The Eastern Han, Wei and Jin dynasties all belonged to Liaoxi County. Northern Qi when the was a Feiru County, Sui when the Lu Longdi. In the early years of Tang Wude, it belonged to Linyu County, then it was changed to Shicheng County, and it belonged to Pingzhou. Liao and Jin were both in Shicheng County. In the early Yuan Dynasty, Shicheng County was incorporated into Yifeng County. In the Ming Dynasty, Yifeng was Yongping Prefecture. Hongwu Yifeng entered Luanzhou in 2. Qing was the land of Luanzhou in Zhili Province. At the beginning of the Republic of China, it belonged to Bohai Road in Zhili Province, followed by Tianjin Sea Road, and belonged to the 8th District of in Luanxian County,. Today, Tangshan is a municipality directly under the Central Government of Hebei Province.

23 August 1995

Mysterious Tuo of Longtan

1.5 kilometers southeast of Xinjuntun Town, Fengrun District, Tangshan City, there is a small village named Longtantuo. About

The name of the village, there are 3 legends.

Niang Niang Temple. According to legend, there was a 3 empress in the Zhao family in the village. After the empress died, in order to commemorate the empress, the family of Zhao built a 3 temple in the village. Therefore, people call this village Niang Temple.

Longtan Tuo. At that time, when the foundation of the temple was excavated, someone dug out an ancient chime. The ancient chime was engraved with the words "Longtan Tuo ". Later, people also called the village Longtan Tuo.

Longtan. It is also said that in ancient times, there was an aunt and sister-in-law in the village who lived together. Her sister-in-law was diligent and thrifty and. Sister-in-law loves to eat fish since childhood, and every meal necessary. Although the family was not well-off, my sister-in-law did everything possible to get fish to make for my sister-in-law. Later, the family was really difficult and could not afford to buy fish, but my sister-in-law did not understand. However, my sister-in-law sat alone in the courtyard at night and cried. When the celestial immortals heard the cry, they were very moved to find out the reason. They handed it to their sister-in-law to 1 a bamboo pole and ordered: When the wants a fish to, he would use the bamboo pole to point to the of the water tank, and the water would rush and the fish would jump. the fish enough, he would lightly and call the "stop" the water. "the water.

The immortal said and floated away. Sister-in-law tried 1 and it worked. As time went by, my sister-in-law was peeked out by sister-in-law fishing fish. One day, while sister-in-law was doing farm work in the fields, my sister-in-law picked up a bamboo pole and pointed at the in the courtyard. I didn't want to. This 1 was extremely difficult. An unfathomable crypt appeared on the flat ground, and 1 shares of groundwater rushed out. Sister-in-law son heard the news and rushed back from the field, desperate to rescue her sister-in-law, but was flooded. After a while, a dragon carrying sister-in-law to free up the water and the sky. At this time, the water on the ground also returned to the cave. For this reason, the cave is called Longtan, and Village is named with the cave, so it is called Longtan Tuo.

These beautiful legends put a layer of mystery on the of Longtan Tuo, a small village in eastern. With the acceleration of the construction of a new socialist countryside, the future of the village will be more charming.

13 September 1995

Qianjin Yecheng Words Past and Present

Guye, now a district of Tangshan City, the ancient solitary bamboo land. According to legend, it is the land of a thousand gold and a city. In the Tang Dynasty, there was a of prosperity here, and there was a of Peking University Temple (the original site is now Beisi Park). From the Liao Dynasty to the Qing Dynasty (907-1911), belonged to Luanzhou,. With the preparation (1879) and commissioning (1889) of Kailuan Linxi Mine, Tangxu Railway was extended to Guye (1889) and Guye Station was built. During the Republic of China, was a in Luanxian County,, and had built a in Guye Town. The current Guye integrates railways, highways, commerce, coal and other industries. It is the largest material distribution center and transportation hub in urban and rural areas in the eastern part of Tangshan City. It is an important town on the 205 national highway and an important section of the Beijing -line. There are special railway lines for large factories and mines under the Kailuan Mining Bureau, such as Linxi, Lujiatuo, Fangezhuang, Tangjiazhuang, and Zhaogzhuang.

Reform and opening up have brought vitality to Guye. In order to make Guye's economy develop faster, the State Council approved the of Guye from the area (office) to the area, and the of the east mining area into the Guye District. It is believed that the ancient ancient ancient metallurgy, which has long been famous at home and abroad, will give full play to its advantages in geography, transportation, energy and popularity, and take off and recreate its glory in the spring tide of the socialist market economy.

12 May 1995

Zunhua yesterday

Today, Zunhua City, a county-level city affiliated to Tangshan City, was called Xu in ancient times. It was established in the Western Han Dynasty (206 BC), and its name was used in the of the Dynasty. By the Northern Zhou Dynasty (557–581 B. C.), the was abandoned to the of County. The new dynasty (Wang Mang for Han Jianxin, AD 8–23) called Beishunting. The Tang Dynasty (AD 618–907) began to build a city with four doors. In order to consolidate the north and indentify its subjects, the court of the five dynasties and the later Tang dynasty (923–936 AD) was named of Zunhua county,, dynasty, which means "observing the and keeping the imperial court indentification". During the reign of Hongwu (1378 A. D.), due to the need of the Ming Dynasty to strengthen the northern rule, the city in Zunhua County was expanded nearly 1 times to the west and north on the original basis. The Qing Dynasty (1644–1911) was renamed Zunhua Zhili Prefecture due to the construction of the Eastern Tombs of the Qing Dynasty in its territory. At this time, Zunhua city prosperity. In order to for Qing imperial courtiers to play, Longquan Park was also built outside the moat in the northeast corner of Zunhua City, which was still alive before the Anti-Japanese War. In the 2nd year of the Republic of China (1913 AD), Zunhua County, was reformed.

Driven by the good situation of reform and opening up, Zunhua has given full play to its advantages in transportation, products, and tourism. The economy has grown rapidly and various industries have flourished. In 1992, the State Council formally approved the withdrawal of Zunhua County and the establishment of a city. Thus, compliance with the to advance at a greater pace on the road of socialism with Chinese characteristics, and will enter the 21st century with a new attitude.

19 May 1995

Shishi City View Abnormal

In Shijiazhuang Zoo, it is needless to say that jackals, tigers and leopards are like lions, bears and. It is enough to say that the in the zoo the Animal Museum, which is enough to make you enjoy it. There are two pavilions for deformed animals.

At the entrance of the first hall is the 1 black and white 5 leg pig, and the fifth leg is long on the right hind leg. next to its side is a black male six-legged cow. The fifth and six leg are on its right front bladder, one large and one small about 1 feet long. The lateral is a female yellow 5-legged bovine with a fifth leg long under its front right armpit. There is also a 1 rooster with a 3 claw, and a third claw is at the base of its right leg and extends outward. Next to it is the of 1 pedestrian chickens. They walk with their heads held high and stand between heaven and earth, just like 1 a deputy husband. There is a three-legged female dog in the second hall. The back is 1 2 the front, and the lower joint of the front leg is bent to the right and landed on the ground. Next to the 3 -legged dog is a 1 three-legged male goat with 1 hind legs and two forelegs. This was followed by a 1 female sheep the 5 leg, and the fifth leg was long at the top right of its head, drooping like an ear. There is also a cattle the 5 leg, with the fifth leg on its left arm. After reading this, I think the creator is fair. Even if it is "extra branches", but let them match left and right. Although more limbs and less feet are, it does not affect their eating, drinking, pulling, scattering, sleeping and other functions of their kind. Here, they are more free from the pain of foraging, housekeeping and labor. When water comes to their mouths, they to eat. They are full of food all day long. They have no intention and are at ease. They are also to.

July 7, 1995

Remembering Wei Chigong's Big Dark Horse Dian

Wei Chi Jingde is a household name in Chinese history. A famous general in the early Tang Dynasty. Wei Chi Jingde (585-658 A. D.) was a famous with words and lines. At the end of the great cause of the Sui Dynasty, he enlisted in the army Gaoyang and followed Liu Wuzhou as a partial general. In the 3 year of Wude of the Tang Dynasty (AD 620), the Tang was and led to the right 1 government army. Once from Li Shimin to attack the Wang Shichong army, participated in the suppression of Dou Jiande, Liu Hei led the Rebels. In the ninth year of Wude (AD 626), the "Xuanwu Gate Change" was awarded the left guard rate in because it helped the King of Qin Li Shimin kill Prince Li Jiancheng and the King of Qi Li Yuanji., he sought promotion to the right General Wuhou and was named the Duke of Wu. In the 19th year of Tang Zhenguan (645 A. D.), Li Shimin, Emperor Taizong of Tang Dynasty, attacked Gaoli with the Emperor Taizong. He was the commander-in-chief of the Taichang Qing, who was by his official. Li Shimin, Emperor Taizong of the Tang Dynasty, cherished the six horses who fought with him all his life. For this reason, he produced the lifelike stone carvings of war horses in the "Six Horses of Zhaoling" with exquisite art. The emperor is so, not to mention the general who "the war loves horses". Wei Chigong is a man who loves horses like a fool. That year, Wei Chigong with the Emperor Taizong Li Shimin imperial drive to the Koryo (now fresh) from the capital Chang'an all the way east, the soldiers to the of Yan's shop in Fengrun District of Tangshan City, imperial orders set up camp, rest and troops, stationed troops here.

One morning, General Wei Chigong got up and walked out of the army's big tent. Suddenly, not far from the south of Daying, there was a tall wild horse of oil and black drinking in the.

In the light of the sun, the wild horse's whole body is black and shining, if it is like a god horse. Immediately General Wei Chigong fell in love with the wild horse at a glance. I thought, what a beautiful and mighty god horse. In ancient times, war generals who galloped on the battlefield loved good horses. This is what they are talking about. As a result, Wei Chigong immediately moved the saddle to the stirrup and flew away on the horse, but the horse had already disappeared. Wei Chigong left with the good news and returned with the bad news. However, from then on, Wei Chigong, who had been thinking more about the gods and horses day and night, was not reconciled to the gods and horses, and vowed not to give up. The soldiers were ordered to build stands high in the camp and take the stage every morning to watch. Presupposing a trap, ambushing soldiers, determined to catch the god horse for their own.

In the early morning of one day, Wei Chigong boarded the earth platform for routine observation. Suddenly, his eyes brightened and he saw God horse drinking water by the pool. Wei Chigong was overjoyed and ordered the ambush to take him, which finally made Wei Chigong get his wish. Later, people built a village at the of Wei Chi Gongnama. In order to commemorate this historical legend, people set up a stone tablet to show that future generations will remember it. More, the name of village was "Namadian". Later, it was more apt to be renamed "Big Dark Horse ".

In ancient times, the Great Black Horse green grass and pure pool water. Until now, the dark horse is still in the deep pool for people to recall, but the stone tablet has long fallen into the deep pool. Today, with the vigorous development of economy, village of big black horse is just like the horse 1, advancing on the broad road of socialist well-off village construction.

13 May 2005

Three Women River

15.4 kilometers west of the south of Fengrun District, Tangshan City, there is a river called River. On the south bank of the river, there is a village Zhuang named "Sannu River". What a warm and beautiful name, but she has experienced a period of pain and bitter past. According to the "Fengrun Geography", the village was built in the early Ming Dynasty. As for the origin of the village name, there are several versions of the legend in the village: in the last years of the Yuan Dynasty, a group of thieves and soldiers had a bestial attack, chasing 3 girls, chasing this place, 3 aunt mother desperate, the front is the river, and then there are prostitutes. In order to clean the body, 3 a girl resolutely threw herself into the river, and got the village name "3 female river ".

Another legend: there was a butcher, his wife died early, and there were 3 daughters in the family. The butcher was so addicted to alcohol that the family's was dilapidated and destitute. In order to enable oneself to often have money to get wine and drink, regardless of family affection, the rate of one by one of the daughters is, regardless of character. The eldest daughter was betrothed to a sick young man, and even she was looking for a body double to get married, but at this time, she suddenly reported "the young master died!" After that, the bride was insulted by her mother-in-law. On a dark night, the bride came to her mother's grave and cried out her sorrow. The husband's family sent someone to find the butcher's dignitaries, but the bride did not follow them. The wanted to to the nunnery and cut her hair. The old nun was afraid of power and refused to accept her. It's really called heaven should not, there is no way to enter the ground, to this point, the bride 1 mercilessly jump into the mud river...

The second daughter was betrothed by a butcher to an old man over 50, but the second daughter, unwilling to fall into the jaws of a tiger, resisted marriage and fled,

find your own love. But the old man sent someone to capture them both and took the 2 girls back to the government, colluding with the government to send the young people to the army. The sweetheart left, and the 2 girl was disheartened and felt that she no longer had the meaning of living. On the wedding day, when the 2 girl was in despair, the 2 girl was waiting for an opportunity to escape, followed the footsteps of her elder sister, and plunged into the mud river ...

3 daughter was betrothed by the butcher to a young man, who later became a county magistrate. People said that this was a good marriage, better than her two sisters. But who knew that this good man had a bad life, and the good scene was not long. This man the of the official the change of love, began to like the new and dislike the old, climbed the golden branch, and married the daughter of the 1 magistrate in the place where he was an official. The 3 girl learned that she went to town to find her husband for questioning, and the wolf-hearted husband put the 3 girl into prison.

Thanks to the kind pawn –in-law sneaking 3 girl out of her cell. The county magistrate had to the to send people to chase all the way. The 3 girl ran to the mud river in a hurry. Looking at the surging river, she looked back at the chief who had caught up. There was no way to go. In a hurry, she threw into the mud river.

Later, out of respect for the three sisters who committed themselves to their loyalty and defiance against feudal marriage, people their intention to commit self-murder. They and the statue of the 3 women in the Guandi Temple in the village, and took the village name "Three Women River".

Today, Sannvhe is not what it used to be. In the 21st century, with the change of Tangshan military airport into a dual-use airport, Tangshan airport has also changed its name to Sannvhe airport. Due to the needs of economic and urban construction development and the coordinated development of Beijing-Tianjin-Hebei, Sannvhe Airport has undergone several renovations and expansions. Sannv River has quickly integrated into the process of Beijing-Tianjin-Hebei integration, plugged in the wings of flying, soaring into the sky with the good wishes of the 3 women in the past, and heading for a better tomorrow.

January 1, 2024

Song Huizong's Remained Da An Le Zhuang

Da 'anlezhuang is a peaceful and peaceful Zhuang name, but she describes a tragic period of resistance to Jin in the Northern Song Dynasty and the yearning of a generation of kings to govern the country.

Da'anlezhuang is located 5.3 kilometers south of the west of Fengrun District, Tangshan City, and faces the Huanxiang River in the north. It is the frontier of the war between the Song and Jin Dynasties years. Legend has it that the Northern Song Dynasty failed to resist the gold, the emperor Song Huizong was captured to the city of 5, in the soldiers and horses accompanied by swords and iron hooves, Song Huizong set foot on the road to the North, when Song Huizong walked on the wooden bridge on the return river, looking at the vast North, looking back at the mountains and rivers of the old country, looking down at the river to the west, thinking of the water is, I can't help but feel.

However, even the emperor who was captured by the Jin army once commanded thousands of troops on the front line to resist the Jin and protect the country. According to the local people, at that time, the Song and Jin dynasties were at war, and the of the Song Huizong camp tour was here. It was in the dead of night, the camp lights were shining, and the family of Wan went into the dream. They sighed with emotion: "East Anle, west peace, south vicissitudes, north return home." As a result, this village, which was originally called Ange Zhuang in ancient, was renamed Anle Zhuang. Later, because a new village was built in the west of the village, the word "Da" was added to the of the name of the village as Da Anle Zhuang. Today's Daanlezhuang has really embarked on the well-off road of building a new socialist countryside, and people have lived a happy and peaceful life.

11 December 1996

Emperor Tang Zong and Qing Dynasty and Diaoyutai

AD 645, that is, the Tang Dynasty Zhenguan nineteen years. In that year, Emperor Taizong Li Shimin personally led more than 100,000 troops on an eastward expedition to Koguryo (now the northern part of the Korean Peninsula). When passing through today's Tangshan city, he was stationed on the 1 mountain to rest and recuperate. Because there is a city on the mountain, it is called Dacheng Mountain, because Li Shimin once stayed here and was later called "Tangshan" by the local people. Dacheng Mountain is both a mountain and a city, so it has been 1379 since Tangshan was founded.

There is a Diaoyutai in Beijing and a Diaoyutai in Tangshan, and Tang Zong and Qing emperors have something to do with it. The Tang Zong here is not the Tang Gaozong, but the latter Tang Mingzong (reigned from 926 to 932 AD) Li Siyuan. He claimed that before the emperor, because of his military service officer to the Han and infantry chief in, he had to station troops in "Tangshan", which is today's Dacheng Mountain in Tangshan City. In his spare and spare, he often came to the foot of the mountain to the steep river hook fishing.

The Emperor of the Qing Dynasty was Emperor Qianlong of the Gaozong of the Qing Dynasty, who was the all-powerful Emperor Qianlong in Chinese history. When Qianlong went on a tour of this place in the 60th year of Qianlong (1795 AD), the accompanying ministers told him about the later Tang Mingzong's fishing here. The legend of the Qing Gaozong was pleasant and gladly named this place

Diaoyutai according to this legend, which is still in use today.

6 July 1997

Nanhai Beishan Ancient Fengrun

Fengrun County was originally a large and ancient county on the land of China. First, King Zhao Wuling of Zhao State, one of the seven heroes of the Warring States Period, obtained a piece of land of Yan State through land exchange between powerful countries, and built a large-scale Tuyin City on it ("Fengrun County Land Name Records" in), which was officially established in the Western Han Dynasty. The Han Dynasty inherited the Qin Dynasty's county system and built Tuyin County, which was located Tuyin City. Today, Yincheng, Fengrun District, Tangshan City, was the location of the then Tuyin County. Legend has it that the of the ancient land Yin City is majestic and spectacular, showing the extraordinary tolerance of a generation of overlord Zhao Wuling King, and the mirage of the mirage of the floor often appeared and became the famous "Yincheng Xiaoshi" in Yanzhao during the Warring States Period ".

In the long history of ancient China, in the continuous wars and dynasties, Fengrun was prospered and abolished several times, and belonged to different counties in different periods. It was not until the sixth year of Jin Shizong's Dading (AD 1166) that the current county was built. Because Fengrun County is located in the Yanshan Alluvial Plain, Ma Pingchuan, with favorable weather and abundant products, it is also named Yongji County. In the first year of Jin Weishao Wang Da 'an (1209 AD), it was renamed "Feng Lean" to avoid the taboo of Wei Shao Wang Wanyan Yongji ". In the first year of Ming Hongwu (1368), it was named "Fengrun", which means "Run, Ze, and beauty. Looking at the "Atlas of Chinese History", we can see that the area of Fengrun County in ancient was vast, and the vast Yanshan Mountains, surging rivers, vast plains, and boundless seas all the of its jurisdiction. From the records of in Fengrun County in the middle of the Ming Dynasty, "Yanshan Barrier County", "Gengshui Chao Jing ", " Dragon Shi Zhaoyu", "Xiandong Title Jin", "Han Shi Yan Run ", "Qinling Jing Fu", "

Chao Feng Yan Moon" and "Belt Hengyun ", we can see the ancient and rich land and rich mountains and magnificent rivers.. Until the Qing Dynasty, the of the county annals during the reign of Guangxu still contained: Fengrun County had two and 21 towns. Today Fengtai Town, Ninghe County,, and today Kaiping, Tangshan, were both rich at that time. In the past, Fengrun County was a large county with an administrative area from the South to the to the Bohai Sea from the North to the Yanshan. The establishment of Tangshan City in the period of the Republic of China, from the of Fengrun County set aside a part. Before the founding of New China in (1937), Wuyang County was established in. From the of Fengrun County in, the southern half to the coast was delineated. After the establishment of the the People's Republic of China, it returned to the of Fengrun County in.

After the establishment of the the People's Republic of China, China's first plain orchard was also the largest plain orchard in Asia, and the construction of that is, the Tang Mountain orchard was set aside from the of Fengrun County,. The establishment of Kaiping District from Fengrun once again set aside a part.

In June 1961, Fengrun Fengnan was divided and conquered again. Because it was the southern half of the of Fengrun County, it was named Fengnan County, which once again divided the of Fengrun County into two, and the southern part of the county and the coast were all returned to Fengnan.

After the Tangshan earthquake, Fengrun New District of Tangshan City was formally established, and Fengrun County designated a of 117.5 square kilometers of to Tangshan City,. Subsequently, the Tanghai County was established in September 1982, and another part of the Fengrun County was allocated to the Tanghai County.

Later, the Tangshan military airport was changed into a dual-use airport for military and civilian use, and the Three Women River was delineated. In 2013, Laozhuangzi Town and Hancheng Town were successively assigned to Tangshan High-tech Development Zone and Tangshan Lubei District. In 2014, Chahe Township was assigned to Fengnan District of Tangshan City.

Today, the scene of Tangshan Fengrun New District and Fengrun County merged into Fengrun District, although the ancient of Fengrun "Yanshan Mountain in the north, Haichuan Mountain in the south, River in the mud in the, and surrounding water" is beyond recognition. Yanshan Mountain is still in the, but Haichuan no longer exists. Fortunately, there are still rivers near the mud and, and the scenery around the water is still an important town in Jingdong. There are also large state-owned enterprises such as China CNR Group (of Tangshan Plant of China Car Group) and Jidong Cement. With a new attitude and pace, she is integrating into the Bohai Rim Economic Circle, following the domestic electrified railway and Beijing-Harbin Expressway, and taking the fast train of China North Group, she is heading for a new world of coordinated development in Beijing, Tianjin and Hebei.

September 3, 1997

Xifengkou -- The Origin of the Broadsword March

Xifengkou, located 31 kilometers north of Chengxing City, Qianxi County, Tangshan City, is an important pass on the Great Wall,. And her name with a scene of historical drama staged and spread in the folk. There is a poem in the Yuan Dynasty: "Heaven teaches that meet here. Father's says that fall from heaven my son." It is said that in the past, there were people who their son to guard the border and did not return home for a long time. My father found him and met him. The with tears. The hugged the and laughed. The died of joy. Therefore, as the story has been spread for a long time, the folk have gradually called the 1 pass of "Song Pavilion Pass" as "Xi Feng Pass.

During the Yongle years of the Ming Dynasty, it was changed to "Xifengkou". In the third year of Ming Jingtai (1452), in order to reach foreign enemies, built a urban construction pass, called Zhenyuan Building, which was 4 feet high. The pass has the of the distant building built during the Jiajing period of the Ming Dynasty. Xifengkou has three closed doors. It is difficult to and attack when it is firmly. It is commonly known as "three closed doors". In ancient times, successive dynasties were heavily guarded. In 1933, when the Japanese army entered the customs, Song Zheyuan's army firmly defended it and launched a fierce hand-to-hand battle with the Japanese army. The Japanese army attacked twice with a large sword of the sharp blade, and the enemy was more than a thousand people. So, at that time people also called "beheading mouth ". The famous anti-Japanese song "Broad Sword March" was created according to this example of the war. In 1944, a platoon on both sides of our ambush Xifengkou wiped out more than 200 Japanese troops.

Today, we revisit the old days of Gu Songting Pass and look back on her glorious course of resisting foreign enemies.

7 October 1997

Zhao Guohua and Xin Xiang Academy

The academy was a special educational organization 1 Chinese feudal society, which began in the Tang Dynasty. At that time, it was a place for collecting and repairing books, and later as a place for giving lectures. There were 10 academies in Tangshan, one of which was founded by Zhao Guohua, a named eunuch in the late Qing Dynasty, Academy.

Zhao Guohua, a native of Dawangzhuang,, Fengrun County,, Zhili Province, the Qing Dynasty. Born in 1838 (the 18th year of Daoguang in Qing Dynasty), he studied hard as a teenager and was admitted to Jinshi in 1863 (the 2 year of Tongzhi). He served as magistrate of a county, Zhizhou and magistrate in Shandong. In the office of self-restraint, the effectiveness of the court. During his time as an official in Shandong, Zhao Guohua went back to his hometown and lived in Dawangzhuang, Xinjuntun,, Fengrun County, for two years. He cared about the education in his hometown and wanted to set up an academy so that he could prepare funds, select teachers, visit the site of the academy, and finally set the site of the academy at Fuxing Temple in Xinjuntun.

In ancient times, Xinjuntun was the largest market town in the southern half of Fengrun County, with cross-shaped blocks, 24 large hutongs, both commercial and agricultural, convenient transportation, Tianjin in the south, Beijing in the northwest, and Shanhaiguan in the east. The academy built in Xinjuntun had advantages in all aspects.

When all the matters of the academy were ready, Zhao Guohua named the academy "Xin Xiang Academy". Xin Xiang Academy was unique among the counties at that time. The academy was completely private. Its purpose was "to our party to live in remote and village schools, limited to square corners of the. to the saying that each should keep a school and, accumulate and extend, and thus be revitalized. Not only the room has a spirit, but also the wings of customs." That is, to exchange ideas, cultivate talents, add honor to the of the township, and for the imperial court. According to the example of other academies in Tangshan, the academy should set up a "mountain chief" to preside over the academy affairs and lectures, while Xinxiang Academy should set up a "division" instead of a "mountain chief". Gu Lin Cang, the first plentiful citizen of Beijing division the national history "Wen Yuan Biography", is listed as the top of the division, and there are 18 sages below.

In 1894 (the 20th century of Guangxu),57-year-old Zhao Guohua died. After the abolition of the imperial examination, Xin Xiang Academy opened a men's teacher training institute in 1923 (the 12th year of the of the Republic of China), which was the first man's teacher education in Fengrun County,. In the 1990 s, Xinjuntun Town, County, Fengrun County, built a five-story modern junior high school teaching building on the original site of Xinjuntun Academy as the second middle school in Xinjuntun Town.

January 8, 2001

Jingjue Temple, which was passed down from Tang to today

Jingye Consciousness Vacuum Temple, which is today's Jingjue Temple, is the 1 plain temple known as Jingdong's First Temple with a history of more than 1000 years. It is located in Manziying Village, Yutian County, Tangshan City. The Qingqing Pomegranate River (a section of the Hometown River, locally called Pomegranate River) flows quietly westward from the front of Jingjue Temple, as if slowly telling the past glory and vicissitudes of Jingjue Temple.

In the long river of history, Jingjue Temple has repeatedly experienced wars. Although it has built several abandoned, it has been easy to rise and fall. To this day, the existing buildings of the entire temple were rebuilt in the first year of Yongzheng in the Qing Dynasty (1723). According to the "Rebuilding the Steles" in the temple in the Qianlong Year of the Qing Dynasty: "Wenzi Jingjue Temple, where the monks and masters live. The began in the Tang Dynasty, and the read the and Five Dynasties, the of the Song Dynasty. The calendar of the Yuan and Ming Dynasties and the of the are now."

Outside the temple, Jingjue Temple is directly seen from a distance. In front of the mountain gate hall is a newly built archway building. All the buildings within the of the mountain gate hall and the temple wall are covered by yellow and green glazed tiles, which look so resplendent in the bright sunshine.

Approaching the mountain gate hall, brick arch, stone round window, the craft is so exquisite. Entering the temple, the brick arch, which was built with Chinese architectural skills special art without beams, was and completely natural. Looking up, it seemed to show people the depth and infinity of the universe. The two tall "hum-ha" 2 in the temple are guarded on both sides of the golden-bellied Maitreya Buddha.

Although the clay sculpture in the Qing Dynasty was destroyed during the "Cultural Revolution" period, the color is still the same, the expression is lifelike, and it is frightening and to feel the loveliness of the clay sculpture Buddha.

The monument between the Shanmen Hall and the main hall downstairs is the Three-way Qing Dynasty "Rebuilding the Monument". Behind the floor of the monument, on the east and west sides are the bell and drum towers with morning bells and evening drums. After the bell tower bell rang, the sound was heavy and distant, and the drum tower drum was ringing.

In front of Xiangfu Palace in the main hall is a pair of tall stone lions, the ridge of the hall is towering, with dragons and phoenixes flying and carving. The tall thousand-handed thousand-eyed Buddha in the temple is golden and the eighteen arhats are in the two compartments. What is even more amazing is the of the side door between the main hall and the east and west distribution rooms. The stone carving are embedded in the wall, and the flowers and birds are like. East and west corner door, east carved dragon, west carved phoenix, carved dragon phoenix vivid, so called "dragon and phoenix gate".

Then there is the magnificent and majestic Hall, with stone pillars holding the mansion in front of the gate, and the lifelike panlong reliefs on the stone pillars of the four major are unique and exquisite, which can be called 1. Within the main hall, there are several golden Buddhas that make people look up.

Walking out of Jingjue Temple and carefully reviewing its temple name was originally the meaning of the vacuum of consciousness the Buddhist Jingye. Looking back again, Jingjue Temple has exquisite and unique, originality and novel and unique style. It is really worthy of being called "Jingdong No.1 Temple.

29 March 1998

The old horse knows the way -- the allusion originates from Tangshan.

The old horse knows the way is an old idiom. Its origin can be found in the 1 section of "The Records of the Eastern Zhou Dynasty-Qi Huangong Set Soldiers to Break the Solitary Bamboo", which specifically describes these 1 idioms and allusions. At that time, the of the State of Zhi (this Qian'an City as the former country) attacked Yan, and Yan asked Qi for help. Qi Huangong's army marched northward and destroyed the country, the monarch fled to the solitary bamboo country. Qi Huangong and soldiers to solitary bamboo country are Wudi city. In order to stop the Qi army, the monarch of the solitary bamboo kingdom used the prime minister's own law and to lure the Qi army into the Valley at dusk, which made the Qi soldiers all shocked and creepy. They disappeared before and did not know where to go after. In a hurry, Qi Xiangguanzhong suggested that the old horse could identify the way to come, so he took off the bridle and let the old horse go one by one. Qi soldiers accompanied him, and finally the brigade of military horses walked out of the lost valley.

Hanhai is a place name, commonly known as Lost Valley. This place is a land of sand moraine. Every evening the evil wind blows, people can't see each other at a distance, and will surely die when they enter this valley. Therefore, the solitary bamboo country in the Qi army lost its way. Today, people use the old horse's knowledge of as a metaphor for experienced people who can play a guiding role in daily work and life. "The old horse knows the way" this 1 code therefore originated in Tangshan this ancient land.

December 27, 1998

The vicissitudes of life return river

Huanxiang River, also known as Xianghe Ring, is 160 kilometers long. Her source is in Quan Zhuang Village, Xinji Township, Qianxi County, Tangshan City, through Xinji, Jiahe, Xinzhuangzi and other villages and towns, a large number of flows to Yankou Village, Fengrun District, Tangshan City into Fengrun, flows to the west into Qiuzhuang Reservoir, then flows south to Fengrun City, and flows west through Baiguan Tun District to Manziying Village, Yutian County into Yutian County, Yutian County, the southwest flows through the first villages and towns of Yahongqiao, Woluogu and He River, and then flows into Ninghe District of Tianjin into Ji Canal. A large section of westward waters is concentrated in the territory of Fengrun, with a total length of 60 kilometers and a drainage area of 460 square kilometers.

In ancient times people called the river water. The water in Shuijingzhu, written by Li Daoyuan of the Northern Wei Dynasty (also known as Geng water, Juliang water), is the Huanxiang River. In ancient times, especially in the Northern Song Dynasty, it has always been an important border area. Today, there are still Dawinggongzhuang and Xiaolinggongzhuang on the south bank of the Huanxiang River. The old "Records of Fengrun County" stated that these two places were guarded by the Northern Song Dynasty's famous general Yang Jiye and his son Yang Yanzhao. By the time of Song Huizong (1101-1125 A. D.), Jin soldiers often went south to burn, kill and loot. Emperor Huizong, who was good at painting and calligraphy, once went on a personal expedition. He camped in the 1 area of Xiaogu and the west of Dongangezhuang on the south bank of the water (the river of returning home). Emperor Huizong lived in Angezhuang, Shayan Temple, and commanded the to resist gold. The old "Records of Fengrun County" introduced: Song Huizong's tour of the camp at night was. There were no chickens barking and barking in the inside and outside the camp. It was very quiet. In his heart, he felt deeply and wrote impromptu poems: "East peace, west peace, south vicissitudes, north return home." Therefore, in order to remember this period of history, Xiaoguzhuang and Ange Zhuang were renamed Taiping Zhuang and Anle Zhuang from now on.

In the 2 year of Jingkang in (1127 A. D.), the Jin soldiers sent troops south again and again. Song Qinzong insisted on making peace, resulting in the prisoners of the Jin soldiers, Song Huizong (Zhao

Ji) and Song Qinzong (Zhao Heng), being taken to 5 Guocheng (now Yilan, Heilongjiang). When Song Huizong rode a horse on the of the Bridge in the water (now 300 meters upstream of the Huanxiang River Bridge), looking back on the rivers and mountains of his country, he felt, sad, and cool. "Yanshan Conglu" recorded: Song Huizong mournfully said: "After crossing the desert, I am as safe as this water to return to the hometown?" Without eating, people also called water to return to the hometown.

A period of history, such as the clouds in front of us. But today the people on the riverside of the return home, building a beautiful home, living a happy and healthy life. , the "homesickness bridge " that made Song Huizong's eyes dim has long ceased to exist. Two 102.6-meter-long, 5-meter-high, and 7-meter-wide bridges fly on both sides of the bridge. There is Zuojiawu Village on the riverside, and it is also brewed with the water from the returning river. "If you don't medicine, don't and cook, you will with deer, and store them in the of the urn. At the beginning of the, there will be a wind to give a speech, and for a long time, you will the wine (the Cao Xueqin wine).

9 June 2001

Liang Jiugong and Bai Guantun

During the Yongzheng period of the Qing Dynasty, Liang Jiugong, who was from a poor family, was selected as her husband (that is, she became a eunuch in the palace) in order to have food, and clothing. He came to the Qing palace from a village called Liangjiafen in, Fengrun County,, to take care of the young Qianlong. With the rise of Qianlong and the accumulation of years, Liang Jiugong's fame has become very big in the imperial court. At that time, there was a saying in folklore: "if you miss the things in the palace, first ask Liang Jiugong." This shows that Liang Jiugong's position in the palace is extraordinary.

Liang Jiugong, who had experienced two generations of emperors, had seen all the splendor and wealth, and had heard about the open and secret struggle for power in the palace, so he couldn't help thinking. As a result, he enlisted the 1 to help his best friend conspire to revolt, usurp power and seize power, and secretly to elect to establish the capital in Fengrun Baiguantun. According to legend, the east gate of the capital is at the Shayan Temple in Linggongzhuang, Fengrun County,, the west gate is at the Yuewang Temple (the site cannot be investigated), the south gate is at the black horse Village in Baiguantun Town, Fengrun County,, and the north gate is at the Fuxing Temple in Tianfuzhuang Township, Fengrun County, Fengrun County,. Because some people in the palace had already noticed this, some loyal officials reported to Emperor Qianlong. Emperor Qianlong made a decisive decision and beheaded Liang Jiugong outside the meridian gate.

March 3, 2002

Two peaches for 3 days

The peaches are delicious, and the "deep state peaches" are even better.

Shenzhou Peach, a famous local product in Shenzhou City, Hebei Province, is famous for its large thin skin and sweet and juicy taste. In the old life, the deep state peach that is the court tribute, the fruit does not fall under the tree, has long been counted, the number of tribute, the working people simply can not eat.

Strange to say, in the deep state, only 3 4 mu of land can really produce this kind of peach. There is also a folk said. Legend has it that once, on the way to meet the Jade Emperor, the heavenly queen felt thirsty because of the hot weather, so she ordered her entourage to stop for a small to rest her and take out the fairy peach the holy fruit to moisten her throat and quench her thirst. St. fruit body big meat fat, juicy sweet, a fruit down the belly, feel satisfied, conveniently threw down the peach pit. Coincidentally, the fruit core fell in the territory of deep state. From then on, this peach pit sprouted and took root here.

Hearing is not as good as seeing. Once, I went to the Shenzhou on a business trip. When I went out for a walk at night, I heard the peddler shouting "Shenzhou Peach" and went forward. I saw the top of the peach is red in, the bottom is yellowish, the size of a small watermelon, a weigh 2kg. I bought two and went back to the hostel. After washing, I 1 eat: zi! 1 strands of peach juice spilled out. Wow, that's sweet!

Deep state peach is worthy of its reputation. The meat is thick and the nucleus is small. I am full after eating half of it. I stayed in the deep state for the 3 day, and it was not until the third day that I finished eating the second big peach. Now I think of deep state peach again, its taste is still so sweet and long, with endless aftertaste.

October 30, 1988

Qingshanguan Sheung Shui Gate Gate

In the rolling green hills of Qingshankou Village, Shangying Township, Qianxi County, Tangshan City, stands 1 majestic Qingshan Pass. It is in this green hill that there is the only preserved 1 "Watergate Gate " in the long Great Wall from Juyong Pass to Laotou ".

The building the water gate gate is an arched gate hole with a height of three zhangs and a width of two zhangs with the help of the natural terrain of a mountain pass. The north and south sides are connected with high city walls. The gate gate is made of brass. Therefore, people call it copper gate. The big gate was put 1, just like a bronze wall and an iron wall, tightly locking Qingshan Pass City within the Great Wall.

The reason why it is called the water gate gate is that it can not only block and store the mountains and rivers coming down from the mountains to the west of the gate, but also open the copper gate discharge the when the mountain torrents come down to the. In addition, one of its important military functions is that it can be used to open the door for flood discharge and flood invading enemies. It can attack and defend freely and be handy. In 1568, the 2 year of Longqing in the Ming Dynasty, Qi Jiguang led troops to rush out of the watergate and the gate to pursue the enemy after attacking the retreating forward on the Qingshan Pass.

In 1644, Aixinjueluo entered from Shanhaiguan, and then unified the whole China. The Great Wall also lost its importance and function to the sun, and so did the watergate gate. Unfortunately, this watergate gate, which can not only store flood and discharge flood, but also prevent the enemy from the enemy, was washed down by the outbreak of mountain torrents in the summer of the 13th year of Guangxu of the Qing Dynasty (1887)., there was no trace of the copper gate. Only the tall and wide doorway was still there, so that people could pay tribute to its former glory.

21 March 2002

Wacky owner's old Wacky Hotel

People have heard of Goubuli steamed buns in Tianjin and Wang pockmarked scissors in Beijing, but they probably don't know there is an "old hotel" in Tangshan.

"Old crooked Hotel" is an individual hotel, located in the town of Xinjuntun. The owner's surname is Li, and his name is Xue Qin. Because his neck was crooked quite like Xu Jiujing, the magistrate of Yutian County in ancient times, he was called "the boss of crooked ". At first, boss Li sounded very embarrassed about this "nickname" and felt very uncomfortable. he spoke with his heart. aren't you talking with the lame? Even some indignant. But over time, the ears are filled with default.

Originally, the old wai hotel did not have this name. it was located on the cross street in the center of xinjuntun town at that time, and later moved to the vicinity of bus stop no 6 in tangshan, east of the town. Happy housewarming, many old customers came to support, suggested that "the new hotel should have a new name". In the noisy discussion, the shopkeeper had a brainwave: yes! Don't you always call me the boss of crooked? I also call it "old crooked hotel. The next day, he asked someone to inscribe the name of the store. In the sound of firecrackers at the opening of the market, he unhurriedly hung up the large horizontal plaque of the "Old Crooked Hotel" and unveiled the big red cloth. The four scarlet characters were extremely eye-catching, attracting many customers who joined in the fun.

"Old crooked Hotel" name crooked real does not crooked. There are ordinary meals and economic snacks in the store, and two cups for commuting workers, especially the service attitude of "crooked boss", which makes customers warm. As a result, business is booming and.

25 January 1987

into Gulangyu Island

Zhang's song "the wave of Gulangyu Island" has aroused many people's infinite yearning for this small island in the South China Sea.

One summer a few years ago, my friends and I took a ferry from Xiamen to Gulangyu, a beautiful island known as the sea garden.

The island is surrounded by the blue sea, under the blue sky and white clouds, the trees are lush and the scenery is beautiful. The buildings here have exotic styles and are different: there are Australian styles, Greek styles, Indonesian styles, and a combination of Chinese and Western styles...

In the past, Gulangyu people went to Southeast Asia, Western Europe, Australia and other places to make a living. When they returned to their hometown, they brought their overseas architectural style here.

Gulangyu around the sound of the waves, as if the never-ending music. Perhaps because of this, people here especially Zhong loves piano, and the per capita ownership rate of piano ranks first in the country. By 2000, there were 600 pianos on the island. Therefore, people also call Gulangyu Island as Qindao. One summer, a square concert was held here. The local government organized a hundred pianos to perform the "The Waves of Gulangyu", allowing people to enjoy the strength of the celestial human piano formed by the sound of the piano and the sound of the waves and the beauty of the string.

Walking on the streets of Gulangyu, you can't see any motor vehicles. Ask the local people to know that the only motor vehicles here are fire trucks and environmental sanitation vehicles. It is only because the local area attaches great importance to environmental protection that it has laid a good foundation for the of environmental protection here.

On a midsummer night, walking under Sunlight Rock, looking at the stars shining all over the, stepping the waves, listening to the sound of the piano, watching the beautiful romantic Gulangyu style of the, 1 is really a kind of transcendent enjoyment.

1 July 2001

The Donkey of Jingzhong Mountain

Born in the plains, I grew up in the plains, but I fell in love with mountain from an early age. I have been to Mount Tai and saw the sweat of Mount Tai's picker carrying a heavy load on his forehead falling to the ground into eight petals on my way up the mountain. After visiting Emei Mountain, I saw the amusing energy and greed of Emei monkeys and people begging for food. However, when I came to Jingzhong Mountain in Qianxi County of Tangshan City as early as 2002, I saw the 1 tenacity, 1 intelligence and 1 understanding of Jingzhong Mountain Donkey.

In the embrace of the vast Yanshan Mountain, Jingzhong Mountain is like a beautiful girl standing there. The green pines of the mountains make me deeply feel the breath of the valley breeze, giving people and infatuation. After listening to people and looking at the history, I learned that Emperor Kangxi of the Qing Dynasty had repeatedly driven Mount Xing Jingzhong. I also heard that there was the Ming Dynasty's "Sanzhong Temple" on the top of the mountain and the magnificent and magnificent Bixia Yuanjun Hall.

Entering the gate of Jingzhong Mountain, climbing up the stairs step by step, passing through the of 4 Shuai Hall, bypassing the Imperial Temple, and slowly marching up the mountain. After walking for a period of time, I felt a little gasping, so I took a rest on a platform. Inadvertently 1 looking back, suddenly saw a donkey standing behind me, 1 team of donkeys coming up the mountain, carrying carpenters on their backs to build the window frame for the house, and the donkeys behind it carrying several buckets of water and rice noodles respectively. I quickly flashed aside to give way, and while I was watching, the owner of the donkey shouted 1 and the donkeys moved on. The head-on donkey first obliquely to the left to pick up the stairs, then walked to a platform and then obliquely to the right. This left-to-right lateral oblique progression is written as one positive and negative zigzag after another. At first, I was absent-mindedly looking at these donkeys who came up the mountain and to down the mountain. Looking at them, I suddenly thought that the people in Jingzhong Mountain were too smart to carry things the mountain and down the mountain. I used donkeys to carry them instead of people to carry them. What a it is. How much hardship has been saved from carrying the blue sky shoulders to carry the burden through the ages. I continued to walk up thoughtfully, and stopped on a platform on the stone steps of the mountain road and rested for a while. Looking around, the mountains near and far are covered with green, which is really refreshing. After enjoying the scenery, I kept thinking about, and then came to the conclusion that it would save energy to go up the mountain. donkey carry heavy loads, if along the stone steps directly upward, will undoubtedly make the object produce vertical downward gravity, there is a sense of heaviness. The oblique sideways detour forward, you can ease or carry on the back to reduce the weight of this vertical pressure, there will be a more relaxed sense of weight. Oh, it turns out that this donkey also has such a well-informed understanding, and in its carrying practice, it can perceive and apply the principles of mechanics. In this way, to avoid the of the heavy and light years, the morning and evening back and forth on the 1872 stone steps of Jingzhong Mountain. From this, I also thought that this ordinary donkey can be smarter than people think. So, since ancient times, people often say "" and "stupid donkey" seems to be getting the right name.

19 December 2004

Wuling Mountain Lange

Wuling Mountain in Xinglong County, Chengde City belongs to the Yanshan Mountains. It is the highest peak of the Yanshan Mountains and the main peak of the Yanshan Mountains. It is a common product of orogeny and Quaternary glaciers more than 0.1 billion years ago. Millions of years of changes in the sea of Sang and the reincarnation of everything that lives and lives have created many majestic and spiritual, mysterious and serene aspects of Wuling Mountain. Travelling through Wuling Mountain, I was deeply infected by its strange.

Qi Yi: Fog Lock "of Crooked Peach" Rises

The "crooked peach peak", which is 2118 meters above sea level, is the main peak of Wuling Mountain. It is named because it looks like a big peach with a crooked mouth from a distance. This is the best place to watch the sunrise in the sea of clouds. at 5: 30 in the morning, men, women, old and young waiting to watch the sunrise in wuling mountain gathered on the crooked peach peak in late summer and early autumn, looking at the vast sea of clouds in wuling mountain in front of them. microwaves rippled and the sea surged up the mountain like water. Standing on the top of the peak and looking around, there is an endless expanse of white, foggy, reckless forests and mountains and ravines, all of which are engulfed by it, and everything seems so majestic. Gradually, the clouds and mist in the east changed from reddish to purplish red clouds, and then half a sunrise appeared in the clouds. The color of the clouds gradually turned to red, followed by 1 rounds of sunrise. At this time, the total area of 14247 hectares of Mist Mountain, shrouded in the sun abbot light. autumn fog is like the sea, Cangshan is reckless, and people see a spectacular sunrise on Mist Mountain.

Qi 2: thorn fog through cloud "fairy tower"

As Wuling Mountain has been formed for a long time, the repeated changes of nature, the passage of time, weathering and erosion have led to the emergence of many strange peaks and rocks in Wuling Mountain, and the "Immortal Tower" is one of the typical examples. The majestic "Fairy Tower" is 48 meters high, 9 meters wide and 5 meters thick across the. It suddenly towered, that is, like Optimus Prime, more like an awe-inspiring fairy, insight into the world. Legend has it that Liu Bowen of the Ming Dynasty sent the subdued black dragon into the sea the eye and planted it the of this tower. People all say that they can live to 99 when they hug the 1 in the face of the Fairy Pagoda. Therefore, all tourists who come here hug 1 the Fairy Pagoda in order to live a long life.

Qi 3: Longtan Waterfall Hangs Cliffs

The dense forests and various vegetation of Wuling Mountain conserve a wealth of water sources, making her streams gurgling and linked to waterfalls, one of which is Longtan Waterfall. It is more than 20 meters high from the water surface of Longtan,, and it pours down from a cliff where grass is not long and there are no trees. Looking up, it looked like a white sail hanging straight. The pool water is clear, standing by the pool, holding a handful to the mouth feel fresh and sweet, full of the taste of Nongfu Spring.

Qi 4: Mist Spirit, Forest and Sea Blurred in Color

The Wuling Mountain area with a forest coverage rate of 80.29 belongs to a temperate forest ecosystem. The is integrated with the beauty of the south and the of the coast in the north. The annual temperature averages 7.6 ℃ or more, and the hottest monthly temperature averages 17.6 to ℃ or. The trees are lush and lush, with more than 1870 kinds of higher plants. From spring to autumn, more than 600 kinds of flowers open one after another, and the fragrance of flowers is unbeaten. It is known as "Species Gene Pool in North China" and "Jingdong Green Pearl". Autumn to Wuling Mountain presents you with a magnificent autumn scenery: majestic mountains, and steep valleys, streams, deep ravines, mountains and mountains, bursts of Lin Tao, and color. From time to time, birds chirp and squirrels jump under trees. The yellow, red, green and purple of all the trees in the mountain will give you infinite intoxication and obsession.

October 24, 2006

Wuling Mountain Upper Eighteen Tam

As the saying goes, the mountain is not high, there is water is spirit. However, the Wuling Mountain I came to is 2118 meters above sea level. It is known as the main peak of Yanshan and the first peak of Jingdong. But 1 mountain is so high, it is still how high the mountain is and how long the water is. From top to bottom, a long history, full of water spirituality, people linger.

Among the more than 100 scenic spots and many pond waterfalls in Wuling Mountain, you can't help but look at the 2 918 pools. Eighteen pools go down the mountain, one pool and one scene, beautiful. In order to facilitate writing, I took out my notebook and wrote down the names of one by one. The first pool is a of Xiangyang pool. Both sides of the pool are full of mountain forests with poplar trees. Under the is a bridge called Maple Leaf Bridge. Autumn tour pool, red-brown maple leaves falling on your shoulders, falling in the pool, full of a romantic interest, oil poetic and rise to. The pool of water flows across the bridge and flows down into a pool-Xietan. The name of pool is self-evident. There is a spring under the. There are willows growing in the dense forest the edge of the spring, so it is called willow spring. Walking through the tower under the willow spring, I saw a pool named Wolongtan. Wolong Lake area is larger, the pool is deeper, so that people always feel that there is a dragon lying inside the pool. This pool homeopathy and straight down the hanging rock endless, become the dry Kun waterfall.

Gankun waterfall more momentum, standing in front of the waterfall, looking at the sky swimming clouds, wide quiet light. Gankun waterfall is the eight-tone waterfall. Standing by the of the Bayin waterfall, listening to the bursts of Lin Tao, the gurgling water, the sound of birds, and the sound of cicadas, I felt that the 1 of nature playing harmoniously a leisurely. Bayin waterfall, through the Bayin bridge into the lake, catalpa bungei forest in the pond luxuriantly growing. Tanshui flows along the bridge of the, and the red letters on the rocks beside the water say "think of the source of drinking water". Next is the word for waterfall, which is named after the word the waterfall is similar in shape. Standing under the of the waterfall, looking up, the swift waterfall is really beautiful like a splash of beads and jade due to the obstruction of rocks. As a result, there was a of flying beads waterfall below, and the splashing of flying beads became a of splashing jade pool. Tanshui hung on the rocks along the flow of the clove bridge, just like the silver dragon landed on the earth, and people gave it a nice name—the silver dragon waterfall. The water of Yinlong waterfall passes through the 1 of the right of the forest bridge and flows up and down the stone. The 1 of the left of the flows into the cave and then flows out, flows into the of the Yin and Yang Lake, and then flows directly under the to form a pool. Due to the wide water surface, the flow rate slows down and appears quiet. This pool is named the slow Lake. Under the of the slow pool is the of the spring, and under the of the fragrant spring is the of the net pool. The edge of the pool is covered with birch trees, and the bottom is the birch bridge. Under the bridge, the ripples of the water gather into the of the new moon pool. Under the new moon pool is the beautiful rainbow pool. The rainbow appears over the, which is a beautiful reflection of the natural phenomenon that water is still in the sky and the sky is still on the ground. The current continued on its way into the of the bath. The water is calm and not deep, hot summer, is a natural good place for bathing. Below is the waterfall pool, Yingyue Lake. Along the way, I recorded the names of all and waterfall in my notebook. The mountains and forests autumn and late, looking at the sky and the world for two months. It is the enjoy 1 kind of beauty.

29 December 2004

Aoan Qingshan Pass

From Laolongtou in the east to Juyongguan in the west, it was built in the Warring States Period, connected to the Qin Dynasty, and finally built and expanded on the eternal Great Wall of the Ming Dynasty. There is a Qingshuan in Qingshankou Village, Shangying Township, Qianxi County, Tangshan City, Hebei Province (in September 1947, the west of Qian'an was designated as Qianxi County). Since Zhu Yuanzhang led the peasant insurrectionary army to push to the Yuan Dynasty, the remnants of the Yuan and Mongolian have repeatedly sought revival based on the Mongolian grasslands and various parts of the northeast, constantly invading the border, disturbing the people and threatening Beijing. In the 38th year of Jiajing's reign (1559), tens of thousands of Mongolian cavalry under the leadership of the chief of Ugliangha Division broke through Panjiakou, crossed the Luanhe River, and carried out crazy looting in Yutian and Qian'an. In 1567, the first year of Mu Zong's ascendancy in the Ming Dynasty, that is, the first year of Longqing (1567), Qi Jiguang, a famous anti-Japanese general, was transferred to the north and appointed him as the commander in chief of Jizhou, Changchang Town and Zhenbao Town, and the premier's military affairs was located in Santun Camp of Qianxi County. When 1 Qi Jiguang arrived, he built and reinforced the Great Wall in this area. The Ming "Qian 'an County Annals" contains: "Tiemenguan, Dongjiakou, Chengziling, Qingshan, Yumu,, Qingyazi and other barriers have been strengthened and raised to the body of the city. Within the barriers, there are additional barriers with garrisoned troops and stone walls, with a height of 56 feet, a circumference of more than 1,000 feet and a small town of 300 or 400 feet." In 1568, in January of the second year when Qi Jiguang Jizhou from Town, the chief of Duoyan Department led soldiers to harass Jizhou Town the dirty fox and the long Ang. Upon hearing the news, Qi Jiguang flew and horses on his body and went straight to Qingshankou to repel the enemy's vanguard. He led his troops out of Qingshan Pass to chase and kill the enemy.

The present Qingshan Pass is a relatively well-preserved pass on the ancient Great Wall. Here, in the rolling mountains from south to north and then to the west, there are still hollow enemy buildings built in the Ming Dynasty. Here the Great Wall rises and falls with the mountains, layer upon layer. The enemy building is built of large pieces of blue bricks and white ash. It can be equipped with people and horses. There are arrows and on all sides. The has a wide of about 16 or 70. From the at the bottom of the platform, Gao can 3 more than ten feet. Here, there is of the only 1 existing water gates on the ancient Great Wall of our country. The local people call it copper gate. The gate is entirely of copper casting. When the gate is put down, the gate is to be flooded, which can store flood and defend the enemy. When the gate is opened, the flood can be discharged and the enemy can be flooded. Unfortunately, this copper gate was washed away by flash floods during the Guangxu years. 4. There is also a well-preserved for moving and pouring wells. It is said that Kangxi used to drink horses here, but he suffered from no bucket. Kangxi ordered the well to be moved down the, Ma went down the slope to drink enough water and carried Emperor Kangxi on. However, during the Japanese invasion of China, the ordered local people to move the down well build it into a shaft. There is a small town in Qingshanguan, called Yuanbao City. This small town built in the Ming Dynasty uses the thick Great Wall across the north and south as a barrier, facing south, and there is a tall arched gate in the north and south. Looking up at the South Gate, it is still clear that the 3 characters "Qingshan Pass" are engraved on the front of the gate. The city gate is magnificent and magnificent, showing the majestic and proud style of the shore. There are also ancient buildings in the town, such as the Qingshan Temple, the soldiers' houses, and the stone mill, which were built in the Ming Dynasty. The small town is not big, but it has experienced the vicissitudes of Chinese history, the division and unification of China.

23 September 2005

Majestic Mount Tai

Tarzan, I walked into you in 1993. In the middle of May 2007, when the flowers of Mount Tai were fragrant, I walked into you again. When I stepped into Zhongtianmen, I still felt so open in front of me. The wild and tumultuous mountains were undulating at my feet. On a huge rock in your mind, there were four powerful characters "Five Mountains alone".

Reading history books can be known, Yue official title and famous mountain mountain name unified and formed a system, began in the Han Emperor, Han Xuandi officially identified the East Yue-Shandong Taishan, West Yue-Shaanxi Huashan, Middle Yue-Henan Songshan, South Yue-Anhui Tianzhu Mountain, North Yue-Hebei Damao Mountain. Later, the Sui Dynasty changed the Nanyue to Hengshan Mountain in Hunan, and the Ming Dynasty changed the Beiyue to Hengshan Mountain in Shanxi. At last, the became the five mountains of today, but since the Han Dynasty, the first of the five mountains has always been you-Mount Tai.

In 1978, Lucas, vice president of the World Conservation Association, was entrusted to visit Mount Tai by UNESCO. After the visit, he praised Tarzan-you as "a model of the integration of natural and cultural heritage". This year, Mount Tai, with its majestic magnificence, beautiful scenery, long history and numerous cultural relics, is not only a symbol of the Chinese nation, but also a local epitome of Chinese history and culture. As one of the important heritage of human culture, Mount Tai has been included in the World Heritage list by the UNESCO Convention for the Protection of the World Cultural and Natural Heritage.

Mount Tai, you have lofty peaks, valleys, pines and cypresses, and Qiong Pavilion. The beauty of your human landscape is reflected in your connotation and external. After Confucius "climbed Dongshan and Xiaolu, climbed Mount Tai and made the world small", your name higher and higher, and you gradually became a symbol of "sublime" and "greatness. The ancients called you "Dai Zong". Only by reading the dictionary can we know that "Dai" means mountain and elder, then you are the elder of Chinese mountain. You occupy the central part of Shandong Province. Although you are 1545 meters above sea level, you are called "the first mountain in the world", and your status is very high among the famous mountains in China. The feudal emperors of all ages regarded you as the incarnation of "God. Historical records: from the Qin Dynasty to the Qing Dynasty, 72 emperors actually sealed you, and most of the literati traveled to Mount Tai as fast as they could, and praised you-Mount Tai with poems, songs and inscriptions. Therefore, in your broad arms left a lot of cultural relics. From the Dai Temple at your feet to the Bixia Temple on the top of the mountain, countless inscriptions and ancient buildings make you 1 a veritable treasure house of cultural relics. The Dai Temple at the foot of the mountain, with a large scale, is one of the few major palace-style buildings in China; Bixia Temple is a unique special building with metal components and civil masonry in China.

Mount Tai, if you want to see your true face, you must climb all the way. In that year, I was determined to from the Dai Zongfang at the foot of your mountain to the Nantianmen Gate. I actually climbed more than 7000 stone steps before reaching the top of the jade emperor and seeing your scenery. To browse your scenic spots and cultural relics and historic sites, I insist on walking around Daimiao,

Dailu, Hongmen Road, Tianwai Village Road, Daiding, Daiyin, Lingyan Temple, Shantong Temple, Lou Jingdong Mountain and Culai Mountain. hard, I have practiced myself. I have also experienced your more than 300 peaks, cliff ridge, more than 260 valleys, waterfalls and flows, 34 ancient temples, more than 110 ancient sites and more than 2500 inscriptions. Mount Tai, the harvest is quite abundant. I was surprised to find that during this period, you have not only the Archaean Cambrian international geological section strata, but also the newly discovered geological-vortex column structure and gravity sliding structure. I saw Zhou Mingtang, the site of the ancient Zhou Tianzi patrolling Mount Tai and the princes of the League-Zhou Mingtang, I also saw the Great Wall of Qi Mount Tai in the Spring and Autumn Period-China's earliest military defense line. I approached the former site of the monarchs of all dynasties, and looked up at China's earliest carved stone of Jigong-Qintai Mountain nearly distance. The "Sutra" carved by the originator of the big character into the scriptures of Shiyu has opened my eyes. Tang Zong's "Ji Yang Taishan Inming; the Four-Gate Pagoda, let me appreciate the elegant demeanour of the earliest existing stone buildings on the ground in China, the Song Tianyi Palace, let me see the magnificence of one of the buildings of the Hall of the Three Palaces in ancient China; the ancient temple Lingyan Temple, let me realize the unique place of the head, which has been called" the Four Wonders in the Domain "since the Tang Dynasty. The highest standard of Dai Temple in the ancestral temple made me know that is worthy of Dongyue House; I saw the most Taoist murals, the" Taishan Shenqi Huiluan Tu ", and also saw the first sculpture in the sea-Lingyan Temple Luohan Color Sculpture. There are also the three treasures of Zhenshan-Chen Xiang Lion, Warm and Cool Jade Gui and Yellow Porcelain Glazed Gourd, etc. In the face of these, Tarzan, you really let me dizzying, linger. My Taishan, in this very short period of time, how can I savor it and chew it slowly?

Mount Tai, the beauty of your natural landscape reflects the height of the mountain and the majesty of the image. You are surrounded by rivers and seas, plains, and the main peak of Mount Tai is abrupt, the mountains are steep, and the mountains are stacked to form a strong contrast, and the high open momentum of "a glance of mountains and small " has emerged. The foundation of Mount Tai for nearly 500 miles is broad and stretches, and the body is concentrated. You 1 me a sense of stability and heaviness, which has achieved my natural psychological feeling of "as stable as Mount Tai" and "as heavy as Mount Tai.

The results of geological archaeology prove that you were submerged by the sea in Archaean 2.5 billion years ago. As time goes by, you gradually rise to the sea. Under the influence of the Himalayan movement in the middle of the Cenozoic 30 million years ago, you have what you are now. I touch you, the oldest rock in the world-Taishan stone, and your mountain is the youngest in the world, never stopped growing and developing, until today, my Taishan, you are still growing at a rate of 0.05mm per year.

Mount Tai, you have come from ancient times. The long history has proved that you are tall and upright, majestic and magnificent, and full of the spirit of the Chinese nation in your. Mount Tai, you are going to the distant future as always, and the endless years will prove that you will be more upright and magnificent, high-spirited and majestic, and stand proudly in the east of the world together with the Chinese nation!

Dalian's Bright Smile

On TV, I often hear Zhang Xing's beautiful and melodious singing: "can't walk out of the clear sky of love for thousands of miles, I am

Dalian's bright smile... "Zhang Xing's singing often leads me to the infinite desire to Dalian.

Brilliant Square

In early June 2007, I finally came to this eye-catching and beautiful city, so that I was able to see the bright smile this city. Dalian is famous for its squares. There are 52 squares in the city, with Xinghai Square topping the list.

Xinghai Square, built on July 30, 1997 when Hong Kong returned to the motherland, is the largest public square in Asia. The inner circle of the square is 199.9 meters in diameter, implying the 100 anniversary of Dalian in 1999. The outer circle is 239.9 meters in diameter, which means Dalian will celebrate its 500 anniversary in 2399. The central part of the square is paved with 999 pieces of marble, drawing on the design concept of Beijing Temple of Heaven round mound. The periphery of the red marble is decorated with large yellow five-pointed stars, with stars and sea, which is the symbol of "Star Bay" Star "and Yellow; the marble surface is carved with patterns such as heavenly stems and earthly branches, 24 solar terms, 12 zodiac signs, etc., and there are also 9 large tripods with different shapes.

Each tripod has a large character of Wei stele on its, which together form" Long live the great unity of the Chinese nation "; The five large palace lanterns around the square, each 12.34 meters high in, are held up by white marble jade pillars...

The square is 500 meters south, which is the blue sea. Linhai is the place where the centennial city sculpture is located. The 100 footprints symbolize the vicissitudes of life that Dalian has gone through. The innocent children's statues hold the hope of Dalian people. The big "book" of stone carving open to the sea shows the city's open and upward mind. The city sculpture is not far from standing a century-old lighthouse.

This a square that not only highlights the ancient Chinese civilization, but also is full of modern consciousness. The Central Avenue is paved with red bricks, and the green grass on both sides is like the sea. Every 20 meters, there is a stone pillar lamp in the shape of a beacon light, symbolizing China Dalian is facing the sea, towards the world, towards a bright tomorrow.

Brilliant North Bridge

There are many bridges in the coastal city of Dalian, but there is a beautiful bridge building that has to be mentioned, and that is the North Bridge. The bridge was built to commemorate the friendship between Dalian, China and Kitakyushu, Japan. The bridge is close to the sea and across the valley. The body of the bridge is white. The bridge shape is both magnificent and novel and unique. Although it is the dry bridge in the 1, it gives people a beautiful view. After the completion of the bridge on May 1, 1987, it became a splendid landscape in the southern coastal scenic area of Dalian.

Brilliant Golden Pebble Beach

58 kilometers away from the center of Dalian, there is a famous golden pebble beach. The stones in the golden pebble beach are more valuable than gold, because it is unique in China and even in the world, extremely rare, and the earth is not renewable. The Golden Pebble Beach is called "the garden of strange stones". Large tracts of pink reefs and golden stones, like huge flowers, are called Rose Garden and Golden Stone Garden respectively.

The pink reef was formed by the accumulation of algae and plant fossils 0.7 billion years ago. The three words "Rose Garden" on the stone tablet were written by the famous Chinese writer Lao She's wife. The rose garden covers an area of more than 1,000 square meters and is composed of more than 100 strange stones as high as several zhangs. When the tide is high, they are lined with blue sea water and reflected in the blue sky with white clouds floating, like flowers blooming particularly eye-catching.

When the, stepping on the pebbles of brilliance as jade, strolled in the meantime, as if walking into a dream-like world.

The Golden Stone Garden was discovered in 1996, and the process of discovering the terracotta warriors was similar that year. The construction unit found that the stones here had special colors and shapes and reported them to the resort committee. As the saying goes: "Sincere to the gold, stone is open". After more than half a year of continuous excavation by Jinshitan people, a piece of sedimentary rock covering an area of 30000 square meters and sleeping underground for more than 0.6 billion years can be seen. The golden rocks, such as like tortoises, are magnificent and colorful and are called "Sea Erosion Zoo". In the garden, the winding path leads to the secluded, and there is no cave. This is the Jinshi Garden, the 1 of the famous natural stone geological landscape Jinshi Beach. Stone garden covers an area of 30000 square meters, for the accumulation of weathered sea rock. There are many strange stones, curved paths and, with different shapes and ingenious workmanship. There are a line of sky, cave and other landscapes, more precipitous and strange.

According to geological scientific research, the Golden Stone Garden was formed in the Sinian period 0.6 billion years ago, which belongs to the same period as the world-famous cracked stone in Jinshitan. The rock composition of Jinshiyuan is quartz sandstone, which belongs to the typical sedimentary layer of coastal island system in the sea advance system. The rock forms are strange, such as turtle like, deer like dog, and is called sea erosion zoo. Because it is golden yellow, so the people of Dalian is called "stone garden".

There are still many splendid scenery and beautiful places to 1 in Dalian. We can "see a leopard" in the above scenic spots ".

Here again mention the beautiful and melodious song of Zhang's: "A thousand miles can't walk out of the clear sky of love, Dalian is my bright smile..." Zhang's song may lead you to be interested in Dalian, give birth to reverie, and then, 1 is a kind of idea that hear is better than see, prompting you to walk into Dalian and catch a glimpse of Dalian's bright smile.

Guandi Temple Jingjue Temple Kakuei Tanaka left a historical passage

Guandi Temple, said here is the founding of the People's Republic of China before the Fengrun County New Juntun North Street Guandi Temple. Through the ages, Fengrun Xinjuntun is not only the place where Cao Cao once stationed troops, but also a central town in Fengrun County. Its geographical location has always been very important since ancient times, and its traffic location advantage has made it a must for military strategists of all ages. After the Japanese invasion of China, they took Xinjuntun as a stronghold, and sent a Japanese detachment to be stationed in the Guandi Temple in the North Street of Xinjuntun. At the same time, they built a gun tower next to the "official well" (water well).

Jingjue Temple is located 44 miles north-southeast of Yutian County since ancient times, to the east of Manziying Village, at the intersection of Huanxiang River and Shaliu River. Jingjue Temple was built in the Tang Dynasty, named after the Buddhist Jingye Consciousness Vacuum. From 1842 to 1855, 4 large-scale reconstruction, expansion and repair were carried out. Existing are built Qing Dynasty. Covering an area of 18540 square meters, it belongs to the royal temple and is known as the "Jingdong First Temple".

Kakuei Tanaka, the captain of the Japanese team stationed at Guandi Temple, North Street, Xinjuntun in 1938, later served as Japanese Prime Minister in the 1970 s. What he never expected was that on July 6 and 7, 1938, the armed uprising in eastern Hebei broke out in Gangbei Village, Luanxian County,, and Yankou Town, Fengrun County,. Then, in the Ji East riot led by Li Yunchang, the Japanese artillery tower beside the "official well" in the north street of Xinjuntun was razed to the ground overnight. The Japanese soldiers died and fled. Tanaka Kakuei was also wounded and fled in a hurry. Tanaka, who was frightened, could not find the north for a while and fled in the direction of Yutian in a panic. In order to divert the attention of the riot members, Tanaka ran for a while, then took a shortcut and ran straight to the Manzi camp in Yutian County. Because he found the resplendent and magnificent Jingjue Temple far away, he went straight to the temple regardless of everything. At that time, the temple gate was just wide open. He hurriedly ran into the mountain gate of the temple. Seeing the ferocious, formidable and tall 2 general in the temple, he couldn't help but feel creepy. Tanaka Kakuei had a brainwave and hid behind the of the's back. The riot team members who arrived afterwards carried out a large-scale search and arrest in every corner of the temple, but no one thought that Tanaka Kok and Rong hid behind the 2 general. The rioters misjudged him to have absconded from the temple the wall and went on to capture him.

Kakuei Tanaka, who slipped through the net this time, later firmly believed in his mind that it was the Hem-Ha 2 in the temple of Jingjue Temple that protected him, so he survived the catastrophe and escaped the 1 to save his life. It is precisely because of this that he will have his future business and political development in the Japanese political arena. He has served as a member of the House of Representatives (No. 16), Minister of Postal Services (12th generation), Minister of Great Tibet (67-69th generation), Minister of Commerce and Industry (33rd generation), Prime Minister of Cabinet Prime Minister of Great (64th and 65th generation). In 1972, Kakuei Tanaka became Prime Minister of Japan. At the end of September of the same year, he visited the People's Republic of China and signed the historic "Japan-China Joint Statement", which realized the normalization of diplomatic relations between China and Japan, and took the initiative to let the Yamato nation and the Chinese nation dilute their grievances and face the future. Join hands in the forest of the world, so it is called "an old friend of the Chinese people".

Late autumn is a time of nostalgia, thoughts and different feelings. Japanese Prime Minister Kakuei Tanaka, who went out of office, is a person who personally experienced the Japanese war of aggression against China and participated in, felt the final defeat of Japanese imperialism, signed the word "Japan-China Joint statement" by hand, and personally witnessed the special experience of the normalization of Sino-Japanese relations.

As a friendly envoy between the People's Republic of China and Japan, Kakuei Tanaka came to China again from Tokyo, Japan, in the late autumn of 1985 with many confessions to the Chinese people, and especially came to Fengrun Xinjuntun where he used to be stationed. Li Baozhong, a villager of Xinjuntun who had worked as a cook for the Japanese army team stationed in Guandi Temple, North Street, Xinjuntun. When parting, Tanaka also presented Li Baozhong with a delicate Japanese-made lighter as a sign of friendship and repentance. Later, Tanaka made a special trip to Jingjue Temple in Yutian County to pay a devout pilgrimage to the 2 General, pursuing the memory that was so shocking that it was hard to erase when he took refuge.

Time has passed to the 21st century. The Guandi Temple and the Japanese artillery tower in the North Street of Xinjuntun have long ceased to exist. However, as an important town in Fengrun District,

Xinjuntun is booming and has become a national key town.

Today, with the rapid economic development of Yutian County, Jingjue Temple has also been well repaired. An elegant ancient archway with beautiful has been erected at the door, and a square of more than 5000 square meters has been laid. Today, this thousand-year-old temple 1 washed the dilapidated dragon clock old state, and it has truly restored its former style and rejuvenated again. The temple is full of cigarettes, and there is an endless stream of people to respect and the Buddha, visit and travel, maintaining the reputation of the first temple in Jingdong.

Kakuei Tanaka, an old friend of the Chinese people who had special experience and made decisive contributions to Sino-Japanese friendship, died of illness in Tokyo, Japan in 1993.

The present and past blacksmith village

The blacksmith Zhuang that these of Zhuang's make people feel real, down-to-earth and hardworking.

It's a long talk about blacksmith's village. According to the Records of Fengrun County in during the seventeen years of Guangxu in the Qing Dynasty, the blacksmith Zhuang was under the jurisdiction of Xugezhuang, County,. According to legend, the original site of the blacksmith village was the grave-watching hut in the graveyard of Dong's family in Donggezhuang. Later, 1 iron-making families moved from other places settled here, and the slowly. The place was also called the blacksmith. That was the 60th year of Kangxi (1721) in the Qing Dynasty.

In modern times, this is not a long historical time, the blacksmith Zhuang repeatedly under the jurisdiction of different periods of the township. In the early of the Republic of, blacksmith Zhuang was an administrative village under the jurisdiction of the third district of in Fengrun County,. In the 36th year of the Republic of China (1947), the government divided the southern half of the original Fengrun County and established Weyang County. In this way, the blacksmith Zhuang was under the jurisdiction of the of Qingzhuang Lake Township, the of Wuyang County. After several changes of affiliation, the blacksmith Zhuang will not be described one by one. Until July 1954, with the new of Fengnan in, it was placed under the of Fengrun County,, and was under the jurisdiction of Fengrun 19 districts in. July, 1956, it was under the jurisdiction of Kuizizizhuang Township,,, Fengrun County,. In September 1958, was under the jurisdiction of Kuizizhuang Management District, Xugezhuang People's Commune,, Fenan, Fenan, Fengrun County, Fengrun County,. June, the blacksmith village is under the jurisdiction of the Kuazizhuang People's Commune in Fengnan County,; in December 1988, the was under the jurisdiction of the of Kuazizhuang Town,, Fengnan County,; in April 1994, the was under the jurisdiction of Yinfeng Town, Fengnan City, Cityunder the jurisdiction of; In 2004, it was under the jurisdiction of, Fengnan Town, Fengnan District,.

In December 2012, Fengnan District Government relocated the original site at the corner of Jingshan Railway, facing Qingnian Road in the east, Xibanqiao Village in the northeast, 100 meters in the west, connected to Kuazizhuang Village in the south, and the blacksmith Village in the north, 500 meters in the north. Most of the villagers moved to Yinfeng Community and a few moved to Jinsheng Huayuan Community. Since then, the blacksmith Zhuang, which has a history of nearly 3 hundred years, has ended its past and integrated into the thriving new urban area.

July 2017

Turnip

Radish Tuo, a name full of the flavor of Chinese farming culture. It used to be a village under the jurisdiction of Fengnan Town in Fengnan District-Radish Tuo Village.

According to the "Fengrun County" contains: "Ming Dynasty built village..." Legend, the Ming Dynasty Zhang surname from Shandong to set up a village. There is also a legend that said: "At that time, there was 1 big radish growing on a high ground near the village of. It was very big. A person had to hoe around it for a day to the hoe around the big radish 1." Therefore, when Zhu Di (reigned from 1402 to 1424), the third-generation emperor of the Ming Dynasty, Emperor Chengzu of the Ming Dynasty, was the Prince of Yan, launched the battle of Jingnan, and started to attack Emperor Jianwen, the nephew of the. After seizing the throne, Gu got the name "Radish Tuo " when he re —and moved to the Zhuang of the people ".

Is such a legendary small village, since ancient times, but frequent changes of affiliation, the Qing Dynasty, radish tuo belong fengrun County jurisdiction of Xugezhuang Town; republic of China period fengrun County the jurisdiction of the third district; after the establishment of the the People's Republic of China, belongs fengrun County district 11 Jurisdiction, 1958 fengrun County xugezhuang Commune small paddy Land Management Area Jurisdiction, 1959 under fengrun County hancheng Commune is under the jurisdiction of 1961 fengrun County under the jurisdiction of the small rice land commune, March 1984 belongs fengrun County small rice field township jurisdiction, March 1993 under fengrun County chahe Town jurisdiction; In June 2009, it was placed under the jurisdiction of Fengnan Town, Fengnan District.

In the unified planning for the construction of Fengnan City, Fengnan District accelerated the process of Tuo Village's rural reconstruction, and started the demolition and reconstruction work on July 13,,. In April 2011, the construction of the villagers' return building officially broke ground, and it was fully completed in June 2013 with extremely fast speed and good quality. Located in the west city of Xugezhuang, a society with 13 residential buildings, ranging from Guowen Road in the east to Yuan Sheng Road in the west, Chunyang Street in the south and Youyi Street in the north, has sprung up the of the new countryside. The former "radish tuo " village, bathed in the bright summer sunshine, turned into "luoxinyuan community".

Meihe Old Railway White Beam Bridge Black Stone Anchor

The Coal River is a coal-carrying river excavated with the approval of the Qing Empire Government in 1878. It has been called the "Coal River" by the official and private people. It is a 35-kilometer-long artificial river located in Jinfengnan. With regard to the of the coal river, the past "Records of Fengrun County," had such a description: "... the long is about 70, the width is more than ten feet, the water of the river is drawn, the water is set up with the tide up and down, the waves are calm, the waves are quiet, and the merchants a passenger ship, the stump is as dense as a forest, the ocean ship, and the ocean ship to travel, dredging place a famous river head, a radius of tens of mu, wave water clarified, both sides of the foreign-style buildings flower dock; The purpose is not to taste the, the is slightly west the bridge, the column is than four scales, the crowd is gathered, incredibly a water land port head also converges."

The coal river was excavated in the spring of 1881, almost at the same time as the Tang Xu railway, which falsely claimed to be "express road", was completed and in the summer of the same year. the bottom of the river was 1.5 zhangs wide, the surface of the river was 6 zhangs wide and 1 zhangs deep. the river course was equipped with iron and stone sluices to control the water level. the total area was about 6500 mu and the project cost 115000 two silver. At this point, the connection between the road and the river has enabled Tangshan to truly walk out of the closure and move towards a broad road of development.

From then on, the charming ring of coal boats on the river, and the sail is elegant. The hustle and bustle of the coal river wharf, the bridge lying on the of the river, and the prosperous of small town in eastern Jidong-river head, which is flourishing due to the of the river.

More than 100 years later, in 2002, Fengnan District completed the 1 phase of the coal river regulation project at a cost of 40 million yuan for two years.

Today, the Coal River, which has experienced a history of 142 years, has a clear water with green and a shallow bottom with fish flying. There are flowers on both sides of the bank, willows and willows. The fitness path is winding and secluded, and it is a beautiful scenery. Ribbon park inlaid with pieces of

4 treasure: the old railway, white beam bridge, black stone tablet, big anchor. It has become a beautiful scenery above the coal river.

Old Railway: the eastern section of Meihe Belt Park, the standard gauge railway with two original pine roads and pillows is still specially reserved. One left and the other right are diagonally displayed in front of people from northeast to southwest. It shows people that China's first quasi- gauge railway was laid and used in Xugezhuang, which is the starting point of China's modern industrial glory. This is a railway built in the seventh year of Guangxu (1881 A. D.) of the Qing Empire from Tangshan to Xugezhuang. Although the ignorant and superstitious Empress Dowager Cixi was afraid that the roar of the locomotive and the sound of the flute would disturb the ancestors who slept underground in the Qing Dongling Mausoleum, the locomotive was not allowed to run at that time, even the horse-drawn carriages full of coal still transported the high-quality Kailuan coal out of the sea. At the same time, the Northern Fleet of the Qing Empire used Kailuan coal. The burning fire inspired warships to rush towards the warships of the Japanese invaders! Looking back at history, the laying and use of the Tangxu Railway not only promoted the advancement of the wheel of history and the development of modern Chinese industry, but also made an indelible contribution to the Chinese people's fight against foreign aggression. This, in a sense, is the great beauty of China and the great of the Chinese nation.

White Beam Bridge: This is a steel structure bridge with a 1 seat lying on the coal river in the north-south direction of Binhe East Road in Xugezhuang. It is built on the of the original bridge. It is white and beautiful from a distance to a close look. It not only improves the grade of the original bridge, but also increases the landscape effect of the bridge.

Black stele: This is the 1 irregular flat and long stele. It is all black stele with smooth and shiny surface. Both the stele body and the inscription are full of dignified and far-reaching. It records the beginning and end of the excavation and future treatment of China's first human dedicated to transporting coal, indicating that this "coal river" is the starting point for China's modern national industrial products to go out of Tangshan and into the world.

Big anchor: the big anchor is located on the opposite side of Fengnan No.1 Middle School across the river. No matter spring summer autumn and winter, wind, frost, rain and snow, the big anchor stand proudly there, standing quietly between heaven and earth. But in its gaze, there are historical clouds, dynasties, ups and downs, honor and disgrace, and a better future.

Memories of Coal River

Coal River. In 1878, with the approval of the government of the Qing Empire, the coal transportation channel was artificially excavated. It was historically known as the "Coal River ". It is located in Fengnan (the of Fengrun County in the Qing Dynasty) in the present of. A 35-kilometer-long artificial river. Today's Xugezhuang Town is adjacent to the original "River Tou" town. " River Tou", as the first coal transportation by Kailuan waterway, had her temporary prosperity. The "River Head" was also the seat of the government of Fengrun County,. With regard to the of the coal river, there was a record in the Records of Fengrun County,: "... the is about 70 in length and more than 10 feet in width. It draws the water of the Luhe River. With the tide going up and down, the gate is set up to the savings. The waves are calm and the waves are calm. The merchants a passenger ship, which is as dense as a forest, and the ocean ship, and the ocean running horse, the famous river in the dredging place has a head, with a radius of tens of mu. The waves of water are clear. The western buildings on both sides of the river are docks. When I was too busy to and taste the, the was slightly west of the bridge, and the was lined up with scales. The crowd gathered, and even the water was converging at the head of the land port."

After the Kaiping coal mine was opened in 1878, Tang Tingshu, then the general office of the Shanghai Shipping Merchants Bureau and alternate Daotai, was entrusted by Li Hongzhang, the prime minister of the imperial court, to take charge of the matter of Kaiping coal mine. However, he had sensitively noticed that the resistance of road construction was enough to kill this emerging industry. He could only redesign and adjust the transportation plan several times, and finally agreed, A 70-mile-long river course was excavated from Xugezhuang to Yan Zhuang, leading Ji canal water. However, the section from Xugezhuang to Tangshan is getting higher and higher, so it is obviously not suitable for water diversion to make river, so the "express road" was modified to connect with it. This was later the Coal River and Tangxu Railway. Coal River was excavated in the spring of 1881, which was almost completed in the summer of the same year at the same time as the Tangxu Railway, which falsely claimed to be "express road". The bottom of the river is 1.5 feet wide, the surface of the river is 6 feet wide and 1 foot deep. The river has iron and stone sluices to control the water level. The total area is about 6500 mu, and the project cost is 115000 two silver dollars. At this point, the connection between the of Road and the river made Tangshan (then Bridge Tunzhen) truly walked out of the closure and moved towards a broad road of development.

On the 144-year-old coal river, the once charming ring the and the elegant charm of the sails. The hustle and bustle of the coal river wharf, the Jiudao bridge lying waves across the river, bustling small town in eastern Jidong-river head, which is flourishing due to the of the river.

From the birth of Meihe in this vibrant land, Fengnan has opened his broad arms and accommodated the flow of people and logistics all over the world with his broad chest skirt. Prosperous shipping has stimulated the rapid development of commerce and industry. Meihe has not only created a rich land, but also nurtured the fighting spirit of Fengnan people who dare to be the first and create great cause. Fengnan cannot without coal river, Fengnan cannot give up coal river! Therefore, more than a hundred years later, in 2002, Fengnan District established the Coal River Management Headquarters, which began the largest scale of Coal River in history. The people of the whole region received more than 3000 million yuan in voluntary donations in just one week. It took two years and a total investment of 40 million yuan to complete the 1 phase of the coal river regulation project.

Today, the Coal River, which has experienced the historical process of the Qing Dynasty, the Republic of China and the Republic of China, has a clear water with green and a shallow bottom of fish. On both sides of the river are ribbon parks with flowers and willows. The fitness path is winding and secluded, with a beautiful scenery.

The sky is long and the history is long. Tangshan, Kailuan and Hetou (Xugezhuang) will never forget this ship that transported high-quality Kailuan coal to Shanghai and sailed overseas. At the same time, the Northern Fleet of the Qing Empire used the coal from the Kaiping Coal Mine, and the raging fire inspired all warships to rush towards the warships of the Japanese invaders! Looking back at history, the excavation and use of coal and rivers have promoted the development of China's modern national industry and made indelible contributions to the Chinese people's fight against foreign aggression. This, in a sense, is the great beauty of China, the great of the Chinese people and. Today, when the Chinese nation is rejuvenating and striving to practice the Chinese dream, we will never forget this river that represents the glory and dreams of country on behalf of the ...

July 2017

big twinkle, exquisite and beautiful Xanadu

In June 2015, I went to live in Yutian rural area for a period of time. In addition to writing, I also had an unexpected harvest, that is, I found the elegant and beautiful countryside of "big twinkle.

It has been a long-standing habit of me to go out every morning. On the evening of June 5, it rained all night and stopped at dawn. At 5 o'clock in the morning on the 6th, I went downstairs to the street and gradually walked to the south of the village. I walked along the country cement road washed clean by rain at night, walking through the fields full of green corn and yellowed wheat. Because it had just rained, the sky was exceptionally clear in the morning. Breathing the fresh air in the fields, I enjoy the idyllic scenery as I walk. As far as the eye can see, there is a high platform with a pavilion on it, which comes into view vaguely. I stand in the distance and look for it on my way. After more than ten minutes of work, I saw the words "Big Ecological Farm" at the door ".

Into the door, look inside, grass, stone carvings, tunnels, weeping willows, ponds, rockery, high platform, pavilions... clean and refreshing.

On both sides of the tunnel weeping willow silk, the door on the right side of the 1 large white marble engraved with: "big ecological farm" golden characters. To the south is the lawn, with willow trees planted in the grass, and scattered stone carvings of different sizes. On the right side of the lawn are 1 neat rows of blue -roofed wooden houses with west to east backs. Further south, there are sika deer, ostrich, peacock, pheasant, pony, dwarf cattle, donkey, goat, chicken, duck, goose, pig and other animal barns. Although they are kept in captivity, they are all kept by special personnel, so they are clean and energetic and very popular.

On the left side of the door is a man-made wooden corridor. In front of the of the corridor is a small man-made lake. The pavilion in the middle of the lake and the boats face each other in the. On the south side of the lake is a man-made rockery. The platform on the mountain has a wall, and on the wall is a wooden pavilion on the platform like the ancient city of. Under the sun, all this is reflected in the lake, it seems quiet and peaceful. Along the water trestle into the pavilion in the center of the lake to look at the water, 1 groups of red carp in the water happily swimming, from time to time out of the water. South rockery on an artificial waterfall straight down, let a person feel 1 shares cool summer. From the center of the lake pavilion to pick up the stage, it is like climbing the of the ancient cong terrace Handan in. When I came to the stage, I looked around and looked up and down, which made my eyes suddenly enlightened. White clouds were floating in the blue sky. In the endless fields below the white clouds, wheat was golden and corn was green. Not far from the field of hope, we can see the rows of new buildings in the new countryside. The red roofs look so bright and beautiful in the morning light...

Standing on the rockery platform, climbing high and looking at the distant scenery is boundless. From the local people's point of view, it is not obvious that they have long been used to it, but for me, a 1 passer-by, it is the discovery of the New World. Unexpectedly, on the land of Xingzhuang in Yutian County, there is such a pleasant environment, quiet and elegant ecological farm, like a paradise. Big twinkle ecological farm-surprise people happy.

North Wudang

Standing at the foot of the mountain, Qianxi Shimen Mountain is unfolding in front of us. The mountain is named Shimen Mountain because it has a huge steep wall to the south resembles a stone gate.

Legend has it that during the Spring and Autumn and Warring States periods, the heroes rose up, the world was contested, and years of scuffles. This place is even more in dire straits, and the people are in dire straits. The Taoist patriarch Lao Zi heard that there were countless treasures hidden in Shimen Mountain, so he wanted to take out the relief to the common people. However, opening the stone door requires a special key. One day, Lao Zi traveled to Shimen Mountain. Under the gourd shelf of the 1 farmer, cast a spell on the strange gourd 1 the and agreed with the farmer to buy it in 749 days.

The farmer was very cunning. Seeing Lao Zi's strange behavior, he guessed Lao Zi's intention to buy the gourd. He picked the gourd at 48 days and opened the stone door while Lao Zi was away. The stone door opened a 1 crack, and the farmer saw that there were countless of wealth treasures in it, and became greedy. For the fear of stone door closed, with a gourd top in the door. The poor gourd did not but broken. The stone door was closed and, and the treasure was not taken out. The next day I came, but the gourd was gone. I learned the details and sighed, "It's a pity that billions of years of opportunities have been lost." then, the 1 god dog, to guard Shimen Mountain all day long.

The years are long, the sun and the moon are reincarnated. Today, Shimen Mountain has another mighty name—North Wudang.

When you stand on the top of the mountain, you will see North Wudang, which is more than 700 meters above sea level. Forty majestic peaks stand in the hinterland of Township,,, watching on the east bank of the Luan River in, nestling Xifeng Xiongguan, on a par with the Great Wall. Climb to the top of the extreme, the painting Li Xiang panoramic view; happy Shuxiong, poetic landscape poured into the heart.

Ancient China, the south of the Yangtze River and the north of the sea, all over the famous mountains of Buddhism and Taoism. Hustle and bustle, full of seeking guest; clouds roll romantic, are for fame and gain trip. However, when you come to and move to Wudang, northwest, you will inevitably feel the following sigh: primitive ecology gives birth to different feelings; To wash away the block in your chest is actually the nature of nature.

Walking in the 50-mile North Wudang Mountain, where there are strange peaks in the array, strange rocks, and eleven natural caves scattered among them, it makes people feel that the scenery is different step by step, and you will hear the legend of 1 scenery. The red granite body here is conspicuous and dazzling. The waterfall spring on the mountain is vacated and. The guard day dog, tireless thousands of years of hard work; Spiritual tortoise, fall to the ground to reflect, ten thousand winter confession no sleep. There are panlong on the mountains. From ancient to modern, Zhang Kun's deeds are still remembered. The mountain is crouching tiger, and Li Guang's majestic style is still evident. The 4 beast from heaven has, as always, guarded the Taoist fairy mountain for thousands of years. The general is with his helmet. In Wuwei world, directly frightens enemies. There are immortals in the immortal cave of the hidden of the, and escape have different world conditions. Xuan the entrance of the cave, leisurely play and two immortals. Under the jade rabbit peak, the sun and moon are two rounds of strange pine in the mountains. Lan the wind to welcome the, Pixia bath fire full of green mountains; At sunset, just like clear water flowing jade flowing jade, it was the afterglow that sent the evening. It is wonderful in every place and beautiful in every day. Avoid the hustle and bustle, get close to the beautiful nature, come to this North Wudang Mountain, look at the scenery, not calm and calm, no more than a fairy.

North Wudang, historic sites full of mountains. Tang Wang Zhengdong, Empress Mountain Birthday Dragon Species; Li Qiu to cultivate immortals and became immortals in the immortal cave. round jue monastery, once saw the incense is exuberant, lingering clouds; Jade Emperor Dojo, and the site reappearance. Laozi mountain like Taozu; Laozi cave like immortal palace. On Xuanwu Peak, the Great Emperor is not old; in Guanyin Mountain, the Bodhisattva is young. Good scenery, step by step change.

A poet praised the of Shimen Mountain: "Look far and near, the side peak cross the ridge gallery. Heavy makeup, light, beautiful scenery and, mistakenly chestnut village as dreamland. "

Down the mountain, turned to look back at the mysterious layers of the mountains, still holding the pipa half cover face. The sunset is brilliant, I am meditating, today's North Wudang, although still hidden in the boudoir unknown, but the bright future is infinite...

5 July 2017

All the way style

On July 26, 2007, our group of 50 people went to Inner Mongolia for a tour, and we went all the way north. From Tangshan City in Hebei Province through Baiyangyu, Chengde Waiba Temple and Saihanba in Qian'an City in Province to the grassland of Gukeshiketeng Banner in Inner Mongolia, people really appreciate the unusual ecology and different customs along the way.

Great Wall Moonlight

Arriving at Baiyangyu in the of Qian'an City, it was already evening. The coach was too big to drive to the top of the mountain. People had to get out of the car, take their bags, and walk to the top of the mountain on the mountain path. On the left side of the mountain road is a high mountain beam. On the mountain beam, a Great Wall lies across it. A sunset hangs on the top right of an arrow tower. It is the years and man-made that make this Great Wall seem lonely and broken today because of. But from another angle, under the sunset, the Great Wall not only let me see her solemn and stirring, but also let me see her pride. In my sight, I could see 5 archery towers, and there were no obvious crenels on the wall between the archery towers. As time goes by, although Arrow House is missing teeth and few mouths, it still stands there, looking tall and inviolable. There are not many trees on the mountain, but the mountain is full of shrubs, which are lush and vibrant.

After dinner, I slept together to play cards. I sat on the stone drum stool in front of the window and looked at the Great Wall in front of me. The Great Wall at night runs from east to west on the mountain ridge. Most of the wheels appear to be a little dim yellow moon in the mountain fog, hanging over the Great Wall in Aries, giving me 1 a sense of desolation in the fog and dim moon. In the Ming Dynasty, the Qin Dynasty, and even the earlier Warring States period, the Great Wall guards had to keep their eyes open all the time, watch all the grass and trees, and be alert to the sound of Hu Ma's iron hooves on such silent nights, either in the wind and snow, or in the thunder and thunder, or in the absence of five fingers. In order to protect our country, we can endure the loneliness and desolation of that side, the loneliness and suffering of that 1. We have worked hard to guard the border along the Great Wall and defend the 5 million square kilometers of rivers and mountains of our country within the Great Wall.

Members of the tour group indulged in singing and singing in the karaoke hall where they lived. On the other hand, I looked at the night sky, mountains, the Great Wall and the moonlight in Baiyangyu, thinking to myself, I wonder if the border guards at that time had bonfire songs, Hu Qin playing and hometown tunes. Aries Valley, you make me think a lot, a lot...

Putuo Dance

The largest royal temple complex in the world is the Outer Eight Temples in Chengde. Of the 40 royal temples in the Qing Dynasty, 32 were in Beijing and the remaining 8 were in Chengde, commonly known as the Outer Eight Temples, which were actually 12. The outer eight temples are the best preserved and largest royal temple complex in the world today. Among them, Putuo Temple is the 1 Tibetan temple with great characteristics. Because its imitation built the Potala Palace in Lhasa, Tibet and is smaller than the Potala Palace, people are used to calling it the Little Potala Palace. Visiting Putuo Temple not only made me feel the architectural style of Tibetan Buddhist temples and the depth of Tibetan Buddhist culture, but also surprised me to enjoy 1 unique Tibetan song and dance performances. During the performance, the loud and high-pitched singing of the Tibetan people's unique plateau nation shocked my soul. The bold and generous, unrestrained and free folk dance of the Tibetan people moved the air and sunshine, as well as the atmosphere on the court and the joy and excitement of the dancers. Through singing and dancing, I have seen the happiness and joy of the Tibetan people today. Through singing and dancing, I saw the Tibetan people's pursuit and yearning for a better.

Grassland gallop

The tour bus started from Chengde and along the Wulie River along the River and to Hebei. It passed through the famous Saihanba National Forest Farm and drove between the forests and seas. We listened to Songtao and watched the birch forest continue to move forward. was not far from the grassland of Shiketeng Banner in, Inner Mongolia Autonomous Region. Keshiketeng Banner is located in the upper reaches of the Xilamulun River in Inner Mongolia, bordering Hebei Province. It was the Keshiketeng Department in the Ming Dynasty and was officially set up in the early Qing Dynasty.

On the prairie, for those of us in Tangshan who came in the same car, we all want to get on the horse 1 try our skills, and experience the feeling of galloping and galloping on the boundless Inner Mongolia prairie. a mongolian woman led a horse from the of the horse stables. maybe it was because ordinary tourists could not ride horses. the owner of the horse would lead the horses rode by tourists to the grassland according to the convention. I can't ride a horse, but I don't want to try my hand 1. As a result, I persuaded the owner of the horse and didn't let the owner of the horse lead me into the grassland., I let the stirrup saddle and turned over to mount the horse. I rode my horse through the north-south avenue and walked towards the grassland. There are more than 20 horses in front of me, carrying tourists on their backs and being pulled forward by their owners. Walking up a mountain bag, I reined in my horse and immediately looked on the high post. I looked forward to the far-reaching prairie. What of this heavenly prairie is so broad, vast and magnificent. All of a sudden, 1 is a kind of bold and unrestrained Mercedes-Benz desire to drive me the can't help blurting out the word "driving", the jujube horse on the crotch trotted immediately. At this time, I remembered the tour guide's words: "When riding a horse, you should point the stirrup on your forefoot, your buttocks are like sitting, and your hands can easily hold the rein ." So, again "drive" 1 sound. The horse accelerated to run, the wind in my ear, the horse quickly ran to the depths of the grassland...

After a long run, I "puffed" a 1 and reined in the horse's reins, and the horse held back the 4 hooves that were scattered. On the vast expanse of the prairie, looking back at the prairie behind me, I saw those Lyler and still walking slowly on quad bikes, dotted in the distance. On the green grassland. I'm a little worried about these brothers and sisters who came with me, even if it happened unexpectedly. As a result, I turned the horse's head around, and the horse held the rein and folded back. Seeing that everyone was safe, my heart was at ease. I smiled at everyone. Happy to turn the horse's head again, his heels 1 and his horse's stomach shouting 1 "drive"! The horse spread its 4 hooves and ran back into the distance...

It is a 1 kind of spiritual agitation, a 1 kind of passion release, and a test of 1 experience and ability to control. I am more cheerful here with a generous personality, and the success of running the horse on the grassland the has strengthened my confidence.

The horse galloped to a lake. I 1 "puff" and the horse stopped. At the edge of the lake, looking at the blue lake and the boundless vast grassland in the distance, the cars scattered among them and the tourists walking on horses one by one, I 1 times rode horses on the return journey. When the sisters and brothers saw my hankiness on horseback, we didn't wave to each other at the same place about.

The prairie where the horse is running, let you run it. As long as you have firm confidence, there is nothing that cannot be done. The ecologically perfect prairie in Keshiketeng Banner, Inner Mongolia, is that you have given me opportunities, success and happiness. You told me: "Confidence will lead to success and persistence in creating eternity."

"days outside the cloud" Saihanba

In June of the midsummer of the lunar calendar, we came to the famous Saihanba Forest Farm. The 12-meter-long bus entered the Saihanba National Forest Park with a total area of 2324 square kilometers, just like a small boat sailing in the vast sea. The car walked through the forest road hidden in the dense forest. I grew up on the plain. I sat in front of the window and looked at the tall and straight pine trees and the and white birch trees on both sides of the road. I felt the coolness and freshness of the vast forest in Saihanba. The trees quickly swept past one by one, and the trees in front of the car window quickly jumped in front of you and then swept past quickly. The car sped forward, and Lin Tao, who constantly dazzled me, the sea of trees, unconsciously reverberated in my ears the modern Peking Opera "Take the Tiger Mountain" Yang "fight the tiger up the mountain", the high-pitched and loud chorus: "cross the forest sea, cross the snow, angry ..." There are 1 kinds of high-spirited and heroic energy.

The tour guide told us that due to the good ecology, the wild animals here include wild boar, black bear, wolf, squirrel and so on. Mountain goods have Ganoderma lucidum, mushrooms and so on. He also introduced to us 1 kind of precious Chinese medicinal materials, the first flower of Saihanba-Trollius chinensis. In the bright summer sunshine, golden flowers open in the green grassland, is very good-looking. He said, "During SARS in, this Chinese herbal medicine was very scarce and expensive. This kind of medicine, as well as clear the throat anti- inflammatory. During the journey of "", the tour guide talked endlessly about the stories of heaven and earth, the classics of the long river of history, the wonders of human geography the wonders of natural environment. Unconsciously, we came to the location of Saihanba Forest Farm. The planning here is still very good. The road is wide, straight and flat, and high-rise buildings, hotels, guesthouses, and commercial buildings abound on both sides. Our car drove into the gold letter "Days Hotel Outside Cloud ". Get out of the car and check into the Museum. Look at the watch on your wrist. It's already over 5 o'clock in the afternoon. Turn on the shower head and wash away all the dust and exhaustion. Lying in bed, relax their muscles and body and mind.

At 7 o'clock in the evening, a 1 of cultural workers came in outside the hotel, all dressed by Mongolian nationality. They spread a red carpet, set up a stereo and set up a drum in the patio of the hotel. We were overjoyed and sat down at 5 tables set up in the courtyard of the hotel a sumptuous banquet. At the beginning, the tall Mongolian boy, wearing a blue-bottomed golden Mongolian robe, opened in Mongolian. The Mongolian girl said in Chinese: "Friends from afar, welcome your arrival. We will dedicate the pure horse milk wine, bold singing, and warm dance to our dear friends, and spend a fiery and warm with you. Bonfire party!"

In the middle of the patio, a bonfire lit up, reflecting the of the heaven, earth and people building in the hotel. After an unrestrained Mongolian dance, a Mongolian girl sang enthusiastically: "Friends from afar, please let me fill you with horse milk wine. This wine is pure, this wine mellow and ..."

The Mongolian girls came to everyone with hada in their hands, silver jugs and silver bowls, and offered us hada one by one and filled them with horse milk wine one by one. According to Mongolian customs, I dipped wine with my middle finger to respect heaven and earth respectively, and then drank all the 1 bowls of mellow horse milk wine filled with national hospitality.

As the party was going on, 1 Mongolian girls from the art troupe came up and sang the song "borrow another 500 years from heaven. I was shocked to find that although she was a girl, she sang this song boldly and spiritually, showing the bearing of the emperor in the prosperous age of Qianlong and relaxing the mighty mind of the overlord emperor. Let me feel the heart tremor, double appreciation. Can't help but applaud her warmly, and then, pick up a bunch of flowers dedicated to the talented singer.

A song was sung leisurely, and a Mongolian young man affectionately performed the famous singer Tengger's "Mongolian" in. This tall Mongolian man, with 1 pair of Mongolian boots, a Mongolian robe and long hair, is soaked in his singing with love and love for his Mongolian hometown. I looked at his expression of pride and praise, listened to his melodious singing, and indulged in 1 kind of deep feeling. I respect his love and love for his hometown very much, because I also have my hometown, and I also have my love and love for my hometown. Therefore, as I was thousands of miles away, I couldn't help up and walked forward to shake hands with the Mongolian singer and took a group photo. At the climax of the party, the members of the cultural and industrial group walked off the stage and held hands with us, surrounded the burning bonfire, and danced a warm and cheerful collective dance. Among our tour members, there are Manchu and Hui members. On this passionate night, we people from the four ethnic groups of Han, Manchu and Mongolian returned to the four ethnic groups. In 1 a smooth, cheerful, warm and friendly atmosphere, we spent a united, beautiful, A night of friendship and harmony. cloud the bonfire outside the sky is particularly red, Saihanba's friendship is particularly strong.

Dream Back to Tang Dynasty

On the west bank of Nanhu Lake in Tangshan, on the southeast side of the intersection of Nanhu Avenue and Xueyuan South Road, the building was built in the era of Emperor of the Tang Dynasty, rebuilt in 2010, completed in 2016 and opened to the outside world at the opening of the 2016 Tangshan World Horticultural Exposition "Tangshan Longquan Temple". On 21 hectares of land, a large temple with a construction area of 41000 square meters has been formed. The whole group of buildings highlights the style of the Tang Dynasty, showing the atmosphere,, heroic style and spirit of the Tang Dynasty country. It stands proudly on the land of Tangshan, where the sun is shining and the spring flowers are blooming in April.

At 10 a.m. the weather was clear and sunny. I came to Tangshan Longquan Temple, standing in front of the temple, looking at this as the of today's eastern Hebei area of Tangshan Longquan Temple, can not help but let me look up and review the past glory of Longquan Temple. Longquan Temple was founded in 644 AD. At this time, the Tang Empire had been established for 27 years. It was during the of the Tang Zhenguan, that is, the 18th year of the Tang Taizong (Li Shimin) Zhenguan. In the Tang Dynasty, the country was strong and the people were healthy. During the period of Emperor Taizong of the Tang Dynasty, Wei Chi Jingde, a powerful general who opened up the territory and expanded the territory, visited the to supervise the repair of the 1 temples of Longquan Temple in. Today, the has a history of more than 1300 years. Over the years, time flies, a big ditch in front of the temple quietly lies there in the east-west direction. Now it is faintly visible. It is the old way to get out of customs since ancient times. This also proves that "the road of a thousand years become a river". The sentence the ancient Chinese discourse is true. Now, the ancient road has become part of the Longquan River.

The Longquan Temple here is an important place for Buddhist activities in ancient northern China, and it has been rebuilt in history. In 1971, when people were demolishing the main hall of Longquan Temple, they found a writing brush on the top of the inlaid of the purlin of the temple: "Renovate in the Ming Dynasty". The following paragraph is 3 personal names, two of which are "Hong X", which may be the Buddha's dharma number. Until one day in the 1930 s, in the 1 fog, the last old monk in the temple passed away in the temple, which ended the history of monks in this ancient temple.

After the reconstruction, the square in front of the mountain gate of Longquan Temple in Tangshan uses the terrain of an existing higher platform to form a distribution space before entering the main body of the temple, and its north side is the main body of the temple. The temple of Longquan Temple is located facing south. The main building is located on a platform about 10 meters higher than the surrounding area. The platform is 300 meters long from north to south and 250 meters wide from east to west. It is said that the current scale is three times larger than the original Longquan Temple. Times. The main buildings from south to north include the mountain gate, the heavenly king hall, the guanyin hall, the main hall and the sutra depository, which form a five-entry temple courtyard in turn, creating a traditional temple space effect. In the architectural style and overall layout of the Tang Empire to maintain the kind of open-minded, generous, sunny, high-spirited momentum. Immersive, nature is surrounded by simple thick and clear atmosphere, infected thinking. Immersed in the architecture of the Tang Dynasty, the colors of the Tang Dynasty, the vegetation of the Tang Dynasty, facing the imposing tall temple of the Tang Dynasty, staring at the door of the bubble nail, looking up at the golden Buddha. Feel the tang dynasty breath, smell the tang dynasty flavor, touch the tang dynasty country.

Before I knew it, I was standing in Longquan Temple in the afternoon, squinting my eyes and looking at the sky. The sun leaped over time and space. From the Tang Dynasty to this day, I have been shining. It makes people feel 1 kind of flying and smooth, as if there is 1 kind of crossing feeling of dreaming back to the Tang Dynasty. 1 is a kind of inspiration that stand and pull proud shore, and exudes 1 kind of the spirit of seizing the day.

Under the bright sunshine, I walked out of the temple, looked back at Tangshan Longquan Temple, admiring the magnificent style of the temple, and felt that is worthy of the 1 large Buddhist ashtra in eastern Hebei. I the spring scenery, Longquan Temple will not only carry forward the past, but also rejuvenate the glory of Tangshan Longquan Temple, an ancient and important place for Buddhist activities in northern China.

Tangshan, take off the phoenix of nirvana

Tangshan has a Phoenix Mountain, which used to be called Shuangfeng Mountain. Because the Tangshan area belonged to the great Liao state a thousand years ago, the Liao sage Zong Yelu Longxu's Rende queen Xiao Shi, the baby name Bodhisattva elder brother, Liao Daozong's Xuan Yi queen Xiao Guanyin. In the middle and late of the Liao, there was an upsurge of worshipping Buddhism. Xiao, who lived in seclusion in the area of Fenghuang Mountain, paid for the construction of a Bodhisattva temple on the mountain, casting a real statue for Xiao Bodhisattva elder brother, and digging caves under the Bodhisattva temple to worship Xiao Guanyin stone elephants. Because they offered sacrifices to the two queens, they named the originally nameless hill Shuangfeng Mountain. It was renamed Phoenix Mountain until the 1970 s.

Tangshan, a heavy industrial city known as Phoenix for more than 100 years, runs through it with the Jingshan Railway, and enterprises from the two major countries Kailuan and steel mills. The two major urban areas are south and north, on the left and right sides, like 1 wings, and Tangshan keeps moving forward. At the time of Tangshan's vigorous development, a 7.8-magnitude earthquake occurred on July 28, 1976, which destroyed Tangshan, but this heroic city, like the Phoenix Nirvana, was reborn from the fire. Today, this city successfully held in 1991. After the second the People's Republic of China City Games, it has successively won the United Nations Habitat Award, China's Excellent Tourist City, National Garden City, National Double Support Model City and other honors. Since the grand opening of the 2016 Tangshan World Horticultural Exposition on April 29, 2016, the 25th Golden Rooster and Hundred Flowers Film Festival, the China-CEEC Local Leaders Meeting, and the China-Latin America Entrepreneurs Summit will also be held in Tangshan in the second half of the year. Held. This opportunity will undoubtedly add invisible wings to Tangshan's economic and cultural and urban construction and development, which will surely help Tangshan take off.

Standing at the No.1 gate of the Expo, looking up to the south, you will feel shocked and the grand design as a whole. Build type, that is, 1 giant phoenix spreading its wings: 13 huge feather-shaped phoenix tails stretch upward, and the architectural shape of Tangshan Planning Exhibition Hall is just like phoenix Body and the wings are full of movement and power. In front, it is that high the phoenix head of Ang, leading the phoenix flying high...

Walking into the citizen square in front of the giant phoenix sculpture, standing on the edge of the south lake, looking around the layout of the 2016 Tangshan world horticultural Expo exhibition park, the two parks at home and abroad are separated by a lake with clear water on the east and west sides. This makes me feel that this is no longer an unintentional coincidence, nor is it a simple graphic design. It is the ingenious design concept of the Expo designers, cleverly using the exquisite intentions of the geographical environment, so that it is 1 pair of ingenious Phoenix wings.

When I boarded the Dragon Pavilion and looked down from a high plane, I couldn't help but marvel at the picture: 1 huge phoenix jumped in front of the, held its head high and fluttered its wings, and flew forward! tangshan ah, tangshan. Aren't you the phoenix that spreads its wings.

The blue sky was extremely clear, and the bright sun was shining just right. The large fountain on the South Lake rises the dance to the sound of music. Good wind with force, sail good sail. Tangshan, the beautiful nirvana phoenix, flying towards a better tomorrow!

April 2016

wind dance autumn sea

At 4 o'clock in the afternoon, the bus was driving on the cement road from Changli County to Beidaihe Beach. The sky was high and the clouds were light and the sky was clear. The branches of weeping willows on both sides of the road are not only like the soft arms of dancer Yang Liping, but also like a horse of green and silk, rippling in the wind, making people feel 1 a wonderful warmth. Unconsciously the car has entered the Gold Coast, through the window and the roadside trees can see the sea, the sea is calm. People at the seaside themselves to play leisurely what they want to play and look at what they want to see. The blue sky, white clouds, blue sea, golden beach and red roof give people a romantic and leisurely feeling. Soon the car arrived at the seaside sanatorium. Here sits north facing south, open the window and see the endless sea by the side of the road, so wide, so broad, the sea breeze blowing is so pleasant.

Beidaihe seashore night moon star sparse, the convalescents some go to the night market, some go to the seaside. I went to the ballroom in the sanatorium to sing and watch dance. The changing lights make people and intoxicated. Sometimes the dance music is lingering or striving for progress, making such a large dance hall sometimes tender and sometimes passionate. All of a sudden, the images and music in the video and sound box were the song "Sleepless Tonight" sung by Zhou Bingqian and her. Suddenly, the whole crowd was excited and danced one after another. The dance steps of men and women were so coordinated and light, and the mood and smile were so cheerful and free and easy. Autumn night, but here the spring breeze.

On the third day of coming here, the institute organized everyone to visit the place where Qin Shihuang asked for immortals to enter the sea. Here, there is a and tall giant stone statue of Emperor Qin Shihuang (259-210 BC), which is so imposing, majestic and majestic. Perhaps, this is the largest 1 statue of Qin Shi Huang in all of China. From 230 BC to 221 BC, the first emperor of China, who conquered all sides of the sea in ten years, faced the vast sea of, not only did he really want to live for another 500 years, but also his ambition to unify the four seas and his overlord's mind. Here, the first emperor looked at him from afar, awe-inspiring...

Under the gaze of the Emperor of Qin, we walked across the trestle and boarded the Qinhuang No. 1 cruise ship and headed deep into the sea. There were also Xinjiang Uygur young men and women performing singing and dancing programs on board, which gave me the honor to see the legacy of singing and dancing in the Western Regions. The cruise ship marched the sea breeze. I held the ship's rail, facing the sea, with my back to the beautiful coast. my teammates took photos of me several times, leaving behind the elegant and romantic wind floating the broad ocean, hair and clothes, and enjoying the, comfortable and pleasant sea breeze autumn.

In the evening, I came to the seaside alone to sit down and watch the people picking shells. fat white Russian woman still swimming in the sea. Not far away, returning ships were busy unloading, and from time to time seagulls danced in the sunset. The waves clatter against the reefs on the shore, leaving footprints on the couple on the beach. The setting sun slanted to the west, and the sea surged flowers...

On the morning of my last day of recuperation, I walked to the seaside to wait for the sunrise. This ancient sea of Qin Emperor's attention to usher in a new round of red sun. Seagulls feed in the shallow sea and visitors wait for the morning sun on the reef. Suddenly someone exclaimed: the sun is out! The flaming sun jumped out of the sea at first half, then 1 the whole of the and then rose. Looking back again, the Qin emperor looked into the wind and left his belt floating. An emperor through the ages is like calling for a new world, reappearing the flourishing age, calling for China to revive its glory and its prestige.

The sea is windy in autumn and the waves are big. The Chinese dream of the great rejuvenation of the Chinese nation is surging and unstoppable!

February 19, 2005

Regression

How can you forget that strongmen trampled on my rivers and mountains, set fire to the Old Summer Palace, humiliated my motherland, and plundered Hong Kong, the son of my mother's—Hong Kong!

The Xiangjiang River flows, and the mother and son are separated for a long time. The wind moves the waves, and the mother and son gazing at each other.

Long years, ardent feelings, deeply looking forward to, the vicissitudes of life is still, from the continuous one and a half centuries of distant homesickness. The national strength is strong, the country is prosperous, the rivers sing, and the sea agitates. Great Britain sighed at the of foreign countries. It closed Hong Kong in 1997. Sun, of Yanhuang, was happy. Shout 1—Hong Kong! You finally realized the longing for too long, return to the motherland, the Pearl of the Orient, you will be more brilliant.

Hong Kong, which is and prosperous, has seen its bauhinia blossom in the past 27 years. The of the Hong Kong–Zhuhai–Macao Supernormal Bridge lies on waves across the ocean, and the country's creation of the Greater Bay Area will lift a more dynamic Hong Kong.

For the return of Hong Kong on 1 7, 1997

Reunification of Hong Kong on 1 7 2024 Revised in 27

Royal Cellar Jinding

Let's start with the story: in April 1681, Emperor Kangxi's northern tour came to today's Jikou, a large in Pingquan, to set up camp and hunt in the ditch of the paddock here. It was near noon when he was chasing the prey, the hungry Kangxi suddenly smelled a fragrance of wine, and looked along the smell. In front of the 1 hut, 1 old man with white beard was making wine. Kangxi rushed over to ask the old man, is there anything to appease his hunger? The old man brought 1 bowls of wine, 1 bowls of mutton and two sesame cakes. Kangxi Dizzla a mouthful of wine and a mouthful of food. Wine fragrance Qin heart spleen, baked wheat cake to fill the belly. Kangxi emperor eat that called a sweet. Kangxi asked the old man, what place is this place called? What's this wine called? The old man replied: This place is called Bagou, and the wine is.

In 1711, Chengde Palace began to take shape. Emperor Kangxi personally named it "Summer Resort". He ordered to a large-scale banquet with Pingquan Bagou wine, which he never forgot, and gave the seal and royal pen the title "old wine in the mountain villa" 4 words. It is also to choose royal wine cellar to store, and a steady stream of Pingquan Bagou old wine is stored in the earliest royal cellar of the Mountain Resort–"with storehouse", and the "royal cellar wine of the mountain resort" comes from this.

Looking back, let's say that on July 26, 2007, 50 of us went to Inner Mongolia for a tour. Halfway through, we take a tour of Chengde Outer Eight Temples, the best-preserved and largest group of royal temples in the world. Of the 40 royal temples in the Qing Dynasty, 32 were in Beijing and the remaining 8 were in Chengde, so they were actually 12. The Outer Eight Temples is the largest royal temple complex in the world today. Among them, Putuo Temple is the 1 Tibetan temple with great characteristics. Because of its imitation of the Tibetan Potala Palace in Lhasa and smaller than the Potala Palace, also known as the Little Potala Palace. Visiting Putuo Temple not only made me feel the architectural style of Tibetan Buddhist temples and the depth of Tibetan Buddhist culture, but also surprised me to enjoy 1 unique Tibetan song and dance performance. During the performance, the loud and high-pitched singing of the Tibetan people's unique plateau ethnic group shocked my soul. The bold and generous, unrestrained and free ethnic dance of the Tibetan people danced the air and sunshine, also the atmosphere on the court and the joy and excitement of the dancers. Through singing and dancing, I have seen the happiness, and joy of the Tibetan people's life today. Through singing and dancing, I have seen the Tibetan people's pursuit and yearning for a better future.

After watching the performance, everyone came to Putuo Temple Jinding to take photos. The golden roof of Putuo Temple is resplendent, glittering and magnificent, and visitors take photos one after another. Everyone take, and naturally I am indispensable. Back against the gold top, hand glazed tile continuous shooting a few, so far treasured.

At that time, visitors could still stay on the Golden Top. (Not now for the protection of ancient buildings and cultural relics.) After visiting several temples in a row, we also felt a little tired, so we spread a piece of cloth on the terrace the top of the golden, took out two bottles of old villa wine from the bag and opened it. The 1 roast chicken was torn apart. The elder brothers narrated in the golden top the magnificence and magnificence of the eight temples outside the. In the mountain villa mountain villa old wine, a taste of wine refreshing, full of good will. Although July of the Gregorian calendar is the sixth month of the lunar calendar and the weather is hot, we are wearing Denim −style wide−brimmed hats, eating hand tearing roast chicken, drinking villa old wine, imagining that Emperor Qianlong was in Putuo Temple, known as the "Little Potala Palace", and warmly entertaining the lively and extravagant grand scene of Tibet's Sixth Panchen Lama with villa old wine. It can be said to be the 1 kind of wisdom of Longdi's close relationship with the leaders of ethnic minorities and the Qing Dynasty. Therefore, "Shanzhuang Laojiu" is worthy of being the "fusion agent" for the harmonious coexistence of multi−ethnic groups in the unified country, and it is also the prosperity of ancient China. The best real material evidence of national unity.

The sky is sunny, Putuo Temple on the old wine back to Gan. Past a paragraph, unforgettable royal cellar gold top drink that paragraph.

Prairie Row: Cambanor, Nantianmen Gate, Wolong Tu, Lightning Lake, Nine Curves and Eighteen Bends

For 3 years, Zhangbei grassland has been planning to visit. The most beautiful period of grassland here is from late July to early August. Xiang Dong, Dianfu, Hai Xia and Chun Lin have also been warmly invited. At 9 o'clock in the morning of August 4, 2023, Xiao Zhang drove us out of the house. The car went to the high-speed intersection and entered the high-speed direct navigation to the outer ring road of Chengde. It went all the way to the north, to the boundary of Chengde and to the west. The destination was Zhangbei Kangbao. We had a dreamy grassland trip.

A five-hour drive to the service area of Qiansongba on the expressway, where we had a rest and had something to eat. The mountains opposite the of the service area are gentle and verdant, which is part of Tianlu. Tianlu stretches for hundreds of miles across Zhangjiakou areas such as Chengde, Beijing, Gu and. Eyes green, very pleasing to the eye, heaven and earth is full of vitality.

After 40 minutes, start the car, go to Guyuan, and run all the way to Kangbao.

Arrive at kangbao county at 3: 30 p. m. and contact Haixia. Haixia contacted us again at 4: 14. She asked us where we are now. After I sent it, Haixia said, "Very good. It will take only 15 minutes. Haixia sent us the location of the hotel we want to stay in. So we navigate 100 forward by location. Twenty minutes later, Hai Xia, Fan Dianfu and Du Xiangdong called one after another to ask where we were. After 40 minutes, 60 minutes, an hour, they felt wrong and kept calling to ask where we were.

Then it was another 20 minutes, 30 minutes, 40 minutes, 50 minutes... In between, our car saw that the showed that it had made a 1 circle around the Zhongdu grassland. On the way, we passed Shagou Town and Gonghui Town in Zhangbei County, Tuchengzi Town in Kangbao County, and so on. Hai Xia and Fan Dianfu. They looked at the position of my hair and suddenly realized that there was something wrong with the position of Hai Xia's hair. However, during the more than two hours of time, we traveled to the grassland highway and toured the grassland, which was an unexpected harvest. At 5: 26 p. m., Haixia sent a location sharing to guide us to the rendezvous site.

Cambalnor

At 6: 11 p. m., Hai Xia, Fan Dianfu, Du Xiangdong and we finally met. Everyone briefly talked about the. Hai Xia suggested that before the sun went down, go to the Cambanor National Wetland Park to have a look and take some photos. The big responded and started the car to go together.

The Cambanor Lake in the Cambanor National Wetland Park is like a mirror of a clean sky. The white clouds and blue sky are reflected in the lake. This is a paradise where gulls. gulls fly in the sky on the lake. It's beautiful.

"Casserole Small Hot Pot"

In the evening, old fan took everyone to a kangbao special restaurant "casserole small hot pot" to rinse kangbao mutton and drink kangbao old cellar wine. The mutton slices are generous and authentic, authentic, well-dipped and delicious. The shop owner is also a Kangbao folk duo actor who has been on CCTV's Avenue of Stars. The boss was very easy-going and had a 1 glass of wine with everyone. He also sang an authentic Kangbao duet for everyone.

Jia Haiyan of the North China Zhangjiakou Branch of Huaxia Fine Literature in Kangbao County saw the photos I sent to my circle of friends on the evening of August 4 by the lake of Kangbanor in Kangbanor National Wetland Park. After calling WeChat to confirm that I had arrived in Kangbao, I came to meet us early on August 5. At 8 o'clock in the morning, in a restaurant in the north of Kangbao City where Kangbao small fat sheep, the eight of us came together to have breakfast. First, we 1 a bowl of hot Kangbao milk tea, with oil flowers floating on the surface of the milk tea. After a sip, it was slightly salty but the was permeated with milk fragrance. After a short while, 1 came up with a plate of two small pieces of white cake (white noodles were on fire), cut the cross with a knife, 4 the flap together, use chopsticks to clip a small piece of white cake, put it in the bowl of milk tea for a while, put it in the mouth to eat, milk tea sesame oil fragrant white cake fragrant sprung up all over the mouth, the taste is very good.

Aobao Meet

After breakfast, the two cars drove forward at full capacity, the destination-Nantianmen. On the way, there was an obo on the side of the road, and the first car stopped, so everyone got out of the car to take pictures.

Nantianmen Gate

Kangbao Yijing Nantianmen Gate. This is a natural stone gate, with two mountains on the left and right. It is empty in the middle. It is a natural gate. Inside the gate is a mountain. The gate faces south, so it is called Nantianmen.

Wolongtu Ecological Oxygen Bar Resort

We hurried through Nantianmen and drove to Wolongtu Ecological Oxygen Bar Resort. Along the way, the grassland scenery is infinite, and the three leaves on the tall and white wind turbine tower are spinning. Grassland, windmill, blue sky, 1 a beautiful picture.

It was already 11:15 a.m. when we arrived at Wolongtu Ecological Oxygen Bar Resort, we hurried into the grassland to smell the fragrance of grass flowers and take a cool photo in the open yurt. Jia Haiyan has been acting as an explanation, introducing us to all kinds of flowers growing on the grassland and grass. These flowers are all Chinese herbal medicines. I wanted to ride a horse, but the horse farm was still at the northernmost end of the grassland. I walked 20 minutes to the stable and asked the owner of the horse how to charge for riding. Ma Lord said: "1 circle 4, 80 yuan." I asked, "Can you ride by yourself?" The horse owner said no. No deal, I came back on foot. Everyone quickly walked out of Wolongtu Ecological Oxygen Bar Resort and took a group photo at the gate. It was already 12:30 after the photo was taken. Everyone hurriedly got on the bus and to catch the to the of Kangbao City. At one o'clock in the afternoon, we arrived in the city, just in time for the Kangbao Grassland Marathon to be held in 2023. The hotels in the city were full. We moved from 1:40 p. m. to 2:20 p. m. and finally sat down on the second floor of a Luo yuedong hotel. Jia Haiyan hosted 1 table of sumptuous Kangbao special lunch. Jia Haiyan, who treated people sincerely, wanted to put all the delicious food in Kangbao on the table. The sincerity was full of touching. After 1 a special and sumptuous lunch, everyone got on the bus at 3: 30 p. m. and drove away from Kangbao to Zhongdu grassland.

Hai Xia sincerely invited a couple in their seventies to join the trip temporarily. Here, I would also like to Shao to their husband and wife: Liu Runjie, 77 years old, Zhang Bei Court, political commissar of the judicial police force, joined the army in 1960, joined the army in 1969, and moved to Wulateqian Banner in Inner Mongolia, Yichang in Hubei, Chengde and Nalati in Xinjiang in a certain army to devote his youth to the construction of China's war preparedness fortifications and Tianshan Highway. Serve as a platoon leader, many times meritorious service. After changing his career, he worked as a bailiff and obtained a trial certificate. After retirement, he still carried forward the spirit of Lei Feng, helped comrades in need, and actively participated in social activities such as literary and artistic propaganda, renovation of old buildings, supporting agriculture and helping agriculture, and was called "living Lei Feng".

Zhao Yuelian, 76 years old, former director of the Zhangbei County Cultural Bureau, went to Zhangbei Normal University in 1965, graduated in 1968 and stayed in Zhangbei to engage in group work for more than 50 years, and now serves as the party branch secretary of retired cadres and the county customs work Committee Deputy director, chairman of the Community Federation of Literary and Art Federation, editor of Zhangbei Normal School Chronicles. Participated in the "Symposium on Chinese Excellent Traditional Culture", the 4th River North Yanzhao Music Culture Seminar.

The warm-hearted couple, we all affectionately call their sister brother-in-law. The couple took us to the Zhongdu Museum, but it was time for the museum to get off work when arrived. So we turned around and headed for the Haige of the prairie to our east cousin.

Beautiful grassland

The two-day gathering along the way, from the Cambanor National Wetland Park to the Kangbao South Tianmen, over the mountains,

To Wolongtu, Zhang Bei Avenue to Jian, the car galloped, 120 miles, sightseeing all the way, grassland endless, sunflower golden yellow, buckwheat white, mountains and hills, long-distance cross-country.

Haige of Grassland

At 4: 20 p. m., our motorcade drove into the Haige in the grassland to the north of Xiao San ying. everyone unloaded their bags and walked into the room to stay in the Haige in the grassland.

Riding

After everyone arranged their accommodation, they came out to feel the sunshine, blue sky and air here.

When the couple heard Hai Xia, president of the Zhangjiakou branch of the, say that I planned to ride a horse, the couple felt that as Zhang Beiren, they should do their best to show the magnanimity and righteousness of Zhang Beiren. They insisted on asking me to go out to ride a horse. After repeated persuasion, they agreed and thanked me. The old brother started the car for 8 minutes and came to the prairie horse racing field opposite the small three camps. Elder sister first swept yards paid for a horse, and I swept another yard to pay for two horses, asking the couple to ride together. The 77-year-old sister and husband not get on the horse, so the 76-year-old sister flew on the horse, and Liang Liping (male) brother also to move the saddle and ride a horse the stirrup. Liang Liping, an optimistic and kind friend, I like it very much. I also to move the saddle on the horse and ride the grassland. This picture of waving immediately was captured by Hai Xia, president of Zhangjiakou Branch.

In the evening, at 6: 20, we rode back and drove into the yard of the Haige on the grassland. We walked into the house, turned on the, took a bath and the nozzle, and washed away the dust all the way.

Grassland Haige Roasted Whole Sheep

In the evening, Du Xiangdong specially prepared roasted whole sheep. Before the opening ceremony, I picked up 1 bowls of milk tea according to Mongolian etiquette, dipped my middle finger in milk and .1 respected the sky, 2 respected the, and 3 respected himself. I also thanked Du Xiangdong for his hospitality and for having this opportunity to gather in the Haige the grassland of Zhongdu grassland. I wish everyone a happy evening, a happy gathering and a happy drink.

Everyone feasted on roasted whole sheep and drank 52-degree Chinese liquor in a large bowl. After a 3 tour, Liu Runjie, a retired brother-in-law from the of the line of the public security war, walked out of the yurt and picked up the microphone. A song "Horse Mercedes-Benz to protect the Frontier" was sung loudly. Although already 77 years old, but the voice is loud, imposing. Brother-in-law's lover, the 76-year-old elder sister Zhao Yuelian, who was formerly the director of the Bureau of and Culture of Zhangbei County in, and has been engaged in group writing for more than 50 years in Zhangbei, immediately danced. A happy couple sang and danced with the style. In those years, the singing was loud and the dancing was beautiful, and everyone praised it.

The 1 table roasted whole sheep, 1 bowls of fragrant milk tea, a song in the heart, everyone ate, drank, and sang, all in infinite joy, singing loudly until midnight.

The prairie moon

Wake up at 4 o'clock in the morning, the bright moon outside the window. The night sky of the grassland is particularly clear, and the moon accompanied by white clouds can be seen at night. I got up and went out in my clothes, and my mobile phone took pictures of the moon in the grassland. Back to the house, old fan's snoring is still. At 4:30, I took a cold shower. At 5 o'clock, I saw Liang Liping (male) old buddy cleaning the car in the yard through the window, so I went out and sat down at the table in the yard. After a while, Liu Runjie and Zhao Yuelian also came out, and we sat at the local table chatting together.

Rushing to the Zhongdu Museum

At 7: 30 in the morning, Du Xiangdong had already made an breakfast outside Haige on the grassland. He called everyone to eat quickly. After the plan was made, he went to Desheng Village, where President Xi Jinping had visited, and then went to Zhongdu Museum. In order to know something about Desheng Village, I first went to Desheng Village on Baidu. The village is very beautiful. However, there was not enough time for the departure 1, so he changed his plan and went directly to the Zhongdu Museum.

Brother-in-law Liu Runjie and elder sister Zhao Yuelian and his wife drove the way, and the four-wheel drive drove 120 miles all the way.

I traveled through time and space here to see the horseback nation, the fast horse machete, swept across Europe and Asia, successively attacked and destroyed the Xiliao, Xixia, Khwarezmo, Jin Dynasty, and created the largest territory in Chinese history. The written description of the Yuan Dynasty, the physical exhibition, and the territory display. If the Yuan Dynasty extended to the Arctic Ocean in the north, there are 22.67 million square kilometers.

Located to the north of Nanshan Road in Zhangbei County and east of Chahar Street, the Yuanzhong Museum, which covers a total area of 69 mu and a construction area of 9202.68 square meters, is the first thematic museum of Mongolian and Yuan history in China, and the first museum with a single dynasty as its theme. The completion of the Museum of Zhongdu in the Yuan is indeed of great significance to the study of the history of the development of the Mongolian Yuan.

After quickly browsing all the contents displayed in the museum and taking photos, I walked out of the Yuan Zhongdu Museum and stood opposite the museum. I looked at the blue sky and white clouds and thought about the grand occasion of the glorious period of the Yuan Empire. So I turned on my mobile phone Baidu. The data showed:

The predecessor of the Yuan Dynasty was the Great Mongolia. When Genghis Khan Temujin founded the country in 1206, it led the desert north and south and the forest area (Nebuchu area). After the management of the Mongolian khan in the past dynasties and the three westward expeditions, the largest territory was as high as 33 million square kilometers.

Starting from the Sea of Japan and the East China Sea in the east, reaching the Black Sea and the Mediterranean region in the west, crossing Siberia in the north and the Persian Gulf in the south, it accounts for 22% of the world's land area, surpassing 1/5, 1.5 times that of the Soviet Union in the 20th century, and 1.9 times that of Russia today. it was a superpower across Asia and Europe at that time.

In 1271 AD, Kublai Khan ordered to change the national title to Yuan. In February of the following year, Kublai Khan changed the national title to Dadu and established the capital here. The Yuan Dynasty still has a huge territory of up to 17.72 million square kilometers. The territory extends from the north to the sea, the Korean Peninsula in the east, the Pamir Plateau in the west, and the northeast of Myanmar and the north of Thailand in the south. The total area is 4.12 million square kilometers larger than that of China now.

According to the map of the Yuan Dynasty, the territory of the Yuan Dynasty mainly includes two countries, namely China and Russia. Russia is the relatively large area of Siberia, and this area is not much cared by the Central Plains dynasty. In addition, there are a small part of the of Myanmar, and many countries in the Indochina Peninsula. South Korea also includes Sikkim, Bhutan, Kashmir and other regions.

After a while, everyone came out of the museum. In my heart, I deeply thank Zhao Yuelian's elder sister and President Hai Xia for creating such a good opportunity and cultural journey for everyone to understand Zhang Bei, Zhongdu and Yuan Dynasty.

From the afternoon of the 4th to the morning of the 6th, I also saw the level, level, contacts and pattern of President Haixia. It makes me firmly believe that there is a very capable president in the branch under the jurisdiction of North China, and that is her.

At about 11 on the morning of August 6, the 3 car finished filling up at the gas station. Brother-in-law Liu Runjie and Elder Sister Zhao Yuelian and his wife were still the first car to open the way. We drove to Sister Zhao Yuelian's home in Zhangbei County. Elder Sister sent me two books her and told me that she would have a meeting in the provincial capital tomorrow, and her husband would drive with us to Guyuan.

Guyuan Lunch

Time was short. We shook hands with our elder sister one by one and said goodbye. Later, our brother-in-law drove forward first. The four-wheel drive drove 120 miles all the way. Arrived at Zhangjiakou Branch Secretary-General Yu Chunlin at 1: 00 p.m. and booked a hotel in Guyuan County. The Secretary-General and the two ministers in the county had been waiting for a long time. After everyone shook hands and got to know each other one by one, they hurried into the restaurant because it was too late. Everyone sat down at the table and filled their glasses with white wine. Chunlin is a former skater, with vision, insight and pattern. She said that because I am the elder brother, let me talk first, then I will talk first: although we are driving at full speed for a moment, it is still late for us to arrive at the first because of the long journey. fortunately, chunlin and the two younger brothers are waiting for us patiently. It is a great fate for everyone to meet for the first time in Guyuan. Therefore, we have come from afar to raise our glasses to Chunlin and our two brothers. Thank you for your and for your and hospitality. We all raise our glasses to celebrate the meeting. After that, Chunlin picked up his glass and said, "I 've been looking forward to Chen Dage coming to the grass. Today I finally arrived. Here, my two good brothers and I raise our glasses to welcome Brother Chen and all the brothers and sisters present here. Let's raise our glasses once again. Since my brother-in-law, Xiao Zhang and Li Ju didn't drink, Xiang Donghe and Dianfu, the two good brothers who took the initiative to take on the role of with spring, pushed a cup for a cup and cheered each other. Before they knew it, they had already drunk 4 cup of wine and had a great time. The atmosphere was very good.

Turning the river upside down

When everyone was drinking, I suddenly felt that my stomach was not strong and felt a dull pain, and then the pain was obviously. However, when everyone is having a good drink, I am not good at affecting the atmosphere. I am silent and pretend to be. It was Chun who drenched and noticed that my face was not right: Brother Chen, I'll pour you a wine bar. At this time, my stomach is churning. I forced myself to stand up and said, "if you don't pour the of spring shower, please drink it slowly. I'll go out first... everyone saw that my face was sallow, so get out of the way and give me a way out. I hurried to the bathroom...

After that, everyone packed up and went outside together. spring shower feel hot, I may be heatstroke, so I brought Huoxiang Zhengqi water to let me drink. Then, everyone got on the bus and went to Guyuan respectively. The car stopped at the side of the road after a short time, Chunlin and Haixia all got off and went to the opposite store. Xiao Zhang said: What did they do in pharmacies and supermarkets? I was groggy in the car and had no time to think about it.

After a while, Chunlin brought Huoxiang Zhengqi Water, Hawthorn Pills and other medicines from the drugstore. Tell me how to take it and let me drink another 1 bottles of Huoxiang Zhengqi water. After that, everyone got on the bus and continued on their way to Guyuan.

Haixia said, I may be taking a cold shower in the morning and it.

Lightning Lake

Lightning Lake, a beautiful and full of reverie and impact of the name. Baidu said: Lightning Lake is located in the source of Gu in Hebei Province. It is the largest lake in the upper reaches of Luan River. It is named after the river before entering the lake is Lightning River. The area of the lightning lake is not small, the lake is not deep, the water is clear to the bottom, the water plants are swaying, occasionally you can see small shrimps swimming freely, black and white water birds rise and fall quickly on the water, the lake in the dusk is decorated vividly, the sun is golden, the grassland is smeared into a golden carpet, alone by the lake, feel the breeze, the heart swayed in such a sunset into the water bottom that and soft aquatic plants. In the sky, the wild grassland flash out such a clear and beautiful lake. High in the sky, she is said to look like a silver bolt of lightning, which the locals call the Lightning Lake or Lightning River. Although the origin of this name can no longer be verified, how can you not marvel at the greatness of nature when there is such a beautiful scenery on the vast and wild grassland.

The motorcade approached the Lightning Lake scenic area, and the high gate of the Lightning Lake scenic area was really full of impact. On top of the mountain

Only the golden eagle spread its wings and wanted to fly. 3 is a big red character below "Lightning Lake.

Arrange accommodation for dinner

We arrived at Lightning Lake at 5: 00 p.m. Chunlin's friend was the manager of Lightning Lake Scenic Area. On the of the east wall the hotel lobby, there was a huge picture of Kunpeng spreading wings and. From this point, we can see that the boss was ambitious, outstanding and ambitious.

The room has been arranged, and the spring shower is very hot to arrange for everyone to drift. I see that it is already over 6 o'clock. I suggest that everyone turn around the scenic spot first.

At 7 o'clock in the evening, everyone gathered at the restaurant for dinner. Chunlin's niece was the restaurant manager. She was warm-hearted and considerate and had excellent service. 1 table sumptuous delicacies, spring shower also specially brought wine for everyone to taste. I poured a glass of water to accompany everyone while joking and eating.

Fever

Chunlin found that I didn't have any food, so he asked me: Mr. Chen, why don't you have food? I said: Because I haven't eaten dinner for a long time, and I also feel a little hot. Chunlin to put his hand on my forehead: Oh, really, Miss Chen you have a fever. The brother-in-law who was drinking looked at me and said, "Brother, it's okay. I have a cold capsule in my car. I'll take it to you and eat it. My brother-in-law quickly brought it to me. I said hello to everyone and let everyone eat and drink well. I retreated first. When I 1 out of the restaurant door, I felt cold and shivering. I told myself in my heart: Chen Xin, you are really ill. On this summer night in Guyuan, I quickly hugged my arms and hurried back to the dormitory. poured of white water, quickly ate two pills cold capsules, and lay on the bed with my clothes covered with my. I was dizzy and.

Brother-in-law called the door

I don't know how long I was confused. I heard someone shouting at the door. I guess I didn't wake up after being called several times in my sleep (later I heard Hai Xia say that my brother-in-law called five or six). At that time, I was lazy and hot all over. I really didn't think of it. Ask: Who is it? Just listen to someone say: check the room. When I heard the voice of my brother-in-law, although I had a high fever, I was still happy, because this was my brother-in-law who had just known me for a day, and when I was in a hotel in a foreign land with a fever, I felt warm in my heart. Staring up and opening the door. The door opened and my brother-in-law looked at me and asked, "how is it now? I said burn. At this time, I felt very hot when my hand touched my thigh.

Spring drenched cake niece sent medicine

Behind her brother-in-law were Chun Lin and Hai Xia. Chun Lin came in with a cake in her with a big smile on her face: Miss Chen, today is my niece's birthday, and my niece specially sent a cake to the teacher.

I was moved to say: thank you for spring shower, and thank your niece, that's great. But spring shower I may be more to burn now. Chunlin touched my forehead 1 with his hand: Oh, my teacher, you are really hot. She picked up her cell phone and dialed her niece's cell phone: do you still have cold medicine? Her niece's voice came from the phone: There are cold particles and ibuprofen, and... Chunyin said: Hurry up, Mr. Chen has a high fever. For a while, Chunlin's niece, niece's girl and a waiter came up together and handed 3 sample medicine to Chunlin. At this time, Xiao Zhang, who came to the grassland with me, also came in. My tears were low. I choked up when I looked at my brother-in-law, Chun, Hai Xia, Chun niece, niece's girl, waiter and Xiao Zhang. Because, this is when I was alone in the Guyuan Flash Electric Lake Scenic Resort Hotel thousands of miles away, everyone saw me coming. Although in the high fever, but this kind of friendship is deeply moved me. But I still have to control. Because, such a big person, can't shed tears, throat a burning. I looked at everyone speechless silence for five seconds: thank you... and can't say it again. It is still spring that drenched quickly: Mr. Chen, I'll take quick pot and give you a 1 pot of boiled water, ready to take medicine. Said to get the quick pot to pick up water.

After sitting on the quick pot, try the temperature of the shower water again. Come back and say: Mr. Chen, the temperature of the shower water is still OK. At this moment, the water also opened. She poured half a cup and said, "Miss Chen will take the medicine just brought up. I think you are not energetic either. Lie down after taking the medicine. Let's go first.

Wake up in the middle of the night

After everyone left, they were very worried and nervous. What if it was too heavy? I haven't Yang in the 4 years since the new crown virus epidemic, is it that Yang has? What will happen tomorrow? Thinking, the bottom of the heart. As a result, when I hated the disease and took medicine, I took some medicine brought by my niece Chun Lin at the same time. I was all weak and dizzy and fell asleep.

Confused, let urine hold awake, up to urinate. After that, I felt that I had roots under my feet. Sit in bed and see if the time is 11:41 at night. In order to get better, I took the medicine 1 times and lay down to sleep.

Morning walk encountered the spring

It was already 5 a.m. when I woke up again, which is the usual time for me to go out for a walk in the morning in summer. When I got out of bed and stood up, I felt much more relaxed than when I got up in the middle of the night. My heart said: It seems that God has eyes, friends are affectionate, and the medicine is powerful. I am not seriously ill. Try waving your arms and kicking your legs feels okay. So, I went into the bathroom and turned on the shower head. The bath water at the right temperature flowed down and washed away my pain and anxiety all night. After washing up, change into clothes, cheer up, put on shoes, go downstairs and stick to the usual outdoor walk and.

The morning of Lightning Lake wetland grassland is very cool. If I were at this temperature last night, I would be shivering with cold. Thank God, friends, cold medicine, together let me restore vitality. I breathe the air that exudes the fragrance of grass the original, and walk with relaxed steps along the of the plank road of the Lightning Lake grassland to the edge of the Lightning Lake.

While walking and browsing the contents of WeChat on my mobile phone, I suddenly saw the breakfast time Chun drenched in the group and thought that she was up. He sent the past few words: where is the spring drenched? I immediately received a reply: I practiced in the small square in front of the entrance to the plank road of Lightning Lake grassland. I saw her waving to me later. I walked back to the spring. She asked me: Miss Chen got up early. How do you feel? I said: It feels okay. Chundrenched said happily: is it really? That's great! I said: see you send a notice in the group, let's have breakfast at 7 o'clock? spring rain said: yes teacher.

Haixia's Kindness

You're practicing here. Where's Hai Xia? I asked spring drenched. She should get up now, too. Miss Chen called and told her that we were here waiting for her to come out. spring drenched said. I dialed my cell phone: Where is Haixia? The other head said: I'm going downstairs. How are you? I said: It's too heavy. I have to go to the hospital. Chunlin take me there. I am preparing to leave. The head said: to the hospital? then wait for me and go with you to take care of you. I said: No, I have to accompany the bed what, trouble, let Chunlin take me alone. The other end was in a hurry: no, how can you go alone? Still burning so badly? I said: Well, come down, Chun and I will wait for you in the small square.

Hai Xia came to us in a hurry and came to see me in the same spirit as yesterday: hey, aren't you going to the hospital? Why do you look like you're okay? I said: You are a blessing god. Thanks to you, I'm fine. Hai Xia said: You are so anxious for me. Still scare me! I said: It is only when one has no preparation that one can show one's true nature.

Although it was a joke, such a temporary dialogue without any psychological and ideological preparation really revealed the original kindness of human nature and the true feelings of friends.

This trip to the grassland, the experience of fever in the Lightning Lake Tourism Resort Hotel made me feel the blessing of God, the true feelings of my friends, and the power of drugs, which I will never forget.

Special thanks

This time the high fever was quickly relieved. I really want to thank my brother-in-law and my niece by Chun for delivering the medicine in time. If not, can imagine the consequences. Therefore, Chen Xin once again said 1 to her brother-in-law and Chun's niece who was drenched in: Thank you! I will never forget!

In the morning, after breakfast, everyone went back to the dormitory to pack their clothes, pack their bags, go downstairs and hand in the card to, ready to leave. This departure also means that he will not go anywhere else, because Xiao Zhang has been out for the fourth day. As a result, we took a picture in front of the supermarket of Guyuan Lightning Lake Scenic Resort Hotel, and got on the bus separately. Or did our brother-in-law drive forward to Luanhe Shenyun Scenic Area, which is the lightning nine curves and eighteen bends.

Luanhe River Charm Scenic Area

Our motorcade drove into the gate of Luanhe Shenyun Scenic Area, and the spring shower took us into the gate of Foshan, turn.

Turn to the Altar of Foshan

We climbed up the mountain for a while to reach the top of the mountain, where we saw the altar built by our ancient ancestors.

The altar in Foshan,, was built about 5000 years ago in the Neolithic period. It was discovered in 2012. The altar is different from the Ao bag. It is built with stones layer by layer higher than layer by layer, and each layer shrinks in. There are flat surfaces about 60cm wide, and each layer is very regular circle.

The altar is the reverence and worship of the sun by primitive people. It is used by the of the source of the to worship the gods of heaven and earth, grass and trees.

The altar adds a testimony of ancient history to the charm of the Luanhe River.

This ancient altar was a place where the ancients worshipped the gods of the mountain and the gods of wind, rain, thunder and electricity. Scientific investigation found that there are a large number of stone tools such as stone mills, stone, hoes,, stone knives and other stone tools on the east bank of grassland lake in the northwest of the mountain, and half-hole houses inhabited by ancient in the southwest of the mountain. These findings fully show that human beings lived here as early as ancient times.

We are here to talk to the ancient ancestors and tell them that we are here. We will take a group photo the altar and let this the ancient mountains and rivers of the and the grasslands remember that we have been here.

Lightning River

The most verve, tourists like weaving, antique pavilions standing in the white clouds, long corridor song leisurely is the best point to watch the verve of the Luanhe River. The Lightning River meanders, nine curves and eighteen bends, like lightning flashing on the grassland. This summer, with abundant rain, the Lightning River is more attractive. In this dreamlike lightning river, the nine bends and eighteen bends, our secretary-general of the North China Zhangjiakou branch of Chinese short literature, Yu Chun, high the banner and the nine bends and eighteen bends of the beautiful lightning river are perfectly combined.

Mend.

Du Xiangdong, deputy secretary-general of the North China Branch of Huaxia Fine and Short

Literature, held high the banner and let our bright red flag fly over the ancient mountains and rivers and grasslands in the of Guyuan.

Turn to the Buddhist Temple

Hai Xia, who has been to Foshan,, many times before 2019, was deeply impressed by the past situation of Foshan and Buddhist temples. According to relevant data, there is a Buddhist temple in the Foshan scenic spot in. The of the Buddhist temple is the of the cattle and sheep temple in Chahar Zhengbai Banner. Built in the 49th year of Kangxi (1710), the Tibetan Buddhist Temple was built by the Lama of Chagangushi. The court named it "Zhenyuan Temple ". transfer Buddhist temple (zhenyuan temple) is called transfer Buddhist temple because there is a transfer Buddhist temple in front of it. temple is built at the foot of mountain. mountain is called transfer Foshan, and the village above is also called transfer Foshan village. It is said that the in front of the original temple the Buddha enshrined in the temple is on the water mill on the channel of the Lightning River, so there is a saying among the people that the water mill the Buddha. The of the Buddhist temple has gone through more than 100 years of ups and downs from its construction to the of the in Guyuan. After the Buddha statue moved to the north, the temple houses were used by the people and were destroyed by wars during the of the period of the Republic of China.

It is regrettable that during the 2020 New Crown epidemic, with the consent of the local government, the transfer was asked to leave. At present, there is no turning Buddha in the turning Buddhist temple, and there is no four –Buddha in the of the turning Buddha pavilion. Even the two dragon beads on the roof of the Great Hall and the pair of stone lions in front of the hall were gone. This is by no means a great loss to the that cannot be calculated by money the inheritance of Guyuan monuments and religious culture.

The wisdom of the ancients can be seen from the original site of the –to –Buddhist temple. Just like the principle of hydropower generation today, the use of lightning to the flow power of the river nine bends and 18 bends and the principle of simple mechanical power conversion prompted the former –to –Buddhist temple to turn the four Buddhas in the of the Buddha pavilion to turn, which had to be praised by the ancients.

Regret and hope

After traveling to the Buddhist temple without Buddha, I returned to the long pavilion on the top of Foshan without Buddha. Looking at the beautiful and graceful lightning river with infinite charm, I couldn't help regretting and losing. Tang Dynasty poet Liu Yuxi's "humble room inscription ", meaning: the mountain does not lie in the height, with the immortal is famous. The pool does not lie in the deep. With the dragon, it seems to have aura. In 1980, a Tang Dynasty stone tablet was found in Guanyin Temple, Zhonghua Forest Farm, Yingshan County, Hubei Province. The first two sentences of the tablet are: "the mountain is not high, but the monk is famous if there is a; the temple is not big, but if there is a god, there is a spirit." On the back of the inscription, the inscription the words "March, the fourth year of Zhenguan in the Tang Dynasty (630), Le Stone. From this, it occurred to me that if, one day, through the attention of cultural and religious departments and the local government, and the persistent running of social sages and people of insight, turn to Buddha and turn back to Buddhist temples, then turn to Foshan will be worthy of the name, and turn to Buddhist temples will be worthy of the name. turn to Buddha pavilion reset the of the four turn to Buddha, and can reproduce the grand occasion of the four Buddha self-turn in the eight bends of the flash river in the in the nine bends, that should be a great good thing for today, for the benefit of future generations, and for the benefit of boundless merit. It can also add a strong stroke to the inheritance of Guyuan monuments and religious culture, and will last forever.

3 Heyuan

Guyuan 3 Heyuan refers to the Luanhe, Heihe and Baihe rivers. Guyuan, a ancient county in the northern part of Hebei Province and on the upper reaches of the Lightning River, is the origin of the Luanhe, Baihe and Heihe rivers, with a total water area of 61000 mu and a wetland area of 700000 mu. It is a zone where nomadic culture and farming culture blend and where nomadic culture and farming culture blend.

The Luanhe River, a river that flows into the sea alone in the Bohai Sea, was known as Kuanshui in ancient times and was named after many hot springs in its birthplace. The is moist. The sounds of the and Luan are similar. After the Tang Dynasty, it evolved into the Luan. The Yuan Dynasty was also called "Yuhe" or "Shangdu River ". Originated in Fengning County, Hebei Province, it flows through Guyuan County, Zhenglan Banner, Duolun County, Longhua County, Luanping County, Chengde County, Xinglong County, Kuancheng Manchu Autonomous County, Qianxi County, Qian'an City, Lulong County, County, Changli County, and in the south of Leting County Dou net Pu into Bohai Sea. The total length of the river is 888 kilometers, according to the website of the Hebei provincial government and 877 kilometers according to the "Hebei Provincial Records of Physical Geography.

The Luan River has a long history and accepts many tributaries along the way, of which 9 have a drainage area of more than 1000 square kilometers, namely the Luan River in, the Xingzhou River in, the Yixun River, the Wulie River, the Launiu River, the Liuhe River, the Waterfall River, the River and the Qinglong River. Among the tributaries, the largest drainage area is the Yixun River, and the largest in length and water volume is the Qinglong River.

The Luanhe River is also the main water source in the northern and eastern part of Hebei Province. There is a famous Luanhe River diversion project, which introduces the river water into the urban area of Tianjin.

Although the data showed that the Luanhe River originated in Fengning, a large stone was on the left side of the west gate of the Zhuanfosi Temple sitting to the east and west, with the words "the source of the Luanhe River" written 3 capital letters. I deeply sigh that the Luanhe River, starting from here, not only moistens Hebei, Inner Mongolia, mountains, rivers and grasslands, but also introduces Tianjin to alleviate the bottleneck of water use in municipalities directly under the Central Government.

The magical and beautiful Lightning River has nine bends and eighteen bends.

Standing on the top of Foshan in the turn of the, looking around the grasslands and rivers at the bottom of the mountain, looking up at the blue sky and white clouds. When we go down the mountain, we will go our separate ways. After a few days of collecting customs and traveling, we will run for thousands of miles, broadening our horizons, increasing our knowledge, enriching our experience, feeling the local conditions and customs, and reaping our true feelings. There are touched, there is happiness, there is enjoyment, there is gain. Unity, friendship and sincerity have made the trip to the grassland. We took a group photo on the plank road to Foshan!

If you want to stay in the grassland for a long time, you can't stop this journey. The schedule was tight, and the planned Zhangjiakou city failed to continue. Good friend Wang Kun, deeply regret. I deeply understand, and please rest assured, long sky clouds, grassland often in. Zhangjiakou Dajingmen, my friend, Wang Kun, will meet later. Elder sister Zhao Yuelian, brother-in-law Liu Runjie, Hai Xia, Du Xiangdong, Yu Chun Lin, Fan Dianfu and Jia Haiyan met in the coming day.

Finally, a section of the lyrics of a soulful and melodious prairie song "Farewell Prairie" ends, and when the wind blows the grass and the horses gallop, it is even more time for everyone to laugh.

parting grassland

Ci: Zhang Feng

Composer: Jia 1

Unforgettable look back on you

Forget your eyes that 1

Unforgettable Grassland Smile

Unforgettable flowers fall and go with the wind

Where did you wake up this night?

It's already a tall building

Not seeing the crescent moon in the sky

Just listen to the noise like flow

Think of the delicate grassland

Walk through that creek

Remember your affectionate retention

Don't forget the tearful charge

How much I want to stay in the grassland for a long time

Can not stop the pace of this trip

Looking forward to seeing each other

Let's stay together

the Russian flavor of "Central Street"

The unit has a 5-day holiday, plus two-day holidays, which is another "seven-day holiday". People like to take a trip to the south in winter, however, I went to Harbin in consultation with my friends.

In Harbin in late November, the temperature was much colder than that in Tangshan. Although I was driving on the highway by bus, I was tired from the journey all the way, so I let everyone take a bath in the hotel and fall asleep in bed after dinner.

First taste of salmon sauce

It has long been said that Harbin's "Central Street" is a street famous for its exotic customs. Since

Saudi Arabia the Russian Empire once occupied Harbin in history, the architecture of this street is full of Byzantine style and Russian style. Especially the delicacy here is full of Russian flavor. Thinking of these, I couldn't help but have a taste, so we, the sleepless buddies, swarmed out. In Harbin at night, men and women old and young people, or stroll under the flashing neon lights, or enter and exit shopping malls, or drink, talk and laugh in food and entertainment venues, a romantic and casual atmosphere.

We walked on the street, in this freezing cold season, actually saw popsicles in the to buy. Everyone passed by a restaurant called "Hua Mei Xi Restaurant". The tour guide told us that it was founded by a Russian Jew named Chu Jill. He also happily told us that the caviar here is relatively cheap.. When it comes to caviar, few of us Tangshan people think of it. Go into the dining room and take your seat and order five breads and caviar. I don't know I call it. I don't know 1 I call it. The world-famous salmon sauce is only here for a 1 of 40 yuan's money. Take a piece of bread, smear it with caviar, sprinkle it with onions and, add a piece of bread and take a bite. Hey! Taste that call a beauty. It is the 1 kind of onion sweet with the smell of fish roe. Do you want to ask why you sprinkle onions foam? It is because the smell of onions can break off the fishy smell of fish roe.

The first time I ate with cream.

Let's put aside the next day's sightseeing and say another delicious thing—with cream. This is another delicacy that Europeans love to eat very much. We came to a restaurant called Portmansi to sit down. When the waiter brought a plate of silver snowfish, he put a small plate in front of each of us. A rectangular container was placed on the small plate. After that, a of silver snowfish were placed inside one by one, and then cream was ordered. The dish was finished. After we opened the Changyu wine we brought and poured a glass of, we ate a tender and sweet silver snow fish with cream, smacked and wine, which felt really different from eating Chinese food.

Out of this Portman Western restaurant, looking at the northern night sky, my heart can not help but feel a sense of desolation. I am thinking that if Tsarist Russia had not forcibly invaded more than one million square kilometers of Chinese territory from the territory of the Qing Empire, the place where we taste Russian flavor today might not be here. I looked up at the moon in the sky, when Chang'e −1 was exploring the moon. Will a strong China one day be able to recover all the Chinese territories occupied by the great powers of the past dynasties? In China, where there were strong Qin, Han Dynasty, prosperous Tang Dynasty and the Great Yuan Dynasty that fought and Europe and Asia, will the descendants of Qin Emperor, Han Wu, Tang Zong, Song Zu and the favored son of heaven one day let all of the states come to and to celebrate China? Are all Chinese children considering this issue today? I think it should be...

Visit Aries Valley in Autumn

In late autumn, he went to Qian'an in eastern Hebei and lived in Baiyangyu Forest Farm for seven days. The sight of the moon sprinkling the Great Wall alone is enough to satisfy one's heart.

Baiyangyu Great Wall, mountain Xiongguan dangerous, since ancient times for the military. Aries Valley, also known as Aries Pass, is famous for its male, and there is a famous marble Great Wall in the area, which is particularly rare.

Today's Baiyangyu mountains and rivers are beautiful, integrating the beautiful scenery of the south of the Yangtze River and the scenery of the north. There are many historic sites and scenic spots, such as "Lixiu Lianzhu", "Xishan Lingwu", "Lingyan Ancient Well" and "Xiandong Stone Bed. As everyone knows, the ancient and vigorous, mighty and vicissitudes of the Great Wall of Aries, has long been integrated and deeply rooted in the hearts of the people.

In the evening, on foot, there is a mountain beam, the Great Wall winding up, the sunset hanging above the 1 enemy tower. This 1 a unique perspective that makes people read the majesty of the ancient buildings. Although the enemy building is old, it is still guarded there. Even if it is far away from the war and the killing, the muscles and bones of the bricks and stones are also tall and majestic and inviolable. This is exactly the embodiment of the strong will of the Great Wall of Steel.

Looking at the Shenwei Building, Zhang Shizhong, a guerrilla general of the Ming Dynasty, had specially inscribed the name of the building. The magic of Shenwei Building is that it does not ride on the city wall like other enemy buildings, but hangs outside the city wall, which highlights the courage and determination of the Ming Dynasty soldiers to resist the invasion of foreign enemies.

On closer inspection, Shenwei Building is the 1 hard mountaintop building with masonry structure, just like 1 two-story building with imitation wood. Its architectural style is peculiar, majestic and unique.

Shenwei upstairs and down, between each piece of green brick, are plastered with lime mud, until the eaves and rafters, which is a typical way of building walls in ancient China. In the middle of the outer wall on the back, an arrow window is opened, which can not only ventilate and light, but also observe the enemy situation, and facilitate the launch of bows and arrows. There are two Dom holes under the arrow window, which are specially used to launch Dom stones and hit the enemy. The arrow window and the Dung stone hole are arranged in a "product shape", which not only has the aesthetic feeling of high and low, but also has the combat practicality.

The next day, we went to the lie city called "Horse Circle" and "Parade City. The morning mist in the mountains is accompanied by heavy moisture. Climbing the commanding heights of the lie city and overlooking the Xiongguan, I couldn't help feeling with emotion. Ancient and modern wind, frost, rain and snow, war and destruction, now the Xiongguan is still there, easy to defend difficult to attack. Stroll through the city and marvel at this distinctive "military pocket city". First of all, it can confuse the enemy; secondly, it is convenient for stationing troops and storing food and grass and horses. This original way of military defense can be called a miracle of Chinese art of war.

Condescending, stop at the throat of Guannei leading to Saibei through the ages, and suddenly feel that this is the real "one man at the gate, ten thousand men do not open it.

There are historical records: Baiyangyu Great Wall was built in the Northern Qi Dynasty (550–577 years). It was made of stone and was only three meters wide. In the early Ming Dynasty, Xu Da built the pass city in Daoai. Later, the governor of Jiliao, Tan Lun, and the commander-in-chief of Jizhen, Qi Jiguang, organized reinforcement for many times. Important sections were covered with bricks, the width increased to five or six meters, and military defense facilities such as enemy buildings and forts were added. Another document says that the Great Wall of Aeyangyu was built by Yan during the Warring States Period and repaired and strengthened during the Ming Dynasty. Among them, there are 21 towers and the well-preserved Great Wall is 4552 meters...

These materials silently tell the story of the past and present of the Great Wall of Aries, of which the most proud is the unique marble Great Wall. The marble Great Wall is about 1.5 kilometers long and is made of brown-red marble as the cornerstone, which is unique in the history of Great Wall architecture. This section of the Great Wall shines brightly at the top of the mountain peaks and has become a wonderful treasure to witness history.

A bright moon, shining on the millennium. The Great Wall, mountains and moonlight of Baiyangyu are still in my mind, which makes people think a lot...

Hebei Daily, October 27, 2023, 11:08

Baiyu Mountain Looking Back at the Blood and Tears of the Past

Climb to the top of Baiyu Mountain and overlook this Lushunkou Military Port, which is surrounded by mountains and the sea, with a pleasant climate and beautiful scenery, and recall its vicissitudes and prosperous years.

Only after opening the chapter of history can we know that Lushunkou was called Ma Shijin in the Eastern Jin Dynasty, Duli Town in the Tang Dynasty, and Shizikou was called by the locals after Liao and Jin dynasties. In the fourth year of Hongwu in the Ming Dynasty (1371 A. D.), Zhu Yuanzhang ordered his generals Ma Yun and Ye Wang to cross the sea from Shandong Peninsula and landed in Shizikou to recover Liaodong Peninsula at one stroke. In order to commemorate the success of the sea crossing, the court issued a decree to change the lion's mouth to Lushun mouth.

Opening the map, you can see that Lushunkou is located at the southernmost tip of the Liaodong Peninsula, protruding between the Yellow Sea and the Bohai Sea, opposite to the Shandong Peninsula across the Bohai Strait, surrounded by the Bohai Sea on three sides, and backed by the Grand Peninsula. It is an excellent seaport. Lvshunkou has always held the throat of the Bohai Sea and has always been strategically important.

Looking back at history, in the fourth year of the reign of Emperor Guangxu of the Qing Dynasty (1880), the Qing Empire, which walked out of the heyday of Kangxi and Qianlong and entered into decay, had to make efforts to strengthen its national strength and strengthen its military power, set up the Beiyang Navy, built a dock in Lushunkou, built a fortress and established a military port. But after 15 years, the Sino-Japanese War of 1894–1895 broke out in the 19th year of Guangxu of the Qing Dynasty. The Japanese army defeated the Chinese guard Xu Bangdao and occupied Lushunkou in 1999 (November 22, 1894) before the end of Qianlong (1795). In the 3 massacre that was tragic day and night, more than 20,000 Chinese people died under the bloody butcher knife of the Japanese. Later, under the interference of Russia, France and Germany, Japan had no choice but to return Lushunkou to China.

Lvshunkou, a battleground for military strategists, can be said to have historically been that the polar bear stepped on the back as soon as the jackal left. In December 1897, a Russian warship of the Tsar suddenly broke into the port of Lushun and forcibly occupied Lushun and Dalian. In January 1898, troops were sent to the grate nest, which is today's picket area to set up a card to collect grain. The Russian army's forced extortion aroused public indignation and the local people rose up to resist. The brutal Russian Maozi was suppressed by force, killing more than 100 Chinese civilians. On March 27, 1898, that is, the 24th year of Guangxu, Tsarist Russia rented Lushun Port as a military port to the Qing government, forcing the Qing government to send Li Hongzhang to sign the "Lushun Lease Treaty" with the Russian agent in China, Baburofu, in Beijing. In April, it sent troops to Jinzhou (now Jinxian County), and on May 7, it signed the Treaty of Renewal Lease in St. Petersburg in St. Petersburg, which further confirmed the Russian Empire's right to build the railway. In November, the Luda lease was planned, thus reducing the entire territory of northeast China to the sphere of influence of tsarist Russia.

However, the little Japanese, who had seized Lushunkou but did not die, were still eyeing the Liaodong Peninsula, especially Lushunkou. The Russo–Japanese War finally broke out in Lvshunkou in the plot that the Japanese longed. During the battle that lasted for more than a year, Japan and Russia suffered heavy losses, and the war was so tragic that the Russian army dismantled the cannons on the warships and used them on the fortifications on the mountain. On January 1, 1905, the war ended and the Japanese occupied Lushunkou. In this war, China, Japan and Russia suffered heavy losses. The Japanese army died more than the Russian side, more than 66800 people. Even Naimu Baodian, the son of the Japanese army commander Naimu Hinori, died here.

In August 1945, the victory of the Anti–Japanese War, Lushunkou returned to the embrace of the motherland. However, it was not until May 1955 that all affairs here were fully managed by China.

Walking down Baiyu Mountain, wandering in the verdant mountains, walking on the refreshing seashore, wandering in the beautiful scenery, there is still a dull pain in my heart. In this unbearable more than one hundred years, the great powers have bullied and humiliated our 5,000-year-old civilization and the Chinese nation one after another. They have left the Chinese people with extremely bitter memories. At the same time, they have already committed genocide and crimes against humanity against China.

In the bright summer sun, standing in front of the ancient cannon of the Sino–Japanese War of 1894–1895, looking forward to the distant sea and frontiers, it is true to think of the saying "if you fall behind, you will be beaten. Only when China is strong and prosperous can it stand in the east of the world, and the Chinese nation can stand up and work hard.

The second series of celebrities on that side

Visiting Cao Gong in the Rain

On the third day when I arrived in Beijing, I always felt that there was one thing that was not right. I must go to see Cao Gong Cao Xueqin, a rich fellow and ancient Chinese literary master. So, in the afternoon, I faced the cold rain and walked to the Beijing Botanical Garden. Cao Gong's former residence is located in the botanical garden. I walked on the corridor in the garden with an umbrella. My trousers and leather shoes were wet by the rain. Unconsciously approached Cao Xueqin's former residence, I stopped under the ancient locust in front of the former residence.

Looking up at the ancient locust, the vicissitudes of the ancient locust are dignified. I wonder if the ancient locust is telling me the past of Cao Gong's "the west window cut the candle the wind the rain and the. Can you let me know about Cao Gong's poor days when "the broken cup is cold and has virtue, which is not as good as writing books in Huang Ye Village.

The willow branches of Huangye Village were fluttering in the rain, and the statue of Cao Gong was wet in the rain, frowning and bowing in meditation. Looking at the statue of Cao Xueqin in the rain, I feel that this is the true reproduction of Cao Gong. Cao Gong is thinking and thinking about life.

Looking back at the rich and powerful childe brothers in the prosperous times of Qianlong, how can they expect their families to fall into the predicament of "family eating porridge and wine on credit" in the "Kangfeng Xuan" in the suburbs of Beijing. However, it is such a wealth of precious human life experience dfd the poor and the superior and the superior, which inspired the inspiration of a generation of literary geniuses, and made the literary pride a great and immortal literary masterpiece "A Dream of Red Mansions" well-known at home and abroad.

In the "anti-wind porch" by the of Mao Xuan, the tile stove rope bed is and cold. That is to say, this kind of human is very cold and, which coruscates the great writer's enthusiasm for writing books, writing immortal skin-cutting works in the world, allowing people to study read and explore from generation to generation.

Cao Xueqin in his flashy days was a piece of "precious jade" in the palm of his ancestors, a "orthodox" young master with the highest status in the clan, and a loving brother in the hearts of all the beauties. Cao Xueqin, whose family was in decline, was not a bachelor in the Hanlin Academy, not a first-grade Taoist platform, not a hereditary official in Jiangnan weaving, but a 1 of the Qing Dynasty. But Cao did not grass, it was not. There is no feudal right but rich experience, there is no feudal degree but rich life experience, there is no feudal horizontal platform but there is a real level. The great understanding of the rich and the poor, the academic title, and the fame are all like smoke. In the difficult environment, the has an immortal chapter of every word, and the words soaked with bitter tears have been painstakingly.

Therefore, Cao Gong is still a well-deserved literary giant until now. Standing at the door of the "Anti-Wind Xuan" in the rain, I watched the ancient Huai Yan Liu and watched Cao Gong. He had no laurel on his head, no money mansion in front of him, and no beautiful car beside him. but Cao Gong, as a thinker and writer, is full of the true scriptures of the universe with a broad mind. The lives in Cherry Valley, a suburb of, "lying the snow Huangye Village, a dream of red mansions endlessly". Superordinary, standing on top of the world to see the world; Living high above life to see life; Standing at the high end of life to observe life. Deep thinking, concentrate on tempering the "stone" text, improve their own ideological realm, artistic realm.

Cao Xueqin (about May 28, 1715-about February 12, 1763) left the sad and sad world on the eve of the 29th year of Qianlong (1763), but Cao Gong's heroic spirit has been in people's hearts for more than 250 years, high for nine days.

Standing in front of Cao Xueqin's former residence in the rain, I couldn't help but read a little poem in my heart: cool wind and cold rain botanical garden, yellow flowers rolled in Huangye village, deserted of Xueqin's former residence, Cao Gong sighed bitterly here, he was in the grass and, light the world, and the local voice from afar cold warm.

"in the rain to visit Cao Gong" published in the "Tangshan Labor Daily", permanent collection in the "Hao Ran Literature Museum".

generation of gifted scholar zhang peilun

In the modern history of China, Zhang Peilun, who was as famous as Zhang Zhidong and Zuo Zongtang and was evaluated by Li Hongzhang as "a rich talent and a ", was praised by the government and the public for his integrity and quick thinking.

Zhang Peilun, a young Qiao with characters, was born in a bureaucratic family in Hangzhou, Zhejiang on November 24, 1848 (the 28th year of Daiguang in Qing Dynasty) in Village, Huanxizhuang Township,, District, Fengrun (Zhili Fengrun in Qing). Father Zhang Yin Tang as early as in Qing Jiaqing Ji Mao, Daguang Yiweinshi. He has served as a magistrate of Jingde, Jiande, Haining and Tonglu in Zhejiang, a magistrate of Hangzhou, and an inspector of Anhui. He is an incorruptible official, upright and clean, and has many favorable policies, which has won the hearts of the people. During the reign of Xianfeng, when Li Hongzhang returned to his hometown to set up a group training, he was supported by the envoy Zhang Yintang. The two could be called family friends. Zhang Pei Lun's father died when he was 6 years old. His widowed mother Mao Shi led Zhang Peilun's six brothers to live in Qituo Village,, Fengrun County,, Zhili, Qing Dynasty,. Perrin ranked 3. He was gifted from an early age and was able to recite more than 100 Tang poems when he was 7 years old. At the age of 9, he worshipped Li, a of Fengrun County, the old man. He was very fond of this smart child and was granted free admission to school. The pro —gave the "Young and ". Teenagers were born when they often went to book stalls to borrow books. After reading, they covered their and rolled them into to recite. When they home, they hand-written books into volumes. Thousands of words of articles were written in one stroke and the numbers were hidden in boxes. In their later years, collected more than 100 volumes of self-recorded by hand. Mr. Li praised Perrin and said: "Zhang's family is lucky to have young !" During the Tongzhi period, there was also a saying among the people that "the romantic talent Zhang Fengrun. Zhang Peilun, a 24-year-old young man, passed the examination as a Jinshi. Later, he served as a teacher, a right concubine son, a left deputy chief censor, a teacher, and a walk in the prime minister's office. When he first entered the official career, he had smooth sailing and made a smooth progress. Together with Baoting, Zhang Zhidong and Chen Baochen, he regarded Li Hongzao, the master of the Tongzhi Emperor, the minister of the Ministry of Industry and the minister of military aircraft as the suzerain, and took it as his duty to be upright and preside over the Qing Dynasty. In the face of corruption in the administration of officials, he dared to speak out, comment on the government, impeach the ministers and denounce corrupt officials. The limelight is healthy, for a time. In just a few years, he Shouci, Minister of the Ministry of, and Dong Xun, Minister of the Ministry of Revenue, were successively and impeached. He also dared to speak up for the protection of the army in the of the Gengchen Meridian case, forcing Empress Dowager Cixi to change her opinion. As a result, people called it "Hanlin 4 remonstrant" and "Qingliu Party". At that time, people attacked Yumo and pointed out in "The Diplomatic View of the Party of the Party": "The of the Party of the Party of the Qing Dynasty is the most prosperous, and it actually has the right to influence the public opinion of the government and the public."

In the early years of Guangxu, Li Hongzhang tried his best to advocate industrial and mining enterprises, and tried to open mines, build railways and other new things, and was heavily besieged by the conservative faction. At this time, Zhang Peilun, together with Zhang Zhidong and others, publicized that "the of difficulties is in urgent, and the Westernization is the big end", stood up to support the proposal of the Westernization faction, and emphasized the need to "adopt Western France to the enemy Western ". Zhang, Pei, Wu Rulun and Liu Mingchuan also drafted the "Preparation of Railways to Build for Self-improvement", and took the lead in proposing the plan of building railways. It played a positive leading role in the railway construction of modern China.

After Zhang Peilun became an official, the Empress Dowager Cixi also summoned him many times in the Hall of Yangxin. Once, the Empress Dowager asked him to recite the "perpetual calendar". He actually recited it like a stream. The Empress Dowager was so happy that he repeatedly praised: "Young Qiao really has no books to read." In 1884 (the tenth year of Guangxu in the Qing Dynasty), due to the increasing tension between China and France, the Battle of Mawei started within half an hour, and the Fujian navy was almost completely shelled and sunk by French gunboats. In 1885 (the 11th year of the reign of Emperor Guangxu of the Qing Dynasty), the imperial court decreed that the 37-year-old Fujian Association, who was in charge of maritime affairs and, was awarded the third rank of. Zhang, who commanded the anti-law affairs together with He Ruzhang, the shipping minister, sent him to Zhangjiakou, Yili and other places strictly, and was commandeered for three years to redeem his crime. At that time, foreign attacks were on the rise, and the court was repeatedly by defeat. The Qing Dynasty was reduced to the point where tens of thousands of people beat the drum. The Japanese minister even made a cursive script to tease the Qing Dynasty: "Zhang Changgong, riding a strange horse, playing a lute, eight tortoise, king on top, single Ge into a war." The Empress Dowager Cixi passed on the full of civil and military forces, but no one was right. Later, Li Hongzhang recommended Zhang Peilun, who had been sent to Yili at that time (1884, the tenth year of Guangxu in the Qing Dynasty). After returning to Beijing from thousands of miles away, Perun immediately issued a lower couplet: "Pseudo, attacking dragon clothes, demons and monsters, 4 little ghosts, ghosts and ghosts live beside, and if you close your hands, you take ." The vast Qing Dynasty let a criminal minister come back to deal with it, and only then did it calculate a mouthful of evil spirit.

In 1888 (the 14th year of Guangxu of the Qing Dynasty), Zhang Peilun finally ended his 3-year exile and returned to Tianjin to work under Li Hongzhang's curtain, in charge of documents. In May of that year, Li Hongzhang betrothed his eldest daughter, Li Ju Ou, to him, and held a grand wedding ceremony for his daughter and Zhang Peilun in Tianjin on November 15. Li Ju Ou was 23 years old when he was, while Zhang Peilun was 40 years old and was a criminal minister who returned from exile with nothing. However, Li Ju Ou chose Zhang Peilun precisely because he admired Zhang Peilun's talent very much before, leaving behind a good story admired by literati at that time.

After marriage, the husband and wife are deeply affectionate. In Zhang Peilun's diary, there are often "home-made wine and bow lotus root for a drink, the moon is round and, the fragrance of flowers is swaying, and the wine is tipsy and ". "have little discomfort, cook medicine, sencha, chess, reading and painting, and talk about it". "birthday, night cook tea talk about history, very happy" such records. It vividly illustrates that the daily life of the two is full of love and interest. In Jinling (Nanjing), the couple, who can be called gifted scholars and beauties, not only gave birth to and one son and two daughters, but also revised and completed the 24 volumes of Guanzi Annotation and 10 volumes of Zhuangzi Ancient Yi written by Zhang Peilun during his exile. He wrote many works such as Jian Yu Ji and Jian Yu Yu Diary, as well as a cookbook and a martial arts novel. In 1903 (the twenty-ninth year of Emperor Guangxu of the Qing Dynasty), Zhang Peilun died of liver disease in Nanjing at the age of 56. His wife Li Ju Ou was buried with him after his death in 1912 at the foot of Mount Qin in Heishangou Village, northeast of, Fengrun County,.

April 17, 1988

Zhang Ailing and the Indissoluble Love in A Dream of Red Mansions

Fengrun-Zhang Ailing-read "Dream of Red Mansions" and study "Dream of Red Mansions"; Fengrun-Cao Xueqin-plan "Dream of Red Mansions" and write "Dream of Red Mansions". Zhang Ailing's ancestors were officials in the Qing government. Cao Xueqin's ancestors were officials in the Qing government in. These factors, which are not closely related but have something in common across the ages, intentionally or unintentionally forged the indissoluble bond between Zhang ailing and A Dream of Red Mansions. From 1934 when she wrote "A Dream of Modern Red Mansions" to the publication of "A Dream of Red Mansions" in 1977, Zhang Ailing has been in love with the Red Mansions for decades, which is amazing.

According to the biography, it is a historical fact that his mother ran away from home and his father Zhang Tingzhong wrote a modern dream of Red Mansions for it. Moreover, Zhang Tingzhong was also the enlightening teacher to explain a dream of Red Mansions to Zhang Ailing. Zhang Ailing herself said: I watched "A Dream of Red Mansions" when I was 12 or 3 years old, and saw less than 80 times, I only felt: "The sky has no light, and it is tasteless in every possible way"! It really shocked people today, and I couldn't help but secretly exclaim. After decades of stupidity, I read Zhang Ailing's book and only the first time I heard people say the eight big words like "the sky has no light, every kind of tasteless" for the time! That is to say, these eight words have made a board for Gao E's pseudo-continuation of "the last 40 rounds.

According to an article, Zhang ailing was born in Shanghai in 1920 and moved to Tianjin in 1922 when she was 3 years old. She lived in Tianjin until she was 9 years old (1928) Fang and returned to Shanghai. During her primary school years, she had enjoyed reading the classical Chinese novels A Dream of Red Mansions and The Romance of the Three Kingdoms. Among the 12-3-year-old girls, it is rare and difficult to find a few examples like Zhang Ailing that can feel the great difference between the original and the pseudo-continuation of "A Dream of Red Mansions" at a glance. It can be seen that her talent is of a high level, and her "function" is a direct sensibility, which is an important "ability" she has alone. Without this ability, she would not have any achievements in creation or research. Zhang Ailing is famous as a writer all over the world. In addition to her superiority in sensory performance, she is also a thinker and scholar. The commendable talents are probably the and beauty who are "versatile" and "do not stick to one " as the most difficult to meet the. Eileen Chang began with "straight feeling", but ended with "scholarship. This fully reflected in her late academic work, A Dream of Red Mansions. By the winter of 1961, Zhang Ailing wrote scripts such as "A Dream of Red Mansions " and "A Family in the North and South of" for the Mao Film Company in Hong Kong.

In 1968, Eileen Chang published "A Dream of Red Mansions" in Taipei's "Crown". In 1969, under the knowledge of Professor Chen Shixiang, he worked at the "China Research Center" of the University of California, Berkeley, and continued the research on "A Dream of Red Mansions.

In 1976, Zhang Ailing published her second collection of essays, "Zhang Watching ", and at the same time published "3 A Dream of Red Mansions". In 1977, Zhang Ailing's "Dream of Red Mansions" review collection "Dream of Red Mansions" was published.

On the night of September 8, 1995, it coincided with the Mid-Autumn Festival, the traditional reunion festival of the Chinese nation. Zhang Ailing, a talented woman who focused on Chinese literature, left alone in her apartment in Ximu District, Los Angeles, USA. She was 74 years old. The curtain was pulled down silently in loneliness. China's talented woman guest died in a foreign country, before her death appointed Lin Shi as the executor of the will. On September 19, the remains were cremated at Rose Hills Cemetery in Whitzel, Los Angeles. On September 30, the ashes were carried out to sea by Lin Tong, Zhang Cuo, Gao Quanzhi, Zhang Shaoqian, Xu Yuanxiang and others and scattered to the vast Pacific Ocean.

China and the world did not have Zhang Ailing before, and there will be no Zhang Ailing in the future. Zhang Ailing is the best in this world! In October 2012, Beijing Art Publishing House also published Zhang Ailing's A Dream of Red Mansions. A Dream of Red Mansions is a gorgeous new edition of the book. Zhou Ruchang, a master of red studies, solemnly recommend: Only Zhang Ailing can be called a bosom friend of Xueqin. I admire her very much now and think that she is a great strange figure in the "history of red studies", which is hard to reach by. Zhang Ailing's wizards, with a very fine heart and strong memory (memory), are extremely difficult to reach. I feel ashamed to be a "red scholar" in vain "!

A Dream of Red Mansions is an important work in Zhang Ailing's life. From 1966 when Zhang Ailing settled in the United States to her death in 1995, she spent ten years studying A Dream of Red Mansions. This book is the academic crystallization of Zhang Ailing's Red Mansions after years of research. The book contains seven research articles, including "A Dream of Red Mansions" Unfinished "," One of the Interludes of "A Dream of Red Mansions", "A Dream of Red Mansions" in the early of "," A Dream of Red Mansions "in the of 2 ", "A Dream of Red Mansions" in the of 3 "" "A Dream of Red Mansions" in the of 5 ".

Some commentators say that "A Dream of Red Mansions" is like a maze, like a jigsaw puzzle, and like a mystery detective story. Zhang Ailing described her textual research "A Dream of Red Mansions" as a 1 crazy situation, so she had to a sentence "Ten years of 1 to be obsessed with textual research and win the name of A Dream of Red Mansions". A Dream of Red Mansions is Zhang Ailing's textual research on A Dream of Red Mansions for more than ten years. A Dream of Red Mansions is a precious work of Redology left by Eileen Chang to the world.

The legendary female writer Zhang Ailing never denied her love for "A Dream of Red Mansions", and even spent ten years writing a "A Dream of Red Mansions". The exquisite textual research and unique perception have surprised many red scholars. Zhang Ailing's familiarity with "A Dream of Red Mansions" is simply staggering. She described it in "The Preface to" A Dream of Red Mansions "," I read it 1 times from the beginning every few years "," My only qualification is Really familiar with "A Dream of Red Mansions", different books don't have to be carefully read, and slightly sighted words will pop out ". This preface is very important. It represents Zhang Ailing's ten-year harvest of Redology and her mood of studying. It is a golden key to understand the writer Zhang Ailing's literary heart. This preface represents her style of writing. The characteristic is that it is very plain, not playing with the of pen and flower, and tweaking some "literary and artistic words words". The real "vernacular", simple heart sound. Zhang Ailing is not only familiar with "A Dream of Red Mansions", but has even regarded "A Dream of Red Mansions" as a good medicine for her life." For such a writer who has been wandering in the fantasy artistic realm of "A Dream of Red Mansions" since childhood, it is only natural that his novel creation is influenced by "A Dream of Red Mansions. At that time, Mr. Zhou Shou, the chief editor of Violet, Mr. Juan, the of the editor-in-chief of Violet, carefully described his feeling when he first read Zhang Ailing's novel "Chenxiang Dipping" in the first of the publication: "One wall reading and one wall hitting the festival, and he thought its style was very similar to the works of the famous British writer Somerset, Maughm, and influenced by some" A Dream of Red Mansions ", no matter what others think after reading it, I am" deeply happy to it. "Because of this, reading Zhang Ailing's novels, there will always be a feeling of deja vu, and even an illusion. There is no doubt that there is a complex in Zhang Ailing's heart, which is the dream of Red Mansions complex. This "emotional entanglement in the heart, the feelings hidden in the bottom of the heart" is the 1 kind of love for "A Dream of Red Mansions" has become the 1 strong feeling lingering in Zhang Ailing's heart, and has deeply affected the creation of her novels.

Zhang Ailing's fans of "A Dream of Red Mansions" 1 an almost crazy state-of reading red and continuing red in. the age of 14 and 5, she wrote "A Dream of Red Mansions", studied Red, and wrote "A Dream of Red Mansions" in ten years. "Nightmare of Red Mansions", thus forming Zhang Ailing's complicated mood. The reasons for the formation of a complex emotion in Dafan are also very complicated. If you use the simplest method to explore the root causes of its formation, you can analyze it from both subjective and objective aspects. Subjectively speaking, Eileen Chang has an unusual family. As we all know, Eileen Chang's life experience is still very prominent, to her father's 1 generation although the family has fallen. The father is a rare figure, and his life is sensual, while the mother is 1. Therefore, such a pair of diametrically opposed couples are destined to end up in divorce, so Zhang Ailing has an unhappy childhood and adolescence. The of Zhang Ailing caused great harm to her parents, and her parents became the first teachers of Zhang Ailing's literary creation at the same time. Although her father Zhang Tingzhong's life was depraved, he had a strong family background and a strong literary foundation. He often explained "A Dream of Red Mansions" to her in his spare time and wrote a review of "A Dream of Modern Red Mansions" for it. Mother Huang Qiong must ask maid to carry Zhang Ailing to her bed for endorsement every morning. Later, she was sent to a new-style primary school, and then she was promoted to a middle school and a university to receive modern education, which made Zhang Ailing influenced by western culture at the same time. In other words, although the Zhang family has a strong feudal atmosphere, it is still affected by the trend of the times. As a result, Eileen Chang not only has a profound Chinese cultural foundation, but also a good geographical understanding of Western culture, which enables her to integrate the two freely and form her own unique style. Objectively speaking, the family's influence on Eileen Chang is much more than that. The Zhang family is a big family. The relationship between members is complicated, parents are divorced, stepmother is introduced, which constitutes a lot of multi-angle relationships that are constantly cut and confused: between father and ex-wife, and, between Zhang Ailing and father and stepmother, between mother and daughter, between sister and brother, between aunt and nephew, plus between relatives, and even between servants in the family, etc., with Zhang Ailing as the core. In reality, the Zhang family, an aristocratic family that has not been, has become a Jia family. Therefore, the complex family growth environment, the experience of large family life, and the strong contrast between wealth and hardship in life later, between the ups and downs of the waves and the bottom of the valley, Zhang Ailing's psychological gap and the perception of the world are much deeper than ordinary people.

Such a special living situation not only makes Zhang Ailing form a unusual character, but also makes it easy for her to find the same feeling as Cao Xueqin in a dream of Red Mansions: the decline and decline can not be covered up in the prosperity of the prosperous times, and the desolation and vicissitudes of life be seen in the of the bustle. How could Eileen Chang not like A Dream of Red Mansions?

Looking at Zhang Ailing's life experience and her temperament similar to Cao Xueqin, it is not difficult to understand Zhang Ailing's extreme love for "A Dream of Red Mansions. The sense of desolation that is penetrating into the common living predicament of human beings, the sense of loss of family of honor and humiliation of the rise and fall of, is the best point for two talented writers to cross time and space, and it is also the natural commonality of their literati character. As the saying goes, "there is no distance between each other, and thousands of miles are still neighbors." therefore, red scholar Zhou Ruchang said with emotion: "only Zhang Ailing."

The article "Zhang Ailing and the Indissoluble Love of A Dream of Red Mansions" is included in the book "A Hundred Years of Chinese Film.

Screenwriter Eileen Chang

Zhang ailing, whose ancestral home is rich in Tangshan, is a rare talented writer and a rare screenwriter.

Zhang Ailing, who lives in a big city, has an indissoluble bond with movies since she was a child. She often mentions movies in novels and essays, and her writing skills are obviously inspired by movies. Her short career as a screenwriter began in post-war Shanghai, where she followed the line of comedy, which turned family ethics from sadness to happiness, humorous but touching. Later, he was a screenwriter for Hong Kong Electric Mao Company. Although the theme is still marriage and family, he builds a completely different world in the film from the novel.

Eileen Chang's novel itself has the characteristics of "paper movie hall". The films written by her are not exactly the same as the novels. The performance of the films is more direct and commercial. In the prosperous of the 20th century, luxury and beauty vividly appeared on the screen.

Eileen Chang screenwriter in Shanghai

Zhang Ailing, who likes watching movies very much, used the protagonist's words as early as in her "Eighteen Springs" to say that the advantages of Shanghai are "1 to buy things, 1 to watch movies". Watching movies is often the scene of the development of her relationship, the turning point even the symbol of a man's reliability. In "Flowers Wither ", she wrote about a terminally ill woman who went out to buy sleeping pills to commit suicide. Before she could buy them, she sat in a rickbait for a circle, had a meal in a western restaurant, and sat in a movie theater for two hours. After that, she changed her mind to see Shanghai again.

Alone quietly observing Shanghai is what Zhang Ailing does most of the time, and with her extremely unique brushwork, she has written a lot of film reviews for the Times and the English monthly magazine Twentieth Century. For example, she said in the article that we are walking in a dead end, such as the movie "Fisherman's Girl" called, because the hero of "Fisherman's Girl" is a special student of fine arts. Western art in China has always been a rich leisure thing. ... The lover of the "fisherman's girl" taught her to read, but the traditional scholar-bureaucrat "taught concubine to read"...

However, in her film review article "Dark Clouds Cover the of the Moon", it aroused her praise. "The title of Chinese films usually either extremely poor or extremely rich, and they seldom touch the life of the middle class. This film is an exception and has a keen description of the life of this class."

After the victory of the Anti-Japanese War in 1946, she turned to film script writing. Through Ke Ling's introduction, she met the director Sang, who was her inspiration in the film industry. In 1947, she wrote "No Love" and "Long Live the Wife". Zhang Ailing wrote the screenplay "No Love" for Sang Arc for the time in early, which was made into the entrepreneurial work of "Wenhua Film Company". She also chose Liu Qiong and Chen Yanyan, the most popular at that time, to perform. The film sold well that year. In the postscript to "Lost in Love", Zhang Ailing wrote: "In 1947, I wrote a movie script for the first time, the title of the film" No Love "..."

At one point, she also completed the script of "The Golden Lock", but the filming was stranded due to the turmoil and the illness of the heroine Zhang Ruifang. Like novels, women are extremely important in these films. In another 1 film review, she jokingly said that if we don't talk about the plot and the attraction of matching, all the Chinese movie stars who really have box office are female.

Sang Arc then asked Zhang Ailing to write the script "Long Live the Wife". Zhang Ailing wrote the family life comedy in a,, and funny way, and incorporated it into a series of misunderstanding, coincidence and funny gimmicks. It is a Hollywood-style "neurocomedy" (Screwball Comedy) of a few Chinese people.

Zhang Ailing left Shanghai in 1952, which was a farewell to Hong Kong. Eileen Chang's screenplay Collection of Eileen Chang Mao in the Hong Kong Film Archive, Volume 1 begins, and the first sentence in the preface is: "Hong Kong is fortunate that there is Eileen Chang's name in the history of literature and film." The first sentence of "Reviewing Love in a Falling City": "In the summer of the year of Pearl Harbor, Hong Kong was still the Rivera of the Far East..." Although Taiwan and Hong Kong were both "border towns" in Eileen Chang's eyes, such a proposition was even more reflected in "Revisiting the Border Town. However, it is the island complex of Eileen Chang's image. Hong Kong is very complex for her. There are many situations comparable to Shanghai, and some life trajectories overlap here. Hong Kong for Zhang Ailing is not only the first time in her life to leave her hometown, nor is it just a short stay in her middle-aged return; for Hong Kong, Zhang Ailing is not only a passer-by of the torrent of the times, but also a part of the island culture. The nearest place to the other side where she has love and hate.

Zhang Ailing came to Hong Kong in economic difficulties and came into contact with movies again. Song, who works for the Mao Company, introduced her to write scripts. Not only can she get the highest remuneration, but she also serves as a member of the script review committee.

In 1957, "Love is like a Battlefield" was adapted from the American stage play "the gentle Trap". The plot is compact and the rhythm is lively. The play is full of love fantasia and suspense, which is in line with Zhang Ailing's idea of love: "I think people are more simple and unrestrained when they are in love than when they are in war or revolution."

Although it is a literati film with characteristics of Dian Mao, it also does as the Romans do and has a strong cultural temperament of Hong Kong citizens. The film is starred by popular stars Lin Dai, Zhang Yang, and Chen. The theme song: "Love is like a battlefield. The battle line is long and long. If you want to win the battle, think about the strategy. If you want to lose the battle, you 'd better surrender first, buy a building and send 1 a car. As long as you are willing to help, you are not afraid that she will not appreciate it... "It was also that time that it was popular in the streets and alleys of Hong Kong. Because of the success of the film, it broke the record of Chinese film in Hong Kong at that time.

When Eileen Chang wrote the script for the, the basic values must first be consistent with the majority of the audience. The reason why she was able to resonate with the Hong Kong audience or simply the people of Hong Kong in some aspects and compose one script after another that they welcomed, first of all, because she knew them. Eileen Chang's plays vividly depict the faces of all beings of "little,, and little, bad ". Here are their smiles, their love, their troubles, and their happiness. Zhang Ailing has a deep understanding of this. It can be said that these scripts show the other side of Zhang ailing: she is not as narcissistic as many people think, she also understands and toleres things that are different from herself, even opposite. Secondly, Eileen Chang is a very good storyteller, and her scripts are really clever. These plays are mostly comedies, from which people can see her playful, relaxed and intelligent.

However, the subsequent adaptation of "A Dream of Red Mansions" made her exhausted, because the boss had not read the original work and only wanted a love story of boys and girls crying and making noise. However, several scripts that were easily written during this period were shot in and sold well at the box office. At that time, when the former actress Li Lihua, who had already become the boss, met Zhang Ailing, she specially dressed up beautifully and received a grand reception. However, the status of Hong Kong screenwriters was not the same as that of the mainland period. The director and the leading actor could ask the screenwriter to revise the script at will. However, even so, from 1956 to 1964, Zhang Ailing wrote ten scripts for Hong Kong Mao Film Company, eight films were filmed, and the scripts have been preserved to this day, namely "Two Deals of Human and Wealth" (released in January 1958, lost of the film), "Love Field Like Battlefield" (released in May 1957), and "Peach Blossom" (1959 It was released in April, the film lost), "June bride" (released in January 1960), "little children" (released in October 1963), "a family in the north and south" (released in October 1962), "unforgettable song" (released in July 1964, the film lost), "happy meeting between the north and the south" (released in September 1964), some of which are original and some are adapted. The "North and South" series of films swept the regions of Hong Kong, Taiwan and. "North and South Harbour" was screened for 60 days and sold for the second place in the year. Of the two films that were not filmed, the original manuscript of "Soul Return to Hate Heaven" is still there. It is a pity that "A Dream of Red Mansions" has been lost. From 1957 to 1965, the wrote the "Mao" for nearly 10 years. Until 1965, Zhang Ailing wrote the final script "Soul Returning to Hate Heaven", which was originally tailored for Ye Feng, who had a wild nature, a difficult and a. However, before it could be handed over to the director, Lu Yuntao, chairman of "Dian Mao ", was hit by an air crash in. "Dian Mao " was changed into "Guotai" and Song Qi left. Zhang Ailing also separated from the screenwriter, into her reclusive life!

Impact of later generations

In 1943, "Love in a Fallen City" was published. This love novel, with 467 pages, is one of Zhang Ailing's most short stories to. It is also the 1 article to explore love, marriage and humanity in the war and before and after, how to survive and struggle works.

"Fallen love" is a beautiful and close to the human story. In "Love in the Fallen City", the tassel that came out of the old family, the baptism of the Battle of Hong Kong did not influence her into a revolutionary woman: the Battle of Hong Kong influenced Fan Liuyuan, and made him turn to a plain life. Finally, he got married, but marriage did not make him a saint, and completely gave up the living habits and style of.

On August 2, 1984, the film "Love in the Fallen City" produced by Hong Kong Shaw Brothers Co., Ltd. was released in Hong Kong. The film is adapted from Zhang Ailing's novel of the same name, "Love in a Fallen City", which tells the love story between Fan Liuyuan and Bai Liusu after the fall of Hong Kong. The film is a romantic film directed by Xu Anhua and starring Chow Yun-Fat and Miao Qian.

In 2009, he was succeeded by Dream as the director and Zou Jingzhi as the screenwriter. Based on Zhang Ailing's novel "Love in the Fallen City" of the same name, he adapted 34 episodes of the TV series "Love in the Fallen City" of the same name, which was broadcast on CCTV 8 (CCTV-8) on March 14 of the same year. starring Chen, Huang Jue, Wang Xuebing and others, the play tells a gorgeous and desolate legendary love story that took place in Shanghai and Hong Kong in the 1930 s.

On the night of September 8, 1995, coinciding with the Mid-Autumn Festival, a traditional Chinese reunion festival, 74-year-old Zhang Ailing died alone in her apartment in Ximu District, Los Angeles, USA. The legend silently drew down the curtain in loneliness. However, as Zhang Ailing's literary works have been adapted into film and television works, her strong artistic vitality is still continuing, and Guanghua is still blooming strongly!

"screenwriter zhang ailing" an article income "one hundred years of chinese film" a book.

Zhang Fengming, the broadsword, was angry with the and hit the horse county magistrate.

During the reign of Emperor Guangxu in the Qing Dynasty (1875-1908), a man named Zhang Fengming in Xiaozhanggezhuang Village,, Fengrun County,, set up a "broadsword Zhang Hebei Bangzi Theater" with 3 40 people in the first year of Guangxu (1875). He was the head of the class and performed in villages and towns in Ninghe, Fengrun, Yutian and other places, which were widely welcomed by the people.

Zhang Fengming learned martial arts from childhood, especially proficient in broadsword techniques. Therefore, people give the nickname "broadsword ".

During the Qing Dynasty, the rural people visited relatives and friends, and most of them went to the market and went to the shops on foot. Those who had transportation were mules, horses, donkeys and other feet. Zhang Fengming always rides a tall white donkey to every time he goes out. Therefore, people also gave him the name of "big white donkey Zhang Fengming. Since Zhang Fengming's martial arts training from an early age, he has developed 1 character of punishing evil and promoting good, drawing out a knife to help when the road is uneven, and his temperament is deeply praised by the village. One day in the 31st year of Guangxu (1905), Zhang Fengming came back from writing plays in Sannvhe Village, Run County, Fengxu. When Zhang Fengming rode a big white donkey to Huanghuagang Village, Fengrun County,, he only heard a gong ringing in front of him. He looked up 1 and saw the chief of the 1 group shouting: "Idle people avoid" while sounding the gong. When Zhang Fengming inquired about it, it turned out that the new head of Fengrun County Ma came to the countryside for inspection. Mention of Ma County Mayor Zhang Fengming has long been heard, this Ma County Mayor is a tyrannical, domineering, fish and meat people of the county magistrate. It happened that when we met across the street on this day, Zhang Fengming was determined not to give way. Ma county magistrate saw that someone dared to get in the way, so he asked the chief officers to call Zhang Fengming to the sedan chair for questioning, "What do you from?" Zhang Fengming said, "I didn't Zhuang."

Ma county magistrate asked again: "what's your name?" Zhang Fengming replied: "head of the black class, no name." Hearing this, the county magistrate ma was clearly a thorn in the head, so he gave an order: "call me!" The yamen swarmed in. However, Zhang Fengming did not change his face and his heart did not jump. He sat on the of a big white donkey and grabbed a chief. He 1 gave up and threw to the ground the plop 1. The opportunity to jump off the big white donkey to display martial arts, a punch to the help of the dog-fighting power of the chief of the army after beating the water, arrow in front of the car, pulled out the horse county magistrate 1 beat. As the head of 1 County, he was beaten by 1. How can he swallow this bad breath. So, after returning to the county government, all the people who raised donkey Fengrun County were arrested and brought to justice. At this time, Zhang Fengming, who was over 50 years old, had to tearfully disband the "Big Dao Zhang Hebei Bangzi Opera", which he had worked so hard for more than 20 years, and went to Kanto alone to avoid disaster. It was not until 1910, after the establishment of the of the Republic of China, that county magistrate Ma was finally transferred from the of Fengrun County in, and Zhang Fengming, an old broadsword, returned to his hometown. Zhang Fengming, a 75-year-old broadsword in the 20 years of the Republic of China (1930), passed away, his story has been passed down to this day.

Cheng Pu and the Three Dynasties of Eastern Wu

China's large-scale reference book "Cihai" has an entry: "Cheng Pu, a native of the Three Kingdoms Right North Pingtuyin. character seeks ." Tuyin in the Western and Eastern Han dynasties, namely Tuyin County, is today's Fengrun District of Tangshan City.

At the end of the Eastern Han Dynasty, the princes rose up, the heroes were in dispute, and each became king. In the end, Wei, Shu, and Wu separated the world, forming such a situation. There was a great general who played an important role in Wu, that is Cheng Pu. Why do you say that Cheng Pugong is indispensable? Because when Cheng Pu was a county official of state in his early years, he with Sun

Jian of Wu (155-191) to suppress the Yellow Turban Army uprising in the first year of Pingzhong (184) and crusade against Dong Zhuo together with Sun Jian.

In the 2 year of Chu Ping (AD 191), when Sun Jian led the army to attack Liu Biao, he was hit by Liu Biao's arrow and killed Huang Zu. After the death of Sun Jian, Cheng Pu Sun Jian's son, Sun Ce (word Bo Fu), as a general. He was named a commander of Wu County because of his repeated achievements in large and small battles. Later moved to Danyang Duwei. Cheng Pu was brave, good at fighting and courageous. Once, Sun Ce's army was besieged by the enemy and was in a very dangerous situation. Cheng Pu led the cavalry to guard the main, Gongsun Ce, and took the lead in the. He fought hard to break through the encirclement. Because Cheng Pu sacrificed his life to the Savior and was meritorious in this battle, he was worshipped as a general in charge of the bandits and led the of the Lingling chief. In the fourth year of Jian 'an (AD 199), Cheng Pu and his Sun Ce conquered Liu Bei and Lujiang County. In the 5 year of Jian'an (AD 200), Sun Ce was assassinated and Cheng Pu assisted Sun Ce's younger brother Sun Quan (word Zhong Mou) to proclaim himself emperor. During Sun Quan's reign, Cao Cao led a large army 200000 to attack Wu in the 13th year of Jian'an (AD 208), hoping to unify China. At this time, Liu Bei and Sun Quan, who occupied the middle and lower reaches of the Yangtze River respectively, joined forces with to reject Cao, and fought a decisive battle with Cao Cao in Chibi (now Lake the northwest of Jiazhuo County, the of North Province) with 50000 troops. Wu Jun's commander-in-chief Zhou Yu and Cheng Pu were the left and right governors of the allied forces. Cheng Pu cooperated with Zhou Yu and other soldiers to use fire attack tactics to break the army of Cao. This is the famous "Battle of Red Cliff" in Chinese history ". Thus, the situation of the three Kingdoms was established. As the founding father of Soochow, Cheng Pu, who was also one of the elders of the three dynasties, was a highly respected and important figure in both the military and political circles in the of Soochow. Therefore, Soochow people respected him as "Cheng Gong".

June 10, 2005

The Reverie under the Giant Buddha of Lusana

I have long wanted to see the world-famous Lusenna Buddha and 1 the eyes of the holy Buddha of the Tang Dynasty. Still in the days of spring breeze, the splendid culture of Longmen Grottoes led me to Longmen Grottoes in Luoyang, Henan Province, to see the face of the Buddha.

Under the clear sky, I stood under the Buddha and looked up at the high Lushena and looked at it carefully. Lushena Buddha sitting posture back to the mountains, facing the world, body, face full, ears and shoulders. The corners of the Buddha's mouth are slightly warped, his eyes are smiling, his head is slightly bent, and his hair is high and combed. The tall Lushuna Buddha has both a lifelike dynamic beauty, and interpretation to 1 a solemn, wise, mysterious, implicit. The Tang Dynasty was a dynasty that advocated light and was full of light. It did not take slenderness and beauty as beauty. The Tang Dynasty was a symbol of the prosperity of China. All these were reflected in Lu the great Buddha. Some people say that Lusana Buddha is Wu Zetian's "of the body image". From this, I think of Wu Zetian (AD 624-AD 705). Wu Zetian named "Zhao" since ". Last name, don't have to distinguish. Then: in the sea of, there is the meaning of is, that is, only, and, if, so, then; Tian: In the sea of words, there are meanings of, heavenly emperor, sky, dependence and spiritual origin. Qu, it goes without saying, light Gankun. And Lusana's translation happens to mean "the light shines all over the ".

When Wu Zetian was 14 years old (during the reign of Emperor Taizong Zhenguan, 638 AD), he was selected by Emperor Taizong (Li Shimin) as a talented person in the palace. Historical data show that Wu Zetian is not only naturally good-looking, but also proficient in literature and history. He also writes and beautiful Zhang Cao characters. In the prosperous Tang Dynasty, Wu Zetian's poems are also good. "All Tang Poems" and other records of Wu Zetian 58 poems. One of them, "Ruyi Niang", reads: "Look at Zhu Chengbi, who is haggard and strapped away to remember him for. If you don't believe it, you will cry often. You will get a pomegranate skirt out of the box." the death of Emperor Taizong (AD 649), Wu Zetian disappeared into the empty door and entered the Ganye Temple. After Tang Gaozong (Li Zhi) came to the throne, in the 5 year of Yonghui (654 AD), Wu Zetian was summoned back to the palace as Zhaoyi, which was in favor of Tang Gaozong. In the sixth year of Yonghui (655 A. D.), Wu Zetian, who was 31 years old at that time, had already been by two emperors, once for and twice for entering the palace. As Tang Gaozong had been ill since his accession to the throne, Wu Zetian participated in the handling and decision-making of the government after he was established as queen. At that time, people called Wu Zetian and Tang Gaozong "two saints". Therefore, Wu Zetian cannot say that he has contributed to the prosperity and development of Datang society.

The Lushena Giant Buddha was excavated in Zhenguan 23rd year (649 AD) in. It was the first year after Emperor Gaozong of Tang ascended the throne. Perhaps this was specially excavated by Tang Gaozong for offering gifts to Wu Zetian. At that time, Zhao Yi, 25-year-old Wu Zetian donated 20,000 to. It cannot be said that there was no 1 tacit understanding between Tang Gaozong and Wu Zetian. The Buddha statue 1 was cut and for 25 years, and it was not completed until the 2 year of Tang Gaozong's Shangyuan (AD 675). This tall Lushena Buddha is the image, appearance and posture of the queen of days. The head of the Buddha is the reproduction of Wu Zetian's appearance when she was 25 years old. At this time, the Queen of Zetian was already fifty years old. Today, it seems that the Lusana Buddha has the majesty and of the world. However, it was not nearly ten years (684 A. D.) after the of the statue of Lushena Giant Buddha, the queen of Zetian, was built that it was. During this period, in the first year of Hongdao (AD 684), Empress Zetian abolished Zhongzong (Li Xian) to set up Ruizong (Li Dan) and then abolished Ruizong to manage the government and change the Yuan Guangzhai. By 690 A. D., Empress Zetian directly called the Holy Emperor from, and the country's name was Zhou. Change yuan day grant. At this time, Wu Zetian had already experienced the 4 emperor of the Tang Dynasty except Tang Gaozu (Li Yuan). Since then, she has become the only female emperor in feudal society and Chinese history. Wu Zetian 1 the courage, wisdom, talent and perseverance of the female emperor of through the ages. With, Wu Zetian assisted Tang Gaozong, Zhongzong and Rui Zong, and personally governed the country for 50 years. It was Emperor Wuzhou who pioneered the palace examination and personally examined the tribute soldiers. It was Emperor Wuzhou who allowed the nine to petty officials and the common people to recommend them on their own. It was Emperor Wuzhou who changed the official system and stipulated that five officials could be promoted to. It was Emperor Wuzhou who reduced taxes and light corvee. It was Emperor Wuzhou who revised the "Surname record". These are the continuation and embodiment of the openness, openness, fairness, justice, social stability and prosperity of the Tang Dynasty. It was not until the late Tang Xuanzong (Li Longji), nearly 50 years after the death of Emperor Wuzhou, that there was an Anshi Rebellion, and the aura of the Tang Dynasty was slightly dimmed.

Everyone has aspirations, and it is even more justifiable to want to be emperor. Everyone wants to be a good emperor, but it is not easy to be an emperor, and it is not easy to be a female emperor. Everyone is enterprising, and no emperor wants to lose his country, rivers and mountains. Emperor

Wuzhou was still like this when he was nearly 80 years old, and maintained a unified, stable and prosperous situation.

Although the sun is red and, there are sunspots. The sun is shining, but there are still moss that cannot be shone. Although Wu Zetian, a generation of female emperors, has experienced many hardships, there are also some shortcomings in trying to run the country. This is exactly what every dynasty is inevitable, because everything is positive and negative coexistence, unity of opposites. The meaning of the word, the meaning of heaven, and the meaning of Lusana all have the meaning of shining light on the sky. This is exactly the original wish of Emperor Wu and the kings of all dynasties.

In Lushena Buddha's kind and amiable, abundant and gentle, beautiful and quiet eyes, there are many people, women, wives, mothers, tens of thousands of people bowing their heads, and the eternal 1 of women emperors, joys and sorrows, joys and sorrows, joys and sorrows, joys and sorrows, joys and sorrows, joys and sorrows, joys and sorrows, joys and sorrows, joys and sorrows, joys, joys, joys, joys, joys, joys, joys. In the sun, looking back at the Lusana Buddha again, I tasted a lot, a lot...

November 11, 2005

Ding Kai and Iron and Blood Meeting

Ding Kaizang, formerly known as Ding Zuo Lin, characters Xiaochuan, was from Zhili Province of the Qing Dynasty (now Village, Tuo, Nanqing, Fengrun District, Hebei Province). He was born in the 9th year of Tongzhi in Qing Dynasty (1870) and died in the 34th year of of the Republic of China (1945). At the age of 20, he was a scholar and later entered the first class of Jingshi University.

In the late Qing Dynasty, Ding Kaizhang was a famous figure in northern China, full of iron and blood feelings and national integrity.

In the 26th year of Guangxu's reign (1900), Tsarist Russia took the opportunity of the Eight-Allied Forces invading China to send troops to occupy the northeast of our country. After that, Japan and Russia went to war. In the second year of the outbreak of the war, Ding Kaizhang with Qin Zongzhou,

Ding and Guan, the leaders of the Iron Society in Zhangjiakou area to further expand the strength of the Iron Society. In 1907, Ding Kaizhang was in the three eastern provinces, Suiyuan, Rehe, Chahar, Inner Mongolia, outer Mongolia (China's historical territorial name, now Mongolia and Tangnuwu Lianghai), Hebei, Shanxi and other places, pendulum fasting sprinkle in the name of the development of iron and blood association organization, but also in the hometown at that time fengrun County nanqing tuo the village was created. North zhenwu Society. The Iron and Blood Association, which was originally designed to fight against Russia, was renamed the Beiyang Iron and Blood Association, with a pro-prime minister. It has four branches, namely Jingdong, Beijing North, Biewai and Kanto, and is divided into 28 leaders. In 1911, the army headquarters of the Iron and Blood Association was established in Xiaobai Building in the French Concession of Tianjin, and four armies with 95000 people were established.

On January 2, 1912, the Iron and Blood Association declared Luanzhou independent. Wang Huaiqing, the commander-in-chief of Qingtong Yongzhen, and Cao, the commander-in-chief of the third town, attacked Luanzhou on January 4. The generals Yue Zhaolin and Zhang Jian's power department defected. The enemy's iron and blood will make great sacrifices and finally fail. When Ding Kaizhang returned to Tianjin, he immediately gathered the generals of the four armies to and discuss the affairs. He decided that at midnight on the New Year's Eve of the New Year of Renzi, he would select the generals of each army to enter the capital, attack the Yamen of the Qing Dynasty respectively, and declare independence by the of the flag where the four armies. On February 3, 1912, Ding Kaizhang changed the military headquarters of the Iron Blood Association to the military government. The officers and soldiers of the Iron Blood Association unanimously elected Ding Kaizhang as the provisional marshal of the northern military government in the of the Republic of China. At that time, China had Sun Yat-sen in the south and Ding Xiaochuan in the north. Under the pressure of the revolutionary situation in the north and south of the country, the Emperor Xuantong of the Qing Dynasty was forced to announce his abdication. At this point, the iron and blood that vowed to be sworn with the Qing court was automatically dissolved in 1913.

24 March 2002

Queen poet Xiao Guanyin

Xiao Guanyin (1040–1075) is a female poet of Liao. In the 22nd year of Xingzong Chongxi (1053), she was the princess of King Yan Zhao (Yelu Hongji). In the first year of Qingning (1055), Yelu Hong Ji succeeded to the throne of Daozong and became queen. In November of the following year, she was named Queen Yide.

On May 5, the 9th year of Chongxi in Da Liao Dynasty (1040), in Youshi, a baby girl came to the world with a crisp cry in the 1 -style building of garden near the palace in Beijing (now Datong) in western Liaoning Province. This baby girl is the younger brother of Liao Xingzong (1032–1055) and Queen Qin Ai (Xiao Zhijin ?–1057); the daughter of uncle Xiao Hui (983–1056) and Xiao Guanyin, wife of Princess Qin—the eldest princess of the state of Jin.

In history, Xiao Guanyin can be regarded as a beautiful and talented woman with bright eyes and white teeth, beautiful and delicate, her eyebrows and are not drawn from black long, and her lips and are not drawn from. She is and, and she is good at piano, chess, calligraphy and painting, riding, archery and drawing a hard bow. Both the talent and appearance of the Central Plains women and the strength of the women in the North. In the history of the great Liao state, Xiao Guanyin was famous for his ability to poetry and martial arts. The poems that have been handed down to this day include "Fu Hulin Should System ", "Comrades Hua Yi and Should System ", " Tongxin Academy Ten ", "Juemong Ci" and so on.

, as Xiao Guanyin grew into a big girl day by day, her beauty and talent spread all over Xijing (now Datong), and the princes and aristocrats also came to ask for relatives. In order to find a suitable husband for her daughter, in the 22nd year of Xingzong Chongxi, when Xiao Guanyin was 14 years old (1053), Xiao Guanyin's parents came up with an idea and set up an examination question to the suitor who came to the door by Xiao Guanyin himself. Whoever the and daughter will be chosen. However, most of the Xijing teenagers were mediocre. After half a month passed, none of them passed. Xiao Guanyin was doubly disappointed and had no intention of taking the exam again. Suddenly one day, 1 people named Han and a dude named Xiao came. Xiao Guanyin looked at them 1. They were all extraordinary in appearance and handsome in spirit. They couldn't help but be overjoyed. So he said, "The little girl likes to recite poems since she was a child. I'll write a few words and ask the two childe to read a poem."

Xiao Guanyin's face was sarcastic, and he wrote with pride and joy: The color is blue and yellow, the is fragrant and, and the wind is for to the.

After Xiao Guanyin finished writing, he said, "this is a Tang poem. As long as the two childe can write this poem, the little girl thinks that the two childe are gifted scholars. But if you don't read Tang poetry well, I'm afraid you can't add to the whole poem."

Not expecting to, Han and Xiao, after taking it over and looking at it, wrote Tang poems quickly and coincidentally: "The grass is green, the is green, the willow is yellow, the peach blossom is messy, the is fragrant with the of Li. The east wind does not blow sorrow away, and the spring day is to resent it."

Xiao Guanyin passed the two examinations of playing the piano (zither) and riding and shooting and carving. Although Han and Xiao were neck and neck, they finally chose Xiao. However, it was unexpected that Xiao was the son of the emperor Liao Xingzong, Yelu Hong, the son of.

Yelu Hong Ji (Dao Zong) succeeded to the throne in the first year of Qingning. In the autumn of the 2 year of Qingning (1056), Dao Zong went to Montenegro with the queen (Xiao Guanyin). In this autumn hunt, Dao Zong 1 tigers and the queen hunted 1 black bears.

Dao Zong was glad to order a banquet. During the banquet, Dao Zong said to the ministers, "Love Qing, I killed the tiger forest today. There is wine and meat on the of the beautiful banquet. How can there be no songs, dances and poems make people of the Southern Dynasty laugh at me. There is no one in the Northern Dynasty?" Then he said to the empress, "Why don't Ai Qing recite a poem to cheer me."

After a little thought, the queen wrote with a brush: ", the mighty wind will shake the of Nanbang, and the yalu river can be to the east. The spirit monster Daqian is with gall, which is called the tiger not to surrender." This is the song that swallows mountains and rivers and looks down upon the world.

This year, Xiao Guanyin was 16 years old. Although she was a young woman, she had such courage and of courage. From the above poem, we fully feel the beauty of the poet's masculinity and courage. However, in Xiao Guanyin's poem "nostalgia", we can fully feel the feminine and soft side of the poetess: "Zhao's house is only counted in the palace, and the of the Han king is lost in the rain and the clouds are lost., only the knows a month, have seen birds enter Zhaoyang." After reading carefully chew taste, we will feel the beauty of a generation of masterpieces. There is also "Ten Poems of the Concentric Institute", which tells us that complaint is and true:

Sweep the deep courtyard, the is closed for a long time the gold to spread the dark. Dust from hairspring caught in the net is as a pile, and the moss is thick order surface at years old. sweep deep courtyard, to wait for your banquet.

Blowing elephant bed, borrow Gao Tang by dream. knock half know concubine lie, the right day out less glow. whisk like a bed, wait for king.

Change the incense pillow, half without brocade. In order to show more in autumn, there are more tears. change pillow, waiting for you to sleep.

Shop Cui is ashamed to kill mandarin ducks. still remember was called acacia, and now alone acacia sleep. Shop Cui, wait for you to sleep.

The gold hook did not dare to go on the embroidery account. solution but four corners luminous beads, do not teach to see sorrow appearance. Embroidered account, to be Jun,.

Brocade bacteria, heavy empty since old. I only wish to be a white jade body, and I don't want to Iraq as a thin lucky person. Broccoli, waiting for King's Landing.

Exhibition Yao seats, flowers smile three Han Bi. laugh concubine Xinpu jade 1 bed, never women Huan not the end of the. exhibition Yao seats, waiting for you to interest.

Tick silver lamp, notice as clear. It is the king who comes to give birth to the color halo and pretends to the green yingying to the concubine. Tick silver lamp, wait for your line.

The hot fumigation stove can the lonely stuffy Su. If Tao concubine's body is filthy and cheap, self-gluing royal fragrance skin. Hot smoker, for your entertainment.

Zhang Ming Zheng, cha cha cha jiao ying. One from playing in the room, often and the wind and rain in front of the window. Zhang Ming Zheng, wait for you to listen.

It is such a graceful and heart-warming beautiful words, unexpectedly to the body. It turns out that only the palace actors (old refers to people who take opera singing as their profession) Zhao, the only one who can play with the palace girl named Shan in the music score of "Tongxin House. On the other hand, Shan's brother Shan Deng was demoted to slave by the family members of Liao traitor with a heavy weight of yuan. The queen thought that she could not be close to royal. Shan Deng held a grudge in his heart, so he took advantage of his sister's adultery relationship with treacherous official Yelu Yixin to falsely claim to her sister that the queen had only fornication with Zhao. The evidence is "Zhao", "Wei" and "1" in the poem "Nostalgia". But the crafty Yeru Yisin believes that this alone cannot cure the queen to death. So he ordered people to fake the "Ten Fragrance Song", which was falsely claimed to be the work of a empress in the of the Song Dynasty. If the empress wrote the imperial book, it would be a double-survival. The kind-hearted and straightforward queen copied "Ten Fragrance Song" and "Nostalgia" together without thinking. As everyone knows, the treacherous official Yelu Yixin was like a treasure, and quickly submitted the empress's handwriting to the Emperor Daozong and slander. All of a sudden, 1 jealousy prompted the angry Taoist clan not to ask questions, not to make calm analysis, to listen to slanderous words, and to believe that the only of the Queen and Zhao had misbehaved. In his great anger, he his imperial power and hanged himself from the queen he once loved deeply. There is no alternative, the beautiful, kind, strong and versatile Empress Xiao, resentful of treacherous court officials, villain side with you, resentful of her husband who did not know good or evil, finished in one go, and resolutely hanged herself after writing "desperate words. Tian Zuo Gan Tongyuan (1101) Zhaoxue in June, and the posthumous "Emperor Xuan Yi" was buried in the of Yongfu Mausoleum. Now Baita Zi North, Balin Right Banner, Inner Mongolia.

The word said: "boyou Xi many lucky, Qiang as a wife Xi the royal family. Chenghao Qiongxi, and recently the moon Xi split the. After the, the are all and, while the is suddenly. Although quarreled tired Xi yellow bed, ordinary innocent Xi ancestral temple. want to cross the fish xi progress, take the yang de xi flying. is no harm to, and no I, obscenity evil Xi the palace. Throw the the heart, from Chen, hope back to shine, the day. Ning Shu female Xi mourn, to the left and right Xi destruction injury. , Xixiao Xi dropped the, suddenly I to Xi Jiao room. call heaven and earth, misery, and, hate ancient and modern, Xi An extremely. Knowing that my is, I will confuse, and I will forever." A good song to tell the clear difference between heaven and earth, but also innocent in the world "the words of the of life" ah, magnanimous lyric, understand to tell God, desolate don't heaven and earth, so that people today read still hate Taoist emperor. Although it is "Breaking Word", it is permeated with evil like hatred, integrity, and the spirit of a female husband; it will never lose atmosphere, pride, and poignant beauty. After reading the volume, I deeply sighed that I did not see the ancients before and those who came after. Reading poetry and talking to the ancients, let a person feel: Xiao Guanyin, beautiful, poetry-more beautiful!

6 April 2007

Lao Li, Yingming Yongzhi

He is Lao Li in "Lao Li and Lao Zhao" sung by Wang Fang in the movie "Heroes and Children. This is what the author heard from the people on the streets of Fengrun Xinjuntun Town in six years ago. So I went to the Glory House of Xinjuntun to interview Lao Li.

Chairman Mao said, "You have done so beautifully"

On December 5, 1948, Chairman Mao of the CPC Central Committee commanded two corps of our army and 1 million local troops to launch the Pingjin campaign. The first battle was the new security battle. At that time, Li (, Lao Li) served as the blasting team leader in, 2nd platoon, 8th company, 59th regiment, 195th division, north China field army. Before the battle, the division chief found Li and said: "Your task is to blow up all the enemy's fortresses and clear the obstacles on the way forward for the general offensive of the large army. The task is very difficult." Li Kezeng immediately replied: "To destroy the enemy and win the battle, you are willing to die!" The chief said happily: "good! Our army needs soldiers like you ."

On December 22, the battle began. Li led the two soldiers to carry four explosive bags and a large iron tongs for pinching barbed wire. They touched the Kuomintang fortress. Our army's machine guns fired fiercely at the enemy to cover their with. them advance. The machine guns in the Kuomintang fortress were shooting frantically. In the rain, Li and his comrades crossed the ditch and crossed the river. They quickly and wittily approached the enemy fortress. Under the roaring machine gun fire of the enemy, the fuse of the explosive package was ignited. With the loud noise of the 1, the of a 3 enemy fort exploded in the darkness of night. Li Ke shook off the stone soil to call his comrades, but there was no echo. Two comrades have died. At this time, there was a enemy fort still firing arrogantly outward to stop our army from advancing. Li kezeng angrily crawled to the enemy's last fort base, put the explosive pack, lit the fuse, and then quickly withdrew. With another loud 1, the last 1 nail in our army's path was pulled out. At this time, it was the time for the general offensive of the large forces. Our army immediately pressed the enemy's position with an overwhelming force, encircling and annihilating the 35th Army headquarters and two divisions of the New Security Kuomintang Army.

The first battle of the Pingjin campaign was won. Chairman Mao of the CPC Central Committee sent a congratulatory message from Xibaipo and specially received members of the combat hero reporting regiment. Chairman Mao held Li Kezeng's hand and said happily, "You did a beautiful job." Li Kezeng replied with spirit: "Chairman, I will definitely finish the task better next time." Chairman Mao kindly patted Li Kezeng on the shoulder and said, "Good!" In recognition of his military exploits, the Military Commission gave Li Ke a great contribution to his. Chairman Mao also personally gave a steel pen and a notebook to Li Ke.

Capture 5 Yankees alive with a pole and a spoon

The author admires this old hero who was in his seventies, and asked him to tell us about his heroic deeds on the battlefield to resist US aggression and aid Korea. When Lao Li talked about the story of Wang Fang singing in the movie "Heroes and Children", he said that he was the cooking squad leader at that time. One day Lao Li and two comrades surnamed Zhao went to deliver food to the soldiers on the position. On the way, they suddenly found that there were 5 American soldiers in front of them. They immediately gently put down the food to observe. From the appearance dynamics, they concluded that these American soldiers with guns on their backs were defeated stragglers, and they could be captured as long as they were outsmart. So, Lao Li took the pole, and the other two soldiers took the spoon and touched it quietly. They were very close, but the enemy did not find them. The three exchanged glances and rushed up to 1 shouting, "Don't kill!" This sudden cry scared the enemy's courage, and the American soldiers obediently put down their guns, raised their hands and became prisoners without daring to return.

The author asked the old hero if anyone had interviewed this story. Li said that when he was in the army, the head of the regiment once interviewed him with a writer.

In 1955, the state arranged a job for Lao Li, but Lao Li insisted on returning to his hometown to participate in the construction of a new socialist rural village. When he got home, he became the production team leader. After the 1976 earthquake, the government took Lao Li, his, to the county and city-level glorious homes to spend his old age in accordance with relevant national regulations, but Lao Li was reluctant to give up the place where he grew up and participated in the revolution, so he lived in the Xinjuntun Glory Home. Here he also took the initiative to plant 3 mu of vegetable garden to ensure the living vegetables of the Glory House.

In order to fully understand Lao Li's glorious past, I recently went to Xinjuntun Glory Institute in Fengrun County to visit him. Regrettably, Lao Li died of illness on December 30, 1997.

Lao Li had nothing else to stay in the world. The author only copied his resume: he was born on the first day of the first lunar month in 1926; joined the Chinese People's Liberation Army in 1947; joined the Communist Party of China in 1948 and served as the blasting team leader; participated in the War to Resist US Aggression and Aid Korea in 1950, Served as a cooking monitor; demobilized and returned to his hometown on January 25, 1955; 48 years of party.

5 November 2000

Hero fearless to eliminate bombs

65 years ago, volunteer Wang Gui successfully defused the bomb. Wang Gui, born in 1929, joined the army in 1948 and became an old soldier of the Chinese people's Liberation Army. He participated in the Chinese people's War of Liberation and the war to resist US aggression and aid Korea to defend his country. He has experienced countless battles, large and small, and there are endless fighting stories.

At 8 o'clock in the morning on June 2, 2017, I once again came to the Glory House of Guoyuan Township to visit the old man Wang Gui and listen to him tell the past battle stories and touching deeds.

When the 89-year-old Wang Gui talked about the fighting years, he was full of energy, very talkative, and told it enthusiastically. It made me feel that a story that was thrilling and dangerous happened during the Korean War. The old man said: "It was one day in September 1952, and what was going on was the battle of the Black Bridge of the Korean ." At that time, Wang Gui was at the headquarters of the 42nd Independent Battalion of the Chinese People's Volunteer Air Force. At about 9 a.m. that day, more than 60 enemy planes flew from the southeast of the battalion. After circling around the battalion for three times, they swooped down and strafed in batches, then climbed back and dropped bombs. Several rounds of dives, strafing, bombs and explosions destroyed the battalion headquarters. After the enemy plane flew away, Wang Gui, who was lying on the ground, stood up and shook off the soil all over his body. He calmed down. Seeing 1 hands exposed in the soil in front of him, he immediately went to to pick up the. It turned out that the operator of the battalion headquarters was buried under the soil lifted by the bomb. Fortunately, the operator did not suffocate. Fortunately, the military vehicles near the battalion headquarters were not blown up. After the battalion count calmed down, everyone found the 1 time bomb poked in the soil not far from everyone. This is an obvious and major hidden danger. If it is not ruled out, it will threaten the lives of all volunteer soldiers. During the war, North Korea had a professional "North Korean people's bomb group ", which was 1 by three people and was responsible for field bomb disposal. But the troops have to contact them and it will be some time before they arrive. At this time, Wang Gui was thinking about the life guarantee of the soldiers of the all-British Volunteer Army. He looked at the time bomb in front of him, and the time passed slowly one by one. He was eager. So he took the initiative to request the battalion commander to personally remove the time bomb. At this moment, the battalion commander looked at Wang Gui, the deputy staff officer of the investigation, and did not agree to his request. However, for the safety of all the volunteer officers and men in the battalion, Wang Gui insisted on repeatedly asking the battalion commander to approve him to remove the time bomb. There was no way, the battalion commander finally asked him, "Are you sure?" Wang Gui said that he had carefully observed the process of the bomb-taking group of the Korean People's Army and kept their methods and steps in mind. "Take care," the battalion commander told him."

Wang Gui paid a standard military salute to the battalion commander. He took the pliers, wrench and hammer needed to disassemble the time bomb and quietly approached the time bomb dropped by the US army. He first picked up the hammer to imitate the movements of the personnel of the bomb-taking group of the Korean People's Army and used the hammer to knock the surface of the bomb under the 3. Then he put his ear close to the bomb and listened to the inside the bomb, after listening for more than a minute, there was no movement inside the bomb. In order to the convenience of the bomb disposal and the safety of everyone's life, in case of accident, he can lie on the time bomb and protect everyone's life with his own life. He puts the time bomb on the ground, then picks up the board and loosens the screw...

Wang Gui carried out the bomb disposal work carefully, and the volunteer officers and men hidden in the distance were sweating for Wang Gui in their palms, because everyone knew that this was 1 a very dangerous thing. Wang Gui, who had never been in contact with the bomb dismantling during the, had sweat on his forehead. Wang Gui knew that the heavy responsibility was on his shoulders and the responsibility was extraordinary. He had only one thought in his heart, that is, to use my own sacrifice in exchange for the safety of all the officers and men in the battalion. Therefore, careful, careful, careful and meticulous safety operation. Slowly and, and slowly, he finally safely removed the detonating rods the time bomb from the body of the time bomb. Until then, Wang Gui wiped the sweat from his face, and then got up. When he stood up and raised the ignition stick of the time bomb, all the warring members of the battalion cheered and ran to hug Wang Gui... The battalion commander also held his hand tightly and said, "You are the most lovely person." After that, the battalion commander stood on the high ground and said loudly to everyone: "We must learn from Wang Gui's spirit of not being afraid of death, for the safety of the big guy's life, and not afraid of sacrificing our fearless spirit!"

Although 65 years have passed since the experience of life and death, the old man Wang Gui still has a happy and happy smile from Hao. Because, in that special era, special environment, and special battle, he really wanted to use his own sacrifice in exchange for the safety of all the commanders and fighters in the battalion. The events in this actual combat story permeate the spirit and essence of a Chinese revolutionary soldier, and I am deeply moved by it.

When the old hero sent me to the five-star red flag in the Glory Courtyard, he told me: "I bought this national flag and flagpole with money. We can't live without a country. The national flag is the symbol of the country. We look at the national flag. I step on it..."

I looked up at the flying national flag and thought to myself that this red flag was soaked in the patriotic mood of the old hero, and even more, it full of the feelings of a Chinese revolutionary soldier who knew the hard-won feelings of the Republic. I look at the old hero, once again deeply moved by it.

June 6, 2017

Li Qingzhao and "Flowers" and "Wine"

Li Qingzhao, a poet of a generation, was once revered as the flower god of lotus root and enshrined in the lotus root shrine on the shore of Daming Lake in Jinan. She once wrote "Like a Dream Order" to describe her happy life in Jinan as a young girl: "I often remember the sunset of Xiting, and I am intoxicated and do not know the way back. Xing back to the boat late and strayed into the depths of lotus flowers. fight to cross the, fight to cross the, startling gulls and herons on 1 Beach." In the Song Dynasty, there was indeed a "Xiting" in the west of Jinan ". Straight down from Tangshan to Jinan to experience Li Qingzhao's flowers and wine.

In Li Qingzhao's works also left us a sweet story of love. This love story, embellished by Li Qingzhao's wonderful pen, has become the spiritual enjoyment of the Chinese people for more than a thousand years. Please look at this song "Magnolia with Decreased Characters": "Sell flowers on the, and buy a spring to release. Tears dye light evenly, still with Tong Xia Xiao dew mark. Afraid lang guessed, slave noodles not as good as flower noodles. Cloud temples oblique hairpin, disciple teach lang compare to see." This is the sweetness of Li Qingzhao's marriage, the coquetry to her husband, and Li Qingzhao's confidence in his beauty.

People can not be without love, flower woman can not be without love, emotional talent can not be without love. Just as her tree of art was thriving under the sap of love, her husband went to the field to become an official. The reunion of husband and wife is inseparable. They do not wait for today's to go and hope that spring will come and return to. Look at this farewell work, "A Cut of Plum": "Red lotus root, fragrant and remnant jade are in autumn, lightly untie their petticoats, and go alone in a blue boat. Who sends the brocade book in the cloud, when the wild goose returns, the moon is full of the west floor. The flowers fall and the water flows, 1 is a kind of acacia, and two are idle and sad. There is no way to eliminate this feeling, so I only brow, but heart."

Don't leave sorrow, love ponder cut, the other 1 a kind of sweet secretly chew. However, Li Qingzhao is by no means an ordinary little woman who only sighs a few words of "cheap concubines guarding the empty room". She is practicing literature in the empty room and has been practicing this art to perfection. Therefore, this most common expression of love has become a proposition creation competition between husband and wife and a record for them to climb to the peak of art. Therefore, she wrote "Drunk Flower Yin-Chongyang": "The mist and thick clouds sorrow will never the day, and the brain will sell gold beasts. The festival is Chongyang again, and the jade pillow gauze kitchen is cool in the middle of the night. Dongli put the wine after dusk, there is a dim fragrance the sleeve. Mo Dao does not enchant, the curtain rolls the west wind, and people are thinner than yellow flowers." This is the 1 Prime Minister's poem sent by Li Qingzhao to Zhao Mingcheng when he was an official in other places. Thoracic love, thoughts of infatuation, through the autumn wind yellow flowers show incisively and vividly. Shi said on the that Zhao Mingcheng, after receiving the word Li Qingzhao, felt it first, and then was excited by the artistic power of the word. He vowed to write a word that surpassed his wife. So on the 3rd, he closed his door and thanked the guest. He got 50 words and mixed Li Qingzhao's words in it. He asked his friend Lu Defu to comment on it. He didn't want Lu Defu to say that there was only 3 excellent sentence: "the is not consumed by Mo Dao, the curtain rolls the west wind, and people are thinner than the Huang flower ." Zhao sighed. This story is very popular, but I want to how Zhao Li husband and wife enjoy the sweetness of Qin Se Xiang in mutual admiration. This also makes all the men and women who have talent and appearance, but can not get the corresponding quality of love feel a little sad.

Li Qingzhao himself recalled that period of life in "The Preface of Jin Shi Lu" and said: "Yu's sexual occasionally memorize. After every meal, he sits back to the hall, referring to the accumulation of books and history, and to say something is in which page and line of a certain volume, and whether wins or fails in the is the order of drinking tea. He raised his glass and laughed, until the tea overturned in his arms, but he could not drink it." This is how happiness, how joy, how a "sweet" word. The honey-like life nourishes her graceful demeanor and exuberant artistic creation.

Li Qingzhao, a lyricist, uses wine to express her feelings, which is her meaningful and beautiful style of lyrics. "Last night, the wind and rain, sleep not residual wine. Ask the roller shutter people, but the Begonia is still the same. Do you know, do you know? Should be green fat red thin!" A good "like a dream" concisely and clearly describes the poet's drunkenness "sleep without residual wine" and his feelings of "should be green, fat, red and thin.

From the passion of writing to the true feelings of drunkenness is a catharsis without affectation. "Where is the hometown, forget unless drunk. Burn when lying in the water, but the incense and wine will not disappear." This song "Bodhisattva Barbarian" is a narration the author has tasted the suffering of war and wandering. The first half of the festival is from winter to spring. Although the sunshine is slightly, the wind is soft. I changed into a clip shirt, there is still a trace of unfinished chill. The plum has withered and my heart is broken. In order to avoid homesickness, I have only drunk. The fire on the has burned out before going to bed, but my wine has not receded. As the poetess, who is known as an amazing last sentence, said, "learning poetry is amazing sentence", she said that a weak woman can only talk on paper and have talent. But now we have to go with the ups and downs of the world!

Speaking of Li Qingzhao's fate in wine, it is also just like the connection between the poet and the ci. This was originally the relationship between the sea of heart and emotion, the integration, and the joyous songs of life and life, which further sublimated Li Qingzhao's character. Although he experienced 1 disasters of remarrying bandits and divorce, Li Qingzhao's will to live was not depressed, and his enthusiasm for poetry creation was even higher. Freed from the pain of a man, she turned her eyes to national affairs. In May of the 3 year of Shaoxing (1133), the court sent Han Xiaozhou, a member of the Privy Council, and Hu Songnian, minister of the Ministry of Industry, to the Jin Dynasty. Li Qingzhao with passion to write an ancient poem and a law poem to see 2 off. In the poem, there is a sentence "I want to send blood and tears to the mountains and rivers, to sprinkle Dongshan 1 soil", which expresses the strong desire to fight back against aggression and recover lost land, and is full of nostalgia for the motherland. 1 a glass of thin wine on short and long, infinite deep feeling to send homesickness. How can these people, who are full of sadness and want to speak a language, the true portrayal of their hometown when they are so that they can do their best to the country and the people in peace! In fact, the graceful lyricist has a bold and unrestrained nature that is not expected by all. "I still think of Xiang Yu and refuse to go to Jiangdong" is her elegant demeanour.

Leave it as a beautiful picture for future generations.

On the northeast side of Baotu Spring Park in Jinan, there is Shuyu Spring, which is one of the 72 famous springs in Jinan. The spring water is crystal clear, and the spring water at the bottom of the pool gushes out continuously. It gently overflows the pool and falls on the stone. The water and stone are excited and gurgling, just like Shuyu. Legend has it that Li Qingzhao used to wash by the spring in his early years, hence the name Shuyu Spring. At the back of Shuyuquan is the memorial hall of Li Qingzhao, a talented woman.

In May 2007, when Sophora japonica was fragrant, I walked into this hall dedicated to a generation of great of Ci with admiration and admiration to see the charm of Ci Poets. In the words left by Ci Poets, I looked for the fragrance of Ci Poets the soul.

The 1 couplet in front of the memorial hall wrote like this: "Daming Lake, Baotu Spring, the former residence is deep in weeping willows; in Jinshilu, the jade is concentrated, and the literary grace has the legacy of the post-master", written by the late old man Guo Moruo. The upper couplet refers to the location of Li's former residence of Qingzhao; the lower couplet is a tribute to his achievements.

According to historical materials, Li Qingzhao was born in an upper family of a scholar and a doctor in the seventh year of Yuanfeng in the Northern Song Dynasty (1084 AD). Li Qingzhao "has a name for poetry since he was a teenager, and his talent is brilliant and close to his predecessors", a famous literary scholar in the Northern Song Dynasty, Chao, praised the of. Around the 3 year of Yuanfu (1100), Li Qingzhao wrote the long poem "Song Poem of Wuxi Zhongxing and Zhang Wenqian", which was well received by people at that time. The sensational Jingshi's "Rumengling" (a note of the sunset of Xiting) was a work of Li Qingzhao when he was more than ten years old. "At that time, the scribes did not hit the festival".

What is called "Yi An Ti" by the world refers to Li Qingzhao's words. When I read them today, I feel a unique and graceful style. The characteristics of creation changed because of the changes of Li Qingzhao's life in the Northern Song Dynasty and the Southern Song Dynasty. Today, we can still clearly see that there are many leisurely lives written in the early stage, and the later works have their own ways, using the form of line drawing to lament their life experience. Although the emotional appeal is sentimental, it also reveals the nostalgia for the Central Plains, but the language is as sonorous and clear as her personality.

In the first year of the founding of Jingguo in the Northern Song Dynasty (1101),18-year-old Li Qingzhao married 21-year-old Zhao Mingcheng, who was a student in Taixue at that time.

In the history of the Song Dynasty, after 167 years of peace and prosperity in the style of "along the River during the Qingming Festival", the Jin Dynasty smashed the Yuyuan on the floor of Qiong in Bianjing (Kaifeng), the capital of, and also looted the Emperors and Qin 2. The Zhao and Song dynasties rushed to and fled south in 1127 AD. Li Qingzhao's love nest in Qingzhou, Shandong Province also scattered, and the family began to live a wandering life. In the second year of Nandu, Zhao Mingcheng was appointed as the magistrate of Jiankang in the capital. He didn't think that 1 national humiliation and family humiliation happened at this time. Late one night, a rebellion broke out in the city. Zhao Mingcheng, as the local governor, did not take the lead in commanding the rebellion, but secretly let the city with a rope and escaped. Therefore, he was removed from office by the imperial court. Li Qingzhao showed great righteousness in this matter, and was very ashamed of her husband's flight. After Zhao was removed from office in, the couple continued to go into exile along the Yangtze River and up to Jiangxi. When he arrived at Wujiang Town, Li Qingzhao, who was of true temperament, learned that this was the place where Xiang Yu was defeated and committed his own suicide. He did not feel the ups and downs of his heart. Facing the vast river, he sang the powerful and unrestrained masterpiece "Summer Judgments": "Life is the to be the hero and, and death is also the ghost hero. Up to now, I think about Xiang Yu and refuse to cross Jiangdong ". The husband listened to the sound of this word and stone behind him, with shame on his face and deep remorse in his heart.

In 1129 AD, what saddened Li Qingzhao most was the death of 49-year-old Zhao Mingcheng on the way to exile. Li Qingzhao, a 46-year-old 1 -generation talented woman, felt lonely and helpless and fell into a painful predicament. Looking back on the past, what she regrets all her life is the memory of spending 29 years with Zhao Mingcheng and the past of mourning.

When Li Qingzhao was lonely, frightened, painful and confused, Zhang Ruzhou, who was to serve Lang at that time, appeared. Li Qingzhao was not better than Zhang Ruzhou's sweet-talking offensive, and he was indeed captured by Zhang Ruzhou. Li Qingzhao experienced a romantic love life like an immortal partner with Zhao Mingcheng, and suffered from the destruction of the country and the family. The huge and difference of fate made her desperately yearn for a sweet and warm family life. In the summer of Shaoxing 2 (1132), Li Qingzhao married Zhang Ruzhou. However, Zhang Ruzhou's pursuit and marriage to the 1 46-year-old Li Qingzhao was definitely not for Li Qingzhao's appearance, nor was it because Li Qingzhao thought that Zhang Ruzhou took a fancy to her incomparable talent, but wanted to get Li Qingzhao's gold and stone collection. Zhang Ruzhou, who was shallow, tyrannical and vulgar in nature, was exposed after marriage, making Li Qingzhao want to cry without tears. Zhang Ruzhou was greatly disappointed when he saw that Li Qingzhao's antique calligraphy and painting were not as rich as he imagined, and Li Qingzhao was still unwilling to give in. Finally, Zhang Ruzhou became angry from embarrassment and began to fight Li Qingzhao. He even wanted to kill her to get rid of the burden of old age and faded and get her property.

In front of the Chinese's account, under the red candle, Li Qingzhao, who has a tenacious, independent, intelligent and resolute character, looked at this cheeky, shameless and little white face, disillusioned and burning with anger. At this time, Li Qingzhao was full of sorrow and hatred, and he thought of Zhang Ruzhou's despicable face when he married Li Qingzhao and was proud of his cheating in the imperial examination. Li Qingzhao was determined to immediately report and accuse Zhang Ruzhou of the crime of using deception to obtain official positions, and to report the scumbag. However, according to the feudal law of the Song Dynasty at that time, a woman who sued her husband, right or wrong, won or lost, would have to go to jail for two years. At this time, Li Qingzhao had no illusions about feelings, and felt that she would never make do in her emotional life. She would rather suffer from flesh and blood than be enslaved by spirit. Once she sees through the other's soul, she shows a relentless of contempt deep remorse. Once the sea was difficult for water, the heart was noble and clean and did not bow. Li Qingzhao regards personality as more precious than life. Where he can suffer from this kind of cowardly spirit, he decided to break up with him. She once wrote in a letter to a friend: "to the evening scene of the mulberry elm, it is to match the material under the driving philistine." She is such a strong-witting person that she would rather go to jail than live in disgrace. She insists on independent personality and high-quality love. At that time, there were still many officials in the Li family and the Zhao family. With their help, Li Qingzhao walked out of the prison after only nine days in prison.

In the autumn of Shaoxing 2 (1132), Li Qingzhao finally achieved his goal and divorced successfully. Li Qingzhao quickly cut the knot and the nightmare marriage of the in the past two months, and devoted himself to the compilation of first husband Zhao Mingcheng's "Jin Shi Lu.

After reading this historical data, I saw a new woman who was anti-feudal in the Song Dynasty a thousand years ago. During the Southern Song Dynasty, Li Qingzhao's works showed a high degree of patriotism. Li Qingzhao pursues national integrity and political firmness from her bones, and pursues a super vulgar personality. She always soberly holds a 1 standard of life and tenaciously keeps her own moral integrity. When she was not in great trouble and her life was relatively stable, she had seen her high standard of personality pursuit. As "life is a hero, death is also a ghost" said. There is also the of the sentence "I want to send blood and tears to the mountains and rivers, and to sprinkle a handful of soil 1 the Dongshan", which expresses her strong desire to fight back against aggression and recover lost land, and is full of nostalgia for the motherland. After that, Li Qingzhao became even more superior to the common people, and he was not stained with the mud in the turmoil of the world. She is standing on the high pavilion, traveling through time and space, looking down on all living beings, so there is a special loneliness that clearly in "Recalling Qin E": "Lingao Pavilion, chaotic mountains, flat wild smoke and thin light. Smoke light thin, roost crow return, twilight day smell horn. broken incense residue wine clear with evil, westerly lining sycamore fall. The phoenix tree falls, it is still autumn, and it is still lonely."

Around the 13th year of Shaoxing (1143), Li Qingzhao, who was about 60 years old, collated and sorted out Zhao Mingcheng's posthumous work "Jin Shi Lu" and showed it into the dynasty. Engraved books in the first year of the jubilee (1205). After more than ten years, about the 26th year of Shaoxing (1156) or later, Li Qingzhao, who had no children and no children, died quietly in extreme loneliness and desolation at the age of at least 73, with the continuous yearning for the dead relatives and the boundless disappointment at the difficult return of his native land.

"Li San thin"

When I arrived in Jinan, I came to visit Li Qingzhao at the Shuyuquan Li Qingzhao Memorial Hall in the north of Baotu Spring. However, it turns out that only Li the "3 thin " in Qingzhao's words, but he did not know that the white marble statue of a generation of lyricist can also be called "3 thin ". neck thin, waist thin, thin body, the nickname "Li San thin". This nickname is rather peculiar and difficult to understand.

Why do people give Li Qingzhao the nickname "Li San and thin? To say "3 thin " must start with Li Qingzhao's words. The reason why "3 thin " is that in Li Qingzhao's words, the word "thin" is into the word to describe the appearance of Hua Rong people, and 3 a moving phrase that has been famous for "thin" has been created through the ages.

Read "Remembering Blowjob on Phoenix":

The incense is cold and golden. After being turned over by the red waves, he gets up and combs his hair. Ren Bao's casket is full of dust, and the curtain hooks on the sun.

Afraid of leaving the bosom don't bitter, how many things, want to say still rest. The new lean, non-dry sick wine, not sad autumn. Hugh!

This back also, thousands of times Yangguan, also difficult to stay. Read Wuling people far away, smoke lock Qin Lou. there is only running water in front of the building, and you should read me and gaze all day long.

Gazing at the place, from now on, a new sorrow.

The of the sentence "new thin, not dry sick wine, not sad autumn" in it made the Qing literati Chen tingzhuo infatuated with, sighed that it was wonderful, and evaluated it as "tactful and tortuous, really wonderful and unique"; Tang guizhang, a contemporary lyricist, also said with and: "the 3 sentence of' new thin', saying don't be bitter and. is more sick wine sad autumn for especially bitter ."

The words mainly describe the themes of spring grievances and boudoir life, especially the sentimental personality of Li Qingzhao, a lyricist. For example, "Dream Order" describes the feelings of cherishing spring and loving flowers:

Last night, the rain was light and the wind was strong, so heavy sleep did not need any wine.

Ask the roller shutter people, but the Begonia is still the same. Know no, know no, should be green fat red thin.

It is this sentence "know or not, know or not, it should be green, fat, red and thin", which makes Huang Liaoyuan say in his "selection of words in Liaoyuan": "green, fat, red and thin" is infinitely sad and melancholy, but it is also subtle, there are countless twists and turns in the short, which is the of words."

When Li Qingzhao's husband Zhao Mingcheng went out for lovesickness, he "Drunken Flower Yin" in words, which is and more sincere and unique. "Drunk Flower Yin" with novel ideas, elegant interest, describes Li Qingzhao in the "festival and double Ninth", feel lonely inner feelings, so self-metaphor Huang Hua said:

The mist is thick and the cloud is sad for the day, and the brain sells gold beasts. The festival is Chongyang again, and the jade pillow gauze kitchen is cool in the middle of the night.

Dongli put the wine after dusk, there is a dark fragrance full sleeve. Mo Dao is not enchanted, the curtain rolls the west wind, and people are thinner than yellow flowers.

This is not the speech body of the average male and female lyricist can be compared with the of complaining words. Legend has it that after Li Qingzhao wrote the 1 words of "Drunk Flower Yin", he sent it to Zhao Mingcheng, husband who lived in two places, "Mingcheng is ashamed of himself and wants to win", so he wrote painstakingly behind closed doors for 3 days and nights, getting 15 words, and mixed with Li Qingzhao's words to invite his friend Lu Defu to appreciate it. After reading and the 3, dev said: "only the sentence" mo dao is not ecstatic, the curtain rolls the west wind, and people are thinner than yellow flowers "3 excellent."

Looking at Li Qingzhao's white marble statue, recalling Li Qingzhao's words "3 thin ", "remembering blowjob on the phoenix stage", "like a dream makes" and "drunk flower yin", every word and sentence, the feeling is cut down to meaning long, how is a "thin" word, it can really be said that people "thin" word "thin" feeling not "thin".

"Li San thin" you let me see your feeling is not "thin".

1 Beach Gull Heron

Li Qingzhao used wine to express his feelings, highlighting his timeless and beautiful style of words. "Ask the roller shutter, but the Begonia is still the same. Do you know, do you know? It should be green, fat, red and thin." This song "like a dream" is concise and vivid, describing the poet's drunkenness of "sleeping without wine". Every sentence is subtle and meticulous, reaching the hearts of the people. "Where is the hometown, forget unless drunk. Burn when lying in the water, but the incense and wine will not disappear." This song "Bodhisattva Man · The wind is soft and the spring is still early" is her confession of suffering from the war. The meaning of the words is implicit and meaningful, showing the grief, anxiety and strong homesickness in the soul of the female lyricist.

The association between Li Qingzhao and poetry originally embodies the blending of life and emotion. Despite the hardships, her will was not depressed. She jumped out of her personal pain and cast her eyes on the affairs of state.

In the spring of 1133, Song Gaozong sent a mission to Jin, and Li Qingzhao wrote a poem to see him off: "I want to send blood and tears to the mountains and rivers to sprinkle a handful of 1 soil on the eastern mountain." With tragic and heroic verses, the author expresses his strong desire to fight back against the enemy and recover lost territory, full of patriotic passion.

Behind Li Qingzhao, a graceful lyricist, there is always an unknown boldness. She wrote "I still think of Xiang Yu and refuse to go to Jiangdong", which once again embodies the heroic spirit of a tender woman.

Screen Uncle Dong Hao

When people in Tangshan talk about Dong Hao, the famous host of CCTV children's programs, everyone can't help but be proud because he is from his hometown. Although Dong Hao was born in Haidian District of Beijing in 1956, his ancestral home is in Fengrun District of Tangshan City. Dong Hao, with the blood of Fengrun, a rich and beautiful land, was born, grew up, went to school, worked and retired in Beijing.

As the host of CCTV children's program, Dong Hao's voice was familiar to children all over the country with Disney's Mickey Mouse and Donald Duck on Chinese TV screens a few years ago. The lovely Mickey Mouse image also left a deep impression on Dong Hao in the minds of children. In the following years, he has been active in children's programs, not only for the national attention, but also by foreign attention. An important factor is that as a male host, he has injected a 1 healthy and open-minded atmosphere into the warm children's world. Dong Hao once said: No matter at home or abroad, most of the people engaged in children's education are women, and their delicacy and kindness have left warm memories for the children. However, society can be maintained not only by warmth, especially in China, the current situation of one-child families 1 more rigid education and influence, and the cultivation of 1 creativity. Otherwise, in the face of a rapidly developing world and increasingly fierce competition, these masters of the 21st century will not be able to shoulder China's future destiny, and society will also be limited by the weakness of the crowd's character. Some foreign media and institutions have also shown great interest and concern. In China, Dong Hao is the second influential male public figure in this field after Sun Jingxiu.

In the early days of the founding of the People's Republic of China, Dong Hao's father, Dong Jingshan, was among the first batch of calligraphers. At that time, Rong Baozhai, a famous calligraphy and painting shop in my country, had his characters. Dong Hao grew up living in such a family, ears, childhood on writing, painting is very interested. However, unexpected circumstances have changed. In 1960, when Dong Hao was just 4 years old, his father died of a sudden myocardial infarction. Fortunately, Dong Hao also has a mother with good artistic skills. His mother taught him to practice calligraphy from an early age. Throughout his childhood, Dong Hao was immersed in the sky of color. At that time, his ideal was to become a calligrapher like his father. But fate is like this. Sometimes it 1 you a dilemma. This choice makes you have to learn to give up one of your loves. In 1977, Dong Hao took part in the Beijing People's Broadcasting Station to recruit announcers. He stood out among more than a thousand candidates and began his broadcasting and hosting career. After that, he became a famous program host, but he did not give up his interest in calligraphy and painting.

Dong Hao has made great progress in news, special topics, and literary broadcasting since 1978, and has won awards nationwide. Before 1987, nearly 20 programs such as newsletters, soundtrack essays, Beijing News, and dialogues were praised by experts from Guangyuan. In addition to being selected as a model teaching material, he also started the practice of continuous broadcasting of novels, essays, short stories, radio dramas, and poetry recitations. After 1980, he began to cooperate with Zheng Rong, Bi Ke, Li Zi, Yang Chengchun, Jin Naiqian, Zhou Zheng, Zhao Zhongxiang, Yakun and other comrades. His hosting and broadcasting style gradually matured and gradually formed Dong Hao's style of "deep but passionate, solemn, humorous, natural and sincere" (teacher Zhang Song's words). His seventy-five lectures "Thorn Birds" (Australian novels) won the "1990 National Novel Recitation Gold Award" and were rebroadcast on the Central People's Broadcasting Station. It was called "the first time that the role of film and television dubbing was performed. A successful example of combining subjective narration".

In 1985, he cooperated with famous voice actors Yang Chengchun and Feng Xianzhen in the poetic novels "Ye Pugeni Onekin", "Yinmeng Lake", "Milton's Lyric Poems", "There is a Blizzard Tonight", "White Beam Black Ears" and other works also won awards.

Since the early 1980 s, he has successively explained large-scale key series of feature films for CCTV: "the spring tide", "out of the trough", "the Nazi crimes of World War II" and "Zhou Enlai" have been praised by the leaders of the Central Literature Research Office, making their own style tend to be stable.

From 1978 to 1989, our uncle Dong Hao successively introduced the series host of "funny head and uncle Dong" (at the end of 1989), which combined the host and doll. This trip was called by experts as "the first perfect combination of human and occasional exercises and language modeling direction". Later, it successively launched "Big Frog Telling Stories", "Mr. Wall Calendar", "Le Baishi Wisdom Palace Fans", and "A New Generation of Movie Fans" "Family Small Court Magic Series", "Peony Paradise", "Zhou Zhou Happy", "Uncle Dong Hao Mailbox" and other national children's favorite programs. Since the end of 1989, he appeared on the screen as "Dong Hao" and officially became "the first uncle in the country", which was loved by children and parents. Therefore, he also rejected the temptation of many adult special topics and artistic programs to transfer work. Vow to be the second "Sun Jingxiu", accumulate virtue and do good deeds, and enjoy yourself.

Uncle Dong Hao planned and organized the "Watch with Mom and Dad" column of the 1 cycle in 1993. Through this year's practice, he improved his ability and prepared for the development of self-writing, self-directing and self-hosting in the future. At the end of 1993, he and the leading comrades of the Central Committee of the Communist Youth League jointly planned and wrote the "policy plan for preparing for the establishment of China children's television station in Guan", which was reported to the Central Committee in the name of the Central Committee of the Communist Youth League. With the strong support and attention of the relevant leaders, it was called the "prelude" of the establishment of the children's channel and fulfilled the obligation of "child leader.

After 1996, he hosted "Big Windmill" in the image of "Windmill King" and performed "Campus Humor Drama" in the image of "Dong Dudu". He also presided over hundreds of issues of "open sesame", which was deeply loved by children and senior students all over the country.

In addition to the column host, Uncle Dong Hao presided over the previous live broadcasts of "June 1 Evening", "Three Excellence Party", "MTV", "Karaoke" and other competition parties, "Luo Huageng Gold Cup" (once every 2 years, hosted 5 times), "Campus Style, National Primary and Secondary School Literature and Art Performance Party" (live broadcast) and other large-scale variety shows, successfully completing the hosting task, all of the above programs won awards.

In 1998, he jointly launched the "CD Stamp Commemorative Card Book for Uncle Dong Hao's Little Wish Friends to Be Talks as Soon as possible" with the Youth Work Committee and the China Youth News Agency. Relevant leaders of the China Care for the Next Generation Committee wrote an inscription according to Wang Hua: "Today's Little Miao and Tomorrow's Pillars". He himself mainly planned and told 6 stories of preaching and moral education, and sang 6 patriotic education songs. This activity was praised by the leaders concerned. His own books and cards were donated to the children in Baise area through the "Hope Project" on June 1, 1998 (in the form of book donation). Uncle Dong Hao has not allowed too much publicity about this.

In November 2009, Dong Hao appeared in Chongqing for the promotion of Astro Boy. Talking about his former CCTV colleagues who were caught in economic disputes, Dong Hao was deeply saddened. Speaking of his secret of life, he revealed that in order to defend his sense of mission to the host's 1 profession, he focused on the circle of children hosting. From 1990 to now, he has pushed off 0.9 billion of his advertising revenue. This allows everyone to see the professional ethics of Uncle Dong Hao and his own moral character.

From 1988 to 2010, Uncle Dong Hao hosted the CCTV "June 1" party "Growing up with the Motherland", bringing endless happiness to young friends. In 2011, he participated in the animation dubbing and project operation of the 100-episode cartoon "Uncle Dong Hao Tells Stories. In January 2012, the host of Liaoning satellite TV children's music growth program "genius children's voice". In 2013, he hosted Xiamen Satellite TV's puzzle challenge program "Eggs Touch Stone". In August 2014, he hosted the "Dad Please Answer" broadcast by Qinghai Satellite TV and Guizhou Satellite TV. In October, he participated in the "Fahrenheit Media College Famous Teachers Celebration Party" held by Beijing Geely College, and was hired as a distinguished professor to teach "Dong Hao Broadcasting and Hosting".

It is the broadcast of these programs that bring knowledge, enlightenment, happiness and life guidance to hundreds of millions of young viewers and parents. Uncle Dong Hao's hard work and hard sweat have won the praise of the majority of film and television audiences, leadership and social recognition, and won many personal honors: in 1985, he cooperated with famous voice actors Yang Chengchun and Feng Xianzhen. Works such as "Yepugeni Onekin", "Yinmeng Lake", "Milton's Lyric", "Snowstorm Tonight" and "White Beem Black Ears" also won awards. "The Story of the Office" won the 1987 "Flying Award" and the best translation award, and "Big Bird in China" also won the award in the international exhibition. 2005 CCTV Top Ten Host. On the evening of November 14, 2009, the 2009 China Broadcasting hosted the "Golden Microphone Award" award ceremony at the Beijing Television Grand Theater. More than a hundred announcers and hosts from all over the country gathered together to celebrate another wonderful appearance of the "Golden Microphone Award. CCTV Zhang Quanling, Yang Rui, Dong Hao, Beijing TV Liu Wenyan, Hebei TV Yu Hui and other 10 people won the TV announcer host award.

In June 2015, in the new version of the Chinese Young Pioneers team song MV, Dong Hao revealed that he would retire in 2015. On the afternoon of January 7, 2016, Dong Hao, the famous CCTV host, announced his retirement in a post, saying "Farewell, Microphone". While saying goodbye affectionately, Dong Hao also posted a photo of tears on the stage in the special retirement farewell program organized by "Echo Loud". Dong Hao wrote with emotion in the article: "Thank you CCTV, thanks to the 70, 80, 90, 00 and all the audience for their love for me! This evening, CCTV's 3 sets of art channels, "Echoes Loud" broadcast at 19:30, produced a special retirement farewell show for me for more than an hour! I sang "applause" and "I love the blue ocean". Li Sisi hugged me on behalf of the children of that year, and I shed tears on the stage! Don't! Microphone! I will give you a new surprise on the painting and calligraphy stage!"

Uncle Dong Hao is Uncle Dong Hao. Uncle Dong Hao who walks off the silver screen will let us see a more open-minded and frank uncle Dong Hao who brings happiness to people on the calligraphy and painting stage in the future.

Sun Fengming, the First to Let Pingju Go Abroad

Sun Fengming (1880-1942), from the 6th year of Guangxu in Qing Dynasty to the 31st year of the of the Republic of China, Qishan on the, nicknamed "Sun Blind ". He is one of the important birthplaces of Chinese Pingju in, Fengrun County, Qing Dynasty, from Port (now Bo Port Village, Daxinzhuang Town, Fengnan District, Tangshan City), and the founder of Pingju in the same period as Cheng Zhaocai. Sun Fengming liked Lotus Flower Fall (the predecessor of Chinese's review of drama) since he was a child. He entered Class 8 of Cui Leting in his teens (this class is the earliest class club) to study art. His ambition was to attack ugly deeds. Because of his witty performance, he his wide belly and got the stage name of "East Shining.

In 1901, at the age of 21, Sun Fengming, together with Cheng Zhaocai and others, went to Beijing to perform and split the play. At the age of 32 in 1912, Sun Fengming, with his 3 younger brothers Sun Fenggang (east hair red), Sun Fengling (fireworks) and Sun Fengli, set up the "Fengming Class

" in Tianjin, also known as the "Sun Family Class ". He performed Pingju in Tianjin and at the same time gave apprentices Hualien, Li Jinshun and Bai Yusheng, she has created the 1 generation of Chinese Pingju actress and a famous actress in Pingju. In 1917, Sun Fengming continued to expand the performance space and went south from Tianjin to Jinan, Shandong, Qingdao and other places to perform.

"Sun Family Class" in 1920 to Dalian was warmly welcomed when he wanted to see their performance, it was 1 a ticket, which made Sun Fengming felt that Dalian was a suitable place for the development of the Fengshui treasure. In 1922, Sun Fengming, after thinking again and again, he led some of the actors in the "Sun Family Class" to "formally take root in Dalian, and change the" Fengming Class "to" the of the Qi Mountain Theater ", which is the famous" Nansun Class "in the history of Chinese drama". The establishment of his own play base, created the first of the Chinese opera to social education class. The characteristics of the "Nansun Class " are that recruit female do not recruit male, and girls are all responsible for the clean and ugly life. Because the success rate of recruiting girls is high, a small number of girls are in the process of training, most of them can become protagonists. The "Nansun Class " in Dalian for 20 years has opened four subjects and trained more than 70 Kun horns, such as Hua Xiaoxian, Hua Yuexian, Hua Lingxia, Bai Yushuang, Xiao Caifeng, Xiao Jin Feng, Xiao Yin Feng, Xiao Yu Feng, Xiao Guihua, Xiao Ma Hong, Xiao Chrysanthemum, Xiao Lihua and others have all become very popular and become famous actors in Chinese Pingju in the future. Among them, Xiao Guihua, Xiao Ma Hong, Xiao Lingzhi, Jin Lingzhi and other famous actors in the history of Chinese Pingju have emerged, which have contributed to the development and prosperity of Pingju. At that time, adult protagonists such as Hua Lianfang, Li Jinshun, Liu Cuixia and Jin Lingzhi, who had already gained a certain reputation in the northeast, only did they dare to and sing Fengtiansuzi outside and become "famous brands" only when they went to the "Nansun Class " to "gild" for further study, obtained the "diploma" of "Nansun Class" and taught masters by their parents ".

At that time, the performance of "5 Women Crying Grave" in Dalian 1 was full. Actors such as Bai Yushuang, Xiao Guihua, Huang Cuifang, Xiao Ma Hong, Xiao Chrysanthemum participated in the performance. On the other hand, the young actors in the small class have solid basic skills, accurate outline accurate words, singing, reading, playing, hand-eye and body-stepping, all of them are good at wherever they go.

The well-known "Nansun " in Dalian is not only famous in the three northeastern provinces, but also goes to Beijing, Tianjin, Shanghai and overseas. Xiao Guihua, Xiao Ma Hong, Xiao Caifeng, Xiao Yufeng and Hua Lingxia of "South Sun Ban " also traveled east to Nagoya and Osaka, Japan in 1929 and 1934, and filled the record company with Pingju records such as "Huang Generation Female Travel

", "Golden Hairpin and Twinkle" and " Pearl. In 1934 and 1935, at the invitation of Japan's Rongli Records, Sun Fengming and Xiao Ma Hong went to Japan twice to make records, recording more than a dozen plays such as "2 Magistrate ", "Huang's Female Youyin ", " Bai Yulou Selling Paintings", "Du Shiniang " and " Qin Xuemei Dao Xiao", which expanded the influence of Chinese Pingju in Japan. It can be said that Sun Fengming's "Nansun Class " took the lead in making Pingju go abroad, and it was Sun Fengming who made Chinese Pingju famous overseas.

In 1942, this master of Pingju, who had made outstanding contributions to the development of Chinese Pingju, died in Xingcheng, Liaoning, at the age of 63.

73 soldiers overlook China in 83 years

In 1941, on the land of eastern Hebei where the war of resistance against Japan was burning more and more vigorously, there was an active force against the Japanese army-the Xinhua army of the Communist Party of China. Under the successive attacks of this force, the Japanese imperialist aggression conspiracy repeatedly failed in our eastern Hebei region. In order to put out the war of resistance against Japan, the Japanese invaders gathered devil soldiers stationed in Shanhaiguan, Tangshan, Beiping (today's Beijing) and other places in this year to carry out an inhuman "May Day" sweep in eastern Hebei. The Xinhua troops of the Communist Party of China, which were active in the areas of Fengrun, Yutian and Ninghe, were ordered to move from Ninghe to the mountainous areas in the north of Fengrun in order to preserve their strength. The captain of the column Li Yunpeng and political commissar Deng Wenbiao led the troops. All the officers and men fought and walked. After seven days and seven nights of hard fighting, on May 11 of that year, they moved from Liqianzhuang Village to Hejiliu Village., the officers and soldiers of the Xinhua troops who had just entered the village had not had time to eat, thousands of ghost soldiers who received secret reports were surrounded by from all directions to Hejiliu village. In order to protect the lives and safety of the people in the village, the army decided to move from the village to the Wei pit in the south of the village to hide. Political commissar Deng Wenbiao led some soldiers to occupy the east kiln pit, and column leader Li Yunpeng led the rest of the army to occupy the south kiln pit. After the Japanese army entered the village, they found that Xinhua troops had occupied the pit of the south kiln, and immediately launched an attack. Under the command of political commissar Deng Wenbiao and lieutenant Li Yunpeng, the soldiers of our army calmly responded to the battle and beat back the Japanese army's repeated attacks.

After many failed attacks, the Japanese army angrily transferred a large number of ghost soldiers from the new military village, the crow hong bridge and other places. after the supported Japanese devils arrived, they immediately occupied two graves in the east of the village of river. under the cover of the Japanese officers the the command of Tian and multiple graves, they launched a more fierce attack on our army. At the critical moment when the enemy was outnumbered, the soldiers of our army became more and more courageous and vowed to stick to their positions to the death. In the fierce battle, our soldiers played their roles in the battlefield, tactfully splashing water on the desks and quilts of the kiln factory to make mobile fortifications to seize the devil's machine guns. When the devil approached our army's position, our army fired machine guns, rifles and grenades at the devil group together, beat back the enemy's three consecutive attacks, and killed the Japanese commander Tada. In the case of great disparity between the strength of the enemy and ourselves, all the soldiers of our army were brave and tenacious and fought hard. In the end, because of the lack of ammunition, the soldiers took bayonets and rushed to the enemy group, and launched a life-and-death struggle with the enemy. Some soldiers actually pulled the grenade and died with the enemy.

The tragic battle continued until more than five o'clock in the afternoon. It rained heavily. The Japanese ghost soldiers could not stand the rain and shrinked into 1 regiments one by one. A battalion of our Xinhua troops took the opportunity to gather and launch a charge in the southeast direction, winning the and breaking through the encirclement from Suo Xinzhuang to Cuijiatun.

In this campaign, more than 350 enemy troops were killed in the River, and 78 soldiers of the Xinhua army, including column leader Li Yunpeng, died heroically, causing the Japanese army to pay a heavy price several times that of our army. In order to commemorate the 73 revolutionary martyrs who died in the war in the of the river (among them, five martyrs including Li Yunpeng of Li Qianzhuang in Fengrun District were buried by their families and returned to their hometown), in 1946, the village of River established the "River Martyrs Cemetery" in the south of the village ".

The cemetery is located in the east and west, covering an area of about 544 square meters. There is a poem at the main gate that says, "for the sake of sacrifice, dare to teach sun and moon to change the new sky. There is a 6-meter-high memorial tower in the middle of the park. The inscription on the tower is "of the heroic spirit tower in the battle of the 73 soldiers of the Xinhua army of the Communist Party of China". There is also the 1 Martyrs Tomb, where the loyal bones of 73 soldiers of the Xinhua Army are buried. In April 1995, it was named as one of the patriotic education bases at the county level by the original Fengrun county party committee and county government.

Eighty-three years have passed since the heroic battle of the of the river. The 73 soldiers of Xinhua troops sleeping in the cemetery overlook the Shenzhou in the of Tian Yingling for 83 years. Every year on Qingming Festival, primary and secondary schools in the surrounding villages and towns organize students to visit the graves and pay tribute to the. While comforting the martyrs, they also make young people not forget history and encourage them to study hard and enhance their skills. Many people also spontaneously expressed their grief in different forms. The base has educated generations of people since it was built in 1946. The Martyrs Cemetery is a patriotic education base in Fengrun District. On the occasion of the 80th anniversary of the victory of the World Anti-Fascist War, its significance is more significant the of the river.

July 2023

Jin Guo Founding Waiting for Broad Sword Wang Xin Tomb Eternally

Today, an ancient village still exists in Xugezhuang Town, Fengnan District, Tangshan City. His village is called 4 Wangzhuang.

According to relevant historical records, this is a village with a long history in the early of Jianzhuang. As early as the era of Emperor Xuanzong of the Tang Dynasty, people settled here to build. According to historical records, in the first year of Emperor Xuanzong of the Tang Dynasty (721 years), village of was established here. Because the village at that time was located between a main road of the Tang Dynasty, the geographical environment was good, the transportation was convenient, and people traveled. It is very convenient, so people named the village "4 to Village" according to these 1 characteristics ". It means starting from here, east, west, north and south.

The continuous development of history continues to write the history and evolution of this village. In the Southern Song Dynasty, Xixia, Jin, Qi, West, Liao, and Dali coexisted in the land of China. Jin, who was strong for a time, went south to attack the Southern Song Dynasty again and again. In the army attacking the Southern Song Dynasty, there was a general who fought bravely and matched him. He repeatedly made military exploits. The general's surname was Wang Mingxin. Time passed to the 11th year of Jin Shizong's decision (1171), Jin Shizong, in order to commend Wang Xin, named Wang Xin the general of the town and the of the founding. However, Wang Xin's hometown is 4 to Zhuang. So far, Zhuang is proud of the general. In order to commemorate this prince, 4 to Zhuang was renamed 4 Wang Zhuang. After Wang Xin's death, the Jin court also built a 1 grand and spectacular mausoleum for Wang Xin in the northwest of his hometown, Wangzhuang,, 4. According to the relevant information and the old people in the village, the mausoleum consists of two tombs in the south and 1 in the north, which are arranged in the shape of 3 tombs. The of tombs is 10 meters high and faces south. In front of the tomb in the north, there is a stone tablet by a turtle, a, and a stone tablet with a height of more than ten feet is engraved with "the of the tomb of Wang Xin, the of the founding of the Jin Kingdom". There is a stone temple on the side of the tomb, and the cemetery also has Shinto. Shinto is on both sides from south to north. The carving technology is superb. Lifelike stone statues are born. Stone sheep, stone horses, stone cattle and stone people stand on both sides. Honor guards generally stand in awe. In particular, the third group of stone carved horses, with round eyes, closed lips, thick 4 hooves, strong and mighty, stood with their heads held high. The fourth group of stone carving military commanders, wearing war helmets and armor, have slightly closed eyes and soft light eyes. The left hand is pressed on the waist, the right hand holds the war knife across the on the right waist, and the feet are in boots, just like 1 majestic general. The fifth group of stone carving literati, wearing official crown, waist carrying sword, feet wearing toward boots, resembling Jin Guo Yipin. However, when the tomb was opened in July 1967, it was found that the two tombs in the south were empty, and the large stone coffin in the 1 tomb in the north had only a piece of blue brick engraved with the name of a person and the remains of a sheep, and there were no other funerals. The mystery of where the owner of the tomb was buried has not been revealed.

The first Han imperial concubine of the Qing Dynasty

In Chinese history, the Manchu entered Beijing in 1644 to establish the Qing Dynasty. In order to show the majesty of the conquerors, the strictly banned Manchu-Han intermarriage. But with the change of the political situation, the Qing imperial court urgently needed to ease the contradiction between Manchu and Han, and stabilize the overall situation of Gyeonggi. In the 5 year of Shunzhi in Qing Dynasty (1648), on August 28 of the lunar calendar, the ancestors of Qing Dynasty, proceeding from long-term peace and stability, resolutely issued an imperial edict: "I want the officials and people of Manchu and Han Dynasty to make and with each other and make and marry each other. ... Later, anyone who the daughter of a Manchurian official and wanted to be a marriage with the Han Chinese must first to the Ming... As the daughter of a Han official, if she wants to marry Manchuria as a, she to report to the ministry; if she is not in office, she does not have to report to the ministry. The Manchurian officials and people who marry the daughter of the Han people are only allowed to marry if they are wives." This was a major move to deal with Manchu-Han relations in the early years of the Qing Dynasty, which had a significant and profound impact on the entire historical process of the Qing Dynasty; and the first Han imperial concubine was elected from, Luanzhou, Jingdong, to marry. She is the granddaughter of Shi Weiyue and the daughter of Shi Shen, the of Mingbei Village (now Luanzhou Town) in Luanzhou. She was later named "Concubine ".

What needs to be explained here is that in the 5 year of Shunzhi, when the emperor of Shunzhi issued the decree of "intermarriage between Manchu and Han", the daughter of Shi Shen, of Luanzhou, was only 7 years old, which was far from the age of marriage. Therefore, the decree specifically stated: "the daughter of Shi Shen, and Chengen."

"Gupta" means that when a girl uses a hair clasp to comb her and tie her hair in a bun; At the age of 15, she is to comb her hair clasp and pull her, and she is an adult and can get married. The imperial edict was announced in advance: when the daughter of Shi Shen in Luanzhou grew up to 15 years old, she would marry into the Palace and bear the royal kindness.

The "Luanzhou Annals" in the Guangxu years of the Qing Dynasty recorded: "Thirteen years of Shunzhi, Bingshen. Shi Shen, a female who served a bachelor, was honored as a noble." ... "After sealing the of the princess". Exactly eight years later.

The imperial edict of the Shunzhi emperor originally stipulated: "Manchurian officials and people marry Han women, but only those who are wives are allowed to marry." It means that Manchu people must as their regular wives (not allowed to marry concubines) to show respect. It is good to prevent the situation of "full wife" bullying "Han concubine" and affecting Manchu-Han relations. However, the emperor himself was not in the list of "officials and people". He had a queen for a long time. According to the palace system, the daughter of the Shi clan in Luanzhou could only the of being a concubine, not a "real wife".

To this end, the Shunzhi emperor "the outside the system to give grace", to the of the imperial concubine to give preferential and courtesy of the:

First, Zhao family, the biological mother of Concubine Ke, was specially designated as "Shu people" and Zhao Shuren was granted permission to enter the palace accompany her female. Second, Zhao, a, was granted permission to enter the palace in a Han–style sedan chair, "entering the sedan chair under Xihua Gate"; Third, Zhao Shuren was granted permission to "honor family gifts" to her daughter. Fourth ", concessionary mother and daughter wear Chinese clothes and eat with Han. This was unthinkable in the "Imperial Palace Omani" where the rank was and strict, and it was an advantage granted by Empress Dowager Xiaozhuang and Emperor Shunzhi.

At that time, even the queen's mother could not enter the palace casually with her female. Even when she was allowed to enter the palace occasionally, she had to kneel down on foot the courtesy of the liege's and kowtow to her daughter first according to the of the palace system. Luanzhou princess mother and daughter can accompany day and night, sit sedan chair into the palace, the family ceremony. The Manchurian and Mongolian women in the West Sixth Palace completely adopted the aristocratic attire before entering the customs, all of which were "two heads" and "with boots at the bottom of the basin". The unique of the imperial concubine mother and daughter wore Han silks and satins, which was really unique and stood out from the crowd.

What is rare is that Luanzhou Concubine in this special of preferential is not arrogant or impetuous, respectful and courteous, fully showing the of Han scholarly family of virtue. Later, she was named "of the Concubine" (Ke, read ke), which means "cautious and, respectful respectful", which is a portrayal of her virtuous character. She is to Han women and Luanzhou people added light.

Emperor Shunzhi, especially his mother, Empress Xiaozhuang, broke through the ancestral system and established this Han imperial concubine for the first time, because he saw the character and performance of the father and ancestor of Concubine and the reputation of Guangyuan. What is more urgent is to bridge the contradiction between Manchu and Han, stabilize the overall situation and calm people's hearts. Therefore, it is urgent to advocate "to collect and the Manchu and Han". However, it is better to "collect and and the Manchu and Han" and go deep into kinship and kinship. Therefore, Shunzhi promulgated the oracle "Manchu-Han Intermarriage" in 5.

So which one to choose? Shi Weiyue was well-known as an official and Qing in the Ming Dynasty, but he was wronged at the end of the Ming Dynasty. The Qing court the funeral of his, and the of his son Shi Shen Gao. Hanlin was entrusted with important tasks. It has been a good story throughout the country and has a wide range of demonstration power. Therefore, the first Han imperial concubine the daughter of Shi Shen's became the first choice. Shi Weiyue was wronged at the end of the Ming Dynasty and the early Qing Dynasty, and Shi Shen was a high-ranking official of the dynasty. His daughter was grateful and naturally came to fruition.

Concubine Ke lived in the Yongshou Palace of the West Sixth Palace. called her "Yongshou Palace Concubine" during her lifetime. The original text of "The Queen of Xiao Xian" written by Emperor Shunzhi reads: "In the spring of the 17th year of Shunzhi (1660), the Yongshou Palace (Concubine) began to suffer from illness. Later (refers to the Queen of Xiao Xian) also bowed to support, 3 forgot to sleep day and. Therefore, the ardent comforting relieving sorrow and sorrow, pre –for treatment, are like serving future (all like serving the queen today), and the clothes made later are still there today." "Queen of filial piety" was Dong Eshi, the daughter of Eshuo, the most beloved Manchu minister in Shunzhi. After his death, he was named "Queen of filial piety and filial piety in and of Xuanren in Zhide ", known as "Queen of filial piety and filial piety". During her lifetime, she was "imperial concubine", and her status was higher than that of "imperial concubine" and "concubine. As an "imperial concubine", she can serve the sick "Yongshou palace concubine" for 3 days and nights, "just like serving the queen of today", comforting and sewing clothes. On the one hand, it reflects the virtuousness of this Concubine Dong E, and on the other hand, it also shows that Concubine Ke is indeed respected in the West Sixth Palace.

Legend has it that Ke Fei, who lives in the Yongshou Palace, often reads and writes. Xiaozhuang queen asked her what is the book? Write what? Princess Ke reported back: This book is called "Motto of Family Management". It is a wise saying which. And read it to Queen Xiaozhuang to listen to the: "should not to the shortcomings of one's own long, should not to the shortcomings of one's own clumsy and avoid the abilities of others", which means: "Don't use one's own strengths to laugh at the shortcomings of others, and don't envy the talents of others just because one's own hands are clumsy."

When Queen Xiaozhuang heard this, she did not realize that she was hooking up in the harem. This motto is great! From then on, Ke Fei taught "Family Motto " and " Daughter Sutra" the harem, and later taught "The Analects of Confucius" and taught writing and painting. In the 18th year of Qing Shunzhi (1661), at midnight on the seventh day of the first month of the first month, Emperor Shunzhi died of illness at the age of 24, and the of Concubine Ke lost her husband young.

In the sixth year of Kangxi's reign of the Qing Dynasty (1667), before the emperor's eastern tour in September, the of the imperial concubine had been infected with the disease, and it was getting worse every day until the 11th.

On the 30th of the month, he unfortunately returned to the west and was only 26 years old.

Gao Di, Experienced Three Emperors of Ming Dynasty

Gao di, whose birth and death are unknown, has data showing that his birth and death is about 1560–1639. he was born in Luanzhou, an ancient of (now an jizhai,, fengnan district, Tangshan city, Hebei province).

According to "Ming Shi Lu" and "Luanzhou Zhi", Chongzhen was put back into Luanzhou in the 12th year (1639). He died shortly after, aged 82. According to the Annals of Fengnan County published by Xinhua Publishing House in June, 1990, "... In the 12th year of Chongzhen (1639), the Baiyun Building was returned to the village and was built as 'Dongshan Villa '. He has written books on the wall, including "Tai Chi Conscience", "Fu Yun Manuscript", "Lai True" (poetry collection), etc. died at the age of 82 ." The above two records have in common that Gao di went back to his hometown in the 12th year (1639) of the of chong Zhen and drove to the west at the age of 82. According to Xinhua Publishing

House's "Fengnan County Records" published in June 1990, it is contained: "Gao di, Zidengzhi, the county has a of people in. The birth and death years were between Ming Longqing (1560) and the early years of Qing Shunzhi (1644)." It is inferred that Gao died at the age of 82 in the 15th year of Chongzhen of the Ming Dynasty, followed the 7th year of Chongde of Jin (Qing Dynasty), that is, 1642, was only one year away from the early year of Shunzhi of the Qing Dynasty (1644) in.

In this way, Gao di caught up with the 5 emperors of the Ming Dynasty: Jiajing, Longqing, Wanli, Tianqi and Chongzhen. In the 17th year of Wanli (1589), he served as a Jinshi of Yichou Branch in Gaodi Middle School, and served as the county magistrate of Linying (now Linying County, Luohe City, Henan Province). In the 12th year of Chongzhen (1639), he was released to the village. He experienced Wanli, Tianqi and Chongzhen 3 emperors on the way to becoming an official in the Ming Dynasty.

Throughout the history of Gao di's official career, although in the summer of the 5 year of the apocalypse (1625), Nurhachi attacked Ningyuan, the border was urgent. Xi sect Gao dijing slightly Ji Liao military. This was a Confucian scholar who did not understand military affairs. After taking office, he took the pretext that he could not defend outside the customs. Without listening to the hard persuasion of Yuan Chonghuan and other main war factions, dismantled the fortifications in Jinzhou, Youtun, Dalinghe and other places. "drove troops into the customs, the Committee abandoned meters millet more than 100,000, while the death carried and cried, the people are angry and the military is sluggish." Yuan Chonghuan insisted on not withdrawing and still clung to Ningyuan. Cui Chengxiu, the main member of the eunuchs party, attended the performance to Xi Zong and Gao Di to retreat in fear of the enemy and was dismissed. From the 17th year of Wanli's reign (1589) when Gao was appointed as the of Linying, to the 5 year of Tianqi's reign (1625) when was, Gao was diligent and honest, dedicated to the public, devoted to his duties, and benefited one party. Especially in the first year of tomorrow (1621), the eunuch Du Jinzhong was in charge of the taxation of Huguang. He levied and extorted money from the people and perverted the law. At this time, Gao Di, who had been promoted to the post of Hu Guang's political affairs, quickly dismissed him and won the hearts of the people. Soon, he was promoted to the positions of Department of Shaanxi Province according to the, left censor of the capital inspection institute, and governor. According to records such as "Yongping Fu Zhi" and "Luanzhou Zhi", he also privately contributed 7,000 taels of silver, helping the of the (supplies) to reward, and had a good reputation in the army and the court. That is to say, during the tour of Datong, Gao di donated money and 7000 from his salary to reward the of soldiers and. Prior to this, in February of the 38th year of Wanli's reign (1610), Gao di was transferred from the prefect of Datong,, to the vice-minister of Shandong province. In March of the 41st year of Wanli's reign (1613), Gao di completed the examination and was promoted from Shandong deputy to Huguang right to participate in politics (from the third grade). As for his deeds during this period, "Hu Guang Tong Zhi" said: "Gao di... was divided into Jingxi, Xuexue Palace, Kuixing Building and Zun Jing Pavilion. Donate money to the district to draw, do not bother the people ", Gao di paid his own money, donated money to help local training of talents. This has a great relationship with Gao di's idea of being an official. In Gao di's heart, he has the ambition to assist the court in governing the country, and he has the idea of clean and honest for officials. This also led to Gao's incorruptible. At the beginning of his official career, he did not unpack the taxes paid at all and sent them directly to Kaifeng government, thus eliminating the malpractice of consuming and envious of. The Ming government at the time stipulated that a certain amount of local taxes collected by magistrates belonged to them. Gao di considered that the country was in the midst of internal and external troubles, and the treasury was empty, so how could he fill his personal pockets? Therefore, the annual silver be paid in full and not taken.

In this way, probably due to the outstanding achievements in taxation, in the 19th year of Wanli (1885), Gao di "transferred the to households to Cao and to discuss the Hu Shu pass", that is, he sent the Suzhou banknote pass to collect business tax.

In the 3 year of the apocalypse (1623), he was promoted to the left assistant minister of the Ministry of War, and in the summer of the 5 year (1625), he was promoted to the minister of the Ministry of War. Nurhachi attacked and hit Ningyuan. When the border was in emergency, the court sent Gao Di to Ji Liao military. However, Gao Di, who did not understand military affairs, ordered to demolish military fortifications in Jinzhou,, and Dalinghe. As a result, Cui Chengxiu, a member of the eunuchs party, to Xizong that Gao Di was afraid of the enemy and to withdraw retreat and was dismissed.

As a result, it affected Gao Di's official career. When the twelfth year of Chongzhen (1639), Gao di returned to his hometown and lived in the "Dongshan Villa" of the Yunlou in Bai. Recalling the three generations of emperors in front of him, he had a clear conscience and wrote a book on the wall. He put a 1 kind of relief in his "Tai Chi Conscience", "Fu Yun manuscript" and " Lai True" (poetry collection).

Nie Er, with the national anthem and forever

Seeing that the National Day is approaching, I can't help thinking of the national anthem, and suddenly I think of going to Yunnan to pay homage to the tomb of Nie, a people's musician,.

Between Taihua Temple and Sanqing Pavilion in Xishan, Kunming, Yunnan Province, there is a gentle slope with pine trees and green trees where 1 great people's musician in China sleeps for a long. He is Nie er, the composer of the the People's Republic of China national anthem -- the March of volunteers.

it was a trip to Yunnan at the turn of summer and autumn in 2007. On the way back to Longmen Scenic Area, I did not follow the tourists. I turned left halfway and walked into a different path. With great reverence, I came to visit Nie Er. At the foot of the mountain, among the green pines and cypresses, the musician's cemetery is in the shape of a piano. The main body is the of piano plates. The tomb the of the piano neck. The seven flower platforms on the road are in the shape of keys, symbolizing seven scales. The 24-level stone steps on the road indicate that he only lived 24 years old. On the top of the piano plate, on seven crystal stones, there are two lines of horizontal writing "people's musician Nie Er's tomb". The design of the cemetery is novel and well conceived, which is both characteristic and solemn.

I stood in front of the tomb of the music giant admiringly, silently reading the life of Nie Er: Nie Er, formerly known as Shouxin, has the meaning of the word, and 1 as a purple art. Born in 1912 in Kunming, Yunnan, a cold home. Love music since childhood, can play a variety of musical instruments. In the middle school, he joined the Communist Youth League of China and participated in revolutionary activities. He went to Shanghai in 1930 and worked as a clerk in a firm. The following year he was admitted to the "Mingyue Song and Dance Club" as a violinist. In 1933 by Tian Han introduced to join the Communist Party of China. Since then, he actively participated in left-wing music, drama, and film work, and published art reviews under the pseudonym "Black Angel", criticized the decadent music, and put forward the idea of "public shouting" for the. In 1935, he went to the Soviet Union via Japan. Unfortunately, he drowned on July 17 while swimming at the seashore of Gumuma, Fujisawa City, Kanagawa Prefecture, Japan.

In memory of Nie Er, the Japanese people established a monument to Nie Er on November 1, 1954 near the death of Nie Er on the coast of, Fujisawa City. In 1963, the granite monument in the shape of "ear" was rebuilt. Guo Moruo's book the six characters "the place where Nie Er finally ". Japanese dramatist Mr. Akita Yuque wrote an inscription introducing Nie Er's life.

Standing in front of the white marble statue of Nie Er, pondering the experiences of great men and the thunder of the son of music. Nie Er's sonorous and powerful songs echoed in his ears: "Volunteer March ", "March Song", "Graduation Song", "Pioneer", "Docker Song", "New Women", etc., concentrated on the performance of that era The suffering and resistance of the workers and peasants under the oppression of the old Chinese class, especially after the "September 18th −18 Incident, awakened the strong will of the Chinese people to resist Japan and save the nation, sound the" horn of the Chinese revolution "and the" drum of the people's liberation ". Among them, the March of volunteers was decided by the first plenary session of the Chinese people's Political Consultative Conference on September 27, 1949 as the the People's Republic of China national anthem. On December 4, 1982, the Fifth Session of the Fifth National People's Congress was officially designated as the the People's Republic of China National Anthem.

"those who hear its voice have no oil, but the patriotic think, Zhuang, however, the spirit of lofty ideals, resolutely and with interest in the common swan. Nie Er is majestic, and it is immortalized with the national anthem. "This is Guo Moruo's perception and affirmation of this song and its creator in" Nie Er Tombstone.

On the blue sky, with the brilliant sunshine, I bowed 3 to Nie Er's tomb again, walked down the steps nostalgically, and fulfilled my wish.

Lu Award for "Good Night" Zhang Chu

Lu Xun Literature Award: one of the literary awards with the highest honor in China today, sponsored by the Chinese Writers Association, selected every four years, has become a yardstick to measure the level of literary creation of a writer and even a region. On August 11, 2014, the Lu Xun

Literature Award was officially announced. Zhang Chu, a writer in Luannan County of our city, won the short story award of the sixth and Lu Xun Literature Award for his short story "good Night.

The award speech of "Good Night": Zhang Chu's narrative is dense, sensitive, lyrical and introverted. He twists and turns in cruelty and tenderness. Although he does not promise to reach warmth every time, he can find the power of the best every time.

"Good Night" describes the touching affection between 1 old man who has a lot of history and is used to seeing the floating and sinking of the world and a boy who has lost his parents suffering from AIDS in a delicate and plain way. In the lonely relationship between the characters, it describes the and of human nature. In the limited scale of a short story, Zhang Chu dramatically presents the complex experience of the moment between day and night, noise and silence, and establishes a desirable spiritual height.

"Good Night" was first published in the summer 2012 issue of "Min Zhi New City Literature", and then published in the 6th issue of "Tianya" in 2012 and the 1st issue of "Novel Monthly" in 2013. The children in "Good Night" are children with AIDS, and women are once popular opera celebrities who suffer from emotional confusion in their lives. For the two, the real "evil time" is everywhere, but they are in Each other's sincerity ushered in the "good night" of the soul ". Reading this novel, like other works, always reads compassion in a miserable and even tragic life, which integrates the writer's outlook on life, and the writer's works reflect the writer's world outlook. "Good Night" describes Cheng Pai Mingdan, who has passed away and still has charm. He is dissatisfied with the weak world and lives in a seclusion in a mountain village. In the confusion and panic of others, he has established the story of forgetting years of friendship with orphans suffering from AIDS. The author approaches the fragility and tenacity, black hole and light of human nature with deep internal strength.

Zhang Chu: Member of Chinese Writers Association. He has published short stories in magazines such as People's Literature, Harvest, October, and Contemporary. Author of a collection of short stories "Cherry". He has won the "Dahongying Literature Award", "people's Literature Award", "Hebei Literature and Art Revitalization Award" and "Hebei Youth Culture Construction Award". In 2011, he was selected as "TOP20 future literature". By the "people's literature" and "southern literature" as 2012 "annual young year writer".

Zhang Chu majored in finance and taxation during his university years. After graduation, he has worked in the of the State Administration of Taxation in Luannan County. Zhang Chu has passed the age of 40. He said that he felt extremely honored to win the Lu Xun Literature Award. 2015 has already begun, and the Spring Festival of the Year of the Goat is approaching. Zhang Chu said that although my

"Good Night", a short story "Wild Mint" and a novella "Seven Peacock Feathers" have attracted a lot of attention in the literary circles inside and outside the province, As a grassroots literary worker, he will continue to take root in life and use honest writing to write the spirit of this land, with a frank and tolerant heart to sing the eternal love and virtue in the world.

Chicken Feathers messenger Li Shengfu

One day in February 1930, a boy was born in a poor family in Cui Tuo Village, Fengnan District, Tangshan City, Hebei Province. In 1938, the little boy became sensible; in March 1942, the Japanese devils entered the village. In August 1942, the boy became the head of the children's team. The boy saw the enthusiasm and vitality of the Eighth Route Army to mobilize the peasants to establish revolutionary bases and establish militia organizations, women's organizations, and children's groups. Also saw the Japanese army in the village to carry out sweeping, everywhere burning, killing, looting, rape all the atrocities. In his young mind, he planted the seeds of hatred for Japanese imperialism. This boy is Li Shengfu, the well-known messenger of chicken feasts in the future. The original form of the head of the hero in the famous movie "letter of chicken feasts" is Li Shengfu.

The old hero was awarded the "Liberation Medal" and was cordially received by the central leadership.

Delivering "Chicken Feather Letter"

During the War of Resistance Against Japan, one of the letters delivered by the Eighth Route Army was called "Chicken Feather Letter", which was to insert a chicken feather in the upper right corner of the envelope to indicate the importance of the letter and must be delivered to the destination quickly. In August 1942, 12-year-old Li Shengfu joined the children's regiment in the liberated area and served as the head of the children's regiment composed of more than 140 children. At that time, under the leadership of Li Shengfu, the children's group was in groups of five every week. No matter day or night, they took turns to be responsible for sending the "Jimaoxin" from the liberated area of Fengnan County to the Eighth Route Army in Luannan County 6 kilometers away. Every time, the children's team members the to deliver the information to their destinations safely and in a timely manner without hesitation, wit and courage. I don't know how many times the children's league members have gone through or how many tests they have gone through. Every time they were very brave and tried every means to send out the letters, providing timely and accurate information for the Eighth Route Army to attack the Japanese army.

On one occasion, when a "chicken feather letter" was about to be sent to the liberated area, Li Shengfu played with three children's League members in dress and went all the way. Just as they were walking halfway, more than 10 Japanese and puppet troops came head-on. In order to keep the intelligence from falling into the hands of the traitors, Li Shengfu tactfully hid the "chicken feather letter" in the grass beside him, and then pretended to dig wild vegetables in the field with three other partners. However, these Japanese and puppet troops did not let them off easily. They also beat Li Shengfu and his partners with wooden sticks, forced them to hand over information and admitted that they were "Xiao Ba Lu". Li Shengfu and his friends, who were choking back the pain, gritted their teeth and said nothing. Finally, the Japanese puppet army could not let pass them helplessly. Seeing that the traitors had gone far away, Li Shengfu and his partners immediately found the "chicken feather letter" buried in the grass, carefully carried it in their arms, and sent the information to the Eighth Route Army as fast as the children could reach at that time. Completed the task.

help to win the battle

The children's regiment led by Li Shengfu, while doing a good job in passing on the "chicken feather letter", also actively assisted the Eighth Route Army to stand posts and watch posts. When the Eighth Route Army was at war with the Japanese aggressors, it helped the carry and ammunition and bandage the wounded. One day in the autumn of 1944, Li Shengfu and the children's team captured 1 Japanese and puppet army spies while standing guard at the head of the village. After interrogation, he was confirmed to be a traitor who committed many crimes and was immediately shot by the Eighth Route Army. In the morning of the next day, due to the traitors, the Japanese aggressors dispatched more than 200 troops to attack the liberated area frantically. The liberated area quickly concentrated its forces and dispatched about 500 Eighth Route Army soldiers from 4 companies to fight the Japanese aggressors. during the battle, li shengfu led the children's group members in braving a hail of bullets to replenish the eighth route army soldiers with ammunition in a timely manner. After more than four hours of bloody fighting, the more than 200 Japanese troops were wiped out. The victory of this battle was due to the children's team members and was praised by the Eighth Route Army in the liberated areas.

Urgent Information

It was the morning of February 27, 1945. The sky in the east was just bright. Li Shengfu and the Eighth Route Army soldiers stationed in the village helped the people sweep the floor and carry water. At this time, the sentry reported that a large number of Japanese cavalry were towards the village in the distance. In the face of a sudden attack, the soldiers of the Eighth Route Army fought bravely in the face of danger. When the bullets were used up, they used bayonets to fight; the soldiers of the cookhouse squad did not have guns, so they stabbed the Japanese aggressors in the chest with the pointed ends of wooden sticks. During the battle, an Eighth Route Army soldier was shot in the head and bleeding. Li Shengfu immediately bandaged his wound. The seriously injured soldier said to Li Shengfu with difficulty: "I am dying. I have a secret information in my pocket. Please hand it over to the party organization." Li Shengfu said to the soldier, "Please rest assured that I will send the information to the party organization." After that, the soldier died. The battle was very cruel. It lasted from 6 a.m. to 3 p.m. before the ended. More than 80 Japanese invaders were killed, and more than 120 Eighth Route Army soldiers participated in the war. In the end, only 9 were left. Li Shengfu, who was filled with righteous indignation, saw the heroic sacrifices of the soldiers one by one, remembered the soldier's entrustment, and was full of hatred for the Japanese devils. He said goodbye with tears, started his way, and quickly sent the secret information to the party organization.

Now the old hero is in the retreat of the Shantou Military Region in Guangdong. Li Shengfu, an 85-year-old retired veteran soldier, is still strong and in good spirits.

August 2015

Xinhua troops break through in the storm

During the Great riot in eastern Hebei in 1938, the Communist Party of China organized a party armed force-the team of the Xinhua Department of the Communist Party of China. It is this anti-Japanese force active on the land of eastern Hebei that has continuously and heavily attacked the Japanese invading army since its establishment, causing the Japanese imperialist conspiracy to invade and occupy China to repeatedly fail in eastern Hebei. It is regarded as an important obstacle to Japan's implementation of the "Greater East Asian Co-Prosperity Circle", and as a thorn in the flesh that must be removed from.

In 1941, in order to put out the raging fire of the War of Resistance against Japan in eastern Hebei, eliminate the Xinhua forces of the Communist Party of China, the effective force against the Japanese militarist army, and crack down on the anti-Japanese spiritual of the people in eastern Hebei. The Japanese invading army carried out a brutal "May 1st" sweep in eastern Hebei, and concentrated on mobilizing ghost soldiers stationed in Beiping (now Beijing), Shanhaiguan, Tangshan and other places to carry out frenzied encirclement and interception of this anti-Japanese team.

Transfer

In order to preserve the anti-Japanese strength, the CPC Jidong Party Organization ordered the Xinhua troops of the CPC to gradually abandon their activities in the plains around Fengrun, Yutian and Ninghe and move from Ninghe County to the depths of Yanshan Mountain in the northern of Fengrun County.

However, the Japanese followed all the way and pursued them. Chief Li Yunpeng (also known as Li Yinpeng) and political commissar Deng Wenbiao led the troops. After seven days and seven nights of hard fighting, all the officers and men fought and walked at the same time. Finally, at 9:00 a.m. on the 11th of the lunar calendar in 1941, they were transferred from Li Qianzhuang Village, of Fengrun County, to Hezhen Village for. However, before the officers and soldiers of the Xinhua army who had just entered the village had time to eat, the sentry reported that the thousands of ghost soldiers who had received the secret report were surrounded by the of the village the river in all directions. In times of crisis, the lives and property of the people are at stake. In order to protect the lives of the people in the village, the army decided to quickly move from the village to the kiln pit south of the village to hide. Political commissar Deng Wenbiao led the and some soldiers to occupy the east kiln pit. Chief Li Yunpeng led the rest of the army to occupy the south kiln pit.

Guild War

After the influx of Japanese troops arrived, they found that the Xinhua troops had occupied the Nanyaokeng, and immediately launched an attack. Under the calm command of the captain Li Yunpeng, the soldiers of the Xinhua troops actively responded to the battle and continuously defeated the Japanese multiple attacks.

After launching many attacks but failed, the Japanese army angrily transferred ghost soldiers from Xinjuntun in Fengrun County, Fengdenwu, Yutian County Rahong Bridge and other places. The reinforcements of the Japanese devils arrived at the battle site and immediately occupied the two graves in the east of Village in the of River. The Japanese officer Tata commanded the Japanese army, under the cover of many graves, they launched an even more fierce attack on the positions of Xinhua troops. In the critical situation of being outnumbered by the enemy, facing the Japanese soldiers with excellent weapons and extremely vicious, the soldiers of the Xinhua troops became more and more brave and vowed to stick to their positions. In the fierce battle, the soldiers played, tactfully the kiln factory's bookkeeping accounts the table, covered them with water-splashed quilts to make mobile fortifications, braved the bullets of the enemy and, and seized the machine guns of the devils. When the devils approached our army's position, the officers and soldiers of the Xinhua army fired machine guns, rifles and grenades at the swarming Japanese devils, he beat back the enemy's attacks three times in a row and killed the Japanese commander, Tsuda. Under the circumstances of the great disparity between the enemy and our forces, all the soldiers of the Xinhua troops of the Communist Party of China were brave and tenacious and fought hard. Because there was not much ammunition, the soldiers finally took up bayonets and rushed to the enemy group, and launched a desperate hand-to-hand battle with the enemy. Some soldiers actually pulled a grenade and died with the enemy. The tragic and fighting continued until more than five o'clock in the afternoon, but at this time it rained heavily and the fighting stopped temporarily.

Breakthrough

The Japanese devils could not stand the lapping of the storm and huddled to avoid the rain. The

Xinhua troops seized this 1 favorable opportunity, and political commissar Deng Wenbiao commanded the assault troops to gather together to launch a fierce charge to the southeast and successfully break through. After that, the soldiers of Xinhua troops, led by a fellow villager 1 the brick kiln, bypassed the enemy's checkpoint and retreated in the direction of Cuijiatun from Suoxinzhuang, Nanbu and Towliu.

More than 350 Japanese troops were killed in the of the River Battle. 78 soldiers of the Xinhua troops of the Communist Party of China, including chief Li Yunpeng, died heroically, causing the Japanese troops to pay a heavy price several times that of us. however, the japanese army also hit a swollen face filled with fat people, everywhere to preach the victory of "all annihilating the xinhua troops. However, only a month later, the Xinhua army, a soldier the people of the eastern of Hebei, not only quickly recovered and grew, but also continued to carry forward the tradition of bravery and good fighting. The heroic galloped and on the great plains of eastern Hebei, hitting the Japanese invaders everywhere.

In order to commemorate the 78 soldiers of the Xinhua troops of the Communist Party of China who died in the breakout of the in the of the river, in 1946, the of Hecheng Village established the "Hecheng Martyrs Cemetery" in the south of the village ". The cemetery is located in the east and west, covering an area of about 544 square meters. There is a poem at the main entrance that says, "Dare to teach the sun and moon to change the sky for the sake of sacrifice. In the middle of the park stands a 6-meter-high memorial tower with the inscription "of the Yingling Tower in the Battle of the Seventy-three Soldiers of the Xinhua Army of the Communist Party of China". There is also the 1 tomb of martyrs, where the loyal bones of 73 soldiers the team of Xinhua department (5 martyrs, including Li Yunpeng of Li qianzhuang in Fengrun district, were buried by their families and returned to their hometown, so they were 73 soldiers), burying this heroic song of anti-Japanese war into the memory of history.

August 3, 2015

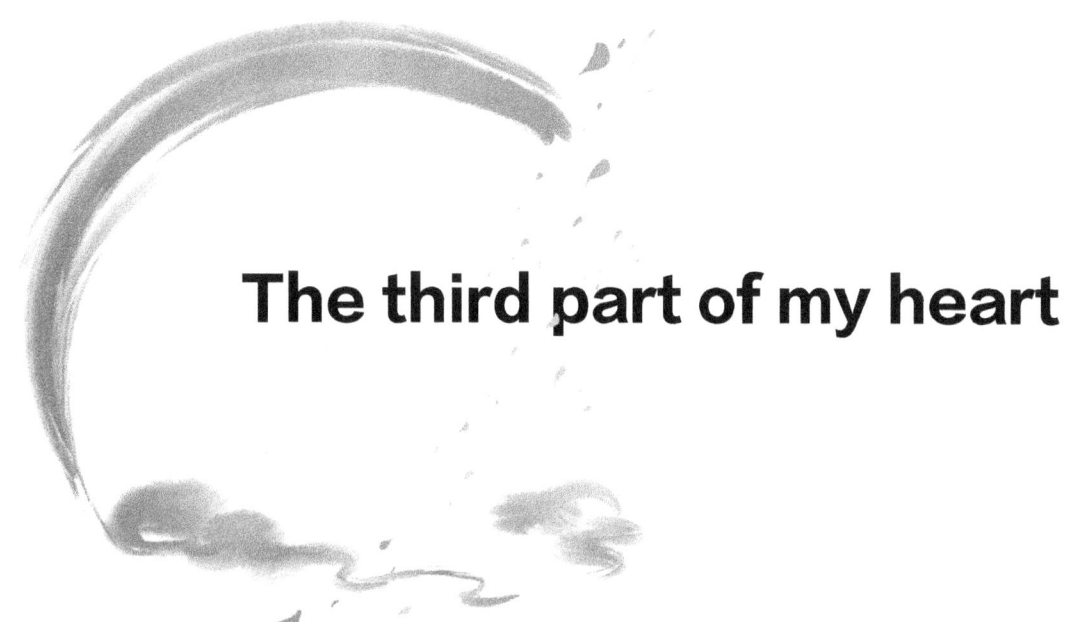

The third part of my heart

When writing into life

The experience of the earthquake has left me endless memories and thoughts. The spirit of Tangshan people's perseverance, perseverance, perseverance, and gratitude to the society has deeply affected my family life.

Because of my work, news writing and literary creation have become a part of my life inadvertently. Because the timeliness of news cannot be delayed, it is only necessary to form a manuscript as quickly as possible. Literary inspiration is all the time, and fleeting, not timely grasp the loss of the source of writing.

In the process of resuming construction after the Tangshan earthquake in the mid-1980s, people's lives are not rich. There is nothing else. Even if I am eating and writing inspiration, I have to put down my bowl and chopsticks and write down a few strokes immediately. My wife, who is not fond of writing, feels that I am very unwilling to integrate my work and creation into my family life. Whenever I see this scene, I will a few white eyes.

Playing cards, smoking, and playing mahjong, I never get involved; books, movies, and TV dramas such as romance, martial arts, and fantasy are never fun for me. It's really okay to sit on the sofa and read books or TV news. Remember once, on Sunday wife to go out shopping. Tell me when I'm leaving the door, plug in the flash heater and get 1 pot of boiling water. After my wife left, I took a kettle of tap water and came to the north balcony. The kettle was plugged into the flash heater and the power plug was plugged in. After that, I went to the South House to read local chronicles. I don't know how long it took, I suddenly smelled the smell of 1 burning plastic. I thumped to think of the water in the thermos in the north balcony. I hurried over to look 1. The plastic shell of the thermos was paralyzed and the hot water in the thermos was still spraying out. I quickly pulled out the bolt of the thermos. But then he did a stupid thing. He even poured the tap water into the boiling kettle after receiving the 1 scoop. The kettle burst immediately, making the balcony full of glass in the kettle. Fortunately, it didn't hurt me.

Another time when I was writing in the room at noon near the, I suddenly heard my wife say, "Chen Xin, go downstairs and buy a bottle of vinegar to. I get fish and have no vinegar ." I was obedient and hurried downstairs, but I happened to see a book stall downstairs. I forgot everything I saw the book. I stopped and squatted in front of the book stall and read the book with all my heart. I don't know how long it took to hear my wife say behind me, "Chen Xin, let's go upstairs for dinner the ." I 1 looked back and suddenly remembered I was asked to buy vinegar. I quickly said, "I haven't bought vinegar you asked me to buy." My wife looked at me with a smile and said, "I stewed the fish. Go upstairs and have dinner." Sitting at the table, we chatted while eating. The wife said, "I watched you go downstairs to the book stand on the platform and stopped. I 1 thinking about it. now you forget about buying vinegar and go. Also don't talk nonsense with you, I turn off the gas stove, go downstairs to buy it yourself. This is not, the fish is stewed, beer is poured for you, reward you forgot to buy vinegar, come on, have a drink..."

In the winter of 1988, when I was waiting for the small train to leave on the platform of Linxi small railway station, where I was picking up and picking up workers from Kailuan Linxi mine and fangezhuang mine, suddenly, there was a noisy shouting in a frozen pit far east of the platform, and many people ran to watch. At this time, the small train whistle started, I got on the train to go to work in the mine. When I came back in the afternoon, I heard that a child playing on the ice fell into the ice. A man jumped into the ice water to save without taking off his clothes. The child was saved, but the man was exhausted and sank to the bottom. Therefore, I wrote the documentary short drama "Tragedy", and in July 1989, my documentary short drama "Tragedy" won the "China's First Miniature Works Editing and Publishing Exhibition" Excellence Award.

My colleague once saved 1 girls bravely. The incident happened suddenly. Two people who did not know each other and did not contact afterwards, but they became husband and wife by mistake. In this regard, I wrote a short novel "Ugly Husband" and won an award in the Correspondence College of Literary Talents in Hainan Province.

In the 1990 s, I entered the peak period of prose poetry creation. In May 1992, I went to Qinhuangdao for a one-day trip to. I saw a young man standing by the seaside and thinking about it... When I came back, I wrote the prose poem "It's Midsummer, Do You Go to See the Sea? Voted to Hong Kong's "World Prose Poetry Writer" magazine. In June 1992, my prose poem "Zhong Xia's feelings" won the first prize of "the first national contemporary literary masterpiece selection competition" held by the editorial department of Hainan Province, and was included in the "thousand Chinese new poets" series edited by Fang Mengquan in, It has also been reprinted by Tianjin economic radio station, Tangshan group news and other media. In 1993, the inaugural issue of the school magazine "Window" of Shaanxi Youth Self-study University published my award-winning prose poem "Midsummer Emotion" in a special edition, as well as my creative talk "Let the light of Emotion shine in the article", and Add editor's note. It is also because this prose poem "Midsummer Love", which won the first prize of the

"National First Contemporary Literary Selection Competition", was founded on October 25, 1949 as the first pure literature journal of New China. In the history of contemporary Chinese literature (new Chinese literature), it can be called the most important, most prominent and most authoritative and representative literary publication "People's Literature" from any aspect. I was also invited to attend the symposium on the 45th anniversary of the founding of the People's Literature.

Every bit of life has inspired my creative inspiration and won honor again and again. Since then, my literary creation has become more and more unacceptable. My works are often published and broadcast in newspapers, magazines, and radio stations at different levels from the country to the local level, and some are included in literary works or awards. Even, in 1993, my prose poem "Midsummer, is it to see the sea? The "you have occupied me" was also published in the fifth and seventh issues of the of the "of World Prose Poetry Writers" in Hong Kong, which was ruled by Britain at that time, and won the Excellence Award of the "Prosperity Cup" World Prose Poetry Competition. My entries have also been included in the list of contemporary poetry lovers edited by the famous poet A Hong (Wang Zhanbiao), the list of unnamed writers and poets edited by the famous writer Yao Xueyin, and the collection of new contemporary literature edited by the famous writer and poet Fang Mengquan. Professor He Shuyun from Fudan University has also been guiding and encouraging me to study in the writer class of the Chinese Department of Fudan University. In 1994, I finished the preparatory class for writers of the Chinese Department of Shanghai Fudan University and was given priority to be admitted as a formal student of the Chinese Department of Shanghai Fudan University.

In 2007, when Guan Renshan, a well-known writer and chairman of the Hebei Writers Association, learned that my "Selected Works of Chen Xin" 1 the was about to be published by the Writers Publishing House, he told me to my face: "After the book is published, you must send me one!" Mr. Tan Ge, a well-known writer and vice chairman of the Hebei Writers Association, wrote the title of the book "Selected Works of Chen Xin" for me. In 2009, the book "Echo of the Years" was printed. During the period from 2015 to 2022, the "Chen Xin News Collection 1 to 4" (1985-2022) will be organized. In January 2017, the 180000-character book "Dream Back to the Tang Dynasty" was published by "Unity Publishing House. In January 2018, the book "A Sunshine with" was published by "Sichuan Nationalities Publishing House. In January 2021, the prose collection "Wind Dance Autumn the Sea" was published by "Beijing Daily Publishing House.

Tangshan City Writers Association, Hebei Province Writers Association, China Coal Mine Writers Association, China Prose Society. This is the home of writers that I have entered and become a member of after the "July 28" Tangshan earthquake in 1976. Writing has accompanied my life, and has become a part of my daily life.

At the beginning of 2023, I suddenly looked back and felt gratified to see the road I had taken. I lamented that persistence can achieve everything. The spirit of a city affects the people of this city. We Tangshan people, with the spirit of earthquake resistance, have been working hard to pursue and struggle to rebuild this home on the ruins into such a beautiful and beautiful coastal city with progress. 48 years ago, I came from the earthquake and then integrated writing into my life. 48 years later, as a Tangshan person who grew up with Tangshan after the earthquake and participated in its construction and development, I feel gratified. Because, there is writing in my life, there are gains and results in writing!

Thank you and yourself.

Today is Thanksgiving Day. I am grateful for the good people I met along the way and for my perseverance in writing.

It was a summer and autumn time in the 1980 s, when the secretary of the branch called me to the branch in the office opposite to him. When I entered the branch, I only heard the secretary say, "Chen Xin, do you know these two elder sisters?" I looked at them and said, "No." "then let me tell you, this is Jia Dajie from the broadcasting station of our mine, and this is Feng, the ." The secretary said. "They 1 come to meet you, 2 they have sent you prizes." Then Jia Dajie said, "Your essay" Iron Horse Knight "is very well written and won the first prize in this essay solicitation activity of the mine radio station. Because I am not familiar with you, I would like to see you today and bring you the prize of this pair of red acrylic pillow towels by the way."

At that time, I had already published many articles in the Kailuan Miners Newspaper. Then, I also kept posting in Tangshan Labor Daily, the municipal party committee organ of the prefecture-level city. The repeated submissions prompted me to put the in China Coal News. As a result, the manuscript was published in the 1 edition of China Coal News in July 1985. I was so happy when I saw the newspaper, because it was published in China Coal News, which is published nationwide. So I called my cousin who was working in Kailuan Mining Bureau at that time and said, "Eldest brother, look for this day's China Coal News. There is my manuscript on the 1 page. This newspaper will be shown to my father when you take a break." It was Sunday off again, and I pretended to be fine and didn't tell my dad anything. After dinner in the evening, my sister whispered to me: "Dad said that your brother's wilted is still in, and it was published in the 1 edition of China Coal News published nationwide..."

Since then, while insisting on news writing, I began to create literature again. In July 1989, my documentary short drama "Tragedy" won the "China's First Miniature Works Editing and Publishing Exhibition" Excellence Award, and the short novel "Ugly Husband" won the award at the Hainan Provincial College of Literary Talents Correspondence.

In the 1990 s, I entered the peak period of prose poetry creation. In June 1992, my prose poem "Zhong Xia's Love" won the first prize in the "National Contemporary Literary Works Trial" held by the editorial department of "Contemporary Literary World" in Hainan Province. The "Thousand Chinese New Poets" series edited by Fang Mengquan has also been reprinted by Tianjin Economic Broadcasting Station, "Tangshan Group News" and other media. In 1993, the inaugural issue of the school magazine "Window" of Shaanxi Youth Self-study University, the special page published my award-winning prose poem "Midsummer Love" and my creative talk "Let the light of Love shine in the article", and add editor's note.

Since then, literary creation has been unacceptable. Works are often published in newspapers, magazines, and radio stations at different levels from the country to the local level, or included in literary works albums or awards. In 1993, my prose poem "Midsummer, do you to see the sea? "You have occupied me" was also published in the fifth and seventh issues of "World Prose Poetry Writers" in Hong Kong under British rule at that time, and won the "Prosperity Cup" World Prose Poetry Competition Award. My entries have also been included in the "List of Contemporary Poetry Lovers" edited by the famous poet A Hong (Wang Zhanbiao), the "List of Unnamed Writers and Poets" edited by the famous writer Yao Xueyin the main, and the "Collection of New People in Contemporary Literature" edited by the famous writer and poet Fang Mengquan and other dictionary books. In 1994, I finished the preparatory class for writers of the Chinese Department of Fudan University in Shanghai, and was given priority to be admitted as an official student of the Chinese Department of Fudan University in the.

In 2007 published "Chen Xin works", in 2009 printed "time echo", I in all levels of newspapers published more than 500 news works editing "New Year manuscript collection"; Join the Tang City Writers Association, Hebei Province Writers Association, China Coal Writers Association, China Prose Society ... All these, now think about it, all of this is really related to good teachers and friends. I remember one day in 1986, I was writing a manuscript in the propaganda department when my colleague said someone called me. I was 1 answering the gentle Mandarin, but I had never met Professor Mou Yunjiang from the Chinese Department of Tangshan Normal University. Professor Mou, who cherishes talents, told me in detail his home address, telephone number and asked me to come and sit at home. It turned out that Professor Mou read my short novel "Spring Plowing Smoke " from the "Miner Newspaper" and was very interested and asked to see me after several inquiries. I was both gratified and embarrassed. I felt that my level was low and it was inconvenient to climb higher. I declined several times. However, Mou always loves talents. Every times he a meeting of Tangshan Writers Association, he personally informed me to attend. In the long run, he became a good teacher and helpful friend for me to strengthen my improvement. Professor He Shuyun from Fudan University has also been guiding and encouraging me to study in the writer class of the Chinese Department of Fudan University. As a result, some famous artists have seen my works before they have a crush on me. Guan Renshan, a well-known writer and chairman of the Hebei Writers Association, when he learned that my "Selected Works of Chen Xin" was about to be published, he told me to my face: "After the book is published, 1 will send me a copy !" Mr. Tan Ge, a famous writer and vice chairman of Hebei Writers Association, was pleased to write these 1 titles for my.

All these achievements have also benefited from the enterprise's exercise and its own persistence. This also fully shows that on the road of growth, no matter what line of love, how to walk their own way, persistence is necessary. Persistence will make achievements, efforts will be rewarded, suddenly looking back, will be pleased with all the results obtained.

Mao Zedong in my heart

Dear friends, do you still remember September 9, 1976. Yes, how can the Chinese forget this painful day? On September 9, this is the 1 special feeling of the Chinese people. I was a middle school student at that time, and was busy rebuilding the campus after the earthquake. Suddenly, the sound of heartbreaking music came from the loudspeaker of the school radio. The old teacher waved to the students who were going to the room and Liang below, asking all the students to gather in the woods on the campus: "The great Marxist-Leninist, the Communist Party of China, the great leader of the Chinese people, and the mentor Chairman Mao Zedong, due to illness The treatment was invalid and died in Beijing at 0:10 on September 9, 1976..."

When the bad news came, every word violently shook our hearts of pure, persistent and loving leaders. The sound of mourning music up, and all the teachers and students cried and burst into tears. My heart was broken at that moment. Has Chairman Mao left us? I silently ask myself in my heart. Great grief surged, and I bit my lip, tears like water that broke the dike. I tearfully looked up at the gray sky, looking for the location of the great constellation...

A female classmate slapped the trunk and cried: "Chairman Mao, Chairman Mao, we have just climbed out of the ruins of the earthquake. The school has not been built yet. Why did you leave? Don't you see our rebuilt campus? ..."

One of my male classmates stood up suddenly and stepped on the ground with his feet and shouted, "Chairman Mao, we love you!" A female classmate who sat side by side with me was named Yang Heyun, a pungent girl who 1 heard this earth-shattering news and shouted 1 bitterly: "Chairman Mao, you can't go!" Then he passed out.

Yes, dear friends, in the 1970 s, the Chinese people loved Chairman Mao very much. Who can restrain this great grief? Especially those of us who survived the "July 28" Tangshan earthquake. We were born in a new society and grew up under China's first five-star red flag in five thousand years. We grew up singing "Dongfanghong. It was Chairman Mao who sent his relatives to the People's Liberation Army. saved Tangshan people from the catastrophe. Chairman Mao left us. How can we not be sad and cry?

The nation mourns the fall of the star. Mount Qomolangma weeps, the Yangtze River sobs, Hulunbeier weeps, and the Tengger Desert whine. In the days of saying goodbye to the leader, the factory could not hear the mechanical singing, the field could not see the tail smoke of the tractor, the barracks were silent, and the school was quiet. the of the mourning flute, the whole territory of China is a sea of mourning.

At this moment, the Chinese people, who are flying at half-mast, have turned their thoughts and grief for the great man into infinite strength, holding the belief that the four modernizations of the motherland must be realized, and the socialist road must go on! Friends, dear friends, have you not forgotten that this was the common aspiration of 0.8 billion Chinese people at that time. In our city, there are tall statues of Chairman Mao in several places. statues are far-sighted and powerful. The leader's style Fan still inspires and inspires hundreds of millions of Chinese people. Every year on September 9, I go to see his old man's house to 1 my grief and memory. On the occasion of the 48th anniversary of Chairman Mao's death, my feelings became stronger and stronger, and my thoughts became stronger and stronger. I once again came to stand in front of Chairman Mao's statue of. For a long time, I stared at Chairman Mao's tall and burly physique, thinking a lot...

Forty-eight years have passed, your brilliant thoughts are still shining, and the people's feelings for you remain unchanged. Chairman Mao, beloved Chairman Mao, you can perceive in the spirit of heaven: this is the prestige of leaders and the charm of great men! Chairman Mao, the people will not forget you, history will not forget you. China will not forget you, and the world will not forget you. you are still with the rivers, with the sun and the moon, life is eternal.

September 9, 4, 202

Dream, lit Phoenix tears

Deep night, made a deep dream, I in the deep river of unremitting excavation of ancient fans, looking for a long source of legends. (want to re-round and warm dream world) I found 1 crystal and translucent colored stone, but I don't know what it should be. I put it under a thousand-fold mirror, which failed to spread the beauty of the stone. I still can't the ugliness of the stone in the past when placed in front of the concave-convex mirror. I put the stone in the sun for a long time and stared at it without change. I concluded that it was just a stubborn stone. The heart moved again and used the condenser mirror to shine unremittingly. The slowly. The stone gradually expanded, expanded, stretched, and finally appeared: Mangyuan, Mao Lin, green mountains and beautiful waters, all things were prosperous, and feathers to celebrate the prosperous times. Suddenly, the sky fell apart, the earth shook, and the Siberian volcano exploded and spewed in historical times. The mountains and rivers were filled, the blocked and the rivers, enveloped the atmosphere, suffocated, suffocated, Baiyu looked up at the phoenix in the struggle, the phoenix fluttered its wings and Li Shuai Baiyu broke through the chaos, but finally exhausted and shed miserable and hopeless tears. tears reflect the desolation, struggle and solemn and stirring, into the volcanic ash, become an ancient amber.

Ah, this ignited the tears of the phoenix, showing prosperity, jubilation and tragedy, and bringing thinking and remembrance. It is said that dinosaurs also became extinct in this devastating volcanic eruption.

1989

Last night's stars

The evening breeze, I sat under the French phoenix tree in autumn, looking up at the bright stars, evoking endless reverie. This vast and deep sky, ah, how many heroic hidden, how many new celestial bodies gave birth, how many vicissitudes of life to see, how many fission polymerization. This vast and infinite starry universe, ah, makes me search up and down, makes me think.

1 a meteor streamed across, trailing its tail and disappearing into the far-reaching night sky. No one knows if it has regrets and wishes. Its fleeting, who knows where it goes, its secret, its joys and sorrows.

The vast sky, the wind and clouds change, the sun and the moon shuttle, the light and dark crisscross; the sun shines, the stars flow; the endless landscape, the endless phenomenon, the endless new discoveries, this is the reciprocating of life, all hope, but also the root of pain.

Looking at the sky full of stars, I think of the ancient new, last night's tonight, the lost future-stars. They have or do not have love, hate, grace, resentment? With or without confusion, confusion, hope? Oh, there is, mixed chaos is hazy, explosion is separation, movement is the birth of combination. All things are the same, there is attraction, there is a combination, there is gestation, there is death ... Last night the stars with all this left, tonight the stars with all this existence.

1989

That year, I donated songs to the disaster area at the Central People's Broadcasting Station.

It was the summer of 1991, when serious waterlogging occurred in Jiangsu, Anhui and other southern provinces. At that time, I was working in the grass-roots trade union of fangezhuang mine of Kailuan Mining Bureau, and I was very concerned about the news. Looking at the screen every day was floods destroyed by the long embankment, fertile fields, villages, can not help but tremble in my heart, more can not help but recall the July 28, 1976, Tangshan earthquake ... 1 kind of sympathy for the, sympathy, support, encourage the affected people's mood arises spontaneously. So I wrote a letter to the "8:30 Tonight Program" of the Central People's Broadcasting Station that I like to listen to, and sent some money, asked to transfer the program to Jiangsu Province, which was the hardest hit by the disaster, and ordered a song for the people in the disaster area. song.

One night 1 weeks later, at 21 o'clock that night, the clock on the radio had just rung, the famous announcer Ya Kun, the host of the Central People's Broadcasting Station,. The solemn and kind voice came from the radio. It was sent to my ear: "Comrade Chen Xin, who works at Fangezhuang Mine of Kailuan Mining Bureau, I wonder if you are listening to our' 8: 30 Tonight Program '. We have received your letter and the remittance to the people in the disaster area, and we will reply to inform you of the handling situation. Here, on behalf of all the comrades in the "8:30 Tonight Program" group and the people in the disaster area, I would like to thank you and play you a song "Dedication of Love" sung by Wei Wei. Please listen with the national audience."

The song sounded, my heart 1 a surge of heat. "As long as everyone gives a little love, the world will become a beautiful world..."

Yes, the world needs love, everyone needs love, everyone has love. As a Tangshan person who has been robbed a major earthquake, a Tangshan person who has received the love and assistance of the people of the whole country, and now a Tangshan person who is helping others, how can this song not be surging? I think that this emotional song must also move and inspire the people in the disaster area to fight and save themselves, and move and inspire all people to give love. In particular, I wrote down this unforgettable moment −21 o'clock on July 23, 1991. Since then, every time I hear the song "Dedication of Love", I always have a different feeling feeling in my heart.

August 20, 1998

Destiny

    I wonder if you could have had such a moment. You, who have long been by the world, your career is bumpy, your bumpy and bumpy collision, and your is exhausted. Like swimmers who are tired and, you would like to find a soft beach and carry it on your back., you would like to a long breath and sigh that people live too tired. This short road of life, you catch up step by step, but step by step, and then appear difficult, lamenting the fate of bad.

    I 've had moments like this. I don't smoke. I don't have the situation of being in the clouds of smoke. I often sit alone in front of the writing desk by the window, looking at the blue sky and clouds outside the window. I envy the carefree, vast, bright and rotten. Unconsciously, the French romantic piano prince Richard Clayderman's heart−shaking "Destiny" piano music echoed around his ears, and he unconsciously pressed the playback button of the combination sound. Suddenly, the space around me was all haunted by the three−dimensional, deep and sonorous melody−Knock Knock Knock Knock Knock... Knock. After that, you will feel bright, smooth and prospective with the relaxation of the rhythm, and even remember the that cannot bear to look back. Finally, you will stop to fight the firm and powerful melody and feel excited. Then, 1 a kind of young ambition not to worry about the feelings of leisurely and rose, stood up and pushed open the window sash, looking at the long sky, thinking that after thunder and lightning flash is not a long haze; After spring, it is not autumn. Only when the mountains are steep can the elegant demeanour of explorers appear. Only when the waves turn over can the show the breadth of the sea. So 1 is a kind of broad and broad filled with your mind, 1 is a kind of vigorous self−confidence filled with your heart, 1 is a kind of bold and unrestrained fearless to make your mighty.

At this moment, you will realize—fate is fighting, the rudder of life luck is in your own hands, only fighting can make progress, and only continuous progress is the meaning of life.

4 January 2003

Conceive a piece on the train

Going out by car is a chore, 1 sitting is hours, even days and nights, monotonous and boring. But I occasionally found that this is a good time to write an article with an idea.

I remember it was the summer of 1984, and the leaders asked me to go to Chifeng, Inner Mongolia, to do business and leave that night. At midnight in Xinghe, the characters were all quiet and, and most of the passengers on the bus fell asleep, but I didn't feel sleepy. Suddenly, I remembered the 1 short story that I wanted to write some time ago, which reflected the life of miners. So I was inspired and began to conceive, the beginning, the end, the level arrangement, the theme, the thought... When I arrived at Chifeng, the draft came out, and named "Spring ploughing smoke ". When I went to the guest house, I immediately started writing, and it was well received after it was published in the "Kailuan Miners News.

Once I went to Jinzhou, it was drizzling. I sat in the seat near the window waiting for the bus to leave. At this time, 1 a couple under the top red and yellow umbrella reluctantly. The siren blew and the train left the station before the girl left the affectionately. These 1 scenes remind me of thousands of miners living in rural areas and even in other provinces. They have been separated from their wives and children for a long time, and only the annual family leave can be reunited. How deep is their love. When they set off to return to the mine, it is not difficult to imagine the feeling of farewell. Once there was a miner's family member, every year when her husband's family leave expired to back to the mine, she always sent ten miles away... Thinking of this, the inspiration came, the car to Jinzhou, the manuscript was completed, and the prose poem "Flute Sound" was written overnight, which was published in "Kailuan Miners' Daily".

As a result, a 1 habit has been formed, and new articles will come out every long distance. The documentary short drama "Tragedy" was formed on the train from Qinhuangdao to Shijiazhuang. The script won the Award in the first China Miniature Literary Works Exhibition Competition. The short novel "Ugly Husband" matured on the train to Taiyuan. After its publication, Hainan Correspondence College of Literary Talents awarded honorary certificates. The prose poem "How many longitude and latitude" was born on the train to Tianjin and was rated as an excellent work of China Cooperative Economic News in 1989. The short poem "Star of Happiness" was conceived on the train bound for Xi'an, was included in the book "Thousand Chinese New Poets", and won the Award for Outstanding Works of Contemporary Poets and Writers.

The idea of riding is a 1 kind of fun and a 1 kind of enjoyment. It has become an integral part of my journey.

20 June 1992

Mai Qiu, those who helped me

The wheat harvest in June 1985 was a golden wheat autumn that I could not forget. This Maiqiu, the second time since the establishment of the the People's Republic of China, has confused me and made me meet many kind-hearted people.

In February 1985, my mother's throat was always abnormal, and she always felt wrong when talking or eating. By the, several hospitals in our Tang Mountain had been checked. Perhaps the medical equipment and technology were not up to standard at that time, and they could not be diagnosed with any disease. Everyone suspected that it was throat cancer, and my mother was under great pressure for this. But up to now, I still remember clearly that in the end, the 1 doctor Chen from Kailuan Hospital suggested that we go to Tianjin General Hospital to check 1. It was already May.

I have five children in my family. Among them, two younger sisters and one younger brother are in school. For several months, I have been running between work and hospital for my mother to see a doctor.

At that time, I was the head of the propaganda and reporting team in the propaganda department, and our state-owned enterprise with more than 10,000 people was still one of the few advanced communication and reporting units in the industry. I'm a strong man, I'm afraid I'll delay my work. In order not to affect the continuity of this work, I explained to the minister that my family was in the countryside, and my mother had to go to Tianjin General Hospital when she got sick. My father raised more than 100 laying hens, and there were still a few acres of land close to Maiqiu. The actual situation put forward the requirement of grassroots work under the to alleviate the leaders' worries about the work. The minister looked at me and said with a smile, I am also an elder at home. I know that it is not easy and hard to be the eldest. I will take care of the work. You can contact Tianjin General Hospital with confidence. How good such a leader is. I deeply realize that it is good to meet a good leader at work.

A colleague of mine approached me when he heard about it and asked, "Is there any connection to Tianjin General Hospital?" "No." "Well, let's see. One of my cousins is a department director there. I'll write you a letter and take it up to find her." In this way, with expectations came to Tianjin General Hospital. "Cousin" is very kind to help us before and after, that is, with the enthusiastic help of "Cousin", through a series of examinations, the mother's condition quickly became clear, it turned out to be a vocal cord polyp, but it had to be removed. In the examination and treatment of my mother's disease, my leaders, colleagues and "cousins" can be said to be my mother's nobles.

At the sight of Mai Qiu, my father sold all the chickens laying eggs to Wanlixiang Roast Chicken Shop and came to Tianjin Hospital to accompany my mother.

Sitting on the train home from Tianjin, I looked at the endless golden wheat waves outside the car window and thought about the wheat in the fields home. I felt a little puzzled, because I had never done any real farm work when I walked out of the school gate and entered the enterprise gate, but I had to do it at this time. At that time, the farmers were very hard, because there was no wheat harvester, and all the wheat was cut from the ground 1 sickle, then loaded into the truck and pulled into the wheat field to thresh with the wheat beater, and then dried on the ground, which was time-consuming, labor-consuming and laborious. I remember that Tie Ning, the chairman of the Chinese Writers Association, once wrote 1 novel called "Wheat Straw Stow", which described the busy of Nong Village, Maiqiu. The next day I was about to go down to the field with my two sisters to cut wheat. just as I was about to go out, 3 of my buddies came into my unit: "eldest brother, our brothers are here to help you cut wheat." Looking at the brothers, my heart a warm. At this point, really good brothers don't say anything. It was the arrival of the brothers that really gave me hope and strength.

The mother and father in the hospital were also thinking about the wheat at home, and the mother hurried back with the throat. When father mother returned home to see the harvested wheat, my heart was at ease...

Annual spring and autumn, annual wheat harvest. At present, it is the wheat harvest season again. Watching large wheat combine harvesters shuttling back and forth across the earth in the wheat field, they are busy harvesting wheat, eating large golden wheat straw ears, but pouring the river of wheat grains flowing into the car hopper of the same trade. It is really time-saving, labor-saving and labor-saving, and all the processes are and. Every time at this time, I feel full of emotion: mechanization is really good, agricultural modernization is really good, and today's era is really good.

Suddenly looking back, this wheat harvest has been more than 30 years. Looking back at that time, I had some pressure both psychologically and ideologically. Because my mother's illness suddenly came, and I didn't have any experience in farm work, I was really afraid. I had to do everything crustily. But through this matter can use two words: "thank you, thanksgiving." Thank you, this wheat harvest has trained me; thank you, Dr. Chen, my minister, colleagues, "wife-in-law", workers, you are all warm-hearted and good people in the world. Dr. Chen, my minister, although you have passed away, I have always remembered you deeply in my heart. Colleagues, "cousins" and co-workers, you are like my brothers to help me through the difficulties. I wish you a happy life and good health.

June 15, 2016

Writing, a writer's precious way of life

A Dream of Red Mansions, which ranks first among the four classic Chinese classics, is a human novel with world influence. It is universally recognized as the pinnacle of Chinese classical novels. It is an encyclopedia of Chinese feudal society that integrates the great achievements of traditional culture. There are not only Tibetan, Mongolian, Uygur, Kazakh, and Korean translations of "A Dream of Red Mansions", which has a circulation of millions in China, but also more than 20 English, French, Japanese, Korean, Russian, German, and Western languages. The selected translation, the translation, and the full translation of "A Dream of Red Mansions" have long become the common spiritual wealth of the people of the world. The 1910 edition of the British Encyclopedia praised: "A Dream of Red Mansions" is a very advanced work, its plot is complex and original. In 2014, the British "Daily Telegraph" published the "Top Ten Asian Novels in History" ranking, and "Dream of Red Mansions" ranked first. In France, which translated the Chinese Yuan song "Orphan of Zhao" as early as the middle and late 17th century, literary critics praised Cao Xueqin for his keen vision, high degree of compassion, quick intelligence and humor, and profound insight and reproduction. The ability of all classes of society from bottom to top.

In the Qing Kangxi and Yongzheng dynasties, the three generations of the Cao family and four grandchildren who had been weaving in Jiangning for 58 years made the Cao family very prosperous. As a teenager, Cao Xueqin experienced a rich and prosperous aristocratic life in Nanjing. The Cao family was confiscated in the sixth year of Yongzheng (1728) because of a deficit. The Cao Xueqin family moved back to Beijing. After returning to Beijing, he once worked as a poor in charge of literature and ink in the "right-wing school" of 1 royal schools. He was in a poor situation and had a difficult life.

In the preface to the first paragraph of the first chapter of "A Dream of Red Mansions", "The Author's Self-Cloud", Cao Xueqin stated that he wrote this book based on the prosperous old dream he experienced in Nanjing in his early years. Because they are living in the western suburbs of Beijing, they are mediocre and accomplished nothing. Facing the leisurely life in the countryside and the scenery is pleasant, recalling all the girls in Cao's mansion when they were young, they feel that their knowledge and talent far exceed their own, and they can't help but deeply and regret. The ancestors worked hard to create this family business. They were in good fortune, but they did not do their jobs properly and did not obey the discipline of their parents and teachers. As a result, they had no skills when they grew up and were down and out for half their lives. The family life in the past is fresh in my mind, everyone has experienced everything, Cao Xueqin, who is modest and ignorant in learning, is unwilling to Jia's government, and everything about his master and servant is annihilated. And this thought, rippling heart, all difficulties are not to mention, Wen thought spring, write like god will this experience and repentance in the vernacular into a novel.

In his later years, he moved to the western suburbs of Beijing and lived a poorer life, "full of penghao" and "family eating porridge". A Dream of Red Mansions was created by Cao Xueqin in poverty. The creation period was from the early years of Qianlong to the thirty years of Qianlong (1737–1765). It is during this period of poverty that Cao Xueqin has added infinite enrichment to the hard and suffering life because of the writing of "A Dream of Red Mansions", and has left a huge cultural heritage to later generations and even all mankind. It has also been in the field of world literature for 300 years. Won unique praise.

The first edition of Tolstoy's novel Anna Karenina was published in 1877. The of Leenin, who led the Russian revolution, read it so repeatedly that it wrinkled the cover. He said: Tolstoy can ask so many important questions in his works, and can achieve such great artistic power, which makes his works occupy a first-class position in world literature. "Anna Karenina " caused "the 1 real social explosion" in Russia of that era. Each chapter of it attracted the attention of all levels of society, as if it were about the most personal issues involving individual. It is recognized by the whole society as a great work, and it has reached a height that has never been reached in the of Russian literature. The writer Dostoevsky commented excitedly: "This is a perfect masterpiece of art. There is no similar thing in modern European literature that can be compared with it!" He even called Tolstoy the "god of art".

In 1870, in the 1870 s, Tolstoy saw the invasion of the Russian countryside by capitalist forces, witnessed the development of activities such as "going to the people", and planned to write a novel about a married woman from a higher society who had lost her feet, and planned to write a pitiful and innocent woman.

In 1872, at a place 5 from Tolstoy's farm, there was a woman named Anazkova. When she found out that her lover had another new love and proposed to her son's governess, she took some to change laundry clothes and went to Tula in a fit of pique. Later, she returned to the village and resolutely threw herself under the wheel of a truck and died. Tolstoy, who witnessed this drama, was deeply touched. So he started writing in 1873 and finished writing Anna Karenina in 1877.

In his writing life, Tolstoy, a parasitic aristocrat living in the countryside, carefully observed and recorded the fierce collision between the rapid collapse of the feudal serfdom of the Russian, the increasingly corrupt and degenerate thoughts of the feudal aristocratic landlords and the humanistic thoughts of the emerging bourgeoisie; he wrote about the rapid changes in the political and economic systems, ideology and moral concepts, the enlightenment of European bourgeois humanistic thought and the awakening of human nature consciously or unconsciously. People demand the liberation of human nature, freedom of love and autonomy of marriage. He frequently visited priests, bishops, monks and hermit monks, and got acquainted with farmers, independent believers • Kang Shustav, fully accepted the patriarchal clan system farmers faith, with perfect and harmonious art, in the epic style in the novel Anna • Karenina, it describes the social life of the countries in Russia and the restlessness of people's inner world under the impact of capitalism, and shows the characteristics of the times that "everything has turned over, everything has just begun to and arranged". It widely shows the Russian society in the period of the transition between the old and the new in the 1870 s. It pushed the critical realism of the 19th century to its peak and set up a towering monument. For more than 100 years, the great success of the writing of Anna Karenina has been continuously affirmed and respected by people. Its achievements and influence are undoubtedly unprecedented in Russia. This is also a full manifestation of the writer's writing life with half the effort.

Midsummer Love

I wandered alone on the beach, the sea breeze blowing, gently lifted my 1 wisps of forehead, like a few I added a few wrinkles. The sentimental waves at my feet, licking wet my shoes and trousers, and the sea surging with waves, looming memories of my past...

Midsummer, to see the sea? As if listening to you again. Yes, it was this romantic season. At the seaside, your songs were like a tide and your feelings were like the sea. the song sings, you expect Prince Charming to come head-on and wander to that distant place together. Therefore, and beautiful things are intoxicating, but they are bookish and do not pay attention to the meaning of drunkards...

Autumn leaves fall and the thatch opens.

It is the warm love in winter that makes the sea not frozen...

Midsummer, to see the sea?

The eardrum agitates all the way through autumn, winter and spring. Suddenly looking back, in the face of the surging ocean, in the face of the red men and green women, excited not to my joyful mood, to lure not a trace of a smile, raised his feet to stare at a loss...

You said I was a strong life. But before the binary equation of love, I was an imbecilar. After the tide ebb, I picked up the 1 gold shell, which you lost to me. Free and easy years have a it, only to wake up Eve emotion... and midsummer today, come to see the sea, I invite you to travel.

Look at the restless sea, the turbulent sea, the turbulent sea...

The sky is blue and, the sea is blue and. The sun is still shining, the beach is still shining, midsummer, here is a bright hope...

The article "Midsummer Love" won the first prize for poetry creation in the first national contemporary literary masterpiece selection competition held by the "Contemporary Literary World" magazine in 1993. Income "China's new poet thousand" series. Broadcast in Tianjin People's Broadcasting Station, "Window" and "Tangshan Mission News " reprinted.

In 1993, the first issue of "Window", the school magazine of Shaanxi Youth Self-study University, published "Midsummer Love" and "Let the Light of Love Shine in the Article" and added editor's note on the special page. Also because of this beautiful article, the author was invited to attend the symposium on the 45 anniversary of the founding of the people's literature.

Fudan University writer class, my heart forever Loulan

During the brilliant Han and Tang Dynasties, on the prosperous Silk Road between Asia and Europe, there was a beautiful and rich western civilization-Loulan, which still the soul of today's people. According to expert research, it is mainly due to man-made changes in the surrounding natural ecosystem and environment, which is one of the reasons for the mysterious disappearance of this beautiful country with its splendid culture. To this day, the old land of Loulan can still be visited, and the ancient land of Loulan has long since disappeared. Although I have long been a member of the Chinese Prose Society, a member of the Hebei Writers Association, and a member of the Tangshan Writers Association, the Chinese Department of Shanghai Fudan University Writers Class, just like this ancient Loulan, will always become the Loulan in my heart.

In June 1992, one of my prose poems entitled "Midsummer Love" won the first prize for poetry creation in the literary masterpiece selection competition held by "Contemporary Literary World" in

Hainan Province, and was included in the Hong Kong Jinling Publishing Company that year. The book "Thousand New Poets in China" published. At that time, the "Tangshan Mission News " also reprinted this prose poem, and Tianjin Economic Radio also broadcast this prose poem. The editor-in-chief of "People's Literature" at that time specially invited me to participate in the literary pen meeting for the 40th anniversary of the founding of "People's Literature" because he saw the prose poem "Zhong Xia Love. Therefore, in 1993, I signed up for correspondence study in the preparatory class for Chinese writers of Fudan University in Shanghai, majoring in poetry creation and emphasizing prose poetry creation. To this day, I still clearly remember that my instructor, Professor He Shu Yun, always carefully reviewed my poems and sent them me. The comments are full of teachings and true feelings, which have benefited me a lot. They have also stimulated and encouraged to work hard. The writing level of prose poems has improved rapidly. This, perhaps let the teacher frequency gratified. Later, I made my dear guidance teacher very sorry, but also let me feel more painful to miss the opportunity, regret.

It was July 1994. According to my study and writing in the preparatory class of Chinese writers in the Chinese Department of Fudan University in Shanghai, after strict examination, examination and selection, I was admitted as a full- student in the Chinese Department of Fudan University in Shanghai. My instructor wrote a letter to congratulate me and sent me the "Admission Notice for of the Writers Class of the Chinese Department of Shanghai Fudan University", "Registration Form for Students of the Writers Class of the Chinese Department of Shanghai Fudan University", etc.

It is not a thing that everyone can have a chance to go to a writer class in a famous Chinese university. I have published literary works of different genres and themes in the newspaper miscellaneous. Although I have made unremitting efforts, I still feel happy and days. But at that time, my family's financial situation could not support my studies, and my mood plummeted. To attend the writer's class, you have to go to Fudan University in Shanghai to study full-time and stay in apartments. if I go to school at my own expense and have no salary, my financial strength will be unbearable. With many contradictions in my heart, I still made a very irresponsible conservative choice after thinking about it-to give up this 1 rare opportunity to go to school for further study.

At the beginning of September 1994, the writer class of the Chinese Department of Fudan University in Shanghai began. Although I filled out and sent the form the students, people did not arrive at school. There is no doubt that the writer's class is looking for me, but also for my instructor to ask clearly. So, my instructor wrote to me, telling me about the beginning of the writer's class, asking why I couldn't come to school to study, and telling me that if I could come, I would come a few days later. At the end of the letter, he wrote politely: "If there are more satisfactory works in the future, you can still send them to me. We will always be friends." I can see that my teacher is full of infinite love and expectation in the silent and regret of the.

When I got home from work, I read the teacher's letter repeatedly. Then, I stood silently in front of the desk by the window, looking up at the sky, but my thinking seemed to be stagnant. For a long time, I pressed the playback button on the stereo. Suddenly, the space around me 4 was all haunted by the powerful melody of the famous piano piece "Destiny" played by Richard Clayderman, the French romantic piano prince. I stared out of the window at the sunset, dusk like blood. In September 1994, I regret for life. Now that I think about it, there are both subjective and objective reasons for the result of this incident, but the most important thing is that I did not dialectically put the's future and studies above the environment and time to think and observe the Chinese Department of Fudan University in Shanghai. The problem of studying in the writer's class. Therefore, I understand that there are not too many opportunities in life, so I should manage and grasp them well, because the rudder of fate is in your own hands.

Perception of Early Winter

After beginning of winter, on November 15, when you look at the 1 of the lunar calendar, it is light snow on November 22. The wind blows in early winter, needless to say, pine trees. There are still many leaves on poplar, willow, phoenix tree, maple and other trees in the city. Yellow poplar leaves and ginkgo leaves float one by one. There are also strings of horns of locust trees hanging between the green leaves in the Chinese leaves. Looking up at the sky, it was blue and still floating with a few clouds. I felt a little thin and cold. Downstairs, the lawn cut by the lawnmower at the end of autumn was spread out like a huge carpet, still with some soft and feeling of hair, some red, yellow, white, purple and rose flowers of various colors in the grass, still unwilling to give up the last 1 wisps of warm sun and blooming tenaciously in the sun. Clusters of western powder lotus red flowers are so eye-catching and affectionate and lively open. The willows weeping along the corridor are swaying in the breeze. On the south side of the small building, the leaves of plants covered with trees are still yellow, green and red due to the arrival of early winter, although some are dark, and still maintain the scenery of late autumn.

Time flies, but this can be said to be a deep autumn scene does not make people feel dilapidated and bleak. Blue sky and white clouds, sunshine, red flowers and green leaves, long willow brush shoulder. At such a time, the flowers are still in their final blooming, full of the desire for the continuation of life, stirring up life and rejuvenating, the frost the leaf rendering, red rippling, how can one not let one's heart sigh with emotion. Looking at the scenery in front of me, I can't help but sigh. It is true that all things grow on the sun. All life in this world will always fight for the day and night. All things in heaven and earth enjoy the sunshine, and their vitality will not be. Have a soft spot for survival, full of desire.

The early winter wind, which was not cold, blew again, bringing thick colors, deep maturity, and endless thoughts. The wind of early winter makes people feel the meaning of life, cherish the feelings of the past, take care of happiness today, and pursue a beautiful future.

Standing in the sky blue, white clouds, ginkgo golden, maple trees red, pine trees green, willow silk swaying sky and earth, leather slightly drum the wind of early winter, the fundus of the still late autumn scenery, feel stirring, mind. Let your thoughts be filled with thoughts of beauty. If the heart is in love, the sunshine in the world will be unbeaten, warmth and beauty the world will always be and.

November 15, 1999

Love is love yourself

"Only learn to love others, can learn to love yourself, others can love you; only learn to care about others, can learn to care about yourself, others can care about you". From the time the children were a little 1 and sensible, my wife and I taught our children, guided them and cared for them. Therefore, children learn to care for others from an early age.

I remember that when my son was just 4 years old, I bought a 1 125 Pearl River motorcycle when I was riding a 50 motorcycle. However, my wife is worried about the field and is most afraid of me riding a fast car. Therefore, every day before I go to work and go out, I say, "Slow down and ride ." I keep saying this day by day, and I remember it. Every morning when I pick up my helmet and want to leave, he follows me to the hall and says, "Dad, your motorcycle slow down you ride ."

Father and son nature, small children are so worried about me, can you not let me double like him? Originally, my son was very lovable, and I liked him even more from the heart he was so good. Every day before riding a bike on the road, my son also asked my mother to hold her to the balcony and lean out and say to me, "goodbye, dad. Come back early."

Riding in the car, I remember my son's words. Childlike innocence, although the words are simple, it is 1 true love and affection, can you not move me? It makes me feel really warm. People have feelings, and they will cherish every 1 of affection and love. What's more, this is the 1 true love of a young son? Therefore, when driving, I always carefully manipulate the gear shift, brake, accelerator, and steering of the motorcycle. Although it is a big car, it is never too fast. I would rather stop for three minutes than grab one second. Because, the innocent and lovely little son is concerned about my safety and looking forward to my early return home. My peace and will bring comfort and joy to his young heart.

"Dad, slow down your motorcycle." I often remember my son's words full of true love. When I come home from work every day, I always gently pick up my son and kiss him, so that the childlike innocence that my son misses will be kindly rewarded.

Now that my son has grown up, there is a big word "love" hanging head–on in front of the teaching building of his school. The great education of "love" may be consistent with my way of education. Sometimes when I am at home, my son often says to me, "Dad, you taught me right. Only love others, to love yourself, others will love you; only care about others, will care about yourself, others can care about you. I gave my classmates love and care, and what my classmates gave me was also love and care. I gave the teacher love and care, and the teacher gave me love and care. Love and care inspire each other, love and care warm us." This is what my son said, did and felt. Because of, my son has won the "Unity and Friendship Award" several times in school.

November 2001

Carry a ray of sunshine to do good

The first sentence of my country's traditional cultural work "Three Character Classic" is: "At the beginning of human beings, nature is good." The words of our ancestors are wise, and as a writer, I have no doubt about it. So, always with good mind.

Good is everywhere. I remember that in the early winter of 1972, my father took me home from Tangshan by bike. When passing a stone bridge in a river, my father saw an old lady picking branches on the bank of the river. she accidentally fell down and rolled down the ditch where the was dry, but she never let go of her hands holding the branches. Dad got on the bicycle ladder went down to the ditch to help the old Mrs. asked her, "Why do you come out to pick up branches when it is so cold?" The old lady said, "There is no more coal at home in winter, pick branches to warm up the Kang." Dad didn't say anything after hearing this. He just took out two dollars from his pocket and said to her, "Go home quickly. it's cold, don't to freeze the. ." Afterwards, I asked my father, "my father helped the old lady up, why did he give her two dollars (two dollars were very useful at that time)?" My father said, "She is poor and hard to live. should help a little bit." I was impressed by my father's kindness.

one morning in the winter of 1988, I took the bus to work. The first bus was crowded. I never grabbed seats with everyone. I was always the last one to get on the bus. The car started and a female passenger called me to give me her seat. I said thank you, you sit, I will not sit. However, she always told me to let me sit down. I couldn't remember who she was 1, but she pulled me over and said, "Brother, do you still know me? Sit down and let me tell you that you are a great patriot of our family... "It made me look at a car full of people, and I was quite upset at that time. I had to sit and listen to her. It turns out that there were also teahouses in the town where I lived when I was a kid. Every morning, my parents asked me to go to the teahouse to have a 1 kettle of boiled water. For 2 cents, the hot water for the family to brush their teeth and wash their faces is enough. One morning I was waiting in line for to get water. There were four or five people in front of me. At this time, 1 woman walked nervously into the teahouse and anxiously asked the people in front of me to let her add a plug-in 1 pot, saying that the child was waiting for boiled water in the hospital, but no one asked her to add plug-in. It's my turn. I said you should call first. She immediately connected the thermos, said thank you three times after the fight, and then went back to the hospital with a jolt. She said: "You let me beat those 1 pots of boiling water first, and saved my son's life... Your appearance has not changed, and you are still the same as when you were a child, so I recognized you at a glance, you are a very good person." I was 9 years old that year, and after 20 years, I didn't think she still remembered me. When she's finished, I really think that in this world, if you do something good for others, they will remember you for a lifetime. It is this incident that deeply touched me and made me firmly insist on doing good deeds. The starting point is very simple, that is: "help others!"

I remember that it was the summer of 1991. Serious floods occurred in southern provinces such as Jiangsu and Anhui. I looked at the TV screen was ravaged by the flood of the long embankment, fertile fields, villages, can not help but tremble in my heart, can not help but recall the July 28, 1976 Tangshan earthquake ... 1 kind of sympathy for the, sympathy, support, encourage the affected people the heart arise spontaneously. So I wrote a letter to the "8:30 Tonight Program" of the Central People's Broadcasting Station that I liked to listen to at the time, and sent some money, asked to transfer the program to Jiangsu Province, which was the hardest hit by the disaster, and for the people in the disaster area. I ordered a song.

One night 1 weeks later, the 21 o'clock clock had just rung from the radio. The solemn and kind voice of Ya Kun, the program host and famous announcer of China National Radio, was sent to my ear from the radio: "Comrade Chen Xin, I wonder if you are listening to our 8: 30 tonight program. We have received your letter and the remittance to the people in the disaster area, and we will reply to inform you of the handling situation. Here, on behalf of all the comrades in the program group at 08:30 tonight, I would like to thank you and play a song "dedication of Love" sung by Wei Wei for you and the people in the disaster area. Please listen with the national audience."

The song sounded, my heart 1 a surge of heat. "As long as everyone gives a little love, the world will become a beautiful world..."

Yes, the world needs love, everyone needs love, everyone has love. As a Tangshan person who has been ransacked by the earthquake disaster, a Tangshan person who has received the love and assistance of the people of the whole country, and now a person who is helping others, how can this song not be surging? The emotional singing must move and inspire people who fight against disasters and save themselves, and move and inspire people to give love. In particular, I wrote down this unforgettable moment −21 o'clock on July 23, 1991. Since then, every time I hear the song "Dedication of Love", I always feel a different kind of feeling in my heart.

In April 2016, the Tangshan World Horticultural Exposition kicked off. I was invited to organize a group of 11 writers, painters and calligraphers to gather the style of the Expo. One day at the World Horticultural Exposition, times to smell the world's fragrance. The flowers are fragrant and the sun is just right. For the world horticultural exposition splash ink painting, wielding calligraphy, inspiring words, writing articles.

We have thus set up a WeChat group "Writers and Artists Sunshine Art Garden". The original intention is to build a sunshine group, gather people who sunshine, create a sunshine atmosphere, and do things that sunshine. While carrying out cultural and artistic exchanges such as literature, calligraphy, traditional Chinese painting and recitation, they also engage in public welfare activities.

In the summer of 2016, some cities and counties in our province were hit by floods. Some writers and artists, members of Sunshine Art Garden, and I resolutely took to the streets to participate in charity sales and disaster relief activities in front of the department store in the center of Tangshan.

In order to stimulate people's patriotic enthusiasm and strengthen people's love for their families, I organized and planned a poetry recital of "Mid-Autumn Festival" on September 25 before the arrival of the ancient traditional festival Mid-Autumn Festival and the National Day of the People's Republic of China in China. Some writers, poets, painters, and calligraphers from various regions of Tangshan gathered in Fengnan Library to express the Mid-Autumn Festival in through the vast of the sky and the autumn wind.

On October 16, when my friend and I went to Qianxi Luotun to see our friends, we heard that a 12-year-old rural girl, Hongying, had myeloma. Her family borrowed 180,000 yuan for treatment and still had no cure. For this reason, my friends and I specially launched the and organized 1 charity charity sale and charity donation activities of "Thanksgiving Life, Set Sail for Love" to raise money to help small Hongying raise medical expenses for the second operation.

In our activity, I was deeply moved by 1 7-year-old girl who came with her mother. She even bought all her 1000 yuan lucky money on the spot. Everyone asked her why she bought all the New Year's money and calligraphy and painting. She said: "I just want to add more money so that my little sister can be cured quickly."

On November 12, 2016, I visited the local people in the old revolutionary base areas to learn about the living conditions of farmers on the spot.

We climbed the mountain and traveled more than 30 miles back and forth, and successively visited several mountain villages such as Pang Zhuang, Liu Zhuang, and Chai Jiawan. As you can see, beside the clear riverside of the hometown and the beautiful Yudai Mountain, it was once a base for eastern Hebei to fight against the Japanese invaders, and the people here have a revolutionary tradition of diligence and courage. However, the living of the people in the mountain villages is not rich. For this reason, everyone also brought rice to the poor households.

In order to stimulate people's confidence and spirit to move forward, on December 18, 2016, which is coming to an end, I launched a large-scale public welfare performance of "singing tomorrow" jointly organized with Fengnan District Cultural Center, so as to stimulate people's yearning for a better life and a better tomorrow, and to move forward with high spirits and full spirit.

Sunshine people, sunshine atmosphere, sunshine heart. Since the establishment of "sunshine art garden for writers and artists" in 2015, sunshine people have been working hard and making progress. While participating in social welfare activities, everyone strives to participate in various literary and artistic activities. Literary works, calligraphy works, and traditional Chinese painting works of various genres and different contents are published in municipal, provincial, and national newspapers and magazines, and are at different levels. The rankings and results were obtained in the competition. More than 26 people published a edition to a special collection of personal literary works. recommend 1309 people have successively joined the Chinese Prose Society, the Chinese Poetry Society, the Chinese Coal Mine Writers Association, the Hebei Writers Association, the Hebei Artists Association, the Hebei Poetry Society, the Tangshan Writers Association, the Tangshan Musicians Association, and the Tangshan Calligraphers Association, Tangshan Artists Association, Tangshan Poetry Society, Huaxia Fine Short Literature Society, etc.

The sky is long and the world is full of love. Although my strength alone is insignificant, I will firmly take the road of combining literature, traditional Chinese painting, calligraphy, reading, singing, performance, dance and other art exchange activities with public welfare, and do my best to bring a of sunshine to the good, extensively unite more people to offer their talents and love, merge into the tide of public welfare, and help more and people enjoy the warm sunshine.

18 January 2024

The fourth series of different feelings

Let the light of emotion flash in the article

Articles, especially lyrical works in literary works, if the author has no true feelings for something, then he cannot write a good work. This is a experience I got through the study and creative practice of Shaanxi Youth Self-study University.

Before I took part in self-study, I mainly wrote news articles or short novels for newspapers. After graduating from 3 years of study, I devoted myself to my own creation. I to write short poems, novels, essays, prose poems, etc., and sometimes I also wrote some for radio, television and newspapers. In daily life, often some things make me produce joys and sorrows, this phenomenon is reflected in the literary works constitute the basis of lyric. For example, when I was on a business trip to Jinzhou, it was drizzling. I was sitting in the seat near the window waiting for the departure. At this time, a couple under a red and yellow umbrella was reluctant to part. The 1 whistle sounded. The train left the station. The girl watched the lover on the train slowly leaving with the train affectionately. These 1 scenes reminded me of thousands of miners living in the countryside or even in other provinces, who had long-term, the family leave once a year can be reunited. How deep their love should be. When they set off to return to the mine, it is not hard to imagine the farewell to their families.

Once there was a miner's wife, every year when her husband returned to the mine after the expiration of the family leave, she always to send her husband ten miles... Thinking of this, the inspiration came, the car to Jinzhou, the manuscript was completed, and she wrote the prose poem "The Sound of the Flute" overnight, published in the "Kailuan Mine Workers Newspaper", in which she wrote the love lover's farewell and psychological state.

In the early summer of 1991, I came to Beidaihe seashore, but I was touched by the scene. I remembered 1 girl who had loved me deeply and. It was on this beautiful seashore that she showed her heart to me, but she did not get her wish. A dream of rose color, she was distressed, because she had secretly loved me for two years. Dream hard, for a spoony girl is a great blow. She hates her incompetence, she hates me incompetence, she hates me heartless, why do people have love and affection! For the sudden awakening of love, it can be said that 1 is a kind of consciousness. When I realized the true meaning, 1 was a good taste in my heart, and I felt guilty, which prompted me to write the prose poem "Midsummer Love" to show my feelings. The first draft is entitled "It's midsummer. Do you to see the sea? Published in the fifth issue of "World Prose Poetry Writers" in Hong Kong in 1991, and later "Midsummer Love", which was polished and renamed by, was included in the book "Chinese Poetry Dictionary" and the book of Thousands of New Poets in China. It won the first prize of poetry creation in the literary masterpiece selection competition organized by Hainan Contemporary Literary Magazine in 1992, and was successively selected and broadcast by Tianjin People's Broadcasting Station Economic Station, "Tangshan Group News.

Through these, I feel that writing with true feelings is the foundation of a beautiful article.

This article is a discussion on the creation of the prose poem "Midsummer Love", which was published in the journal "Window" of Shaanxi Youth Self-study University.

Tracing the Origin of 5 Chinese Surnames

According to the latest research results of Mr. Du Ruofu, a researcher at the Institute of Genetics of the Chinese Academy of Sciences, the 5 with the largest number of people in China today are Li, Wang, Zhang, Liu, and Chen. The culture of surname is an integral part of the culture of our ancient civilization. The origin and evolution of surnames are complex and diverse, generally related to ancient feudal states, official names, numbers, nature, utensils, colors, and days, stems, and branches.

The first ancestor of the surname Li is Gao Tao, a descendant of Emperor Shaohao. Gao Tao was the judicial director of Yao's–Dali. During the Shang Dynasty, Gao Tao's descendant Li Zheng was executed for law enforcement and offended Zhou Wang. Li's wife and his son Lizhen escaped. It was the season when plums were ripe and. The mother and son, who were hungry and free of choice, ran all the way to keep their alive with plums full belly. After the disaster, in order to thank Li for her kindness, the mother and son changed their surname Li to Li, and from then on they had Muzi's surname "Li.

There are different opinions on the origin of Wang's surname, and various materials are different.

One came from Ji's surname, after Bi Gong, the 15th son of Zhou Wenwang, Gao. One comes from Gui's surname, after Yu Shun, the emperor. The other is from's surname, after being the prince of Shang dynasty.

Zhang's ancestor should be the son of Shao Hao-wai.

When he was a child, he wielded knives and guns, and he was extremely smart and brave. He invented the most important weapon in ancient wars–the bow, and was therefore named "Bow Zheng" to supervise the manufacture of bows and arrows, and his surname was Zhang.

Liu said there was a 2. The theory originated from Qi.

Emperor Yao's surname was Yi Qi. One of his descendants took Qi as his surname and was sealed Liu. Therefore, these descendants took Liu as his surname. After the death of Duke Xiang of Jin, the son was still young, and the courtiers appointed Duke Xiang's younger brother Yong as the king, and sent 1 people to the of Qin to pick up Yong and return to the Jin, the widow of the of Nangong Miao Ying crying every day, making the ministers at a loss, only to make Prince Yi Gao the king. Zhao Dun, the ruling minister, also had to lead the army to stop Yong from the Qin Hui Jin. The Qin army who escorted the Yong Hui Jin saw this unjust thing, and met with each other. However, after losing the battle, the would also flee to Qin with the Qin army. A few years later, he returned to the of Jin to work as a taxi club, but left his home in the State of Qin, and later became the Liu family–meaning "stay".

Chen's ancestor should be Shun. Before Shun became the son of heaven, Yao married his two daughters. His descendants lived along the riverside of Gui Ne in, and took Gui as their surname. King Wu cut down Zhou and destroyed Shang, and sealed Gui Man, a descendant of Shun, as the of Chen Hou, and his domain as the land of ancient Chen State. Later generations took Chen as their surname.

April 26, 1995

Collection of letters, don't have fun

I the of collecting letters, which was triggered by learning. In the past, I took part in the study of the University of Science and Technology and the People's Literature Creation Center. Every time the tutor sent back homework and comments, I always studied carefully and understood the true meaning from it. Over time, the number of replies from tutors increased. It suddenly occurred to me that this is the teacher's lecture record, which is of great benefit to keep, so I paid attention to collecting it.

My name was included in several lists because I went to school and often published and won awards in some books, newspapers and magazines. Then, some business, information, newspapers, publishing, solicitation, recruitment, free reading, pen and other letters have flown in. In this way, I have expanded the scope and content of the letter collection. At present, my letter collection can be roughly divided into study, communication, essay solicitation, pen notification, free reading, friends and poetry, friendship, love, family letter,, which is more than. It is precisely because these letters are in hand that some kind of emotion often comes up one day. When you are nostalgic for a certain period of time and feelings in the past, you will read the relevant letters for comfort.

In addition, you can easily check the correspondence addresses, postcodes, and telephone numbers of some provinces, cities, newspapers, magazines, and various friends. These letters are accompanied by my life, but it is also beautiful and fortunate.

29 September 1995

Reading

I want to read books 1 I am free. Most of the street is to go to the book market and bookstore, or read a book. I especially like to read history books, so I don't have time to read them 1, which makes my wife really angry.

It was a Sunday. I was reading local chronicles at home while boiling water with a fast heater. The thermos was placed behind the north balcony and plugged in the electricity to read in the south room. No, I forgot the water as soon as I read the book. It was not until I smelled the burnt plastic in the room that I suddenly remembered the water and hurried out to unplug the power. However, the rapid heater has completely burned out, leaving only two metal poles and the water has dried up. To make matters worse, I was stupid. I took 1 scoops and poured cold water into the thermos to cooling. It backfired. With a bang of 1, the thermos burst and the balcony was full of mercury glass fragments. Fortunately, didn't hurt me. At this time, his wife came up from downstairs. seeing this, she couldn't help but say loudly, "you are reading again. Well, I really can't. You forget everything when you see a book. Wow ". It can be said that his wife's words changed, "anyway, everything is broken. OK, I'll clean it up."

Another Sunday. At noon, my wife was stewing fish and suddenly called me to go to the store downstairs to get a bottle of vinegar. I ran down the floor and saw a book seller. hey, I forgot everything. I squatted on the side of the road and saw it. I don't know how long I watched it. my wife came down and stood behind me: "you are really rare! Let you buy vinegar and read." "Yo, my fault, I'll buy it." "I bought it a long time ago, I 1 thought you were reading it. Go home quickly."

When he came to the upstairs room, his wife brought fish and said seriously: "first, you burned my kettle and quick; second, you delayed me stewing fish, you did a lot of credit, say, what should I do today?" I see 1 my wife happy.

His wife added, "Well, in order to reward you for your mistakes, I give 1 beer. In the future, can't you 1 to read the book and be a mistake? "I nodded and said" yes ", secretly praising my wife's magnanimity and tolerance.

19 March 2001

Mountain Village Sunset

It was the turn of summer and autumn. I stayed in a small hotel in a mountain village on business. There is a mountain not far from the west of the hotel. In the evening, I walked to the mountain with my colleagues. In front of a high-lying rock, I saw smoke curling the house of the mountain people, yellow cattle and white geese, daiwa white wall, green trees sunset ... The sight is like 1 a quiet and leisurely beautiful beautiful traditional Chinese painting, which makes people taste endless.

Suddenly, my line of sight into a girl's beautiful image. But she on a right crutch and looked slender in a white black grid coat and a pair of cool-toned trousers under her. She stood on the side of the mountain, motionless staring at the sun and the brilliant sunset in the sky over the west. I don't know how long, when we walked down the mountain, she was still standing in place, her expression ten minutes of concentration and a trace of sadness.

We stayed in the hotel for 1 weeks. The weather was very good. Every day when we went up the mountain, we could see the girl watching the sunset. I can't help but wonder, why does she stand alone on this mountain road every day to watch the sunset? The writer's searching heart decided me to ask her why.

"Girl, the evening scenery here is very good." I said softly. The girl smiled at me and said with sadness a little, "The sunset here is good, and the sunset here is red." The girl held the small pine tree beside her and said, "I have been watching the sunset with it for 3 years." Speaking of this, the girl's eyes turned tears.

"Why?" I asked in surprise.

"one evening three years ago, the tractor that we used to pull mountain goods suddenly failed to brake and rushed down the mountain road. just when I was frightened and at a loss, uncle shan er who was sitting in the truck suddenly pushed me off the tractor. however, at the same time, the tractor, the driver and uncle shan er were all..."

After a moment of silence, the girl adjusted her mood and said, "at that time, I only had a fracture in my right leg, but the second uncle of lost his life in the valley. If it weren't for Uncle Shan, I wouldn't be standing here today. Therefore, the injury a little better, and as soon as I was able to get out of bed,

I planted this pine tree for Uncle of Mountain where the tractor rolled down the valley, and watched the sunset with it every evening."

I looked at the girl, the little pine tree, the valley, the sunset all over the sky. I didn't ask about uncle 2 the mountain. I only felt that the sunset was full of the mourning of the living for the dead, and the sunset was full of the hope of the dead for the living. Only think that 1 a pure human affection, sublimation in the sunset.

24 August 1997

I give dad a leaf ordinary boat

The advertisement on TV kept shouting every day: "My parents don't accept gifts this year. Which should I give platinum brain ." A pair of little dummy children jump on the TV screen and say this every day, which makes people annoyed and angry. I give gifts to my parents, but this year I just don't give platinum.

the age of 23, my news articles have been adopted by many radio, television, newspapers and other news media at or above the municipal level, and many literary works have been published. Once my father asked me, you wrote it all the time and also wrote a novel for me. At that time, I said confidently, "Write, that's hard to say." Several novels were published later. Every time my father looked at it, he always smiled. Last year, the Year of the Monkey, August 18 of the lunar calendar, was my father's 72-year-old birthday. At the banquet, I said to my father, "I want to give you a 1 gift when it comes to the New Year's Eve. Can you guess what it is?" Dad looked at me and couldn't guess. I said to send you a book, the name of the book is called "Chen Xin collected works". In the past, you have not read my published works one by one. This time, you can sit at home and systematically look at what I have written. This may be a comfort to you, dad you say OK? My father, who had suffered from cerebral thrombosis for more than ten years, touched his white hair and said, "Medium, medium." A few days ago, I finally sorted out some works through and computer. The cover design was simple and unpretentious.

A line of small characters was written on it: "The sea is flowing, and an ordinary leaf a small boat". The below the "Chen Xin Collected Works" in large characters.

On January 12, 2005, I printed and bound it into a book. At noon on New Year's Eve, I poured my father a 1 glass of wine, and then said to my father, "This color-printed and illustrated" Collected Works of Chen Xin "is for you as a New Year gift. It is the result you expect. You can watch it when you are free." Dad picked up the book and said, "Yes, yes, I have to have a good look." Looking at the rare happy appearance of my father since his illness, my heart was very relieved.

Idle Cloud Solitary Crane

Usually I have a hobby-go to the bookstore. In the afternoon, I walked into a bookstore and saw a CD called "going my own way" on the shelf in the video department.

I suddenly remembered that there was an introduction in the "Electronic News", but it was five years ago. This time I caught it and bought it without hesitation. Back home in the afternoon, immediately put in the CD player. When the music sounded, 1 was a feeling that I had for a long time against the. So I started to listen to it 3 4 times. It was not until my wife told me to eat that it came to an end.

I especially like the song "idle cloud solitary crane". The guqin music is supplemented by some western musical instruments, the arrangement of the music, the compatibility of the musical instruments, and the exquisite playing skills of the musicians, so that the desolate and poignant artistic conception in the music is reflected,, and transparent.

The rhythm and charm of the song make people feel so resentful and moving, just like a fairy music, with notes drifting in gently from the ears, and then slowly falling into the hearts of the appreciators, and 1 rippling streams flow through the whole body along the blood vessels, making people feel slightly cool and a trace of bitterness. The song is like a word from the graceful school, sorrow and, bitterness and loneliness; it is also like 1 prose to express homesickness, so you can't bear to let go and look; it is more like the 1 landscape scroll painted by the, in which the mountains and clear waters are painted, and the lone boat fishing alone ... Fully demonstrates the unique charm of the national musical instrument, the "Idle Clouds and Lonely Crane", but also shows the author's 1 unusual feelings. It makes people deeply understand the meaning of "don't plucking the string, complain about the extreme string can say.

Immersed in the artistic conception of the music, it is like seeing 1 old man who lives in a shack in the mountains but has the world in mind.

Listening to this song, it seems that the old man is sitting in front of you, telling you a and painful life course: when he was young and, he the cold window to reflect the snow and read all over the books. After going through hardships in the middle age, he was able to show his talents. Later, he was demoted and returned to Shan Ye because of the backfire. He even stood alone and lost everything. He was quite desolate and had no way to serve the country. After all, the old man's heart is quiet as autumn water but occasionally ripples. The old man's eloquent words come, the climax is exciting and surging, and when you are depressed, you feel disappointed, which makes you sigh for the old man.

The Lonely Crane in Clouds is like a clear spring of 1, purifying my complicated mood. In the past few days, the deep and inspirational sound of the guqin lingered in my ears from time to time, which made me know at the beginning of the exquisiteness of the ancient words "three days around the beam.

Outside the window, the sun set the, giving the world the unshackled light.

December 24, 2005

For the little girl on the other side of Castle Peak

On the morning of January 19, 2002, the sky was already bright at 6 o'clock. Guo Shiyin, driver of Kailuan Group Donghuantuo Mining Company's car team, has already driven on the way to Qianxi. This is a way for him to show his love and hope to the out-of-school children in the mountain village. He has driven more than once.

One day in early 2000, Guo Shiyin had just sponsored 1 poor students to attend Hebei University. He also heard that a little girl named Wang Yingchun was out of school in Qingshankou Village, Shangying Township, Qianxi County. So, drove more than 100 kilometers to the little girl's home to understand the situation. When she learned that the little girl dropped out of school because her father was sick and could not afford to pay the tuition, she felt a burst of discomfort. She couldn't help but take out 500 yuan and put it in the hands of the little girl's father, Wang Zhenfeng, and said, "Let the children go to school." In the days that followed, Guo Shiyin subsidized Wang Yingchun to go to school with 1,000 yuan a year, and often bought some school supplies and clothes so that the little girl could learn better. The party committee and trade union of Kailuan Group Donghuantuo Mining Company also paid attention to this matter. On this day, Li Dawei, deputy secretary of the party committee of Donghuantuo Mining Company, and Sun Yanbin, of the propaganda minister of the party committee, and Guo Shiyin drove more than 170 kilometers to Shangying Township, Qianxi County, located at the foot of Qingshan Pass of the Great Wall of China. A little girl named Wang Yingchun's home in Qingshankou Village sent the little girl two down jackets and schoolbags, pens, pens, pens, pens, paper and books to keep out. Li Dawei, deputy secretary of the party committee of Donghuantuo Mining Company of Kailuan Group, and other sat on Wang Zhenfeng's adobe kang, with the little girl and her parents who her, while learning about the little girl's study. When everyone learned that the little girl ranked in the top six among the 150 students in the second grade of junior high school this year, they were all happy for the little girl and her parents. Li Dawei earnestly told the little girl: "to study hard, there is no culture in the future, we should make further progress in learning, and strive to be admitted to key universities in the future." When the little girl on the bright red down suit bought for her by Guo Shiyin, Wang Zhenfeng and his wife said excitedly: "You said this, we had never known each other before, had no relatives for no reason, did not say how to subsidize school, and bought these for Yingchun. Yingchun said that we should repay the kind-hearted people with good academic results. To be honest, we are very grateful..."

When everyone got up to leave, the Wang Zhenfeng family had to leave everyone at home for dinner. Finally, Deputy Secretary Li Dawei said: "we will not eat meal. As long as the little girl's academic performance is good, it is the best reward for us and our greatest wish. wish little girl learning progress. By the way, I'd like to give you years earlier and wish your family happiness."

The family reluctantly sent the kind-hearted people out of the farmyard, and everyone drove back with their best wishes for the little girl and her family. The car gradually went away, but everyone left a piece of good hope and blessing for the little girl in the small mountain village, in the green mountains of Qingshankou Village carrying the Great Wall...

Poetry-my lover, my love

When I was still young, the poems of predecessors such as Ai Qing and He Jingzhi and the recitation of Mao Zedong's poems by teacher Xia Qing inspired my hazy love for poetry. After entering the society, I read and write poems, but I write novels when I fail to write poems. After the novels are published, I still write poems again. Published, won awards, and then realized that poetry-is the best way for me to express my emotions. Recalling these scenes, bitterness, joy, sweet and spicy came to my mind again, as if they were right in front of my eyes. Now, we can say that the spring of poetry has arrived. The open era has emancipated the mind and liberated the creation of poetry. Social needs to develop, the times need to develop, these developments, are accompanied by the prosperity and development of poetry.

The Chinese nation has made several brilliant contributions in the history of human cultural development. Today, our motherland is experiencing a 1 great rejuvenation, which requires a large number of singers the times. The tide of reform is stirring China's Shenzhou, and the of the times is full of calls and innovations.

Dear friends, the singing of the tide can't let the singers lead the, nor can we let those people of the moment go to the to show their romance alone. We should merge into the tide to develop fantasies, express romantic feelings, face the colorful sunshine, open up bright and set up rainbows, and let the dream of prosperous Tang Dynasty come true again!

Dear friends, the endless ocean tide ups and downs, is a good world to make the tide; look a long way to go, a long way to go. While we are full of passion, contribute to the prosperity of poetry.

China has a long history of 5,000 years. There is no period when there is no depression and melodious poetry accompanying the rolling wheels of history. The period of 1 without is not full of the poet's boldness, sadness, desolation and passion.

These are fully reflected in the works of the Book of Songs, Chu Ci, Tang Poetry, Song Ci and later times. Their worries come from the country's broken mountains and rivers, and the city's spring grass and trees are deep. Their boldness comes from the open Chinese sitting and watching all directions to congratulate them. Today, coinciding with the era of China's take-off, we should suck the rich nutrition of Chinese poetry, accumulate sincere love for the motherland, inject our creative heart, write gorgeous poems and chapters, and enrich the Chinese Garden of Eden.

Dear friends, October frost dyed Wanheavy Mountain, watching the red leaves of Xiangshan Mountain and sitting in the evening of Love Maple Forest. This is the season of maturity, this is the season of harvest, this is the season of poetry, let's pick up the pen, face the country of 5,000 years of poetry, dedicate the and persistent love of our, write the of playing songs of the times, depict beauty and write beautiful poems!

October 1989

Father and son deep

I am busy at work every day, and I go 1 for one day. Only in the evening do I have a 1 hot reunion dinner with my wife and son. It gets dark early in winter, and it gets dark at 5: 30 p. m. One evening when I got home, my son, who was watching a cartoon in the of the house, heard the sound and shouted that his father ran out. I picked up my son and kissed him. my wife was busy cooking, I felt relieved lying on my back in bed. My son sat on the sofa again and continued to watch cartoons. I closed my eyes and closed my eyes. After a while, my son turned his face and put his little mouth on my face and kissed me, then said, "Dad, why don't you keep your eyes open?" Listening to my son's questions after careful observation, I admired my son for his care and wanted to tease. So he pretended to be listless and said, "Dad is going to die." "Why did Dad die?" "I'm tired of making money for you every day." "I won't let you die!" "If you don't let me die, I will die." This worried his son. He stopped watching the pictures moving. He opened the door and ran into the north room. He lay on the bed and cried. The wife heard her son crying and ran into the north room from the balcony and asked her son what he was crying about. The son wiped away tears and sobbed, "My father said he was going to die!" Hearing this, the wife picked up her son and came to the south room and said, "your father is playing with you. do you think your father is happy!"

I was also busy saying, "son, dad is playing with you, good son, dad has a good son like you, how can dad die? Come on, dad hug." After some explanation, my son stopped crying and wiped his tears on my shoulder.

His wife blamed him and said, "The child only sees you all day long. He is so close to you. In the future, you should not the with the child." I think so, my son is less than 5 weeks old, and I go to work every morning before he wakes up, but my son son, even if he is still in the of the, he has to say 1 in a formulaic way: "goodbye, dad, come back early." But I have been looking forward to to stay with my father for a while until the evening. How can his young heart not suffer when he hears such words. On second thought, this is the of father-son affection.

March 31, 2000

Bitter and Happy Obsession Tao Poetry Heart

Five thousand years of Chinese civilization has created our country of ancient and great poetry. From "The Book of Songs" to "Li Sao", from Tang poetry to Song Ci, all are the pride and treasures of our Chinese nation. However, these bright flowers of civilization are like the fragrant white rice in front of us: "who knows that every grain of Chinese food is hard."

From ancient times to the present, there have been countless poets and lyricists of the Chinese nation, but in their beautiful poems that have been passed down through the ages, they are all soaked 1 the painstaking efforts of every hard-working author. In their arduous writing practice, they deeply the hard work of writing poems, and also appreciate the joy and comfort of the 1 when they get satisfactory works after the of mood into poetry and the of words.

Poet Liu Wei has a poem about "all through painstaking efforts, has proved that the former sages do not have the heart" of the search; Lu Yanrang wrote a "Yin An word, twist a number of stems and whiskers" of the contemplation; Li also said that "only the 5 word, with to break a lifetime of heart" a good bitter poetry heart; du Xun He obsessively wrote the poet's unremitting poem heart that "life should have no end, death is not the when chant. Jia Dao couldn't help but show the joy of "two sentences 3 years old, 1 singing and two tears flowing", which is like a child coming late. And monk to benevolence is full of a poem of complacence forget all worries: "every day is a poem of bitterness, who talk about spring and autumn; A couplet of is like a of complacence, and everything is forgotten."

Looking back at the Spring and Autumn and Warring States Period, the heroes competed for hegemony. Strong Qin and Han Dynasty, Tang Zong and Song Zu; A scene of prosperity, scenes of poetry. In the romantic feelings of three thousand feet of white hair and lofty sentiments rushing to the sky, sing about the ups and downs of the Chinese nation's, the ups and downs of the, and the bitter and happy feelings of poets writing poems also accompany among them.

Huan Mine Reading

Huan Mine, people say, you gave birth to fragile hope before you were pregnant. Indeed, you were planned by the state during the planned economy period, by the Kailuan construction during the reform and opening up period, and on the road of production and construction during the market economy period.

Huan mine, you once stood alone on the yellow land. Because of geological, hydrological, technical, financial and other difficulties, you once struggled to endure the pain before the "abortion. Thinking about it once made me teary-eyed.

Huan mine, see you tall and straight today. I want to say, you are like a bean sprout, weak and tortuous, and then a strong indomitable. From 1976 to 1994 (the mine was built on August 18, 1994), from the grand design with an annual output of 4 million tons, to the suspension of loans, to the mine production, after 18 years of eagerness.

Huan mine is an eagle who does not want to fly, but its feathers fail to plump its wings. Ready to go, in order to rush to the far ahead of the goal. Annual output of 500000 tons, 800000 tons, 1 million tons, 1.2 million tons, 1.85 million tons... but also to chase the glory of 3 million tons. Although this is only an ordinary step by step, you are a new force for Kailuan to become bigger and stronger. It heralds a majestic march that will be sung over the yellow land!

Huan mine, you give me endless imagination.

that 1 care.

tianqi111 is not normal, so that many people have a cold. Maybe I have a cold, too. I feel bad all over during the day, and even feel uncomfortable when I go home at night after dinner, so I went to sleep without even watching the news broadcast.

the wife, who did not notice in advance, tidied up the tables, chairs, bowls and chopsticks and came to the house to see that I was asleep before she felt something was wrong. Busy asked: "dude, do you have a cold?" I said: "may be, where are not strong." my wife was in a hurry, brought me cold medicine to eat one by one, and let me drink some plain boiled water, which was a lot more at ease.

At more than two o'clock in the middle of the night, I suddenly coughed badly. Not only did I cough and wake up, but also my sleeping wife woke up. wife quickly got up and poured water, and gave me some busy work. When I settled down, my wife sat by my bed and said, "How can I be good? I'm an old wife. I'm a wife who wants to treat you as husband's child and treat you as a child. I'm really worried about ."

The wife's words reminded me of the words in a book: the bride, since she married her husband, has replaced husband's mother-in-law to her duty of care and care for the. There is also a book that says: In fact, the role of a wife is twofold. She is both a wife and a mother. In the unconsciousness of daily life, she brings her wife's love and mother's love to her husband at the same time.

Think about it, the book is right. For this love, can not say that this love is precious, great.

Guansong, Jingzhongshan

I came to Jingzhong Mountain in Qianxi County to catch the temple fair, but the pine trees all over the mountain attracted me deeply. The only place I could see was pine. Whether it is steep cliffs, deep canyons, or small pavilions on both sides of the mountain road, the green mountains are all pine, and green has become the keynote of Jingzhong Mountain.

Walking along the forest path, the breeze in the valley mixed with the aroma of pine cones gently swept over my cheeks, making me feel the softness of the wind and smell the fragrance of pine. In the meantime, people feel detached, calm and relaxed.

The mountain wind blows slowly, bringing the vitality and beauty of the pine, as well as the gentle vitality of the wind. The strong spirit, and of the mountain are quite. Mountain wind pine day into one, making this picturesque scenery, people obsessed with intoxication.

A proud fairy rat pine, resolutely standing in the steep mountain road in a piece of only flat place, upright.

The tall canopy leans to the side of the stone steps, showing its characteristic noble green. There is no thousand-year-old pine comparable to it around it, only 1 groups of uneven small pine trees, looking up their heads, as if expecting its care. the fairy rat pine led the children to look down at the foot of the mediocre tree, with its tenacity against the glitz of the world.

Its robust root system, quietly embedded in the rocks, leaving the noise of the world, sucking the masculinity of the mountain, so that life can be uncompromising continuation. The green pine needles of the 1 are scattered and folded into the shape of a squirrel. From a distance, they look like 1 fairy rat with their tails cocked up and delicious food in, making people and love. The strong trunk of the tree makes people feel 1 a kind of proud wind, stepping on the green hills and the sky above their heads. With its tall, stand up the right path in the world to see the vicissitudes of years. I don't know how many years of wind and rain the fairy rat pine has gone through before it is as resolute as it is today. despite the of the mountain and the of the mountain and the strong wind, the root is still firmly planted in the crevices of the mountain. The trunk is still tall and straight. The crown is still thick and large, covering the and 1 sunshine for tourists, blocking the wind and rain in the, witnessing the summer and the bustling, and the bustling of the morning bell and the.

Yushan, Jingzhong, 7, 2003

The beauty of the miners is precious

In the history of human development, coal miners are the great power to create photothermal civilization.

In the colorful world, human civilization is also diverse, but human hearts are interlinked, and beauty can be together. The miners I have met in different coal mines in different provinces and regions have different backgrounds, local languages, respective qualities, and years of experience in the coal industry, but their desire for a bright, warm, happy, and peaceful life is There is no 2 difference. This can be fully demonstrated by their simple and honest smiles, eyes, and their friendliness to people. This makes me feel and more in other places, underground, on the mine car in the big tank, and in the karaoke canteen. It also makes me full of confidence and hope for the warmth, kindness, understanding and harmony between people.

Miners are pursuers of light and heat, excavators, creators and devotees. They enrich the world and illuminate people's hearts with their hard work, courage, kindness and wisdom, perseverance, sincerity and generosity, and with their hard work, black face, bright eyes, open and generous external beauty.

Over the years, I feel very relieved to be able to often contact and feel the beauty of different styles of miners. At the same time, I also sigh for the colorful beauty. The beauty of miners is precious.

On July 28, 1976, miner Li Yulin drove alone to Beijing to report the disaster of Tangshan earthquake to Chairman Mao of the CPC Central Committee. His actions made me feel the beauty 1 a kind of broad love and the beauty 1 a sense of national responsibility in an emergency.

In 1979, Liu Shaoyun, an underground worker named Liu Shaoyun in the fangezhuang mine in Kailuan, resolutely shouted, "I am a Communist Party member, you should withdraw first!" Everyone withdrew, but he had his kidney smashed. I was moved by his to save others. That's the beauty of a 1 hero.

On the morning of June 2, 1984, Ordovician fresh water, which had been sealed underground for more than 0.5 billion years, suddenly, with the mining surface the roof of the old pond, fell on the 2171 working face and surged out. At that time, the captain of the fourth fully mechanized mining team of Fangezhuang Mine often came. When organizing the working face workers to withdraw to a safe place to count the number, he found that the old worker Ceng Xianyi had not come up and immediately returned to the to look for it. When Chang came to pull Lao Zeng to the point where the underground water in the windward channel was, the gushing water column thicker than the waist blocked the way. At the moment of life and death, Chang Lai resolutely pushed Lao Zeng across the water column with both hands and shouted at the same time: "Lao Zeng, hurry up..." "Often... often... often... often..." Lao Zeng and the miners shouted at the top of their voices for thousands of times, and were swallowed up by the turbulent and cruel current. In order to save the miners brothers and sleep forever in the depths of the coal sea, I feel the beauty of the image of a front-line cadre in coal mine production who is selfless for the people.

All this, in the mine life on the road to hear the encounter there are still many beauty. There are miners who are bold and unrestrained, honest and trustworthy, beautiful and; there are pioneers and tunnelers who are determined to forge ahead and the beautiful; there are coal cutters who look focused and can control the iron horse knight beautiful; there are hydraulic support workers who indomitable, iron palm holding the beauty of the sky; there are miner lamp female workers smile like silver bell, body light beauty; there are young miners singing "Long live the miners" all the way...

Looking back on the individual and the things we have experienced, we taste different kinds of beauty, and deeply feel that these beauties are precious in the long river of life. I can't help but deeply thank those miners, who made me feel the beauty of miners in different places, different environments, different ages, different cultures, and different accomplishments, and urged me to write them down with a pen and record their beautiful life fragments. Looking at the miners walking in front of me, going down, working, living, drinking and singing... I sincerely wish them happiness and wish the mine full of beauty.

Mom made pumpkin flowers with salty food

The production team is undoubtedly an unfamiliar vocabulary for today's children, and it is also a distant era, but for the children of that era-we, there are also different memories in the young mind. Among them, I have a childhood memory can still bring me a good aftertaste.

In the era of agricultural production teams, farmers all worked in the production teams to earn their work points to support their families. The parents of rural children all to go to the fields to do farm work, and my mother was no exception.

When I was 5 years old, my mother had to go to work in the production team during the day. I had to stay at home by myself, but there was nothing interesting in the family at that time. every day a child did not fall at home (l ao), and the lively nature of the child had to disappear in loneliness. Therefore, whenever my mother wants to go out to work, I reluctantly drag her skirt and look at her with a small face. I am the eldest son of the first born in the family. Of course, my mother also misses me from the heart, but at that time it was for the sake of making a living. I always tell me that my children listen to my mother and come back from work my makes good food for you. But this will work for two days a day, and it will not work well 1 a long time. In midsummer, large crops such as corn and sorghum in the field need people to weed and fertilize. Labor is scarce and mothers cannot go to work. When my mother picked up the hoe and had to go to work for the next half day, I looked at my mother helplessly. I didn't want her to go. My mother coaxed me into doing nothing. My mother helplessly looked at the courtyard under the scorching sun in the south of the main room. Now that I think about it, my mother's love for her son and her hard work for life must have been fighting the fierce. It is this kind of psychological struggle, prompted the mother in a hurry. Son, do you see the pumpkin flowers there? Small I nodded. Mom gave you the salty food pumpkin flowers. you eat in the?? In. As a result, my mother quickly put down her hoe and ran to the south courtyard, pinched three tender yellow pumpkin flowers, washed 1 scallions, chopped them up quickly with a knife, beat the batter, put the spiced noodles and salt noodles (there was no chicken essence or monosodium glutamate at that time) and stirred them together. a firewood fire was lit under the big pot, and some oil was poured into the pot. when the oil was hot, the noodles were 1. A little while, with a shovel 1 turn, wow! oil yellow, fragrant 1 large pieces of pumpkin flowers salty food looks delicious. The mother shoveled the salty food on the plate and said, son, wait until it is cold to eat. After that, he picked up the hoe, locked the door and hurried to work.

Time flies, and decades have passed in a flash. Although time flies, the salty food of the pumpkin flower that my mother ate at a young age has always felt very delicious and fragrant. After getting married, I often think of this delicious food in my daily life, and I have asked my wife to share salty food to eat several times. However, the tender yellow pumpkin flowers cannot be found in the high-rise buildings in the city, so the salty food of the fragrant pumpkin flowers has never been eaten again.

Mother's kindness, childhood memories, delicious memories, has been wrapped in my heart and lingering. The other day, when I went back to my hometown to see my mother, I talked about it with my mother. My mother, who is nearly 80 years old, is still as happy as she was then to say that she will go out and pinch some pumpkin flowers for you, cut up scallions, put spiced noodles and salt noodles, and then spread out a large piece of pumpkin flowers for my son to eat salty food. On a hot day, another firewood was lit under the big pot in the main room. A little oil was poured into the same pot. The oil was hot. My mother still put the batter mixed with pumpkin flowers, scallion flowers, spiced noodles and salt noodles into the pot to spread the evenly as when she was young. A little while, with a shovel 1 turn, wow! It was 1 big piece of oil yellow, fragrant pumpkin flowers salty food, mother shoveled the salty food or on the plate and said, son, wait until it is cold to eat. However, this time I tasted the salty food of pumpkin flowers with my mother and recalled the scene of that year. It's just that the scene of my mother who spent her old age in peace picking up a hoe, locking the door and rushing to work is long gone. Japanese melon flowers salty food, childhood delicious, mother's love, forever in my heart.

Happy 5 August

"so bright a gleam on the foot of my bed, could there have been a frost already? lifting myself to look, I found that it was moonlight, and bowed their heads to think of my hometown." China's great reality romantic poet Li Bai's immortal poems, which have been passed down through the ages, have condensed the feelings of homesickness of many travelers, and have gathered more and less the expectations and staring eyes of relatives in their hometown.

It is human nature to think twice about one's family during the festive season. It's just that everyone misses different people. Every year in the section of the big festival, what I miss and miss most is my mother. It has been seven or eight years since my father died, and my mother is alone at home. My mother is 78 years old, but the old man has a good spirit, a good memory and a good body. With these good things, I am very satisfied as a son. Because the health of the elderly is the blessing of their children.

In China, most of the old people of their mother's age have experienced China's War of Resistance against Japan, the War of Liberation, the War to resist US aggression and Aid Korea, and 3 years of serious difficult, commonly known as "melon and vegetable generation." it has also experienced the Tangshan earthquake, the distribution of fields to households in the new period, reform and opening up, and the construction of a new countryside. With so many experiences and experiences, all of them are the precious spiritual wealth and life wealth of their generation, which also makes them open-minded, indifferent and emotionally accessible. Because they have experienced different periods of life and death, right and wrong, chaos and noise, truth reflection. I cherish my mother's experience and life, and respect my mother for people and life.

As a son, the only best reward for his mother is one word: "filial piety". Simple and clear, the way for people. As the saying goes: "Seventy has a home, eighty has a mother ." This is really true. A person from small to large, until the white hair, no matter when and where, the world's most miss you, or a mother. No matter when, my mother's heart caring and thinking about her son can't let go. This, I am quite feeling and experience. Therefore, I serve my mother sincerely and earnestly. Whenever I talk with my mother, I feel steadfast, happy and happy to see such a scene. Every time I go back to my hometown and sit on the kang with my mother and talk face to face, I always have to say to my mother: "mom my mother and my mother are talking like this. how nice it is for you to look at ." Indeed, a mother is good. Can talk, can let rely on, can pretend lazy; Can get mother's kindness, understanding and love. There is only a good mother in the world. Although it is sung in a song, it is an unbreakable truth.

My mother is very self-reliant and does not live with us. She insists on eating and living by herself. I can't help but rely on my mother, but I will often pick up my mother to stay at home. Every time my mother comes, I try my best to make my mother eat, live and play well. From brushing my teeth, washing my face and eating in the morning, to soaking my feet, making my bed, taking urine cans and in the evening, I have done well. My mother always thinks that I am a big masterpiece and won't let me do this for my mother. But I am a son and should do for mom mom. After a long time, my mother will not say anything. One day my mother said to me, "son, your brothers and you are careful. They are all like this to your parents. My mother knows your heart and it is quite good."

before the Mid-Autumn Festival last year, I took my mother home. My wife is also busy taking care of eating, and drinking every day. My mother is very happy. At noon on August 15, the family sat around and faced a table full of delicious food. I poured wine for my mother, and my wife and son picked up their glasses. On the occasion of the arrival of the traditional Chinese reunion festival, we wished my mother good health and a happy Mid-Autumn Festival! The mother raised her cup happily, looked at her son, daughter-in-law and grandson and said happily, "Good. I also wish you a happy holiday and my grandson's progress in his studies!"

On the night of August 5, the Mid-Autumn Festival party of CCTV started on time. My mother and we sat on the sofa. Sweet Hami melons, crisp and sweet golden jujube, and fragrant melon seeds filled the tea table. CCTV's program is lively and cordial, and the atmosphere at home is full of affection. During this period, my mother and I came to the balcony and looked at the round moon in the sky. I said to my mother, "you always look at the, the festival is good, the full moon is good, the family is good, we have a mother is better." Mother said: "is good, look at my son's family, eat well live in a good mood good for my mother, mother's mood is better..." I looked at my mother, thought, mother happy happy. The full moon is in the sky, reflecting my mother's joyful smiling face. I also wish my mother good health and longevity in my heart.

On the 5 of August 10, the mother, son, daughter-in-law, grandson and the league members were happy, full of happiness and happiness.

26 September 2015

Miss childhood "well Beier cool"

The place where my grandfather lived has a long history and is an ancient town. It is clearly recorded that it was founded in the Eastern Han Dynasty, where Cao Cao, the prime minister of the Eastern Han Dynasty, established the army. However, a village has been formed here for a long time, and it has been a long time cannot be tested. It can be said that it began in the Eastern Han Dynasty, flourished in the Ming Dynasty and flourished in the Qing Dynasty. Until the 1970 s, the style of the ancient town remained, with Big Cross Street, which extends in all directions, and 32 hutongs. After the city gate was closed, the residents in the city were able to move freely and orderly, and the Ming and Qing buildings on the of town remained. Unfortunately, when the Tangshan earthquake in 1976, it was in ruins, making everything the ancient town gone. However, there is still a trace of my childhood memories. That is "well Beier cool soda" by "Tricks".

"Tricks", real name Cui Wenguang, one-armed, burly body. Smile often hung on the face, a pair of lovely smile, talk humorous. Because the has a Marxist beard, people give the good name "Trex".

In the midsummer of childhood, the cold summer products on the market "ice cream" and "popsicles". Two cents 1 root. The cold drink is "iced soda", 1 bottles for five minutes. It's a big basin with bottles of soda chilled in a. Although the material was not rich in those days, "popsicles" and "iced soda" were monotonous and simple, but they were very popular. People loved to eat such "popsicles" and drink such "iced soda".

Every summer, "popsicles" and "iced soda" are sold in front of shops and outlets on Street in 4 of the town. People from south to north also stopped to buy "popsicles" and "iced soda" to quench their thirst and heat.

In front of the gate of Cui's courtyard facing the street on the north side of Dashiqiao in the east street of the ancient town, under the white pergola on the 1, there was a square eight immortals table with four old-fashioned stools on all sides and several old-fashioned benches behind it. In front of the of the cloth shed, there was a cardboard sign with the words "well Beier cool soda", which was very eye-catching and especially inviting. This is Tricks's "well cool soda". The special thing about people is not ice, but water town. Most of the people walking, doing business and passing by on the street stop and sit in the arbor and drink a bottle of "well cool soda" to relieve thirst, and heat.

Why is the soda sold by "Trex" called "well times cool soda? It turned out that "Cui Kesi", that is, Cui Wenguang's father, made a big deal in the old society. Therefore, the Cui Family Courtyard was a residence for buyers and sellers, and it was a five-entry courtyard facing south. There is a deep of a large stone well in the courtyard. The water in the deep well is naturally cool. Sink the soda in an iron bucket into the well for a period of time and then bring it up. People drink it really cool. When I was a child, I specialized in the hot sun. I ran from South Street to East Street and spent 5 cents selling 1 bottles of "Well Beier Cool Soda" to drink addiction.

Nowadays, after the red warning of high temperature in Beijing, Tianjin and Hebei, the high temperature still continues. It is really hot in summer, and the heat wave rolls. At this time, I really miss the "well Beier cool soda" I bought in "Tricks" when I was a child ". Today, although society has progressed, science and technology have developed, and living standards have improved, the taste of 1 pure natural and pollution-free "Jingbeier cool soda" is completely gone. Now, although decades have passed, the scene of a little boy, wearing the "plastic sandals" of that era, wearing underpants and vest, Mimi with a pair of small eyes and a person's burning sun, ran from the south street of the ancient town to the east street to buy 1 bottles of "jingbeier cool soda" to drink is still clearly in front of us.

48 years ago, we were the first middle school student earthquake relief team in Tangshan.

Forty-eight years have passed with a flick of my finger, but Tangshan people will never forget the unforgettable day of great disaster that nature 1 caused destruction and destruction to Tangshan. The sun and the moon shuttled back and forth, but July, 1976. 28, is a day that I will never forget in my life.

Having personally experienced the rare earthquake in Tangshan on July 28, 1976, my still feels trembling. The earthquake not only left me with a heart tremor, mental panic and the pain of losing loved ones. Moreover, it made me deeply feel that a minor, when the disaster came, was separated from his family, alone to bear the panic, desolation, loneliness, self-reliance, and expectation brought about by the catastrophe of the collapse of the sky., Unease, miss. Whenever I think of the scene of extreme horror and helplessness, I always have a kind of unspeakable taste and feeling.

Nantuo Village

On the 3 day before the Tangshan earthquake in 1976, that is, on July 25, the school organized more than 400 teachers and students to come to Nantuo Village, Xiaozhanggezhuang Commune, Fengrun County, to take part in (weeding) work. It is to compete with God for time and give the production team to pull the wild weeds in the cotton fields.

Here, it was once the manor of a famous big landlord family in the southern half of Fengrun County, County, which flourished in the Qing Dynasty and the Republic of China. The manor building looks tall and imposing. In the deep mansions in the manor, the -made stone moon doors 1 holes are still so exquisite. The long stone walkways are still lying there cleanly and neatly, with large blocks of blue bricks on both sides. The horse-tying stones and water well platforms in the yard are carefully carved and still look so pleasing. The platform bases of the buildings in the manor are high. The building forms of the houses are all in front of the corridor. The traditional cornices are arched, carved beams and painted buildings. The shapes of all wooden doors and windows are full of 1 antique Chinese beauty. Even the chimney on the house is an exquisite design of the eaves pavilion. In the yard and under the cloister, the large porcelain vats and flowerpots placed in those years were still placed intact, making people vaguely see the wealth and glory of the manor owner in the past.

I was in this ancient land to enthusiastically participate in the agricultural labor here, shed sincere sweat, experienced the unprecedented Tangshan earthquake, and our team of agricultural labor students, after the earthquake occurred The first time it became an earthquake relief team, where the first student earthquake relief the Tangshan earthquake was carried out, and eight of my Senior high school classmates died in that ancient village.

An instant of misery

In this big landlord manor in Nantuo village, there are eight independent courtyards, which is the 1 large manor called "eight halls" in the late Qing Dynasty. Although it is surrounded by the weeping willow river on the Changdi, the special and hot on the midsummer night of July 27, 1976 still made it difficult to sleep for a long time. After midnight, four male students supporting agriculture and I lay on the kang in the east room of the house of, the deputy secretary of the village party branch, dragging our tired bodies and falling asleep in the hot wind outside the window. In my sleep, many black mud jars and mud cans on the board cabinet near the north wall in the house yards to the roof suddenly crackled and fell to pieces. I woke up with a start because I didn't know it was an earthquake at that time. I thought it was a big dark day when bandits were beating and smashing the north window of the. Then the entire north wall of the 3 bungalow crumbled outward. Lin xiuliang, the team leader, was still clear-headed: "earthquake, quickly and get off the kang!" And jumped down to open the door, rushed to the courtyard, several of our students also ran out. The deputy secretary of the village branch of Westinghouse broke out of the window, and his calf was cut by the window glass, bleeding bright red. His's wife and son were also in the courtyard. Only his daughter, dressed in underpants and bra, was ashamed to see some of us young boys. She held her shoulders and arms in her hands and refused to come out. The deputy secretary shouted anxiously, "come out quickly, don't come out again, the house inverted i'll kill you!" The deputy secretary's wife was also shouting: "girl, come out quickly. what time is it? don't worry about it wear don't wear clothes, obedient quickly come out, or wait a while shock the house fell down and you buried inside." The girl had no choice but to come out of the house shyly, still holding her shoulders and breast, barefoot.

I looked at the village in the twinkling of an eye, the huge manor under the misty sky was rampant, the smoke was filled with dust, and a shrill mess like the howling of ghosts and wolves. In the past, the magnificent thousands of high-rise buildings and deep mansions of the Manor 1 swept away the and collapsed on the trembling earth. This sudden disaster made me feel the creepy of extinction for the first time in my life, the power of destruction for the first time, and the irresistible and natural disasters for the first time...

Put into rescue

The gray sky was drizzling with a cool rain. The safety of the landlord's family reassured us 5 a student. Xiuliang and I thought of the classmates and teachers who lived in all parts of the village, so we brought to change clothes and looked for them. The two of us came to the kitchen where we were cooking for the teachers and students supporting agriculture at that time. We were seeing a man with a bare backbone shouting for help at the top of his voice, trying to pry 1 a very heavy beam. Xiuliang and I picked two big rafters and punted inlay help the man pry the heavy beams. Sure enough, Liang's head cocked, and the man took advantage of the opportunity to get into the upper body and pulled up his

80-year-old mother who was panting. After that, we carried the old man to the clearing together. The man pulled out a mat from the ruins and covered it over his old mother's naked body. took our hand again and said, thank you two little brothers, otherwise my mother should have let the big beam be crushed to death...

We were just about to step away when the math teacher Yaoshuxing suddenly came head-on and hugged Xiuliang and our tightly in his arms: "Oh, my children,, are you all right, my children..."

This kind of sincere love between teachers and students still makes me very touched when I think about it. The teacher asked us what to do? We both said to look for other students and see how they are. The teacher said, go ahead, I will also look for other students.

We went west to 1 the broken wall and saw 1 group of girls squatting together crying. We approached the 1 and asked whether the two boys were still buried under the ruins. I am anxious: you still cry this time! Get! Hurry! The girls woke up at this moment, and one by one, they did not care to wear only underwear vests and quickly picked up the side by side with us to. Because the houses here are old, the bricks are heavy, the tiles are heavy, and we don't have shovel and pick tools in our hands, our hands are all bleeding, but we finally pulled out a male classmate. His face was blue and his mouth, nose and ears were and unconscious. And hurry to pick up the second male classmate, I don't know how long, very easy to pick out, as if already hopeless. A girl said, "Look, if you wake up and cry, you will be saved." Sure enough, the boy woke up slowly and cried that I was looking for my mother... Everyone shed tears and breathed a sigh of relief, but also put the hanging heart down. In the cold, a female classmate named Yang Heyun quickly me with a dacron sweatshirt tied around my waist and covered her youthful breast peak under the. Smiling at me, Chen Xin this undershirt I to wear.

Xiu Liang's two clothes were given to the other two female classmates respectively. After that, we looked elsewhere. As we were walking, a female teacher wearing only underpants came towards us: "Chen Xin, what clothes are you holding in your hand?" I said pants. "Give it to me." After saying this, the female teacher pulled her pants over and pushed them up twice. "Ah! tight, make do with it, you go." The two of us went on and ran into my junior high school deskmate Zuo Xiangyang. In the fallen manor, he came out of the panic of the collapse of the house and cried bitterly like seeing his own brother: "Chen Xin, my sister was killed." I asked, has it been stripped out? Left Xiangyang said, stripped out. I hugged Zuo Xiangyang, looked at entire destroyed manor, patted Zuo Xiangyang on the shoulder and comforted helplessly: "Then don't cry, Xiangyang, this is a natural disaster, we can't help it..."

It was already bright, and the sky was still raining, and it was raining heavily. The whole village, both teachers and students, braved the rain to find and rescue the villagers buried under the collapsed houses and in the ruins. This is the first team to be involved in earthquake relief at the first time when the Tangshan earthquake occurred, and it is also a team for middle school students to fight against the earthquake. This group of more than 400 teachers and students who did not know the life and death of their relatives in the family, selflessly rescued the villagers in the place in the rain, and searched for the fathers and villagers who were killed in the rubble.

Lu Fengan, Pei Fengwu, Han Guangxin, Zhang Zhigang and Wang Junqi live in a green brick house, the landlord's family lives in the East House, and several of their students live in Westinghouse. The strong earthquake woke them up from their sleep. Several students jumped out of the window one after another. The house collapsed, but fortunately it was not buried.

After the earthquake, the village immediately cried and shouted into a piece. The children of the landlord of the east house tore their hearts and cracked their lungs in the ruins and cried. several of their classmates hurriedly and picked people from the rubble. When they removed the beams, purlins,, etc., what they saw was a horrible scene: the landlord and his wife were hit in the head by the same purlins and died, and the two children survived the 1 because of their parents' physical support.

After they rescued the two children, the children kept shouting and crying "Mom". After a short time, 1 aunt who was in her fifties came. Seeing this, she cried a few times and took the two children with a wooden expression. It turned out that this was the child's grandmother.

Several of them walked to the team site of the production team. Wang Junqi's family in their dormitory came to see him, only to learn that his mother had been killed in the earthquake. Wang Junqi's home is in Zhuangwu Village, Qingqing, 500 meters east of Nantuo Village. The two villages are connected. At noon on the 27th, several of their classmates also went to Wang Junqi's house. His mother picked a lot of tomatoes to entertain them. Unexpectedly...

Xiu Liang and I continued to look forward. Suddenly we saw a 1 of people around us. Approaching the 1, 1 "barefoot medical student" in the village was giving a shot in the arm to our female classmate who had just been pulled out of the ruins. As she pushed the medicine in the needle tube, she said helplessly, "It's hopeless, so give me an injection." It means dedicated. The rain in the sky kept hitting her face condensed in her youth at the age of 17.

Just as fellow-townsmen and classmates were sorry for it, suddenly someone cried out: "Oh my son, your sister was killed..." Hearing this, everyone immediately looked back 1 and saw a middle-aged man holding his son crying. It turned out that he came by bike from Xinjuntun to see that his son was all right in the of Tuo in Nan. He suddenly the pain of losing his and hugged his son and cried loudly. The students gathered around and asked how Xinjuntun and Xinjuntun Middle School were doing. The middle-aged man sat slumped on the ground and cried and said, "the children, the of Xinjuntun is flat and ." This suddenly the mood of the students suddenly boiling nervous, because the students are all family members of all the circumstances are not known, eager, looking forward to return, thinking, anxiety, anxiety... heart mixed taste.

In Huanxi Village, east of Nantuo, teacher Zhang Yuchen also led more than 20 students in the village to carry out rural work,, research and activities. On the night of July 27, the boys were naked on a hot and muggy day. Two students, Liu Ruichun and Zhang Aiguo, who live with the teacher's 1 room. I washed all my clothes and slept naked on the kang.

the teacher slept relatively lightly and woke up as soon as the earthquake 1 trembled. He immediately called them to get up and jumped out of the open south window together. As soon as the man landed, he heard the muffled sound of the 1 behind him. Looking back, he saw that the wall in the middle of the house patted on the kang where they were sleeping. If you come out one second late, the consequences will be unimaginable. The two students were safe and sound, but the teacher's buttocks were cut deep by the gate under the window, and his underpants were also scratched.

The old lady, the landlord at Westinghouse, had fainted from the shock of the earthquake. Under certain circumstances, Liu Ruichun and Zhang Aiguo ran naked into the half-collapsed house and carried the old lady to the yard.

The tension was slightly calm. It was already 4 o'clock in summer and it was dawn. Standing in the yard and looking at the whole village, Huanxi Village was all. The three of them, teachers and students, hurried to help neighboring people and pick up people from the ruins. Under a collapsed house of a villager, they and their fellow villagers picked up an old man under the purlin of the house and carried him to the open space. He may have suffered serious internal injuries and soon died. They went to look for other students. A house where a girl lived collapsed, and a female classmate was buried inside. As the house collapsed and the underpants could not be found to protect the body, Liu Ruichun and Zhang Aiguo found two female classmates' jackets tied at the waist to cover their lower bodies and grabbed them together. It took five or six students a long time to pull the female student out of the ruins, but she was hopeless.

Shu Hai and the four classmates who lived together all ran out, and the house collapsed after they ran out. They rushed to the hometown's house to help the pick up people. A family was picking up child buried in the rubble. They saw the boy's face when they picked it up. Everyone stepped up to pick up the and finally pulled it out. However, the 13-year-old boy died due to suffocation for a long time.

Sweat, tears and life are dedicated to this soil and water.

In the rain, it was already afternoon in the earthquake relief, which was very tense without eating or drinking. The disaster relief here basically came to an end. Teachers and students covered in muddy water to the playground of Tuo Village Primary School in the south. All teachers and students counted and verified that 8 students were killed, and more than 20 teachers and students were seriously injured, with many minor injuries. The names of the eight students who died in the earthquake were Li Bao, Zuo Huifang, Tang Yumei, Feng Ruiyan and Zhao Guifen. The names of several other students can no longer be recalled. They were only 17 years old and died in these two ancient manors and villages with historical records from the Ming Dynasty. In the past, the eight students who lived together day and night, at this time, their bodies lay quietly in the heavy rain for a moment, and the tears of the teachers and students supporting the farmers dripped into the land of the manor together with the rain.

Standing in the rain, Principal Zhou Shangyi said loudly: "Teachers, classmates, the folks here will not forget us. Because we not only supported the farmers here to participate in the heavy labor in the fields, but also actively rescued the people buried in the collapsed houses when the earthquake occurred. Now most of the teachers and students are out of danger. Except for all the teachers and disabled teachers and students of the party members, the rest of the students can go home on the road..."

Our group of 16-or 17-year-old students, like little swallows who could not find a home, looked at the destroyed villages, unaware of the life and death of their parents, brothers and sisters, and eagerly embarked on the way home.

48 years ago, we had no cars or bicycles. We only remembered the direction of our mother in our hearts. With tears in our eyes, we shouted to our mother, spread our legs, and ran frantically in one direction. On the way home, the air echoed with us high school students calling eagerly for their loved ones...

In the villages we passed, the disaster situation of each village was not the same. In some villages, very few houses collapsed, and most of the villages were severely affected. On both sides of the street, there were the remains of the victims by the of the kang mat. There were groans of the injured and cries of family members after losing their loved ones. Some of the villagers in these villages are using livestock carts, stretchers or directly carrying people to transport the wounded to schools or brigade sites. Some are using bamboo poles, wooden sticks, kang mats, plastic sheets and other things to build simple small sheds to shelter from the wind and rain. On the dirt road leading to a big ditch in a village, we saw 1 ox carts pulling many corpses, some wrapped in reed mats, some wrapped in plastic sheets, followed by several young adults with shovels and picks. At that time, because there was no means of transport, several families used the 1 vehicle of the production team to bury the remains of their loved ones.

At that time, some students were less than 16 years old, it was raining all the time, and the road was muddy. Because there were no shoes, they didn't get home after 3 pm. Although thirsty and hungry, but homecoming, and did not walk the feeling. On the way, Lu Fengan and Pei Fengwu walked to a sweet potato field and saw no one around. Each of them secretly picked up a sweet potato and ate it while walking. In those days, it was also a shame for innocent students to steal a piece of sweet potato. At 4 p.m., most of the students finally returned home to be reunited with their families.

Forty-eight years have passed since the "July 28" Tangshan earthquake. People will not forget that the Tangshan earthquake with a magnitude of 7.8 on the Richter scale killed more than 242000 people, seriously injured more than 194000 people, killed more than 7200 families, disintegrated tens of thousands of families, and orphaned 4204 children.

In the great disaster, we and Huanxi Village in South Tuo. "July 28 ", we Tuo and Huanxi Village in South China. This ancient village

Garden and village, we will never forget. "July 28", we are Tangshan's first student earthquake relief team!

July 28, 2024

Moonlight Great Wall

I came to Baiyangyu in September 2007 and lived in Baiyangyu Forest Farm for seven days. Looking at the Great Wall, climbing the Great Wall and shooting the Great Wall, the whole was more satisfied.

Love the Great Wall of Aeyangyu, 1 the Great Wall of Aeyangyu mountain Xiongguan dangerous, can be called the second pass in the world. 2 is the famous marble Great Wall here, Wanli Guanshan is very rare, is the essence of the Great Wall.

Although today's Aeyangyu is a beautiful mountain and water, it integrates the beautiful scenery of the south of the Yangtze River and the scenery of the north, adding radiance to each other.

Twenty-eight scenes are dotted with scenery, step by step, and the scenery is pleasant. There are monuments and scenic spots such as "Lixiu Lianzhu, Xishan Lingling Fog, Lingyan Ancient Well, Xiandong Stone Bed, Dry Tortoise Drain, Jiulongxizhu, Sanyang Kaitai, Stone Monkey Climbing, Qisong Climbing High, Phoenix Falling Wutong. But what I take a look at is the ancient and vigorous, mighty and vicissitudes of the Great Wall of Aries.

Arriving at Baiyangyu is already one evening in September, hiking the mountain road to the mountain's residence. As you walk, you look to the left of the mountain road. There is a high mountain beam. On the mountain beam, a Great Wall lies across it. A sunset hangs on the right above an enemy building on the Great Wall in Aries. It is the years and human factors that make this Great Wall seem a little lonely and broken. But from another point of view, under the sunset, the Great Wall not only makes people see its solemn and stirring, but also makes people see its pride. 5 enemy buildings could be seen in the line of sight, and there were no obvious crenels on the wall between the enemy buildings. As the years passed by, the enemy building was still standing there, tall and inviolable.

There are not many trees on the mountain, but the mountain is full of trees and looks lush. It's really twilight. Look at Jin Song, towering and long

In the sunset of the city.

Our residence was on the hillside on the west side of the ancient Great Wall's Baiyang River. The next day I got up early and stood at the door of my residence and looked at the Great Wall to the south. There is a Ming Dynasty guerrilla general Zhang Shizhong inscribed the name of the Shenwei building.

The of Shenwei Building really had its magic. It didn't ride on the wall like other enemy buildings, but hung outside the wall of City (north side), which highlighted the courage and determination of the soldiers of Ming Dynasty to resist the invasion of foreign enemies. In people's eyes, from the structural point of view, it looks like the 1 house the brick imitation wood hard mountain top added to the nearby wall. From a distance, it looks like the 1 ancient generation imitation wood two-story building. Among the many enemy buildings, the Shenwei Building is peculiar and majestic, unique, and impressive. The place I could see was the of Shenwei Building, so I had already dressed up and prepared to go up the mountain to see Shenwei really face.

When I approached the Shenwei Building, I saw that every green brick up and down the Shenwei Building, there were stained and the white plaster plastered by the builders of the Ming Dynasty, all the way to the eaves and rafters, which was a typical ancient Chinese way of building walls. I saw that an arrow window was opened in the middle of the outer wall on the back, which was ventilated and daylighting, observing the enemy's situation, firing bows at the enemy, firing cannons and firing guns. It was a place where the 1 window used more. There are also two thunder holes under the arrow window, which are specially used to launch thunder holes to attack enemies close to the downstairs of the. arrow holes and thunder holes are arranged in finished shapes, which not only have architectural aesthetic feeling, but also have neat sense of height and height and practicality of fighting. Inside the building, there was a stone plaque embedded in the door on the of the simple arch. The inscription of regular script "Shenwei Building" 3 a large character. The upper left "Guerrilla General Zhang Shizhong", and the lower right "Wanli Bingshen Midsummer Jili". Looking at the big characters and withdrawals, I feel 1 is a kind of might in front of me, 1 is a kind of national spirit rising, and 1 is a kind of pride in my heart. There is a shadow wall on the wall of opposite the ticket, with a sumeru seat under it and a monument inlaid.

Walking out of Shenwei Building, stood in the sun and looked at the of Shenwei Building. The unique and majestic Shenwei Building still stands on the ridge after more than 400 years of wind and rain. The of Shenwei Building did not use 1 wood except doors and windows, and there was not a piece of green tile on the roof, but the imitation wood structure made of brick was so lifelike that it increased the firmness of the enemy building. In my opinion, this not only show that the Ming Dynasty's defense projects were beautifully designed, well-formed, sturdy, and practical and humanized, but also showed the Chinese people's architectural wisdom and superb architectural skills.

The next morning, I went out again to the lie city, which was called "horse circle" and "of the parade city. In the morning of the mountain, I was accompanied by fog. When I reached the top of the mountain, the fog had soaked my hair and shirt. The lie city on the commanding heights on the east side of the ancient white sheep water pass of the great wall in Aries, standing before the long xiongguan pass, can't help but let my heart sigh with emotion. Suddenly feel, despite the ancient and modern wind, rain and snow, war and robbery, but now lie city majestic, easy to defend difficult to attack, can not be expected. Walk in the city and stroll in the space of 3000 square meters. Let me see that this is the 1 military pocket city that can be used to confuse the enemy on the one hand, and can store food and grass, horses, and soldiers on the other. It is worthy of the 1 original creation in the defense system of the Great Wall in Aeyangyu, and it is also the Chinese. The surprising use of military tactics.

I was condescending, looking down at the dangerous of Xiongguan the mountain of Baiyangyukou. In this throat place leading to the north of the Great Valley through the ages, I felt the momentum of "one man at the gate. Looking around the mountain peak danger, the Great Wall winds above the mountain top, and the ancient border defense systems such as beacon tower (horse circle), Shuiguan and

Duchayuan gather here completely.

At the end of the day's study, after dinner and sleeping together to play cards, I sat on the stone drum stool in front of the window and looked at the Great Wall in front of the. The Great Wall at night runs from east to west on the mountain beam. Most of the wheels appear to be a little dim yellow moon in the mountain fog, hanging over the Great Wall in Aries, giving me 1 a foggy and desolate feeling. Think of Yan and Qin dynasties...

The soldiers guarding the border here until the Ming Dynasty, just in such a quiet night, or wearing stars and moon, or the wind and snow, or lightning and thunder, or stretching their hands and fingers, should always open their eyes and ears, watching the enemy's movements outside the Great Wall, and be alert to the sound of running horses and iron shoes. In order to protect our country, we can endure the loneliness and desolation of that side, the loneliness and suffering of that 1, the loneliness and, and that 1 a kind of hardship and persistence. Brave garrison along the Great Wall, defending the country's rivers and mountains within the Great Wall.

Tourists living in Baiyangyu Forest Farm indulge in singing and singing in the karaoke hall where they live. I pondered the account of the Great Wall of Aries under the moon in the mountains. Some sources say: "When the Baiyangyu Great Wall was built in the Northern Qi Dynasty (550-577 AD), it was all made of stone and was only 3 meters wide. After the Northern Zhou extermination of the Northern Qi slightly repaired. In the early Ming Dynasty, Xu Da set the in the key pass to build the of the city. During the ten thousand years of, Tan Lun, Liu Yingjie and other Jiliao governors, Qi Jiguang and other Jizhen officers organized several reinforcements. Important sections were covered with bricks, the width increased to 5-6 meters, and military defense facilities such as enemy buildings and forts were added." Another source said: "The Great Wall of Baiyangyu was built by Yan during the Warring States Period and repaired and strengthened during the Ming Dynasty. Among them, there are 21 towers and the well-preserved Great Wall is 4552 meters."

I will not explore which 1 is right or wrong, but the common point of the two statements is that "the long city was repaired and strengthened in the Ming Dynasty". What we are most proud of is the "Marble Great Wall" that makes the Great Wall of Baiyangyu extra glorious ".

This 3-mile-long marble Great Wall, made of precious brown-red marble as the cornerstone, is unique in the construction of the Great Wall of China. It is the essence of the Great Wall and a treasure in today's words. The Great Wall was built with marble from local materials. The commanders and builders of the Great Wall at that time probably did not expect that the section of the Great Wall they built was both generous and beautiful and. The, and spectacular and strong Great Wall was built on the top of the dangerous peaks. It is neat and shining, and it can be called the 1 of the Great Wall. Today, it has become a gorgeous treasure within the scope of national and even world defense projects.

Looking at the night sky, mountains, the Great Wall, moonlight and the deep valley of Baiyangyu, I was thinking in my heart that Baiyangyu, a place that has always been a battleground for military strategists, has always been the main road in the Spring and Autumn and Warring States periods, the Great Qin Dynasty and the of Hungary, the Qing soldiers entering the customs, the army entering the customs, and the Japanese aggressors entering the customs. Through the ages, the history is boundless and the years are long. The Great Wall has traveled through time and space for nearly 3000 years. The vicissitudes of life the sun, moon and stars. The bright moon has been shining from the Warring States Period to this day. I wonder if the border guards in different historical periods have ever had bonfire songs, zither piano playing, drinking wine, hometown minor and wild dancing. The moonlight of the Great Wall in Aeyangyu, the moonlight of the Great Wall in Aeyangyu, you make me think a lot...

The spring water of Aries Valley gushes out like pearls, and a clear and quiet Aries River passes through the pass from north to south, flowing for a long time in all seasons. Looking at the green mountains and green waters of Baiyangyu, the majestic and beautiful scenery, and the picturesque landscape of Xiongguan, I really sigh that Baiyangyu is worthy of the reputation of "the south of the north. With the prosperity of people's life, with the efforts of the local government and people of insight, Baiyangyu has become more and more magnificent, simple and elegant. Aries Valley has entered a new realm, showing a good scenery. I saw the elegant demeanor of Xiongguan in the past, which is stepping into a well-off era with the "Chinese Dream" of the Chinese people and the take-off of Qian'an, towards a better future!

Unforgettable father played "clouds chasing the moon"

As I grow older, I miss my father more and more strongly. In many childhood memories, one of them is always like a movie, lingering in my mind from time to time, flashing in front of my eyes and echoing in my ears.

In the 1960 s, there were big trees in the north and south courtyards of my hometown. It was not until the end of the 1970 s that trees were cut down. The trees became shade. On summer nights, people enjoyed chatting under the trees. My father, who works in the tax office, sometimes after dinner with colleagues, will gather under the big tree in my south courtyard, and sit on the big mat on the ground with several adults talking about topics I don't understand. Sometimes my father will play or erhu or dulcimer to his colleagues. Everyone likes to listen to his father's instruments. One night, my father and his colleagues came home together after dinner. After a few simple words, they took the mat and went to the ground under the big tree the south courtyard. Several colleagues of their father sat on it. The father happily took the violin and stood under the tree. He put the violin between his left shoulder and left jaw, smiled at everyone and played the violin. When my father played the piano, he was free and easy and elegant. he bowed on the string, and the sound of the piano turned and. Everyone was intoxicated.

At that time, I had no idea what the tune was, only that it was very nice and beautiful. It was not until the 1980 s that I knew that this one played by my father was first seen in the Qing Dynasty. It originated from the Guangdong folk Cantonese music in the Qing Dynasty. It is the famous Cantonese music "Caiyun Chasing the Moon". Its style is light and unique. It describes the relaxed freehand brushwork of ordinary life of ordinary citizens and highlights the typical Guangdong folk music style. When Li Hongzhang was the governor of Guangdong and Guangxi, he copied this song to Ounai for performance.

In the 1930 s, Chinese composer Ren Guang (1900–1941) rearranged and rearranged it into a in 1935.

In 1960, Peng Xiuwen was re-orchestrated according to the orchestra of the Central Broadcasting

National Orchestra.

"Colorful Clouds Chasing the Moon", my father played this famous Chinese song describing the wonderland of the Moon Palace in people's minds with a violin. I have always remembered it, but my father is already in heaven. In memory of my father, I think that this beautiful piece of music may be played in heaven...

The look in my father's eyes before 48

It has been 48 years since the Tangshan earthquake, but I have never forgotten the look in my father's eyes when he stood on Cross Street on the afternoon of July 28, 1976, looking forward to my safe return.

When the earthquake occurred, my classmates and I were taking part in agricultural support work in Fengrun Nantuo Village. On the of July 27, 1976, the weather was particularly sultry on this midsummer night. It was not until after midnight that my five students supporting agriculture in the same room and I gradually fell asleep in the hot wind outside the window. In my sleep, there was a loud noise. The whole north wall the three bungalows where we were located all crashed out. Several of our classmates also ran out quickly.

The deputy secretary of the village party branch who lives in Westinghouse has broken the window and his calf has been cut by the window glass. The wound is rolled and bloody. The deputy secretary's wife, son, and daughter are all safe and sound.

My classmate Lin Xiuliang and I thought of the classmates and teachers who lived in different parts of the village, so we went to find them. The two of us passed by the kitchen where we were cooking for the teachers and students supporting agriculture at that time. We were seeing a man with a light backbone shouting for help at the top of his voice, and trying to pry 1 a very heavy beam. Xiuliang and I picked up two big rafters and put inlay on them. helped the man pry heavy beams. This 1 trick really worked, Liang's head cocked, the man took advantage of the situation to get into the upper body, pulled out his panicked 80-year-old mother. After that, we carried the old man to the clearing together. In the drizzle, the man took our hand and said, thank you, little brothers. if it weren't for your help, my mother would have been crushed to death by the big beam ...

We walked west through the 1 wall and saw 1 group of girls squatting together crying. We approached the 1 and asked whether the two boys were still buried under the ruins. As soon as I heard this, I was anxious: "You still cry this time! Get! Save someone!"

At this moment, they woke up like a dream and quickly picked up the side by side with us. Because the old of the house, the bricks were, the tiles were heavy, and we did not have shovel and pick tools in our hands, our hands were all bloody, but we finally pulled out a male classmate. His face was blue and his mouth, nose and ears were covered with and he was unconscious. We also hurry to pick up second male classmate, I do not know how long, very easy to pick out, as if is already dead. A girl hesitated and said, "I heard adults say that if you cry, you will be saved." The miracle really happened. The boy woke up slowly. The 1 of "wow" cried and said, "I'm looking for my mother..." Everyone breathed a sigh of relief and put the heart hanging in the throat back to its original place.

As we walked further, we met my junior high school deskmate Zuo Xiangyang on the road. In this stricken manor, he came out in horror of the collapse of the house and hugged me tightly as if he had seen his brother: "Chen Xin, my sister sister was killed." I hurriedly asked: "did you pull it out?" zuo xiangyang said: "did you pull it out..." I reluctantly comforted him and said: "xiangyang, this is a natural disaster, we also have no way, you don't cry..."

We continued to look forward and suddenly saw a bunch of people gathered together. In the past, 1 saw that it was the "barefoot doctor" in the village who was giving a shot in the arm to a female classmate who had just been pulled out of the rubble. As she pushed the medicine in the needle tube, she 1 the and said helplessly as she: "It's hopeless, so give me an injection." It means dedicated. The female classmate was lying on the ground, and the rain in the sky kept falling on her face her 17 -year-old youth.

By the afternoon, the disaster relief and rescue work had basically come to an end. Mud-covered teachers and students gathered at the exercise in Tuo Village Primary School. The bodies of Li Bao, Zuo Huifang, Tang Yumei, Feng Ruiyan four students who died in the earthquake were also carried. In the misty rain, the headmaster said forcefully: "teachers, students, the masses here, the villagers here will not forget us. Because we not only supported agriculture here and participated in the heavy labor in the fields, but also rescued the people buried in the collapsed houses in time when the earthquake occurred. Now most of the teachers and students are out of danger. After research and decision, the party and League members will stay and continue to participate in rescue and disaster relief. All the teachers stayed and also took part in the rescue and disaster relief. Injured teachers and students to prevent the deterioration of the injury also have to stay, waiting for treatment. The rest of the students can go home to ..."

On the way home, we had no car, no bicycle, only the concern for our family, only tears soaked in our eyes, and ran towards home with our legs spread. In the gloomy sky, we students are eager to call for our relatives...

When I came back, I 1 see that there were no upright houses in ruins everywhere. Fortunately, the streets of the past were still clear. I saw my father standing on the cross street looking around from a distance. I ran over and saw my father holding a stick in his hand, and then saw wrapped in gauze on his right foot. It turned out that when my grandfather was from the ruins, the let the date pit nail penetrate the sole of his foot. However, he was overjoyed to see his son come back. Take a closer look at me and say, it is good to come back...

For 48 years, my father's look of looking forward to his son's return often appeared in front of my eyes. I understand that my father, who was worried at that time, did not know how his son was doing, but he was injured and could not move. All he could do was wait and hope. Therefore, I have never forgotten my father's eager eyes 48 years ago when he was looking forward to his son's return.

2024

flute sound

Early in the morning, under the light rain. People came in and out of the station with umbrellas of all colors. In the station, the electric locomotive whistle, from time to time...

On the concrete floor of the platform, two lines of footprints with rain, time is sparse and time is dense, like a poem, like a song...

Ling looked up and looked at Hua with affectionate eyes. Hua, a young miner, also looked down at Ling's affectionate eyes, which reminded him once again of the crystal grains of Wujin. Hua wanted to smile at Ling. Suddenly he saw the "particles" overflowing with 1 "clear water". The smile suddenly disappeared on his face. Ling lowered her head, her bangs covered her eyes, and tightly Hua.

Hua wanted to say something to Ling, but he couldn't find the topic for a while. Light rain drifted between heaven and earth, falling on the platform ... flute sound. Ling thought: if the departure of the flute will never sound; the car will never enter the station, then I... they think so in their hearts, who also dare not look at each other first, silent rain, silent people, any time minutes and seconds of the passage of time...

In the window, Hua smiled at the "black particles.

Ling raised her hand, like 1 bright miner's lamp, Hua raised her arm, like the high-pitched coal cutter rocker arm...

10 July 1986

The song black -for the miners

Those who burn coal all their lives do not necessarily know what miners look like, and those who know miners do not necessarily know that the sea of coal is deep thick and chest. All I know is that without the burning of coal, there would be no warm hall like spring, no rushing steel flow and steel flowers in full bloom...

Miners like the sun, but every day in the sun by can to the underground, and the rumbling of machinery, mining rolling black gold shining.

If it is said that the hottest red in the sky is the sun, the hottest red on the earth is the heart of the miners. The busy miners on the palm face, are they like a round of the sun emitting light and heat?

Summer season, leisurely people in the karaoke bar dashing, romantic seaside red men and green women. On the ground of the mining area, derricks are towering, and one by one, ships are flying, like 1 ships, sailing away.

On the 30th of the year, there is no delicacies or wine, no firecrackers and fireworks, and no light singing and dancing in the underground. But there are coal cutters singing, but there are mine trucks full of raw coal, but there are miners flying...

In fact, miners are like sailors on the sea, busy in spring, summer, autumn and winter. In the sea what kind of magnificent, what kind of difficulties and obstacles, what kind of tragic and passionate will encounter. When you listen carefully to the deep and passionate songs of the miners, you will feel twists and turns, imagining and stirring.

the warm hearts in rainy days

Every morning, I insisted on walking. At 5 o'clock in the morning on July 4, 2023, I walked out of the gate of the community and walked slowly to the north as usual. No, an hour and a half later, on the way back home, it began to rain lightly. I hid under the tree for a 1. I met the rain and came to a park pavilion nearby to take shelter from the rain. It was during the rain that there were three conversations that made me feel warm.

After walking for about 40 minutes, I reached the riverside bridge and walked down the corridor. 1 I looked up and saw the trees beside the riverside and the corridor. As I was just planted, I tied a wooden frame to the trunk to prevent it from being blown down by the wind, and attached three wooden sticks as support. A few years have passed, and the trees are growing well, and the pine sticks that support the trees have disappeared, but the wooden sticks tied to the trunks are tied to the trunks with iron wires the 4 frame. The trees grow fast, but the section with wooden sticks the 4 frame is obviously trapped. The upper and lower ends of the wooden sticks the 4 frame highlight bulges, while the places bound by the wooden sticks the 4 frame cannot grow normally, and even the iron wire has into the trees. Seeing this scene, my heart couldn't help feeling a painful struggle and uncomfortable feeling, so my mobile phone took it and sent it to the circle. Unexpectedly, 1 kind micro- friend saw the lens of the circle of friends and called to agree to drive me to the river tomorrow morning to solve the pain of trees being tied up. This phone call, let me feel warm and gratified for trees.

Make an appointment to do good things together, good people, good hearts.

Friends say hello to each other early in the morning, every day. No exception, rainy days are also uninterrupted. Just as I had just entered the park pavilion to take shelter from the rain and sit down to watch my cell phone, a morning greeting and blessing appeared. My usual voice reply: "Good morning auspicious! When I came back from my walk, it began to rain. Take shelter from the rain in the park pavilion. It's cool. I wish you a happy day!"

In the pavilion, I looked through the information in various groups on my mobile phone. The rain outside the pavilion was lingering. After a while, the phone rang: "Hello, brother, where are you now? I just came out to do something. I'll pick you up and take you home by the way." The wind brought by the rain is cool, but at this moment, receiving such a word really makes my heart hot. In the wind and rain, my friend will pick me up and drive me home. What a friendship this is. But I couldn't bear to let my friend pick me up in the rain and send me off, so I said, I will go home after the rain stopped. Thank you, don't drive, I'll wait a little longer...

A sincere person, a friendly heart, and a warm heart of friendship, rain or shine.

Put down your cell phone and look at the sky. The rain is still falling and there is no sign of stopping. Think about it is not far from home, take a few steps to the to catch. However, I don't know if I can't get out of the pavilion. 1 I got out of the pavilion, I felt that the light rain was quite. I hurried to walk under the big sycamore tree on the side of the road. However, the rain for a long time. The sycamore tree was also dripping rain. Fortunately, the city of the future, not far from home, was ahead and came to a corridor. Just standing still, the phone rang: where is dad? I said it was under a corridor in our neighborhood opposite the future city on the north of the road. I said. OK, then I won't move the car. I'll walk over and deliver the umbrella. said the son.

After a while, in the dense rain, I saw my son, who was one meter eight tall, with his trousers a white T-shirt, an umbrella in his left hand and a 1 umbrella in his right hand, walking towards me across the road. See me and say: my father, see the weather is bad, take an umbrella out. Well, I'm afraid you're cold. Bring it a long-sleeved shirt and put it on. Give you the big umbrella and let's go home.

The children who come in the rain, the sensible ones, 1 a heart that loves the of the Father.

Untie the tree

I insisted on walking every morning. At 5: 00 a.m. on July 4, I left the gate of the community and walked slowly to the north as usual. After walking for about 30 minutes, I came to the south bank of Longquan River under the south slope of Nanhu Avenue and walked down along the curved path beside the Bridge. 1 I looked up and saw the torch trees beside the river and the corridor. As I was just planted to prevent them from being blown down by the wind, people tied wooden frames to the tree trunks, and attached three pine sticks below them as support and fixation. Several years have passed, and the trees have grown very fast. The pine sticks that support the trees have disappeared, but the sticks tied to the trunks are still tied to the trunks by iron wires in the of 4 frames. Other parts of the trunk are growing as usual, but the the 4 frame with wooden sticks is obviously bound and cannot grow normally. The upper and lower ends of the of the 4 frame wooden sticks highlight bulges. Even worse, some iron wires have been deeply into trees. It makes people feel like people are tied up, and the rope is to the bone. See this scene, my heart can not help but have a painful struggle very uncomfortable feeling.

So, the next day, that is, in the early morning of July 5, 2023, I came to the river with a screwdriver at 5: 30 on time, and removed the wooden frames tied to the trunks one by one, so as to solve the pain of binding the trees.

During the time I was dismantling the wooden frames on these tree trunks, from time to time people walking to and from the river stopped to watch. When they understood that I was loosening the of trees, some smiled kindly to me, some gave me a thumbs up, and some said, "1 see that you are a kind person. Although these trees cannot speak, your goodness can be learned from heaven and earth. I would like to praise you !" In the face of these friendly people, I also smiled to show my gratitude and continued to relieve the of trees from binding. Although my head was stained with a lot of leaves and dust, the handle of the screwdriver was tied tightly by the wire, and the tight was broken by the difficulty of the tree trunk, and my right thumb was bleeding. However, after more than two hours, the pain of being bound was relieved for 17 torch trees. From now on, they will no longer be bound, can let go of the free growth.

At 5: 30 a.m. on July 7, 2023, I brought electrician pliers to the river again and continued to tear down the wooden frames tied to the trunk of the tree one by one for the fire torch the tree. In the meantime, an old man walking by the river stopped and asked me, "Are you a gardener?" I said no. "Then why do you care about this?" I said, "I feel bad watching these trees suffer. The old man smiled and said, "You are really a good man." Thumbs up and said, "You are the one. As the saying goes, when people are doing it, the sky is watching. You are such a good man. There must be a good return." Say that finish smiled and left. I also relieved the remaining few torch trees from being tied up. Have a good heart, do good deeds, good deeds. Great goodness is silent and exists in heaven and earth.

Finally, return to the side of the road to complete the most difficult task of untying the trees. Because, here the tree tall tree thick, wire tension more tight. It takes time and effort to untie the seven trees I don't know here. Two big blisters are also worn out on the middle finger and ring finger of my right hand, but I still insist on loosening tying for them.

I put down my pliers and stood by the big tree. Looking at the trees in front of me, I also felt happy and relieved for these trees. Said to himself, you are free, thrive in the days to come...

On the way home, the sky was blue and the sun was shining, and my heart was full of bright sunshine...

The fifth series of songs to the sun

To the east

It is also the morning sun reflecting the brilliant blue sea, walking alone on the beach, sending I am glad to want to go, stand the blue shore, slender figure. Sing a song to the east, stirring the heart. Ah, my sun.

1983

Midsummer Rising Sun

In the early morning of midsummer, I stood on the reef by the sea, looking out over the horizon, with an ardent expectation–to see the sun out.

The sound of the sea waves in front of the pigeon nest on the beidaihe seashore, destroying the hour hand of the clock, exciting people's hearts and calling to the red sun.

The ancient sea, hundreds of millions of years of depth, hundreds of millions of years of selflessness, hundreds of millions of years of kindness; gave birth to the cells of life, dedicated to the son of the sun, the ship entrusted to the survival of mankind.

Sun, moon and stars, day and night back and forth, only the sun the earth and the sea. In front of the sea restless, a round of sunrise spurting out, slowly rising, the crowd the sea jubilant. The rosy clouds are gorgeous, the sun rises, and people walk forward under her light, leaving a beautiful heart. The sun is the reddest, the sun is the warmest, and the sun is shining and the mountains and rivers are magnificent.

Midsummer sunrise, I will never forget.

1985

The Sun in July

On the first morning of July, a sunrise glorified the east of the sky.

I stand on the seaside rocks, the sea level line overlooking, watching the sunrise, is I with a fervent expectation.

Sun, moon and stars, day and night back and forth, only the sun the earth and the sea.

Ears gently the waves, more like the South Lake on the Communists in a leisurely paddle.

In front of Columbus called "the of the city of gold " a round of rising sun, under the agitation of the sea spurted out, and ran up.

The crowd boiled and the sea boiled. People cheered to see the sea sunrise, the sea cheered this is the light.

The Communist Party is like the sun, shining wherever it goes.

The lyrics were filled in the songs of the old farmers in northern Shaanxi, and from then on, the "East is Red" was so loud and clear.

The sun in July is brilliant. In this season, the Communist Party of China was born.

The sun gradually rose, shining Jinggangshan, Yan'an, Xibaipo, Tiananmen Gate Tower a brilliant sunshine.

Hong Kong bauhinia in full bloom, Macao lotus in full bloom, the western region ancient country reappears enchanting, people in her light heart left beautiful, joy to the front.

The sun is the most red, the sun is the most warm. In the 21st century, the land of China is especially enchanting, with more magnificent rivers and mountains and more prosperous ancient countries in 5,000 years.

The sun in July, I will never forget.

Won the first prize of the poetry competition held by China Development News in 7, 1989.

You have occupied me

In the romantic season, unexpectedly meet a natural and graceful you, want to know you, doubt this is love at first sight, but did not approach you. After ten centuries, the environment has gathered me and you. although things changed, the video of memory has not erased you. the wind and frost of the years have not withered you. you are still a free and easy, beautiful and lovely you. Perhaps the preference of life, in that tasteless summer, I saw a unwilling to be lonely, unwilling to do nothing, unwilling to be depressed, youthful you. I don't know because of me, I don't know because of you, you and I meet always so warm and sweet. What I imagine is you, what I love and admire is you, what I want to help is you, what I want to talk to is you, what I want to is you. You, you, you, let me forget you.

Published in Hong Kong in 1992, "World Prose Poetry Writer".

know my heart

Facing the eastern red sun, I stared for a long time. You are brilliant and attractive. At the beginning of the confided to you that I was so pure that I would to you a cavity of my blood and virginity.

Along the arc of taking off from you, I went through the wilderness, jungle, mountains and rivers, sea and rivers, and tasted hardships...

After years of nostalgia and hard pursuit, I also rejoice and worries.

The time and space that have been cloudy for a long time have collapsed my missing, making me unable to bear your heavy weight. I love and treasure it to you, but my heart is broken...

A bright and sunny day, seeing that your love is still bright and beautiful, said that you have not forgotten all the time, inviting me to deviate from the cold, winter and seasons at the same time. My dead heart is rekindled by your love, I embrace you through broken windows, and I look forward to a better tomorrow. But I a heart, I feel tired in my longing, and I don't want to roam in the ocean of prayer and waiting, although you are my love.

1993

total solar eclipse

After 2,500 years of waiting, in the snowy region of the ice sheet, the hour hand is filtering the black sun on the cold sky screen, allowing me to carefully analyze your internal organs and desires. Numb legs support my eyes full of god, listening attentively to your emotional story...

Deep under the sunglasses, taste your lonely feelings, realize you save a long hope, unexpectedly shattered in an instant, behind the moon looming your eager and unbearable past. more epiphany, you gave me so many long and helpless waiting. Slowly comeback, symbolizing the of your bloody bumpy heart...

The sun, the moon, the, the, and the earth (the sun, the moon, the comet, and the earth appear in this total solar eclipse) will have to wait two and five thousand years. I understand your magnificent past, your boundless state of mind, innocence, loss, confidence, unrestrained... Ah, my sun, let everything be silent...

9 March 1997

Tiangou

After a consummation, the moon fades a little, the sun mashes my heart, and the painful tears into red blood...

Why do you want to turn infatuation into bubble, red sun, you are a brilliant devil, I want to be a dog, devour your remnants

Cool, the arrival of the total solar eclipse, that is, the breeze to send the moon...

1994

No longer follow.

Looking at the setting sun from afar, I hobbled along the path paved with the world of mortals. ah, how many years have I been infatuated with the sun. when your light first appeared, my heart surged and I yearned for your brilliance. You seem simple and honest. You can kiss across the sea, but you to rise I go into the sea. Then you are lofty, scorching and volleyed in everything. I gallop to the top of the hill and start, conceiving the route you take off. Spring, summer, autumn and winter with my lone sail boat shadow.

Looking at the sunset the fiery red sunset and the sunset, I am helpless and glad that your has not. This will make you calm and, sink your and thinking, and realize that it is not extraordinary. Perhaps, in the Ming Dynasty, you are brilliant again, but it is difficult to start my sad and painful heart car and there is no idle speed to follow.

30 August 2001

Sunset

Meng Chun, a young man on a distant island, stands. The clouds on the red day of the western red sun reflect red, and the face of the young man is more reflected. Everything is as brilliant as a rose. Midsummer dusk, the setting sun hanging on the edge of the earth, delaying the falling moment, a young man in a long way.

In the sunset in the autumn of the year, the sun setting is like blood, the maple is red, the grass is green, and the aspen leaves are golden. The young look at the end of the world, and the clouds are and soaked in the evening to feelings. It can't be said that the days melancholy, leaving silence, loneliness and deep feeling. There is only one young year in the world.

Yuanmingyuan

Yuanmingyuan, I gaze in front of you, you desolate overlook, bright and bright. Yuanmingyuan, Venus left a concept: lonely beauty, will be humiliated; peerless purity will be raped. Yuanmingyuan, great pain, magnificent sorrow, you tearful attention, broken virginity, longing for sunshine warm jade body, re-leading coquettish, brilliant 21st century.

Written in 1, 1994, the 45th anniversary of the founding of People's Literature

The longitude and latitude are still

Looking at the sky and clouds, I am looking for the season when your songs linger the blue sky and the clouds.

Soft wind, grass, running water, have eavesdropping on you and me, hiding the footprints of you and me, and secretly recording the touching kisses of you and me. Suddenly the hurricane came, lost your shadow.

Witnessing the loneliness of the setting sun, hearing the sadness of the 1 returning birds, and experiencing the long and eager thoughts of the winter night, I my to save the fire the remnant flooded and hope for a warm one. How many times wandering in the wind, how many times flying in the rain, how many times the sun looking far away under the light.

A line of geese the spring red sun flying in. 1 wild goose drew its neck and fluttered its wings. asked me what longitude and latitude it should be?

Yo, this long-lost voice is the inquiry of how many days and nights I have lost love, and how many years I have been worried about.

North, latitude and longitude still, still.

1986

Elf

A cosmic spirit, drifting in the vastness of space, echoing the call of search.

Pangu opened the of heaven and earth, that is, turned into mountains and rivers. Eve gave birth to all living beings and disappeared. Mummies were under the pyramids. Thousands of troops and horses were amazed by the edge of the tomb of the Qin Emperor. Babylon declined and the Mayans fell. Spaceships, UFOs, relentless search.

Wandering, wandering, tens of thousands of light years a day, but I can't see the birthplace of my kind, can't see the light of the crown of civilization.

There was a city of gold in the distance, whose shone the sky and ran to her, telling all doubts.

Note: When Columbus was looking for India, he called the sun gold city at sea.

30 August 2001

The 1 award-winning prose poem made a good marriage.

In 1993, in the essay contest for the national contemporary literary masterpiece held by the "Contemporary Literary World" magazine, my essay poem "Midsummer Love" won the first prize for poetry creation the essay contest. However, it was this award-winning work that led to a story from 2000.

I went to work just after the Spring Festival that year. At that time, I was working in the Propaganda Department of the Party Committee. I was about to go downstairs to the cafeteria for lunch when the telephone on my desk rang. Pick up the phone and answer: "Is Chen Xin there, please?" I said I am, and you are? "I am 2 Xing to pay New Year's greetings to my eldest brother." He is the younger brother of a friend of mine, Xing. Originally, there was not much contact. I hurried downstairs to and him and went to the hotel...

We chatted while eating at the dinner table. He said, "Brother, do you know why I have been to you for years?" I said, "Brother, don't know. For so many years, your brother and I have been coming and going frequently. What are you doing today?

He said with joy on his face, "Elder brother, I came here specially to thank you." What do I say is worth making my brother such a sacred ritual? He said: "It's worth it. Some time ago, I got along with 1 girlfriend. We have a good relationship with each other. She is nice and kind to me. After a long time, I slowly to think of getting married. But after she told her family, her parents disagreed, saying that I can't afford a house. Where will I live when I get married? elder brother you know my situation, I really can't afford a house. This is indeed a problem, and I don't blame her parents. But also helpless, who let me have no money, my heart is very depressed. After working all day 1, I lay bored in bed and blindly and looking through things aimlessly. Suddenly I turned to the prose poem written by Brother you in 1993, which was the prose poem "Midsummer Love" which was the first prize of the National Contemporary Literary Essay Contest in by Brother. Do you remember it? "I said I remember it. "elder brother, you said I this poor boy that is toad want to eat swan meat, lying on the bed board, looking at the roof, no money to buy a house also loathe to give up the beloved girl, how to do? What should we do ?? your brother, I looked at the prose poem "Midsummer Love" my hand, and suddenly had a brainwave. The content of poem by elder brother fully expresses my feelings. I know clearly that I have nothing at this time. I have only 1 sincere heart for my beloved girl. I have only one heart to impress her. Thinking about it, determined to fight. In the evening, I went to the phone booth to call at her home and asked her to come out after dinner. I my in my heart and finished with her. She arrived as promised, and we came to the steep river to walk and talk, and found a place with grass to sit down. I said to her, I really can't afford a house, this is indeed a problem, I don't blame your parents. But I also really loathe to give up you ah, really want you, in my heart how also can't put down, that also helpless, only my heart depressed, wrote a poem miss to you. After listening, you can go your way. I just keep my love for you in my heart. As I read, she listened quietly, and listened as she cried: Did you write this? Then don't read, with your heart, our family opposes me to marry you. Without a house, we can work together to earn money and save money to buy in the future. I will be satisfied with your love..."

In October 1999, they got married and gave me a New Year greeting on the first month of the lunar calendar. He also told his wife the truth: that 1 poem that touched you was written by 1 of my good brothers, and the content represented my heart, so I borrowed it to express my love to you.

After listening to his story, although he deceived the world, I still can't help but feel gratified. My prose poem "Midsummer Love", which won the first prize in the contemporary literary essay contest, has actually completed a good marriage. It is also a 1 good thing!

The Light of Humanity

The "Journey of Discovery" column of CCTV Channel 4 once reported that during the archaeological excavation of the old course of the Yellow River, Chinese archaeologists were surprised to find a scene of human civilization solidified more than 7,000 years ago: a woman knelt on her knees and looked up at the sky with her head in horror. Her arms held a young child in her arms, and her hands held the young child tightly. The of the young child nestled in her arms.

According to the archaeological environment, people infer that this is the time when human beings encountered a sudden attack can not resist the natural disaster-catastrophic flood. But the human instinct, especially the maternal instinct, is to protect the child. Therefore, this great maternal nature, who lived far away from today's civilized society more than 7,000 years ago, instinctively protected her children from harm when facing the disaster of extinction. Although, to this day, mother and son only exist in bones, they still shine with the light of ancient human nature...

Time flies, 14: 28 on May 12, 2008, a moment remembered by the world. A similar scene reappeared in a family in Beichuan, Wenchuan County, Sichuan Province: when the building collapsed, 1 mother knelt on her knees and leaned forward, supporting the ground with her hands to protect her child. At noon on May 13, 2008, when the rescue team carried out the rescue under the ruins, they saw this moving scene. Although her mother had stopped breathing, a little girl 3 four months on the ground was safe. It was her mother who held up the falling sky with her body. This scene was fixed in the moment of history. How could everyone who saw not be moved, how could they not tremble, and could they not cry...

Rescuers found a mobile phone in the child's little flower quilt, and the screen of the mobile phone kept the last words written by the mother to the child: "Dear baby, if you want to live, please remember that I love you ..." Seeing this, I can't help but shout: Mother is great, humanity is great! Humanity shines forever!

In 1 schools in Wenchuan County, Sichuan Province, at a critical moment when landslides and ground cracks, houses collapse, and the lives of teachers and students are extremely threatened in class, the teacher on the podium called on the students to escape and save their lives. At the moment when the building collapsed, he was still calling the students to hide under the podium. The lives of the four students were saved, but the posture and life of the teacher's hands calling the students were never solidified at this 1 moment.

, I saw in the TV report that 1 citizen who was hit by the earthquake and suffered a fracture sent a little girl about one year old to a temporary hospital. When the little girl's biological parents came to the hospital, people were shocked to know that the little girl was with her grandmother when the earthquake occurred. It was only at the moment of the tragedy that the grandmother tried her best to throw the little girl out of the to save the young life, but the old man was killed.

December 18, 2023 23:59. A 6.2-magnitude earthquake occurred in Jishishan County, Linxia Hui Autonomous Prefecture, Gansu Province. At about 14:00 on December 21, at the of a residential house at No. 2, Caotan Village, Haidong Citizen and County, fire officers and fighters worked to dig and search for missing persons. Later, a sad scene appeared. In the mud, three adults formed a circle and seemed to be protecting something. Rescuers quickly dug the surrounding mud and water with their hands. After lifting out the three adults, they found that they were using two children wrapped in quilts.

Seeing this 1 behind the scenes, the fire rescue personnel present could not restrain their grief, with faint tears in their eyes, carefully holding out the muddy water with their hands, but afraid of being too slow, they could only speed up the hand planing. After all the personnel were dug out, the scene held a collective silence.

One by one, one by one, through the ages, from present to ancient, in the process of human development and growth, all flashing the light of human nature. Human nature is born with life and passed on from generation to generation. The reason why human beings have multiplied to this day is closely related to the existence of human nature. It is the light of human nature that shines on the night sky of disaster and guides the growth of life. It is the same strain that human nature passes through and time and space. Only then can we have the high hymn of eternal life.

friend, I want to say to you

    I often hear people say and write like this. What kind of life is like a song and years are like water. To me, this is still like a song in to accomplish one thing. A few years have passed in the twinkling of an eye, and suddenly looking back, the idea of writing a book is the same as before. At the end of 2006, the senior leaders of the company paid attention to this matter from the perspective of friends, and gathered all parties with great enthusiasm to the publication and distribution of mass support books. This is 1 kind of invisible inspiration to me. Because, a writer, his greatest hope is to bring his observation, understanding, and search of things to his readers, using his own language and expression to tell. As I wrote in the preface of "Selected Works of Chen Xin": "Heaven has given me moist rain and dew and warm sunshine. Traveling in the clouds gives me yearning and reverie. The earth gives me the grains I need for growth. The mountain peaks make me appreciate the tall and high. The river let me know that the blood flow is long. However, I this 1 very little cosmic dust, take what to dedicate to you—God, the earth. Only when I have this trivial cognition, understanding, emotion, and 1 a grateful heart, I will flow to the end of the pen and offer it piously..."

    Publishing a book, for the writer, is not only a summary of his own account to the reader, but also a phased summary of himself. However, from planning to publishing a book to actually publishing a book, in this process, I made a lot of friends. From the writers' associations at all levels to the publishing house, the behavior of my friends made me feel that everyone paid me too. A lot of hard work. At the same time, I have accepted the help, support and encouragement of many warm-hearted friends. Now, book has been published by Publishing House. In the face of my sincere friends, I keep asking myself: what do I give to you? After thinking about it, I 'd better say 1 a sincere sentence to express it: "only by putting my insignificant cognition, understanding, emotion, and 1 grateful heart into the pen and offering it piously."

Pick up the seven steps have dry Kun

On the Shili Cultural Street that runs from east to west in Xugezhuang, where Fengnan District is located in Tangshan City, there is a building full of cultural colors-Qipu Building, which is very conspicuous in the winter sun.

Standing in front of the seven-step building with four floors above the ground, but the outer walls of the middle two floors are decorated with nearly a hundred different styles of calligraphy "Ancient Xuan Museum", 1 is an irresistible cultural atmosphere. Come, make people feel unique! Looking at the near, I saw the signs of the North China Branch of Huaxia Fine and Short Literature Association, Fengnan District Cultural Post Station, Fengnan District Intangible Cultural Heritage Living Room and Fengnan Calligraphers Association hanging at the gate of the seven-step building. Unconsciously, the attraction of 1 shares hit strongly. I couldn't help but pick up the grade and push open the door in seven steps and walk into the "seven step floor " 1 to see what happened. On the left side of the door is the exhibition room of Zhai's Curium Porcelain. On both sides of the of Road, there are Tianhu Painting Academy, Fengnan Wenyuan and Writer Wenyuan Editorial Department. looked straight into the and saw a 4 carved wooden door full of Chinese architectural features in ancient and ancient colors. See these, let you suddenly feel, here is like the ancient and modern intersection, is a cultural gathering place.

Under the guidance of the guide, I came to Fengnan Antique City, which filled the gap in the antique market in Fengnan District, under the of the seventh step building. Here, gold, stone and jade, antique books, cultural relics ornaments, piano, chess, calligraphy and painting, ancient and modern modern handicrafts, pearlescent treasures, and dazzling, dazzling. Here, people can see that cultural relics have come to life and the long history has stood. Also let people see, here is the traditional craft and modern culture display platform. There are also ancient teahouses for people to rest and drink tea and talk about the past and the present. Think about the past, think about the future.

From the underground antique city to the second floor above ground, the lights are bright and the vision is wide. As soon as I entered the door, an amazing scene appeared in front of me. The ceramic collections of different ages, large and small, tall and short, were all over the floor of the whole floor, which was dizzying. Arranged neatly, comparable to the terracotta warriors. Even the famous Redology expert Wang Jiahui and the famous Chinese writer Zhang Jinchi were deeply shocked after visiting here.

There are two bright spots in the ceramic collection here. 1 is that the "Tangshan Kiln " ceramic collection here is the most complete, and the and Tangshan ceramic porcelain painting with the theme of the Red Mansion Dream are extremely rare, and some can be called orphans. The 2 is an exhibition of curium porcelain by the representative inheritor of Zhai's curium porcelain in, Tangshan City, Hebei Province, Intangible Heritage Project, Tangshan City, Hebei Province. The ancient curium porcelain technique reproduces the broken and damaged ancient and modern porcelain in good condition, so that the "curium work" of the soon-to-be-lost porcelain can be inherited and continued. It is worth mentioning 1 that Zhai's Curium Porcelain also held the only Curium Porcelain Exhibition in the country.

There are also collections and displays of utensils, articles, books, daily necessities, signs, books, newspapers and periodicals from the founding of the People's Republic of to the 1990 s. Let people relive the lost years, the past time and life.

The 3 building, which has entered another 1 style, is a collection of conference rooms, Ming and Qing furniture, precious utensils, ceramics, and documents. It is magnificent, luxurious, graceful and fashionable, showing the charm of traditional and modern civilization. Into such a situation, let a person feel worthwhile, rare!

Walking into the 4 floor, this is a multi-functional living and dynamic room integrating learning and training, cultural activities, meetings, lectures and 4 floors! Lighting, sound, venues, everything.

With the rise of the "Seven Steps Building ", Fengnan District of Tangshan City has an additional place where ancient and modern blend, traditional culture and modern culture coexist. It has become the highlight of cultural industry, leisure and entertainment, and cultural communication in Fengnan area, Tangshan city and even Hebei province. With the continuous expansion of influence, literature and history, culture, painters, calligraphers, tourists and players from all over the country come here to visit and exchange.

Xugezhuang, where the "Qipu Building " is located, has a history of more than a thousand years. There was a Hongyang Temple in the town, which was built during the reign of Emperor Taizong of the Tang Dynasty (627-649 AD). Famous and influential. And as early as the Xianfeng period of the Qing Dynasty, it became the largest bristle processing and export base in northern China, and the "Torch" brand bristles produced were well-known overseas. In the 2 year of Guangxu of the Qing Dynasty (1876), Beiyang Minister Li Hongzhang appointed Tang Tingshu, the general office of Shanghai Shipping and Investment Promotion Bureau, to establish Kaiping Mining Co., Ltd. in the form of official supervision of and commercial offices. In order to facilitate the transportation of coal, the coal river was excavated in

Xugezhuang in the spring of 1881. At the same time, some civilian ships took advantage of the of the coal river to carry lime, ceramics, grain and other daily necessities between Tianjin and Tang, which became the transportation artery at that time. In 1990, Xugezhuang ranked among the top 100 townships in the country, and ranked first in the ranking of 100 million yuan townships in Hebei Province in 1991.

In 2006, the National Bureau of Statistics assessed the comprehensive development level of small towns in the country as the tenth "thousand strong towns", becoming the only township in the north of the Yangtze River to enter the top ten, known as the "first town in Jiangbei". In 2008, it ranked eighth in the evaluation of the top in the comprehensive strength 500 of the of Town, Township, China.

Here, is the cradle of modern Chinese industry. China's first standard gauge railway-Tangxu Railway, extends far from here! Xugezhuang locomotive repair shop, produced China's first steam locomotive-"Dragon" locomotive. On November 8, 1881, the Tangxu Railway from Tangshan to Xugezhuang was officially opened to traffic. With the continuous extension of the two ends, constitute a railway artery extending in all directions. The construction of Tangxu Railway greatly promoted the development of modern Chinese national enterprises and opened the prelude to China's railway construction. Xugezhuang was the hardest hit area of the Tangshan earthquake in 1976, and it was also the focus of world attention at that time...

After the snow, the sun was shining. Walk out of the "seven-step floor " and look at the "seven-step floor" in the warm winter sun next, "seven

The "Step Building "is a new landmark building in the cultural and creative circles of Fengnan District. The "Seven-Step Building" will also inherit the splendid culture of the past and the.

carry it forward. Bathing in the light of Chinese culture, blooming the flower of romantic culture!

Yishou Garden Sings Beauty

By chance, we broke into "Yishou Garden", a large-scale indoor ecological health park covering an area of 6500 square meters, also known as "Subtropical Room Garden.

In the garden, 1 is a rockery facing east and back west. The waterfall on the top of the mountain is pouring down. On the north side of the mountain, is a welcoming pine with good 1 to greet everyone. At the foot of the mountain artificial lake lake water red, flowers, white, gold and other ornamental fish, come and go swimming in the lake and garden inner ring water system, so leisurely.

As people walk up to the small bridge, see the water under the bridge clear. I wonder where this water came from? people around you a sign: the water sources of the hot spring pavilion and the water system in the garden are all water the deep layer of more than 400 meters below the Tangshan Water Source Reserve, which is rich in sodium, oxide, bicarbonate, sulfate, magnesium, calcium carbonate, strontium, calcium, iron, selenium, potassium and other minerals and trace elements beneficial to the human body, it has good curative effect on arthritis, cardiovascular and cerebrovascular diseases, neurofunctional diseases, etc., as well as whitening and skin care, delaying skin aging, etc., and has extremely high health care physiotherapy value. I didn't expect that there was such a good water source in this great plain?

After crossing the small bridge, there is the of Yixian pavilion with cornices hanging from its feet, giving people the feeling of time passing through and sunshine flying in the sky. As soon as people enter the park, the scene they see is like a fairyland. Wandering in the garden, pavilion a small rest, enjoy the beautiful scenery, like a god like an immortal. "Yixian Pavilion "the famous sentence in "Preface to Tengwang Pavilion" by Bo, the king of the, " painting Liang Chaofei Nanpu cloud, bead curtain dusk rolls the rain in the western mountains". It is a perfect match with all the scenery of the left water, right mountains and flowers and trees in the garden. Walking in the corridor makes people feel like walking through the years of history.

Looking back to the south, Tingnan is relatively an antique nine-song corridor with red columns and tiles, winding and full of architectural beauty Chinese classical gardens. A gold plaque of "Health Corridor" is hung on the painted head-on beam of the corridor. The "Health Corridor" is matched with Baduanjin, Wuqinxi and other Chinese health-preserving materials painted, so that people can exert a subtle influence on the and of health-preserving ears and eyes. The couplet written on the red cylinder is written by Zhao Puchu, "the same practice is benevolent and virtuous, saving the world and keeping in good health" complement each other.

The park uses landscape and water system to create a harmonious environment between man and nature, full of subtropical natural customs. The scenery is beautiful, the scenery is pleasant, the vegetation is luxuriant, the seasons are spring-like, the water, air and humidity in the garden are all excellent, because the is completely based on subtropical climate, the temperature in the garden has been kept at C of 18 −25, C and humidity of 40%−70% RH, which can be called: the unity of heaven, earth and man, and are in a natural environment, it is also a paradise hidden in the busy city.

The pavilion, which is located in the middle of the garden, is to welcome the morning and evening. It has a wide field of vision, pleasant scenery and free heart. Facing the university for the elderly, the flowing water around the pavilion. The is like a song and the sings in a shallow way. The fish swims at the shallow bottom and is at ease. The pavilion is called "Singing Night Pavilion" and is accompanied by a couplet of "Fishery Songs Sing Smoke at Night, Morning Bell Songs Sing and Songs". It has excellent artistic conception.

There is a badminton and table tennis field in the north of the park, which makes people feel full of vitality. On the west side of the park is the fitness area. The existence of various fitness machines gives people the feeling of moving up. The Garden a small central square on the south−central side, surrounded by and lawns in the subtropical. The southernmost part of the garden is the chess and card room, the painting and calligraphy room, and the video room, which satisfy people's pursuit of spiritual entertainment today.

After a tour, I will go back. When I came to the gate of the garden, I saw the name "Yishou Garden" the garden ". When you are in this place, you can cultivate your body and enjoy yourself. You can also strengthen your body and prolong your life. The setting sun is gorgeous, the sunset clouds cover the of the Yishou Garden, and the fragrance of flowers and birds is extremely pleasant.

That year to "people's literature" to participate in the pen

thing still needs to start in April 1992. The editorial department of Hainan Province's "Contemporary Literary World" magazine sent me a letter of invitation for the "National First Contemporary Literary World Trials. At that time, I didn't have any ready−made works on hand, and I didn't have any inspiration when I suddenly received about draft letters from. The draft letter was in the desk drawer.

a few days later, when I was looking for materials in the scattered file column in the upper right corner of my desk, I 1 a printed prose poem "Midsummer, do you want to see the sea? appear in front of us. Take it over and look at it 1. I think it is good to it as an essay. Take a closer look, I also want to reconsider the topic. As a result, the idea of a few days topics are not satisfied. One day, a brainwave came to mind, and an ideal title "Midsummer Love" appeared in my mind. With a burst of joy, I immediately took out a ballpoint pen from my pocket and wrote it on the palm of my hand. Come to the office to turn on the computer, immediately put "midsummer, go to see sea? "The title of this 1 was revised to" Midsummer Love ", quickly packed the envelope, wrote the receiving address and sent it to the editorial department of Hainan Province's" Contemporary Literary World "magazine.

One day in June 1992, I received a good news book from the editorial department of "Contemporary Literature" in Hainan Province. The prose poem "Zhong Xia's Love" won the first prize in the "National First Contemporary Literary Masterpiece Selection Competition" held by the editorial department of "Contemporary Literary World" in Hainan Province, and was included in the "Chinese Song " edited by Fang Mengquan. "Thousand Chinese New Poets" series. The prose poem "Midsummer Love" has also been reprinted by Tianjin Economic Radio Station, "Tangshan Mission News " and other media. In 1993, the inaugural issue of the school magazine "Window" of Shaanxi Youth Self-study University, the special edition published my award-winning prose poem "Midsummer Love", and my creative talk "Let the Light of Emotion Shine in the Article", and added the editor's note. It is also because this prose poem "Midsummer Love", which won the first prize of "the first national contemporary literary masterpiece selection competition", was founded on October 25, 1949 as the first pure literary journal of New China. In the history of Chinese contemporary literature (new Chinese literature), no matter from which aspect, it can be called the most important, most prominent and most authoritative and representative literary publication "People's Literature", I was also invited to Beijing to attend a symposium on the 45th anniversary of the founding of People's Literature.

It was in early December 1993, and the editorial department of "People's Literature" sent me an invitation letter for the "People's Literature" pen meeting (and the "People's Literature" 45th Anniversary Symposium). On Saturday afternoon, January 1, 1994, more than 370 experts, professors, writers, poets, critics, journalists and editors from all over the country except Taiwan gathered in the Party School of the Ministry of Railways at that time. At the meeting held in the auditorium of the Ministry of Railways that night, everyone introduced themselves on the stage one after another. The stage of the auditorium was very large. When I introduced myself on stage and wanted to walk off the stage, 1 big editor with glasses stopped me and motioned me to go there. I walked over and shook his hand on the rostrum seat behind the on the big stage. He smiled and said, "Hello, Chen Xin. I am Green Wind, editor of people's literature and prose poems. I 'd like to introduce you to the leaders. This is Liu Baiyu and Cheng Shuzhen, chief editors of People's Literature, Cui Daoyi and Wang, deputy chief editors, and this is the critic Leida and Lu Tongliu... "After I shook hands with all the famous artists one by one, the teacher Green Feng said," Why is it so to invite Chen Xin? "He stunned me, and I said no. He smiled again and said, "No? did you receive the invitation letter last year's Kyoto Spring PEN? "I said I did. "you received the invitation letter for Kyoto Summer PEN?" "Yes." "Have you received the invitation to the Kyoto Autumn PEN?" "Yes." "Have you received the invitation letter of Kyoto Winter PEN?" "Yes." "Then why didn't you come?" "The unit was busy and came out 1 week without the approval of the leader." "Then why is it this time?" "Because" People's Literature ", the first literary magazine in New China, I love it so much. In addition, the reportage "Goldbach Conjecture" published in "People's Literature" is too well written!" This is how we ask and answer. Editor-in-chief Liu Baiyu and Cheng Shuzhen, deputy editor -in-chief Cui, Wang Fu, critic radar and Lu Tong all smiled at us. "Chen Xin, know where I find you?" "I don't know." he took out a copy of "a thousand families of new poets", "you wrote the" midsummer love "in this book, right?" "oh, yes." He smiled, "How do you write so well? Because of your article. Won I must call you to Beijing for the prose poem that won the first prize!" I suddenly smiled, "thank you teacher!" "Well, let's go back to our seats under the stage and take time for me to go to your dormitory." green the wind teacher said with a smile.

The People's Literature Pen Conference and Symposium were held in Beijing for a week. During the period, they listened to lectures, held seminars, went to the Old Summer Palace, the Summer Palace, and the Great Wall to collect styles. After that, each person wrote 1 literary works and finally got together.

It is the prose poem "Midsummer Love", which won the first prize of the "National First Contemporary Literary Works Selection Competition" held by the editorial department of "Contemporary Literary World" in Hainan Province in,, and created a relationship with "People's Literature" Editor-in-chief and deputy editor-in-chief, famous Chinese critics such a good opportunity to have close contact.

Often recall the love of father

Father's Day is coming, which reminds me of the 1 thing when I was a child. I remember that it was one morning during the summer vacation when I was in the 3 grade of primary school. I wanted to get up when I was sleeping alone, but somehow, my legs couldn't get back to the bend these, and my knees covered with and still painful. I called dad, dad 1 look also don't know what is going on. Asked me where it hurt, I said my knees and legs hurt. So, my father gave me a good time to rub the muscles, legs and knees, just a little better. I got up and dressed, washed and ate.

For this reason, my father didn't go to work that day and took me to the second hospital, which is now Tangshan orthopedic hospital. Tangshan before the earthquake did not have so many large and small hospitals today. My father and I went to the second hospital and waited in line for a period of time. finally, it was the doctor's turn to see me. the doctor looked left and right. he also knocked on various parts of my leg with a small hammer. finally, he pushed the glasses on the bridge of his nose and said, "did you go to take a bath in the river yesterday? it's all right. it was just a little cold. Remember, don't play in the water for too long in the future, or you will get joint and rheumatism." I looked at the doctor and nodded. Dad listened to this to see me laugh. Now that I think about it, it may be that my father didn't know what was going on with my leg at that time. The doctor's heart was bright when he said this, and the 1 cloud of doubt dispersed, so he smiled happily.

It was noon when I came out of the second hospital. My father led me around to play and came to the restaurant across from the old long-distance bus station in the south of Xishankou. My father looked at the restaurant and said to me, "My father and son will not go home for lunch. You can tell my father what you want to eat ." To be honest, every family before the reform and opening up was not wealthy. My father worked alone in the industrial and commercial office, and the life of the family of seven was not relaxed. The children of that time were not like the children of today. They ate all the delicacies. Because I haven't eaten anything delicious, I can't say what I want to eat, that is, I don't know what is delicious. Dad looked at me blankly and said, "Then I'll give you a big cake and a fat sausage." Oh, these pig sausage can only be eaten during the Chinese New Year. Without hesitation, I said, "Medium."

Dad bought big cakes and rolled them up and handed them to me: "son, eat. It smells good." "Dad won't eat?" "Son, there's stewed pie Dad." "Then we cannot father 1 half of us." "Silly son, when you grow up to my age, you will know dad's heart. Eat, you still have to grow." a mouthful of pie fat sausage chew in my mouth, incense in my heart. Today, every time I think back to my father's loving and happy appearance at that time, I feel a burst of acid and want to cry. As the saying goes, "Father and son nature." When I also had a son, I deeply understood the rich meaning of this old saying. Although my father has passed away, my father's 1.1 drops of father's love are reflected through small things, which I still remember in my heart today. Before Father's Day, I bought fat sausage on the of the pie roll and put it in front of my father's portrait to respectfully send his grief and thoughts to his old man's house.

The pancakes are rolled with fat sausage and taste really delicious. While the fragrance flutters, it is bathed in the light of fatherly love. I have often mentioned this long past to my son 1.

From "Selected Works of Chen Xin" to "Wind, Dance and Autumn Sea"

From 2007 to 2024, I successively published 5 books: Selected Works of Chen Xin, Echo of Time, Dream Back to the Tang Dynasty, with a Sunshine of, Wind Dance and Autumn the Sea. He also sorted out the news manuscripts published in newspapers at all levels from 1984 to 2023, edited and collected the "Chen Xin Manuscript Collection" 1 to the 4 episode.

In the 1990 s, I entered the peak period of prose poetry creation. In June 1992, my prose poem "Zhong Xia's Love" won the first prize in the "National Contemporary Literary Works Trial" held by the editorial department of "Contemporary Literary World" in Hainan Province. The "Thousand Chinese New Poets" series edited by Fang Mengquan has also been reprinted by Tianjin Economic Broadcasting Station, "Tangshan Group News" and other media. In 1993, the inaugural issue of the school magazine "Window" of Shaanxi Youth Self-study University published my award-winning prose poem "Midsummer Emotional Thinking" in a special edition, as well as my creative talk "Let the

Light of Feeling in the Article", and Add editor's note. It is also because this prose poem "Midsummer Love", which won the first prize of the "National First Contemporary Literary Selection Competition", was founded on October 25, 1949 as the first pure literature journal of New China. In the history of contemporary Chinese literature (new Chinese literature), it can be regarded as the most important, most prominent and most authoritative and representative literary publication "People's Literature" from any aspect. I was also invited to attend the symposium on the 45th anniversary of the founding of the People's Literature.

Since then, my literary creation has become more and more unacceptable. My works are often published and broadcast in newspapers, magazines, and radio stations at different levels from the country to the local level, and some are included in literary works or awards. Even, in 1993, my prose poem "Midsummer, do you to see the sea? "you have occupied me" was also published in the fifth and seventh issues of the world prose poetry writer in Hong Kong, which was ruled by Britain at that time, and won the "prosperity Cup" world poetry competition excellence award. My entries have also been included in the list of contemporary poetry lovers edited by the famous poet A Hong (Wang Zhanbiao), the list of unnamed writers and poets edited by the famous writer Yao Xueyin, and the collection of new contemporary literature edited by the famous writer and poet Fang Mengquan. Professor He Shuyun from Fudan University has also been guiding and encouraging me to study in the writer class of the Chinese Department of Fudan University. In 1994, I finished the preparatory class for writers of the Chinese Department of Shanghai Fudan University and was given priority to be admitted as a formal student of the Chinese Department of Shanghai Fudan University.

In 2007, when Guan Renshan, a well-known writer and chairman of the Hebei Writers Association, learned that my "Selected Works of Chen Xin" 1 the was about to be published by the Writers Publishing House, he told me to my face: "After the book is published, you must send me one!" Mr. Tan Ge, a well-known writer and vice chairman of the Hebei Writers Association, wrote the title of the book "Chen Xin's Selection" for me. In 2009, the book "Echo of the Years" was printed. Especially on March 26, 2018, the 180000-character book "Dream Back to the Tang Dynasty" was officially published by Unity Publishing House. In July 2019, "with a ray of sunshine" was published by Sichuan Nationalities Publishing House. In January 2021, the prose collection "Wind Dance Autumn the Sea" was published by Beijing Daily Edition. In the past four years, I have published three books. During this period, he also organized the editing of "Chen Xin Manuscript Collection 1 to 4" (1984-2022).

On the morning of July 24, 2022, the first "Ma Hsi Literature Award" award ceremony of Tangshan City was held in Fengnanbin Hall. Member of the Presidium of the Chinese Writers Association,

Chairman of the Hebei Writers Association, and famous writer Guan Renshan attended the event and delivered a speech. Then, awards will be given to winners in fiction, documentary literature and prose.

My prose collection "Wind, Dance and Autumn Sea" won the first "Ma Hsi Literature Award" in Tangshan City ". The award speech reads: "Chen Xin's prose collection" Wind and Dance Autumn the Sea "is a deep and timeless work. The book has the vicissitudes of time, the tenderness of small bridges and flowing water, the surging passion, and the touching light of fraternity! The book covers a wide range of subjects and is rich in themes. The 1 book has pearlescence in hand, which makes people feel 1 a kind of persistent persistence and 1 a kind of vigorous and upward spirit!" Guan Renshan, member of the presidium of the Chinese Writers Association, chairman of the Hebei Writers Association, and a famous writer, presented me with an honorary certificate and trophy.

In January 2024, at the request of domestic readers, the book "Wind Dance Autumn Sea" was republished by Beijing Daily Publishing House. Guan Renshan, a member of the presidium of the Chinese Writers Association, chairman of the Hebei Writers Association, and a famous writer, also reprinted "Wind Dancing Autumn Sea" and personally made a preface entitled "Docking with the Times, Sympathy with the Times.

Tangshan Writers Association, Hebei Writers Association, China Coal Mine Writers Association, China Prose Society, this is after I experienced the 1976 "7 28 • " Tangshan earthquake, on the long road of writing, continue to write at the same time, one after another into the home of writers and become its members.

suddenly look back, look at the road they have come to feel gratified, lamenting that persistence can achieve everything. The spirit of a city affects the people of this city. We Tangshan people, with the spirit of earthquake resistance, have been working hard to pursue and struggle to rebuild this home on the ruins into such a beautiful, progressive and civilized coastal economy. Strong city. 48 years ago, I came from the earthquake. 48 years later, as a Tangshan person who grew up with Tangshan after the earthquake and participated in its construction and development, I am proud, and I am even more proud of Tangshan. I wish Tangshan, a strong economic city around the sea that has created the miracle and dream of Phoenix Nirvana, will transform and develop. Tangshan to the sea, phoenix dance autumn the sea, carry on the past, to the beautiful new generation.

Writer Chen Xin Literature and Art Achievement Index

On July 15, 1989, the documentary short drama "Tragedy" won Gansu Province xifeng City (now Xifeng District) held "China's first micro-works editing and publishing exhibition" race award of Excellence.

In July 1989, the short novel "Ugly Husband" was awarded the "Certificate of Honor" by the Correspondence Institute of Literary Talents in Hainan Province ".

1989 July, the poem "July Sun" won the "China Development News" held poetry contest first prize.

In February 1992, Hainan Province, China National Culture City Academic Creation Center as "91 Chinese Laurel Poems".

In March 1992, it was rated as "91 Chinese Poetry Star" by Hainan Province's "Great Special Zone Poetry Journal".

In June 1992, the prose poem "Midsummer Love" won the first prize for poetry creation in the "First National Contemporary Literary Works Selection Competition" organized by the editorial department of "Contemporary Literary World" in Hainan Province. The prose poem was included in the "Thousand Chinese New Poets" series edited by Fang Mengquan. The prose poem "Midsummer Love" was also broadcast by Tianjin People's Broadcasting Station and reprinted by "Tangshan Group News.

In August 1992, the prose poem "Midsummer, go to see the sea? "Published in the fifth issue of" World Prose Poetry Writers "in Hong Kong, and won the" Prosperity Cup "World Prose Poetry Competition Excellence Award.

In October 1992, the prose poem "You have occupied me" was published in the seventh issue of "World Prose Poetry Writers" in Hong Kong.

In 1993, the first issue of the school magazine "Window" of Shaanxi Youth Self-study University, published the award-winning prose poem "Zhong Xia's Emotion" and the creation talk "Let the Light of Emotion Shine in the Article" and added editor's note on the page of the Chronicle Edition.

In January 1994, due to the article "Midsummer Love", Chen Xin was specially invited to Beijing to participate in the 45th anniversary symposium of the founding of "People's Literature.

In 1996, the prose "The Documentary of the Manor of the Eight Hall on July 28 " was included in the book "The Story of My Heart" published by China International Statistics Publishing House.

2000 May 29, the prose "Looking at Xinjiang" by the Xinjiang Radio and Television adopted.

In July 2007, "Selected Works of Chen Xin" was published.

In October 2009, "Echo of the Years" was printed.

1985-2015 group collection "New Year's Manuscript Collection".

In November 2010, "Tangshan Earthquake First Earthquake Relief Student Team" won the Tangshan City Propaganda Department's "Love Tangshan" Excellent Essay Award, and "Human Light" won the Tangshan City Propaganda Department's "Love Tangshan" Essay Commemorative Award.

In December 2010, the party committee of Kailuan group company named "2009 outstanding news propaganda worker title".

In December 2011, he was named "2010 Outstanding News and Propaganda Worker" by the Party Committee of Kailuan Group Company ".

On October 27, 2014, the documentary "Harmony Liu Xianzhuang Elderly Happiness Paradise" was published on Xinhua (15: 05:55).

On October 27, 2014, Harmony liu Xianzhuang happy Paradise for the Elderly "in China Daily Online published (15:13:00).

On November 12, 2014, the documentary "Entering the of Liu Xianzhuang-the of Liu Xianzhuang and Zhuang New Countryside Construction and Practicing Socialist Core Values" (16000. words) was published on Hebei Communist Party Member Network (15:49:37).

In April 2016, published in "Tangshan Labor Daily Wen Hui", the essay "in the Rain Visits Cao Gong in" was in the permanent collection of "Haoran Literature Museum.

In July 2016, the documentary "40 years, I came from Tangshan's first student earthquake relief team" (9285 words), "Jia Bang friend: earthquake, leading underground miners safely into the well is my duty" (4096 words) was included in the Tangshan Municipal Party Committee Propaganda Department's "40, expressing feelings" book.

In August 2016, "Zhang Ailing's Love and Hate" (3280 words) and "Uncle Dong Hao" (3026 words) were included in the book "Tangshan and Chinese Film" published by China Film Publishing House.

On the of 2017 June, in the "Miner Brother" magazine published the novel "True Life Lover".

In September 2017, the article "Tangshan Earthquake, the First Student Earthquake Relief Team" was included in the book "Heart Traces " edited by the Writers Association of Tangshan Fengrun

District.

In March 2018, the book "Dream Back to Tang Dynasty" was published by Unity Publishing House.

In July 2019, A Sunshine with was published by Sichuan Nationalities Publishing House.

In October 2019, the free verse "China's Glory" was included in the book "Long Song" (published by Shanhua Magazine).

On the of January, 2021, the prose collection "Wind, Dance Autumn and the Sea" was published by Beijing Daily Press.

2021 september 17 day −31 the novel is true. Life lover "at Philadelphia's Haihua Metropolis Daily • Literature world the world is serialized. And published in the "writer Wen Yuan" newspaper.

In October 2021, the short novels "Xianyang has a ", "Little Yingzi", "Song Love ", "Spring Plowing Smoke ", "Huai" and "Getting Back together" were published in the "Writer Wenyuan" newspaper.

In November 2021, the novel "Tiger Girl" was serialized in "Writer Wenyuan" (to be continued).

In July 2022, the prose collection "Wind, Dance and Autumn Sea" won the first Ma Hsi Literature Award in Tangshan.

On January 9, 2023, the short novel "Imperial City " won the first prize in the "Contemporary Writers" Cup Literature and Art Competition.

On June 18, 2023, the prose "Royal cellar gold top diet" won the "I and the Royal cellar story" second prize.

On October 7, 2023, Hebei Daily published the essay "Autumn Visits Baiyangyu" on.

On December 24, 2023, he was awarded the honorary title of "Person of the Year" by the Writers Association of Fengnan District, Tangshan City.

On December 29, 2023, Hebei Daily published the essay "1 Beach Gull Heron" on.

In January 2024, the prose collection "Wind Dance Autumn Sea" was reprinted by Beijing Daily News Publishing House.

Postscript

The prose collection "Wind, Dance, Autumn, Sea" has been published since 2021. Readers across the country who have not received the book "Wind, Dance,, Autumn Sea" have requested a reprint. Thank you for your encouragement and encouragement. Today, the book "Wind, Dance, Autumn, Sea" is finally republished and ready. It contains some of the different themes that I published in newspapers, magazines, and radio stations at home and abroad from the 1980 s to 2023. Prose works. For some time, the 1 thing on my mind has finally been settled. I would like to thank Guan Ren, chairman of the of Hebei Writers Association, for his concern and strong support and help. He has asked about the arrangement of the book many times and personally the preface to the edition of "Wind Dance Autumn the Sea. Here, thank you again!

I think that what is written in the book can be beneficial to the society and the readers, and then resonate and identify with it. That will be my pleasure.

Chen Xin

6 January 2024

www.ingramcontent.com/pod-product-compliance
Lightning Source LLC
Chambersburg PA
CBHW081151070526
44583CB00021B/2796